Renzi

MASS SOCIETY IN CRISIS

BERNARD ROSENBERG
The City College, New York

ISRAEL GERVER
John Jay College of Criminal Justice, City University of New York

F. WILLIAM HOWTON
The City College, New York

MASS SOCIETY IN CRISIS

Social Problems and Social Pathology

SECOND EDITION

The Macmillan Company, New York
Collier-Macmillan Limited, London

Preface to the Second Edition

Six years—and as many eternities—have passed since the first edition of this book appeared. To be sure, mass society is still with us, and it seems to be at least as deep in crisis as ever. Yet we return to our task a second time somewhat prayerfully and hope that despite the tremendous velocity of contemporary social change, things will not so worsen that our work will be obsolete before students and scholars can come properly to grips with the problems we take to be significant.

Some of them are the same problems, only more pressing. If racial conflict loomed large in the 1960's, it looms even larger in the 1970's. On this matter, complacency in every quarter has been dispelled. Real and illusory progress notwithstanding, the rage of oppressed minorities is at a fever pitch. The Walker Report and the Kerner Report are but two of the superabundant sources on which we have drawn in this new edition to suggest the nature and basis of that rage. An excerpt from *The Autobiography of Malcolm X*, basic reading for those who would understand the mind and point of view of the new Black militant leadership, provides still another index. Over the recent past, resegregation has outpaced desegregation. Seldom in American history have the races been more fatefully polarized than they are at this moment. Tension mounts, violence leads to counterviolence, Black nationalism and Black capitalism emerge only to produce an unmistakable backlash—which further poisons an already noxious atmosphere.

All three editors of this collection are old enough to remember Hiroshima and Auschwitz. Insofar as they can, they do not propose to let the young forget those horrors. A-bombs and death factories have set the stage for the mainstream of events ever since. The scene before us will remain forever unintelligible to those who turn away from mankind's recent debasement and recurring barbarism. We therefore have retained our focus on the painful past and have brought some of the material more or less up to date. We need to record that as of this writing, twenty-five years after the end of World War II, our government is still unwilling to sign an international pact to outlaw genocide. And we cannot refrain from raising Louise Howton's question about the North American Indian ("Is he a victim of genocide?") if only to answer with a qualified "No" or "Not quite."

We made our first collection of materials on social problems against the backdrop of a national tragedy. When John F. Kennedy died senselessly, something snapped in the collective consciousness and the nation went into shock. Who could have foreseen then that Robert F. Kennedy and Martin Luther King would soon meet with an identical fate, that political assassination would make quite a few people shockproof and hence insensitive to the progressively brutalized world around them?

In the last edition, we chided the conventional sociologist for his failure to show more professional interest in these matters. This time the admonition is not necessary; sociologists are sufficiently immersed—if not overimmersed—in the struggle of modern man to confront and cope with the really fundamental problems of modern society, to "overcome" and build a world fit to live in.

B. R.
I. G.
F. W. H.

Preface to the First Edition

No one taking a cool view of our time can find much comfort in it. And our view is far from cool. We do not claim to be disinterested observers of the tragicomic scene before us, Olympian scientists above the melée, removed, disengaged, value-free. The present state of affairs troubles us greatly—else we would not have bothered to put this book together.

Civilization may be *in extremis*; human sensibility is under fire; we are threatened on every side. At such a time, he who remains in his accustomed groove could indeed find that it will be his grave.

What follows was selected, arranged, commissioned, and written with much soul searching over a period of years. The reader should not expect to find in these pages a comprehensive reflection of social science literature bearing on all our pathology; we have tried to incorporate the fundamentals, however, and to emphasize critical evaluation. Our basic intent has been to redirect the student of society from paying exclusive attention to a range of social problems limited by the perspective of an earlier generation of sociologists who set and defined it. In the light of present concerns what was of indisputably central importance thirty years ago includes much that can only be called trivial today and leaves out matters that are at the very heart of our vital interests in the '60's.

Another bone we have to pick with the conventional approach to the study of social problems is that it sometimes fosters in the mind of the public an over-confidence in the efficacy of social science. Deflating this illusion is part of our task. When given the chance they clamor for, economists seldom perform wonders in helping us grapple with our ailing economy—or psychologists with mental disorder or sociologists and criminologists with juvenile delinquency. Investing quite limited means with magico-religious power does service neither to science nor society. If in seeking his lost faith secular man succeeds in deifying science he will destroy it, especially a science still in swaddling clothes. There are stirrings in sociology, unmistakable signs of growth; but making a god-hero out of the infant is more likely to produce a monster than to speed its moral and intellectual development.

We gratefully acknowledge the help of our wives in producing this book: Sarah Rosenberg, Joan Gerver, and Louise Howton. Their advice and criticism did much to sustain the whole enterprise, as did our shared hopes of a better world for our children: Deena, Daniel, Jane, Michael, Erica, and two Josephs. We would like also to express our sense of solidarity with members of the Humanistic Underground, as one of them has dubbed that segment of our profession. Thanks, then, for inspiration and friendship, to: Joseph Bensman, Judith Kramer, Dennis Wrong, Arthur Vidich, Lewis Coser, Albert Salomon,

Reinhard Bendix, and Hans Gerth. Donna Whiteman ably assisted with typing and other essential tasks. Finally, we thank our Macmillan editor, John Dennis Moore, for his help and forbearance.

B. R.
I. G.
F. W. H.

Contents

The Morning After / Howard Nemerov / xiii
Introduction / 1

PART ONE: EXTREME SITUATIONS / 7

1 : TOTAL INSTITUTIONS / 11
   The Insanity Bit / Seymour Krim / 11
   The Moral Career of the Mental Patient: The Inpatient Phase /
      Erving Goffman / 16
   The Totalitarian State, I: The Totalitarian Secret Police /
      Hannah Arendt / 31
   The Totalitarian State, II: "Thought Reform" in Communist China /
      Robert J. Lifton / 45

2 : MASS TERROR / 53
   Daily Routine in Buchenwald / Eugen Kogon / 53
   Prisoner Behavior and Social System in the Nazi Concentration
      Camps / Elmer Luchterhand / 59
   Patterns of Unlawful Police Violence in the U.S. / National Advisory
      Commission on Civil Disorders and the United States Civil Rights
      Commission / 85

3 : GENOCIDE / 104
   Auschwitz: A Transport Arrives / Tadeusz Borowski / 104
   The Destruction of the European Jews / Raul Hilberg / 107
   Genocide and the American Indian / Louise G. Howton / 144

4 : THERMONUCLEAR WAR / 151
   Hiroshima Diary / Michihiko Hachiya / 151
   A Hypothetical Thermonuclear Strike / Leiba Brown and
      Ruth Leeds / 157
   Fallout: I Feel It in My Bones / Isaac Asimov / 162
   Theses for the Atomic Age / Gunther Anders / 172
   The Nuclear Revolution in Military Power—Overkill /
      Seymour Melman / 184

PART TWO: APPROACHES / 187

1: BIOLOGISM / 193
   Crime and the Man / Earnest Albert Hooton / 193
   Crime and the Anthropologist / Robert K. Merton and
     M. F. Ashley-Montagu / 196

2: ECONOMISM / 212
   Crime and Poverty / W. A. Bonger / 212
   White-Collar Criminality / Edwin H. Sutherland / 216

3: PSYCHOLOGISM / 227
   Crime and the Psychoanalyst / Franz Alexander / 227
   Psychoanalysis and Crime / David Feldman / 231

4: SOCIAL PSYCHOLOGISM / 240
   The Primacy of Primary Groups / Charles H. Cooley / 240
   The Functions of Small-Group Research / Lewis A. Coser / 245

5: SOCIOLOGISM / 253
   The Professional Ideology of Social Pathologists / C. Wright Mills / 253
   A New Look at Mills' Critique / Emil Bend and
     Martin Vogelfanger / 271
   Social Structure and Anomie / Robert K. Merton / 282
   Evaluating Juvenile Delinquency Research /
     Louise G. Howton / 290
   Varieties of Delinquent Experience / Bernard Rosenberg and
     Harry Silverstein / 294

PART THREE: ENDEMIC CONDITIONS / 309

1: DEVIANCE / 313
   On Thieves and Flowers / Jean Genet / 313
   Crime and Conformity / Emile Durkheim / 315
   Mental Health in the Metropolis / Lee Srole, Thomas S. Langner,
     Stanley T. Michael, Marvin K. Opler, and Thomas A. C. Rennie / 320
   Drug Addiction: Enforcement and/or Treatment / Charles Winick / 329

2: DISCRIMINATION / 333
   "White Devils" and Liberal Myths / Malcolm X / 333
   Ethnic Liberalism and Employment Discrimination in the North /
     Bernard Rosenberg and F. William Howton / 341
   Negro Life and Social Process / Sethard Fisher / 354

3: RATIONALIZATION / 367

Individual Initiative and the Problem of Bureaucracy /
    Reinhard Bendix / 367
Some Uses and Abuses of Statistical Recording Procedures in a
    Government Agency / Harry Cohen / 369
Man, Work, and the Automated Feast / Ben B. Seligman / 381

4: ALIENATION / 399

Apathy and Involvement in the Political Process / David Riesman and
    Nathan Glazer / 399
Democracy and Political Participation in the Emerging Nations /
    Seymour Martin Lipset / 424
The Intellectual and the Language of Minorities / Melvin Seeman / 428
Crisis at Columbia / The Cox Commission / 442

PART FOUR: SOLUTIONS / 459

1: CAUSE AND CURE: MATCHING LEVELS / 466

Strategies in Delinquency Prevention / Thomas Gladwin / 466
The Professionalization of Reform / Daniel P. Moynihan / 472
Social and Physical Planning for the Elimination of Urban Poverty /
    Herbert J. Gans / 482
Minority Group Leadership: The Advantages of the Disadvantages /
    Seymour Leventman / 498

2: ACTION AND NONACTION: APPRAISING NEED / 508

Some Sociological Factors in Drug Addiction Control in England and
    Wales / Leslie T. Wilkins / 508

The Morning After
November 23, 1963

As though a diamond were to split apart and show
Its central core was soft with pus that all the glitter
Could not at last contain, could not at last disguise
Or keep from stinking, is that how it is with us?
The mighty civilization, racing to the moon,
Pressing the money from the chambers of its heart?

Now, citizen, consider. It will do no good
To say the man who pulled the trigger was insane
Or Communist-inspired. That excuse may serve by day,
But what of the night, the evil hatred born of fear
That eats the heart? Did that man, by his distant kill,
Reflect the people of our country to themselves?

Another man, having as yet much life to live,
Rich yet ambitious, honorable even in
The ways of power, one elected by the people
To express the intricacies of their will through tangled paths
In the mechanical jungle of this world, has died
Of his election. Does that death express our will?

Our will to hatred and the arrogance of wealth,
To smugness and expediency and want of charm,
To politics as foolish as intemperate,
And, product of these, our will to be indifferent
To sufferings that enduring wrong permissively
Sustains among our own, excluded and kept poor,

Despised and beaten for the color of their skins,
And savagely deprived of even the little learning
Our universities afford—all this because
Their ancestors were haled to us in prison-holds,
In chains, in filth; thus we rewrite the Word of Christ:
"If once you smite a man, give him the other fist."

Our will, I mean, to money and armor more than all,
Our stingy computation of the overcost
Of charity, or kindness, or common honesty,
Our deathy phantasies about "Defense" and that

"Security" that could not, when the moment came,
Secure the life of the one man who stood for us.

The people elevated him; it is fair to say
He died because of all the people, of his party
And of the party opposed. As though the nation's will,
So evenly divided and balanced as to be
Near paralyzed, as in a catatonic state,
Had suddenly expressed itself as trigger-happy.

Sorrow, America, sorrow has always been
Easy for us because we love ourselves so well,
And it may be we love ourselves so well because
We're always able to dredge up the extra tear
In favor of survival, after we have made
The great refusals that leave survivors blind with grief.

Sorrow is easy, America, we are a people
Quick to the handkerchief. Maybe our tears can be
Impounded behind a dam and used to turn the wheels
Of some concern whose wastes will more pollute the waters.
Maybe our tears will poison all the Russians. Maybe.
Sorrow, America, and while you sorrow, think.

—HOWARD NEMEROV

(Reprinted from the *New Leader*, December 9, 1963. Used by permission.)

INTRODUCTION

We are living in a demented world. And we know it. It would not come as a surprise to anyone if tomorrow the madness gave way to a frenzy which would leave our poor Europe in a state of distracted stupor, with engines still turning and flags streaming in the breeze, but with the spirit gone.

Everywhere there are doubts as to the solidity of our social structure, vague fears of the imminent future, a feeling that our civilization is on the way to ruin. They are not merely the shapeless anxieties which beset us in the small hours of the night when the flame of life burns low. They are considered expectations founded on observation and judgment of an overwhelming multitude of acts. How to avoid the recognition that almost all things which once seemed sacred have now become unsettled, truth and humanity, justice and reason? We see forms of government no longer capable of functioning, production systems on the verge of collapse, social forces gone wild with power. The roaring engine of this tremendous time seems to be heading for a breakdown.

But immediately the antithesis forces itself on our minds. Never has there been a time when men were so clearly conscious of their commanding duty to cooperate in the task of preserving and improving the world's well-being and human civilization. At no time has work been so much honored as it is today. Man has never been so ready to apply all his powers to a common cause. At least hope has not yet been lost.

If, then, this civilization is to be saved, if it is not to be submerged by centuries of barbarism but to secure the treasures of its inheritance on new and more stable foundations, there is indeed need for those now living fully to realize how far the decay has already progressed. . . .

Between the extremes of despairing pessimism and the belief in imminent deliverance stand all those who see the grave evils and shortcomings of our time, who do not know how they are to be remedied and overcome, but who hope and work, who strive to understand and are ready to bear.

—J. H. Huizinga[1]

Crisis is a medical concept that originated with Hippocrates. When modern man speaks of political, economic, social, religious, or esthetic crisis, he proceeds metaphorically, and nowhere more than in sociology. Beginning more than a century ago, when Auguste Comte first baptized the discipline, sociology has been animated by a profound sense of crisis in every sphere of life. Indeed, the presence of disease and disorder, and the need to ameliorate them for man's survival, brought sociology into existence and has sustained it ever since. At first, as one brilliant sociologist, Albert Salomon, has put it, there was "the nineteenth-century intellectual's eschatological vision of a dying world."[2] Among those mentioned by Salomon is Jacob Burckhardt, who wrote in 1846, "I have no hope at all for the future. It is possible that

---

[1] Reprinted from *In the Shadow of Tomorrow* by J. H. Huizinga by permission of W. W. Norton & Company, Inc. Copyright 1936 by W. W. Norton & Company, Inc. Copyright renewed © 1964 by J. H. Huizinga.

[2] Albert Salomon, *The Tyranny of Progress* (New York: Noonday, 1955), p. 84.

a few half endurable decades may still be granted us, a sort of Roman imperial time. I am of the opinion that democrats and proletarians must submit to an increasingly harsh despotism. . . ."[3] and Proudhon, "All traditions are abused, all beliefs abolished, while the new gospel has not yet entered the mind of the masses. That is what I call the dissolution."[4]

Such are the origins of sociology as a field of study or a point of view, cradled in Europe and nurtured on crisis. That these origins have never been systematically studied (beyond the brilliant though as yet fragmentary contribution of men like Salomon) is cause for regret. They require intensive scholarly study by the historian of ideas and the sociologist of knowledge. Meanwhile, it may be said that the sociologist arose out of feverish change, revolutionary ferment, and the accompanying hope that perhaps he might equip himself to survive amidst all the wreckage.

Comte's view of the situation was relatively parochial and so was that of his great successor, Emile Durkheim. Both of these men were wracked with anxiety for their Motherland. It was the future of France, under successive republics and in her time of troubles, that passionately concerned them. They felt apprehensions of doom but did not look far beyond their own borders. It took Oswald Spengler to dramatize a greater fear that welled up in the twentieth century: *The Decline of the West*—or translated more precisely, *The Destruction of the West*—as his masterwork is entitled. Only a few decades later, Spengler strikes us as having written an optimistic book, since it only envisages *Der Untergang des Abendlandes* at a time when, not Western man alone, but mankind at large faces the possibility of universal extinction.

Is it any wonder that in a prophetic series of lectures years ago Huizinga said:

> In the social and cultural domain no metaphor is more apt than the pathological one. No doubt our time is full of fever. Growing pains? Possibly. There is raving; there are phantasms and senseless oppression. Or is it more than a passing overstimulation of the brain? Is there reason to speak of a derangement caused by a serious lesion of the nerve center? Every one of these metaphors has its weight of meaning when applied to the various aspects of the present state of our culture.[5]

Technically, that is, academically, social pathology is, at present, a subdivision of sociology. We treat it as such in this book. However, for long periods of time from their stormy inception, the two fields have been indistinguishable. Since Comte and St. Simon, the subject matter of one has been substantially that of the other. As the crisis deepens, notwithstanding a certain euphoria which is itself symptomatic, this virtual identity of interests becomes more apparent. To the pioneer sociologist, and he is not much more than that today, society always was the *patient*.

---

[3] *Ibid.*, quoted by Salomon, p. 6.
[4] *Ibid.*, quoted by Salomon, p. 75.
[5] *Loc. cit.*

For some time, thoughtful Europeans have felt that their world was collapsing. But what of Americans? Optimism is deeply ingrained in our national character. We are suspicious of nay-sayers and skeptics, and the "worry-bird" is a disgraceful symbol. Yet nowhere has sociology flourished as in the United States, and nowhere has it been more clearly oriented to social problems. The pragmatic attitude created by a feeling that society was out of kilter found its ultimate expression in American sociology, which begins and ends with specific social problems. In point of fact, an excessive preoccupation with "problems" has often blinded American sociologists to the larger framework without which these problems could not be grasped. We must nevertheless face the paradox of a habitually optimistic people that produces a social science focused upon pathological behavior.

It was a contemporary *American* social philosopher, Charles Frankel, who recently observed, *a propos* the story *Frankenstein*, "In the twentieth century version Frankenstein and his monster keep house together and work out an uneasy *modus vivendi*." It is to the exorcism of this monster in his innumerable forms that the American sociologist has addressed himself from first to last, that is, from Lester Frank Ward to Robert K. Merton and beyond. The dark side of American civilization, so elusive in surface manifestations, can be seen not only in American literature, which has remained as perversely gloomy in Faulkner as it was in Melville and Hawthorne, but also in its peculiar social science. At the same time, Americans like "to do something" about their "problems," and the emphasis in sociology is fully harmonious with that trait.

To this day the sociology curriculum in American institutions of higher learning is heavily weighted with courses called Social Problems and Social Disorganization, whose unit of study may be anything from the hobo and cripple to the causes of war. We favor a different, but not altogether unpopular, name and a more coherent definition of the field. The name, if not the concept it embodies, should be given short shrift. There are persuasive reasons, based on premises already suggested, to organize relevant data under the heading Social Pathology, but it will be no more offensive to us by any other name. For we agree with Humpty Dumpty :

"There's glory for you."
"I don't know what you mean by glory," Alice said.
Humpty Dumpty smiled contemptuously. "Of course you don't—till I tell you. I meant, There's a nice knock-down argument for you!"
"But glory doesn't mean a nice knock-down argument," Alice objected.
"When *I* use a word," Humpty Dumpty said, in a rather scornful tone, "it means just what I choose to mean—neither more nor less."

By calling it Social Pathology, we choose to mean a tremendous but finite segment of the social scene. Yet our decision is a little less capricious than Humpty Dumpty's, because it rests on a solid and usable tradition.

To date, most of us have studied the darker side of social life, in one of four ways. We have subsumed the subject under these headings: pathology, problems, deviation, and disorganization. None will do; each is defective; all have been criticized. Deviation for one man is conformity for another; problems in one context are solutions in another. Our standpoint will determine whether the same activity is viewed as disorganized or highly organized.

Other equally important strictures apply to the concept of pathology. Like crisis it is a medical metaphor with the special discursive hazard that human society may at first be likened to, and then mistaken for, an organism. Our sociological forefathers were often subject to that illusion which has for long been dismissed as "organicism," a quaint conceit of the Social Darwinists who were swept aside along with their too literal analogy. We still have evolutionists, but none who seriously claim that culture is analogous to the human nervous system, with its own social cerebrum, cerebellum, and medulla oblongata. Because no one is now taken with that theoretical extravagance, we think it is safe and even advantageous to revive the old concept without any nineteenth-century trappings. Put to current use, the idea that there are pathological circumstances of a specially forbidding nature abroad in our world is given the centrality it deserves.

Next to pathology, the term *dysfunction*, which is so fashionable in sociology these days, takes on a pallid coloration. Habits are dysfunctional when they create upsets, cause perturbations, produce conflict, provoke strife, or foster discontent. But shall we say of mass terror, wholesale imprisonment, brainwashing, death factories like Auschwitz, the incinerators of Hiroshima and Nagasaki—mounting to global delirium in the prospect of race suicide—that they are "dysfunctional"? As well shall we say they are signs of impropriety?

The contemporary crisis is of a different magnitude from problems like organized crime. By the same token, it has nothing to do with "the human predicament," the perennial and irremediable troubles that always beset us, our finite state, the curse of consciousness and its agonies. Men are born, they suffer, and die as "discontinuous beings," in Georges Bataille's phrase, "individuals who perish in isolation in the midst of an incomprehensible adventure. . . ." [6] The possible abrupt termination of that adventure is our reality. We cannot but view it as profoundly pathological, although to do so is no more (nor less) "scientific" than to view it through other, likewise imperfect, sociological lenses.

Delimiting and defining the field is a more formidable matter, one with which we propose to deal throughout the text that follows. At this juncture, one or two guiding principles may be set forth. For example, it is not our intention to encompass all current problems, or even to explore any one

---

[6] Georges Bataille, *Death and Sensuality* (New York: Walker, 1962), p. 15.

problem exhaustively. The major weakness of existing perspectives is their omnivorousness: not only do they take in too much, but also they take it in from too many angles.

A glimpse of some fairly recent books will immediately establish that the social pathologist in this country chronically overreached himself and operated at an intolerably low level of abstraction. We should like to eschew these tendencies. About them more will be said subsequently. On the positive side, we take one simple proposition for granted and thereby differentiate this text from much of the literature, namely, *that social problems can only be understood by the sociologist in social terms.* This is, if you like, the credo of Emile Durkheim, and with certain minor qualifications, we shall adhere to it. Before doing this we must examine the work of other schools (Part Two of this book) and determine whether to reject them completely or to retain whatever is salvable.

This does not mean that we adhere to a rigid sociological determinism. Rather, we propose a certain structural and holistic emphasis in our analysis of social problems. The analysis of social problems in social terms—whether these problems appear in the domain of human extinction, mental disorder, or deviant behavior—means that we engage in certain procedures that will aid in obtaining analyzable data. Ideally, the sociological analysis of social problems requires information about (1) the distribution of the phenomenon throughout the population, (2) the differential distribution of the problem throughout subgroups of the population, (3) the institutional features of society that contribute to perpetuation of the problem, and (4) the cultural values that provide ideological support for the persistence of the problem.

Our social problems are often only incidentally conceived of as having their sources in social life. The popular preference is to ascribe their existence to external or extraneous sources, biological defects, personality disorders, or a lack of positive thinking and optimistic faith in the future of humanity. As a result of this mystical and seemingly simpler causal analysis, meliorative efforts, those aimed at some kind of solution, are rarely successful.

In casting about for a solution to a complex social problem that may have been erroneously defined in the first place, we tend to seek quick results even at the risk of acting on a misapprehension of its causes. Our American inclination is to do something in a hurry rather than to assess the sources of a problem with great care and with a view to the likeliest solution. This inclination is itself a social problem of some significance—and we treat it as such in our final section.

A Chilean politician once said, "There are two kinds of political problems: those that solve themselves and those for which there is no solution." Does the apothegm have any relevance for us? More, perhaps than we like to admit as North Americans given over to activism. To be sure, we cannot preserve our manhood and relinquish all hope for a rational solution to the problem of international tension, to the danger of thermonuclear war, of atmospheric *or* cultural fallout, the risk of being physically extinguished or spiritually anesthetized. Yet the matter of survival is so precarious that despite its urgency we are often better advised to embrace immobilism, to do nothing at all, than to act in reckless and precipitate haste.

If there is some truth to the Chilean attitude on matters of cultural life and death (the theme of Part One), then there is much more truth in it for "traditional" problems (such as those discussed in Part Three). Part Two of this book is a critical examination of several, mostly monocausal, approaches to social pathology in its most conventional sense. Part Four rounds out the picture foreshadowed in Part Two. For every theory of the origin of social problems, with all its deficiencies, there is an accompanying panacea, whose implementation promises to generate more problems than it allays. Everyday problems are serious and vexatious, but we have not begun to understand them any better than those that threaten us with the apocalypse. Learning what we do not know and what we cannot do is the precondition for extricating ourselves from an otherwise hopeless impasse.

PART ONE

EXTREME SITUATIONS

The term *extreme situations* was introduced into the social science literature by Bruno Bettelheim, a psychologist who was interested in explaining why some individuals confined in Nazi concentration camps were better able to survive than others. Drawing from his own experience as a former inmate, he noted that the extreme harshness of camp life killed off a high proportion of new prisoners within months. He concluded that those who survived either were capable of great self-discipline (such as Bettelheim himself), or else were able to accept being remade morally in the image of the SS guards and commanders.

The Bettelheim thesis has been criticized by other camp survivors and social scientists. Luchterhand (p. 59) interviewed fifty-two individuals in depth. He concluded, contrary to Bettelheim, that the individuals most likely to survive extreme situations are those who have established a strong personal bond with another individual. This sometimes makes it possible for him to enter a wider network of sustaining and nurturing social relationships.

What makes the situation of the concentration camp inmate extreme is that typically he is deprived of practically everything he needs to live and to make him want to go on living: food, rest, warmth, health care, and the social and psychological amenities that make life worthwhile. He is continuously in danger of deteriorating, mentally and morally as well as physically. What he wanted in the German camps, above all else, was to come out alive and *unchanged*. The special agony he had to endure was that often he had to choose between survival and self-alteration.

Extreme situations take on a new dimension of sociological interest when they are considered in relation to what Erving Goffman (p. 16) calls total institutions : jails, prisons, mental hospitals, military barracks, ships at sea, convents, monasteries, boarding schools—and, of course, concentration camps.

The mental patient's situation is less extreme than the camp inmate's, but the two are similar enough in character to be of the same species. Goffman describes the patient's "moral career" in a way that strikingly recalls the concentration camp literature. The "unmanageable" patient is punished repeatedly until he learns to accept the role laid out for him. He goes through "degradation ceremonies"—and witnesses others—as part of a process whose end result is sociological reincarnation: a *patient* is born. The same thing happens in some degree in all total institutions, even boarding schools. A staff of functionaries oversees in intimate, totalitarian detail the daily lives of a body of inmates, with the objective of changing them.

The distinguishing feature of the functionary-inmate relationship is that, in logic, the inmate is not a person but a thing: a horse to be trained, "broken" to saddle or harness, or a block of wood to be carved into a useful implement. Any legal or moral restraint on the functionary's freedom to reshape the inmate is an obstacle to be worked around: Civil rights are a nuisance, administratively speaking, and moral scruples against treating a human being as a thing are a deplorable source of inefficiency. Rationality in operations— functional rationality—can be realized only to the extent that the functionary's freedom to act in a way that manifests the logic of his situation is unhindered.

The term *institution* is fruitfully ambiguous in sociology. An institution such as a school, a hospital, or a military installation is an organization of people— staff and inmates, or clients—that has a certain character and makes use of certain facilities. Monogamous marriage, slavery, and the American two-party system in politics are examples of institutions in a different sense: they are established ways of doing things in a given society at a given moment in its history. The common quality is that each is an established way of acting, in accord with the values a society upholds and the material conditions of its existence. An institution, whether as organizational instrument or social pattern, exists because it has been found workable and morally acceptable. As it changes it reflects new features of both technology and the moral order. New ways of doing things become available, and demands arise for doing old things differently and for trying new things previously thought out of reach. Evidently the conception of extreme situations can be broadened to cover a wider range of human experience than Bettelheim had in mind. *Total institutions breed extreme situations*. The whole institutional character of modern society tends to be totalitarian. Extreme situations are not confined within total institutions like jails but are found everywhere—their quality of extremeness varying as a function of the totalness of the environing institutional structure. The point requires some development.

The special quality of the functionary-inmate relationship in a (relatively) total institution makes for the (relatively) extreme situation in which the individual inmate finds himself. However, an inmate is only a special kind of client (a client in general is one who has something done *to* him in the course of having something done *for* him). What happens when the citizen becomes a client, as in a totalitarian state like Nazi Germany or Maoist China or in the Stalinist period of the Soviet Union? He loses his political existence as a subject and becomes an acted-for or acted-upon object; he loses his civil rights and liberties. The people he formerly related to as elected officials and civil servants are now caretakers ("leaders") and state functionaries, and he has undergone a metamorphosis from constituent to client.

Hannah Arendt makes it clear (p. 31) that the existence of a totalitarian secret police puts everyone within its reach, at least latently, into an extreme situation. The Nazi doctrine that Jews are "objectively criminalistic" had its echo in the Communist doctrine, in the USSR under Stalin and in China under Mao (Lifton, p. 45), that to be of the bourgeoisie is to be categorically an "enemy of the state." In the United States the genocidal doctrine of the nineteenth century that "the only good Indian is a dead Indian" (Howton, p. 144) and the institutionalized police vigilantism in the South and parts of the North (with its rationale that "you've got to keep the nigger in his place" (p. 85)) remind us that the United States has not been backward in producing its share of the extreme situation breeding structural totalitarianism.

Finally, extreme situations are found in a third mode: that generated by the existence of the weapons and techniques of thermonuclear war.

Wars of extermination against whole populations are as old as history. But never before has it been possible, as it is now, to strike one massive blow and be certain that it will effectively achieve that end. Instant genocide is forestalled only by the "balance of terror": our thousands of hydrogen-bomb-tipped ballistic missiles hold the Soviet Union's cities in hostage, just as the Soviet Union's retaliatory force threatens our cities. Neither the United States nor the Soviet Union can strike the other without being struck back with catastrophic force. (Brown and Leeds, p. 157.)

The functionary-inmate or the broader functionary-client model does not at first seem to fit very well into a scheme that postulates that total weapons as well as total institutions produce extreme situations. But then we reflect that an actual relationship between persons is not essential. What makes a situation extreme is the fact that the individual is encompassed in the (collective) object of a collective someone who may want to kill him (it) and can, and is not bound by legal or moral considerations in deciding whether or not he should.

Functional rationality is concerned with means, not ends, with "how," not "what." The way the system is supposed to operate is that functionary types man it, but the signal to "go" is the exclusive prerogative of a level of command above and apart from operations. Statesmen decide whether and when, after making a rational calculation of self-interest. But in practice the advance of technology tends to shrink the statesman's sphere and extend effective responsibility for deciding to act to the functionary. (The case of the Sentinal or Safeguard anti-ballistic missile [ABM] system is illustrative. If it is to work, reaction time will have to be so short that the decision to fire an interceptor missile will be shifted down to an operational-level functionary—ultimately a machine, the computer.)

The logic and the ethic of functional rationality erodes even self-interest as a factor inhibiting action. The ultimate horror is not so much that the thermonuclear holocaust may be triggered by a strategic mistake as that it may be triggered by a "computer malfunction," if we bear in mind that the logic of computer operation and the logic of functionary operation are substantially the same.

The worldwide proliferation of thermonuclear weapons and the corresponding advance in technology of their control and delivery systems must result in placing everyone on the globe in an extreme situation: man is a hostage to a functionary who takes him into account not as a human being with existence and rights and a claim to compassion but as a cipher in a projection of probable megadeaths.

CHAPTER 1

TOTAL INSTITUTIONS

The Insanity Bit

SEYMOUR KRIM

——

I was as wrong as you can be and still live to tell about it. In the summer of 1955, when I was 33, the thousand unacknowledged human (not literary!) pressures in my being exploded. I ran barefooted in the streets, spat at members of my family, exposed myself, was almost bodily thrown out of the house of a Nobel Prize-winning author, and believed God had ordained me to act out every conceivable human impulse without an ounce of hypocritical caution. I know today that my instinct was sound, but my reasoning was self-deceptive. It was not God who ordained me, but I who ordained God for my own under-standable human purposes. I needed an excuse to force some sort of balance between my bulging inner life and my timid outer behaviour, and I chose the greatest and most comforting symbol of them all. He was my lance and my shield as I tore through the New York streets acting out the bitter rot of a world-full of frustrations that my human nature could no longer lock up. I was finally cornered on the 14th floor of the St. Regis Hotel by two frightened friends and another brother; and with the aid of handcuffs seriously-humorously clipped on by a couple of bobbies I was led off to Bellevue, convinced all along that I was right. I tolerated those who took me away with the kindly condescension of a fake Jesus.

From Bellevue I was soon transferred to a private laughing academy in Westchester and given insulin-shock treatments. No deep attempt was made to diagnose my "case"—except the superficial and inaccurate judgment that I had "hallucinated." Factually, this was not true; I did not have visual images of people or objects which were not there; I merely believed, with the beautiful relief of absolute justice which the soul of man finds when life becomes un-bearable, that God had given me the right and the duty to do everything openly that I had secretly fantasied for years. But this distinction was not gone into by my judges and indifferent captors. They did not have the time, the patience, or even the interest because work in a flip-factory is determined by mathematics;

Source: Seymour Krim, "The Insanity Bit," in Seymour Krim (ed.), *The Beats* (New York: Fawcett, 1960). Reprinted by permission.

you must find a common denominator of categorization and treatment in order to handle the battalions of miscellaneous humanity that are marched past your desk with high trumpets blowing in their minds.

Like all the other patients, I was considered beyond reasoning with and was treated like a child; not brutally, but efficiently, firmly and patronizingly. In the eyes of this enclosed world I had relinquished my rights as an adult human being. The causes for my explosion were not even superficially examined, nor was the cheek-pinching house psychiatrist—with a fresh flower in the button hole of his fresh daily suit—truly equipped to cope with it even if he had tried, which he did not. Private sanitariums and state institutions, I realized much later, were isolation chambers rather than hospitals in the usual sense; mechanical "cures" such as the one I underwent in a setup of unchallenged authority, like the Army or a humanitarian prison, slowly brought 75 per cent of the inmates down to a more temporarily modest view of reality. Within nine or ten weeks I too came down, humbled, ashamed, willing to stand up before the class and repeat the middle-class credo of limited expressiveness and the meaning of a dollar in order to get my discharge.

In three months' time I was out, shaken, completely alone, living in a cheap Broadway hotel-room (having been ashamed to go back to Greenwich Village) and going to a conventional Ph.D. psychologist (I had been to three medically trained therapists in the preceding decade) as a sop to both my conscience and family. I had broken beyond the bounds of "reality"—a shorthand word which is used by the average psychiatrist for want of the more truthfully complex approach that must eventually accommodate our beings' increasing flights into higher altitudes—and come back to the position I was in before. But once again the causes that had flung me into my own sky continued to eat me up. Sexually unconfident, I went to whores, ate my meals alone, and forced myself to write a few pieces in that loneliest of places, a tiny blank hotel-room in the middle of nowhere. For the first time in my life the incentive to live, the isolation and frustration of my existence, grew dim; while the psychologist smiled and smoked his pipe—and did the well-adjusted, tweedy, urbane act behind his tastefully battered desk as he ladled out platitudes—I was saving up the sleeping bombs, and when I had enough to do the trick I burned the letters I had received through the years from the several men and women I had loved, destroyed my journal of fifteen years' standing, and one carefully chosen night went to a hotel in Newark, N.J.

My plan was to take the pills and slowly conk out in the full bathtub, ultimately drowning like Thomas Heggen; if one missed the other would work. I splurged on a beautiful deathroom in a modernistic hotel, one that included a bathroom with the biggest tub in the house. But it was too small to fit my long body. The idea of not being able to drown and of surviving the pills afterwards, perhaps to become a burden or an invalid, began to scar what seemed like the paradise of suicide. I went instead to a Polish bar in downtown Newark, vaguely seeking the eternal anodynes of snatch and booze while I mentally played with my fate.

I found the booze, and saw a coarse, ignorant Polish girl do such a life-giving, saucy, raucous folk-dance (on the small dance-floor to the right of the bar) that I broke into loving sobs like prayers over my drink. The sun of life blazed from her into my grateful heart. I went back to the beautiful hotel-room, poured the pills down the toilet, and went to sleep. The next morning I returned to Manhattan a chastened man, shaking my head at how close I had come to non-being.

When I told my tale to Mr. Pipe, my psychologist, he speedily hustled me off to a legitimate head-doctor who doped me until a private ambulance came. Very much in my right and one and only mind but too paralyzed by drugs to move, I was once again taken on the long ride—this time to another hedge-trimmed bin in Long Island. I was helpless to protest, mainly because of the shame and guilt I felt for even contemplating suicide. Obviously I was not crazy, mad, psychotic, out of my mind, schizophrenic, paranoiac. I was simply a tormented man-kid who had never steeled himself to face the facts of life—who didn't know what it meant to have principles and live by them come grief or joy—and who thought that human worth and true independence comes as easily as it does in the movies we were all emotionally faked on. As a sputtering fiction-writer and fairly active literary critic, I had had occasional peaks of maturity and illumination; but as a man I was self-deceptive, self-indulgent, crying inwardly for the pleasures of a college-boy even while in my imagination I saw myself as another Ibsen or Dreiser. Ah, the extraordinary mismating of thoughts in the mind of the modern American literary romantic, as fantastic and truly unbelievable a stew of unrelated dreams as have ever been dreamt, believe me!

Once again I was on the human assembly-line: electric shock clubbed my good brain into needless unconsciousness (and I walked to my several executions like a brave little chappie instead of questioning them) and unquestioned Old Testament authority ruled our little club. Good-natured, but mostly cowlike and uneducated male orderlies carried out the orders from above; and apart from the mechanical treatment and the unimaginative grind of occupational therapy, each patient was left completely on his or her bewildered own, a sad and farcical sight when one considered the $125 per week that their frightened families were paying.

I saw now that nine-tenths of the people I was quartered with were not "insane" by any of the standards a normally intelligent person would use: the majority had lost confidence in their own ability to survive in the world outside, or their families were *afraid* of them and had palmed them off on "experts," but positively no serious effort was being made to equip them to become free and independent adults. This was their birthright—beyond country and society, indeed an almost religious obligation—but they were palliated with pills or jolted with shock, their often honest rage echoed back to them as a sign of their "illness." Some of them must have been "sick," you say. I answer: Who can not be conceived as such in a world so complex ("The truth is there is a truth on every side"—Richard Eberhart) that each group has its own method for judging manners, behaviour, ideas, and finally the worth of human values? What was more important was that I, a person from a hip milieu and with a completely opposite set of values, could see their so-called sickness with the human sensibility that an immersion in literature and experience had given to me—rather than as a clinical manifestation. When I later recognized the objective provinciality of many psychiatrists in precisely the humanistic areas that could cover the actions of the majority of the inmates without finding it "psychotic," I realized that the independent thinker and artist today must learn to be resolute towards a subtle, socially powerful god-father who often drips paternalism: namely, the newly-enthroned psychiatric minority that has elevated itself to a dangerous position of "authority" in the crucial issues of mind, personality, and sanity.

I now began to fight persistently—but still with shakiness—for my release; my life was my own; it did not belong to the cliches of the salesman-aggressive, well-barbered, Jewish refugee (my brother, my enemy!) house psychiatrist or to my smiling, betweeded nonentity of a psychologist, who paid me diplomatically inscrutable visits like a Japanese ambassador. Even if I had been or if there were such a reality as a "raving maniac"—which, perhaps childishly, I implore the over-imaginative, zeitgeist-vulnerable reader to believe is an impossible conception today—I would and should have fought for my release. What the institution-spared layman does not realize is that a sensitive and multiple-reacting human being remains the same everywhere, including a sanitarium, and such an environment can duplicate the injustice or vulgarity which drove your person there in the first place. By this I mean that a mental hospital is not an asylum or a sanctuary in the old-fashioned sense: it is just a roped-off side-street of modern existence, rife with as many contradictions, half-truths and lousy architecture as life itself.

Both of the sanitariums I was in were comparable to Grossinger's, in that they took in only financially comfortable, conventionally middle-class, non-intellectual people. By every human standard my being there was life's sarcastic answer to whatever romantic ideas I had about justice. Since the age of 19 I had deliberately led an existence of experimentation, pursuit of truth, bohemianism, and non-commercialism: fate's punishment for my green naivete was for me to recover my supposed mental health in this atmosphere of uncriticizable authority, air-conditioned by just the whiffs of truth that are perfumed and bland, and based on a pillar of middle-class propriety with the cut-throat reality of money underneath. Could I accept my former life, which had produced some good work, as a lie to myself—which the house-psychiatrist wanted me to do (in effect) in his one psychotherapeutic pass at me (he left me alone after this)?

I could not and never would: not only for myself but for the great principles and accomplishments of others, both living and dead, which had been my guide throughout my adult life. I might fail—but why go on having an identity at all if in a crisis you will throw away not only your past years, but the moral achievements of rare souls who have shared in your emotional and intellectual experience and whose own contributions to existence are also at stake?

When I heard this second house-psychiatrist literally equate sanity with the current cliches of adjustment and describe Greenwich Village as a "psychotic community," I saw with clarity that *insanity* and *psychosis* can no longer be respected as meaningful definitions—but are used by limited individuals in positions of social power to describe ways of behaving and thinking that are alien, threatening, and *obscure* to them. (A year later when I took a psychiatrist friend of mine to the San Remo, she told me with a straight face that it reminded her of the "admission ward in Bellevue," where she had interned. This was her analogy on the basis of accurate but limited experience, that increasing chasm which separates intelligent people from understanding each other. I realized with a sense of almost incommunicable hopelessness that the gap between her and the well-known poet with whom I had had a beer at the Remo two weeks before was tremendous, and that between these two poles of intelligence the neutral person—who could see the logic of each—was being mashed up with doubt and conflict. The poet was at home, or at least the heat was off, there; while the psychiatrist felt alien and had made a contemptuous psycho-sociological generalization. There was little bond of shared values and therefore genuine communication between both of these intelligent and honest human beings, each of whom contributed to my life.)

To finish with my four months in the sanitarium: I argued and reasoned for the basic right to the insecurity of freedom, and finally a good friend did the dirty in-fighting of getting me out. Had I to do it over again, I believe I would now have the guts to threaten such an institution or psychologist with a law suit, ugly as such a procedure can be to a person already vulnerable with the hash-marks of one legally defined "psychotic episode" and the contemplation of the criminal act of suicide. But I had been—as so many of Jack Kerouac's subterraneans are when faced with the machinery of official society—milk and sawdust when, in such situations, you must be iron and stone in spite of your own frailty. It is not that the present-day authorities of mental life want to railroad anyone, as in your Grade C horror movie; it is merely that as one grows older it becomes clear that there are almost unremediable differences between people in the total outlook towards life.

Mine had hardened as a result of my experiences, and I realized it was better to die out in the world, if need be, than be deprived of the necessity to confront existence behind the cheap authority of a lock and key. The majority of people who stay in mental institutions for any length of time do not want to return to the uncertain conditions outside the walls: which in our time spells out to emotionally anarchic, multi-dimensional, brain-trying, anxiety-loaded, and—O hear me mortality, from the year one!—ultimate and divine life.

The Moral Career of the Mental Patient: The Inpatient Phase

ERVING GOFFMAN

The last step in the prepatient's career can involve his realization—justified or not—that he has been deserted by society and turned out of relationships by those closest to him. Interestingly enough, the patient, especially a first admission, may manage to keep himself from coming to the end of this trail, even though in fact he is now in a locked mental-hospital ward. On entering the hospital, he may very strongly feel the desire not to be known to anyone as a person who could possibly be reduced to these present circumstances, or as a person who conducted himself in the way he did prior to commitment. Consequently, he may avoid talking to anyone, may stay by himself when possible, and may even be "out of contact" or "manic" so as to avoid ratifying any interaction that presses a politely reciprocal role upon him and opens him up to what he has become in the eyes of others. When the next-of-relation makes an effort to visit, he may be rejected by mutism, or by the patient's refusal to enter the visiting room, these strategies sometimes suggesting that the patient still clings to a remnant of relatedness to those who made up his past, and is protecting this remnant from the final destructiveness of dealing with the new people that they have become.[1]

Source: Erving Goffman "The Moral Career of the Mental Patient," *Psychiatry,* 22 (1959), pp. 123–142. Copyright by The William Alanson White Psychiatric Foundation, Inc. Reprinted by special permission of The William Alanson White Psychiatric Foundation, Inc.

[1] The inmate's initial strategy of holding himself aloof from ratifying contact may partly account for the relative lack of group formation among inmates in public mental hospitals, a connection that has been suggested to me by William R. Smith. The desire to avoid personal bonds that would give licence to the asking of biographical questions could also be a factor. In mental hospitals, of course, as in prisoner camps, the staff may consciously break up incipient group formation in order to avoid collective rebellious action and other ward disturbances.

Usually the patient comes to give up this taxing effort at anonymity, at not-hereness, and begins to present himself for conventional social interaction to the hospital community. Thereafter he withdraws only in special ways—by always using his nickname, by signing his contribution to the patient weekly with his initial only, or by using the innocuous "cover" address tactfully provided by some hospitals; or he withdraws only at special times, when, say, a flock of nursing students makes a passing tour of the ward, or when, paroled to the hospital grounds, he suddenly sees he is about to cross the path of a civilian he happens to know from home. Sometimes this making of oneself available is called "settling down" by the attendants. It marks a new stand openly taken and supported by the patient, and resembles the "coming-out" process that occurs in other groupings.[2]

Once the prepatient begins to settle down, the main outlines of his fate tend to follow those of a whole class of segregated establishments—jails, concentration camps, monasteries, work camps, and so on—in which the inmate spends the whole round of life on the grounds, and marches through his regimented day in the immediate company of a group of persons of his own institutional status.

Like the neophyte in many of these total institutions, the new inpatient finds himself cleanly stripped of many of his accustomed affirmations, satisfactions, and defenses, and is subjected to a rather full set of mortifying experiences: restriction of free movement, communal living, diffuse authority of a whole echelon of people, and so on. Here one begins to learn about the extent to which a conception of oneself can be sustained when the usual setting of supports for it are suddenly removed.

While undergoing these humbling moral experiences, the inpatient learns to orient himself in terms of the "ward system."[3] In public mental hospitals this usually consists of a series of graded living arrangements built around wards, administrative units called services, and parole statuses. The "worst" level often involves nothing but wooden benches to sit on, some quite indifferent food, and a small piece of room to sleep in. The "best" level may involve a room of one's own, ground and town privileges, contacts with staff that are relatively undamaging, and what is seen as good food and ample recreational facilities.

---

[2] A comparable coming out occurs in the homosexual world, when a person finally comes frankly to present himself to a "gay" gathering not as a tourist but as someone who is "available." See Evelyn Hooker, "A Preliminary Analysis of Group Behavior of Homosexuals," *Journal of Psychology*, XLII (1956), pp. 217–225; see especially p. 221. A good fictionalized treatment may be found in James Baldwin's *Giovanni's Room* (New York: Dial, 1956), pp. 41–57. A familiar instance of the coming-out process is no doubt to be found among prepubertal children at the moment one of these actors sidles *back* into a room that had been left in an angered huff and injured *amour propre*. The phrase itself presumably derives from a *rite-de-passage* ceremony once arranged by upper-class mothers for their daughters. Interestingly enough, in large mental hospitals the patient sometimes symbolizes a complete coming out by his first active participation in the hospital-wide patient dance.

[3] A good description of the ward system may be found in Ivan Belknap, *Human Problems of a State Mental Hospital* (New York: McGraw-Hill, 1956), ch. ix, especially p. 164.

For disobeying the pervasive house rules, the inmate will receive stringent punishments expressed in terms of loss of privileges; for obedience he will eventually be allowed to acquire some of the minor satisfactions he took for granted on the outside.

The institutionalization of these radically different levels of living throws light on the implications for self of social settings. And this in turn affirms that the self arises not merely out of its possessor's interactions with significant others, but also out of the arrangements that are evolved in an organization for its members.

There are some settings that the person easily discounts as an expression or extension of him. When a tourist goes slumming, he may take pleasure in the situation not because it is a reflection of him but because it so assuredly is not. There are other settings, such as living rooms, which the person manages on his own and employs to influence in a favorable direction other persons' views of him. And there are still other settings, such as a work place, which express the employee's occupational status, but over which he has no final control, this being exerted, however tactfully, by his employer. Mental hospitals provide an extreme instance of this latter possibility. And this is due not merely to their uniquely degraded living levels, but also to the unique way in which significance for self is made explicit to the patient, piercingly, persistently, and thoroughly. Once lodged on a given ward, the patient is firmly instructed that the restrictions and deprivations he encounters are not due to such blind forces as tradition or economy—and hence dissociable from self—but are intentional parts of his treatment, part of his need at the time, and therefore an expression of the state that his self has fallen to. Having every reason to initiate requests for better conditions, he is told that when the staff feel he is "able to manage" or will be "comfortable with" a higher ward level, then appropriate action will be taken. In short, assignment to a given ward is presented not as a reward or punishment, but as an expression of his general level of social functioning, his status as a person. Given the fact that the worst ward levels provide a round of life that inpatients with organic brain damage can easily manage, and that these quite limited human beings are present to prove it, one can appreciate some of the mirroring effects of the hospital.[4]

The ward system, then, is an extreme instance of how the physical facts of an establishment can be explicitly employed to frame the conception a person takes of himself. In addition, the official psychiatric mandate of mental hospitals gives rise to even more direct, even more blatant, attacks upon the inmate's view of himself. The more "medical" and the more progressive a mental hospital is— the more it attempts to be therapeutic and not merely custodial—the more he

---

[4] Here is one way in which mental hospitals can be worse than concentration camps and prisons as places in which to "do" time; in the latter, self-insulation from the symbolic implications of the settings may be easier. In fact, self-insulation from hospital settings may be so difficult that patients have to employ devices for this which staff interpret as psychotic symptoms.

may be confronted by high-ranking staff arguing that his past has been a failure, that the cause of this has been within himself, that his attitude to life is wrong, and that if he wants to be a person he will have to change his way of dealing with people and his conceptions of himself. Often the moral value of these verbal assaults will be brought home to him by requiring him to practice taking this psychiatric view of himself in arranged confessional periods, whether in private sessions or group psychotherapy.

Now a general point may be made about the moral career of inpatients which has bearing on many moral careers. Given the stage that any person has reached in a career, one typically finds that he constructs an image of his life course—past, present, and future—which selects, abstracts, and distorts in such a way as to provide him with a view of himself that he can usefully expound in current situations. Quite generally, the person's line concerning self defensively brings him into appropriate alignment with the basic values of his society, and so may be called an apologia. If the person can manage to present a view of his current situation which shows the operation of favorable personal qualities in the past and a favorable destiny awaiting him, it may be called a success story. If the facts of a person's past and present are extremely dismal, then about the best he can do is to show that he is not responsible for what has become of him, and the term sad tale is appropriate. Interestingly enough, the more the person's past forces him out of apparent alignment with central moral values, the more often he seems compelled to tell his sad tale in any company in which he finds himself. Perhaps he partly responds to the need he feels in others of not having their sense of proper life courses affronted. In any case, it is among convicts, "winos," and prostitutes that one seems to obtain sad tales the most readily.[5] It is the vicissitudes of the mental patient's sad tale that I want to consider now.

In the mental hospital, the setting and the house rules press home to the patient that he is, after all, a mental case who has suffered some kind of social collapse on the outside, having failed in some over-all way, and that here he is of little social weight, being hardly capable of acting like a full-fledged person

---

[5] In regard to convicts, see Anthony Heckstall-Smith, *Eighteen Months* (London: Allan Wingate, 1954), pp. 52–53. For "winos" see the discussion in Howard G. Bain, "A Sociological Analysis of the Chicago Skid-Row Lifeway" (Unpublished M.A. thesis, Department of Sociology, University of Chicago, September 1950), especially "The Rationale of the Skid-Row Drinking Group," pp. 141–146. Bain's neglected thesis is a useful source of material on moral careers.

Apparently one of the occupational hazards of prostitution is that clients and other professional contacts sometimes persist in expressing sympathy by asking for a defensible dramatic explanation for the fall from grace. In having to bother to have a sad tale ready, perhaps the prostitute is more to be pitied than damned. Good examples of prostitute sad tales may be found in Henry Mayhew, *London Labour and the London Poor*, Vol. IV, *Those That Will Not Work* (London: Charles Griffin and Co., 1862), pp. 210–272. For a contemporary source, see *Women of the Streets*, edited by C. H. Rolph (London: Secker and Warburg, 1955), especially p. 6: "*Almost always, however, after a few comments on the police, the girl would begin to explain how it was that she was in the life, usually in terms of self-justification. . . .*" Lately, of course, the psychological expert has helped out the profession in the construction of wholly remarkable sad tales. See, for example, Harold Greenwald, *The Call Girl* (New York: Ballantine Books, 1958).

at all. These humiliations are likely to be most keenly felt by middle-class patients, since their previous condition of life little immunizes them against such affronts, but all patients feel some downgrading. Just as any normal member of his outside subculture would do, the patient often responds to this situation by attempting to assert a sad tale proving that he is not "sick," that the "little trouble" he did get into was really somebody else's fault, that his past life course had some honor and rectitude, and that the hospital is therefore unjust in forcing the status of mental patient upon him. This self-respecting tendency is heavily institutionalized within the patient society where opening social contacts typically involve the participants' volunteering information about their current ward location and length of stay so far, but not for reasons for their stay—such interaction being conducted in the manner of small talk on the outside.[6] With greater familiarity, each patient usually volunteers relatively acceptable reasons for his hospitalization, at the same time accepting without open immediate question the lines offered by other patients. Such stories as the following are given and overtly accepted.

I was going to night school to get a M.A. degree, and holding down a job in addition, and the load got too much for me.
The others here are sick mentally but I'm suffering from a bad nervous system and that is what is giving me these phobias.
I got here by mistake because of a diabetes diagnosis, and I'll leave in a couple of days. [The patient had been in seven weeks.]
I failed as a child, and later with my wife I reached out for dependency.
My trouble is that I can't work. That's what I'm in for. I had two jobs with a good home and all the money I wanted.[7]

The patient sometimes reinforces these stories by an optimistic definition of his occupational status. A man who managed to obtain an audition as a radio announcer styles himself a radio announcer; another who worked for some months as a copy boy and was then given a job as a reporter on a large trade journal, but fired after three weeks, defines himself as a reporter.

A whole social role in the patient community may be constructed on the basis of these reciprocally sustained fictions. For these face-to-face niceties tend to be qualified by behind-the-back gossip that comes only a degree closer to the "objective" facts. Here, of course, one can see a classic social function of informal networks of equals: they serve as one another's audience for self-supporting tales—tales that are somewhat more solid than pure fantasy and somewhat thinner than the facts.

---

[6] A similar self-protecting rule has been observed in prisons. Thus, Alfred Hassler, *Diary of a Self-Made Convict* (Chicago: Regnery, 1954), p. 76, in describing a conversation with a fellow prisoner: "*He didn't say much about why he was sentenced, and I didn't ask him, that being the accepted behavior in prison.*" A novelistic version for the mental hospital may be found in J. Kerkhoff, *How Thin the Veil: A Newspaperman's Story of His Own Mental Crack-up and Recovery* (New York: Greenberg, 1952), p. 27.

[7] From the writer's field notes of informal interaction with patients, transcribed as nearly verbatim as he was able.

But the patient's apologia is called forth in a unique setting, for few settings could be so destructive of self-stories except, of course, those stories already constructed along psychiatric lines. And this destructiveness rests on more than the official sheet of paper which attests that the patient is of unsound mind, a danger to himself and others—an attestation, incidentally, which seems to cut deeply into the patient's pride, and into the possibility of his having any.

Certainly the degrading conditions of the hospital setting belie many of the self-stories that are presented by patients, and the very fact of being in the mental hospital is evidence against these tales. And of course there is not always sufficient patient solidarity to prevent patient discrediting patient, just as there is not always a sufficient number of "professionalized" attendants to prevent attendant discrediting patient. As one patient informant repeatedly suggested to a fellow patient: "If you're so smart, how come you got your ass in here?"

The mental-hospital setting, however, is more treacherous still. Staff have much to gain through discreditings of the patient's story—whatever the felt reason for such discreditings. If the custodial faction in the hospital is to succeed in managing his daily round without complaint or trouble from him, then it will prove useful to be able to point out to him that the claims about himself upon which he rationalizes his demands are false, that he is not what he is claiming to be, and that in fact he is a failure as a person. If the psychiatric faction is to impress upon him its views about his personal make-up, then they must be able to show in detail how their version of his past and their version of his character hold up much better than his own.[8] If both the custodial and psychiatric factions are to get him to co-operate in the various psychiatric treatments, then it will prove useful to disabuse him of his view of their purposes, and cause him to appreciate that they know what they are doing, and are doing what is best for him. In brief, the difficulties caused by a patient are closely tied to his version of what has been happening to him, and if co-operation is to be secured, it helps if this version is discredited. The patient must "insightfully" come to take, or affect to take, the hospital's view of himself.

The staff also have ideal means—in addition to the mirroring effect of the setting—for denying the inmate's rationalizations. Current psychiatric doctrine defines mental disorder as something that can have its roots in the patient's earliest years, show its signs throughout the course of his life, and invade almost every sector of his current activity. No segment of his past or present need be defined, then, as beyond the jurisdiction and mandate of psychiatric assessment. Mental hospitals bureaucratically institutionalize this extremely

---

[8] The process of examining a person psychiatrically and then altering or reducing his status in consequence is known in hospital and prison parlance as bugging, the assumption being that once you come to the attention of the testers you either will automatically be labeled crazy or the process of testing itself will make you crazy. Thus psychiatric staff are sometimes seen not as discovering whether you are sick, but as making you sick; and "Don't bug me, man" can mean, "Don't pester me to the point where I'll get upset." Sheldon Messinger has suggested to me that this meaning of bugging is related to the other colloquial meaning, of wiring a room with a secret microphone to collect information usable for discrediting the speaker.

wide mandate by formally basing their treatment of the patient upon his diagnosis and hence upon the psychiatric view of his past.

The case record is an important expression of this mandate. This dossier is apparently not regularly used, however, to record occasions when the patient showed capacity to cope honorably and effectively with difficult life situations. Nor is the case record typically used to provide a rough average or sampling of his past conduct. One of its purposes is to show the ways in which the patient is "sick" and the reasons why it was right to commit him and is right currently to keep him committed; and this is done by extracting from his whole life course a list of those incidents that have or might have had "symptomatic" significance.[9] The misadventures of his parents or siblings that might suggest a "taint" may be cited. Early acts in which the patient appeared to have shown bad judgment or emotional disturbance will be recorded. Occasions when he acted in a way which the layman would consider immoral, sexually perverted, weak-willed, childish, ill-considered, impulsive, and crazy may be described. Misbehaviors which someone saw as the last straw, as cause for immediate action, are likely to be reported in detail. In addition, the record will describe his state on arrival at the hospital—and this is not likely to be a time of tranquillity and ease for him. The record may also report the false line taken by the patient in answering embarrassing questions, showing him as someone who makes claims that are obviously contrary to the facts:

Claims she lives with oldest daughter or with sisters only when sick and in need of care; otherwise with husband, he himself says not for twelve years.

Contrary to the reports from the personnel, he says he no longer bangs on the floor or cries in the morning.

. . . conceals fact that she had her organs removed, claims she is still menstruating.

At first she denied having had premarital sexual experience, but when asked about Jim she said she had forgotten about it 'cause it had been unpleasant.[10]

Where contrary facts are not known by the recorder, their presence is often left scrupulously an open question:

The patient denied any heterosexual experiences nor could one trick her into admitting that she had ever been pregnant or into any kind of sexual indulgence, denying masturbation as well.

Even with considerable pressure she was unwilling to engage in any projection of paranoid mechanisms.

No psychotic content could be elicited at this time.[11]

---

[9] While many kinds of organizations maintain records of their members, in almost all of these some socially significant attributes can only be included indirectly, being officially irrelevant. But since mental hospitals have a legitimate claim to deal with the "whole" person, they need officially recognize no limits to what they consider relevant, a sociologically interesting licence. It is an odd historical fact that persons concerned with promoting civil liberties in other areas of life tend to favor giving the psychiatrist complete discretionary power over the patient. Apparently it is felt that the more power possessed by medically qualified administrators and therapists, the better the interests of the patients will be served. Patients, to my knowledge, have not been polled on this matter.

[10] Verbatim transcriptions of hospital case-record material.

[11] Verbatim transcriptions of hospital case-record material.

And if in no more factual way, discrediting statements often appear in descriptions given of the patient's general social manner in the hospital:

When interviewed, he was bland, apparently self-assured, and sprinkles high-sounding generalizations freely throughout his verbal productions.

Armed with a rather neat appearance and natty little Hitlerian mustache this 45-year-old man who has spent the last five or more years of his life in the hospital, is making a very successful hospital adjustment living within the role of a rather gay liver and jim-dandy type of fellow who is not only quite superior to his fellow patients in intellectual respects but who is also quite a man with women. His speech is sprayed with many multi-syllabled words which he generally uses in good context, but if he talks long enough on any subject it soon becomes apparent that he is so completely lost in this verbal diarrhea as to make what he says almost completely worthless.[12]

The events recorded in the case history are, then, just the sort that a layman would consider scandalous, defamatory, and discrediting. I think it is fair to say that all levels of mental-hospital staff fail, in general, to deal with this material with the moral neutrality claimed for medical statements and psychiatric diagnosis, but instead participate, by intonation and gesture if by no other means, in the lay reaction to these acts. This will occur in staff-patient encounters as well as in staff encounters at which no patient is present.

In some mental hospitals, access to the case record is technically restricted to medical and higher nursing levels, but even here informal access or relayed information is often available to lower staff levels.[13] In addition, ward personnel are felt to have a right to know those aspects of the patient's past conduct which, embedded in the reputation he develops, purportedly make it possible to manage him with greater benefit to himself and less risk to others. Further, all staff levels typically have access to the nursing notes kept on the ward, which chart the daily course of each patient's disease, and hence his conduct, providing for the near present the sort of information the case record supplies for his past.

I think that most of the information gathered in case records is quite true, although it might seem also to be true that almost anyone's life course could yield up enough denigrating facts to provide grounds for the record's justification of commitment. In any case, I am not concerned here with questioning the desirability of maintaining case records, or the motives of staff in keeping them.

---

12 Verbatim transcriptions of hospital case-record material.

13 However, some mental hospitals do have a "hot file" of selected records which can be taken out only by special permission. These may be records of patients who work as administration-office messengers and might otherwise snatch glances at their own files; of inmates who had elite status in the environing community; and of inmates who may take legal action against the hospital and hence have a special reason to maneuver access to their records. Some hospitals even have a "hot-hot file," kept in the superintendent's office. In addition, the patient's professional title, especially if it is a medical one, is sometimes purposely omitted from his file card. All of these exceptions to the general rule for handling information show, of course, the institution's realization of some of the implications of keeping mental-hospital records. For a further example, see Harold Taxel, "Authority Structure in a Mental Hospital Ward" (Unpublished M.A. thesis, Department of Sociology, University of Chicago, 1953), pp. 11–12.

The point is that, these facts about him being true, the patient is certainly not relieved from the normal cultural pressure to conceal them, and is perhaps all the more threatened by knowing that they are neatly available, and that he has no control over who gets to learn them.[14] A manly looking youth who responds to military induction by running away from the barracks and hiding himself in a hotel-room clothes closet, to be found there, crying, by his mother; a woman who travels from Utah to Washington to warn the President of impending doom; a man who disrobes before three young girls; a boy who locks his sister out of the house, striking out two of her teeth when she tries to come back in through the window—each of these persons has done something he will have very obvious reasons to conceal from others, and very good reason to tell lies about.

The formal and informal patterns of communication linking staff members tend to amplify the disclosive work done by the case record. A discreditable act that the patient performs during one part of the day's routine in one part of the hospital community is likely to be reported back to those who supervise other areas of his life where he implicitly takes the stand that he is not the sort of person who could act that way.

Of significance here, as in some other social establishments, is the increasingly common practice of all-level staff conferences, where staff air their views of patients and develop collective agreement concerning the line that the patient is trying to take and the line that should be taken to him. A patient who develops a "personal" relation with an attendant, or manages to make an attendant anxious by eloquent and persistent accusations of malpractice, can be put back into his place by means of the staff meeting, where the attendant is given warning or assurance that the patient is "sick." Since the differential image of himself that a person usually meets from those of various levels around him comes here to be unified behind the scenes into a common approach, the patient may find himself faced with a kind of collusion against him—albeit one sincerely thought to be for his own ultimate welfare.

In addition, the formal transfer of the patient from one ward or service to

---

14 This is the problem of "information control" that many groups suffer from in varying degrees. See Goffman, "Discrepant Roles," in *The Presentation of Self in Everyday Life* (New York: Anchor Books, 1959), ch. iv. pp. 141–166. A suggestion of this problem in relation to case records in prisons is given by James Peck in his story, "The Ship that Never Hit Port," in *Prison Etiquette*, edited by Holley Cantine and Dachine Rainer (Bearsville, N.Y.: Retort Press, 1950), p. 66:

"*The hacks of course hold all the aces in dealing with any prisoner because they can always write him up for inevitable punishment. Every infraction of the rules is noted in the prisoner's jacket, a folder which records all the details of the man's life before and during imprisonment. There are general reports written by the work detail screw, the cell block screw, or some other screw who may have overheard a conversation. Tales pumped from stoolpigeons are also included.*

"*Any letter which interests the authorities goes into the jacket. The mail censor may make a photostatic copy of a prisoner's entire letter, or merely copy a passage. Or he may pass the letter on to the warden. Often an inmate called out by the warden or parole officer is confronted with something he wrote so long ago he had forgot all about it. It might be about his personal life or his political views—a fragment of thought that the prison authorities felt was dangerous and filed for later use.*"

another is likely to be accompanied by an informal description of his characteristics, this being felt to facilitate the work of the employee who is newly
responsible for him.

Finally, at the most informal of levels, the lunchtime and coffee-break small
talk of staff often turns upon the latest doings of the patient, the gossip level
of any social establishment being here intensified by the assumption that
everything about him is in some way the proper business of the hospital
employee. Theoretically there seems to be no reason why such gossip should
not build up the subject instead of tear him down, unless one claims that talk
about those not present will always tend to be critical in order to maintain the
integrity and prestige of the circle in which the talking occurs. And so, even
when the impulse of the speakers seems kindly and generous, the implication of
their talk is typically that the patient is not a complete person. For example, a
conscientious group therapist, sympathetic with patients, once admitted to his
coffee companions:

I've had about three group disrupters, one man in particular—a lawyer [*sotto voce*]
James Wilson—very bright—who just made things miserable for me, but I would
always tell him to get on the stage and do something. Well, I was getting desperate and
then I bumped into his therapist, who said that right now behind the man's bluff and
front he needed the group very much and that it probably meant more to him than
anything else he was getting out of the hospital—he just needed the support. Well, that
made me feel altogether different about him. He's out now.

In general, then, mental hospitals systematically provide for circulation about
each patient the kind of information that the patient is likely to try to hide.
And in various degrees of detail this information is used daily to puncture his
claims. At the admission and diagnostic conferences, he will be asked questions
to which he must give wrong answers in order to maintain his self-respect, and
then the true answer may be shot back at him. An attendant whom he tells a
version of his past and his reason for being in the hospital may smile dis-
believingly, or say, "That's not the way I heard it," in line with the practical
psychiatry of bringing the patient down to reality. When he accosts a physician
or nurse on the ward and presents his claims for more privileges or for discharge,
this may be countered by a question which he cannot answer truthfully without
calling up a time in his past when he acted disgracefully. When he gives his
view of his situation during group psychotherapy, the therapist, taking the role
of interrogator, may attempt to disabuse him of his face-saving interpretations
and encourage an interpretation suggesting that it is he himself who is to blame
and who must change. When he claims to staff or fellow patients that he is
well and has never been really sick, someone may give him graphic details of
how, only one month ago, he was prancing around like a girl, or claiming that
he was God, or declining to talk or eat, or putting gum in his hair.

Each time the staff deflates the patient's claims, his sense of what a person

ought to be and the rules of peer-group social intercourse press him to reconstruct his stories; and each time he does this, the custodial and psychiatric
interests of the staff may lead them to discredit these tales again.

Behind these verbally instigated ups and downs of the self is an institutional
base that rocks just as precariously. Contrary to popular opinion, the "ward
system" insures a great amount of internal social mobility in mental hospitals,
especially during the inmate's first year. During that time he is likely to have
altered his service once, his ward three or four times, and his parole status
several times; and he is likely to have experienced moves in bad as well as good
directions. Each of these moves involves a very drastic alteration in level of living
and in available materials out of which to build a self-confirming round of
activities, an alteration equivalent in scope, say, to a move up or down a class
in the wider class system. Moreover, fellow inmates with whom he has partially
identified himself will similarly be moving, but in different directions and at
different rates, thus reflecting feelings of social change to the person even when
he does not experience them directly.

As previously implied, the doctrines of psychiatry can reinforce the social
fluctuations of the ward system. Thus there is a current psychiatric view that
the ward system is a kind of social hothouse in which patients start as social
infants and end up, within the year, on convalescent wards as resocialized
adults. This view adds considerably to the weight and pride that staff can attach
to their work, and necessitates a certain amount of blindness, especially at
higher staff levels, to other ways of viewing the ward system, such as a method
for disciplining unruly persons through punishment and reward. In any case,
this resocialization perspective tends to overstress the extent to which those
on the worst wards are incapable of socialized conduct and the extent to which
those on the best wards are ready and willing to play the social game. Because
the ward system is something more than a resocialization chamber, inmates
find many reasons for "messing up" or getting into trouble, and many occasions,
then, for demotion to less privileged ward positions. These demotions may be
officially interpreted as psychiatric relapses or moral backsliding, thus protecting the resocialization view of the hospital; these interpretations, by implication, translate a mere infraction of rules and consequent demotion into a
fundamental expression of the status of the culprit's self. Correspondingly,
promotions, which may come about because of ward population pressure, the
need for a "working patient," or for other psychiatrically irrelevant reasons,
may be built up into something claimed to be profoundly expressive of the
patient's whole self. The patient himself may be expected by staff to make a
personal effort to "get well," in something less than a year, and hence may be
constantly reminded to think in terms of the self's success and failure.[15]

In such contexts inmates can discover that deflations in moral status are not

---

[15] For this and other suggestions, I am indebted to Charlotte Green Schwartz.

so bad as they had imagined. After all, infractions which lead to these demotions cannot be accompanied by legal sanctions or by reduction to the status of mental patient, since these conditions already prevail. Further, no past or current delict seems to be horrendous enough in itself to excommunicate a patient from the patient community, and hence failures at right living lose some of their stigmatizing meaning. And finally, in accepting the hospital's version of his fall from grace, the patient can set himself up in the business of "straightening up," and make claims of sympathy, privileges, and indulgence from the staff in order to foster this.

Learning to live under conditions of imminent exposure and wide fluctuation in regard, with little control over the granting or withholding of this regard, is an important step in the socialization of the patient, a step that tells something important about what it is like to be an inmate in a mental hospital. Having one's past mistakes and present progress under constant moral review seems to make for a special adaptation consisting of a less than moral attitude to ego ideals. One's shortcomings and successes become too central and fluctuating an issue in life to allow the usual commitment of concern for other persons' views of them. It is not very practicable to try to sustain solid claims about oneself. The inmate tends to learn that degradations and reconstructions of the self need not be given too much weight, at the same time learning that staff and inmates are ready to view an inflation or deflation of a self with some indifference. He learns that a defensible picture of self can be seen as something outside oneself that can be constructed, lost, and rebuilt, all with great speed and some equanimity. He learns about the viability of taking up a standpoint—and hence a self—that is outside the one which the hospital can give and take away from him.

The setting, then, seems to engender a kind of cosmopolitan sophistication, a kind of civic apathy. In this unserious yet oddly exaggerated moral context building up a self or having it destroyed becomes something of a shameless game, and learning to view this process as a game seems to make for some demoralization, the game being such a fundamental one. In the hospital, then, the inmate can learn that the self is not a fortress, but rather a small open city; he can become weary of having to show pleasure when held by troops of his own, and weary of having to show displeasure when held by the enemy. Once he learns what it is like to be defined by society as not having a viable self, this threatening definition—the threat that helps attach people to the self society accords them—is weakened. The patient seems to gain a new plateau when he learns that he can survive while acting in a way that society sees as destructive of him.

A few illustrations of this moral loosening and moral fatigue might be given. In state mental hospitals currently a kind of "marriage moratorium" appears to be accepted by patients and more or less condoned by staff. Some informal peer-group pressure may be brought against a patient who "plays around" with more than one hospital partner at a time, but little negative sanction seems to be attached to taking up, in a temporarily steady way, with a member of the opposite sex, even though both partners are known to be married, to have children, and even to be regularly visited by these outsiders. In short, there is licence in mental hospitals to begin courting all over again, with the understanding, however, that nothing very permanent or serious can come of this. Like shipboard or vacation romances, these entanglements attest to the way in which the hospital is cut off from the outside community, becoming a world of its own, operated for the benefit of its own citizens. And certainly this moratorium is an expression of the alienation and hostility that patients feel for those on the outside to whom they were closely related. But, in addition, one has evidence of the loosening effects of living in a world within a world, under conditions which make it difficult to give full seriousness to either of them.

The second illustration concerns the ward system. On the worst ward level, discreditings seem to occur the most frequently, in part because of lack of facilities, in part through the mockery and sarcasm that seem to be the occupational norm of social control for the attendants and nurses who administer these places. At the same time, the paucity of equipment and rights means that not much self can be built up. The patient finds himself constantly toppled, therefore, but with very little distance to fall. A kind of jaunty gallows humor seems to develop in some of these wards, with considerable freedom to stand up to the staff and return insult for insult. While these patients can be punished, they cannot, for example, be easily slighted, for they are accorded as a matter of course few of the niceties that people must enjoy before they can suffer subtle abuse. Like prostitutes in connection with sex, inmates on these wards have very little reputation or rights to lose and can therefore take certain liberties. As the person moves up the ward system, he can manage more and more to avoid incidents which discredit his claim to be a human being, and acquire more and more of the varied ingredients of self-respect; yet when eventually he does get toppled—and he does—there is a much farther distance to fall. For instance, the privileged patient lives in a world wider than the ward, containing recreation workers who, on request, can dole out cake, cards, table-tennis balls, tickets to the movies, and writing materials. But in the absence of the social control of payment which is typically exerted by a recipient on the outside, the patient runs the risk that even a warmhearted functionary may, on occasion, tell him to wait until she has finished an informal chat, or teasingly ask why he wants what he has asked for, or respond with a dead pause and a cold look of appraisal.

Moving up and down the ward system means, then, not only a shift in self-constructive equipment, a shift in reflected status, but also a change in the calculus of risks. Appreciation of risks to his self-conception is part of everyone's moral experience, but an appreciation that a given risk level is itself merely a social arrangement is a rarer kind of experience, and one that seems to help to disenchant the person who undergoes it.

A third instance of moral loosening has to do with the conditions that are often associated with the release of the inpatient. Often he leaves under the supervision and jurisdiction of his next-of-relation or of a specially selected and specially watchful employer. If he misbehaves while under their auspices, they can quickly obtain his readmission. He therefore finds himself under the special power of persons who ordinarily would not have this kind of power over him, and about whom, moreover, he may have had prior cause to feel quite bitter. In order to get out of the hospital, however, he may conceal his displeasure in this arrangement, and, at least until safely off the hospital rolls, act out a willingness to accept this kind of custody. These discharge procedures, then, provide a built-in lesson in overtly taking a role without the usual covert commitments, and seem further to separate the person from the worlds that others take seriously.

The moral career of a person of a given social category involves a standard sequence of changes in his way of conceiving of selves, including, importantly, his own. These half-buried lines of development can be followed by studying his moral experiences—that is, happenings which mark a turning point in the way in which the person views the world—although the particularities of this view may be difficult to establish. And note can be taken of overt tacks or strategies —that is, stands that he effectively takes before specifiable others, whatever the hidden and variable nature of his inward attachment to these presentations. By taking note of moral experiences and overt personal stands, one can obtain a relatively objective tracing of relatively subjective matters.

Each moral career, and behind this, each self, occurs within the confines of an institutional system, whether a social establishment such as a mental hospital or a complex of personal and professional relationships. The self, then, can be seen as something that resides in the arrangements prevailing in a social system for its members. The self in this sense is not a property of the person to whom it is attributed, but dwells rather in the pattern of social control that is exerted in connection with the person by himself and those around him. This special kind of institutional arrangement does not so much support the self as constitute it.

In this paper, two of these institutional arrangements have been considered, by pointing to what happens to the person when these rulings are weakened. The first concerns the felt loyalty of his next-of-relation. The prepatient's self is described as a function of the way in which three roles are related, arising and declining in the kinds of affiliation that occur between the next-of-relation and the mediators. The second concerns the protection required by the person for the version of himself which he presents to others, and the way in which the withdrawal of this protection can form a systematic, if unintended, aspect of the working of an establishment. I want to stress that these are only two kinds of institutional rulings from which a self emerges for the participant; others, not considered in this paper, are equally important.

In the usual cycle of adult socialization one expects to find alienation and mortification followed by a new set of beliefs about the world and a new way of conceiving of selves. In the case of the mental-hospital patient, this rebirth does sometimes occur, taking the form of a strong belief in the psychiatric perspective, or, briefly at least, a devotion to the social cause of better treatment for mental patients. The moral career of the mental patient has unique interest, however; it can illustrate the possibility that in casting off the raiments of the old self—or in having this cover torn away—the person need not seek a new robe and a new audience before which to cower. Instead he can learn, at least for a time, to practise before all groups the amoral arts of shamelessness.

DOING RESEARCH IN THE DISTURBED WARD: INITIATION AND CULTURE SHOCK

My initial period at the hospital was one of disorientation, shock, and disequilibrium. It lasted for about three or four weeks and was highlighted by my need and attempt to find firm ground upon which to stand and to reconstitute an integrated "self" with which to operate.

Although I had previously done some research in mental hospitals, I was utterly unprepared for the impact of the hospital and especially the ward. The intensity of emotion expressed, the incomprehensible behavior of patients, the unreality of the context (the locked doors and closed world), the psychoanalytic language and interpretations that always "looked behind" the apparent and surface transaction and gave it an "odd twist," the eerie silence of apathy and the penetrating shrieks of a disturbed patient in a panic, all combined to produce a form of culture shock. In addition, my own fears and insecurities about interacting with these strange people, about the direction and success of the research enterprise, and about my personal capacity to cope contributed to a disequilibrium of self and to my disorientation as observer.

Life on the ward appeared at first as a continuous flow of confused transactions, eruptions of intense feelings, unpredictable behaviors, and obscure processes caught in some primitive mold with a contemporary façade. I simply could not sort it out. I did not know where to look, what to concentrate on, how to make some order out of the chaos. At this point I had not as yet acquired the confidence that the fog would lift in time, that directions for ordering and organizing myself and the research would emerge, and that I would develop some perspective on the situation. I felt that the experience was so complex, intense, confused, and disorienting that perhaps I should give up. But I did not, perhaps out of stubbornness—once you start a venture like this you simply do not quit—or refusal to take the easy way out.

Source: Morris S. Schwartz, "The Mental Hospital: The Research Person in the Disturbed Ward," in Arthur J. Vidich, Joseph Bensman, and Maurice R. Stein, eds., *Reflections on Community Studies* (New York: Wiley, 1964), p. 87. Reprinted by permission.

The Totalitarian State, I: The Totalitarian Secret Police

HANNAH ARENDT

▬

Up to now we know only two authentic forms of totalitarian domination: the dictatorship of National Socialism after 1938, and the dictatorship of Bolshevism since 1930. These forms of domination differ basically from other kinds of dictatorial, despotic or tyrannical rule; even though they have developed, with a certain continuity, from party dictatorships, their essentially totalitarian features are new and cannot be derived from one-party systems. The goal of one-party systems is not only to seize the government administration but, by filling all offices with party members, to achieve a complete amalgamation of state and party, so that after the seizure of power the party becomes a kind of propaganda organization for the government. This system is "total" only in a negative sense, namely, in that the ruling party will tolerate no other parties, no opposition and no freedom of political opinion. Once a party dictatorship has come to power, it leaves the original power relationship between state and party intact; the government and the army exercise the same power as before, and the "revolution" consists only in the fact that all government positions are now occupied by party members. In all these cases the power of the party rests on a monopoly guaranteed by the state and the party no longer possesses its own power center.

The revolution initiated by the totalitarian movements after they have seized power is of a considerably more radical nature. From the start, they consciously strive to maintain the essential differences between state and movement and to prevent the "revolutionary" institutions of the movement from being absorbed by the government.[1] The problem of seizing the state machine without amalgamating with it is solved by permitting only those party members whose importance for the movement is secondary to rise in the state hierarchy. All

---

[1] Hitler frequently commented on the relationship between state and party, and always emphasized that not the state, but the race, or the "united folk community," was of primary importance (cf. the afore-quoted speech, reprinted as annex to the *Tischgespräche*). In his speech at the Nuremberg Parteitag of 1935, he gave this theory its most succinct expression: "It is not the state that commands us, but we who command the state." It is self-evident that, in practice, such powers of command are possible only if the institutions of the party remain independent from those of the state.

real power is vested in the institutions of the movement, and outside the state and military apparatuses. It is inside the movement, which remains the center of action of the country, that all decisions are made; the official civil services are often not even informed of what is going on, and party members with the ambition to rise to the rank of ministers have in all cases paid for such "bourgeois" wishes with the loss of their influence on the movement and of the confidence of its leaders.

Totalitarianism in power uses the state as its outward façade, to represent the country in the nontotalitarian world. As such, the totalitarian state is the logical heir of the totalitarian movement from which it borrows its organizational structure. Totalitarian rulers deal with nontotalitarian governments in the same way they dealt with parliamentary parties or intraparty factions before their rise to power and, though on an enlarged international scene, are again faced with the double problem of shielding the fictitious world of the movement (or the totalitarian country) from the impact of factuality and of presenting a semblance of normality and common sense to the normal outside world.

Above the state and behind the façades of ostensible power, in a maze of multiplied offices, underlying all shifts of authority and in a chaos of inefficiency, lies the power nucleus of the country, the superefficient and supercompetent services of the secret police.[2] The emphasis on the police as the sole organ of power, and the corresponding neglect of the seemingly greater power arsenal of the army, which is characteristic of all totalitarian regimes, can still be partially explained by the totalitarian aspiration to world rule and its conscious abolition of the distinction between a foreign country and a home country, between foreign and domestic affairs. The military forces, trained to fight a foreign aggressor, have always been a dubious instrument for civil-war purposes; even under totalitarian conditions they find it difficult to regard their own people with the eyes of a foreign conqueror.[3] More important in this respect, however, is that their value becomes dubious even in time of war. Since the totalitarian ruler conducts his policies on the assumption of an eventual world government, he treats the victims of his aggression as though they were rebels, guilty of high treason, and consequently prefers to rule occupied territories with police, and not with military forces.

Even before the movement seizes power, it possesses a secret police and spy service with branches in various countries. Later its agents receive more money and authority than the regular military intelligence service and are frequently

---

[2] Otto Gauweiler, *Rechseinrichtungen und Rechtsaufgaben der Bewegung*, 1939, notes expressly that Himmler's special position as Reichsfuehrer-SS and head of the German police rested on the fact that the police administration had achieved "a genuine unity of party and state" which was not even attempted anywhere else in the government.

[3] During the peasant revolts of the twenties in Russia, Voroshilov allegedly refused the support of the Red Army; this led to the introduction of special divisions of the GPU for punitive expeditions. See Anton Ciliga, *The Russian Enigma*, London, 1940, p. 45.

the secret chiefs of embassies and consulates abroad.[4] Its main tasks consist in forming fifth columns, directing the branches of the movement, influencing the domestic policies of the respective countries, and generally preparing for the time when the totalitarian ruler—after overthrow of the government or military victory—can openly feel at home. In other words, the international branches of the secret police are the transmission belts which constantly transform the ostensibly foreign policy of the totalitarian state into the potentially domestic business of the totalitarian movement.

These functions, however, which the secret police fulfill in order to prepare the totalitarian utopia of world rule, are secondary to those required for the present realization of the totalitarian fiction in one country. The dominant role of the secret police in the domestic politics of totalitarian countries has naturally contributed much to the common misconception of totalitarianism. All despotisms rely heavily on secret services and feel more threatened by their own than by any foreign people. However, this analogy between totalitarianism and despotism holds only for the first stages of totalitarian rule, when there is still a political opposition. In this as in other respects totalitarianism takes advantage of, and gives conscious support to, nontotalitarian misconceptions, no matter how uncomplimentary they may be. Himmler, in his famous speech to the Reichswehr staff in 1937, assumed the role of an ordinary tyrant when he explained the constant expansion of the police forces by assuming the existence of a "fourth theater in case of war, internal Germany."[5] Similarly, Stalin at almost the same moment half succeeded in convincing the old Bolshevik guard, whose "confessions" he needed, of a war threat against the Soviet Union and, consequently, an emergency in which the country must remain united even behind a despot. The most striking aspect of these statements was that both were made after all political opposition had been extinguished, that the secret services were expanded when actually no opponents were left to be spied upon. When war came, Himmler neither needed nor used his SS troops in Germany itself, except for the running of concentration camps and policing of foreign slave labor; the bulk of the armed SS served at the Eastern front where they were used for "special assignments"—usually mass murder—and the enforcement of policy which frequently ran counter to the military as well as the Nazi civilian hierarchy. Like the secret police of the Soviet Union, the SS formations usually arrived after the military forces had pacified the conquered territory and had dealt with outright political opposition.

In the first stages of a totalitarian regime, however, the secret police and the party's elite formations still play a role similar to that in other forms of dictatorship and the well-known terror regimes of the past; and the excessive cruelty of

---

[4] In 1935, the Gestapo agents abroad received 20 million marks while the regular espionage service of the Reichswehr had to get along with a budget of 8 million. See Pierre Dehillotte, *Gestapo*, Paris, 1940, p. 11.

[5] See *Nazi Conspiracy*, U.S. Government, Washington, D.C., 1946, IV, 616 ff.

their methods is unparalleled only in the history of modern Western countries. The first stage of ferreting out secret enemies and hunting down former opponents is usually combined with drafting the entire population into front organizations and re-educating old party members for voluntary espionage services, so that the rather dubious sympathies of the drafted sympathizers need not worry the specially trained cadres of the police. It is during this stage that a neighbor gradually becomes a more dangerous enemy to one who happens to harbor "dangerous thoughts" than are the officially appointed police agents. The end of the first stage comes with the liquidation of open and secret resistance in any organized form; it can be set at about 1935 in Germany and approximately 1930 in Soviet Russia.

Only after the extermination of real enemies has been completed and the hunt for "objective enemies" begun does terror become the actual content of totalitarian regimes. Under the pretext of building socialism in one country, or using a given territory as a laboratory for a revolutionary experiment, or realizing the *Volksgemeinschaft*, the second claim of totalitarianism, the claim to total domination, is carried out. And although theoretically total domination is possible only under the conditions of world rule, the totalitarian regimes have proved that this part of the totalitarian utopia can be realized almost to perfection, because it is temporarily independent of defeat or victory. Thus Hitler could rejoice even in the midst of military setbacks over the extermination of Jews and the establishment of death factories; no matter what the final outcome, without the war it would never have been possible "to burn the bridges" and to realize some of the goals of the totalitarian government.[6]

The elite formations of the Nazi movement and the "cadres" of the Bolshevik movement serve the goal of total domination rather than the security of the regime in power. Just as the totalitarian claim to world rule is only in appearance the same as imperialist expansion, so the claim to total domination only *seems* familiar to the student of despotism. If the chief difference between totalitarian and imperialist expansion is that the former recognizes no difference between a home and a foreign country, then the chief difference between a despotic and a totalitarian secret police is that the latter does not hunt secret thoughts and does not use the old method of secret services, the method of provocation.[7]

Since the totalitarian secret police begins its career after the pacification of the

---

[6] This is supported by Hitler's statements during the war, quoted by Goebbels (*The Goebbels Diaries*, ed. Louis P. Lochner, 1948) to the effect that "the war had made possible for us the solution of a whole series of problems that could never have been solved in normal times," and that, no matter how the war turned out, "the Jews will certainly be the losers" (p. 314).

[7] Maurice Laporte, *Histoire de l'Okhrana*, Paris, 1935, rightly called the method of provocation "the foundation stone" of the secret police (p. 19).

In Soviet Russia, provocation, far from being the secret weapon of the secret police, has been used as the widely propagandized public method of the regime to gauge the temper of public opinion. The reluctance of the population to avail itself of the periodically recurring invitations to criticize or react to "liberal" interludes in the terror regime shows that such gestures are understood as provocation on a mass scale. Provocation has indeed become the totalitarian version of public opinion polls.

country, it always appears entirely superfluous to all outside observers—or, on the contrary, misleads them into thinking that there is some secret resistance.[8] The superfluousness of secret services is nothing new; they have always been haunted by the need to prove their usefulness and keep their jobs after their original task had been completed. The methods used for this purpose have made the study of the history of revolutions a rather difficult enterprise. It appears, for example, that there was not a single anti-government action under the reign of Louis Napoleon which had not been inspired by the police itself.[9] Similarly, the role of secret agents in all revolutionary parties in Czarist Russia strongly suggests that without their "inspiring" provocative actions the course of the Russian revolutionary movement would have been far less successful.[10] Provocation, in other words, helped as much to maintain the continuity of tradition as it did to disrupt time and again the organization of the revolution.

A PREMONITION OF TOTALITARIANISM

Then—this is all what you say—new economic relations will be established, all ready-made and worked out with mathematical exactitude, so that every possible question will vanish in the twinkling of an eye, simply because every possible answer to it will be provided. Then the "Palace of Crystal" will be built. Then . . . In fact, those will be halcyon days. Of course there is no guaranteeing (this is my comment) that it will not be, for instance, frightfully dull then (for what will one have to do when everything will be calculated and tabulated?), but on the other hand everything will be extraordinarily rational. Of course boredom may lead you to anything. It is boredom sets one sticking golden pins into people, but all that would not matter. What is bad (this is my comment again) is that I dare say people will be thankful for the gold pins then. Man is stupid, you know, phenomenally stupid; or rather he is not at all stupid, but

---

[8] Interesting in this respect are the attempts made by Nazi civil servants in Germany to reduce the competence and the personnel of the Gestapo on the ground that Nazification of the country had been achieved, so that Himmler, who on the contrary wanted to expand the secret services at this moment (around 1934), had to exaggerate the danger coming from the "internal enemies." See *Nazi Conspiracy*, II, 259; V, 205; III, 547.

[9] See Jean Gallier-Boissière, *Mysteries of the French Secret Police*, 1938, p. 234.

[10] It seems, after all, no accident that the foundation of the Okhrana in 1880 ushered in a period of unsurpassed revolutionary activities in Russia. In order to prove its usefulness, it had occasionally to organize murders, and its agents "served despite themselves the ideas of those whom they denounced. . . . If a pamphlet was distributed by a police agent or if the execution of a minister was organized by an Azev—the result was the same" (M. Laporte, *op. cit.*, p. 25). The more important executions moreover seem to have been police jobs—Stolypin and von Plehve. Decisive for the revolutionary tradition was the fact that in times of calm the police agents had to "stir up anew the energies and stimulate the zeal" of the revolutionaries (*ibid.*, p. 71).

See also Bertram D. Wolfe, *Three Who Made a Revolution: Lenin, Trotsky, Stalin*, 1948, who calls this phenomenon "Police Socialism."

he is so ungrateful that you could not find another like him in all creation. I, for instance, would not be in the least surprised if all of a sudden, apropos of nothing, in the midst of general prosperity a gentleman with an ignoble, or rather with a reactionary and ironical, countenance were to arise and putting his arms akimbo, say to us all: "I say, gentlemen, hadn't we better kick over the whole show and scatter rationalism to the winds, simply to send these logarithms to the devil, and to enable us to live once more at our own sweet foolish will!" That again would not matter; but what is annoying is that he would be sure to find followers—such is the nature of man. And all that for the most foolish reason, which, one would think, was hardly worth mentioning: that is, that man everywhere and at all times, whoever he may be, has preferred to act as he chose and not in the least as his reason and advantage dictated. And one may choose what is contrary to one's own interests, and sometimes one *positively ought* (that is my idea). One's own free unfettered choice, one's own caprice—however wild it may be, one's own fancy worked up at times to frenzy—is that very "most advantageous advantage" which we have overlooked, which comes under no classification and against which all systems and theories are continually being shattered to atoms. And how do these wiseacres know that man wants a normal, a virtuous choice? What has made them conceive that man must want a rationally advantageous choice? What man wants is simply *independent* choice, whatever that independence may cost and wherever it may lead. And choice, of course, the devil only knows what choice. . . .

Source: Fyodor Dostoyevsky, *Notes from Underground*, Constance Garnett, trans. (New York: Dell, 1960).

This dubious role of provocation might have been one reason why the totalitarian rulers discarded it. Provocation, moreover, is clearly necessary only on the assumption that suspicion is not sufficient for arrest and punishment. None of the totalitarian rulers, of course, ever dreamed of conditions in which he would have to resort to provocation in order to trap somebody he thought to be an enemy. More important than these technical considerations is the fact that totalitarianism defined its enemies ideologically before it seized power, so that categories of the "suspects" were not established through police information. Thus the Jews in Nazi Germany or the descendants of the former ruling classes in Soviet Russia were not really suspected of any hostile action; they had been declared "objective" enemies of the regime in accordance with its ideology.

The chief difference between the despotic and the totalitarian secret police lies in the difference between the "suspect" and the "objective enemy." The latter is defined by the policy of the government and not by his own desire to overthrow it.[11] He is never an individual whose dangerous thoughts must be provoked or whose past justifies suspicion, but a "carrier of tendencies" like the carrier of a disease.[12] Practically speaking, the totalitarian ruler proceeds like a man who persistently insults another man until everybody knows that the latter is his enemy, so that he can, with some plausibility, go and kill him in self-defense. This certainly is a little crude, but it works—as everybody will know who ever watched how certain successful careerists eliminate competitors.

The introduction of the notion of "objective enemy" is much more decisive for the functioning of totalitarian regimes than the ideological definition of the respective categories. If it were only a matter of hating Jews or bourgeois, the totalitarian regimes could, after the commission of one gigantic crime, return, as it were, to the rules of normal life and government. As we know, the opposite is the case. The category of objective enemies outlives the first ideologically determined foes of the movement; new objective enemies are discovered according to changing circumstances: the Nazis, foreseeing the completion of Jewish extermination, had already taken the necessary preliminary steps for the liquidation of the Polish people, while Hitler even planned the decimation of certain categories of Germans;[13] the Bolsheviks, having started with descendants of the former ruling classes, directed their full terror against the kulaks (in the early thirties), who in turn were followed by Russians of Polish origin (between

---

[11] Hans Frank, who later became Governor General of Poland, made a typical differentiation between a person "dangerous to the State" and a person who is "hostile to the State." The former implies an objective quality which is independent of will and behavior; the political police of the Nazis is concerned not just with actions hostile to the state but with "all attempts —no matter what their aim—which in their effects endanger the State." See *Deutsches Verwaltungsrecht*, pp. 420–430. Translation quoted from *Nazi Conspiracy*, IV, 881 ff.—In the words of Maunz, *op. cit.*, p. 44: "By eliminating dangerous persons, the security measure . . . means to ward off a state of danger to the national community, independently of any offense that may have been committed by these persons. [It is a question of] warding off an *objective* danger."

[12] R. Hoehn, a Nazi jurist and member of the SS, said in an obituary on Reinhard Heydrich, who prior to his rule of Czechoslovakia had been one of the closest collaborators with Himmler: He regarded his opponents "not as individuals but as carriers of tendencies endangering the state and therefore beyond the pale of the national community." In *Deutsche Allgemeine Zeitung* of June 6, 1942; quoted from E. Kohn-Bramstedt, *Dictatorship and Political Police* London, 1945.

[13] As early as 1941, during a staff meeting in Hitler's headquarters, it was proposed to impose upon the Polish population those regulations by which the Jews had been prepared for the extermination camps: change of names if these were of German origin; death sentences for sexual intercourse between Germans and Poles (*Rassenschande*); obligation to wear a P-sign in Germany similar to the Yellow Star for Jews. See *Nazi Conspiracy*, VIII, 237 ff., and Hans Frank's diary in *Trial, op. cit.*, XXIX, 683. Naturally, the Poles themselves soon began to worry about what would happen to them when the Nazis had finished the extermination of the Jews (*Nazi Conspiracy*, IV, 916). [Nor were the Germans themselves exempt.] Hitler contemplated during the war the introduction of a National Health Bill: "After national X-ray examination, the Fuehrer is to be given a list of sick persons, particularly those with lung and heart diseases. On the basis of the new Reich Health Law . . . these families will no longer be able to remain among the public and can no longer be allowed to produce children. What will happen to these families will be the subject of further orders of the Fuehrer." It does not need much imagination to guess what these further orders would have been. The number of people no longer allowed "to remain among the public" would have formed a considerable portion of the German population (*Nazi Conspiracy*, VI, 175).

1936 and 1938), the Tartars and the Vulga Germans during the war, former prisoners of war and units of the occupational forces of the Red Army after the war, and Russian Jewry after the establishment of a Jewish state. The choice of such categories is never entirely arbitrary; since they are publicized and used for propaganda purposes of the movement abroad, they must appear plausible as possible enemies; the choice of a particular category may even be due to certain propaganda needs of the movement at large—as for instance the sudden entirely unprecedented emergence of governmental antisemitism in the Soviet Union, which may be calculated to win sympathies for the Soviet Union in the European satellite countries. The show trials which require subjective confessions of guilt from "objectively" identified enemies are meant for these purposes; they can best be staged with those who have received a totalitarian indoctrination that enables them "subjectively" to understand their own "objective" harmfulness and to confess "for the sake of the cause."[14] The concept of the "objective opponent," whose identity changes according to the prevailing circumstances—so that, as soon as one category is liquidated, war may be declared on another—corresponds exactly to the factual situation reiterated time and again by totalitarian rulers: namely, that their regime is not a government in any traditional sense, but a *movement*, whose advance constantly meets with new obstacles that have to be eliminated. So far as one may speak at all of any legal thinking within the totalitarian system, the "objective opponent" is its central idea.

Closely connected with this transformation of the suspect into the objective enemy is the change of position of the secret police in the totalitarian state. The secret services have rightly been called a state within the state, and this not only in despotisms but also under constitutional or semiconstitutional governments. The mere possession of secret information has always given this branch a decisive superiority over all other branches of the civil services and constituted an open threat to members of the government.[15] The totalitarian police, on the contrary, is totally subject to the will of the Leader, who alone can decide who the next potential enemy will be and who, as Stalin did, can also single out cadres of the secret police for liquidation. Since the police are no longer permitted to use provocation, they have been deprived of the only available means of perpetuating themselves independently of the government and have become entirely dependent on the higher authorities for the safeguarding of their jobs.

---

[14] F. Beck and W. Godin, *Russian Purge and the Extraction of Confession* (1951), p. 87. Beck and Godin speak of the "objective characteristics" which invited arrest in the USSR; among them was membership in the NKVD (p. 153). Subjective insight into the objective necessity of arrest and confession could most easily be achieved with former members of the secret police. In the words of an ex-NKVD agent: "My superiors know me and my work well enough, and if the party and the NKVD now require me to confess to such things they must have good reasons for what they are doing. My duty as a loyal Soviet citizen is not to withhold the confession required of me" (*ibid.*, p. 231).

[15] Well known is the situation in France where ministers lived in constant fear of the secret "*dossiers*" of the police. For the situation in Czarist Russia, see Laporte, *op. cit.*, pp. 22.23: Eventually the Okhrana will wield a power far superior to the power of the more regular authorities. . . . The Okhrana will inform the Czar only of what it chooses to."

CONVERSATION IN A SOVIET FORCED LABOR CAMP

"Alyoshka," Shukhov said, . . . "I'm not against God, understand. I believe in God, all right. But what I don't believe in is Heaven and Hell. Who d'you think we are, giving us all that stuff about Heaven and Hell? That's the thing I can't take."

Shukhov lay back again and dropped the ash of his cigarette between the bunk and the window, careful so's not to burn the Captain's stuff. He was thinking his own thoughts and didn't hear Alyoshka any more, and he said out loud: "The thing is, you can pray as much as you like but they won't take anything off your sentence and you'll just have to sit it out, every day of it, from reveille to lights out."

"You mustn't pray for that." Alyoshka was horror-struck. "What d'you want your freedom for? What faith you have left will be choked in thorns. Rejoice that you are in prison. Here you can think of your soul. Paul the Apostle said: 'What mean you to weep and to break my heart? for I am ready not to be bound only, but also to die for the name of the Lord Jesus.'"

Shukhov looked up at the ceiling and said nothing. He didn't know any longer himself whether he wanted freedom or not. At first he'd wanted it very much and every day he added up how long he still had to go. But then he got fed up with this. And as time went on he understood that they might let you out but they never let you home. And he didn't really know where he'd be better off. At home or in here.

But they wouldn't let him home anyway. . . .

Alyoshka was talking the truth. You could tell by his voice and his eyes he was glad to be in prison.

"Look, Alyoshka," Shukhov said, "it's all right for you. It was Christ told you to come here, and you are here because of Him. But why am *I* here? Because they didn't get ready for the war like they should've in forty-one? Was that *my* fault?"

Source: Alexander Solzhenitsyn, *One Day in the Life of Ivan Denisovich*, Max Hayward and Ronald Hingley, trans. (New York: Frederick A. Praeger, 1963), pp. 205–206. Reprinted by permission.

Like the army in a nontotalitarian state, the police in totalitarian countries merely execute political policy and have lost all the prerogatives which they held under despotic bureaucracies.[16]

[16] "Unlike the Okhrana, which had been a state within a state, the GPU is a department of the Soviet government; . . . and its activities are much less independent" (Roger N. Baldwin, "Political Police," in *Encyclopedia of Social Sciences*).

The task of the totalitarian police is not to discover crimes, but to be on hand when the government decides to arrest a certain category of the population. Their chief political distinction is that they alone are in the confidence of the highest authority and know which political line will be enforced. This does not apply only to matters of high policy, such as the liquidation of a whole class or ethnic group (only the cadres of the GPU knew the actual goal of the Soviet government in the early thirties and only the SS formations knew that the Jews were to be exterminated in the early forties); the point about everyday life under totalitarian conditions is that only the agents of the NKVD in an industrial enterprise are informed of what Moscow wants when it orders, for instance, a speed-up in the fabrication of pipes—whether it simply wants more pipes, or to ruin the director of the factory, or to liquidate the whole management, or to abolish this particular factory, or, finally, to have this order repeated all over the nation so that a new purge can begin.

One of the reasons for the duplication of secret services whose agents are unknown to each other is that total domination needs the most extreme flexibility: to use our example, Moscow may not yet know, when it gives its order for pipes, whether it wants pipes—which are always needed—or a purge. Multiplication of secret services makes last-minute changes possible, so that one branch may be preparing to bestow the Order of Lenin on the director of the factory while another makes arrangements for his arrest. The efficiency of the police consists in the fact that such contradictory assignments can be prepared simultaneously.

Under totalitarian, as under other regimes, the secret police has a monopoly on certain vital information. But the kind of knowledge that can be possessed only by the police has undergone an important change: the police are no longer concerned with knowing what is going on in the heads of future victims (most of the time they ignore who these victims will be), and the police have become the trustees of the greatest state secrets. This automatically means a great improvement in prestige and position, even though it is accompanied by a definite loss of real power. The secret services no longer know anything that the Leader does not know better; in terms of power, they have sunk to the level of the executioner.

From a legal point of view, even more interesting than the change from the suspect to the objective enemy is the totalitarian replacement of the suspected offense by the possible crime. The possible crime is no more subjective than the objective enemy. While the suspect is arrested because he is thought to be capable of committing a crime that more or less fits his personality (or his suspected personality),[17] the totalitarian version of the possible crime is based

---

[17] Typical of the concept of the suspect is the following story related by C. Pobyedonostzev in *L'Autocratie Russe: Mémoires politiques, correspondance officiele et documents inédits . . . 1881–1894*, Paris, 1927: General Cherevin of the Okhrana is asked, because the opposing party has hired a Jewish lawyer, to intervene in favor of a lady who is about to lose a lawsuit. Says the General: "The same night I ordered the arrest of this cursed Jew and held him as a so-called politically suspect person. . . . After all, could I treat in the same manner friends and a dirty Jew who may be innocent today but who was guilty yesterday or will be guilty tomorrow?"

on the logical anticipation of objective developments. The Moscow Trials of the old Bolshevik guard and the chiefs of the Red Army were classic examples of punishment for possible crimes. Behind the fantastic, fabricated charges one can easily detect the following logical calculation: developments in the Soviet Union might lead to a crisis, a crisis might lead to the overthrow of Stalin's dictatorship, this might weaken the country's military force and possibly bring about a situation in which the new government would have to sign a truce or even conclude an alliance with Hitler. Whereupon Stalin proceeded to declare that a plot for the overthrow of the government and a conspiracy with Hitler existed.[18] Against these "objective," though entirely improbable, possibilities stood only "subjective" factors, such as the trustworthiness of the accused, their fatigue, their inability to understand what was going on, their firm conviction that without Stalin everything would be lost, their sincere hatred of Fascism—that is, a number of factual details which naturally lacked the consistency of the fictitious, logical, possible crime. Totalitarianism's central assumption that everything is possible thus leads through consistent elimination of all factual restraints to the absurd and terrible consequence that every crime the rulers can conceive of must be punished, regardless of whether or not it has been committed. The possible crime, like the objective enemy, is of course beyond the competence of the police, who can neither discover, invent, nor provoke it. Here again the secret services depend entirely upon the political authorities. Their independence as a state within the state is gone.

Only in one respect does the totalitarian secret police still resemble closely the secret services of nontotalitarian countries. The secret police has traditionally, *i.e.*, since Fouché, profited from its victims and has augmented the official state-authorized budget from certain unorthodox sources simply by assuming a position of partnership in activities it was supposed to suppress, such as gambling and prostitution.[19] These illegal methods of financing itself, ranging from friendly acceptance of bribes to outright blackmail, were a prominent factor in freeing the secret services from the public authorities and strengthened their position as a state within the state. It is curious to see that the

---

[18] The charges in the Moscow Trials "were based . . . on a grotesquely brutalized and distorting anticipation of possible developments. [Stalin's] reasoning probably developed along the following lines: they may want to overthrow me in a crisis—I shall charge them with having made the attempt. . . . A change of government may weaken Russia's fighting capacity; and if they succeed, they may be compelled to sign a truce with Hitler, and perhaps even agree to a cession of territory. . . . I shall accuse them of having entered already into a treacherous alliance with Germany and ceded Soviet territory." This is I. Deutscher's brilliant explanation of the Moscow Trials in *Stalin: A Political Biography* (New York and London, 1949), p. 377.

A good example of the Nazi version of the possible crime can be found in Hans Frank, *op. cit.*: "A complete catalogue of attempts 'dangerous to the State' can never be drawn up because it can never be foreseen what may endanger the leadership and the people some time in the future." (Translation quoted from *Nazi Conspiracy*, IV, 881.)

[19] The criminal methods of the secret police are of course no monopoly of the French tradition. In Austria, for example, the feared political police under Maria Theresa was organized by Kaunitz from the cadres of the so-called "chastity commissars" who used to live by blackmail. See Moritz Bermann, *Maria Theresa und Kaiser Joseph II*, Vienna-Leipzig, 1881. I owe this reference to Robert Pick.

financing of police activities with income from its victims has survived all other changes. In Soviet Russia, the NKVD is almost entirely dependent upon the exploitation of slave labor which, indeed, seems to yield no other profit and to serve no other purpose but the financing of the huge secret apparatus.[20] Himmler first financed his SS troops, who were the cadres of the Nazi secret police, through the confiscation of Jewish property; he then concluded an agreement with Darré, the Minister of Agriculture, by which Himmler received the several hundred million marks which Darré earned annually by buying agricultural commodities cheaply abroad and selling them at fixed prices in Germany.[21] This source of regular income disappeared of course during the war; Albert Speer, the successor of Todt and the greatest employer of manpower in Germany after 1942, proposed a similar deal to Himmler in 1942; if Himmler agreed to release from SS authority the imported slave laborers whose work had been remarkably inefficient, the Speer organization would give him a certain percentage of the profits for the SS.[22] To such more or less regular sources of income, Himmler added the old blackmail methods of secret services in times of financial crisis: in their communities SS units formed groups of "Friends of the SS" who had to "volunteer" the necessary funds for the needs of the local SS men.[23] (It is noteworthy that in its various financial operations the Nazi secret police did not exploit its prisoners. Except in the last years of the war, when the use of human material in the concentration camps was no longer determined by Himmler alone, work in the camps "had no rational purpose except that of increasing the burden and torture of the unfortunate prisoners."[24]

However, these financial irregularities are the sole, and not very important, traces of the secret police tradition. They are possible because of the general contempt of totalitarian regimes for economic and financial matters, so that methods which under normal conditions would be illegal, and would distinguish the secret police from other more respectable departments of the administration, no longer indicate that we are dealing here with a department which enjoys

[20] That the huge police organization is paid with profits from slave labor is certain; surprising is that the police budget seems not even entirely covered by it; Kravchenko (Victor Kravchenko, *I Chose Freedom* [New York, 1946]) mentions special taxes, imposed by the NKVD on convicted citizens who continue to live and work in freedom.

[21] See Fritz Thyssen, *I Paid Hitler* (London, 1941).

[22] See *Nazi Conspiracy*, I, 916–917.—The economic activity of the SS was consolidated in a central office for economic and administrative affairs. To the Treasury and Internal Revenue, the SS declared its financial assets as "party property earmarked for special purposes" (letter of May 5, 1943, quoted from M. Wolfson, *Uebersicht der Gliederung verbrecherischer Nazi-Organisationen. Omgus*, December, 1947).

[23] See Kohn-Bramstedt, *Dictatorship and Political Police* (London, 1945), p. 112. The blackmail motive is clearly revealed if we consider that this kind of fund-raising was always organized by local SS units in the localities where they were stationed. See *Der Weg der SS*, issued by the *SS-Hauptamt-Schulungsamt* (undated), p. 14.

[24] *Ibid.*, p. 124.—Certain compromises in this respect were made for those requirements pertaining to the maintenance of the camps and the personal needs of the SS. See Wolfson, *op. cit.*, letter of September 19, 1941, from Oswald Pohl, head of the WVH (*Wirtschafts-und Verwaltungs-Hauptamt*) to the Reichskommissar for price control. It seems that all these economic activities in the concentration camps developed only during the war and under the pressure of acute labor shortage.

independence, is not controlled by other authorities, lives in an atmosphere of irregularity, nonrespectability, and insecurity. The position of the totalitarian secret police, on the contrary, has been completely stabilized, and its services are wholly integrated in the administration. Not only is the organization *not* beyond the pale of the law, but, rather, it is the embodiment of the law, and its respectability is above suspicion. It no longer organizes murders on its own initiative, no longer provokes offenses against state and society, and it sternly proceeds against all forms of bribery, blackmail and irregular financial gains. The moral lecture, coupled with very tangible threats, that Himmler could permit himself to deliver to his men in the middle of the war—"We had the moral right . . . to wipe out this [Jewish] people bent on wiping us out, but we do not have the right to enrich ourselves in any manner whatsoever, be it by a fur coat, a watch, a single mark, or a cigarette"[25]—strikes a note that one would look for in vain in the history of the secret police. If it still is concerned with "dangerous thoughts," they are hardly ones which the suspected persons know to be dangerous; the regimentation of all intellectual and artistic life demands a constant re-establishment and revision of standards which naturally is accompanied by repeated eliminations of intellectuals whose "dangerous thoughts" usually consist in certain ideas that were still entirely orthodox the day before. While, therefore, its police function in the accepted meaning of the word has become superfluous, the economic function of the secret police, sometimes thought to have replaced the first, is even more dubious. It is undeniable, to be sure, that the NKVD periodically rounds up a percentage of the Soviet population and sends them into camps which are known under the flattering misnomer of forced-labor camps;[26] yet although it is quite possible that this is the Soviet Union's way of solving its unemployment problem, it is also generally known that the output in those camps is infinitely lower than that of ordinary Soviet labor and hardly suffices to pay the expenses of the police apparatus.

Neither dubious nor superfluous is the political function of the secret police, the "best organized and the most efficient" of all government departments,[27]

---

[25] Himmler's speech of October, 1943, at Posen, *International Military Trials*, Nuremberg, 1945–1946, Vol. 29, p. 146.

[26] "Bek Bulat (the pen name of a former Soviet professor) has been able to study documents of the North Caucasian NKVD. From these documents it was obvious that in June, 1937, when the great purge was at its apex, the government prescribed the local NKVDs to have a certain percentage of the population arrested. . . . The percentage varied from one province to the other, reaching 5 per cent in the least loyal areas. The average for the whole of the Soviet Union was about 3 per cent." Reported by David J. Dallin in *The New Leader*, January 8, 1949.—Beck and Godin, *op. cit.*, p. 239, arrive at a slightly divergent and quite plausible assumption, according to which "arrests were planned as follows: The NKVD files covered practically the whole population, and everyone was classified in a category. Thus statistics were available in every town showing how many former Whites, members of opposing parties, etc., were living in them. All incriminating material collected . . . and gathered from prisoners' confessions was also entered in the files, and each person's card was marked to show how dangerous he was considered; this depending on the amount of suspicious or incriminating material appearing in his file. As the statistics were regularly reported to higher authorities, it was possible to arrange a purge at any moment, with full knowledge of the exact number of persons in each category."

[27] Baldwin, *op. cit.*

in the power apparatus of the totalitarian regime. It constitutes the true executive branch of the government through which all orders are transmitted. Through the net of secret agents, the totalitarian ruler has created for himself a directly executive transmission belt which, in distinction to the onion-like structure of the ostensible hierarchy, is completely severed and isolated from all other institutions.[28] In this sense, the secret police agents are the only openly ruling class in totalitarian countries and their standards and scale of values permeate the entire texture of totalitarian society.

From this viewpoint, it may not be too surprising that certain peculiar qualities of the secret police are general qualities of totalitarian society rather than peculiarities of the totalitarian secret police. The category of the suspect thus embraces under totalitarian conditions the total population; every thought that deviates from the officially prescribed and permanently changing line is already suspect, no matter in which field of human activity it occurs. Simply because of their capacity to think, human beings are suspects by definition, and this suspicion cannot be diverted by exemplary behavior, for the human capacity to think is also a capacity to change one's mind. Since, moreover, it is impossible ever to know beyond doubt another man's heart—torture in this context is only the desperate and eternally futile attempt to achieve what cannot be achieved—suspicion can no longer be allayed if neither a community of values nor the predictabilities of self-interest exist as social (as distinguished from merely psychological) realities. Mutual suspicion, therefore, permeates all social relationships in totalitarian countries and creates an all-pervasive atmosphere even outside the special purview of the secret police. . . .

---

[28] The Russian secret-police cadres were as much at the "personal disposal" of Stalin as the SS Shock Troops (*Verfügungstruppen*) were at the personal disposal of Hitler. Both, even if they are called to serve with the military forces in time of war, live under their own special jurisdiction. The special "marriage laws" which served to segregate the SS from the rest of the population, were the first and most fundamental regulations which Himmler introduced when he took over the reorganization of the SS. Even prior to Himmler's marriage laws, in 1927, the SS was instructed by official decree "never [to participate] in discussions at membership meetings" (*Der Weg der SS, op. cit.*). The same conduct is reported about the members of the NKVD, who kept deliberately to themselves and above all did not associate with other sections of the party aristocracy (Beck and Godin, *op. cit.*, p. 163).

The Totalitarian State, II: "Thought Reform" in Communist China

ROBERT J. LIFTON

—

I had the opportunity to study this process ["thought reform"] in Hong Kong over a period of seventeen months, working with twenty-five Westerners who had been in Chinese prisons,[1] and with fifteen Chinese intellectuals who had undergone the type of process I am going to describe.

Although I could occasionally conduct interviews in English, where the subject had been exposed to a Westernized education (generally in mission-endowed institutions), I usually worked through interpreters. That set up a very complicated three-way communication system, which I won't discuss now. I found that it was very important to work with a subject over a long period of time, and the most meaningful data that I was able to obtain came through working with people for over a year. There is a very simple reason for this. It is a Chinese—and East Asian—cultural trait to say what one thinks the listener wants to hear, as a form of politeness and propriety. So I would first encounter many cliché anti-Communist statements; one could only get into the real areas of conflict when there developed a meaningful and trusting relationship, and when the subject could realize that I wanted to know about his true feelings.

Who attends a revolutionary college? Students are drawn from many divergent sources: former Nationalist officials and affiliates, teachers who had been associated with the old regime, Communist cadres who had demonstrated significant "errors" in their work or thoughts, party members who had spent long periods of time in Nationalist areas, students returning from the West, and finally, arbitrarily selected groups of university instructors or recent graduates. Many in these groups came in response to thinly veiled coercion—

Source: Robert J. Lifton, "Methods of Forceful Indoctrination: Psychiatric Aspects of Chinese Communist Thought Reform," in Maurice R. Stein, Arthur J. Vidich, and David Manning White (eds.), *Identity and Anxiety in Mass Society* (New York: Group for the Advancement of Psychiatry, Inc., 1960), pp. 480–492. Reprinted by permission.
[1] R. J. Lifton, "Thought Reform of Western Civilians in Chinese Communist Prisons," *Psychiatry,* XIX (1956), pp. 173–195. R. J. Lifton, "Chinese Communist Thought Reform: The Assault Upon Identity and Belief," presented before the American Psychiatric Association, May, 1956.

the strong "suggestion" that they attend; but others actively sought admission on a voluntary basis, in order to try to fit in with the requirements of the new regime, or at least to find out what was expected of them.

The college itself is tightly organized along Communist principles of "democratic centralism." One center may contain as many as 4,000 students, subdivided into sections of about 1,000 each, then into classes of 100 to 200 each, and finally into six- to ten-man groups. The president of the institution may be a well-known scholar serving as a figurehead; technically below him in rank are a vice-president and the section heads, who are likely to be Communist party members, and exert the real authority at the center. Under their supervision are the class-heads, each of whom works with three special cadres.

These cadres, usually long-standing and dedicated party workers, play a central role in the thought reform process: they are the connecting link between the faculty and the students, and it is they who perform the day-to-day leg work of the reform process. The three cadres of each class may be designated according to function: the executive cadre, concerned essentially with courses of study; the organizing cadre, most intimately involved with the structure and function of the small group and the attitudes of the individual students who make them up; and the advisory cadre—the only one of the three who may be a woman—offering counsel on personal and ideological "problems" which come up during this arduous experience.

I have divided the "thought reform" process into three stages, referring to the successive psychological climates which are created. These are my subdivisions, but I believe that they are very much in keeping with the Communist view of their own process: first, the Great Togetherness—the stage of Group Identification; second, the Closing in the Milieu—the stage of Emotional Conflict; and third, Submission and Rebirth—the Final Confession.

THE GREAT TOGETHERNESS—GROUP IDENTIFICATION

New students approach the course with a varying mixture of curiosity, enthusiasm, and apprehension. When a group of them arrives, their first impression is likely to be a favorable one. They encounter an atmosphere which is austere, but friendly—an open area of low-slung wooden buildings (frequently converted from military barracks) which serve as living quarters and class rooms—old students and cadres greeting them warmly, showing them around, speaking glowingly of the virtues of the revolutionary college, of the Communist movement, of the new hope for the future. Then, after a warm welcoming speech by the president of the college, they are organized into ten-man study groups. And for a period of from a few days to two weeks they are told to "just get to know each other."

Students are surprised by this free and enthusiastic atmosphere: some among the older ones may remain wary, but most are caught up in a feeling of camaraderie. Within the small groups they vent their widely shared hostility towards the old regime—an important stimulus to the thought reform process. There is a frank exchange of feeling and ideas, past and present, as they discuss their background experiences, and hopes and fears for the future. There is an air of optimism, a feeling of being in the same boat, a high *esprit de corps*.

Let me illustrate this with a few sentences quoted directly from one of my subjects:

> Everyone felt a bit strange at first, but we soon realized that we were all in the same position. We all began to talk freely and spontaneously; we introduced ourselves to each other, and talked about our past life and family background. . . . The Revolutionary College seemed to be a place which brought together young people from all over with a great deal in common. We ate, slept, and talked together, all of us eager to make new friends. I had very warm feelings towards the group, and towards the school. . . . I felt that I was being treated well in a very free atmosphere. I was happy and thought that I was on my way to a new life.

Next, through a series of "thought mobilization" lectures and discussions, the philosophy and rationale of the program are impressed upon the individual student: the "old society" was evil and corrupt; this was so because it was dominated by the "exploiting classes"—the landowners and the bourgeoisie; most intellectuals come from these "exploiting classes" (or from the closely related *petite bourgeoisie*) and therefore retain "evil remnants" of their origins and of the old regime; each must now rid himself of these "ideological poisons" in order to become a "new man" in the "new society." In this way, he is told, the "ideology of all classes" can be brought into harmony with the changing "objective material conditions."[2]

Also quoted invariably is a highly significant speech of Mao Tse-tung, the chairman of the Communist party in China:

> . . . our object in exposing errors and criticizing shortcomings is like that of a doctor in curing a disease. The entire purpose is to save the person, not to cure him to death. If a man has appendicitis, the doctor performs an operation and the man is saved. If a person who commits an error, no matter how great, does not bring his disease to an incurable state by concealing it and persisting in his error, and in addition if he is genuinely and honestly willing to be cured, willing to make corrections, we will welcome him so that his disease may be cured and he can become a good comrade. It is certainly not possible to solve the problem by one flurry of blows for the sake of a moment's satisfaction. We cannot adopt a brash attitude towards diseases of thought and politics, but must have an attitude of saving men by curing their diseases. This is the correct and effective method.[3]

This illustrates the tone with which thought reform is presented to the

---

[2] Ssu-Ch'i Ai, "On Problems of Ideological Reform," *Hsueh Hsi*, III (January 1, 1951).
[3] C. Brandt, B. Schwartz, and J. K. Fairbank, "Correcting Unorthodox Tendencies in Learning, the Party, and Literature and Art," in *A Documentary History of Chinese Communism* (1954), p. 392.

student. What we see as a coercive set of manipulations, they put forth as a *morally uplifting, harmonizing, and therapeutic experience.*

Then the formal courses begin—the first usually entitled the History of the Development of Society (to be later followed by Lenin—the State, Materialistic Dialectics, History of the Chinese Revolution. Theory of the New Democracy, and Field Study—visits to old Communist workshops and industrial centers). The subject matter is introduced by a two- to six-hour lecture delivered by a leading Communist theorist. This is followed by the interminable *hsueh hsi* or study sessions within the six- to ten-man group, where the real work of thought reform takes place. Discussion of the lecture material is led by the group leader who has been elected by its members—usually because of his superior knowledge of Marxism. At this point he encourages a spirited exchange of all views, and takes no side when there is a disagreement. The other students realize that the group leader is making daily reports to a cadre or to the class head, but the full significance of these is not yet appreciated; they may be viewed as simply a necessary organizational procedure. Most students retain a feeling of pulling together towards a common goal in a group crusading spirit.

THE CLOSING IN OF THE MILIEU—THE PERIOD OF EMOTIONAL CONFLICT

About four to six weeks from the beginning of thought reform—at about the time of the completion of the first course—a change begins to develop in the atmosphere. With the submission of the first "thought summary" (these must be prepared after each course) there is a shift in emphasis from the intellectual and ideological to the personal and the emotional. The student begins to find that he, rather than the Communist doctrine, is the object of study. A pattern of criticism, self-criticism, and confession develops—pursued with increasing intensity throughout the remainder of the course.

Now the group leader is no longer "neutral"; acting upon instructions from above, he begins to "lean to one side," to support the "progressive elements"; to apply stronger pressures in the direction of reform. He and the "activists" who begin to emerge, take the lead in setting the tone for the group. The descriptions of the past and the present attitudes which the student so freely gave during the first few weeks of the course now come back to haunt him. Not only his ideas, but his underlying motivations are carefully scrutinized. Failure to achieve the correct "materialistic viewpoint," "proletarian standpoint," and "dialectical methodology," is pointed out, and the causes for this deficiency are carefully analyzed.

Criticisms cover every phase of past and present thought and behavior; they not only "nip in the bud" the slightest show of unorthodoxy or nonconformity, but they also point up "false progressives"—students who outwardly express the "correct" views without true depth of feeling. Group members are constantly on the lookout for indications in others of lack of real emotional involvement in the process. Each must demonstrate the genuineness of his reform through continuous personal enthusiasm, and active participation in the criticism of fellow students. In this way he can avoid being rebuked for "failure to combine theory with practice."

Standard criticisms repeatedly driven home include: "individualism"—placing personal interests above those of "the people"—probably the most emphasized of all; "subjectivism"—applying a personal viewpoint to a problem rather than a "scientific" Marxist approach; "objectivism"—undue detachment, viewing oneself "above class distinction," or "posing as a spectator of the new China"; "sentimentalism"—allowing one's attachment to family or friends to interfere with reform needs, therefore "carrying about an ideological burden" (usually associated with reluctance to denounce family members or friends allegedly associated with the "exploiting classes"). And in addition: "deviationism," "opportunism," "dogmatism," "reflecting exploiting class ideology," "overly technical viewpoints," "bureaucratism," "individual heroism," "revisionism," "departmentalism," "sectarianism," "idealism," and "pro-American outlook."

The student is required to accept these criticisms gratefully when they are offered. But more than this, he is expected to both anticipate and expand upon them, through the even more important device of *self-criticism*. He must correctly analyze his own thoughts and actions, and review his past life—family, educational, and social—in order to uncover the source of his difficulties. And the resulting "insights" are always expressed within the Communist jargon—corrupt "ruling class" and "bourgeois" influences, derived from his specific class origin.

The criticism and self-criticism process is also extended into every aspect of daily life, always with a highly moralistic tone. Under attack here are the "bourgeois" or "ruling class" characteristics of pride, conceit, greed, competitiveness, dishonesty, boastfulness, and rudeness. Relationships with the opposite sex are discussed and evaluated solely in terms of their effects upon the individual's progress in reform. Where a "backward" girl friend is thought to be impeding his progress, a student may be advised to break off a liaison; but if both are "progressive," or if one is thought to be aiding the other's progress, the relationship will be condoned. Sexual contacts are, on the whole, discouraged, as it is felt that they drain energies from the thought-reform process.

The student must, within the small group, *confess* all of the "evils" of his past life. Political and moral considerations here become inextricably merged; especially emphasized are any "reactionary" affiliations with the old regime or with its student organizations. Each student develops a "running confession," supplemented by material from his self-criticisms and "thought summaries"; its content becomes widely known to students, cadres, and class heads, and it serves as a continuous indicator of his progress in reform.

Most are caught up in the universal confession compulsion which sweeps the environment: students vie to outdo each other in the frankness, completeness, and luridness of their individual confessions; one group challenges another to match its collective confessions; personal confession is the major topic of discussion at small group meetings, large student gatherings, informal talks with cadres, and in articles in wall newspapers. Everywhere one encounters the question: "Have you made your full confession?"

Confession tensions are brought to a head through a mass, pre-arranged, revival-like gathering where a student with a particularly evil past is given the opportunity to redeem himself. Before hundreds or even thousands, of fellow students, he presents a lurid description of his past sins: political work with the Nationalists, anti-Communist activities, stealing money from his company, violating his neighbor's daughter. He expresses relief at "washing away all of my sins," and gratitude towards the Government for allowing him to "become a new man."

As the months pass, "progressives" and "activists" take increasing leadership, aided by group manipulations by cadres and class heads. Where a group leader is not sufficiently effective, if his reports to the class head are not considered satisfactory, or where there is a general "lagging behind" in a particular group, a reshuffling of groups is engineered from above. The weak group becomes reinforced by the addition of one or two "activists," and the former group leader, in his new group, is reduced to the level of an ordinary student. Although group leaders may still be elected by students, these shifts can insure that this position is always held by one considered "progressive" and "reliable."

At the same time, "backward elements"—students with suspicious backgrounds, whose confessions are not considered thorough enough, who do not demonstrate adequate enthusiasm in reforming themselves and criticizing others, whose attitudes are found wanting—are singled out for further attention. Such a student becomes the target for relentless criticism in his group; and during odd hours he is approached by other students and cadres in attempts to persuade him to mend his ways. Should he fail to respond, friendliness gives way to veiled threats, and he may be called in to receive an official admonition from a class head. As a last resort, he may be subjected to the ultimate humility of a mass "struggle" meeting: in ritualistic form, he is publicly denounced by faculty members, cadres, and fellow students, his deficiencies reiterated and laid bare. It becomes quite clear that his future in Communist China is indeed precarious, and the ceremony serves as a grim warning for other students of questionable standing.

In response to all of these pressures, no student can avoid experiencing some degree of fear, anxiety, and conflict. Each is disturbed over what he may be hiding, worried about how he may come out of this ordeal. Some, recalling either stories they have heard or personal experiences, find revived in their minds images of the extreme measures used by the Communists in dealing with their enemies. All are extremely fearful of the consequences of being considered a "reactionary."

I can again illustrate this through the feelings expressed by another one of my subjects:

Towards the middle of the semester the intensity of my anti-Communist thoughts greatly increased. I developed a terrible fear that these thoughts would come out and be known to all, but I was determined to prevent this. I tried to appear calm but I was in great inner turmoil. I knew that if I kept quiet no one would know the secret which I had not confessed. But people were always talking about secrets. In small group meetings or large confession meetings, everyone would say that it was wrong to keep secrets, that one had to confess everything. Sometimes a cadre or a student would mention secrets during a casual talk, and I would feel very disturbed. Or at large meetings someone would get up and say, "There are still some students in the University who remain 'anti-organization.'" I knew that no one else was thinking specifically of me, but I couldn't help feeling very upset. The secret was always something that was trying to escape from me.

Students who show signs of emotional disturbance are encouraged to seek help by talking over their "thought problem" with the advisory cadre, in order to resolve whatever conflicts exist. Many experience psychosomatic expressions of their problems—fatigue, insomnia, loss of appetite, vague aches and pains, or gastrointestinal symptoms. Should they take their complaints to the college doctor, they are apt to encounter a reform-oriented and psychosomatically sophisticated reply: "There is nothing wrong with your body. It must be your thoughts that are sick. You will feel better when you have solved your problems and completed your reform." And indeed, most students are in a state of painful inner tension; relief is badly needed.

SUBMISSION AND "REBIRTH"—THE FINAL CONFESSION

The last stage—that of the over-all thought summary or final confession—supplies each student with a means of resolving his conflicts. It is ushered in by a mass meeting at which high Communist officials and faculty members emphasize the importance of the final thought summary as the crystallization of the entire course. Group sessions over the next two or three days are devoted exclusively to discussions of the form this summary is to take. It is to be a life history, beginning two generations back and extending through the reform experience. It must, with candor and thoroughness, describe the historical development of one's thoughts, and the relationships of these to actions. It is also to include a detailed analysis of the personal effects of thought reform.

The summary may be from five to twenty-five thousand Chinese characters (roughly equivalent numerically to English words) and require about ten days of preparation. Each student then must read his summary to the group, where he is subjected to more prolonged and penetrating criticism. He may be kept under fire for several days of detailed discussion and painful revision, as every group member is considered responsible for the approval of each confession presented, and all may even have to place their signature upon it.

The confession is the student's final opportunity to bring out anything he has previously held back, as well as to elaborate upon everything he has already said. It always includes a detailed analysis of class origin. And in almost every case, its central feature is the denunciation of the father, both as a symbol of the exploiting classes, and as an individual. The student usually finds the recitation of his father's personal, political, and economic abuses to be the most painful part of his entire thought reform. He may require endless prodding, persuasion, and indirect threats before he is able to take this crucial step. But he has little choice and he almost invariably complies.

The confession ends with an emphasis of personal liabilities which still remain, attitudes in need of further reform, and the solemn resolve to continue attempts at self-improvement and to serve the regime devotedly in the future. When his confession is approved, the student experiences great emotional relief. He has weathered the thought reform ordeal, renounced his past, and established an organic bond between himself and the Government. His confession will accompany him throughout his future career as a permanent part of his personal record. It is his symbolic submission to the regime, and at the same time his expression of individual rebirth into the Chinese Communist community. . . .

CHAPTER 2

MASS TERROR

Daily Routine in Buchenwald

EUGEN KOGON

———

The camp was awakened by whistles, in the summer between four and five o'clock, in the winter between six and seven o'clock. Half an hour was allotted to washing, dressing, breakfasting and bed-making, sometimes an impossible job within that period.

A number of camps insisted on morning calisthenics, performed winter and summer at break-neck pace for half an hour before the regular rising time. They consisted mostly of everlasting push-ups in the snow and muck. Because of numerous fatal cases of pneumonia, this practice never persisted for very long.

Breakfast consisted of a piece of bread from the ration issued for the day and a pint of thin soup or so-called "coffee," without either milk or sugar. The bread ration was issued at different times to different barracks. Those who had got it at night and had immediately eaten it up had no bread for breakfast.

Next came morning roll call. On a signal the prisoners from each barracks fell in on the camp street and marched eight abreast to the roll-call area. Thousands of zebra-striped figures of misery, marching under the glare of the floodlights in the haze of dawn, column after column—no one who has ever witnessed it is likely to forget the sight.

Each barracks had its own assigned place in the roll-call area. The entire strength of the camp was counted, and this roll call usually took an hour, until it was light enough to start work. Morning roll call was not as important as its evening counterpart, still to be discussed, for little change was likely to take place overnight—deaths during the night were reported ahead of time from the prisoner hospital. After roll call came a thunderous command from the Roll Call Officer over the public-address system, addressed to the army of shorn men: "Caps off!" and "Caps on!" This was the morning salute for the Officer-in-Charge. If it was not executed smartly enough, it had to be repeated again

Source: Reprinted from *The Theory and Practice of Hell* by Eugen Kogon, by permission of Farrar, Straus & Company, Inc. Published in 1950 by Farrar, Straus & Company, Inc. Also reprinted by permission of Martin Secker & Warburg Limited, London.

and again, to the accompaniment of such comment as this: "You god-damned ass-holes, if you're too lazy to ventilate your filthy pates, I'll make you practice till the juice boils in your tails, you sons of bitches!"

Now came the dreaded call: "Prisoners under orders to the gatehouse!" It affected all those who had received a slip from the Orderly Room the night before. In Buchenwald six numbered signs were mounted at the wall of the left wing of the gatehouse. There the prisoners had to await the nameless terror about to engulf them. When they had painfully come to learn which number meant a summons before the Political Department, and which indicated more harmless matters—records, signatures, notarizations, etc,—the assignment of the numbers would be suddenly changed. The prisoners often had to wait for hours, haunted by uncertainty. If their families had only known the fear they could engender by routine inquiries and business matters! It was impossible to evade such a summons, and the waiting prisoners were at the mercy of the SS men who always loitered near the gatehouse.

Often prisoners so summoned were not given notice the night before at all. Their numbers were simply called out at the end of morning roll call and they were ordered to report to such-and-such a sign. I can state from personal experience that such an unexpected announcement of one's number was like a stab in the heart, regardless of what was involved.

The next command was "Labor details—fall in!" There was a wild milling about, as the prisoners moved to their assigned assembly points with all possible speed. The camp band, in the winter-time scarcely able to move its fingers, played merry tunes as the columns moved out five abreast. At the gatehouse caps had to be snatched off again, hands placed at the trouser seams. The details then marched off in double time, the prisoners compelled to sing.

Work continued until late afternoon, with half an hour for lunch, out in the open. For a long time the prisoners were not permitted to carry bread with them. Under an alternate plan, the details marched back into camp at noon, for half an hour or three-quarters, to bolt down their lunch. This hot meal, the only one all day, generally consisted of a single dish—a quart of soup or broth often very thin and devoid of nourishment. The work schedule differed from camp to camp, but by and large it followed the schemes here described.

In the winter work ended around five o'clock, in the summer, around eight— between March and November the time was periodically shifted by half-hour intervals. At the conclusion of the work day the prisoners were marched back to camp, past the band, again ordered to play sprightly tunes. Then came evening roll call.

In every camp this head count was the terror of the prisoners. After a hard day's work, when ordinary men look forward to well-deserved rest, they had to stand in ranks for hours on end, regardless of rain or storm or icy cold, until the SS had tallied its slaves and established that none had escaped during the day. The preliminary work for these roll calls often had to be done by prisoner clerks, since few SS men were capable of making an accurate tabulation. The prisoners always endeavored to avoid the slightest error, especially in counting the numerous inmates on "permanent detail," whose work brooked no interruption and who therefore never appeared in line, though they were, of course, counted. Any slip, even though not a man was missing, was likely to result in hours of checking and delay, depriving the exhausted prisoners of the last shreds of leisure. So long as the number of prisoners to be accounted for did not exceed 5,000 to 7,000, any absence was quickly noted. It was a different matter when the number swelled to 20,000, to say nothing of 50,000. A great many non-German inmates looked on this roll call as just another form of Prussian drill, to be evaded whenever possible. On many occasions a shirker would simply sleep away roll call in some hiding place, while tens of thousands of his fellows stood in stupor and agony until the culprit was found. (His would be an unenviable lot—no one took pity on him!) If a single prisoner was absent, hundreds of names and numbers from various barracks had to be called out— Polish names, Russian names, French names that could be pronounced only with the aid of interpreters. The SS men would lose their tempers, bellow, and let their fists and boots fly. Few roll calls took less than an hour and a half.

Whenever a prisoner actually escaped, the whole camp was kept on its feet until he was recaptured, often a matter of many hours. Guards were kept posted around the entire camp area during roll call, to insure that no prisoner could lurk about the headquarters area. The search within this guard line was

PENAL LABOR

The idea has occurred to me that if one wanted to crush, to annihilate a man utterly, to inflict on him the most terrible of punishments so that the most ferocious murderer would shudder at it and dread it beforehand, one need only give him work of an absolutely, completely useless and irrational character. . . . [If the convict laborer] had to pour water from one vessel into another and back, over and over again, to pound sand, to move a heap of earth from one place to another and back again—I believe the convict would hang himself in a few days or would commit a thousand crimes, preferring rather to die than endure such humiliation, shame, and torture. Of course such a punishment would become a torture, a form of vengeance, and would be senseless, as it would achieve no rational object. But as something of such torture, senseless humiliation, and shame is an inevitable element in all forced labour, penal labour is incomparably more painful than any free labour—just because it is forced.

Source: Fyodor Dostoyevsky, *The House of the Dead,* Constance Garnett, trans. (New York: Dell, 1959), pp. 48–49.

the job of the Senior Block Inmates, the Barracks Orderlies, the Prisoner Foremen and the Camp Police. Successful escapes drew such savage punishment upon the entire camp, especially in the early years, that the political prisoners renounced even the attempt until the final months. Then a few escapes, undertaken with the approval of the underground leadership, proved necessary in order to establish contact with the approaching Allies.

During evening roll call on December 14, 1938, two convicts turned up missing at Buchenwald. The temperature was 5° above zero and the prisoners were thinly clad—but they had to stand in the roll-call area for nineteen hours. Twenty-five had frozen to death by morning; by noon the number had risen to more than seventy.

During the fall of 1939 there was another occasion when the entire camp was kept standing for eighteen hours on end, because two convicts had hidden in the pigsty. Oh, it is easy enough to write about now—standing like that, after a full day's work, throughout the night and until next noon, without food! The cold death figures can be set down—but not the permanent damage suffered by hundreds who later perished of the after effects. What a relief when the war in the air forced even the SS to black out, when the floodlights could no longer be turned on! From that time onward, roll call simply had to be called off after a certain period, whether there were any absences or not. In the complete blackout the SS would have lost control of the camp, would have had good reason for fear in its own ranks.

From time to time the Block Leaders were ordered to "frisk" the inmates during roll call. Pockets had to be emptied and the contents were examined by the SS, a process during which as a rule much money and tobacco simply disappeared. One Sunday in February (!) 1938, the prisoners were compelled to stand stripped to the skin for three hours on such an occasion. The wife of Commandant Koch, in company with the wives of four other SS officers, came to the wire fence to gloat at the sight of the naked figures.

Roll call was a time for many special tortures. Often, following the head count, the command would be heard, "All Jews, remain behind"—to sing over and over again deep into the night the vile jingles known as the "Jew song":

> For years we wreaked deceit upon the nation,
> No fraud too great for us, no scheme too dark.
> All that we did was cheat and lie and swindle,
> Whether with dollar or with pound or mark.

It ended with the following verses:

> But now at last the Germans know our nature
> And barbed wire hides us safely out of sight.
> Traducers of the people, we were fearful
> To face the truth that felled us overnight.

And now, with mournful crooked Jewish noses,
We find that hate and discord were in vain.
An end to thievery, to food aplenty.
Too late, we say, again and yet again.

This choice product of Nazi culture was the work of one of the "asocials" who sought to insinuate himself into the favor of the SS. Rödl, a man who could hardly be described as very discriminating, had the Jews sing it twice and then even he had enough. He forbade it. It was Officers-in-Charge Florstedt and Plaul, vicious anti-Semites, who restored it to Nazi honors. An especially popular procedure for entertaining visitors to the camps was to have the Jews line up in the roll-call area to the left of the tower and sing the vile tune.

Everyone had to appear for roll call, whether alive or dead, whether shaken by fever or beaten to a bloody pulp. The only exceptions were inmates on permanent details, and those in the prisoner hospital. The bodies of men who had died during the day, either in the barracks or at work, had to be dragged to the roll-call area. During particularly virulent sieges, there were always dozens of dying and dead laid in neat "rank and file" beyond the block formations, to answer the final roll call. For the SS exacted order and discipline down to the last breath. Not until after roll call could the dying be taken to the hospital, the dead to the morgue.

Once evening roll call was over, with the commands of "Caps off!" and "Caps on!" there usually followed another command: "Left face!"—and the public punishments, yet to be discussed in a separate chapter, were meted out.

FROM THE PREFACE TO *UNDER TWO DICTATORS*

From 1935 to 1937 . . . [my husband and I] both worked in Moscow as translators. During those two years we were already political outcasts and really prisoners in all but name. Our every movement was watched and everything we said in public was noted. In April, 1937, he was finally arrested by the N.K.V.D., the Soviet Secret Police, now the M.V.D., but better known as the G.P.U., by which initials I propose to refer to it. In June, 1938, my turn came. In 1940, after imprisonment in Moscow and in a Soviet concentration camp in Siberia, I was handed over to the German Gestapo during the period of the Russo-German friendship pact. I then spent five further years in the notorious German concentration camp at Ravensbrueck.

This book is the plain story of my experiences at the hands of both Russian and German secret police. . . .

Source: Margarete Buber, *Under Two Dictators*, Edward Fitzgerald, trans. (New York: Dodd, 1949), pp. xi, xii.

Or one of the Officers-in-Charge might call for a song. It might be raining or storming. The prisoners might scarcely be able to keep to their feet. All the more reason for exacting a song, as much as possible at odds with the situation— once, three times, five times in succession—"I saw a little bird flying," or "Something stirs in the forest." Most of the camps had songs of their own, written and composed by prisoners, on command. Some of these have become widely known, notably "The Peat-Bog Soldiers" and "The Buchenwald Song."

It might have been thought that once the final "Fall out!" had sounded the day's torments were over and the prisoners could sit down to eat and rest at leisure. But often they returned to the barracks, only to be confronted by the results of the inspection conducted during the day by the Block Leaders— lockers overturned, their contents scattered in every direction. The search for one's mess kit often led to savage clashes among the prisoners, driven beyond the limits of human endurance.

When the prisoners worked through the day, the main meal was issued at night. Of course it was cold by the time a protracted roll call was completed. The remaining ration, when issued at night, consisted of bread, a dab of margarine, and a bit of sausage or possibly a spoonful of cottage cheese. At any moment during "dinner" the Barracks Orderly might suddenly sing out: "Attention! B-wing of Barrack X reporting! One hundred and thirty-five prisoners at mess!" Some SS sergeant had conceived the notion to pay a visit. Not yet through the door, he would bellow: "Get under the tables, you swine!" Benches would be overturned, mess gear clatter to the floor. Still, there were always a few left over who, try as they might, could not find room under the tables and became the particular whipping boys. There were many variations on this tune. A Block Leader might simply order a barracks cleared during the meal, having the prisoners execute some senseless command, such as standing on their heads in the snow. To execute a headstand is not the easiest thing, even for a youngster. But even the aged and decrepit had to do it as a matter of course, just as they might have to double-time endlessly round the barracks. Any hesitation drew kicks and beatings. Even when nothing whatever happened in the barracks after roll call, the prisoners were obsessed by the fear that lightning might strike at any moment.

If roll call had been concluded with reasonable dispatch, work had to be continued for several hours deep into the night by certain prisoner groups. The rest might stroll about the camp streets, in front of the barracks, in the washrooms or toilets—unless they preferred to retire immediately. When taps sounded—between eight and ten o'clock, according to season—everyone except those on detail had to be indoors, half an hour later in bed.

Prisoners were permitted to wear only their shirts while sleeping, even in the deep of winter, when the barracks grew bitter cold and the damp stone walls often coated with ice at the windows and corners. Block Leaders frequently conducted night inspections, ordering all the inmates in a barracks to line up beside the beds or even outdoors, in order to catch those who might be wearing an additional garment. Whoever was found in socks or underwear could expect merciless punishment. On occasion an entire barracks was chased around the block for as much as an hour, barefoot and dressed only in shirts.

These nocturnal invasions did not occur regularly. They came from time to time, at irregular intervals, unexpectedly, generally when the Block Leaders were drunk. But they *could* happen at any moment. The threat was ever-present. Mercifully, the prisoners were far too exhausted to brood on the danger. For a few short hours each night sleep spread its balm over the misery. Only the aged, the fretful, the sick, the sleepless, lay awake in a torment of worry, awaiting the ordeal of another day.

Prisoner Behavior and Social System in the Nazi Concentration Camps

ELMER LUCHTERHAND

■■■

ABSTRACT

Until recently, American theory and discussion on prisoner behavior in the Nazi concentration camps differed in important ways from most European work. The American peculiarities stem from two main sources. First, there were gross reporting errors which added to the common difficulties in making sense of the camp system and genocide. Second, before the end of World War II and after, there was quick publication of poorly-grounded theories, reflecting concern with narrowly psychodynamic processes, rather than social processes.

The present paper reviews study findings on the importance of human groups in the struggle for survival. Particular attention is given to the emergence of a prisoner social system and to the normative aspects of such a system. Along with references to the relevant work of others, the author deals at some length with his own early research, involving intensive interviews with fifty-two camp survivors who emigrated to the United States. In that study, data were gathered on

Source: Elmer Luchterhand, "Prisoner Behavior and Social System in the Nazi Concentration Camps," *International Journal of Social Psychiatry*, Vol. 13, No. 4 (Fall 1964). Reprinted by permission.

changes with time in the camps in (1) patterns of interpersonal relations, (2) sharing with other prisoners and assisting them, and (3) thefts from other prisoners.

The paper considers several propositions on human behavior in extreme situations. These include the proposition by Bruno Bettelheim that the longer prisoners were confined, the more they identified with the SS; that "a prisoner had reached the final stage of adjustment to the camp situation when he had changed his personality so as to accept as his own the values" of his captors.

The paper summarizes the author's findings on prisoner behavior in especially extreme situations such as prolonged punishment assemblies and wintertime transports of Auschwitz evacuees; on the attitudes of respondents toward "old" prisoners and toward members of prisoner underground organizations; and on the length of imprisonment of members of various national and international camp committees.

Evidence is offered which suggests that "stable" pairing was the most common type of interpersonal relationship pattern and that most survivors had a sharing relationship of mutuality with one or more persons; that the pair was the basic unit of survival.

Respondents showing decline in sharing behavior were in the camps substantially less time than those showing "no change." Those respondents who showed greater and more stable general social participation were in the camps considerably longer than those whose participation declined. Respondents showing decline in thefts (taking from other prisoners only) or consideration of theft, were in the camps longer than those showing increasing theft behavior.

The study findings offered conflict at many points with narrowly psycho-dynamic interpretations of prison behavior. It is concluded that in the camps the human group and social system emerge as the most fruitful foci for scientific analysis.

INTRODUCTION

This paper is concerned with prisoner behavior and survival in the Nazi camps, and the ways in which human groups affected survival chances. Theodore Abel states that "all of the special topics of the sociology of the concentration camp system can be focused upon one basic issue, . . . the problem of survival. . . . The material abundantly shows that only in rare instances was survival a purely individual achievement. In most cases, survival was due to the operation of social factors. . . ."[1] It is a sociological truism, as Abel notes, that ". . . society is a means of survival for the individuals in whom it is manifest. . . ."[2] Some limited evidence will be adduced of the importance of human groups for

---

[1] Abel, Theodore: "The Sociology of Concentration Camps." A paper prepared for the Netherlands State Institute for War Documentation, Amsterdam, 1950 (mimeographed), p. 3.
[2] *Loc. cit.*

survival chances, and of the emergence of a prisoner social system in the face of the most awesome deterrents.

The extensive literature on the Nazi concentration camps consists largely of personal accounts of survivors. Among these are a few which are organized around some kind of conceptual framework from medicine, psychiatry, politics and, in several instances, the social sciences. With the deepest respect for the richness and worth of these accounts, only a few of the writers were so situated that it was at all possible to penetrate deeply the social and psychological complexities of the horror that engulfed them. Among these few are Eugen Kogon,[3] David Rousset,[4] Benedikt Kautsky,[5] Elie A. Cohen,[6] and also Bruno Bettelheim.[7] In recent years, works by non-prisoner scholars have begun to appear.[8] Among these, the historical study by Raul Hilberg[9] stands as a model of painstaking research. His analysis of the destructive procedures instituted by the Nazi regime, and the role of bureaucracy in genocide, seems nowhere to be excelled, and removes some major obstacles to historical interpretation of the Third Reich itself.

The peculiarities of the camp system for its survivors, and the strangeness, the seeming incomprehensibility of camp phenomena to the rest of the population are major obstacles to the post-camp adjustments of the survivors and to the development of effective help for them. In recent years various writings have appeared, which reduce somewhat this strangeness by showing the continuities between camp and non-camp society in the modern world. Among these might be mentioned the autobiography of Rudolf Hoess, commandant of Auschwitz.[10] Here one meets the insensitive, loyal, Nazi bureaucrat, busy with his genocidal work. The second is a long essay by the American sociologist, Erving Goffman,[11]

---

[3] Kogon, Eugen: *Der SS-Staat. Berlin*: Verlag des Druckhauses Tempelhof, 1947. This work has been translated into English under the title *The Theory and Practice of Hell*. New York: Farrar, Straus & Co. (date omitted from publication).

[4] Rousset, David: *The Other Kingdom*. New York: Reynal and Hitchcock, 1947, translated from the French by Ramon Guthrie. Also see the novel by Rousset: *Les Jours de Notre Mort*. Paris: Editions du Pavois, 1947.

[5] Kautsky, Benedikt: *Teufel und Verdammte*, Zürich: Büchergilde Gutenberg, 1946.

[6] Cohen, Elie A.: *Human Behavior in the Concentration Camps*. New York: W. W. Norton, 1953.

[7] Bettelheim, Bruno: "Individual and mass behavior in extreme situations." *Journal of Abnormal and Social Psychology*, 38, 417–452. Also see the revised and shortened version of this article in Newcomb, T. M., Hartley, E. L. and others (eds.), *Readings in Social Psychology*. New York: Henry Holt, 1947, and in succeeding editions of the *Readings* . . . Other writings of Bettelheim include "Concentration Camps, German," in *Ten Eventful Years*. Chicago: Encyclopedia Britannica, 1947 Vol. 2; *The Informed Heart*. Glencoe, Ill.: The Free Press, 1960.

[8] Of special interest is the monograph by Eberhard Kolb, *Bergen-Belsen*. Hannover: Verlag für Literatur and Zeitgeschehen, G.m.b.H., 1962. The comprehensive bibliography by Jacob Robinson and Philip Friedman, *Guide to Jewish History under Nazi Impact*. New York: Yivo Institute for Jewish Research, 1960, includes recent long studies by a number of non-prisoner scholars in Europe.

[9] Hilberg, Raul: *The Destruction of the European Jews*. Chicago: Quadrangle Books, 1961.

[10] Hoess, Rudolf: *Commandant of Auschwitz*. New York: The World Publishing Co., 1960.

[11] Goffman, Erving: *Asylums*. Garden City: Doubleday, 1961. Since this paper was presented, Peter Weiss' play, *The Investigation* has been performed in many countries and has further reduced the strangeness of the camp system by suggesting various continuities between camp and non-camp society.

relating the Nazi camp system to other varieties of total institutions in modern society.

Until recently, American theory and discussion on the camps differed in important ways from most European work. The American peculiarities stemmed from two main sources which have been mentioned elsewhere. *First,* gross reporting errors were added to the common ". . . difficulty of making sense of the strange world of the camps. *Second,* at the war's end there was quick publication of poorly grounded theories. *Third,* and this is a point made by the sociologist, Paul Foreman[12] in . . . 1959, 'early American discussions are conforming and tend to seal off major sociological interests.'"[13]

Here extended consideration is given to various propositions by Bettelheim. In one of the earliest systematic treatments of behavior in the camps,[14] he claims that the longer prisoners remained in the camps the more they identified with the Gestapo, that "old" prisoners, as distinct from new ones (i.e., prisoners confined three or more years as against those confined one year or less), tended to identify with the SS. It is maintained that this adjustment was accomplished in a series of stages.[15]

In more recent work Bettelheim reaffirms his earlier propositions and dismisses consideration of prisoner behavior in the extermination camps as "offering less of psychological interest"[16] than behavior in other camps. In this work he ignores completely the literature on prisoner behavior during the last years of the camp system—a period when underground organizations, including the formation of small, national and international camp committees, developed in most of the base camps and some of their older affiliates.

Formal Organization and Survival

It is important to recognize that survival is not a unitary concept. There is psychological survival, but which ends in death due to physical breakdown. There is physical survival, for a limited time, accompanied by more or less severe "mental disorder." The distinction has some merit, even though death was the common outcome of both. Jackman,[17] basing himself solely on prisoner accounts, is concerned with the factor of group identification in survival and

---

[12] Foreman, Paul B.: "Buchenwald and modern prisoner-of-war detention policy." *Social Forces,* 37, 4, 289.

[13] Luchterhand, Elmer: "Survival in the concentration camp: an individual or a group phenomenon?" in Bernard Rosenberg, Israel Gerver and F. William Howton (eds.), *Mass Society in Crisis.* New York: The Macmillan Co., 1964, p. 223. That brief paper includes critical comments on an article by Herbert A. Bloch, "The Personality of Inmates of Concentration Camps." *American Journal of Sociology,* 52, 4. Bloch interviewed survivors at several locations shortly after liberation. On the basis of his knowledge of prison life, Bloch characterized the camps as "modern feral communities."

[14] Bettelheim: The work cited first in ref. 7.

[15] *Ibid.,* p. 420 and *passim.*

[16] Bettelheim: *The Informed Heart.* Glencoe, Ill.: The Free Press, 1960, p. 248.

[17] Jackman, Norman R.: "Survival in the concentration camp," in *Human Organization,* Summer 1958, 17, 2, 23.

specifically with the relevance of reference group theory. He notes the importance of large political and religious membership and reference groups, and poses the following questions:

1. Was the individual's reference group present or absent for the camp?
2. If the individual's reference group was outside of the camp how closely integrated was that group?[18]

Jackman says that the answers to these two questions indicate respectively, the probabilities (1) of physical and psychological survival and (2) of "psychological survival until death."[19] He explains the relative durability of left politicals as due to the presence in the camp of their reference group. He explains the relative psychological durability of the Jehovah's Witnesses—until death—by the existence of a closely integrated reference group outside the camps. The fact is, however, that the reference groups of both the Jehovah's Witnesses and the left politicals were substantially inside. The Nazis could not stand it otherwise. The point has been well documented by Bettelheim[20] and others that the regime started the camp system by incarcerating its avowed political enemies. While doctrinally the Witnesses were apolitical, by their behavior they also challenged the Nazi power.

Although Jackman's speculations thus run into difficulties, they are none the less interesting. Unlike the Witnesses, the most implacable of the left politicals were equipped with tactical and combative skills specific for coping with the SS; their presence was more observable than that of the Witnesses because it had campwide social effects. There is also the further point that the left politicals were not visibly distinguishable, within the ideologically heterogeneous population of "politicals," since all of them wore similar identifying red triangles, despite their different reference groups. This fact provided strategic opportunities and protection for the left politicals, and probably led to some changes in prisoners' reference groups in ways that improved survival chances.

A Research Approach to Prisoner Social System

Further speculations about large formal groups and reference group theory would lead away from the central purpose of this paper. (Something will be said later about the "old" prisoners as reference individuals for new ones.) Here the concern is with evidence relative to the emergence of a prisoner social system, and with the normative aspects of such a system.[21] The terror within the camp

---

[18] *Ibid.*, p. 25.
[19] *Loc. cit.*
[20] Bettelheim, Bruno: "Concentration camps, German," in *Ten Eventful Years*. Chicago: Encyclopedia Britannica, 1947, Vol. 2.
[21] Prisoner norms are treated here as integral parts of the prisoner social system, whatever its state of development in one or another camp. To deal with religious behavior, sharing, "organizing" (camp language for taking or getting things by sharp practice from anyone but a prisoner) and stealing (taking from another prisoner) apart from the social system is to invite misunderstanding. In simplest terms, the concept of social system includes the notions of role, status, authority, rights, objectives, norms and territory.

system makes it critically important to examine relationships within small groups and pairs. These relationships also provide the testing ground for interpretations of behavior which emphasize social system, as against those in which the emphasis is more narrowly psychodynamic. The central hypothesis of the research reported here arises out of such conflicting interpretations. This hypothesis may be stated in general terms as follows: The new and "old" types of Nazi concentration camp prisoners advanced by Bruno Bettelheim, and his stage theory of prisoner adjustment, fail to fit the behavior of a considerable part of the prisoner population.

Two other hypotheses are offered: (1) Different types of camp situations produced widely different predominant effects. With regard to interpersonal relations, these effects varied from violent conflict to cooperation, and with regard to the prisoner social system, from extreme destructiveness to constructiveness. (2) The leadership of underground prisoner organizations consisted primarily of "old" and "very old" prisoners, contrary to what would be predicted from the Bettelheim propositions.

Bettelheim does not deal explicitly with the prisoner social system, as a system. Unlike Kogon, he makes only brief reference to the workings of camp organization, and to prisoner organization within it. The implications of his position, however, are quite clear. The effects of camp administration were such that no countervailing set of social influences had any significant effect on the drift of prisoners, with time, into utter moral degradation, i.e., into identification with the SS. He writes *as though* no prisoner social system existed or could exist.

Even such an acute observer as Cohen, while taking a stand which is far removed from that of Bettelheim, concludes his chapter on the "Psychology of the Prisoner" by saying that ". . . the prisoner's behavior cannot but be individual. . . ."[22] He then amends this by a reference to ethnic allegiance, and to ties based on common experiences.[23] It must be said, however, that Cohen, writing in 1952, generally provides strong support for the position of Kogon, Rousset and Kautsky, who wrote in the late forties, and who still stand among the major contributors to understanding of the social processes in the camps. The bulk of the research findings to be presented here were obtained at the time Cohen wrote, and are being examined here in the light of other studies of camp phenomena.

It was manifestly impossible to get a probability sample, either of the universe of prisoners (the vast majority were killed), or of the universe of survivors (the social disruption after the war made this impossible). Given a set of virtually unqualified generalizations, such as Bettelheim's, one feasible research approach was to apply them to a purposively selected population of camp veterans and see how well they might stand up.

---

[22] Cohen, Elie A.: *op. cit.*, p. 210.
[23] *Loc. cit.*

The Sample

The names of camp veterans were obtained with help from two sources: (1) newly formed survivor groups, and (2) health and social work professionals having extensive contact with camp survivors. The undertaking of a comprehen-

INDIVIDUAL SURVIVAL IN AN EXTREME SITUATION

The author spent approximately one year in the two biggest German concentration camps for political prisoners, at Dachau and at Buchenwald. . . . [He] had studied and was familiar with the pathological picture presented by certain types of abnormal behavior. During the first days in prison, and particularly during the first days in the camp, he realized that he behaved differently from the way he used to. At first he rationalized that these changes in behavior were only surface phenomena, the logical result of his peculiar situation. But soon he realized that what happened to him, for instance, the split in his person into one who observes and one to whom things happen, could no longer be called normal, but was a typical psychopathological phenomenon. So he asked himself, "Am I going insane, or am I already insane?" To find an answer to this urgent question was obviously of prime importance. Moreover, he saw his fellow prisoners act in a most peculiar way, although he had every reason to assume that they, too, had been normal persons before being imprisoned. Now they suddenly appeared to be pathological liars, to be unable to restrain themselves, to be unable to make objective evaluations, etc. So another question arose, namely, "How can I protect myself against becoming as they are?" The answer to both questions was comparatively simple: to find out what had happened in them, and to me. If I did not change any more than all other normal persons, then what happened in me and to me was a process of adaptation and not the setting in of insanity. So I set out to find what changes had occurred and were occurring in the prisoners. By doing so I suddenly realized that I had found a solution to my second problem: by occupying myself during my spare time with interesting problems, with interviewing my fellow prisoners, by pondering my findings for the hours without end during which I was forced to perform exhausting labor which did not ask for any mental concentration. I succeeded in killing the time in a way which seemed constructive. To forget for a time that I was in the camp seemed at first the greatest advantage of this occupation. As time went on, the enhancement of my self-respect due to my ability to continue to do meaningful work despite the contrary efforts of the Gestapo became even more important than the pastime.

Source: Bruno Bettelheim, "Individual and Mass Behavior in Extreme Situations," *Journal of Abnormal and Social Psychology,* **38** (October 1943), pp. 421–422. Reprinted by permission.

sive enumeration of camp veterans residing in New York and Chicago—two major centers of settlement in the United States at the time of the study—was considered, but was judged to be unfeasible.

With the advice of the most knowledgeable persons in the service fields mentioned, and among the heads of survivor organizations, fifty-two respondents were chosen whose social characteristics were regarded as approximating those of camp veterans residing in the two cities. Table 1 summarizes, for the beginning of respondents' imprisonment, the data on age, sex, marital status, occupation, social class position, country and-place of longest residence, and religious orientation.

Table 1 / Social Characteristics of 52 Veterans of Nazi Concentration Camps at Time of Imprisonment

Category	No. of Cases	Percentage of Cases
Age		
15–19	12	23
20–29	21	40
30–39	12	23
40–49	6	12
58	1	2
Sex		
Male	35	67
Female	17	33
Marital Status		
Single	35	67
Married	17	33
Married with children	8	
Occupation		
Business manager	6	
Housewife	5	
Office worker	5	
Salesman	5	
Student	5	
Teacher (University, college)	3	
Artist	2	
Electrician	2	
Farm laborer	2	
Sewing machine operator	2	
Shoe worker (skilled)	2	
Social worker	2	

Category	No. of Cases	Percentage of Cases
Beautician	1	
Butcher workman	1	
Dress designer	1	
Factory supply clerk	1	
Farm operator	1	
Journalist and writer	1	
Mechanic	1	
Musician	1	
Plumber	1	
Political party functionary	1	
Tool and die maker	1	
Class position		
Upper class	1	2
Middle class	39	75
Working class (skilled)	12	23
Country of longest residence		
Germany	31	60
Others	21	40
Poland	9	
Austria	7	
Czechoslovakia	3	
Netherlands	1	
Hungary	1	
Place of longest residence		
Cities over 100,000	35	67
Berlin	11	
Vienna	6	
Breslau	3	
Frankfurt on the Main	3	
Düsseldorf	2	
Krakow	2	
Prague	2	
Amsterdam	1	
Cologne	1	
Dortmund	1	
Essen	1	
Hamburg	1	
Nürnberg	1	
Other cities (2,500–100,000)	11	21
Towns (1,000–2,500)	4	8

Category	No. of Cases	Percentage of Cases
Villages (under 1,000)	2	4
Religious orientation		
Jewish	41	79
Protestant	2	4
Catholic	2	4
Agnostic	1	2
Atheist	6	12

The respondents spent time in seventy-one different Nazi concentration camps, in the area of six pre-war European countries. The total of seventy-one is exclusive of time spent in Nazi ghettos, assembly compounds and prisons. Also omitted from the total of seventy-one are several organizationally atypical camps in occupied countries, and several camps mentioned repeatedly by respondents, but whose exact locations could not be determined. Allowing for some mis-classification and identification problems with the 800 camps (counting separate installations rather than base-camp clusters) in the geographic areas where respondents were imprisoned, the camp experience of respondents extended to roughly 10 per cent of the camps in the network, and to *all* of the major base camps.

In order to explore the hypothetic propositions stated previously, it was necessary to select respondents who had been in the camps for periods varying

Table 2 / Length of Imprisonment of 52 Respondents, Beginning with Arrest

Imprisonment Time		No. of Respondents
In months	In years	
0–11	Under 1	4
12–23	1 to 2	12
24–35	2 to 3	15
36–47	3 to 4	11
48–59	4 to 5	2
60–71	5 to 6	4
72–83	6 to 7	2
84–95	7 to 8	1
144	12	1
	Total	52

from a few months to the maximum of twelve years. Only one 12-year veteran was found. He and probably those in the five-to-eight year category over-represent the long-term veterans residing in the two cities. Table 2 shows the distribution of respondents by imprisonment time in months and in years.

The Interviews

A rather long interview guide was used with sample members[24] to get the following kinds of data:[25]

(a) Changes with time in the camp in (1) interpersonal relationship patterns, (2) sharing with other prisoners and assisting them, and (3) theft behavior.
(b) Changes in prisoner behavior in special extreme situations, such as prolonged assemblies, punishment details and transports.
(c) Characterization and length of imprisonment of "old" prisoners, and in particular, of members of prisoner underground organizations.
(d) Gross variations in the frequency of suicides and of "mental disorder" cases, by camp situation.

An imprisonment calendar was made up for each respondent at the beginning of the interview in order to locate individuals and events by *time, type of camp,* and *situation.*

In this study interview material, which was gathered from survivors at eight locations after liberation,[26] personal accounts, and studies by survivors were used chiefly for validation. Some of the central findings from the data indicated under (a) and (c) will be offered in this paper, together with brief references to findings from the data indicated in (b).

Patterns of Association

The following patterns of association ordered by size were used in analyzing interviews:

---

[24] From forty-seven of the fifty-two respondents, data were gathered by the use of a lengthy interview guide. Special guides were designed for the remaining five interviews dealing with selected extreme situations, the roles of "old" prisoners and other areas of study.

[25] In addition, data were sought on a wide range of prisoner behavior. Questions were asked about feelings of rage and panic; becoming a *Muselman*; preoccupation with suicide; reactions to mass debasement routines; religious participation before and after imprisonment; participation in sabotage; reactions to punitive prisoner assemblies; participation in *Sonderkommandos*; special physiological effects; differences in survival of men and women; and various other areas.

[26] At the time of liberation or immediately after, survivors were interviewed informally by the author at the following camps and locations: Ohrdruf Nordlager, Buchenwald, Hersbruck-Happurg, Gusen No. 1, Mauthausen, Wanfried (small factory prison and camp), and one prison-barracks in a factory. Survivors were also interviewed several months after liberation at Dachau, and at the displaced persons camp at Feldafing, Germany. In addition, the partially destroyed installations at Gusen No. 2 were examined.

Pattern	Distinguishing Characteristics
I. Lone wolf	All pair relations and ties with prisoner groups unstable.
II. Stable pairs	Stable[27] pair relations with one or more individual prisoners, but not with groups.
III. Small groups	Stable pair relations, plus participation[28] in one or more groups of three to eight prisoners.
IV. Large groups	Small group relations, plus participation in one or more groups of nine or more prisoners.

Respondents were classified according to the pattern which was most characteristic of the *first* half of their imprisonment careers. The results are summarized in Table 3. The four of our respondents classified as lone wolves were in the camps 21.8 months on the average, while large-group participants were in twice as long. The Table indicates a high association between length of imprisonment and size of pattern. Since all patterns except "lone wolf" involve stable pairing, the Table shows that forty-three of the respondents (91.5 per cent) developed such relationships. As one might expect, participation in "large" groups was severely limited: only a fourth of the sample (27.7 per cent) participated in such groups.

Table 3 / Mean Imprisonment Time of 47[a] Respondents Classified by Pattern of Association

Pattern Association	No. of Cases	Per cent of Total	Mean Imprisonment Time (Months)
Lone wolf	4	8.5	21.8
Stable pairs	10	21.3	31.2
Small groups	20	42.6	39.0
Large groups	13	27.6	43.0
Totals	47	100	

[a] From 47 of the 52 respondents, data were gathered by the use of a lengthy interview guide. Special guides were designed for the remaining five interviews dealing with selected extreme situations, the roles of "old" prisoners and other areas of study. Only the data from the 47 regular interviews are included in this table.

---

[27] Pairs were treated as stable if they persisted without breaking up until the partners were separated by events beyond their control. Brief friendships that continued without conflict, but which involved only slight interaction were not included.

[28] Persons who maintained regular contact with small or large groups of prisoners without conflict for several months, and whose separation from the group was not initiated by it, were classified as participants.

The Friendly and the Exploitative Relationships

While there were no clearly criminalistic prisoners among the respondents (as immigrants they were a select group), the relationships of some tended to be exploitative rather than friendly, and some established expedient ties with "greens" and with SS men. Table 4, like Table 3, shows a high association between length of imprisonment and size of pattern. However, Table 4 shows a

Table 4 / Mean Imprisonment Time of 47 Respondents Classified by Pattern of Association and by General Quality of Relationships

Pattern of Association	*Friendly*		*Exploitative*	
	No. of Cases	*Mean Imprisonment Time (Months)*	*No. of Cases*	*Mean Imprisonment Time (Months)*
Lone wolf	2	20.0	2	23.5
Stable pairs	6	31.8	4	30.5
Small groups	14	32.0	6	46.0
Large groups	8	39.0	5	47.0
Totals	30		17	

generally longer imprisonment time for those whose interpersonal relations were classified as exploitative rather than friendly in the first half of their imprisonment careers.

Changes in Interpersonal Relationship Patterns

The concern here is with changes—long-time shifts rather than fluctuations—in a respondent's pattern of association. Behavior during the first half of imprisonment was compared with that of the second half. With regard to association patterns, a shift toward the large groups end of the series is defined as positive change; negative change means a shift toward the lone wolf pattern. Within any of the four patterns, a shift toward exploitativeness is defined as negative change.

With regard to interpersonal relationships, Table 5 shows that a much higher percentage of "exploitative" than "friendly" respondents changed negatively (35 per cent, compared with 13 per cent); and a much lower percentage changed positively (6 per cent, as against 27). The Table shows a tendency for a higher percentage of participants in the larger patterns of association to change positively than for those whose participation was limited to the smaller patterns.

Pairing As a Response to Massive Stressor Situations

The major obstacles to the development of a full-blown prisoner social system were the rapid turnover of population due to death or transports;

Table 5 / Mean Imprisonment Time and Change in Adjustment[a] by
Interpersonal Relationship Pattern of 47 Prisoners

Interpersonal Relationship Pattern (First Half of Imprisonment)	Totals			Change in Adjustment								
				Positive Change			No Change			Negative Change		
	No.	Total	%	No.	Total	%	No.	Total	%	No.	Total	%
Lone wolf		4	100	0	—		0	—		4	100	
Exploitative	2		100	0		—	0		—	2		100
Friendly	2		100	0		—	0		—	2		100
Stable pairs		10	100	1	10		4	40		5	50	
Exploitative	4		100	0		—	1		25	3		75
Friendly	6		100	1		16.7	3		50	2		33.3
Small groups		20	100	4	20		16	80		0	—	
Exploitative	6		100	0		—	6		100	0		—
Friendly	14		100	4		28.6	10		71.4	0		—
Large groups		13	100	4	30.8		8	61.5		1	7.7	
Exploitative	5		100	1		20	3		60	1		20
Friendly	8		100	3		37.5	5		62.5	0		—
Totals		47	100	9	19.1		28	59.6		10	21.3	
Exploitative	17		100	1		5.9	10		58.8	6		35.3
Friendly	30		100	8		26.7	18		60	4		13.3

[a] For this table a positive change in adjustment means a shift away from the lone-wolf end of the pattern series, and toward the large-groups pattern; negative change means a shift in the reverse direction, or within patterns, a shift from "friendly" to "exploitative."

sudden changes in camp function; the extreme nature of the deprivation and terror climaxed by extermination; and the inclusion of a high proportion of criminalistic persons who were incapable of responsible participation in any ordinary social group. The data which have been offered on pairing are interpreted partly as a response to massive stressor situations.

One of the common phenomena of the camps was the swiftness with which replacement occurred in event of death of one partner or separation by transport, change of work detail, or quarreling. Much information was obtained about stable friendship pairs of real mutuality within the camps that were in effect repudiated after liberation, and which would have been most unlikely in pre-camp life. *These so-called incompatible pairings are important clues to the supportive nature of some aspects of camp life.*

It is striking how often bereavement in such an "incompatible" pair was swiftly made good by another, equally "impossible" partner. The peculiar speed of replacement suggests (1) the intense affectional needs caused by the continuing and universal bereavement, and (2) ease of replacement. It is not only that there were many partners to choose from but that many of the masks and other impediments of social interaction in pre-camp life were swept away in the fearful levelling of induction to the system.

The interview material is full of accounts of the friendships of these dedicated "incompatibles." By way of illustration, passing mention is made of such friendships of four respondents. These were parallel types of interview situations, but none of the respondents knew each other. There were two gracious, well-schooled, women interviewees whose best friends in the camps were women from the tough parts of Berlin and Warsaw, occupations unknown. During informal discussions after the interviews, the husbands, who had never been in camps but had been introduced by their wives to their best friends of camp days, interjected good-natured comments that friendship of any kind with such a person was an utter impossibility, let alone friendship of richness and depth.

There were also two men respondents, each of whose *best* friends in the camps belonged to a party of the left, which each man referred to in terms of "enemy." In each of the two interviews, there was more than a trace of awkwardness at the instant of emotional re-instatement when friendships were discussed. Only after some obvious fumbling in both interviews were the *politically* objectionable friendships of camp days re-defined as only expedient alliances.

It may be mentioned that among psychoanalytically oriented interpreters there have been several who have speculated about widespread homosexual attachments of prisoners. However, there is such uniform agreement on the virtual disappearance of sexual feelings among ordinary prisoners (not among the privileged prisoners, however) that this speculation suggests, not the prevalence of homosexual patterns, but ubiquitous pairing.

The data on "stable" pairing are congruent with evidence presented in the next section that a substantial part of the prisoner population developed a sharing relationship with one or more prisoners.

Sharing

As used here, the term sharing includes various forms of assistance to fellow prisoners. In instances of continuing relationships, sharing was usually reciprocal, and in the long run, did not involve sacrifice. It should be noted that there were occasional instances of sharing by our respondents under conditions of the most extreme deprivation when only a small minority survived and any thought of *quid pro quo* dealings would have been completely unrealistic. It must be kept in mind that the usual state of camp life was one of more or less rapid starvation for the great mass of prisoners and that an act of sharing, at the instant it occurred, was apt to appear as a sacrifice.

The analysis was concerned with long-time shifts, rather than with fluctuations in behavior. Sharing for the first half of a person's imprisonment was compared with that of the second. If a person shared more frequently, either with the same person(s) or a greater number of persons, he was classified as showing positive change; in the reverse instance, as showing negative change. As with other behavior areas examined, the "no-change" category here is a misnomer in that it leaves out of account relatively brief shifts.

Only three persons showed positive change, thirty-five showed no change, and nine persons showed negative change. The small number of positive-change cases hardly permits interpretation, but imprisonment time averaged 28 months and there were no extreme cases in this trio. More meaningful is the difference in means for the no-change and negative-change cases. For the no-change cases, the mean is 39.6 months; for the negative-change cases, 26.1. The direction is what one would normally expect in the development of social systems. It should be noted also that the negative-change cases fail to include a single person whose pattern of association included participation in "small" or "large" groups.

When one considers the progressive shift toward more extreme deprivation throughout the history of the camp system, the low number of positive-change cases makes sense, and the high total of no-change cases argues for the development of norms of mutual support within the dreary limits set by the camp system.

The no-change category includes persons who showed positive change in their association patterns. Whether under conditions of less severe deprivation such persons would have shown positive change in sharing, or whether they would have remained in the no-change category, cannot be known.

Respondent Steve, hospital secretary for many months at one of the notorious base camps and an expert on ecclesiastical law, observed, "There were two kinds of prisoners. One was a good fellow. It was most important to be recognized as a good fellow. The other was a *Speckjaeger*. When he had something to share, he gave to no one. He was selfish and had no real friends. Speckjaegers died early. They are dead. One could not exist in the camp without participating somehow in a sharing relationship." The extreme deprivation usually restricted sharing to one's best friend, and occasionally to one or two others. This, incidentally, was a factor which tended to restrict the size of prisoner groups. It is clear, however, that the general trend was a higher proportion of negative change in sharing than in association patterns, and in theft behavior, which will be considered next.

Thefts

The nature of the respondents' reference to thefts (i.e., taking from another prisoner) indicates that enforcement of the prisoners' code against stealing involved extreme moral condemnation, as well as severe physical punishment often resulting in death. Many respondents used the term "bread thief" with tones as condemnatory as those used for rape or armed robbery in non-camp society. Gathering data on thefts therefore required the development of a special procedure. It consisted of two carefully selected "confessions," one from a camp prisoner quoted by Bloch,[29] and one from a respondent in this study. These were written for use as thematic statements. They were presented in such

---

[29] See Bloch, Herbert: "The Personality of Inmates of Concentration Camps." *American Journal of Sociology*, January 1947, 52, p. 338.

a way that respondents could, with a minimum of stress, relate their own theft behavior, if any, to that described in one statement, while rejecting that described in the other statement completely. Questions on theft were constructed so that the interviewee could respond in terms of increasing or decreasing *consideration* of theft rather than theft, if he so wished. The interviews were accordingly analyzed in terms of increasing or decreasing consideration of theft as well as outright thefts.

Conditions were so severe during transports and in the camps, and prisoners were moved so often from camp to camp, that it is hard to imagine conditions more conducive to thefts. In the face of these conditions, only nine of our respondents admitted thefts, and only five others said they had considered thefts.

Can this be explained on the basis that the sanctions mentioned above were effective? Or shall we assume that our returns understate the extent of thefts? We have no way of knowing the answers to these questions. Table 6 indicates

Table 6 / Mean Imprisonment Time of 46 Respondents[a]
by Change in Theft Behavior

Change in Theft Behavior	No. of Respondents	Mean Imprisonment Time (Months)
Increasing theft behavior (negative change)	5	31.0
No theft behavior	33	34.7[b]
Decreasing theft behavior (positive change)	8	35.1[c]
Total	46	

[a] Among the 47 regular informants, one person stole at infrequent intervals throughout imprisonment. Since there seemed to be no change in frequency, she was omitted from the tabulations.
[b] This mean was computed without the extreme value, 144.
[c] This mean was computed without the extreme value, 78.

that the mean imprisonment time for our no-theft-behavior cases and our positive-change cases is practically identical. The negative-change cases were in the camps 31 months, substantially less than the others.

Prisoner Cleavages

One of the central points to emerge from Bettelheim's stage interpretation of prisoner behavior is the cleavage between new and "old" prisoners. From our sources it seems clear that this emphasis distinguishes Bettelheim's views from that of most other interpreters. Other writers refer in passing to strains between newcomers and old-timers. With few if any exceptions, all other writers see the cleavage between the "politicals" and the criminalistic prisoners (who wore green triangular insignia) as the all-important one which decisively affected behavior and social system.

The literature on the early days of Buchenwald, Dachau, Sachsenhausen and other camps makes it quite clear that the "green" prisoners, many of whom were originally installed by the SS in leading positions in the camps, maintained their grip by out-and-out terror. Thus Kautsky states, "if the concentration camp was generally hell, then the camps under the control of criminals were hell multiplied a thousand times." [30] ‑

Cohen takes a similar position. He says: "In order to avoid any misunderstanding it must be pointed out that generally there was a very great difference between the 'green' and the 'red' Kapos. In those camps in which the 'reds,' the political prisoners, held the leading functions, there was as a rule more justice and less corruption than in those where the 'green' prisoners were in control." [31]

Our interviews show that the prisoner cleavage which had the most fateful effects on the development of the prisoner social system was that between the criminal prisoners and those in the various non-criminal categories, generally including the Jews, "politicals," Jehovah's Witnesses and others. Bettelheim, on the other hand, basing his position on psychodynamic notions, sees the main cleavage as that between the new prisoners and the "old," and completely ignores differences between prisoners belonging to the several distinct categories.

Respondents' attitudes toward "old" prisoners were examined. Of 108 "old" prisoners who were well known to our respondents, 87 were liked and 21 disliked by them. All but two were trusted. The short-term respondents who had "old" prisoner acquaintances were more often favorably disposed toward them than long-term respondents, but they also had fewer acquaintances among the "old" prisoners.

The respondents who expressed dislike of *certain* "old" prisoners (not all of them) included the two interviewees with the longest imprisonment times, 144 and 85 months, and two others who were in camps 68 and 60 months. "Old" prisoner Richard said of the International Camp Committee members in Buchenwald, "I did not *like* any of them, but I *trusted* them all completely." On the other hand, respondent Frank, who spent 73 months in Buchenwald, the camp with the most highly developed prisoner social system, offered the following impressions as part of a lengthy written statement:

Let me sum up my impressions of the "old" prisoners. A very substantial fraction of them were or became firm fighters against the SS and all the SS stood for, never succumbed to the power ideal of their "masters" and never accepted, even unconsciously, their values. They survived Buchenwald not by assimilating themselves to the camp, but by assimilating Buchenwald, in spite of everything, to themselves; by conquering it instead of submitting. Misery became a challenge, abasement a spring to

---

[30] Kautsky, *op. cit.*, p. 203.
[31] Cohen, *op. cit.*, p. 200.

activity. These "old" prisoners, and not prominent newcomers, became in all national groups the representatives of their compatriots. Take for instance the list of fifteen men in Kogon's book and to whom he read his manuscript because they were either members of the Camp Committee or representatives of certain political groups: there is among them not a single one who came to the camp after 1942, they are all "old" prisoners. . . . If it were not for those "old" prisoners I should not be alive today, and tens of thousands of my fellow-prisoners with me.

A number of factors must be considered in interpreting the attitude of respondents toward "old" prisoners:

1. More or less severe strains arose in camps between new and "old" prisoners.
2. The nature of camp life created obstacles of many kinds to communications between new and "old" prisoners.
3. The introduction of "old" criminals into the system into positions of prisoner leadership had a corrosive effect on all relationships.
4. As "old" prisoners (including "old" politicals) moved into positions of greater influence within the system, they became involved in dealings with "greens," and with the SS camp complement as required by camp routines. Those who withstood the corrupting influences of the system often became organizers of the underground.

"Old" Prisoners and the Underground

More important than the scattered instances of rebellious behavior and organization (mentioned by several of our respondents and in published accounts) is the development of underground committees of nationals, and international camp committees towards the end of the system. In this study, respondents reported on the make-up of the Czech and the Polish camp committees, as well as on the International Camp Committee in Mauthausen and on various committees in Buchenwald. Other reports were obtained on the length of imprisonment of members of the International Camp Committee in Flossenburg and in Dachau. These data are summarized in Table 7.

On a visit to Dachau three months after liberation, an officer of the U.S. Army indicated that he had come to know most of the "eighteen" members of the International Camp Committee before their repatriation. In the course of several references to them he stated that they were all "old-timers." A non-commissioned officer, who had been stationed in Dachau immediately after liberation of the camp, was interviewed in the United States regarding the length of imprisonment of members of the International Camp Committee. He said, "A couple of them were in from the beginning (of the camp, E. L.). The others were *there* at least several years, and I don't know where else."

Table 7 shows that five members of these leading underground groups were in the camps only two years, and that the time of a sixth was estimated to be just under three years. Thus, out of roughly 60 prisoners included in the individual and group estimates, only about 10 per cent were "new" prisoners.

Table 7 / Summary of Interview Data on Length of Imprisonment of
Members of National and International Camp Committees of
Three Base Camps—Buchenwald, Mauthausen, and Flossenburg[a]

Buchenwald[b]		Mauthausen[b]		Flossenburg[c]	
Prisoner	Time in Months	Prisoner	Time in Months	Prisoner	Time in Months
B	46	A	72	Z	60
D	58	C	45	Z	60
D	58	C	42	G	108
F	46	C	42	G	108
F	34	C	41	G	108
G	96	C	24	G	108
G	96	C	24	P	42
G	96	P	72	P	42
G	96	P	60	P	42
Y	46	P	48	R	24
Y	46	P	42	R	24
Y	46	P	42	R	24
Several[c] Austrians	76 plus				
Several[c] Poles	64 plus				

[a] Prisoners are designated by a letter to indicate nationality: A, Austrian; B, Belgian; C, Czech; D, Dutch; F, French; G, German; P, Polish; R, Russian; Y, Yugoslav; and Z, nationality unknown. In estimating imprisonment time, respondents sometimes took the beginning date of a wave of arrests. This unavoidably results in some overestimation of imprisonment time, since a prisoner may have evaded arrest for a while. Because of the highly organized nature of Nazi round-ups the errors introduced in this way are probably small. When respondents used a time interval in making their estimate, such as "the year 1939," the mid-point of the interval was used in estimating months of imprisonment.

[b] The Buchenwald and Mauthausen columns include members of various national committees of prisoners, and of the International Camp Committee in each. The Flossenburg column includes only members of the International Camp Committee.

[c] These group estimates are based on respondent Frank's statement. Details for individual Austrians and Poles belonging to both types of committees were not obtained.

INTAKE AT POSTON

The new arrivals, coming in a steady stream, were poured into empty blocks one after another, as into a series of bottles. The reception procedure became known as "intake" and it left a lasting impression on all who witnessed or took part in it.

Picture the brightness of the morning and a sun that heats the earth and beats down on rubbish piles and row after row of even, black tar-papered barracks. There is the sound of hammers and the hum of motors in trucks, cars, bulldozers, tractors, pumps, and graders. In the single wooden building that houses the administrative offices, desks are jammed together and the members of the departments of law, housing, supply, and transportation bump into each other as they go about their business and try to shout above each other's noise. . . .

It is almost 6 when someone shouts that the first bus is coming, and it can be seen plowing through the dust, like a ship on a choppy sea. . . .

One of the volunteers gets into the bus and makes a short speech in Japanese and then in English. He tells them that everyone understands that they have just had a long hot train ride, that the Administration therefore will try to send them through the necessary routine in the shortest possible fashion, and that as soon as it is over, food will be served. In the allotment of apartments, they are told that, if there are less than five in a family, they must be prepared to have others living with them.

They begin to file out of the bus, clutching tightly to children and bundles. Military Police escorts anxiously help, and guides direct them in English and Japanese.

They are sent into the mess halls where girls hand them ice water, salt tablets, and wet towels. In the back are cots where those who faint can be stretched out, and the cots are usually occupied. At long tables sit interviewers suggesting enlistment in the War Relocation Work Corps. Overhead is a placard stating briefly in Japanese the main points of the enlistment application.

Men and women, still sweating, holding on to children and bundles try to think.

A whirlwind comes and throws clouds of dust into the mess hall, into the water, and into the faces of the people while papers fly in all directions.

Order is restored again.

The new arrivals are constantly urged to be quick.

Source: Alexander H. Leighton, *The Governing of Men* (Princeton, N.J.: Princeton University Press, 1945, 1949; Princeton Paperback, 1968), pp. 63–64.
Editors' Note: The federal government ordered all persons of Japanese ancestry, native born citizens, naturalized citizens, and noncitizens alike, to be removed from the Pacific coastal region during the Second World War, and detained in "relocation centers" for the duration of the national emergency. Poston, Arizona was the site of one such center.

Respondents provided information on several, less developed underground groups in smaller camps administered from the base camps of the system. One example, typical of this interview material, is offered here. Stella reported being unacquainted with five prisoners in the Brunnlitz camp who belonged to the leading underground group. It coordinated activities of the Czech and Polish underground members operating within the camp, and collated information gleaned from various sources, including the ex-Nazi director of the factory which adjoined the camp. In function, this group of five resembled the more developed international camp committees of the base camps included in Table 7. Stella said the five prisoners "were very likeable and good to others," but that one was "ambitious" for prominent positions in the camp. She added that she has "never trusted anyone more than these five people." They were in the camps about four and a half years.

Pairs and the Underground: Interpretation

Despite the apparently total destruction of prisoner resistance in some camps, in the system as a whole a precarious kind of resistance politics developed. Here and there, with the uneven development of the prisoner social system, it gained noteworthy strength.

For many people the impulse to reject any consideration of the politics of camp prisoners is overwhelming. Yet, in the abstract, this politics makes as strong a claim on thought and interest as any other. The goal of the complex grouping known as the "politicals," in its deadly warfare with the "greens," was nothing less than life itself.

The hazards were extreme in building an underground organization that could provide some protection for individuals and groups, and on the eve of liberation, for *all* prisoners. So great were the hazards that they effectively precluded the functioning of organizations as reference groups except in a few camps in the last months—Buchenwald, Mauthausen, Dachau, Flossenburg and others. What there was of organization, manifested itself primarily in pair relations with political individuals.

The same hazards that hindered the functioning of organizations as reference *groups*, obstructed prisoner recognition of those who might have served as reference *individuals*. There was no medium to sponsor a favorable image of a prisoner leader, in fact, hardly the possibility for him to make himself known. By undermining or destroying the prisoners' pre-camp group and individual references and by effectively preventing camp groups and individuals from functioning as references, the regime set in motion, and on a vast scale, socially destructive processes which Rosenberg, Gerver and Howton refer to as "denormatization." [32] The interaction between the regime and its victims was "carried on without effective governance by societal norms." [33] Humane sentiments were eliminated and "law, in the form of guarantees of civil rights," was ruled out. [34] In the language of psychology, one behavioral response to denormatization was regression.

---

[32] See Bernard Rosenberg, Israel Gerver and F. William Howton (eds.), *Mass Society in Crisis*. New York: The Macmillan Co., 1964, p. 161.

[33] *Loc. cit.*

[34] *Loc. cit.*

In Kogon's work[35] and in the discussion paper by Jackman referred to previously, there is much emphasis on the value for survival of camp and pre-camp memberships in well-integrated groups that continued to oppose the regime. Vast numbers of prisoners had no such reference groups. Much of this paper deals with the ways in which survival chances of such prisoners were affected by pairing and by the formation of larger groups.

From the data of this study, much of the strength for survival—psychic and physical—seems to have come from "stable" pairing. With all of the raging conflicts in the camps, it was in the pairs, repeatedly disrupted by transports and death, and paradoxically restored in the general bereavement, that the prisoner kept alive the semblance of humanity. The pairs gave relief from the shame of acts of acquiescence and surrender. The pairs produced expertness in the survival skills known as "organizing." For the minority that had some contact with an underground, it was in the pair that man and organization usually met. In the pair, the politics of resistance survived, found form and technique, and in some places began to grow.

Effects of Special Extreme Situations on Behavior and Social System

Four respondents were interviewed regarding a prolonged punishment assembly in bitter winter weather. Bettelheim[36] who was at that assembly also, reported that a feeling of indifference to torture and threat of death arose among most prisoners after some hours had passed. Some of our interview material also indicates loss of fear and the emergence of we-feeling among the prisoners. However, Bettelheim's claim that a mood of "quasi-orgiastic happiness"[37] swept the prisoners, suggests an intensity and uniformity of response in the assembly which is not supported by our interview material. Nevertheless, these observations of Bettelheim, which seem to be unique in the literature, provide an instance of "productive error of investigation."

Our regular respondents who participated in prisoner assemblies called to witness executions and other punishments, generally responded with anger against the SS. The repeating of mass-debasement routines commonly led from initially severe shock to indifference. Particularly arduous foot marches frequently resulted in increased we-feeling and cooperation.

Ten of our forty-seven regular respondents were evacuees of Auschwitz camps who marched on foot to Gleiwitz, Silesia in January 1945 where they were loaded into roofless, low-sided (gondola) freight cars, and taken to various camps within the boundaries of pre-war Germany. Because of the demands of

---

[35] Kogon's approach to survival, and that of others in the underground, has been summed up by Foreman (*op. cit.*, p. 293). He says that they "... placed their faith for survival in organization, infiltration of functionary statuses, systematic intelligence within the camp, mutual aid, ruthless discipline of confederates, control of other *Kazets*, collective action, and, when possible, liaison with outside underground or military power."

[36] Bettelheim: *The Informed Heart.* Glencoe, Ill.: The Free Press, 1960, pp. 136–138.

[37] *Loc. cit.*

the military on the battered German railroad system, transports were side-tracked for long periods and were detoured crazily off direct routes. As a result prisoners were enroute as many as fourteen days in cold winter weather. The emotional and social system compensations that occurred in some other situations were generally absent in these gondola car transports. This was manifested by recurrent melees, i.e., of confused, general, hand-to-hand fighting, to such an extent, and with fatal results for so many prisoners, that the occasional presence of an SS man, was an unsung blessing. Substantial evidence was found of the maintenance of defensive relationships, however, and of the continuance or reemergence, in some degree of acts of sharing and cooperation among the handfuls of survivors in each car.[38]

DISCUSSION AND CONCLUSIONS

Nothing in their pre-camp lives, not even the pogroms and violent seizures of anti-Nazis, enabled the respondents to make much sense of camp situations. For many, induction to the camp system was so violent that traumatization of a massive character can be assumed. Family and friends were gone and local communities in shambles. After 1939 Europe was at war, and homelands of many were gutted. In the camps, extreme violence and deprivation were matters of administrative design, arbitrariness of camp functionaries, and of essentially planless conjunction of military with other events.

The late psychophysical effects on camp veterans of stressor situations in the camps is an area of continuing study in medicine, psychiatry and social science. This paper deals with response in terms of prisoner organization and individual behavior. Included are part of the data and findings of an early study by the author exploring the emergence—unevenly and in the most places feebly—of a prisoner social system.

It has already been suggested that one effect of stressor situations was to inhibit the reference function for prisoners, of outstanding *individuals* among them, and of resistance *organizations* until the last year of the system. It was suggested also that such situations necessarily led to denormatization, as that term is used by Rosenberg, Gerver and Howton. In psychological terms, one outcome for the individual of the socially disruptive processes of denormatization, was regression. Special attention has therefore been given to the data on what may be called re-norming, in particular to the data on sharing with other prisoners, and on theft behavior.

Patterns of association of respondents were classified as lone wolf, "stable" pairs, small groups and large groups, with the last two patterns defined as

---

[38] For a fuller report of research findings on these especially extreme situations see Elmer Luchterhand. "The Gondola-Car Transports," in *The International Journal of Social Psychiatry*, 1967, 13, 1.

including "stable" pairing. Those respondents who showed greater and more stable general social participation were in the camps longer than those whose participation declined. This finding runs counter to the Bettelheim conclusion that "It seemed easier to resist the pressure of the Gestapo if one functioned as an individual . . ." [39] On its face, this statement is open to various interpretations. The one that is relevant here is contained in a summary by Foreman of Bettelheim's views on prisoner survival:

(1) Survival in a concentration camp is primarily a matter of self-discipline. (2) One must resist desocialization in the face of chronic terror and deprivation. (3) This resistance is most effective where inmates function as individuals avoiding all interpersonal entrapments. [40]

Obviously other personality characteristics besides friendliness and acceptance of duties and rights in pair relations figured in survival chances. The interpersonal relationship patterns of thirty respondents were classified as "friendly" and seventeen as "exploitative" in the first half of imprisonment. Eleven "exploitative" respondents who were classified as small-groups and "large-groups" participants had a much longer mean imprisonment time than the twenty-two friendly respondents having similar association patterns. From a re-examination of interview protocols, it is concluded that the "exploitative" ones with the small- and "large-group" patterns of association, seemed to have some of the manipulative skills that form part of the stereotype of the aggressive politician in non-camp society.

Despite fearful deterrents to the development of some kind of social system among prisoners, various bases existed for the development of conduct norms. Some highly integrated resistance groups continued to exist outside and in the camps and helped to maintain norms. The carry-over by individual prisoners of pre-camp beliefs and attitudes also helped. Finally the very nature of human socialization assisted re-norming by the common tendency, in all but the most anti-social prisoners, for reciprocal acceptance of duties and rights in pair relations.

Much evidence was found of widespread opposition to criminalistic prisoner officials. The inclusion of a large criminal population among the prisoners eliminated from practical consideration the course of nonparticipation by the noncriminalistic in the special "self-government" procedures set up by the Nazis. All of the evidence of this study shows that it was the cleavage between criminalistic and non-criminalistic prisoners, rather than that between new and "old" prisoners, which most decisively influenced development of the prisoner

---

[39] Bettelheim: "Individual and Mass Behavior in Extreme Situations," in Harold Proshansky and Bernard Seidenberg (eds.), *Basic Studies in Social Psychology*. New York: Holt, Rinehart and Winston, 1965, p. 637. This is the same shortened version of Bettelheim's 1943 paper which has been republished in the several editions of *Readings in Social Psychology* as mentioned in ref. 7.
[40] Foreman, *op. cit.*, pp. 292–293.

social system. In camps where the prisoner social system was rather highly developed (e.g., Buchenwald and Mauthausen) it was common for criminalistic prisoners to be pushed to peripheral positions or outside the system. Thereafter some of them moved toward the social system of the SS camp complements.

The data show considerable trust, by both new and "old" prisoner respondents, in "old" prisoner acquaintances. However, few of the latter were defined as heroes. There was much awareness of the saving role of the underground as the allied advance brought danger of final annihilation. The favorable attitudes of respondents toward "old" prisoner acquaintances and the underground may have arisen partly from that fact that almost all of the respondents witnessed the end of the camp system—a time when the underground surfaced skillfully in some of the base camps and their affiliates.

In clarifying different effects of camp situations on prisoners, Bettelheim's observations on a prolonged punishment assembly at Buchenwald are in *general* accord with others offered in this paper.

The stage theory of prisoner adjustment advanced by Bettelheim seems to have much more limited relevance than he implies. His statement that "a prisoner had reached the final stage of adjustment to the camp situation when he had changed his personality so as to accept as his own the values of the Gestapo,"[41] may apply to criminalistic prisoners in some degree but is considered generally inapplicable to others.

In sum, the findings offered here are in conflict at critical points with narrowly psychodynamic interpretations of prisoner behavior. It is concluded that in the camps—the most awesome of all contrivances for the destruction of freedom and man—the human group and social system emerge as the most fruitful foci for scientific analysis.

---

[41] Bettelheim, *op. cit.*, p. 636.

Patterns of Unlawful Police Violence in the U.S.

NATIONAL ADVISORY COMMISSION ON CIVIL DISORDERS AND THE UNITED STATES CIVIL RIGHTS COMMISSION

———

I. OVERREACTION AND EXCESSIVE FORCE

On Thursday, inflammatory leaflets were circulated in the neighborhoods of the Fourth Precinct. A "Police Brutality Protest Rally" was announced for early evening in front of the Fourth Precinct Station. Several television stations and newspapers sent news teams to interview people. Cameras were set up. A crowd gathered.

A picket line was formed to march in front of the police station. Between 7:00 and 7:30 P.M. James Threatt, Executive Director of the Newark Human Rights Commission, arrived to announce to the people the decision of the mayor to form a citizens group to investigate the Smith incident, and to elevate a Negro to the rank of captain.

The response from the loosely milling mass of people was derisive. One youngster shouted "Black Power!" Rocks were thrown at Threatt, a Negro. The barrage of missiles that followed placed the police station under siege.

After the barrage had continued for some minutes, police came out to disperse the crowd. According to witnesses, there was little restraint of language or action by either side. A number of police officers and Negroes were injured.

As on the night before, once the people had been dispersed, reports of looting began to come in. Soon the glow of the first fire was seen.

Source: Report of the National Advisory Commission on Civil Disorders (New York: Bantam, 1968), pp. 63–69, 301–306. © 1967 by the New York Times Company. Reprinted by permission. United States Commission on Civil Rights, *Justice*, Report No. 5, 1961 (Washington, D.C.: U.S. Government Printing Office, 1961).

Editors' Note: The first two parts of this section are taken from the report of the National Advisory Commission on Civil Disorders in 1967, and the third is from a document issued by the U.S. Civil Rights Commission in 1961. Putting together excerpted materials this way raises the question of scholarly objectivity: Each of the parts is taken out of its larger context, the sequence is rearranged, and the first and second parts are given new subtitles. Inescapably, old meanings are changed and new ones are introduced. But the critical reader should bear in mind that each excerpt is exactly what it purports to be: a portion of an official document, with nothing attributed to either of the two commissions that they did not publish (except the subtitles of the first and second parts, as noted); and that the objective of choosing and arranging the excerpts is to identify patterns of violence and to suggest how they are causally linked. It is not to bring a wholesale indictment of "the police," but to understand the social conditions that put police officers under pressure, at some times and places and in some situations, to overreact, to harass, or to enforce segregation.

Without enough men to establish control, the police set up a perimeter around a two-mile stretch of Springfield Avenue, one of the principal business districts, where bands of youths roamed up and down smashing windows. Grocery and liquor stores, clothing and furniture stores, drug stores and cleaners, appliance stores and pawnshops were the principal targets. Periodically police would appear and fire their weapons over the heads of looters and rioters. Laden with stolen goods, people began returning to the housing projects.

Near midnight, activity appeared to taper off. The Mayor told reporters the city had turned the corner.

As news of the disturbance had spread, however, people had flocked into the streets. As they saw stores being broken into with impunity, many bowed to temptation and joined the looting.

Without the necessary personnel to make mass arrests, police were shooting into the air to clear stores. A Negro boy was wounded by a .22 caliber bullet said to have been fired by a white man riding in a car. Guns were reported stolen from a Sears Roebuck store. Looting, fires, and gunshots were reported from a widening area. Between 2:00 and 2:30 A.M. on Friday, July 14, the mayor decided to request Governor Richard J. Hughes to dispatch the state police, and National Guard troops. The first elements of the state police arrived with a sizeable contingent before dawn.

During the morning the governor and the mayor, together with police and National Guard officers, made a reconnaissance of the area. The police escort guarding the officials arrested looters as they went. By early afternoon the National Guard had set up 137 roadblocks, and state police and riot teams were beginning to achieve control. Command of anti-riot operations was taken over by the governor, who decreed a "hard line" in putting down the riot.

As a result of technical difficulties, such as the fact that the city and state police did not operate on the same radio wavelengths, the three-way command structure—city police, state police and National Guard—worked poorly.

At 3:30 P.M. that afternoon, the family of Mrs. D. J. was standing near the upstairs window of their apartment, watching looters run in and out of a furniture store on Springfield Avenue. Three carloads of police rounded the corner. As the police yelled at the looters, they began running.

The police officers opened fire. A bullet smashed the kitchen window in Mrs. D. J.'s apartment. A moment later she heard a cry from the bedroom. Her 3-year old daughter, Debbie, came running into the room. Blood was streaming down the left side of her face: the bullet had entered her eye. The child spent the next two months in the hospital. She lost the sight of her left eye and the hearing in her left ear.

Simultaneously, on the street below, Horace W. Morris, an associate director of the Washington Urban League who had been visiting relatives in Newark, was about to enter a car for the drive to Newark Airport. With him were his two brothers and his 73-year old step-father, Isaac Harrison. About 60 persons had been on the street watching the looting. As the police arrived, three of the looters cut directly in front of the group of spectators. The police fired at the looters. Bullets plowed into the spectators. Everyone began running. As Harrison, followed by the family, headed toward the apartment building in which he lived, a bullet kicked his legs out from under him. Horace Morris lifted him to his feet. Again he fell. Mr. Morris' brother, Virgil, attempted to pick the old man up. As he was doing so, he was hit in the left leg and right forearm. Mr. Morris and his other brother managed to drag the two wounded men into the vestibule of the building, jammed with 60 to 70 frightened, angry Negroes.

Bullets continued to spatter against the walls of the buildings. Finally, as the firing died down, Morris—whose stepfather died that evening—yelled to a sergeant that innocent people were being shot.

"Tell the black bastards to stop shooting at us," the sergeant, according to Morris, replied.

"They don't have guns; no one is shooting at you," Morris said.

"You shut up, there's a sniper on the roof," the sergeant yelled.

A short time later, at approximately 5:00 P.M., in the same vicinity a police detective was killed by a small caliber bullet. The origin of the shot could not be determined. Later during the riot a fireman was killed by a .30 caliber bullet. Snipers were blamed for the deaths of both.

At 5:30 P.M., on Beacon Street, W. F. told J. S., whose 1959 Pontiac he had taken to the station for inspection, that his front brake needed fixing. J. S., who had just returned from work, went to the car which was parked in the street, jacked up the front end, took the wheel off and got under the car.

The street was quiet. More than a dozen persons were sitting on porches, walking about, or shopping. None heard any shots. Suddenly several state troopers appeared at the corner of Springfield and Beacon. J. S. was startled by a shot clanging into the side of the garbage can next to his car. As he looked up he saw a state trooper with his rifle pointed at him. The next shot struck him in the right side.

At almost the same instant, K. G., standing on a porch, was struck in the right eye by a bullet. Both he and J. S. were critically injured.

At 8:00 P.M., Mrs. L. M. bundled her husband, her husband's brother, and her four sons into the family car to drive to a restaurant for dinner. On the return trip her husband, who was driving, panicked as he approached a National Guard roadblock. He slowed the car, then quickly swerved around. A shot rang out. When the family reached home, everyone began piling out of the car. Ten-year-old Eddie failed to move. Shot through the head, he was dead.

Although, by nightfall, most of the looting and burning had ended, reports of sniper fire increased. The fire was, according to New Jersey National Guard reports, "deliberately or otherwise inaccurate." Major General James F. Cantwell, Chief of Staff of the New Jersey National Guard, testified before an Armed Services Subcommittee of the House of Representatives that "there was too much firing initially against snipers" because of "confusion when we were finally called on for help and our thinking of it as a military action."

"As a matter of fact," Director of Police Spina told the Commission, "down in the Springfield Avenue area it was so bad that, in my opinion, Guardsmen were firing upon police and police were firing back at them . . . I really don't believe there was as much sniping as we thought . . . We have since compiled statistics indicating that there were 79 specified instances of sniping."

Several problems contributed to the misconceptions regarding snipers: the lack of communications; the fact that one shot might be reported half a dozen times by half a dozen different persons as it caromed and reverberated a mile or more through the city; the fact that the National Guard troops lacked riot training. They were, said a police official, "young and very scared," and had had little contact with Negroes.

Within the Guard itself contact with Negroes had certainly been limited. Although, in 1949, out of a force of 12,529 men there had been 1,183 Negroes, following the integration of the Guard in the 1950's the number had declined until, by July of 1967, there were 303 Negroes in a force of 17,529 men.

On Saturday, July 15, Spina received a report of snipers in a housing project. When he arrived he saw approximately 100 National Guardsmen and police officers crouching behind vehicles, hiding in corners and lying on the ground around the edge of the courtyard.

Since everything appeared quiet and it was broad daylight, Spina walked directly down the middle of the street. Nothing happened. As he came to the last building of the complex, he heard a shot. All around him the troopers jumped, believing themselves to be under sniper fire. A moment later a young Guardsman ran from behind a building.

The director of police went over and asked him if he had fired the shot. The soldier said yes, he had fired to scare a man away from a window; that his orders were to keep everyone away from windows.

Spina said he told the soldier: "Do you know what you just did? You have now created a state of hysteria. Every Guardsman up and down this street and every State Policeman and every city policeman that is present thinks that somebody just fired a shot and that it is probably a sniper."

A short time later more "gunshots" were heard. Investigating, Spina came upon a Puerto Rican sitting on a wall. In reply to a question as to whether he knew "where the firing is coming from?" the man said:

"That's no firing. That's fireworks. If you look up to the fourth floor, you will see the people who are throwing down these cherry bombs."

By this time four truckloads of National Guardsmen had arrived and troopers and policemen were again crouched everywhere, looking for a sniper. The director of police remained at the scene for three hours, and the only shot fired was the one by the Guardsman.

Nevertheless, at six o'clock that evening two columns of National Guardsmen and state troopers were directing mass fire at the Hayes Housing Project in response to what they believed were snipers.

On the tenth floor, Eloise Spellman, the mother of several children, fell, a bullet through her neck.

Across the street a number of persons, standing in an apartment window, were watching the firing directed at the housing project. Suddenly several troopers whirled and began firing in the general direction of the spectators. Mrs. Hattie Gainer, a grandmother, sank to the floor.

A block away Rebecca Brown's 2-year old daughter was standing at the window. Mrs. Brown rushed to drag her to safety. As Mrs. Brown was, momentarily, framed in the window, a bullet spun into her back.

All three women died.

A number of eye witnesses, at varying times and places, reported seeing bottles thrown from upper story windows. As these would land at the feet of an officer he would turn and fire. Thereupon, other officers and Guardsmen up and down the street would join in.

In order to protect his property, B. W. W., the owner of a Chinese laundry, had placed a sign saying "Soul Brother" in his window. Between 1:00 and 1:30 A.M., on Sunday, July 16, he, his mother, wife, and brother, were watching television in the back room. The neighborhood had been quiet. Suddenly B. W. W. heard the sound of jeeps, then shots.

Going to an upstairs window he was able to look out into the street. There he observed several jeeps, from which soldiers and state troopers were firing into stores that had "Soul Brother" signs in the windows. During the course of three nights, according to dozens of eye witness reports, law enforcement officers shot into and smashed windows of businesses that contained signs indicating they were Negro owned.

At 11:00 P.M., on Sunday, July 16, Mrs. Lucille Pugh looked out of the window to see if the streets were clear. She then asked her 11-year-old son, Michael, to take the garbage out. As he reached the street and was illuminated by a street light, a shot rang out. He died.

By Monday afternoon, July 17, state police and National Guard forces were withdrawn. That evening, a Catholic priest saw two Negro men walking down the street. They were carrying a case of soda and two bags of groceries. An unmarked car with five police officers pulled up beside them. Two white officers got out of the car. Accusing the Negro men of looting, the officers made them put the groceries on the sidewalk, then kicked the bags open, scattering their contents all over the street.

Telling the men, "Get out of here," the officers drove off. The Catholic priest went across the street to help gather up the groceries. One of the men turned to him: "I've just been back from Vietnam two days," he said, "and this is what I get. I feel like going home and getting a rifle and shooting the cops."

Of the 250 fire alarms, many had been false, and 13 were considered by the city to have been "serious." Of the $10,251,000 damage total, four-fifths was due to stock loss. Damage to buildings and fixtures was less than $2 million.

Twenty-three persons were killed—a white detective, a white fireman, and 21 Negroes. One was 73-year-old Isaac Harrison. Six were women. Two were children.

POLICE VIOLENCE

. . . in the front rank, a little ahead. They were crossing the bridge. They were walking on cobbles on a badlylighted street under an elevated structure. Trains roared overhead. "Only a few blocks from Charlestown jail," a voice yelled.

This time the cops were using their clubs. There was the clatter of the horses' hoofs on the cobbles and the whack thud whack thud of the clubs. And way off the jingle jangle of patrolwagons. Mary was terribly scared. A big truck was bearing down on her. She jumped to one side out of the way behind one of the girder supports. Two cops had hold of her. She clung to the grimy girder. A cop was cracking her on the hand with his club. She wasn't much hurt, she was in a patrolwagon, she'd lost her hat and her hair had come down. She caught herself thinking that she ought to have her hair bobbed if she was going to do much of this sort of thing.

"Anybody know where Don Stevens is?"

Don's voice came a little shakily from the blackness in front. "That you, Mary?"

"How are you, Don?"

*   *   *

Much I thought of you when I was lying in the death house—the singing, the kind tender voices of the children from the playground where there was all the life and the joy of liberty—just one step from the wall that contains the buried agony of three buried souls. It would remind me so often of you and of your sister and I wish I could see you every moment, but I feel better that you will not come to the death house so that you could not see the horrible picture of three living in agony waiting to be electrocuted.

The Camera Eye (50)

they have clubbed us off the streets   they are stronger   they are rich
    they hire and fire the politicians the newspapereditors the old judges the small men with reputations the collegepresidents the wardheelers (listen businessmen collegepresidents judges   America will not forget her betrayers) they hire the men with guns   the uniforms the policecars the patrolwagons

all right you have won   you will kill the brave men our friends tonight
there is nothing left to do   we are beaten   we the beaten crowd
together in these old dingy schoolrooms on Salem Street   shuffle up and
down the gritty creaking stairs sit hunched with bowed heads on benches and
hear the old words of the haters of oppression   made new in sweat and agony
tonight
      our work is over   the scribbled phrases   the nights typing releases
the smell of the printshop the sharp reek of newsprinted leaflets the rush for
Western Union stringing words into wires the search for stinging words to
make you feel who are your oppressors America
      America our nation has been beaten by strangers who have turned our
language inside out who have taken the clean words our fathers spoke and
made them slimy and foul
      their hired men sit on the judge's bench they sit back . . .

Source: *The Big Money* by John Dos Passos. Copyright by John Dos Passos. Published by
Houghton Mifflin Company, 1946. Reprinted by permission.

II. PREVENTIVE HARASSMENT[1]

In an earlier era third-degree interrogations were widespread, indiscriminate
arrests on suspicion were generally accepted, and "alley justice" dispensed with
the nightstick was common. Yet there were few riots, and the riots which did
occur generally did not arise from a police incident.

Today, many disturbances studied by the Commission began with a police
incident. But these incidents were not, for the most part, the crude acts of an
earlier time. They were routine, proper police actions such as stopping a motorist
or raiding an illegal business. Indeed, many of the serious disturbances took
place in cities whose police are among the best led, best organized, best trained
and most professional in the country.

Yet some activities of even the most professional police department may
heighten tension and enhance the potential for civil disorder. An increase in
complaints of police misconduct, for example, may in fact be a reflection of
professionalism; the department may simply be using law enforcement methods

---

[1] In performing this task we wish to acknowledge our indebtedness to and reliance upon the
extensive work done by the President's Commission on Law Enforcement and Administration
of Justice (The "Crime Commission"). The reports, studies, surveys, and analyses of the Crime
Commission have contributed to many of our conclusions and recommendations.

which increase the total volume of police contacts with the public. The number of charges of police misconduct may be greater simply because the volume of police-citizen contacts is higher.

Here we examine two aspects of police activities that have great tension-creating potential. Our objective is to provide recommendations to assist city and police officials in developing practices which can allay rather than contribute to tension.

Police Conduct

Negroes firmly believe that police brutality and harassment occur repeatedly in Negro neighborhoods. This belief is unquestionably one of the major reasons for intense Negro resentment against the police.

The extent of this belief is suggested by attitude surveys. In 1964, a New York Times study of Harlem showed that 43 percent of those questioned believed in the existence of police "brutality."[2] In 1965, a nationwide Gallup Poll found that 35 percent of Negro men believe there was police brutality in their areas; 7 percent of white men thought so. In 1966, a survey conducted for the Senate Subcommittee on Executive Reorganization found that 60 percent of Watts Negroes aged 15 to 19 believed there was some police brutality. Half said they had witnessed such conduct. A University of California at Los Angeles study of the Watts area found that 79 percent of the Negro males believed police lack respect for or use insulting language to Negroes and 74 percent believed police use unnecessary force in making arrests. In 1967, an Urban League study in Detroit found that 82 percent believed there was some form of police brutality.

The true extent of excessive and unjustified use of force is difficult to determine. One survey done for the Crime Commission suggests that when police-citizen contacts are systematically observed, the vast majority are handled without antagonism or incident. Of 5,339 police-citizen contacts observed in slum precincts in three large cities, in the opinion of the observer, only 20—about three-tenths of 1 percent—involved excessive or unnecessary force. And although almost all of those subjected to such force were poor, more than half were white. Verbal discourtesy was more common—15 percent of all such contacts began with a "brusque or nasty command" on the part of the officer. Again, however, the objects of such commands were more likely to be white than Negro.

Such "observer" surveys may not fully reflect the normal pattern of police conduct. The Crime Commission Task Force concluded that although the study gave "no basis for stating the extent to which police officers used force, it did confirm that such conduct still exists in the cities where observations were made."

Physical abuse is only one source of aggravation in the ghetto. In nearly every city surveyed, the Commission heard complaints of harassment of interracial couples, dispersal of social street gatherings, and the stopping of Negroes on

---

[2] The "brutality" referred to in this and other surveys is often not precisely defined, and covers conduct ranging from use of insulting language to excessive and unjustified use of force.

foot or in cars without obvious basis. These, together with contemptuous and degrading verbal abuse, have great impact in the ghetto. As one Commission witness said, these strip the Negro of the one thing that he may have left—his dignity, "the question of being a man."

Some conduct—breaking up of street groups, indiscriminate stops and searches—is frequently directed at youths, creating special tensions in the ghetto where the average age is generally under 21. Ghetto youths, often without work and with homes that may be nearly uninhabitable, particularly in the summer, commonly spend much time on the street. Characteristically, they are not only hostile to police, but eager to demonstrate their own masculinity and courage. The police, therefore, are often subject to taunts and provocations, testing their self-control and, probably, for some, reinforcing their hostility to Negroes in general. Because youths commit a large and increasing proportion of crime, police are under growing pressure from their supervisors—and from the community—to deal with them forcefully. "Harassment of youths" may therefore be viewed by some police departments—and members even of the Negro community—as a proper crime prevention technique.

In a number of cities the Commission heard complaints of abuse from Negro adults of all social and economic classes. Particular resentment is aroused by harassing Negro men in the company of white women—often their light-skinned Negro wives.

"Harassment" or discourtesy may not be the result of malicious or discriminatory intent of police officers. Many officers simply fail to understand the effects of their actions because of their limited knowledge of the Negro community. Calling a Negro teenager by his first name may arouse resentment because many whites still refuse to extend to adult Negroes the courtesy of the title, "Mister." A patrolman may take the arm of a person he is leading to the police car. Negroes are more likely to resent this than whites because the action implies that they are on the verge of flight and may degrade them in the eyes of friends or onlookers.

In assessing the impact of police misconduct we emphasize that the improper acts of a relatively few officers may create severe tensions between the department and the entire Negro community. Whatever the actual extent of such conduct, we concur in the Crime Commission's conclusion that:

. . . all such behavior is obviously and totally reprehensible, and when it is directed against minority-group citizens it is particularly likely to lead, for quite obvious reasons, to bitterness in the community.

Police Patrol Practices

Although police administrators may take steps to attempt to eliminate misconduct by individual police officers, many departments have adopted patrol practices which in the words of one commentator, have ". . . replaced harassment by individual patrolmen with harassment by entire departments."

These practices, sometimes known as "aggressive preventive patrol," take a number of forms, but invariably they involve a large number of police-citizen contacts initiated by police rather than in response to a call for help or service. One such practice utilizes a roving task force which moves into high-crime districts without prior notice, and conducts intensive, often indiscriminate, street stops and searches. A number of persons who might legitimately be described as suspicious are stopped. But so also are persons whom the beat patrolman would know are respected members of the community. Such task forces are often deliberately moved from place to place making it impossible for its members to know the people with whom they come in contact.

In some cities aggressive patrol is not limited to special task forces. The beat patrolman himself is expected to participate and to file a minimum number of stop-and-frisk or field interrogation reports for each tour of duty. This pressure to produce, or a lack of familiarity with the neighborhood and its people, may lead to widespread use of these techniques without adequate differentiation between genuinely suspicious behavior, and behavior which is suspicious to a particular officer merely because it is unfamiliar.

Police administrators, pressed by public concern about crime, have instituted such patrol practices often without weighing their tension-creating effects and the resulting relationship to civil disorder.

Motorization of police is another aspect of patrol that has affected law enforcement in the ghetto. The patrolman comes to see the city through a windshield and hear about it over a police radio. To him, the area increasingly comes to consist only of law breakers. To the ghetto resident, the policeman comes increasingly to be only an enforcer.

Loss of contact between the police officer and the community he serves adversely affects law enforcement. If an officer has never met, does not know, and cannot understand the language and habits of the people in the area he patrols, he cannot do an effective police job. His ability to detect truly suspicious behavior is impaired. He deprives himself of important sources of information. He fails to know those persons with an "equity" in the community—homeowners, small businessmen, professional men, persons who are anxious to support proper law enforcement—and thus sacrifices the contributions they can make to maintaining community order.

Recommendations

Police misconduct—whether described as brutality, harassment, verbal abuse, or discourtesy—cannot be tolerated even if it is infrequent. It contributes directly to the risk of civil disorder. It is inconsistent with the basic responsibility and function of a police force in a democracy. Police departments must have rules prohibiting such misconduct and enforce them vigorously. Police commanders must be aware of what takes place in the field, and take firm steps to correct abuses. We consider this matter further in the section on policy guidelines.

Elimination of misconduct also requires care in selecting police for ghetto areas, for there the police responsibility is particularly sensitive, demanding and often dangerous. The highest caliber of personnel is required if police are to overcome feelings within the ghetto community of inadequate protection and unfair discriminatory treatment. Despite this need, data from Commission investigators and from the Crime Commission disclose that often a department's worst, not its best, are assigned to minority group neighborhoods. As Professor Albert Reiss, Director of the Center for Research on Social Organization, University of Michigan, testified before the Commission:

. . . I think we confront in modern urban police departments in large cities much of what we encounter in our schools, in these cities. The slum police precinct is like the slum school. It gets, with few exceptions, the worst in the system.

Referring to extensive studies in one city, Professor Reiss concluded:

In predominantly Negro precincts, over three-fourths of the white policemen expressed prejudice or highly prejudiced attitudes towards Negroes. Only one percent of the officers expressed attitudes which could be described as sympathetic towards Negroes. Indeed, close to one-half of all the police officers in predominantly Negro high crime rate areas showed extreme prejudice against Negroes. What do I mean by extreme racial prejudice? I mean that they describe Negroes in terms that are not people terms. They describe them in terms of the animal kingdom. . . .

Although some prejudice was displayed in only 8 percent of police-citizen encounters:

The cost of such prejudiced behavior I suggest is much higher than my statistics suggest. Over a period of time, a substantial proportion of citizens, particularly in high crime rate areas, may experience at least one encounter with a police officer where prejudice is shown.

To ensure assignment of well-qualified police to ghetto areas, *the Commission Recommends*:

—Officers with bad reputations among residents in minority areas should be immediately reassigned to other areas. This will serve the interests of both the police and the community.

—Screening procedures should be developed to ensure that officers with superior ability, sensitivity and the common sense necessary for enlightened law enforcement are assigned to minority group areas. We believe that, with proper training in ghetto problems and conditions, and with proper standards for recruitment of new officers, in the long run, most policemen can meet these standards.

—Incentives, such as bonuses or credits for promotion should be developed wherever necessary to attract outstanding officers for ghetto positions.

The recommendations we have proposed are designed to help ensure proper police conduct in minority areas. Yet there is another facet of the problem: Negro perceptions of police misconduct. Even if those perceptions are exaggerated, they do exist. If outstanding officers are assigned to ghetto areas, if acts of misconduct, however infrequent, result in proper—and visible—disciplinary action, and if these corrective practices are made part of known policy, we believe the community will soon learn to reject unfounded claims of misconduct.

▄▄▄▄▄▄

III. PATTERNS OF POLICE BRUTALITY: ENFORCEMENT OF SEGREGATION OR SUBORDINATE STATUS

THE KILLING OF A NEGRO IN GEORGIA: 1943.—In the early morning of January 30, 1943, Manley Poteat responded to a call for an ambulance at the jail in Newton, Baker County, Georgia. He explained in sworn testimony that he found an "unconscious" man crawling around in a pool of blood on the floor of a cell.[1] The man was a young Negro, Bobby Hall, a skilled mechanic who was married and had one child. He was taken to a hospital in Albany, 22 miles away, where he died approximately 1 hour after his arrival. When Walter Poteat, Manley's father, embalmed the body, he observed that it had been brutally beaten.[2]

The authorities in Albany, which is not in Baker County, were notified and saw the body; photographs were made; and the matter soon came to public attention. Sheriff Claude M. Screws—and other officers—who beat and killed Hall were later prosecuted by the Federal Government for violation of an 1866 statute that makes it a Federal crime for an officer of the law to interfere with the constitutional rights of any person.[3] In beating and killing young Hall without justification, a Federal grand jury in Macon charged, the sheriff had deprived the victim of a number of constitutional rights including the right not to be subjected to punishment except after a fair trial and the right to equal protection of the laws. Screws was convicted, and eventually appealed to the Supreme Court, challenging the constitutionality of the statute. In the landmark decision of *Screws* v. *United States*,[4] the Supreme Court in 1945 upheld the statute, construed it strictly, and overturned the conviction because it had not been established that in killing Bobby Hall, Screws had intended to deprive him of a constitutional right.[5] Screws was later tried again under the standard set forth by the Supreme Court and acquitted.[6]

While this example of police brutality took place almost two decades ago it is still a classic case. Recent complaints coming to the attention of this Commission contain allegations that bear a striking similarity to it. For this reason the case will be described in detail.

Sheriff Screws testified at his first trial that the trouble began late that January evening in 1943 when he asked night patrolman Frank E. Jones and Deputy

---

[1] Record, p. 109, *Screws* v. *United States*, 325 U.S. 91 (1945).
[2] *Ibid.*, at 114.
[3] 14 Stat. 27 (1866), 18 U.S.C. sec. 242 (1958).
[4] *Screws* v. *United States*, *supra*, note 6.
[5] A full discussion of the statute, the *Screws* case, and other aspects of the enforcement of the Civil Rights Acts are found in ch. 4 *infra*.
[6] *United States* v. *Screws*, Crim. No. 1300, M.D. Ga., Nov. 1, 1945.

Sheriff Bob Kelley to serve a warrant of arrest on Bobby Hall for theft of a tire. The two men brought the Negro back to Newton in the Sheriff's car. Screws continued:[7]

> I opened the door and I said, "All right, Bobby, get out" and I noticed he wasn't in any hurry to get out when he, when I did see him come out, I saw something coming out ahead of him like that (indicating) and I discovered it was a gun; and he said; "You damn white sons"—and that is all I remember what he said. By that time I knocked the gun up like that and the gun fired off right over my head; and when it did he was on the ground by then and me and Kelley and Jones ran in to him and we all were scuffling and I was beating him about the face and head with my fist. I knew Jones had a blackjack and I told him to hit him and he hit him a lick or two and he didn't seem to weaken and I said, "Hit him again!" When he fell to the ground, we didn't hit him on the ground.

*   *   *

> At no time when I saw the deceased or Bobby Hall did he have any handcuffs on him.

The only colored prosecution witness who observed a crucial part of this event was Mrs. Annie Pearl Hall, the wife of the victim. She contradicted, in part, one vital item in the defendant's case: Mrs. Hall stated after the victim left their home under arrest, "they were handcuffing him when I went to the door."[8] All three of the officers said that he had never been handcuffed and was, therefore, able to grab the shotgun from the front seat of the car and attack them with it.

While there are many similarities between this case and others in Commission files, there is one major difference. A number of white people observed the beating of Bobby Hall and events connected with it—and appeared at the trial as witnesses. Their stories supported one another and directly contradicted that of Screws. The testimony of these witnesses may be summarized as follows: Screws and his companions had threatened to get a "nigger" that night; they took Hall to an open area in the center of town near the public pump; the three men beat him to the ground and continued for 15 to 30 minutes to pound him with a heavy object—which was later found to be a 2-pound metal blackjack; the victim was handcuffed during all of these proceedings; after the beating the shotgun was fired once—not by the unconscious victim but apparently by one of the officers for some unknown reason.[9]

One of the white eyewitnesses who appeared at the trial and swore to these facts was Mrs. Ollie Jernigan. Her husband, J. H. Jernigan, did not see the incident, but he testified that he was walking through town one day and

---

[7] Record, *supra*, note 6, at 171.

[8] *Ibid.*, at 60.

[9] This description is based primarily on the testimony of these white eyewitnesses: Mr. A. B. Edwards (*ibid.*, at 79–82), Mrs. A. B. Ledbetter (*ibid.*, at 83–85), Mr. A. B. Ledbetter (*ibid.*, at 85–89), Mrs. Mabel Burke (*ibid.*, at 105–106), and Mrs. Ollie Jernigan (*ibid.*, at 89–92).

Sheriff Screws called him over to his car where the following conversation took place:[10]

"Herschell, you know those FBI men are down here investigating that case?" He said, "Well, I understand that your wife saw it." I told him "Yes." He says, "Well, you know we have always been friends and I want us to continue to be friends." I told him, "Well, I hoped we could."

The dynamics of combined prejudice and violence in this case are suggested in the testimony of James P. Willingham, a white man, who said that shortly after the killing he had a talk with his friend, Officer Frank Jones:[11]

[H]e told me that the Negro had a mighty good pistol and they had taken it away from him and the Negro acted so damn smart and went before the Court in some way trying to make them give it back to him . . . and that they went out there that night with a warrant and arrested him and handcuffed him and brought him to town and the Negro put up some kind of talk about wanting to give bond or something to that effect and they beat hell out of him; then, that when they got him up to the well they whipped him some more and he died shortly afterwards. He said the Negro attempted to shoot them at the well; said the Negro attempted to shoot them at the well with a shotgun and said he hit him with a blackjack pretty hard and I asked him about how in the world did the Negro try to shoot you and you had him handcuffed and he said well we finished him off and that is all.

Bobby Hall apparently was considered a somewhat "uppity" Negro. Evidence produced at the trial indicated that the tire theft charge was a sham for, as suggested in the Willingham testimony, Hall's major "crime" was to challenge the power of the sheriff to confiscate his pistol. Bobby Hall was not accused of any crime in connection with the weapon. He needed it, he claimed, for protection. In attempting to exercise not his civil rights but his property rights, Hall contacted a lawyer and even went before a local grand jury. But he did not recover his pistol.[12] And, while he never challenged the system of segregation, he was something of a leader among Negroes.[13]

No State or local action was taken against the alleged offenders. Prosecution by the State—which has the power to impose the supreme penalty—may be blocked in cases of this type by the fact that the potential defendant is the person who must start up the machinery of the criminal law. While the district solicitor general in the *Screws* case had formal power to prosecute, he repeatedly felt "helpless in the matter" because he had "to rely upon the sheriff and policemen of the various counties of his circuit for investigation."[14] In the absence of an investigation and a complaint from Sheriff Screws, or by another police officer implicating Screws, no prosecution was commenced. In police brutality cases

---

[10] *Ibid.*, at 93.

[11] *Ibid.*, at 120.

[12] *Ibid.*, at 67–68.

[13] Special Agent Marcus B. Calhoun of the FBI office testified at the trial that, "Mr. Screws . . . told me that he had had trouble with Bobby Hall, that he seemed to be a leader or denominated himself as such and that when a Negro got in trouble with the law that he, Bobby Hall, would advise him as to what action he should take." Record, *supra*, note 6, at 78.

[14] Information from the Department of Justice, as quoted in Carr, *Federal Protection of Civil Rights* 107 (1947).

where the potential defendant is not the *chief* law enforcement officer of the county, there is a greater possibility of criminal or disciplinary action by local authorities. But even in such situations, local action against officers of the law is not common.[15]

Neither Screws nor any of his associates was ever punished. They experienced the difficulty and expense of months of litigation but a second Federal jury acquitted them. The episode did not seriously tarnish the reputation of Claude M. Screws. In 1958 he ran for the State Senate and was elected.

THE KILLING OF A NEGRO IN GEORGIA: 1958.—The town of Dawson in Terrell County, Ga. is approximately 30 miles south of Newton. There on April 20, 1958, James Brazier, a Negro in his thirties, suffered a beating at the hands of officers of the law (from which he later died)—in circumstances similar to those in the *Screws* case.[16]

According to the police account, the incident started in the early evening of Sunday, April 20, 1958, when Dawson Police Officer "X" arrested James Brazier's father on a charge of driving under the influence of alcohol. When the elder Brazier resisted, he was subdued by a blackjack. James Brazier protested and, according to the policemen, threatened the officer who later returned with Officer "Y" and arrested the younger Brazier, allegedly with a warrant, for interfering with an arrest. He resisted violently and was subdued with a blackjack. Shortly thereafter he was taken to jail and examined by a local physician who found no serious injury.[17]

Brazier died 5 days later at a hospital in Columbus, Ga. from brain damage and a fractured skull. He had four to six bruised spots on his scalp from a blunt instrument which apparently also caused the skull fracture.[18] The police claimed that Brazier was hit only once or twice at the time of the arrest.

In a sworn statement to Commission representatives Mrs. Hattie Bell Brazier, the widow of the victim, claimed that this affair had actually started months earlier. Mrs Brazier explained that she and her husband had purchased a new Chevrolet in 1956—and another in 1958.[19] In November of 1957 James Brazier

---

[15] See Ch. 6 at 79 *infra*.

[16] The description of the Brazier case is largely based on evidence gathered in an investigation by Commission representatives in late August, 1960 and incorporated into a Commission document entitled *Report on Field Investigation in Terrell County, Georgia*. Four Negro eyewitnesses to various parts of the Brazier incident were interviewed and statements taken from them. In addition, statements were received from other Negro eyewitnesses who were not then available to be interviewed. Four white people were interviewed regarding the case.
In addition to the Brazier incident other cases in Terrell County involving alleged Police brutality to Negroes were investigated on this field trip. The evidence supporting complaints in these cases was not as strong as that in the Brazier case.

[17] *Ibid.*, at 10–12.

[18] This information comes from the Certificate of Death of James Brazier and from an interview with a doctor who attended the victim at the Columbus Medical Center, *Report on Field Investigation in Terrell County, Georgia, supra*, note 21, at 18.

[19] Affidavit of Mrs. Hattie Bell Brazier, and *Report on Field Investigation In Terrell County, Georgia, supra*, note 21, at 14. Although their hourly wages were not high, Mrs. Brazier explained, she had three jobs and her late husband, two. They sometimes worked at menial tasks from early morning until late night. This allowed them to purchase the automobiles. Interview With Mrs. Hattie Bell Brazier, Albany, Ga., August 23, 1960.

had been arrested on a speeding charge. According to Mrs. Brazier, her husband told her that Dawson Officer "Y" took him to jail, and that:[20]

"When I first entered the door of the jail, ["Y"] hit me on the back of the head and knocked me down and said, 'You smart son-of-a-bitch, I been wanting to get my hands on you for a long time.' I said, 'Why you want me for?' ["Y"] said, 'You is a nigger who is buying new cars and we can't hardly live. I'll get you yet.'"

Officer "Y" then allegedly hit Brazier several more times, put his foot on the small prostrate Negro's back (Mrs. Brazier said she saw the footprints there later), and warned him, "You'd better not say a damn thing about it or I'll stomp your damn brains out." After his release from jail, Brazier was bleeding from his ear and vomiting blood. From this time in the fall of 1957 until the second incident in April of 1958, James Brazier was under the care of a local white doctor because of these injuries. Officer "X", the policeman who accompanied "Y" during the arrest in April 1958, also allegedly made a remark about the new car at some time previous to the fatal incident.[21] It appears that James Brazier of Terrell County, like Bobby Hall of Baker County, was considered an "uppity" Negro.

The story of the fatal incident in 1958 as told by Mrs. Brazier and several other colored witnesses contradicts the account given by the officers. In her affidavit Mrs. Brazier stated that her husband had been beaten brutally by the arresting officers in full view of numerous colored people, including herself and her four children. No warrant was presented by the officers, nor was any paper observed in their hands. The officers, she said, simply ran out of their car and roughly grabbed her husband. While pulling him toward the police car, "Y" beat him repeatedly with a blackjack. Mrs. Brazier's affidavit continued:[22]

["Y"] then said, "You smart son-of-a-bitch, I told you I would get you." James said, "What do you want to hurt me for? I ain't done nothing. I got a heap of little chillun. [sic]." ["Y"] said, "I don't give a goddamn how many children you got, you're going away from here" . . . ["Y"] pulled out his pistol and stuck it against James' stomach and said, "I oughta blow your goddamn brains out."

Then these events allegedly occurred: James Brazier's 10-year-old son pleaded with the officers to stop beating his father and was knocked to the ground by "Y";[23] the victim was thrown onto the floor of the police car with his legs

---

[20] Affidavit of Mrs. Hattie Bell Brazier, and *Report on Field Investigation in Terrell County, Georgia, supra*, note 21, at 12–13.

[21] Earlier in the Spring of 1958 Mrs. Brazier alleged that Officer "X" saw the Brazier's new car and asked them how they managed to purchase it. James Brazier replied flippantly, "I works for what I gets." And "X" countered in a threatening tone, "You'll never remember paying for it." Mrs. Brazier said that this took place in her presence, and it is set out in her affidavit and in *Report on Field Investigation In Terrell County, Georgia, supra*, note 21, at 14.

[22] Affidavit of Mrs. Hattie Bell Brazier and *Report on Field Investigation in Terrell County, Georgia, supra*, note 21, at 15.

[23] Affidavit of Mrs. Hattie Belle Brazier, Affidavit of James Brazier, Jr. (aged 10), and *Report on Field Investigation in Terrell County, George, supra*, note 21, at 16. Mrs. Brazier explained in a subsequent interview that the shock of this incident brought on a nervous condition in James, Jr., and forced her to send the boy to live with his grandmother in the North. Interview with Mrs. Hattie Bell Brazier, Albany, Ga., August 23, 1960.

dangling outside; "Y" kicked him twice in the groin; slammed the car door on his legs; threw a hat full of sand into his bloody face, and drove off.[24]

When Brazier reached the jail, he was bloody but conscious and apparently not seriously injured by the beating he had received. Yet, when he was taken to court the next morning, he was virtually unconscious. The question that arises is whether Brazier was beaten during the interval between his arrival in jail at approximately 7 P.M. and his appearance in court at approximately 9 A.M. the next day. There is evidence that he was. It comes from several witnesses, one of whom has since died [25] and may be identified—Marvin Goshay, a Negro who was 23 years of age when he signed an affidavit on August 24, 1960 during an interview with Commission representatives in Albany, Ga. Goshay was in jail on a charge of assault and battery when Brazier was incarcerated. The story, as Goshay saw it, is as follows: When James Brazier was brought into the jail he was fully dressed in suit, shirt, tie, and shoes. He talked coherently to Goshay (describing his arrest consistently with Mrs. Brazier's later testimony). Several hours later—probably around midnight—he was ordered out of the cell by Officers "X" and "Y." "They took Brazier out again," Goshay stated in his affidavit. "He asked them to wait because he wanted to put on his shoes. The police said, 'You won't need no shoes.'" This was the last time that Goshay saw him that night. Goshay next saw Brazier on the following morning. His affidavit continued:

He had on pants, a torn undershirt, no coat, no tie, no white shirt. The last time I saw him, he had on a blue suit, white shirt, and tie. He looked worse on his head than when I saw him also . . . it was beaten worse than when I first saw him. On his back were about four long marks about a foot long. They looked reddish and bruised. His head was bleeding. We had to carry [him] to the car because he couldn't walk. He was slobbering at the mouth. When we got to the car. James, who was dazed but not completely out, didn't know enough to get in the car. Mr. ["Z"—a Dawson police officer] said if he didn't get in, he'd beat him with his blackjack.

More than a year after Brazier's death Sheriff Z. T. Mathews of Terrell County allegedly made the following statement to Mrs. Brazier:[26]

I oughta slap your damn brains out. A nigger like you I feel like slapping them out. You niggers set around here and look at television and go up North and come back and do to white folks here like the niggers up North do, but you ain't gonna do it. I'm gonna carry the South's orders out like it oughta be done.

---

[24] In addition to the affidavit of Mrs. Brazier this story is supported by several colored eyewitnesses interviewed by Commission representatives in Georgia. *Report on Field Investigation in Terrell County, Georgia, supra*, note 21, at 16.

[25] See note 30, *infra*.

[26] Affidavit of Mrs. Hattie Bell Brazier, and *Report on Field Investigation in Terrell County, Georgia, supra*, note 21, at 20. Mayor James Griggs Raines of Dawson reported in an interview with two Commission representatives that he felt that Sheriff Mathews was a bad influence on Dawson policemen. "In my opinion the Sheriff, Mathews, is unfit and has violated the Civil Rights Acts. I've seen him beat a pregnant Negro woman. He's unfit to hold office. You can quote me," the Mayor stated. *Ibid.*, at 40.

Also, Sheriff Mathews told reporter Robert E. Lee Baker, "You know, Cap, . . . there's nothing like fear to keep niggers in line. I'm talking about 'outlaw' niggers." [27]

No local disciplinary or criminal action was taken against any of the officers involved. The attitude of local authorities toward police was protective in this and several other cases of alleged brutality that occurred within a brief period in Dawson. Indeed, there was indignation when Negroes claimed they were "living in an atmosphere of fear." [28] As in the *Screws* case the Department of Justice was sufficiently impressed with the results of an FBI investigation to authorize Civil Rights Acts prosecutions. From August 4 to 8, 1958, the local United States Attorney presented witnesses to a Federal grand jury in Macon and requested indictments in five cases of alleged police brutality against policemen "X," "Y," and another Dawson officer.[29] The grand jury returned no indictments.[30]

In the 15 years between the death of Bobby Hall and the death of James Brazier the world had changed in many ways. But in Terrell and Baker, as in some other rural southern counties,[31] the economy, the social system, and racial attitudes remained virtually what they had been. James Griggs Raines who owns many of the buildings in Dawson and has been its Mayor, explained in a 1960 interview that, "This is a feudalistic system. But I don't know if, or how, it will be changed."[32] Few Negroes vote in these counties and in most ways they are deprived and subordinate. Officers of the law sometimes enforce this status by illegal or violent methods.[33]

Not long after Brazier died, police officer "Y" was promoted to Chief of the

---

[27] Washington Post, June 8, 1958, p. A–12.

[28] Atlanta Constitution, June 9, 1958, pp. 1–5; June 10, 1958, pp. 1, 8.

[29] The Government contended that the officers had violated 18 U.S.C. sec. 242 because by these acts of brutality they had "under color of law" interfered with the constitutional rights of the victims.

[30] Although Marvin Goshay was subpenaed by the Federal Government to testify before the grand jury sitting in Macon, he did not appear. In his sworn statement to a Commission representative Goshay explained that shortly after he received the subpena, Officer "Y" found him walking on the street in Dawson and ordered him to jail. When the Negro asked why he was being incarcerated, "Y" replied, "You just need to be in jail." The young man was kept prisoner for 1 week, during which time the Federal grand jury met and refused indictments. One week later, "Officer ['Y']" came in and told me I could go on home," Goshay explained. "I never was brought to . . . court during this time. I just stayed in jail. I can only guess, although no one ever told me, that the only reason I was locked up was because they didn't want me to go to Macon." Goshay was slated to be a witness in a pending Federal civil suit for $177,000 brought by Mrs. Brazier against Officer "Y" and others. On March 14, 1961, Marvin Goshay was found dead—apparently of asphyxiation—in a Dawson undertaking parlor. An FBI investigation failed to uncover evidence of foul play.

[31] Those rural, southern counties which have a high percentage of nonwhites in their population are the subject of a separate and detailed analysis in this report. See part III, *supra.*

[32] *Report on Field Investigation in Terrell County, Georgia, supra,* note 21, at 5.

[33] In addition to the Brazier case, there are recent cases containing similar allegations in the files of the Commission. Some of these have been referred to the Department of Justice for possible prosecutive action.

Dawson Police Department. Z. T. Mathews at this writing is still sheriff of Terrell County.

The Hall and Brazier cases are more dramatic than most, partly because they resulted in death. But the Commission has reviewed complaints and reports of similar incidents. Reports of some of the most heinous of these have come to the Commission from the Mississippi State Advisory Committee which says that it has received "many and at times almost unbelievable reports of atrocities and brutalities" perpetrated by law enforcement officials.[34] As with many other current complaints, these are now under investigation by the Department of Justice and for that reason will not be considered here.

Some of the worst complaints of police brutality have included allegations that the officers involved expressed some racial motive for their conduct. The extensive violence found in the Hall and Brazier cases, for example, is rarely seen in incidents where there is no element of racial hate. . . .

---

[34] Report of the Mississippi Advisory Committee to the Commission on Civil Rights, *The 50 States Report* 315, 317 (1961). . . .

CHAPTER 3

GENOCIDE

Auschwitz: A Transport Arrives

TADEUSZ BOROWSKI

PROLOGUE OR ANTICIPATION OF THE "TRANSPORT"

Greeks are sitting around us, moving their jaws voraciously like huge in-human insects, greedily eating moldy clods of bread. They are uneasy; they don't know what they'll be doing. Rails and planks worry them. They don't like heavy hauling.

"Was wir arbeiten?" they ask.

"Niks. Transport kommen, alles Krematorium, compris?"

"Alles verstehen," they answer in crematorium esperanto. They calm down; they won't be loading rails on trucks, or carrying planks.

ACT I, OR THE ARRIVAL OF THE "TRANSPORT"

A striped crowd lay near the tracks in the long strips of shade. It breathed heavily and unevenly, spoke lazily in its own tongues and gazed indifferently

Source: Reprinted from *The Captive Mind* by Czeslaw Milosz, by permission of Alfred A. Knopf, Inc. Copyright 1951, 1953 by Czeslaw Milosz. Also, by permission of Martin Secker & Warburg Ltd., London. (From a story by Tadeusz Borowski. The adapted version reprinted here first appeared in English translation, attributed to an anonymous Polish author, in Czeslaw Milosz, *The Captive Mind*, trans. by Jane Zielenko. Its authorship became known to English-speaking readers when the complete story, "This Way for the Gas," trans. by Barbara Vedder, appeared in *Commentary* (July 1962), pp. 39–47.)

Editors' Note: This is a fictional account of actual events, written by an eyewitness and participant. Czeslaw Milosz introduces it in these words: "In the abundant literature of atrocity of the twentieth century, one rarely finds an account written from the point of view of an accessory to the crime. Authors are usually ashamed of this role. But collaboration is an empty word as applied to a concentration camp. The machine is impersonal; responsibility shifts from those who carry out orders to those higher, always higher. ... [This story] should, I believe, be included in all anthologies of literature dealing with the lot of men in totalitarian society, if such anthologies are compiled." His judgment carries weight; it is that of one who has lived under and knows intimately the totalitarianism of Communist Poland as well as Nazi Germany.

at the majestic people in green uniform, at the green of the trees, near and unattainable, at the steeple of a distant little church which at that moment was tolling a late angelus.

"The transport is coming," someone said, and everyone stood up in expectation. Freight cars appeared around the curve as the train backed in. The trainman standing in the caboose leaned out, waved his hand, whistled. The locomotive screeched, wheezed and the train trundled slowly along the station. Behind the tiny barred windows one could see human faces, pale, crumpled, disheveled, as if they were sleepy—frightened women, and men who, exotically, had hair. They passed slowly, gazing at the station in silence. Then something started to boil inside the wagons and to beat against their wooden walls.

"Water! Air!" Despairing, hollow cries burst out.

Human faces pressed to the windows, lips desperately gasping for air sucked in a few gulps, vanished; others struggled into their place, then they too vanished. The shrieks and moans grew steadily louder.

ACT II, OR THE SEGREGATION (A FEW SCENES WILL SUFFICE)

Here comes a woman walking briskly, hurrying almost imperceptibly yet feverishly. A small child with the plump, rosy face of a cherub runs after her, fails to catch up, stretches out its hands, crying, "Mama, mama!"

"Woman, take this child in your arms!"

"Sir, it isn't my child, it isn't mine!" the woman shouts hysterically, and runs away covering her face with her hands. She wants to hide; she wants to reach those who won't leave in a truck, who will leave on foot, who will live. She is young, healthy, pretty, she wants to live.

But the child runs after her, pleading at the top of its voice, "Mama, mama, don't run away!"

"It's not mine, not mine, not . . .!"

Until Andrej, the sailor from Sevastopol, overtook her. His eyes were troubled by vodka and the heat. He reached her, knocked her off her feet with a single powerful blow and, as she fell, caught her by the hair and dragged her up again. His face was distorted with fury.

"Why you lousy fucking Jew-bitch! Jebit twoju mat'! You'd run away from your own child! I'll show you, you whore!" He grabbed her in the middle, one paw throttling her throat which wanted to shout, and flung her into the truck like a heavy sack of grain.

"Here! Take this with you, you slut!" And he threw her child at her feet.

"Gut gemacht. That's how one should punish unnatural mothers," said an SS man standing near the van.

A pair of people fall to the ground entangled in a desperate embrace. He digs his fingers into her flesh convulsively, tears at her clothes with his teeth. She screams hysterically, curses, blasphemes until, stifled by a boot, she chokes and falls silent. They split them apart like a tree; and herd them into the car like animals.

Others are carrying a young girl with a missing leg; they hold her by her arms and by her one remaining leg. Tears are streaking down her face as she whispers sadly, "Please, please, it hurts, it hurts . . ." They heave her into a truck among the corpses. She will be burned alive, together with them.

ACT III, OR THE CONVERSATION OF THE WITNESSES

A cool and starry evening falls. We are lying on the tracks. It is infinitely silent. Anemic lamps burn on high poles behind the circles of light.

"Did you exchange shoes?" Henri asks me.

"No."

"Why not?"

"Man, I have enough, absolutely enough!"

"Already? After the first transport? Just think, me—since Christmas maybe a million people have passed through my hands. The worst are the transports from Paris: a man always meets friends."

"And what do you say to them?"

"That they're going to take a bath, and that we'll meet later in the camp. What would you say?"

EPILOGUE (MANY TRAINS CAME TO AUSCHWITZ THAT EVENING. THE TRANSPORT TOTALED 15,000 PEOPLE)

As we return to the camp, the stars begin to fade, the sky becomes ever more translucent and lifts above us, the night grows light. A clear, hot day announces itself.

From the crematoriums, broad columns of smoke rise steadily and merge above into a gigantic, black river that turns exceedingly slowly in the sky over Birkenau and disappears beyond the forests, in the direction of Trzebinia. The transport is already burning.

We pass an SS squad, moving with mechanized weapons to relieve the guard. They march evenly, shoulder to shoulder, one mass, one will.

"Und Morgen die ganze Welt . . ." they sing at the top of their lungs.

The Destruction of the European Jews

RAUL HILBERG

<hr>

1. THE PERPETRATORS

The Germans killed five million Jews. A process of such magnitude does not come from the void; to be brought to a conclusion in such dimensions an administrative undertaking must have meaning to its perpetrators. To Adolf Hitler and his followers the destruction of the Jews had meaning. To these men, the act was worthwhile in itself. It could not be questioned. It had to be done. When half of Europe lay conquered at Germany's feet, the uniqueness of the opportunity became compelling. The chance could not be missed. At that moment the German bureaucrat beckoned to his Faustian fate. The scope of human experience was to be widened as never before. Inevitably, at this point the German machine of destruction had to attempt the ultimate, for when a generation seeks to accomplish more than its scientific and artistic heritage has equipped it for, its path to fulfilment lies only in destruction. The process of creation is tedious and long; destruction alone is both swift and lasting.

Let us point out at once that the Germans have not been the only ones in history who have had a reason to embark upon a destructive course of action. When we examine the world historical scene, we may note that many times, in many countries, bureaucracies have launched the opening phases of a destruction process. Even now, in the Union of South Africa and elsewhere specialists are selecting, exploiting, and concentrating new victims. Very often, seemingly harmless bureaucratic activities—such as the definition of a particular group and the exclusion of its members from office—contain the seeds of administrative continuity. Potentially, these measures are steppingstones to a killing operation, but as a rule insurmountable barriers from without and within arrest and disrupt the destructive development. Externally, the opposition of the victims may bring the process to a halt; internally, administrative and psychological obstacles may

<hr>

Source: Raul Hilberg, *The Destruction of the European Jews* (Chicago: Quadrangle, 1961), pp. 639–669. Reprinted by permission.

Editors' Note: All footnotes have been preserved. Unless otherwise noted, page references are to *The Destruction of the European Jews.*

bar the way. The discriminatory systems of many countries are the leftovers of such disrupted destruction processes.

The German destruction of the Jews was not interrupted. That is its crucial, decisive characteristic. At the threshold of the killing phase the flow of administrative measures continued unchecked. Technocratic and moral obstacles were overcome. An unprecedented killing operation was inaugurated, and with the beginning of this operation the Germans demonstrated once and for all how quickly even large groups, numbering in the millions, could be annihilated.

How this was done?

THE DESTRUCTIVE EXPANSION

The German destructive effort may be likened to a three-dimensional structure which was expanding in all three directions. In one direction we can see an alignment of agency after agency in a machinery of destruction. In another direction we note the development, step by step, of the destruction process. In the third we can observe an attempt to set up multiple processes aimed at new victims and pointing to a destruction, group by group, of all human beings within the German reach.

Let us examine first the horizontal expansion at the base: the growth of the machinery of destruction. We know that as the process unfolded, its requirements became more complex and its fulfilment involved an ever larger number of agencies, party offices, business enterprises, and military commands. The destruction of the Jews was a total process, comparable in its diversity to a modern war, a mobilization, or a national reconstruction.

An administrative process of such range cannot be carried out by a single agency, even if it is a trained and specialized body like the Gestapo or a commissariat for Jewish affairs, for when a process cuts into every phase of human life, it must ultimately feed upon the resources of the entire organized community. That is why we found among the perpetrators the highly differentiated technicians of the armament inspectorates, the remote officials of the Postal Ministry, and—in the all-important operation of furnishing records for determination of descent—the membership of an aloof and withdrawn Christian clergy. The machinery of destruction, then, was structurally no different from organized German society as a whole; the difference was only one of function. The machinery of destruction *was* the organized community in one of its special roles.

As the apparatus expanded, its potential increased—the wider the base, the farther the reach. When the machine was finished, so was the process. But now we may ask: What determined the order of involvement? What determined the sequence of steps? We know that the bureaucracy had no master plan, no basic blueprint, no clear-cut view even of its actions. How, then, was the process regulated? What was the key to the operation?

FACT SHEET ON GENOCIDE

MEANING OF GENOCIDE

The cornerstone of all human rights is the right to exist. Yet, since time immemorial, entire groups of people — racial, religious, national — were put to destruction either by ruthless governments or by groups blinded by hatred and intolerance. For these victims, guarantees of free speech were meaningless, while their torturers were cutting out their tongues. The guarantees of free worship by national constitutions meant nothing while their churches were razed through organized fury. Millions of Christians were slaughtered in the Balkans; more than a mi
of Maronites were levelled
Iraq. Out of 80,000 Hereros
extermination campaign led
million Jews under Nazi o

This is genocide — the d
linguistic and political grou

I. Introduction
  A. What is Genocide
  B. Genocide is Not
  C. A Matter of Dom
  D. International Cri
II. Action by the United N
  A. Question first Br
  B. General Assembl
    Draft Conventio
  C. Draft Convention
  D. Consideration by
    in 1947
  E. Establishment in
    Draft a Convent
  F. Draft Convention
  G. Consideration by
    Its Seventh Sess
  H. Consideration by
    Its Third Sessic
III. Summary of the Provi
IV. Significance of the Cor
V. Question of Reservatic
  A. Consideration by
    in 1950

united nations
work for human rights

A clearly written account of United Nations
achievements during ten years toward the
promotion and protection of human rights
throughout the world. It provides informati

THE CRIME OF GENOCIDE

REPORT

OF THE

INTERNATIONAL LAW

COMMISSION

COVERING ITS SECOND SESSION
5 JUNE — 29 JULY 1950

GENERAL ASSEMBLY
OFFICIAL RECORDS: FIFTH SESSION
SUPPLEMENT No. 12 (A/1316)

UNITED   NATIONS

FACT SHEET ON GENOCIDE

REPORT OF THE AD HOC COMMITTEE ON GENOCIDE
5 April to 10 May 1948

A destruction process has an inherent pattern. There is only one way in which a scattered group can effectively be destroyed. Three steps are organic in the operation:

Definition

|

Concentration (or seizure)

|

Annihilation

This is the invariant structure of the basic process, for no group can be killed without a concentration or seizure of the victims, and no victims can be segregated before the perpetrator knows who belongs to the group.

There are, of course, additional steps in a modern destructive undertaking. These added steps are not required for the annihilation of the victim, but they are dictated by considerations of cost and economy. These are expropriations. In the destruction of the Jews expropriatory measures were introduced after every organic step. Thus dismissals and Aryanizations came after the definition; exploitation and starvation measures followed concentration; and the confiscation of personal belongings was incidental to the killing operation. In its completed form a destruction process in a modern society will consequently be structured as shown in the accompanying chart.

The sequence of steps in a destruction process is thus determined. If there is an attempt to inflict maximum injury upon a group of people, it is therefore inevitable that a bureaucracy—no matter how decentralized its apparatus or how unplanned its activities—should push its victims through these stages.

This is a twofold destructive expansion: the growth of the machine of destruction and the development of the destruction process. Today we know of a destructive expansion upon still another plane: as the machine was thrown into high gear and as the process accelerated toward its goal, German hostility became more generalized. The Jewish target became too narrow. More targets had to be added. This development is of the utmost importance, for it casts a revealing light upon the perpetrators' fundamental aim.

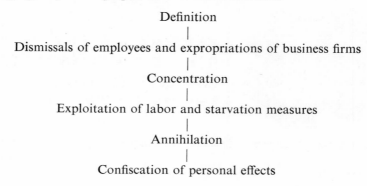

Definition

|

Dismissals of employees and expropriations of business firms

|

Concentration

|

Exploitation of labor and starvation measures

|

Annihilation

|

Confiscation of personal effects

If a group seeks merely the destruction of hostile institutions, the limit of its most drastic action would be drawn with the complete destruction of the bearers of the institutions. The Germans, however, did not draw the line with the destruction of Jewry. They attacked still other victims, some of whom were thought to be like Jews, some of whom were quite unlike Jews, and some of whom were Germans. The Nazi destruction process was, in short, not aimed at institutions; it was aimed at people. The Jews were only the first victims of the German bureaucracy; they were only the first caught in its path. That they should have been chosen first is not accidental—historical precedents, both administrative and conceptual, determined the selection of the people which for centuries had been the standby victim of recurring destructions. No other group could fill this role so well. None was so vulnerable. But the choice could not be confined to the Jews. Three illustrations will make this more clear.

Example I. The destruction process engulfed a group which was classified as a parasitical people leading a parasitical life: the Gypsies.[1] There were 34,000 to 40,000 Gypsies in the Reich. In accordance with a Himmler directive the Criminal Police were empowered to seize all persons who looked like Gypsies or who wandered around in "Gypsie-like" manner. Those who were seized were classified as follows:

Z   Full Gypsy (Zigeuner)
ZM+ Gypsy *Mischling*, predominantly Gypsy
ZM   Gypsy *Mischling* with equal Gypsy and German "blood-shares"
       (*Blutsanteile*)
ZM− Gypsy *Mischling*, predominantly German
NZ   Free of Gypsy blood (*Nicht Zigeuner*)

The victims in the first three categories were subjected to special wage regulations, taxes, and movement restrictions. Special provisions were made for "privileged Gypsy mixed marriages," etc.[2] In the 1940's the Germans went one step further: mobile units of the Security Police in Russia killed roving Gypsies;

---

[1] In the past the Gypsies had been linked to the Jews in popular belief as well as scholarly investigation. A seventeenth-century German writer, Johann Christof Wagenseil, wrote a thesis to prove that "the very first Gypsies were Jews who stemmed from Germany [*die allerersten Ziegeiner sind aus Teutschland gebürtige Juden gewesen*]." Wagenseil, *Der Meister-Singer Holdseligen Kunst* (in the introduction), printed 1697. The Nazis were not so sure of the Gypsy origins; however, it was thought that there was some racial affinity to the Jews. Two agencies were engaged in research on the subject: the *Reichszentrale zur Bekämpfung des Zigeunerwesens* and *Rassenhygienische Forschungsstelle* of the *Reichsgesundheitsamt*. H. Küppers, "Die Beschäftigung von Zigeunern," *Reichsarbeitsblatt*, V (March 25, 1947), 177, reprinted in *Die Judenfrage* (*Vertrauliche Beilage*), April 15, 1942, pp. 30–31.
[2] Küppers in *Reichsarbeitsblatt*, V, 177. Circular decree by Sauckel, June 24, 1942, in *Ministerialblatt des Reichs- und Preussischen Ministeriums des Innern*, July 22, 1942, p. 1488.

the military commander in Serbia concentrated Gypsies and shot them; and in Auschwitz several thousand Gypsies were gassed.[3]

Example II. The Poles in the territories incorporated by the Reich were in a rather precarious position. It had been planned to shove them into the *Generalgouvernement*, while the incorporated provinces to the west were to have become purely German. But that program, like the forced emigration of the Jews from Europe, collapsed. In the back of some people's minds a "territorial solution" now loomed for these Poles. On May 27, 1941, an interministerial conference took place under the chairmanship of Staatssekretär Conti of the Interior Ministry. The subject of discussion was the reduction of the Polish population in the incorporated territories. The following proposals were entertained: (1) no Pole to be allowed to marry before the age of twenty-five; (2) no permission to be granted unless the marriage was economically sound; (3) a tax on illegitimate births; (4) sterilization following illegitimate birth; (5) no tax exemptions for dependents; and (6) permission to submit to abortion to be granted upon application of the expectant mother.[4]

One year later, on May 1, 1942, Gauleiter Greiser of the incorporated Wartheland reported to Himmler that the "special treatment" of 100,000 Jews in his *Gau* would be completed in another two or three months. Greiser then proceeded in the same paragraph to request Himmler's permission for the use of the experienced (*eingearbeiteten*) *Sonderkommando* at Kulmhof in order to liberate the *Gau* from still another danger which threatened "with each passing week to assume catastrophic proportions." Greiser had in his province 35,000 tubercular Poles. He wanted to kill them.[5] The suggestion was passed on to health expert Blome (Conti's deputy) who wanted to refer the matter to Hitler. Months passed without a decision. Finally Greiser expressed his disappointment to Himmler. "I for my person do not believe that the Führer has to be bothered with this question again, especially since he told me only during our last conversation, with reference to the Jews, that I may deal with those in any way I pleased."[6]

Example III. In consequence of an agreement between Himmler and Justice Minister Thierack, so-called asocials were transferred from prisons to concentration camps. On November 16, 1944, after the transfer of the "asocials" had largely been completed, the judiciary met to discuss a weird subject: ugliness.

---

[3] Lengyel, *Five Chimneys*, pp. 68, 112–113, 121. The Gypsies had been brought to Auschwitz from the Reich-Protektorat area, Poland, France, and Hungary. A Gypsy transport was also brought to Lodz. See pp. 142–144. Gypsies were concentrated in a number of camps. Note reference to Lackenbach (Austria) in letter by Deputy Gauleiter Gerland of Niederdonau to Himmler, August 24, 1942, NO–39. In the Orleans area (France), Jaregeau had 600 Gypsies. Oberstabsarzt Sonntag to *Chef, Militärbezirk A* (Glt. von der Lippe), October 2, 1942, NOKW–1516. In general, see also Dora E. Yates, "Hitler and the Gypsies—The Fate of Europe's Oldest Aryans," *Commentary*, November, 1949, pp. 455–459.
[4] Reich Chancellery memorandum, May 27, 1941, NG–844.
[5] Greiser to Himmler, May 1, 1942, NO–246. Greiser was also *Reichsstatthalter*.
[6] Greiser to Himmler, November 21, 1942, NO–249. The Poles were ultimately spared.

The phrase on the agenda was "gallery of outwardly asocial prisoners [*Museum äusserlich asozialer Gefangener*]." The summary of that conference states:

During various visits to the penitentiaries, prisoners have always been observed who —because of their bodily characteristics—hardly deserve the designation human [*Mensch*]; they look like miscarriages of hell [*Missgeburten der Hölle*]. Such prisoners should be photographed. It is planned that they too shall be eliminated [*auszuschalten*]. Crime and sentence are irrelevant. Only such photographs should be submitted which clearly show the deformity.[7]

THE OBSTACLES

We have talked so far about a destructive expansion which is unparalleled in history. An entire bureaucratic network was involved in these operations; a destruction process was brought to its final conclusion; and a veritable target series was established in a first attempt at unlimited destruction. The German bureaucracy, however, did not always move with unencumbered ease. From time to time barriers appeared on the horizon and caused momentary pauses. Most of these stoppages were occasioned by those ordinary difficulties which are encountered by every bureaucracy in every administrative operation: procurement difficulties, shortages, mixups, misunderstandings, and all the other annoyances of the daily bureaucratic process. We shall not be concerned with these occurrences here. But some of the hesitations and interruptions were the products of extraordinary administrative and psychological obstacles. These blocks were peculiar to the destruction process alone, and they must therefore claim our special attention.

ADMINISTRATIVE PROBLEMS.—The destruction of the Jews was not a gainful operation. It imposed a strain upon the administrative machine and its facilities. In a wider sense it became a burden which rested upon Germany as a whole.

One of the most striking facts about the German apparatus was the sparseness of its personnel, particularly in those regions outside the Reich where most of the victims had to be destroyed. Moreover, that limited manpower was preoccupied with a bewildering variety of administrative undertakings; upon close examination the machinery of destruction turns out to have been a loose organization of part-timers. There were at most a handful of bureaucrats who could devote all their time to anti-Jewish activities. There were the "experts" on Jewish affairs in the ministries, the mobile killing units of the RSHA, the commanders of the killing centers. But even an expert like Eichmann had two jobs: the deportation of Jews and the resettlement of ethnic Germans; the

---

[7] *Generalstaatsanwalt* (chief prosecutor), *Oberlandesgericht Bamberg*, to Generalstatasanwalt Helm in Munich, November 29, 1944, enclosing summary of conference held under the chairmanship of Ministerialdirektor Engert on November 16, 1944, NG–1546.

mobile killing units had to shoot Jews, Gypsies, commissars, and partisans alike; while a camp commander like Höss was host to an industrial concentration next to his gas chambers.

In the totality of the administrative process the destruction of the Jews presented itself as an additional task to a bureaucratic machine already over-burdened and strained to the utmost by war preparations and by war itself. To grasp this fact, we need think only of the railroads or of the armies which moved east into Russia.[8] The German administration, however, was not deterred by the pressures of other assignments; it never resorted to pretenses, like the Italians, it never took token measures, like the Hungarians, it never procrastinated, like the Bulgarians. The German bureaucrats worked efficiently, in haste, and with a sense of urgency. Unlike their collaborators, the Germans never did the minimum. They always did the maximum.

Indeed, there were moments when an agency's eagerness to participate in the decision-making led to bureaucratic competition and rivalry. Such a contest was in the offing when Unterstaatssekretär Luther concluded an agreement with the RSHA to preserve the Foreign Office's power to negotiate with Axis satellites in Jewish matters. Again, within the SS itself, a jealous struggle was waged between two technocrats of destruction, Obersturmbannführer Höss and Kriminalkommissar Wirth, over the replacement of carbon monoxide with Zyklon B in the killing centers. We have observed this bureaucratic warfare also in the attempt of the judiciary to conserve its jurisdiction in Jewish affairs. When that attempt was finally given up, Justice Minister Thierack wrote to his friend Bormann:

> I intend to turn over criminal jurisdiction against Poles, Russians, Jews, and Gypsies to the *Reichsführer-SS*. In doing so, I base myself on the principle that the administration of justice can make only a small contribution to the extermination of these peoples.

This letter reveals an almost melancholy tone. The judiciary had done its utmost; it was no longer needed.

The bureaucrats did not spare themselves; neither could they spare the economy. Just how expensive was the destruction of the Jews? What were the effects of this cost? Table 1 reveals the financial aspects of the operations.[9]

Upon analysis of Table 1, we observe two important trends: with the progress of the destruction process, gains declined; on the other hand, expenditures tended to increase. Looking at the table horizontally, we thereupon discover that in the preliminary phase (above the dividing line) financial gains, public or private, far outweighed expenses, but that in the killing phase (below the

---

[8] "In the Reich only the most vitally important transports are run." Präsident Emrich in traffic conference held on December 9, 1942, in Paris; summary, dated December 12, 1942, in Wi/I 2.10. . . .

[9] Aryanization differentials, Reich property tax, and confiscations under the 11th Ordinance listed in letter from *Restverwaltung des ehemaligen Reichsfinanzministeriums* to Allied Control Commission, November 14, 1946, NG–4906. . . .

dividing line) receipts no longer balanced losses. Let us examine the cost of this killing phase a little more closely.

Table 1 / The Cost of Destroying the Jews

Receipts, Gains, Savings	Expenditures and Losses
Net profits to industry from purchase and liquidations of Jewish enterprises: ca. one-fourth to one-half of value of Jewish business property in Reich-Protektorat area. These profits probably amounted to billions of reichsmark.	Loss of markets abroad in consequence of buyers' resistance and boycott: no estimates.
Aryanization differentials paid by companies to Reich: 49,000,000 reichsmark.	
Reich Flight Tax: 900,000,000 reichsmark.	
Reich Property Tax (fine): 1,127,000,000 reichsmark.	
Wage differentials and other industry savings as result of employment of Jewish labor: probably in tens of millions.	
Wage differentials, special income tax, and other wage savings accruing to Reich: probably in tens of millions.	Direct expenditures for *a.* personnel and overhead (prior to killing phase)
Confiscations under the eleventh ordinance (securities and bonds): 186,000,000 reichsmark.	*b.* personnel and overhead (in killing operations) *c.* Transport *d.* Camp installations (in hundreds of millions)
Confiscations under the eleventh ordinance and other measures (not including securities and bonds): 592,000,000 reichsmark.	Extraordinary direct expense for razing of Warsaw ghetto: 150,000,000 reichsmark.
Miscellaneous confiscations not booked by Finance Ministry in above figures: possibly hundreds of millions.	Loss of Jewish production in consequence of the "final solution": ca. 3,000,000,000 reichsmark.

Receipts (last three items in the left column) were meager. This is explained by the fact that in occupied and satellite territories the Germans did not engage in extensive confiscations. In the interest of a "final solution" in these areas the German perpetrators had to leave most of the Jewish property to their non-German collaborators.

Losses, however, were high. How do we explain those figures? Direct expenditures (here estimated in the hundreds of millions) were comparatively small. They represent a remarkable attempt at economizing. We have seen how sparingly personnel were used, both in the killing units and in the killing centers. The deportation trains (*Sonderzüge*) were made up of freight cars, and several thousand Jews could be transported in one train. The killing centers were extraordinarily cheap, notwithstanding Speer's complaint that Himmler was using scarce building materials too extravagantly. The installations were built with camp labor, and the inmates were housed in huge barracks with no light and no modern toilet facilities. The investment in gas chambers and ovens was not very great, either. Why all this economizing? The answer is simple. In all these cases savings did not reduce efficiency; they might even have promoted the smooth implementation of bureaucratic measures. The destruction process was oriented not to cost but to efficiency. Not money but time was of the essence.

This point is even more sharply illustrated when we examine the next two items. The razing of the Warsaw ghetto ruins after the battle of April–May 1943, was a Himmler project for which the Finance Ministry received a bill in the amount of 150,000,000 reichsmark. Himmler felt that a park should obliterate the site of the ghetto, lest Warsaw grow back to its former size.

The last item in the expense column—the loss of Jewish war production—is a glaring illustration of the triumph of speed over cost. Himmler never made any pretense that for him the destruction of the Jews had priority even over armaments. When he was overwhelmed with arguments in favor of the war effort, Himmler had only this reply: "The argument of war production, which nowadays in Germany is the favorite reason for opposing anything at all, I do not recognize in the first place."[10] In the measured language of the Ministry for Eastern Occupied Territories, the priority of the destruction process was phrased as follows: "Economic questions should not be considered in the solution of the Jewish question." Let us now explore the consequences entailed by the loss of the Jewish labor force.

The war economy lost the aggregate value of those products which two or three million workers in Germany and in the occupied countries could produce in two or three years. This loss was total because the destruction process had removed the Jewish labor force without replacement from going concerns. This does not imply that in individual plants or warehouses Jews were not replaced;

---

[10] In his pronouncements, *passim*.

it does mean that in the total production picture the loss of Jewish labor could never be made up, in spite of all labor recruitment drives by Plenipotentiary for Labor Allocation Sauckel, for in 1944 the shortage of workers had reached a total of not less than 4,000,000.

What was the value of that lost production? In military terms the loss cannot be calculated, but in monetary terms it is possible to make some estimates. Economy Minister Funk estimated after the war that the total value of war production in Germany, from 1941 through 1943, was 260 billion reichsmark. The amount produced in the occupied territories he estimated (for the same period) at 90 billion marks.[11] If we consider that in Germany about 0.5 per cent of the labor force engaged in war production was Jewish, and that in the occupied territories about 2 per cent were Jews, the value of Jewish war production lost is approximately 3 billion reichsmark. This figure swamps the entire income derived from the destruction process after the "final solution" had started, and it proves that whenever it was not efficient to be thrifty, the implementation of the operations could be extravagant in the extreme.

PSYCHOLOGICAL PROBLEMS.—The most important problems of the destruction process were not administrative but psychological. The very conception of the drastic "final solution" was dependent on the ability of the perpetrators to cope with weighty psychological obstacles and impediments. The psychological blocks differed from the administrative difficulties in one important respect: an administrative problem could be solved and eliminated; the psychological difficulties had to be dealt with continuously. They were held in check but never removed. Commanders in the field were ever watchful for symptoms of psychological disintegration. In the fall of 1941 Higher SS and Police Leader Russia Center von dem Bach shook Himmler with the remark:

Look at the eyes of the men of this *Kommando*, how deeply shaken they are. These men are finished [*fertig*] for the rest of their lives. What kind of followers are we training here? Either neurotics or savages [*Entweder Nervenkranke oder Rohlinge*]!

Von dem Bach was not only an important participant in killing operations. He was also an acute observer. With this remark he pointed to the basic psychological problem of the German bureaucracy: the German administration had to make determined efforts to prevent the breakdown of its men into either "savages" or "neurotics." This was essentially a dual task—one part disciplinary, the other moral.

The disciplinary problem was understood clearly. The bureaucrats were fully aware of the dangers of plundering, torture, orgies, and atrocities. Such behavior was first of all wasteful from an administrative point of view, for the destruction process was an organized undertaking which had room only for organized tasks. Moreover, "excesses" attracted attention to aspects of the destruction process

---

[11] Testimony by Funk, *Trial of the Major War Criminals*, XIII, 129–130.

which had to remain secret. Such were the activities of Brigadeführer Dirle-wanger, whose rumored attempts to make human soap drew the attention of the public to the killing centers.

Indeed, atrocities could bring the entire "noble" work into disrepute. What was wasteful administratively was dangerous psychologically. Loose behavior was an abuse of the machine, and a debauched administration could disintegrate. That was why the German administration had a certain preference for quick, blow-type (*schlagartige*) action. Maximum destructive effect was to be achieved with minimum destructive effort. The personnel of the machinery of destruction were not supposed to look to the right or to the left; they were not allowed to have either personal motives or personal gains. An elaborate discipline was introduced into the machine of destruction.

The first and most important rule of conduct of this discipline was the principle that all Jewish property belonged to the Reich. So far as Himmler was concerned, the enforcement of that rule was a success. In 1943 he told his Gruppenführer:

> The riches which they [the Jews] owned we have taken from them. I have given strict orders which Obergruppenführer Pohl has carried out, that this wealth should naturally [*selbstverständlich*] be delivered to the Reich. We have taken nothing. Individuals who have transgressed are being punished in accordance with an order which I gave in the beginning and which threatened that anyone who takes just one mark is a condemned man. A number of SS men—not many—have transgressed against that order, and they will be condemned to death mercilessly. We had the moral right vis-à-vis *our* people to annihilate [*umzubringen*] *this* people which wanted to annihilate us. But we have no right to take a single fur, a single watch, a single mark, a single cigarette, or anything whatever. We don't want in the end, just because we have exterminated a germ, to be infected by that germ and die from it. I will not stand by while a slight infection forms. Whenever such an infected spot appears, we will burn it out. But on the whole we can say that we have fulfilled this heavy task with love for our people, and we have not been damaged in the innermost of our being, our soul, our character.[12]

There is, of course, considerable evidence that more than a few individuals "transgressed" against the discipline of the destruction process. No estimate can be formed of the extent to which transport *Kommandos*, killing units, the ghetto and killing center personnel, and even *Kommando* 1005—the grave-destruction *Kommando*—filled their pockets with the belongings of the dead. Moreover, we should note that Himmler's rule dealt only with *unauthorized* takings by participating personnel in the field. It did not deal with *authorized* distributions to the participants.

The essence of corruption is to reward people on the basis of their proximity to the loot—in a corrupt system, the tax collectors become rich. In the course of the destruction process many distributions were made to the closest partici-

---

[12] Speech by Himmler to *Gruppenführer* meeting at Poznan, October 4, 1943, PS–1919.

pants. We need remind ourselves only of the Finance Ministry's appropriation of fine furniture during the deportations of Jews from Germany, the distribution of better apartments to civil servants, the cuts taken by the railways, SS and Police, and postal service in the allocation of the furniture of the Dutch, Belgian, and French Jews, the "gifts" of watches and "Christmas presents" to SS-men and their families. The destruction process had its own built-in corruption. Only unauthorized corruption was forbidden.

The second way in which the Germans sought to avoid damage to "the soul" was in the prohibition of unauthorized killings. A sharp line was drawn between killings pursuant to order and killings induced by desire. In the former case a man was thought to have overcome the "weaknesses" of "Christian morality"; in the latter case he was overcome by his baseness. That was why in the occupied USSR both the army and the civil administration sought to restrain their personnel from joining the shooting parties on the killing sites.

Perhaps the best illustration of the official attitude is to be found in an advisory opinion by a judge on Himmler's Personal Staff, Obersturmbann-führer Bender. Bender dealt with procedure to be followed in the case of unauthorized killings of Jews by SS personnel. He concluded that if purely political motives prompted the killing, if the act was an expression of idealism, no punishment was necessary unless the maintenance of order required disciplinary action or prosecution. However, if selfish, sadistic, or sexual motives were found, punishment was to be imposed for murder or for manslaughter, in accordance with the facts.[13]

The German disciplinary system is most discernible in the mode of the killing operation. At the conclusion of the destruction process Hitler remarked in his testament that the Jewish "criminals" had "atoned" for their "guilt" by "humane means." The "humaneness" of the destruction process was an important factor in its success. It must be emphasized, of course, that this "humaneness" was evolved not for the benefit of the victims but for the welfare of the perpetrators. Time and again, attempts were made to reduce opportunities for "excesses" and *Schweinereien* of all sorts. Much research was expended for the development of devices and methods which arrested propensities for uncontrolled behavior and which lightened, at the same time, the crushing psychological burden on the killers. The construction of gas vans and of gas chambers, the employment of Ukrainian, Lithuanian, and Latvian auxiliaries to kill Jewish women and children, the use of Jews for the burial and burning of bodies—all these were efforts in the same direction. Efficiency was the real aim of all this "humaneness."

So far as Himmler was concerned, his SS and Police had weathered the destruction process. In October, 1943, when he addressed his top commanders, he said to them:

---

[13] Memorandum by OStubaf. Bender, October 22, 1942, NO–1744.

Most of you know what it means when 100 corpses lie there, or when 500 corpses lie there, or when 1000 corpses lie there. To have gone through this and—apart from a few exceptions caused by human weakness—to have remained decent, that has made us great. That is a page of glory in our history which has never been written and which is never to be written. . . .[14]

However, the descent into savagery was not nearly so important a factor in the destruction process as the feeling of growing uneasiness that pervaded the bureaucracy from the lowest strata to the highest. That uneasiness was the product of moral scruples—the lingering effect of two thousand years of Western morality and ethics. A Western bureaucracy had never before faced such a chasm between moral precepts and administrative action; an administrative machine had never been burdened with such a drastic task. In a sense, the task of destroying the Jews put the German bureaucracy to a supreme test. The German technocrats solved also that problem and passed also this test.

To grasp the full significance of what these men did, we have to understand that we are not dealing with individuals who had their own separate moral standards. The bureaucrats who were drawn into the destruction process were not different in their moral makeup from the rest of the population. The German perpetrator was not a special kind of German. What we have to say here about his morality applies not to him specially but to Germany as a whole. How do we know this?

We know that the very nature of administrative planning, of the jurisdictional structure, and of the budgetary system precluded the special selection and special training of personnel. Even the killing units and the killing centers did not obtain professional killers. Every lawyer in the RSHA was presumed to be suitable for leadership in the mobile killing units; every finance expert of the WVHA was considered a natural choice for service in a death camp. In other words, all necessary operations were accomplished with whatever personnel were at hand. However one may wish to draw the line of active participation, the machinery of destruction was a remarkable cross-section of the German population. Every profession, every skill, and every social status was represented in it. We know that in a totalitarian state the formation of an opposition movement outside the bureaucracy is next to impossible; however, if there is very serious opposition in the population, if there are insurmountable psychological obstacles to a course of action, such impediments reveal themselves *within* the bureaucratic apparatus. We know what such barriers will do, for they emerged clearly in the Italian Fascist state. Again and again the Italian generals and consuls, prefects and police inspectors, refused to co-operate in the deportations. The destruction process in Italy and the Italian-controlled areas was carried out against un-remitting Italian opposition. No such opposition is to be found in the German area. No obstruction stopped the German machine of destruction. No moral problem proved insurmountable. When all participating personnel were put to

---

[14] Himmler speech, October 4, 1943, PS–1919.

the test, there were very few lingerers and almost no deserters. The old moral order did not break through anywhere along the line. That is a phenomenon of the greatest magnitude.

Just how did the German bureaucracy overcome its moral scruples? We know that it was something of a struggle; we know also that the struggle was won only with the employment of the most complex psychological tools fashioned during centuries of German cultural development. Fundamentally, the psychological defense arsenal consisted of two parts: the repressive mechanism and the system of rationalizations.

First of all, the bureaucracy wanted to hide its deeds, it wanted to conceal the destruction process, not only from all outsiders but also from the censuring gaze of its own conscience. The repression proceeded through five stages. The first was secrecy.

As we might expect, every effort was made to hide the ultimate aim of the destruction process from Axis partners and from the Jews. Inquiries such as Hungarian Prime Minister Kallay put to the Foreign Office about the disappearance of European Jewry, or questions which foreign journalists in Kiev asked army authorities about mass shootings, could obviously not be answered. Rumors which could spread like wildfire had to be smothered. "Plastic" evidence, such as "souvenir" photographs of killings, mass graves, and the wounded Jews who had risen from their graves, had to be destroyed. All these efforts were an administrative necessity. However, beyond that, they were necessary also for psychological reasons. The extreme care with which the machinery of destruction, and particularly the SS and Police, guarded the secrecy of its operations betrayed uncertainty, worry, and anxiety. In May, 1944, the RSHA complained to the Justice Ministry that the *Landgericht* in Vienna was making too many inquiries to elicit the whereabouts of deported Jews for the purpose of rendering decisions in proceedings involving proof of descent (*Abstammungsverfahren*). The *Landgericht* had been told repeatedly, said the complaint, that no information could be given about deportees, but the court had persisted in making inquiries. Quite apart from the fact that the "Jews" (that is, the persons seeking clarification of their status) had been given plenty of time to clear questions about their descent, these people were only trying to hide their ancestry, anyway, in order to remove themselves from the effect of "Security Police measures" (*sicherheitspolizeiliche Massnahmen*). For these reasons, and because of more pressing war work, the Security Police could not furnish replies, etc., etc.[15]

Thus the first stage in the repression was to shut off the supply of information from all those who did not have to know it. Whoever did not participate was not supposed to know. The second stage was to make sure that whoever knew would participate.

---

[15] RSHA to Justice Ministry, May 3, 1944, NG–900.

There was nothing so irksome as the realization that someone was watching over one's shoulder, that someone would be free to talk and accuse because he was not himself involved. This fear was the origin of what Leo Alexander has called the "blood kit," [16] the irresistible force that drew every official "observer" into the destruction process. The "blood kit" explains why so many office chiefs of the RSHA were assigned to mobile killing units and why staff officers with the killing units were ordered to participate in the killing operations. The "blood kit" also explains why Unterstaatssekretär Luther of the Foreign Office's *Abteilung Deutschland* insisted that the Political Division countersign all instructions to embassies and legations for the deportation of Jews. Finally, the "blood kit" explains the significant words spoken by General-gouverneur Frank at the conclusion of a police conference in Krakow:

> We want to remember that we are, all of us assembled here, on Mr. Roosevelt's war-criminals list. I have the honor of occupying first place on that list. We are therefore, so to speak, accomplices in a world-historical sense.

The third stage in the process of repression was the prohibition of criticism. Public protests by outsiders were extremely rare; the criticisms were expressed, if at all, in mutterings on the rumor circuit. It is sometimes hard, even to distinguish between expressions of sensationalism and real criticism, for often the two were mixed. One example of such mixed reactions is to be found in the circulation of rumors in Germany about the mobile killing operations in Russia. The Party Chancellery, in confidential instructions to its regional machinery, attempted to combat these rumors. Most of the reports, the chancellery stated, were "distorted" and "exaggerated." "It is conceivable," the circular continued, "that not all of our people—especially people who have no conception of the Bolshevik terror—can understand sufficiently the necessity for these measures." In their very nature, "these problems," which were sometimes "very difficult," could be solved "in the interest of the security of our people" only with "ruthless severity."

In the German documents we found a singular example of a genuine public protest. A Catholic priest named Lichtenberg, prayed for the Jews in open services at St. Hedwig's Cathedral in Berlin. He prayed not only for baptized Jews but for all the Jewish victims. Placed in custody, he pronounced himself a foe of National Socialism and declared that he wanted to share the fate of the Jews in the East, in order to pray for them there. Released from prison, Lichtenberg died on the way to a concentration camp.

Within the bureaucracy we find a few more examples of criticism, though again it was very seldom outspoken protest. Of course, it was permissible to criticize measures from the viewpoint of German welfare. We have seen the unbelievable amount of discussion about the *Mischlinge* and Jews in mixed

---

[16] Leo Alexander, "War Crimes and Their Motivation," *Journal of Criminal Law and Criminology*, XXXIX (September–October 1948), 298–326.

marriages—that is, persons against whom action could not be taken without hurting Germans. Again, we have noted the voluminous correspondence, dealing with the adverse effects of anti-Jewish measures on the war effort. Once in a while it was permissible even to mention the harmful psychological effects of killings on the perpetrators, but a sharp line was drawn between such criticisms and the implication that the destruction process itself was intrinsically wrong.

A Director of the Reichsbank, Wilhelm, overstepped the line when he cautioned his chief, Puhl, not to visit concentration camps and when he announced his refusal to participate in the distribution of Jewish belongings with the words: "The Reichsbank is not a dealer in second-hand goods." Generalkommissar Kube of White Russia violated the injunction against moral condemnations by making accusations against the KDS in White Russia, Strauch. Kube implied that Jews—at least those Jews who had come from Germany ("from our own cultural level")—were human beings and that Strauch and his killers were maniacs and sadists who had satisfied their sexual lust during shootings. Strauch did not take kindly to such criticism. In a complaint against Kube he wrote that "it was regrettable that we, in addition to having to perform this nasty job, were also made the target of mud-slinging." In the Interior Ministry the expert on Jewish affairs, Ministrialrat Lösener, was disturbed by reports of killings which had occurred in Riga; he began to put questions to his chief, Staatssekretär Stuckart, and requested a transfer. After a while a colleague asked Lösener to stop pestering the Staatssekretär, for Stuckart's position was difficult enough.[17]

On the highest level, the following story was told by Gauleiter Schirach's secretary: While Schirach's wife was staying in a hotel in Amsterdam, she watched a roundup of Jews at night. The Jewish women "screamed terribly." Mrs. Schirach's nerves were so much on edge that she decided to tell her husband about it. The *Gauleiter* advised her to tell the story to Hitler himself, since the Führer would not tolerate such "abuses" (*Missstände*). During their next visit to Hitler Mrs. Schirach told the story. Hitler listened "ungraciously," interrupting several times and telling her not to be so sentimental. Everyone present found the exchange between Hitler and Mrs. Schirach "very embarrassing" (*äusserst peinlich*). The conversation broke down, no one spoke, and Mr. and Mrs. Schirach left the room. The Schirachs departed the next day without saying good-bye.[18]

In its fourth stage repressive mechanism eliminated the destruction process as a subject of social conversation. Among the closest participants it was considered bad form to talk about the killings. This is what Himmler had to say on the subject in his speech of October 4, 1943:

---

[17] Affidavit by Lösener, February 24, 1948, NG–1944–A.
[18] Affidavit by Maria Höpken, January 19, 1946, Schirach–3. Affiant was not a witness but claims that the identical story was told to her on separate occasions by Schirach and his wife.

I want to mention here very candidly a particular difficult chapter. Among us it should be mentioned once, quite openly, but in public we will never talk about it. Just as little as we hesitated on June 30, 1934, to do our duty and to put comrades who had transgressed [the brown shirts] to the wall, so little have we talked about it and will ever talk about it. It was with us, thank God, an inborn gift of tactfulness, that we have never conversed about this matter, never spoken about it. Every one of us was horrified, and yet every one of us knew that we would do it again if it were ordered and if it were necessary.

I am referring to the evacuation of the Jews, to the extermination of the Jewish people. . . .[19]

This, then, was the reason why that particular "page of glory" was never to be written. There are some things that can be done only so long as they are not discussed, for once they are discussed they can no longer be done.

We know, of course, that among those who were not quite so close to the killing operations the sensations of the destruction process were irresistible. The rumor network was spread all over Axis Europe. One Foreign Office official stationed in Rome mentions that he discussed details of the killings with at least thirty of his colleagues.[20] But the urge to talk was not so deep in men who were heavily involved in the destruction process. Höss, the Auschwitz commander, says that he never spoke about his job even to his wife. She found out about what he was doing because of an inadvertent remark by a family friend, Gauleiter Bracht. The Treblinka guard, Hirtreiter, never spoke of his task at all.

The fifth and final stage of the repressing process was to omit mention of "killings" or "killing installations" even in the secret correspondence in which such operations had to be reported. The reader of these reports is immediately struck by their camouflage vocabulary: *Endlösung der Judenfrage* ("final solution of the Jewish question"), *Lösungsmöglichkeiten* ("solution possibilities"), *Sonderbehandlung* (or SB—"special treatment"), *Evakuierung* ("evacuation"), *Aussiedlung* (same), *Umsiedlung* (same), *Spezialeinrichtungen* ("special installations"), *durchgeschleusst* ("dragged through"), and many others.

There is one exchange of correspondence in which knowing officials carried the game of pretense to the point of distortion and outright falsification: In 1943 the Foreign Office inquired whether it would be possible to exchange 30,000 Baltic and White Russian Jews for Reich Germans in Allied countries. The Foreign Office representative in Riga replied that he had discussed the matter with the Security Police commander in charge; the BdS had felt that the "interned" Jews could not be sent away for "weighty Security Police reasons." As was known (*bekanntlich*), a large number of Jews had been "done away with" in "spontaneous actions." In some places these actions had resulted in "almost total extermination" (*fast völlige Ausmerzung*). A removal of the

---

[19] Himmler speech, October 4, 1943, PS–1919.
[20] Affidavit by Vortragender Legationsrat Dr. Ulrich Dörtenbach, May 13, 1947, NG–1535.

remaining Jews would therefore give rise to "anti-German atrocity propaganda," etc.[21] Thus even in 1943 an internal secret letter could claim that the Jews in the East had all been victims of pogroms.

A particularly revealing example of disassociation may also be found in a private letter written by a sergeant of the Rural Police to a police general. The sergeant, at the head of 23 German gendarmes and 500 Ukrainian auxiliary policemen, had killed masses of Jews in the Kamenets Podolski area. These are excerpts from his letter.

Naturally we are cleaning up considerably, especially among the Jews. . . .
I have a cozy apartment in a former children's asylum. One bedroom and a living room with all of the accessories. Practically nothing is missing. Naturally, the wife and the children. You will understand me. My Dieter and the little Liese write often, after their fashion. One could weep sometimes. It is not good to be a friend of children as I was. I hope that the war, and with it the time of service in the East, soon ends.[22]

The process of repression was continuous, but it was never completed. The killing of the Jews could not be hidden completely, either from the outside world or from the inner self; therefore the bureaucracy was not spared an open encounter with its conscience. It had to pit argument against argument and philosophy against philosophy. Laboriously, and with great effort, the bureaucracy had to justify its activities.

Psychological justification is called rationalization. The Germans employed two kinds of rationalizations. The first was an attempt to justify the destruction process as a whole; it was designed to explain why the Jews had to be destroyed. It was focused on the Jew. The other explanations served only to justify individual participation in the destruction process: a signature on a piece of paper or the squeeze of a trigger. They were focused entirely on the perpetrator. Let us consider first the broad rationalizations which encompassed the whole destruction process. In the formation of these justifications old conceptions about the Jew—reinforced and expanded by new propaganda—played an important role. Precisely how did German propaganda function in this process?

The Germans had two kinds of propaganda. One was designed to produce action. It exhorted people to do things, for instance, to come to a mass meeting, to boycott Jewish goods, or to kill Jews. This type of propaganda—the command propaganda—does not concern us here since it was confined, on the whole, to the incitement of boycotts and pogroms, the so-called *Einzelaktionen*. But the Germans also engaged in a campaign which consisted of a series of statements, for example, allegations which implied that the Jew was bad. This propaganda had a very important place in the arsenal of psychological defense mechanisms.

The function of declarative propaganda is to act as a storehouse which may be drawn upon according to need. The statement "the Jew is bad" is taken from the storehouse and is converted in the perpetrator's mind into a complete

---

[21] Windecker to Foreign Office, April 5, 1943, NG–2652.
[22] Meister der Gendarmerie Fritz Jacob to OGruf. Rudolf Querner, May 5, 1942, NO–5654.

rationalization: "I kill the Jew because the Jew is bad." To understand the function of this propaganda is to realize why it was continued until the very end of the war, and, surreptitiously, even after the end of the war. Propaganda was needed to combat doubts and guilt feelings wherever they arose—whether inside or outside the bureaucracy—and whenever they arose—before or after the perpetration of the acts.

In fact, we find that in April, 1943, after the deportations of the Jews from the Reich had largely been completed, the press was ordered to deal with the Jewish question continuously and without letup.[23] In order to build up a storehouse the propaganda had to be turned out on a huge scale. "Research institutes" were formed,[24] doctoral dissertations were written,[25] and volumes of propaganda literature were printed by every conceivable agency. At times this activity even led to bureaucratic competition. Thus Unterstaatssekretär Luther of the Foreign Office had to assure Obergruppenführer Berger of the SS-Main Office that the Foreign Office's pamphlet *Das russische Tor ist aufgestossen* ("*The Russian Gate is Thrown Open*") in no way competed with Berger's masterpiece *Der Untermensch* ("*The Subhuman*").[26]

What did all this propaganda accomplish? How was the Jew portrayed in this unending flow of leaflets and pamphlets, books and speeches? How did the propaganda image of the Jew serve to justify the destruction process?

First of all, the German map drew a picture of an international Jewry ruling the world and plotting the destruction of Germany and German life. "If international-finance Jewry," said Adolf Hitler in 1939, "inside and outside of Europe should succeed in plunging the nations into another world war, then the result will not be the Bolshevization of the earth and, with it, the victory of the Jews, but the annihilation of the Jewish race in Europe." In 1944 Himmler said to his commanders: "This was the most frightening order which an organization could receive—the order to solve the Jewish question," but if the Jews had still been in the rear, the front line could not have been held, and if any of the commanders were moved to pity, they had only to think of the bombing terror, "which after all is organized in the last analysis by the Jews."[27]

The theory of world Jewish rule and of the incessant Jewish plot against the German people penetrated into all offices. It became interwoven with foreign policy and sometimes led to preposterous results. Thus the conviction grew that foreign statesmen who were not very friendly toward Germany were Jews, part-Jews, married to Jews, or somehow dominated by Jews. Streicher did not hesitate to state publicly that he had it on good Italian authority that the Pope

---

[23] Instructions by Reich Press Chief, April 29, 1943, NG–4705.

[24] Notably, the Institut zur Erforschung der Judenfrage in Frankfurt, under Dr. Klaus Schickert. Steengracht to Rosenberg, January 22, 1944, NG–1689.

[25] Dr. Hans Praesent, "Neuere deutsche Doktorarbeiten über das Judentum," *Die Judenfrage*, November 15, 1943, pp. 351–353.

[26] Luther to Berger, June 22, 1942, NG–3304.

[27] Himmler speech, June 21, 1944, NG–4977.

had Jewish blood.[28] Similarly, Staatssekretär Weizsäcker of the Foreign Office once questioned the British chargé d'affaires about the percentage of "Aryan" blood in Mr. Rublee, an American on a mission in behalf of refugees.[29]

This type of reasoning was also applied in reverse. If a power was friendly, it was believed to be free of Jewish rule. In March 1940, after Ribbentrop had succeeded in establishing friendly relations with Russia, he assured Mussolini and Ciano that Stalin had given up the idea of world revolution. The Soviet administration had been purged of Jews. Even Kaganovich (the Jewish Polit-bureau member) looked rather like a Georgian.[30]

The claim of Jewish world rule was to be established irrefutably in a show trial. Toward the end of 1941 the Propaganda Ministry, the Foreign Office, and the Justice Ministry laid plans for the trial of Herschel Grynzpan, the man who had assassinated a German Embassy official (vom Rath) in Paris in 1938.[31] The trial was to prove that Grynzpan's deed was part of a "fundamental plan by international Jewry to drive the world into a war with National Socialist Germany," [32] but it was never held, because the Justice Ministry in its eagerness had made the fatal mistake of adding homosexuality to the indictment. At the last moment, it was feared that Grynzpan might reveal "the alleged homosexual relations of Gesandtschaftsrat vom Rath." And so the whole scheme was dropped.[33]

When Germany began to lose the war at Stalingrad, the propaganda machine sought to make up in sheer volume of endless repetition for the "proof" it had failed to obtain in the ill-fated Grynzpan trial. The Jew was now the principal foe, the creator of capitalism and Communism, the sinister force behind the entire Allied war effort, the organizer of the "terror raids," and, finally, the all-powerful enemy capable of wiping Germany off the map. By February 5, 1943, the press had to be cautioned not to "over-estimate the power of the Jews." [34] On the same day, however, the following instructions were issued:

---

[28] Memorandum by Ribbentrop, November 18, 1938, on the Italian protest in the Streicher affair, *Documents on German Foreign Policy 1918–1945*, Ser. D, IV, 524–525. The pontiff in question was the "temperamental Pope," Pius XI, not the "diplomatic Pope," Pius XII.

[29] Weizsäcker to Wörmann, Dg. Pol., trade and legal divisions, *Referat Deutschland* (Aschmann), November 7, 1938, NG–4686. The British diplomat replied that he didn't think Rublee had any Jewish blood.

[30] Summary of conference between Ribbentrop, Mussolini, and Ciano, May 10, 1940, PS.2835.

[31] Ministerialrat Diewerge (Propaganda Ministry) to Gesandter Dr. Krümmer (Foreign Office), December 22, 1941, NG–971. Krümmer to Foreign Office press division, January 2, 1942, NG–971. Summary of interministerial conference, January 23, 1942, NG–973. Rintelen to Weizsäcker, April 5, 1942, NG–179. Krümmer via Luther to Weizsäcker, April 7, 1942, NG–179. Schlegelberger to Göbbels, April 10, 1942, NG–973. Memorandum by Diewerge, April 11, 1942, NG–971.

[32] Rintelen to Weizsäcker, quoting Ribbentrop's views, April 2, 1942, NG–179.

[33] Summary of Grynzpan conference, January 23, 1942, NG–973. Louis P. Lochner (ed.), *The Goebbels Diaries*, entries for February 11, 1942, and April 5, 1942, pp. 78, 161. After the trial was dropped, Grynzpan was kept "on ice." He was discovered in 1957, living quietly in Paris. Kurt R. Grossmann, "Herschel Gruenspan lebt!" *Auf bau* (New York), May 10, 1957, pp. 1, 5–6.

[34] *Zeitschriften Dienst* (Propaganda Ministry), February 5, 1943, NG–4715.

Stress: If we lose this war, we do not fall into the hands of some other states but will all be annihilated by world Jewry. Jewry firmly decided [*fest entschlossen*] to exterminate all Germans. International law and international custom will be no protection against the Jewish will for total annihilation [*totaler Vernichtungswille der Juden*].[35]

How was this theory applied to justify specific operations? The "Jewish conspiracy" was used over and over again. We find the theory in the correspondence of the German Foreign Office, which pressed for deportations in Axis countries on the ground that the Jews were a security risk. The Jews were the spies, the enemy agents. They could not be permitted to stay in coastal areas because in the event of Allied landings they would attack the defending garrisons from the rear. The Jews were the inciters of revolt; that was why they had to be deported from Slovakia in 1944. The Jews were the organizers of the partisan war, the "middle men" between the Red Army and the partisan field command; that was why they could not be permitted to remain alive in partisan-threatened areas. The Jews were the saboteurs and assassins; that was why the army chose them as hostages in Russia, Serbia, and France. The Jews were plotting the destruction of Germany; and that was why they had to be destroyed. In Himmler's words: "We had the moral right vis-à-vis our people to annihilate this people which wanted to annihilate us." In the minds of the perpetrators, therefore, this theory turned the destruction process into a kind of preventive war.

However, the Jews were portrayed not only as a world conspiracy but also as a criminal people. This is the definition of the Jews, as furnished in instructions to the German press:

Stress: In the case of the Jews there are not merely a few criminals (as in every other people), but all of Jewry rose from criminal roots, and in its very nature it is criminal. The Jews are no people like other people, but a pseudo-people welded together by hereditary criminality [*eine zu einem Scheinvolk zusammengeschlossene Erbkriminalität*]. . . . The annihilation of Jewry is no loss to humanity, but just as useful as capital punishment or protective custody against other criminals.[36]

And this is what Streicher had to say:

Look at the path which the Jewish people has traversed for millennia: Everywhere murder; everywhere mass murder![37]

A Nazi researcher Helmut Schramm, collected all the legends of Jewish ritual murder.[38] The book was an immediate success with Himmler. "Of the book *The Jewish Ritual Murders*," he wrote to Kaltenbrunner, "I have ordered a large number. I am distributing it down to *Standartenführer* [SS-colonel]. I am sending you several hundred copies so that you can distribute them to your *Einsatz-*

---

[35] *Deutscher Wochendienst*, February 5, 1943, NG–4714.
[36] *Deutscher Wochendienst*, April 2, 1943, NG–4713.
[37] Speech by Streicher during dedication of Wilhelm Gustloff Bridge in Nuremberg, September, 1937, M–4. Gustloff, the AO *Landesgruppenleiter* in Switzerland, had been assassinated by a Jew.
[38] Helmut Schramm, *Der Judische Ritualmord—Eine historische Untersuchung* (Berlin, 1943).

kommandos, and above all to the men who are busy with the Jewish question." [39] *The Ritual Murders* was a collection of stories about alleged tortures of Christian children. Actually, hundreds of thousands of Jewish children were being killed in the destruction process. Perhaps, that is why *The Ritual Murders* became so important. In fact, Himmler was so enthusiastic about the book that he ordered Kaltenbrunner to start investigations of "ritual murders" in Roumania, Hungary, and Bulgaria; he also suggested that Security Police people be put to work tracing British court records and police descriptions of missing children, "so that we can report in our radio broadcasts to England that in the town of XY a child is missing and that it is probably another case of Jewish ritual murder." [40]

How the theory of Jewish criminality was applied in practice may be seen in the choice of some of the expressions in the reports of killing operations, such as the term "execution" (in German, *hingerichtet, exekutiert, Vollzugstätigkeit*). In correspondence dealing with the administration of the personal belongings taken from dead Jews, the WVHA used the cover designation "utilization of the property of the Jewish thieves [*Verwertung des jüdischen Hehler- und Diebesgutes*]."

A very striking example of how the theory invaded German thinking is furnished in the format of portions of two reports by the army's Secret Field Police in occupied Russia: [41]

Punishable Offenses by Members of the Population:	
Espionage	1
Theft of ammunition	1
Suspected Jews (*Judenverdacht*)	3
Moving about with arms (*Freischärlerei*)	11
Theft	2
Jews	2

In the culmination of this theory to *be* a Jew was a punishable offense (*strafbare Handlung*); thus it was the function of the rationalization of criminality to turn the destruction process into a kind of judicial proceeding.

There was a third rationalization which was focused on the Jew: the conception of the Jew as a lower form of life. Generalgouverneur Frank was given to the use of such phrases as "Jews and lice." In a speech delivered on December 19, 1940, he pointed out that relatives of military personnel surely were sympathizing with men stationed in Poland, a country "which is so full of lice and

---

[39] Himmler to Kaltenbrunner, May 19, 1943, NG–4589.
[40] *Ibid.*
[41] GFP Group 722 to 207th Security Division Ic, February 23, 1943, NOKW–2210. GFP Group 722 to 207th Security Division Ic, March 25, 1943, NOKW–2158.

Jews." But the situation was not so bad, he continued, though of course he could not rid the country of all lice and Jews in a year.[42] On July 19, 1943, the chief of the *Generalgouvernement* Health Division reported during a meeting that the typhus epidemic was subsiding. Frank remarked in this connection that the "removal" (*Beseitigung*) of the "Jewish element" had undoubtedly contributed to better health (*Gesundung*) in Europe. He meant this not only in the literal sense but also politically: the re-establishment of sound living conditions (*gesunder Lebensverhältnisse*) on the European continent.[43]

In a similar vein Foreign Office Press Chief Schmidt once declared during a visit to Slovakia, "The Jewish question is no question of humanity, and it is no question of religion; it is solely a question of political hygiene" (*eine Frage der politischen Hygiene*).

In the terminology of the killing operations the conception of Jews as vermin is again quite noticeable. Dr. Stahlecker, the commander of *Einsatzgruppe A*, called the pogroms conducted by the Lithuanians "self-cleansing actions" (*Selbstreiningungsaktionen*). In another report we find the phrase "cleansing-of-Jews actions" (*Judensäuberungsaktionen*). Himmler spoke of "extermination" (*Ausrottung*). Many times, the bureaucracy used the word *Entjudung*; this expression, which was used not only in connection with killings but also with reference to Aryanizations of property, means to *rid* something of Jews.[44] Again, we discover the term *judenrein*, which in exact translation means "clean of Jews." Finally, in the most drastic application of this theory, a German fumigation company, the Deutsche Gesellschaft für Schädlingsbekämpfung, was drawn into the killing operations by furnishing one of its lethal products for the gassing of a million Jews. Thus the destruction process was also turned into a "cleansing operation."

In addition to the rationalizations which were used to justify the whole undertaking as a war against "international Jewry," as a judicial proceeding against "Jewish criminality," or simply as a "hygienic" process against "Jewish vermin," there were also those rationalizations which were fashioned in order to enable the individual bureaucrat to justify his individual task in the destruction process. It must be kept in mind that most of the participants did not fire rifles at Jewish children or pour gas into gas chambers. A good many, of course, also had to perform these very "hard" tasks, but most of the administrators, and most of the clerks did not see the final, drastic link in these measures of destruction.

Most bureaucrats composed memoranda, drew up blueprints, signed correspondence, talked on the telephone, and participated in conferences. They could destroy a whole people while sitting at their desks. Except for inspection

---

[42] Speech by Frank to men of guard battalion, December 19, 1940, Frank diary, PS–2233.
[43] Summary of *Generalgouvernement* health conference, July 9, 1943, Frank diary, PS–2233.
[44] Compare Entlausung ("ridding of lice") and *Entwesung* ("ridding of vermin," or "fumigation").

tours, which were not obligatory, they never had to see "100 bodies lie there, or 500, or 1000." However, these men were not stupid; they realized the connection between their paper work and the heaps of corpses in the East. And they realized, also, the shortcomings of those rationalizations which placed all evil on the Jew and all good on the German. That was why they were compelled to justify their individual activities. Their justifications contain the implicit admission that the paper work was to go on, regardless of the actual plans of world Jewry and regardless of the actual behavior of the Jews who were about to be killed. We can divide the rationalizations focused on the perpetrator into five categories.

The first rationalization was the oldest, the simplest, and therefore the most effective: the doctrine of superior orders. First and foremost there was discipline. First and foremost there was duty. No matter what objections there might be, orders were given to be obeyed. A clear order was like absolution; armed with such an order, a perpetrator felt that he could pass his responsibility and his conscience upward. When Himmler addressed a killing party in Minsk, he told his men that they need not worry. Their consciences were in no way impaired, for they were soldiers who had to carry out every order unconditionally.

Every bureaucrat knows, of course, that open defiance of orders is serious business, but he also knows that there are many ingenious ways of evading orders. In fact, the opportunities for evasion and hesitation increase as one ascends in the hierarchy. Even in Nazi Germany orders were disobeyed, and they were disobeyed even in Jewish matters. We have mentioned the statement of Reichsbankdirektor Wilhelm, who would not participate in the distribution of "second-hand goods." Nothing happened to him. A member of the RSHA, Sturmbannführer Hartl, simply refused to take over an *Einsatzkommando* in Russia. Nothing happened to this man, either.[45] Even Generalkommissar Kube, who had actually frustrated a killing operation in Minsk and who had otherwise expressed himself in strong language, was only warned.

The bureaucrat clung to his orders not so much because he feared his superior (with whom he was often on good terms) but because he feared his own conscience. The many requests for "authorization"—whether for permission to mark Jews with a star or to kill them—demonstrate the true nature of these orders. When they did not exist, the bureaucrats had to invent them.

The second rationalization was the administrator's insistence that he did not act out of personal vindictiveness. In the mind of the bureaucrat duty was an assigned path; it was his "fate." The German bureaucrat made a sharp distinction between duty and personal feelings; he insisted that he did not "hate" Jews, and sometimes he even went out of his way to perform "good deeds" for Jewish friends and acquaintances. When the trials of war criminals started, there was hardly a defendant who could not produce evidence that he had

---

[45] Affidavit by Albert Hartl, October 9, 1947, NO–5384.

helped some half-Jewish physics professor, or that he had used his influence to permit a Jewish symphony conductor to conduct a little while longer, or that he had intervened on behalf of some couple in mixed marriage in connection with an apartment. While these courtesies were petty in comparison with the destructive conceptions which these men were implementing concurrently, the "good deeds" performed an important psychological function. They separated "duty" from personal feelings. They preserved a sense of "decency." The destroyer of the Jews was no "anti-Semite."

Staatssekretär Keppler of the Office of the Four-Year Plan was interrogated after the war as follows:

QUESTION [by Dr. Kempner of the prosecuting staff]: Tell me, Mr. Keppler, why were you so terribly against the Jews? Did you know the Jews?

ANSWER: I had nothing against the Jews.

QUESTION: I am asking for the reason. You were no friend of the Jews?

ANSWER: Jews came to me. Warburg invited me. Later Jews looked me up in the Reich Chancellery and asked me to join the board of directors of the Deutsche Bank.

QUESTION: When were you supposed to join the board of directors?

ANSWER: I didn't want to; it was in 1934, they wanted to give me a written assurance that I would be a director in half a year. If I had been such a hater of Jews, they would not have approached me.

QUESTION: But you transferred capital from Jews into Aryan hands.

ANSWER: Not often. I know the one case of Simson-Suhl. Also the Skoda-Wetzler Works in Vienna. But it turned out that was no Jewish enterprise.

Keppler was then asked whether he had not favored the "disappearance" of the Jews from Germany. The Staatssekretär fell back on Warburg, with whom he had once had an "interesting discussion." The interrogator broke in with the remark that "now we do not want to talk about anti-Semitism but about the final solution of the Jewish question." In that connection, Keppler was asked whether he had heard of Lublin. The *Staatssekretär* admitted hesitantly that he had heard of Lublin and offered the explanation that he was "deeply touched by this matter" (*dass mich das furchtbar peinlich berührt*). What did Keppler do when he was touched like this? "It was very unpleasant for me, but after all it was not even in my sphere of jurisdiction." [46]

Another defendant in a war-crimes trial, the former commander in Norway, Generaloberst von Falkenhorst, offered the following explanation for his order to remove Jews from Soviet prisoner-of-war battalions in his area. Falkenhorst pointed out that, to begin with, there were no Jews among these prisoners, for the selection had already taken place in Germany (i.e., the Jewish prisoners had already been shot as they were shuttled through the Reich). The order was consequently "entirely superfluous and might just as well not have been included. It was thoughtlessly included by the officer of my staff who was working on it, from the instructions sent to us, and I overlooked it." The general then continued:

---

[46] Interrogation by Kempner of Keppler, August 20, 1947, NG–3041.

For the rest it may be inferred from this that the Jewish question played as infamous a part in Norway as elsewhere, and that I and the Army were supposed to have been particularly anti-semitic.

Against this suspicion I can only adduce the following: First, that in Scandinavian countries there are only very few Jews. These few are hardly ever in evidence. The sum total in Norway was only about 350. [Actual figure, 2000.] A negligible number among two or three million Norwegians. These [Jews] were collected by [Reichskommissar] Terboven and according to orders despatched to Germany by steamship. In this manner the Jewish problem in Norway was practically solved [i.e., by deportation to Auschwitz].

As regards myself, I made at this time an application to Terboven at the request of the Swedish Consul, General Westring, in Oslo, who did not much like visiting Terboven, for the release of a Jew of Swedish nationality and of his family with permission to leave the country, gladly and, as a matter of course, fulfilling the Consul's wish to facilitate the return of these people to Stockholm.

If I had been a rabid anti-semite I could, without further ado, have refused this request, for the matter did not concern me in the slightest.

On the one hand, however, I wanted to help the Swedish Consul, and, on the other hand, I have nothing against the Jews. I have read and heard their writings and compositions with interest, and their achievements in the field of science are worthy of the highest respect. I have met many fine and honorable people among them.[47]

How widespread the practice of "good deeds" must have been may be gauged from the following remark by Heinrich Himmler:

And then they come, our 80,000,000 good Germans, and each one has his decent Jew. It is clear, the others are swine [*Schweine*], but this one is a first-class Jew. Of all those who speak thus, no one has seen it, no one has gone through it.[48]

But even if Himmler regarded these interventions as expressions of misplaced humanity, they were necessary tools in the attempt to crystallize one of the important justifications for bureaucratic action—duty. Only after a man had done "everything humanly possible" could he devote himself to his destructive activity in peace.

The third justification was the rationalization that one's own activity was not criminal, that the next fellow's action was the criminal act. The Ministerialrat who was signing papers could console himself with the thought that he did not do the shooting. But that was not enough. He had to be sure that *if* he were ordered to shoot, he would not follow orders but would draw the line right then and there.

The following exchange took place during a war-crimes trial. A Foreign Office official, Albrecht von Kessel, was asked by defense counsel (Dr. Becker) to explain the meaning of "final solution."

---

47 Affidavit by von Falkenhorst, July 6, 1946, in *Trial of Nikolaus von Falkenhorst* (London, 1949), p. 25.
48 Speech by Himmler, October 4, 1943, PS–1919.

INTELLECTUAL PREPARATION FOR GENOCIDE

It was in recognition of the cultural importance of the Jews that the Nazis almost immediately after achieving power sought to combat them intellectually. Quite early they established a special Jewish-research division in their Reichs-institut für Geschichte des neuen Deutschlands in Munich. This was followed by the Institut zur Erforschung der Judenfrage in Frankfort, the directorship of which was entrusted to the leading ideologist of the Nazi movement, Alfred Rosenberg. The Institut worked hard to assemble a library of Judaica and Hebraica which could be used for attacking the Jewish people and its religion. After confiscating many German and French collections, including the Roths-child archives and the library of the Alliance Israélite Universelle, the Frankfort institution brought together by 1941 some 350,000 volumes which could serve to support whatever distortions of the Jewish past were dictated by the Nazi ideology. Even the vulgar antisemite Julius Streicher, who needed no "scholarly" evidence for his pornographic attacks on the Jews, assembled a substantial collection of Hebraica, most of which is now in New York, on which he em-ployed a number of so-called experts to find passages usable in his anti-Jewish propaganda. With the spread of the New Order, the Germans saw to it that similar institutes for the study of "the Jewish question" were also established in Paris, where it was affiliated with the Department of Jewish Affairs, and in Lodz. The Institut für deutsche Ostarbeit, founded in Cracow in 1940, likewise concerned itself with Jewish matters, as did a special professorship in Jewish history and languages attached to the newly established University of Poznan in 1941. Under Nazi prompting, Italy made available in 1942 research facilities for the study of race and Jewish matters at the universities of Florence, Bologna, Milan, and Trieste.

Source: Salo Baron, *European Jewry Before and After Hitler* (New York: American Jewish Committee, 1962), pp. 37–38.

ANSWER: This expression "final solution" was used with various meanings. In 1936 "final solution" meant merely that all Jews should leave Germany. And, of course, it was true that they were to be robbed; that wasn't very nice, but it wasn't criminal.

JUDGE MAGUIRE: Was that an accurate translation?

DR. BECKER: I did not check on the translation. Please repeat the sentence.

ANSWER: I said it was not criminal; it was not nice, but it was not criminal. That is what I said. One didn't want to take their life; one merely wanted to take money away from them. That was all.[49]

[49] Testimony by Albrecht von Kessel, Case No. 11, tr. pp. 9514–9515.

The most important characteristic of this dividing line was that it could be *shifted* when the need arose. To illustrate: Once there was a Protestant pastor by the name of Ernst Biberstein. After several years of ministering to his congregation, he moved into the Church Ministry; from that agency he came to another office which was also interested in church matters—the Reich Security Main Office. That agency assigned him to head a local Gestapo office. Finally he became the chief of *Einsatzkommando* 6 in southern Russia. As commander of the *Kommando*, Biberstein killed two or three thousand people. These people, in his opinion, had forfeited the right to live under the rules of war. Asked if there were Jews among his victims, he replied: "It is very difficult to determine that. Also, I was told at that time that wherever there were Armenians, there were not so many Jews."[50] To Biberstein the moral dividing line was like the receding horizon. He walked toward it, but he could never reach it.

Among the participants in the destruction process there were very few who did not shift the line when they had to cross the threshold. One reason why the person of Generalkommissar Kube is so important is that he had a firm line beyond which he could not pass. The line was arbitrary, and very advanced. He sacrificed the Russian Jews and fought desperately only for the German Jews in his area. But the line was fixed. It was not movable, it was not imaginary, it was not self-deceptive. We have indicated that the destruction process was autonomous, that it could not be stopped internally; the adjustable moral standard was one of the principal tools in the maintenance of this autonomy.

There was a fourth rationalization which implicitly took cognizance of the fact that all shifting lines are unreal. It was a rationalization of more sophisticated people and was built on simple premise. No man alone can build a bridge. No man alone can destroy the Jews. The participant in the destruction process was always in company. Among his superiors he could always find those who were doing more than he; among his subordinates he could always find those who were ready to take his place. No matter where he looked, he was one among thousands. His own importance was diminished, and he felt that he was replaceable, perhaps even dispensable.

In such reflective moments the bureaucrat quieted his conscience with the thought that he was part of a tide and that there was very little a drop of water could do in such a wave. When Werner von Tippelskirch, a Foreign Office official, was interrogated after the war, he pointed out that he had never protested against the killing of Jews in Russia because he had been "powerless." His superiors, Erdmannsdorff, Wörmann, and Weizsäcker, had also been "powerless." All of them had waited for a "change of regime." Asked by Prosecutor Kempner whether it was right to wait for a change of regime "and in the meantime send thousands of people to their death," von Tippelskirch replied, "A difficult question."[51]

---

[50] Interrogation of Biberstein, June 29, 1947, NO–4997.
[51] Interrogation by Kempner of Werner von Tippelskirch, August 29, 1947, NG–2801.

The fifth rationalization was the most sophisticated of all. It was also a last-ditch psychological defense, suited particularly to those who saw through the self-deception of superior orders, impersonal duty, the shifting moral standard, and the argument of powerlessness. It was a rationalization also for those whose drastic activity or high position placed them out of reach of orders, duty, moral dividing lines, and helplessness. It was the jungle theory.

Oswald Spengler once explained his theory in the following words: "War is the primeval policy of all living things, and this to the extent that in the deepest sense combat and life are identical, for when the will to fight is extinguished, so is life itself." [52] Himmler remembered this theory when he addressed the mobile killing personnel at Minsk. He told them to look at nature: wherever they would look, they would find combat. They would find it among animals and among plants. Whoever tired of the fight went under.

From this philosophy Hitler himself drew strength in moments of meditation. Once at the dinner table, when he thought about the destruction of the Jews, he remarked with stark simplicity: "One must not have mercy with people who are determined by fate to perish [*Man dürfe kein Mitleid mit Leuten haben, denen das Schicksal bestimmt habe, zugrunde zu gehen*]." [53]

2. THE VICTIMS

So far we have pointed out how the Germans overcame their administrative and psychological obstacles; we have dealt with the internal problems of the bureaucratic machine. But the internal technocratic and moral conflicts do not fully explain what happened. In a destruction process the perpetrators do not play the only role; the process is shaped by the victims, too. It is the *interaction* of perpetrators and victims that is "fate." We must therefore discuss the reactions of the Jewish community and analyze the role of the Jews in their own destruction.

When confronted by force, a group can react in five ways: by resistance, by an attempt to alleviate or nullify the threat (the undoing reaction), by evasion, by paralysis, or by compliance. Let us consider each in turn.

The reaction pattern of the Jews is characterized by almost complete lack of resistance. In marked contrast to German propaganda, the documentary evidence of Jewish resistance, overt or submerged, is very slight. On a European-wide scale the Jews had no resistance organization, no blueprint for armed action, no plan even for psychological warfare. They were completely unprepared. In the words of Anti-Partisan Chief and Higher SS and Police Leader Russia Center von dem Bach, who observed the Jews and killed them from 1941 to the end:

---

[52] Oswald Spengler, *Der Untergang des Abendlandes* (Munich, 1923), II, 545–546.

[53] Henry Picker (ed.), *Hitler's Tischgespräche im Führerhauptquartier 1941–1942* (Bonn, 1951), entry for April 2, 1942, p. 227. The entries are summaries by Picker of "Hitler's remarks at the dinner table."

Thus the misfortune came about. . . . I am the only living witness but I must say the truth. Contrary to the opinion of the National Socialists that the Jews were a highly organized group, the appalling fact was that they had no organization whatsoever. The mass of the Jewish people were taken completely by surprise. They did not know at all what to do; they had no directives or slogans as to how they should act. That is the greatest lie of anti-Semitism because it gives the lie to the old slogan that the Jews are conspiring to dominate the world and that they are so highly organized. In reality they had no organization of their own at all, not even an information service. If they had had some sort of organization, these people could have been saved by the millions; but instead they were taken completely by surprise. Never before has a people gone as unsuspectingly to its disaster. Nothing was prepared. Absolutely nothing. It was not so, as the anti-Semites say, that they were friendly to the Soviets. That is the most appalling misconception of all. The Jews in the old Poland, who were never communistic in their sympathies, were, throughout the area of the river Bug eastward, more afraid of Bolshevism than of the Nazis. This was insanity. They could have been saved. There were people among them who had much to lose, business people; they didn't want to leave. In addition there was love of home and their old experience with pogroms in Russia. After the first anti-Jewish actions of the Germans, they thought now the wave was over and so they walked back to their undoing.[54]

The Jews were not oriented toward resistance. They took up resistance only in a few cases, locally, and at the last moment. Measured in German casualties, Jewish armed opposition shrinks into insignificance. The most important engagement was fought in the Warsaw ghetto (16 dead and 85 wounded on the German side, including collaborators). In Galicia sporadic resistance resulted in some losses to SS and Police Leader Katzmann (8 dead, 12 wounded). In addition, there were clashes between Jewish partisans and German forces in other parts of the East, and occasional acts of resistance by small groups and individuals in the ghettos and killing centers. It is doubtful that the Germans and their collaborators lost more than a few hundred men, dead and wounded, in the course of the destruction process. The number of men who dropped out because of disease, nervous breakdowns, or court martial proceedings was probably greater. The Jewish resistance effort could not seriously impede or retard the progress of destructive operations. The Germans brushed that resistance aside as a minor obstacle, and in the totality of the destruction process it was of no consequence.

The second reaction was the attempt to avert the full force of the German destructive measures. This attempt was carried out in three forms. One was the petition—the appeal. By appealing, the Jews sought to transfer the struggle from a physical to an intellectual and moral plane. If only the fate of the Jews could be resolved with arguments rather than with physical resources and physical combat—so Jewry reasoned—there would be nothing to fear. In a petition by Rabbi Kaplan to French Commissioner Xavier Vallat this Jewish mentality becomes absolutely clear. Among other things, the Rabbi pointed out that a

---

[54] Von dem Bach made this statement to Leo Alexander, who quoted it in his article "War Crimes and Their Motivation," *Journal of Criminal Law and Criminology*, XXXIX, 315.

pagan or an atheist had the right to defame Judaism, but in the case of a Christian, did not such an attitude appear "spiritually illogical as well as ungrateful?" To prove his point, Kaplan supplied many learned quotations. The letter is as though it were not written in the twentieth century. It is reminiscent of the time toward the close of the Middle Ages when Jewish rabbis used to dispute with representatives of the Church over the relative merits of the two religions.

Yet in various forms, some more eloquent than others, the Jews appealed and petitioned wherever and whenever the threat of concentration and deportation struck them: in the Reich, in Poland, in Russia, in France, in the Balkan countries, and in Hungary. Everywhere the Jews pitted words against rifles, dialectics against force, and everywhere they lost. The reliance upon petitions became so great that internal struggles developed over the formulation and timing of the appeals.

When the petition system is unsuccessful, when an appeal fails to save the whole group, there is a tendency to appeal for part of the group. In the minds of the drafters, these appeals therefore become life-and-death matters. Whoever is excluded is given up. We may cite as an example the conflict in the Vienna Jewish community over the petitioning for exemptions from deportations. At the end of 1941, when the community organization (*Kultusgemeinde*) made an "agreement" with the Gestapo about "exempt" categories, the head of the Jewish war invalids, who had been left out of the "negotiations," accused the deportation expert of the *Kultusgemeinde* of "sacrificing" the disabled veterans. Later on, when the war invalids were pressed to the wall, the leaders of the veterans' organization discussed the advisability of presenting an independent petition. One of the war-invalid chiefs remarked, "Fundamentally, I am of the opinion that we cannot afford a war with the *Kultusgemeinde*." Another commented: "The *Hauptsturmführer* will say to himself 'These are Jews, and those are Jews. Let them fight among themselves. Why should I worry about that?' He [the *SS-Hauptsturmführer*] will eventually drop us in this matter [*Er wird uns in dieser Frage eventuell fallen lassen*]." Thereupon the head of the war veterans said, "My answer is that in such an eventuality it will be time to disband our organization."

Sometimes the Jews appealed not with words but with personal gifts; they attempted to bribe individual Germans. But these attempts were also largely unsuccessful: the German officials accepted the gifts but these Germans were not bought. Even the few Jewish girls who offered themselves to policemen on the eve of ghetto-clearing operations were killed on the next day. The bribery *did* worry Himmler, but it had no effect on the progress of the operations.

There was a second way in which the Jews tried to avert disaster: by judicious compliance with orders, and sometimes by anticipatory compliance with orders not yet issued. The most conspicuous example of anticipatory compliance was the decision of the Jewish community leaders in Poland to organize a forced labor system. Another anticipatory move was made by the Jewish leadership in Kislovodsk (Caucasus), where, in full awareness of the German threat, the *Judenrat* confiscated all Jewish valuables—including gold, silver, carpets, and clothing—and handed the property to the German commander.[55] A third example of anticipatory compliance may be found in the minutes of a discussion held in the Shavel *Judenrat* (in Latvia) on March 24, 1943. The *Judenrat* had been asked three times whether any births had occurred in the ghetto, and each time it had denied that there were any births. Now, however, the Jewish leadership was confronted with twenty pregnancies. It decided to use persuasion and, if need be, threats on the women to submit to abortions. One woman was in her eighth month; the *Judenrat* decided that in this case a doctor would induce premature birth and that a nurse would kill the child (a doctor objected to doing the job himself). The nurse would be told to proceed in such a way that she would not know the nature of her act.[56]

In one respect this Jewish co-operation created administrative problems within the machinery of destruction. The zeal with which the Jews applied themselves to the German war effort accentuated the differences of interests which paired industry and the armament inspectorates against the SS and Police, but these differences were ultimately resolved to the disadvantage of the Jews. And insofar as the Jews co-operated in other ways, the attempts at forestalling not only availed nothing but actually fitted into German plans. Playing into German hands, they speeded the process of destruction.

The third alleviation attempt may be noted in the system of relief and salvage, from the elaborate social services of the ghetto communities to the primitive "organization" in the killing centers.[57] The relief system was basically the product of a calculation of time, the hope or expectation that the liberation would come before the destruction process could consume itself. We know, simply by counting the relative handful of survivors, that this attempt failed also.

The basic reactions to force are fundamentally different from each other. Resistance is opposition to the perpetrator. Nullification or alleviation is opposition to the administrative enactment. In the third reaction, evasion, the victim tries to remove himself from the effects of force by fleeing or hiding. The phenomenon of flight is most difficult to analyze. We know that the emigration of approximately 350,000 Jews from Germany and German-occupied Czechoslovakia before the war was forced. In many cases the emigrating Jews had been deprived of their livelihood, and they reacted to the consequences of anti-Jewish measures rather than in anticipation of disaster. The flight of the

[55] Protocol by Prof. P. A. Ostankov and others, July 5, 1943, USSR–1 A (2–4).

[56] Minutes of the Shavel *Judenrat*, March 24, 1943, found by the Red Army and turned over to the Soviet Extraordinary State Commission, in Jewish Black Book Committee, *The Black Book* (New York, 1946), pp. 331–333.

[57] To "organize" in a camp meant to take a bit of food or some item of clothing wherever it could be found.

Belgian and Parisian Jews in 1940 and the evacuation of Soviet Jews a year later was compounded with mass migrations of non-Jews. Here again, the flight was not a pure reaction to the threat of the destruction process but also a reaction to the war. We know that only a few thousand Jews escaped from the ghettos of Poland and Russia, that only a few hundred Jews hid out in the large cities of Berlin, Vienna, and Warsaw, that only a handful of Jews escaped from camps. Von dem Bach mentions that in Russia there was an unguarded escape route to the Pripet Marches, but few Jews availed themselves of the opportunity.[58] In the main, the Jews looked upon flight with a sense of futility; the great majority of those who did not escape early did not escape at all.

There were instances when in the mind of the victim, the difficulties of resistance, undoing, or evasion were just as great as the problems of automatic compliance; in such instances the futility of all alternatives became utterly clear, and the victim was paralyzed. Paralysis occurred only in moments of crisis. During ghetto-clearing operations many Jewish families were unable to fight, unable to petition, unable to flee, and also unable to move to the concentration point to get it over with. They waited for the raiding parties in their homes, frozen and helpless. Sometimes the same paralytic reaction struck Jews who walked up to a killing site and for the first time gazed into a mass grave half-filled with the bloodied corpses of those who had preceded them.

The fifth reaction was automatic compliance. Much has been said and much has been written about the *Judenräte*, the informers, the Jewish police, the *Kapos*—in short, all those persons who deliberately and as a matter of policy co-operated with the Germans. But these collaborators do not interest us so much as the masses of Jews who reacted to every German order by complying with it automatically. To understand the administrative significance of this compliance, we have to see the destruction process as a composite of two kinds of German measures: those which perpetrated something upon the Jews and involved only action by Germans, such as the drafting of decrees, the running of deportation trains, shooting, or gassing, and those which required the Jews to do something, for instance, the decrees or orders requiring them to register their property, obtain identification papers, report at a designated place for labor or deportation or shooting, submit lists of persons, pay fines, deliver up property, publish German instructions, dig their own graves, and so on. The successful execution of these latter measures depended on action by the Jews. Only when one realizes how large a part of the destruction process consisted of the fulfilment of these measures can one begin to appraise the role of Jews in their own destruction.

If, therefore, we look at the whole Jewish reaction pattern, we notice that in its two salient features it is an attempt to avert action and, failing that, automatic compliance with orders. Why is this so? Why did the Jews act in this way? The

---

[58] Statement by von dem Bach in *Aufbau* (New York), September 6, 1946, p. 40.

Jews attempted to tame the Germans as one would attempt to tame a wild beast. They avoided "provocations" and complied instantly with decrees and orders. They hoped that somehow the German drive would spend itself.

This hope was founded on a two-thousand-year-old experience. In exile the Jews had always been in a minority; they had always been in danger; but they had learned that they could avert danger and survive destruction by placating and appeasing their enemies. Even in ancient Persia an appeal by Queen Esther was more effective than the mobilization of an army. Armed resistance in the face of overwhelming force could end only in disaster.

Thus, over a period of centuries the Jews had learned that in order to survive they had to refrain from resistance. Time and again they were attacked; they endured the Crusades, the Cossack uprisings, and the Czarist persecution. There were many casualties in these times of stress, but always the Jewish community emerged once again like a rock from a receding tidal wave. The Jews had never really been annihilated. After surveying the damage, the survivors had always proclaimed in affirmation of their strategy the triumphant slogan, "The Jewish people lives [*Am Yisrael Chaj*]." This experience was so ingrained in the Jewish consciousness as to achieve the force of law. The Jewish people could not be annihilated.

Only in 1941, 1942, and 1943 did the Jewish leadership realize that, unlike the pogroms of past centuries, the modern machine-like destruction process would engulf European Jewry. But the realization came too late. A two-thousand-year-old lesson could not be unlearned; the Jews could not make the switch. They were helpless.

Let us not suppose, however, that compliance was easy. If it was difficult for the Germans to kill, it was harder still for the Jews to die. Compliance is a course of action which becomes increasingly drastic in a destruction process. It is one thing to comply with an order to register property but quite another to obey orders in front of a grave. The two actions *are* part of the same habit—the Jews who registered their property were also the ones who lined up to be killed. The Jews who lined up on a killing site were the ones who had registered their property. Yet these two activities are very different in their effects. Submission is altogether more burdensome in its last stages than in its beginning, for as one goes on, more and more is lost. Finally, in the supreme moment of crisis the primeval tendency to resist aggression breaks to the surface; resistance then becomes an obstacle to compliance, just as compliance is an obstacle to resistance. In the Jewish case the co-operation reaction was the stronger one until the end. The Jews consequently dealt with their resistance in much the same way as the Germans dealt with their consciences.

The major obstructions faced by the Jews in their course of submission were never physical ones. No major administrative encumbrances were encountered by the surrendering victims. Only a resistance organization with sufficient power to interfere with surrender can erect such obstructions. This kind of resistance organization could not be formed, and this kind of organized resistance could therefore not occur. However, there were significant psychological blocks on the path to capitulation, blocks which revealed themselves clearly in the victims' repressions and rationalizations.

People do not easily accept the fact that they are going to be killed; if they have the know-how to resist, they will defend themselves as best they can. If, on the other hand, they have unlearned the art of resistance, they will repress their knowledge of the true situation and will attempt to go on as though life could not change. The Jews could not resist. In complying with German orders they therefore tried, to the utmost of their ability, to ignore all evidence of danger and to forget all intimation of death. They pretended that nothing unusual was happening to them, and that belief became so crucial that they did anything to perpetrate it.

One is struck by the fact that the Germans repeatedly employed very crude deceptions and ruses. The Jews were bluffed with "registrations" and "resettlements," with "baths" and "inhalations." At each stage of the destruction process the victims thought that they were going through the last stage. And so it appears that one of the most gigantic hoaxes in world history was perpetrated on five million people noted for their intellect. But were these people really fooled? Or did they deliberately fool themselves?

We have evidence that even in the absence of misleading promises the Jewish victims managed to repress their awareness of catastrophe and to substitute for that knowledge a mere illusion. In survivors' accounts we find long descriptions of the elaborate educational programs for the children, and one survivor tells us that in the closing days of the Kaunas ghetto the slogan of the victims was "life for an hour is also life [*A sho gelebt is oich gelebt*]." [59]

The Jews, in short, did not always have to be deceived; they were capable of deceiving themselves; the Jewish repressive mechanism could work independently and automatically. In the minutes of the Vienna Jewish war invalids' conferences we discover the same significant absence of direct references to death and killing centers that we have already noted in German correspondence. The Jewish documents abound with such roundabout expressions as "favored transport" (meaning Theresienstadt transport), "I see black," "to tempt fate," "final act of the drama," etc. The direct word is lacking.

Moreover, the attempt to repress unbearable thoughts was characteristic not only of the ghetto community but of the killing center itself. In Auschwitz the inmates employed a special terminology of their own for killing operations: a crematory was called a "bakery"; a man who could no longer work—and who was therefore destined for the gas chamber—was designated a "Moslem"; and the depot holding the belongings of the gassed was named "Canada." [60] These,

---

[59] Samuel Gringauz, "The Ghetto as an Experiment in Jewish Social Organization," *Jewish Social Studies*, XI (1949), 17.

[60] On "bakery," see Lengyel, *Five Chimneys*, p. 22. On "Moslem" (*Muselmann*), see report by commander's office, Auschwitz III, May 5, 1944, NI–11019. On "Canada," see Sehn, "Oswiecim," in *German Crimes in Poland*, p. 41.

it must be emphasized, are not Nazi terms; they are expressions by the victims. They are the counterparts of the Nazi vocabulary, and, like the German euphemisms, they were designed to blot out visions of death.

There were moments, of course, when the issue could not be evaded, when forgetting was no longer effective. In such moments of crisis the victims, like the perpetrators, resorted to rationalizations. The Jews, too, had to justify their actions. It is interesting to note how the two principal rationalizations emerged directly from the repressive pattern.

The Germans were notably successful in deporting Jews by stages, for always those who remained behind could reason that it was necessary to sacrifice the few in order to save the many. The operation of that psychology may be observed in the Vienna Jewish community, which concluded a deportation "agreement" with the Gestapo, with the "understanding" that six categories of Jews would not be deported. Again, the Warsaw ghetto Jews argued in favor of co-operation and against resistance on the ground that the Germans would deport sixty thousand Jews but not hundreds of thousands. The bisection phenomenon occurred also in Salonika, where the Jewish leadership co-operated with the German deportation agencies upon the assurance that only "Communist" elements from the poor sections would be deported, while the "middle class" would be left alone. That fatal arithmetic was also applied in Vilna, where *Judenrat* chief Gens declared: "With a hundred victims I save a thousand people. With a thousand I save ten thousand."[61]

In situations where compliance with death orders could no longer be rationalized as a life-saving measure there was still one more justification: the argument that with rigid, instantaneous compliance unnecessary suffering was eliminated, unnecessary pain avoided, the necessary torture reduced. The entire Jewish community, and particularly the Jewish leadership, now concentrated all its efforts in one direction—to make the ordeal bearable, to make death easy.

This effort is reflected in the letter which the Jewish Council in Budapest sent to the Hungarian Interior Minister on the eve of the deportations: "We emphatically declare that we do not seek this audience in order to lodge complaints about the merit of the measures adopted, but merely ask that they be carried out in a humane spirit."

The effort is also illustrated in the following statement, which the chief of the Reich Association of the Jews in Germany, Rabbi Leo Baeck, made after the war:

I made it a principle to accept no appointments from the Nazis and to do nothing which might help them. But later, when the question arose whether Jewish orderlies should help pick up Jews for deportation, I took the position that it would be better for them to do it, because they could at least be more gentle and helpful than the Gestapo and make the ordeal easier. It was scarcely in our power to oppose the order effectively.[62]

---

[61] Philip Friedman, "Two 'Saviors' Who Failed," *Commentary*, December 1958, p. 487.
[62] Leo Baeck in Eric H. Boehm (ed.), *We Survived* (New Haven, 1949), p. 288.

When Baeck was in Theresienstadt, an engineer who had escaped from Auschwitz informed him about the gassings. Baeck decided not to pass on this information to anyone in the ghetto city because "living in the expectation of death by gassing would only be the harder."[63]

The supreme test of the compliance reaction came in front of the grave; yet here, too, the Jews managed to console themselves. From one of the numerous German eyewitness reports comes the following typical passage:

> The father was holding the hand of a boy about ten years old and was speaking to him softly; the boy was fighting his tears. The father pointed to the sky, stroked his head, and seemed to explain something to him. . . . I remember a girl, slim and with black hair, who passed close to me, pointed to herself, and said, "Twenty-three." . . . The people, completely naked, went down some steps which were cut in the clay wall of the pit and clambered over the heads of the people lying there, to the place where the SS-man directed them. Then they lay down in front of the dead or injured people; some caressed those who were still alive and spoke to them in a low voice. Then I heard a series of shots.[64]

The German annihilation of the European Jews was the world's first completed destruction process. For the first time in the history of Western civilization the perpetrators had overcome all administrative and moral obstacles to a killing operation. For the first time, also, the Jewish victims—caught in the strait jacket of their history—plunged themselves physically and psychologically into catastrophe. The destruction of the Jews was thus no accident. When in the early days of 1933 the first civil servant wrote the first definition of a "non-Aryan" into a civil service ordinance, the fate of European Jewry was sealed.

---

[63] *Ibid.*, pp. 292–293.
[64] Affidavit by Hermann Friedrich Graebe, November 10, 1945, PS–2992.
Source: Prepared especially for this volume.

Genocide and the American Indian

LOUISE G. HOWTON

Genocide a quarter of a century ago had a reasonably clear meaning. After the revelations of 1945 that in fact there had been a system of Nazi "death camps," and the findings of the Nuremburg trials that the German government under Hitler had deliberately, planfully destroyed the Jews of Europe, no informed person could doubt that the killing of *a people* by *a state* could happen and must be condemned as criminal by all who consider themselves civilized.

The memory of that holocaust has faded somewhat, but paradoxically the interest in genocide as a sort of super crime has increased in the past decade. Third world ideologues charge the "imperialist" powers with continuing genocidal policies even after they have withdrawn from direct political control. New-left radicals and black militants in the United States assert that racial minorities in this country—Indians, Negroes, Mexicans, Puerto Ricans—have been victims of genocide for generations and still are.

Finally there is Vietnam. Former "hawks" who changed their minds did so, in many instances, because they came to see genocide as the only solution that would bring victory—"bomb them back to the Stone Age," in the words of U.S. Air Force General (Ret.) Curtis LeMay—and rejected it. "Doves" argued all along that massive counterguerilla warfare could only end with such vast social wreckage that the result would be genocide.

Evidently genocide in the '70s means something different than it did in the '40s. The plan of this paper is to clarify the concept by examining U.S. government policy in relation to the Indians, sketchily, but in some historical depth. The focus is on what has been called cultural genocide, the form of greatest interest now.

THE PROBLEM OF DEFINITION

The killing of a man is homicide. The killing of a people is genocide. But are the two acts really analogous? "A people" is an organized human collectivity with a common heritage and in some sense a life of its own. Killing people, therefore, is an event of a different order than killing *a* people. Destroying most or all of the individual members of the group is a sure way of destroying the life of the group (as the Nazis did of the European Jews and Gypsies), but it is not the only way. The same result can be achieved without bringing physical harm to a single person: through dispersal, relocation, or imposed conditions of life so oppressive that the group falls apart.

The societal group lives on regardless of the fate of particular individuals, and the individual can live biologically regardless of the fate of the group. But the life of the group and the welfare of the individual tied to it is more than a matter of simple survival. A human being is more than a biological entity. Harm to the group inevitably entails harm to the individual: he may not die, but socially, culturally, and therefore psychologically, he is made to suffer and may be maimed.

The term *genocide* was coined by Raphael Lemkin, a specialist in international law, who tried, through the League of Nations and then the United Nations, to get the destruction of a human group recognized as an international crime. The U.N. Ad Hoc Committee on Genocide proposed that the definition of genocide, following Lemkin, encompass ". . . deliberate acts committed with the intent to destroy a national, racial, religious, or political group"[1] whether through physical means (killing), biological means (prevention of reproduction by sterilization or gross interference with family life), or cultural means (destruction of the moral and spiritual life of a group by denying the means of worship, education, scholarship, and preservation of the artifacts and symbols of its heritage).[2]

This was the proposal. The version adopted by the U.N. General Assembly in 1948 omitted those parts that referred to genocide by cultural means on the grounds that it more properly belonged in a separate convention dealing with the protection of human rights.[3] (There was a consideration of political feasibility as well as principle. It seemed quixotic to try to get the United States to stop its efforts to bring Amish children into the public school system, for example, or to persuade the Soviet Union to establish effective freedom of worship.)

A sociological conception of genocide has to go beyond a legal definition if it is to be useful, however; cultural genocide as a phenomenon was not made meaningless by act of the General Assembly. The problem for sociology is to devise a concept narrow enough to be precisely defined, but broad enough to encompass acts that have the effect of destroying the life of a human group regardless of the means used.

A REVISED CONCEPTION OF GENOCIDE

Genocide in sociological perspective is a patterned series of events in time that constitutes the natural history of the relations between a destroyer and a victim as social groups. It is a multidimensional process: the intentions and capabilities of the destroyer vary, as do the character and effectiveness of the means used.

The case of the American Indians in the United States is illustrative. We posit three types of genocide: primary, secondary, and tertiary. The *primary* type is one in which the social group (an Indian tribal society) is utterly destroyed, through physical means, by an agency of government (the military), following a policy of extermination. In the *secondary* type the means employed are mainly cultural: the policy of the government (through the Bureau of Indian Affairs) is to destroy "barbaric customs" and "civilize the savages." The *tertiary* type occurs in the absence of an explicitly genocidal policy. Cultural and physical means are used by a host of agencies and forces, public and private, that effectively destroy the life of the victim group because they are unrestrained by a weak or negligent legal authority.

---

[1] United Nations, Ad Hoc Committee on Genocide, *Report to the Economic and Social Council of the Meetings of the Committee Held at Lake Success*, New York, April 5 to May 10, 1948, Third Year: Seventh Sess., Suppl. No. 6 (Lake Success; N.Y.: 1948), p. 18.

[2] *Ibid.*

[3] Political groups were also omitted from the revised definition.

INDIANS AND THE U.S. GOVERNMENT: VICTIM AND DESTROYER

The question, it has been said, is "whether the Indian tribes are communities of people or hills of ants. They should not have to live in perpetual fear that the federal foot is going to squash them to death. Yet this is the situation in which they exist under an on-again off-again application of federal pressures that would be considered intolerable by any white community."[4]

The United States government has always claimed jurisdiction in dealing with the aboriginal inhabitants of its territory. It has never been sure of its role, however, and several times changed its conception in a fundamental way.

One of the few elements of continuity is that the Euro-Americans have never denied the doctrine, inherited from the British and laid down by the first U.S. Secretary of War, that the intention of the Republic was not to destroy the Indians but to make just and binding treaties with them. In the view of Secretary Knox, they "possess the right of the soil," and this "cannot be taken from them unless by their free consent, or by right of conquest in case of a just war." They "ought to be considered as foreign nations, not as subjects of any particular state."[5] More than a generation later, in 1832, Chief Justice Marshall called them "distinct, independent, political communities,"[6] not subject to the laws of the various states of the Union.

Federal policy in the early period was not genocidal, but federal authority was weak. Local governments were often free in fact to carry out acts of genocide, some planned, some sporadic, some inadvertent. Georgia affords an example. Responding to population pressure and political agitation by land speculators, the state obtained federal military action to remove Indians from lands the whites wanted. Most of the Cherokee nation in 1838 was forced to march from its homeland to "the Indian Line" in the far distant Oklahoma territory. The hardships they endured were severe—a quarter of the population perished—and the episode has since become known as the "Trail of Tears."

In 1849 the Bureau of Indian Affairs was transferred from the War Department to the Department of the Interior, but the policy it undertook to pacify the Indians scarcely changed in character. Some forty-five wars, massacres, and major "actions" were recorded in a period of thirty years. The character of these encounters is evident in the report of a military eye witness:

"We arrived at the Indian village about daylight. . . . Colonel Chivington moved his regiment to the front, the Indians retreating up the creek, and hiding under the banks. . . . White Antelope ran towards our columns unarmed, and with both arms raised, but was killed. Several others of the warriors were killed in like manner. The women

---

[4] LaVerne Madigan, executive director of the Association on American Indian Affairs, quoted in Edmund Wilson, *Apologies to the Iroquois* (New York: Vintage Books, Alfred A. Knopf and Random House, 1966), p. 278.

[5] Jack D. Forbes (ed.), *The Indian in America's Past* (Englewood Cliffs, N.J.: Prentice-Hall, 1964), p. 99.

[6] *Ibid.*, p. 105.

and children were huddled together, and most of our fire was concentrated on them. . . . I estimated the loss of the Indians to be from one hundred and twenty-five to one hundred and seventy-five killed; no wounded fell into our hands and all the dead were scalped. The Indian who was pointed out as White Antelope, had his fingers cut off."

Summing up, Lt. Cramer said, "Our force was so large that there was no necessity of firing on the Indians. They did not return the fire until after our troops had fired several rounds." He tried to stop the commander. "I told Colonel Chivington . . . that it would be murder, in every sense of the word, if he attacked those Indians. His reply was, bringing his fist down close to my face, 'Damn any man who sympathizes with Indians' . . . he had come to kill Indians and believed it to be honorable to kill Indians under any and all circumstances."[7]

Pacification was completed by the early 1880s. The Indians were confined to reservations. Unable to find subsistence, they soon became dependent on the federal dole. The Bureau of Indian Affairs fed its wards, and then from 1870 to 1934, took on the infinitely larger task of trying to remake them into replicas of whites.

FROM COERCED ACCULTURATION TO COMMUNITY SELF-DEVELOPMENT

During the 1870–1934 period children were rounded up and confined in boarding schools, native religion was banned, and even such trivial expressions of a sense of group heritage as long hair were forcibly restricted—in some instances haircuts were carried out at the point of a gun. The rationale was that "everything native had to be destroyed, even if the process sometimes meant destroying the native himself."[8] The U.S. Commissioner of Indian Affairs said in 1887 that the perpetuation of tribal languages was to be discouraged: "Teaching an Indian youth in his own barbarous dialect is a positive detriment to him."[9] A special college for Indians was set up. It was no small disappointment to the Bureau that the graduates more often than not went "back to the blanket." The effort to destroy native religion was no more successful. In 1926 the entire governing body of the Taos Pueblo in New Mexico was jailed for violating the Bureau's religious crime codes.

These harsh, self-righteous policies were relaxed in 1934, when the Bureau philosophy shifted from coerced acculturation to community self-development. One of the unanticipated consequences, however, was that racial consciousness grew faster than community consciousness. The effort of the Eisenhower

---

[7] *Ibid.*, p. 47.
[8] *Ibid.*, p. 113.
[9] *Ibid.*, pp. 113–114.

administration in the late 1950s to end the special responsibility of the federal government—in effect to turn Indian affairs over to the states—gave unexpected impetus to the national red power movement. One of its first successes was in stopping some of the promiscuous taking of Indian lands for reclamation projects or for private business exploitation. Through court action and lobbying the movement won important victories, and Indian spokesmen for Indian interests and movement leaders for civil rights and political power have become noticeable on the national scene within the past ten years.

REVIEW AND CONCLUSIONS

There can be no doubt that the American Indians have been off-and-on victims of genocide: direct and indirect, planned and spontaneous, calculated and inadvertent, systematic and casual, physical and cultural, depending on circumstances and the temper of the times. At different places and at different moments in history they have been cast in the role of honorable foes, nuisances, beggars and thieves to be held in check, mad dogs to be hunted down, protected wards of the government, savages to be civilized, living relics to be preserved, miniature national communities with a right to exist, and underprivileged citizens of the Republic.

There has been virtually no primary genocide in its pure form. It never was avowed public policy to exterminate Indians, as individual communities or as a racial category of people. On the other hand there have been in fact numerous campaigns against Indian tribes, with the tacit or open support of public officials (conspicuously the U.S. Cavalry in the period just after the Civil War), ostensibly to subdue or contain the tribes but actually to wipe them out. However, these were formally illegal actions. Lt. Cramer's account of the Sand Creek massacre became part of the public record because Colonel Chivington was court-martialled for exceeding his authority. "The only good Indian is a dead Indian" was an ethical norm held by many white people, and acted upon by some, including public officials, but it was not public policy. To the extent that primary genocide occurred it was sporadic, furtive, and exceptional.

The same cannot be said of secondary and tertiary genocide.

"The Indian problem" became something larger than a matter of making and enforcing treaties and protecting white settlers when the federal government took formal responsibility, in 1849, for the welfare of the Indians as well as for the safety of the whites. Pacified and contained on reservations, the Indians became dependents, and the question of what to do with them in the long run became urgent. High officials concluded that they must be civilized and assimilated into the mainstream of American life, if necessary by forcible means. Their language, institutions, ways of thought, and behavior had to be destroyed (the victim suffers loss of his identity and heritage as he becomes engulfed by the destroyer).

Secondary genocide following this pattern was confined mostly to the period 1849–1934. Tertiary genocide was endemic throughout. The white settlement process was so overwhelming, regardless of the intention of governments or paragovernments, that one after another of the six hundred indigenous tribal societies found it impossible to carry on. Many perished. Others (notably the Navahoes and the Pueblo group in the desert regions of the southwest) were favored by isolation and kept enough of the old ways to maintain a group life, but by and large the remnant has accommodated so radically to the dominant white culture that the little communal life and sense of separate identity they still retain has been warped and fragmented almost beyond recognition.

Cultural Genocide: Indians and Negroes

The difficulty with the concept of cultural genocide is that it makes it hard to differentiate between a benign process of assimilation and a malignant process of mental and moral destruction, intended or not, of a victimized minority by an oppressive majority. It is indispensable, nonetheless, to make the distinction because it calls attention to the realities of power and its role in the process of group change that the value-neutral concept of assimilation does not.

In the case of the American Indians cultural genocide is abundantly evident.[10] The group life and heritage has been ruined, occasionally by physical means and with intent (primary genocide), but more often by cultural means with or without intent (secondary and tertiary genocide).

The case of black Americans, Negroes, is more complex. Brought to this continent in a socially and culturally fragmented condition, their life as slaves until the Civil War made it very difficult to develop a distinctive group life and culture. The process of building a black heritage was greatly hastened by the ending of slavery, but even more by the economic, social, and cultural freedom that followed from the emigration of black people to the urban North, where they formed self-nurturing communal enclaves in the big cities.

White America has followed a policy of forcible assimilation or coerced acculturation—not integration—in regard to Negroes as well as Indians, but in different ways: the red man's heritage and much of his identity has been taken from him, whereas the black man has been denied the liberty and the means to build his own. Cultural genocide does apply, used in this limited and cautious way, and can serve to sensitize us to the realities of the process by which minorities can be and have been victimized or destroyed by the majority. Used loosely, as a slogan and a substitute for precise thought, it is a tool in the service of ideology rather than sociology.

---

[10] A recent author has reminded us of the danger of using terms that imply a set of values and standards accepted in the present time to actions that occurred in an earlier period when the moral definitions were different. Hence, the difficulty of calling ancient wars genocidal. See Bruno Cormier, "On the History of Men and Genocide," *The Canadian Medical Assoc. Journal*, **94** (February 1966), pp. 276–291.

CHAPTER 4

THERMONUCLEAR WAR

Hiroshima Diary

MICHIHIKO HACHIYA

▬▬

6 AUGUST 1945

The hour was early; the morning still, warm, and beautiful. Shimmering leaves, reflecting sunlight from a cloudless sky, made a pleasant contrast with shadows in my garden as I gazed absently through wide-flung doors opening to the south.

Clad in drawers and undershirt, I was sprawled on the living room floor exhausted because I had just spent a sleepless night on duty as an air warden in my hospital.

Suddenly, a strong flash of light startled me—and then another. So well does one recall little things that I remember vividly how a stone lantern in the garden became brilliantly lit and I debated whether this light was caused by a magnesium flare or sparks from a passing trolley.

Garden shadows disappeared. The view where a moment before all had been so bright and sunny was now dark and hazy. Through swirling dust I could barely discern a wooden column that had supported one corner of my house. It was leaning crazily and the roof sagged dangerously.

Moving instinctively, I tried to escape, but rubble and fallen timbers barred the way. By picking my way cautiously I managed to reach the *roka* and stepped down into my garden. A profound weakness overcame me, so I stopped to regain my strength. To my surprise I discovered that I was completely naked. How odd! Where were my drawers and undershirt?

What had happened?

All over the right side of my body I was cut and bleeding. A large splinter was protruding from a mangled wound in my thigh, and something warm trickled into my mouth. My cheek was torn, I discovered as I felt it gingerly, with the lower lip laid wide open. Embedded in my neck was a sizable fragment of glass which I matter-of-factly dislodged, and with the detachment of one stunned and shocked I studied it and my blood-stained hand.

Source: Michihiko Hachiya, *Hiroshima Diary* (Chapel Hill, N.C.: University of North Carolina, 1955). Reprinted by permission.

Where was my wife?

Suddenly thoroughly alarmed, I began to yell for her: "Yaeko-san! Yaeko-san! Where are you?"

Blood began to spurt. Had my carotid artery been cut? Would I bleed to death? Frightened and irrational, I called out again: "It's a five-hundred-ton bomb! Yaeko-san, where are you? A five-hundred-ton bomb has fallen!"

Yaeko-san, pale and frightened, her clothes torn and blood-stained, emerged from the ruins of our house holding her elbow. Seeing her, I was reassured. My own panic assuaged, I tried to reassure her.

"We'll be all right," I exclaimed. "Only let's get out of here as fast as we can."

She nodded, and I motioned for her to follow me.

The shortest path to the street lay through the house next door so through the house we went—running, stumbling, falling, and then running again until in headlong flight we tripped over something and fell sprawling into the street. Getting to my feet, I discovered that I had tripped over a man's head.

"Excuse me! Excuse me, please!" I cried hysterically.

There was no answer. The man was dead. The head had belonged to a young officer whose body was crushed beneath a massive gate.

We stood in the street, uncertain and afraid, until a house across from us began to sway and then with a rending motion fell almost at out feet. Our own house began to sway, and in a minute it, too, collapsed in a cloud of dust. Other buildings caved in or toppled. Fires sprang up and whipped by a vicious wind began to spread.

It finally dawned on us that we could not stay there in the street, so we turned our steps toward the hospital.[1] Our home was gone; we were wounded and needed treatment; and after all, it was my duty to be with my staff. This latter was an irrational thought—what good could I be to anyone, hurt as I was.

We started out, but after twenty or thirty steps I had to stop. My breath became short, my heart pounded, and my legs gave way under me. An overpowering thirst seized me and I begged Yaeko-san to find me some water. But there was no water to be found. After a little my strength somewhat returned and we were able to go on.

I was still naked, and although I did not feel the least bit of shame, I was disturbed to realize that modesty had deserted me. On rounding a corner we came upon a soldier standing idly in the street. He had a towel draped across his shoulder, and I asked if he would give it to me to cover my nakedness. The soldier surrendered the towel quite willingly but said not a word. A little later I lost the towel, and Yaeko-san took off her apron and tied it around my loins.

Our progress towards the hospital was interminably slow, until finally, my legs, stiff from drying blood, refused to carry me farther. The strength, even the will, to go on deserted me, so I told my wife, who was almost as badly hurt

---

[1] Dr. Hachiya's home was only a few hundred meters from the hospital.

as I, to go on alone. This she objected to, but there was no choice. She had to go ahead and try to find someone to come back for me.

Yaeko-san looked into my face for a moment, and then, without saying a word, turned away and began running towards the hospital. Once, she looked back and waved and in a moment she was swallowed up in the gloom. It was quite dark now, and with my wife gone, a feeling of dreadful loneliness overcame me.

I must have gone out of my head lying there in the road because the next thing I recall was discovering the clot on my thigh had been dislodged and blood was again spurting from the wound. I pressed my hand to the bleeding area and after a while the bleeding stopped and I felt better.

Could I go on?

I tried. It was all a nightmare—my wounds, the darkness, the road ahead. My movements were ever so slow; only my mind was running at top speed.

In time I came to an open space where the houses had been removed to make a fire lane. Through the dim light I could make out ahead of me the hazy outlines of the Communications Bureau's big concrete building, and beyond it the hospital. My spirits rose because I knew that now some one would find me; and if I should die, at least my body would be found.

I paused to rest. Gradually things around me came into focus. There were the shadowy forms of people, some of whom looked like walking ghosts. Others moved as though in pain, like scarecrows, their arms held out from their bodies with forearms and hands dangling. These people puzzled me until I suddenly realized that they had been burned and were holding their arms out to prevent the painful friction of raw surfaces rubbing together. A naked woman carrying a naked baby came into view. I averted my gaze. Perhaps they had been in the bath. But then I saw a naked man, and it occurred to me that, like myself, some strange thing had deprived them of their clothes. An old woman lay near me with an expression of suffering on her face; but she made no sound. Indeed, one thing was common to everyone I saw—complete silence.

All who could were moving in the direction of the hospital. I joined in the dismal parade when my strength was somewhat recovered, and at last reached the gates of the Communications Bureau.

Familiar surroundings, familiar faces. There was Mr. Iguchi and Mr. Yoshi-hiro and my old friend, Mr. Sera, the head of the business office. They hastened to give me a hand, their expressions of pleasure changing to alarm when they saw that I was hurt. I was too happy to see them to share their concern.

No time was lost over greetings. They eased me onto a stretcher and carried me into the Communications Building, ignoring my protest that I could walk. Later, I learned that the hospital was so overrun that the Communications Bureau had to be used as an emergency hospital. The rooms and corridors were crowded with people, many of whom I recognized as neighbors. To me it seemed that the whole community was there.

My friends passed me through an open window into a janitor's room recently converted to an emergency first-aid station. The room was a shambles; fallen plaster, broken furniture, and debris littered the floor; the walls were cracked; and a heavy steel window casement was twisted and almost wrenched from its seating. What a place to dress the wounds of the injured.

To my great surprise who should appear but my private nurse, Miss Kado, and Mr. Mizoguchi, and old Mrs. Saeki. Miss Kado set about examining my wounds without speaking a word. No one spoke. I asked for a shirt and pajamas. They got them for me, but still no one spoke. Why was everyone so quiet?

Miss Kado finished the examination, and in a moment it felt as if my chest was on fire. She had begun to paint my wounds with iodine and no amount of entreaty would make her stop. With no alternative but to endure the iodine, I tried to divert myself by looking out the window.

The hospital lay directly opposite with part of the roof and the third floor sunroom in plain view, and as I looked up, I witnessed a sight which made me forget my smarting wounds. Smoke was pouring out of the sunroom windows. The hospital was afire!

"Fire!" I shouted. "Fire! Fire! The hospital is on fire!"

My friends looked up. It was true. The hospital *was* on fire.

The alarm was given and from all sides people took up the cry. The high-pitched voice of Mr. Sera, the business officer, rose above the others, and it seemed as if his was the first voice I had heard that day. The uncanny stillness was broken. Our little world was now in pandemonium.

I remember that Dr. Sasada, chief of the Pediatric Service, came in and tried to reassure me, but I could scarcely hear him above the din. I heard Dr. Hinoi's voice and then Dr. Koyama's. Both were shouting orders to evacuate the hospital and with such vigor that it sounded as though the sheer strength of their voices could hasten those who were slow to obey.

The sky became bright as flames from the hospital mounted. Soon the Bureau was threatened and Mr. Sera gave the order to evacuate. My stretcher was moved into a rear garden and placed beneath an old cherry tree. Other patients limped into the garden or were carried until soon the entire area became so crowded that only the very ill had room to lie down. No one talked, and the ominous silence was relieved only by a subdued rustle among so many people, restless, in pain, anxious, and afraid, waiting for something else to happen.

The sky filled with black smoke and glowing sparks. Flames rose and the heat set currents of air in motion. Updrafts became so violent that sheets of zinc roofing were hurled aloft and released, humming and twirling, in erratic flight. Pieces of flaming wood soared and fell like fiery swallows. While I was trying to beat out the flames, a hot ember seared my ankle. It was all I could do to keep from being burned alive.

The Bureau started to burn, and window after window became a square of flame until the whole structure was converted into a crackling, hissing inferno.

Scorching winds howled around us, whipping dust and ashes into our eyes and up our noses. Our mouths became dry, our throats raw and sore from the biting smoke pulled into our lungs. Coughing was uncontrollable. We would have moved back, but a group of wooden barracks behind us caught fire and began to burn like tinder.

The heat finally became too intense to endure, and we were left no choice but to abandon the garden. Those who could fled; those who could not perished. Had it not been for my devoted friends, I would have died, but again, they came to the rescue and carried my stretcher to the main gate on the other side of the Bureau.

Here a small group of people were already clustered, and here I found my wife. Dr. Sasada and Miss Kado joined us.

Fires sprang up on every side as violent winds fanned flames from one building to another. Soon, we were surrounded. The ground we held in front of the Communications Bureau became an oasis in a desert of fire. As the flames came closer the heat became more intense, and if someone in our group had not had the presence of mind to drench us with water[2] from a fire hose, I doubt if anyone could have survived.

Hot as it was, I began to shiver. The drenching was too much. My heart pounded; things began to whirl until all before me blurred.

"*Kurushii*," I murmured weakly. "I am done."

The sound of voices reached my ears as though from a great distance and finally became louder as if close at hand. I opened my eyes; Dr. Sasada was feeling my pulse. What had happened? Miss Kado gave me an injection. My strength gradually returned. I must have fainted.

Huge raindrops began to fall. Some thought a thunderstorm was beginning and would extinguish the fires. But these drops were capricious. A few fell and then a few more and that was all the rain we saw.[3]

The first floor of the Bureau was now ablaze and flames were spreading rapidly towards our little oasis by the gate. Right then, I could hardly understand the situation, much less do anything about it.

An iron window frame, loosened by fire, crashed to the ground behind us. A ball of fire whizzed by me, setting my clothes ablaze. They drenched me with water again. From then on I am confused as to what happened.

I do remember Dr. Hinoi because of the pain, the pain I felt when he jerked me to my feet. I remember being moved or rather dragged, and my whole spirit rebelling against the torment I was made to endure.

My next memory is of an open area. The fires must have receded. I was alive. My friends had somehow managed to rescue me again.

A head popped out of an air-raid dugout, and I heard the unmistakable voice

---

[2] The water mains entered the city from the north and since the Communications Bureau was in the northern edge of the city, its water supply was not destroyed.

[3] There were many reports of a scanty rainfall over the city after the bombing. The drops were described as large and dirty, and some claimed that they were laden with radioactive dust.

of old Mrs. Saeki: "Cheer up, doctor! Everything will be all right. The north side is burnt out. We have nothing further to fear from the fire."

I might have been her son, the way the old lady calmed and reassured me. And indeed, she was right. The entire northern side of the city was completely burned. The sky was still dark, but whether it was evening or midday I could not tell. It might even have been the next day. Time had no meaning. What I had experienced might have been crowded into a moment or been endured through the monotony of eternity.

Smoke was still rising from the second floor of the hospital, but the fire had stopped. There was nothing left to burn, I thought; but later I learned that the first floor of the hospital had escaped destruction largely through the courageous efforts of Dr. Koyama and Dr. Hinoi.

The streets were deserted except for the dead. Some looked as if they had been frozen by death while in the full action of flight; others lay sprawled as though some giant had flung them to their death from a great height.

Hiroshima was no longer a city, but a burnt-over prairie. To the east and to the west everything was flattened. The distant mountains seemed nearer than I could ever remember. The hills of Ushita and the woods of Nigitsu loomed out of the haze and smoke like the nose and eyes on a face. How small Hiroshima was with its houses gone.

The wind changed and the sky again darkened with smoke.

Suddenly, I heard someone shout: "Planes! Enemy planes!"

Could that be possible after what had already happened? What was there left to bomb? My thoughts were interrupted by the sound of a familiar name.

A nurse calling Dr. Katsube.

"It is Dr. Katsube! It's him!" shouted old Mrs. Saeki, a happy ring to her voice. "Dr. Katsube has come!"

It was Dr. Katsube, our head surgeon, but he seemed completely unaware of us as he hurried past, making a straight line for the hospital. Enemy planes were forgotten, so great was our happiness that Dr. Katsube had been spared to return to us.

Before I could protest, my friends were carrying me into the hospital. The distance was only a hundred meters, but it was enough to cause my heart to pound and make me sick and faint.

I recall the hard table and the pain when my face and lip were sutured, but I have no recollection of the forty or more other wounds Dr. Katsube closed before night.

They removed me to an adjoining room, and I remember feeling relaxed and sleepy. The sun had gone down, leaving a dark red sky. The red flames of the burning city had scorched the heavens. I gazed at the sky until sleep overtook me.

A Hypothetical Thermonuclear Strike

LEIBA BROWN AND RUTH LEEDS

■

Instants after the bombs exploded at the earth's surface at each of the 224 target locations, balls of fire formed, emitting highly destructive thermal radiation. Nuclear reactions causing the explosions were accompanied by damaging radiation, much of which remained as part of the fall-out. Minutes after the explosion, a destructive shock wave formed in the air, moving rapidly away from the fireballs and leveling everything in its path. The fireballs excavated highly radioactive craters where they came to rest, and, as if they possessed a magic wand, all they touched vaporized.

EFFECTS ON PHYSICAL STRUCTURES

BLAST DAMAGE. Throughout the country, a quarter of the homes— 11,800,000 dwelling units—were completely demolished. Another eight million were badly damaged but could be made habitable again with major repairs. Still another 500,000 buildings sustained light damage. In buildings where total destruction had not reaped its toll, the shock wave broke gas lines and fuel tanks, upset stoves and furnaces, and short-circuited wiring, so that severe fire damage also resulted from the blast.

Thriving cities were reduced to rubble within seconds. When a ten-megaton bomb exploded in New York at Rockefeller Center, all buildings without steel supports, within a radius of seven and a half miles collapsed completely. Multistory brick apartment houses were mowed down. Wood-frame houses and stores within a nine-mile radius fell like the proverbial house of cards. Bridges

Source: Leiba Brown and Ruth Leeds, "What the Bombs Can Do," in Amitai Etzioni, *The Hard Way to Peace* (New York: Collier Books, 1962), pp. 270–275. Reprinted by permission.

Editors' Note: Based on testimony by military and scientific experts who were asked by a Congressional committee to describe the effects of a possible attack. It was assumed that enemy bombs (atomic and thermonuclear) with explosive force equivalent to 1,500 megatons of TNT were dropped on 71 urban areas within the continental United States, plus 153 other strategic targets, on October 17, 1958. Casualties, as calculated, totalled 70 million—23 million killed instantly, 28 million wounded who later died of their injuries, and 19 million wounded who recovered. (Joint Committee on Atomic Energy, Congress of the United States, *Biological and Environmental Effects of Nuclear War* [Washington, D.C.: U.S. Government Printing Office, 1959].)

within a three-and-a-half-mile zone were destroyed and, within ten miles, telephone and power lines were out of commission. In short, most buildings and communication and transportation networks, so vital for survival and evacuation, were demolished.

EFFECTS OF THERMAL RADIATION. The heat emitted by the fireball ignited most combustible materials within the destruction zone (up to twenty-five miles for a ten-megaton bomb). Any accessible paper, trash, window curtains, awnings and leaves caught fire immediately. Flames spread rapidly through the crowded wholesale districts and the slums. In some areas, depending on local weather and terrain, "fire storms" raged with unconquerable fury through woods and towns.

EFFECTS OF THE CRATER. Where the fireball touched the earth, it sucked up all beneath it, leaving a cavernous hole. All underground shelters, subways and other subterranean installations within the quarter-mile radius of the crater were destroyed, for the crater at its deepest was 240 feet.

EFFECTS OF FALL-OUT. Many buildings that were left standing were contaminated by radiation and thereby rendered temporarily useless for human purposes. The radioactive fall-out affected about thirteen million homes, making them uninhabitable for at least two months.

The physical damage caused by the attack, although far-reaching in its impact, did not turn the United States into the utter wasteland it became in Nevil Shute's *On the Beach*. Roughly one-third of the homes were still intact, and many of the roads could be used for travel. But our economic, political, cultural, religious, and medical centers, as well as our communications system, were ruined.

EFFECTS ON MAN

Casualties caused by the impact of the air shock waves could not be so isolated from deaths and injuries by fire and radiation. The blast directly hit persons close to ground zero, inflicting serious injury to lungs, stomach, intestines, eardrums, and the central nervous system. These same persons were also the most likely to be hit by flying debris, trapped by fire, or buried by collapsing buildings. Within a seven-mile radius of a ten-megaton burst, the secondary effects of blast accounted for many deaths.

THERMAL EFFECTS. Within a twenty-five mile radius of ground zero, any survivor who was out of doors when the bomb exploded sustained second-degree flash burns on his exposed skin. The thermal radiation ignited his clothing as well, causing severe flame burns. While the fire storms raged, many were trapped in burning buildings, suffocating from the inhalation of acrid fumes.

RADIATION EFFECTS. Nuclear radiation is measured in rems. A rem is that amount of radiation required to produce a biological effect equivalent to that of one roentgen of x-ray. A single dosage of up to 220 rems will cause nausea and vomiting for about a day, but it is not fatal. If a population is exposed to a dosage of 270 to 330 rems, about 20 per cent of the group will die within two to six weeks following exposure. The remaining 80 per cent will recover, following a three-month bout with radiation sickness. With a dosage of 550 rems or more, chances of survival are very slim, and recovery takes about six months for those few who do survive. A dosage of 1000 rems is virtually lethal.

The number of rems released in a nuclear explosion is determined by its location (air, surface, or underground) its tonnage, and its "cleanliness." The so-called clean nuclear warheads do not release enough energy to explode the highly destructive element, Uranium 238, but they do explode other elements that yield radioactive particles of Carbon 14 and Strontium 90. The "dirty" bombs, on the other hand, have the capacity to unleash Uranium 238. Once exploded, U-238 releases additional energy and an immense quantity of exceedingly poisonous fall-out. Thus, a "dirty" ten-megaton bomb gives off enough rems to kill a man within 140 miles of ground zero if he remains outside for thirty-six hours. The fifteen-megaton "superbomb" tested at Bikini in 1954 contained U-238, and its fall-out was responsible for the radiation sickness of the Japanese fishermen eighty miles from the test site. (Although the Congressional report on which our account is based did not state explicitly whether clean or dirty bombs were used, the weight of current reputable information suggests that most of the weapons tested, if not all, were dirty bombs. The report's fall-out statistics hold only for dirty bombs.)

The bombs the United States is likely to be bombed with will probably not be "clean," because Russia—as far as we know—does not know how to produce "clean" bombs, and the West refused to tell her how to "clean" them.

Initial nuclear radiation effects. Each ten-megaton explosion instantaneously released 700 rem, covering a two-mile radius from ground zero. All unsheltered and unshielded persons within this area received a lethal dose of radiation. But anyone this close to ground zero was equally likely to succumb to blast or fire.

Local fall-out effects. Local fall-out is caused by those radioactive particles which descend to earth within several hundred miles of ground zero and within a few days of the explosion. Its damaging effects are greatly influenced by local weather, altitude, and terrain, and must be calculated separately for each region of the country.

Regardless of local conditions, the effects of fall-out were not felt immediately. The unsheltered and unshielded persons within 150 miles downwind from ground zero and within twenty-five miles of the crosswinds around the crater received at least 450 rems within forty-eight hours. These were the persons most likely to die or to be seriously ill for many months. But those who were able to spend the few days following the explosion indoors or could leave the areas vulnerable to fall-out had a good chance for survival, and, if taken ill, had a relatively quick recovery.

Worldwide fall-out. The effect of worldwide fall-out cannot be calculated precisely even for a specific set of conditions, with place, time, weather, altitude, terrain, density of buildings, and the like held constant. We do know that world-wide fall-out leads to additional deaths by increasing a person's long-term susceptibility to such diseases as cancer. Long after the nuclear attack, then, the survivors continue to be exposed to additional radiation, which would eventually shorten the lives of some of them.

Genetic effects. Approximately four out of 100 babies presently are born with defects, some of which were caused by damaged genes. To prevent an increase in the present 4 per cent rate of defective births, each person's gonads should sustain less than ten roentgens of radiation during his first thirty years of life, and no more than ten roentgens during each succeeding decade. Should radiation dosages increase on a mass scale, so that every American receives the ten-roentgen limit, the rate of defective births would increase by four per thousand in the first generation and by four per hundred in future generations.

The amount of cumulative radiation experienced by each of the survivors of the October 17 nuclear attack was about 250 to 500 roentgens. If we assume that genetically defective births increase at the same rate as the increase in exposure to radiation, then the rate of defective births would increase by at least 25 per cent. Furthermore, the genes damaged by fall-out would continue to be inherited by the next twenty to forty generations, carrying the curse of fall-out from generation to generation until we are remembered only as the children-torturer generation.

HOW FAR AWAY IS "SAFE"?

When we played hide-and-seek as children, the closer to base we hid, the easier it was to come home safely. But in a nuclear bombardment, as the figures in Table 1 indicate, "safe" is relatively far from ground zero.

Let us suppose Rockefeller Center was ground zero for a ten-megaton bomb. To be safe from initial nuclear radiation, one would have to be at least as far downtown as the garment district, or as far uptown as the Museum of Natural History, or as far across town as the other side of the East River. To escape falling buildings and flying debris, one would have to be at least as far as the Bronx Zoo, the Statue of Liberty, or Forest Hills. To be spared second-degree burns, one would have to be as distant as Jones Beach or Greenwich, Connecticut. For safety from local fall-out, one would have to be in Rutland, Vermont, or Fort Ticonderoga, New York, to the north, or Lewistown, Pennsylvania, to the west, or the Atlantic Ocean to the east. One would not be safe south of New York, for then one would suffer the effects of the bombs dropped on Philadelphia, Baltimore, and Washington, D.C.

If one were in Rutland, Lewiston, or Ticonderoga, one would probably escape direct personal injury. The likelihood of getting radiation sickness from local fall-out is comparatively slight. Moreover, if one's home is in one of these towns, it will be untouched by blast or fire. But a "safe" distance from ground

Table 1 / The Distance to Safe Territory (Figures are estimates, calculated on the basis of weather conditions for October 17, 1958)

	Distance from Ground Zero	
Effect	*One Megaton*	*Ten Megatons*
Inanimate objects		
Crater (dry soil)	Radius 650 feet Depth 140 feet	Radius 1,250 feet Depth 240 feet
Brick apartment houses collapse	Radius 3 miles	Radius 7 miles
Ignition of light kindling materials	Radius 9 miles	Radius 25 miles
Man		
Blast injury (flying debris)	Radius 3 miles Area 28 square miles	Radius 7 miles Area 150 square miles
Second degree burns on bare skin	Radius 9 miles Area 250 square miles	Radius 25 miles Area 2,000 square miles
Initial nuclear radiation (700 rem)	Radius 1½ miles Area 7 square miles	Radius 2 miles Area 12½ square miles
Fallout: 15 knot winds (450 rem in 48 hours), no shielding	40 miles downwind 5 miles crosswinds Area 200 square miles	150 miles downwind 25 miles crosswinds Area 2,500 square miles

zero by no means assures immunity from the effects of nuclear war. The lucky people live in one of those towns not hit, out of the blow of the fall-out carrying winds, and are not on a business trip or vacation in a target area when the bombs come. That is, such persons' bone structure and tissues will not suffer, but they will still never be the same again. Less fortunate relatives—perhaps brothers, sisters, parents—will have perished in a thermonuclear cloud; many millions of one's fellow citizens will have vanished; America will be lying in ruins. Actually, a survivor might not consider himself lucky at all.

Editors' Epilogue: What happens when the bombs get bigger? Under certain conditions, as the authors point out, a 100 mt bomb (only half again as powerful as the one the Russians exploded over Siberia in 1961) could set off a fire storm capable of engulfing 11,000 square miles, an area larger than the state of Vermont. Aside from thermal and blast effects—and 100 mt is by no means the technological upper limit on size—radiation yield could be greatly stepped up by building the completely feasible "dirty" bomb (with a shell of cobalt, sodium oxide, or similar substances), or the as yet-undeveloped neutron bomb. And delivery systems are constantly being improved: the newer missiles are larger, less vulnerable, and more reliable than earlier generations, and they require less reaction time. Above all, of course, not only are *their* numbers increasing, but the number of political sovereignties that possess bombs and the means of delivering them is almost certain to increase. Terrible as it was, the hypothetical attack described above is based on assumptions long since obsolete.

Fallout: I Feel It in My Bones

ISAAC ASIMOV

The presidential campaign of 1956 introduced a new word to the American public: *strontium-90*. And ever since then, the sound of the word has been growing louder and louder.

What exactly is strontium-90? Or, to begin with, what exactly is strontium?

Strontium is a chemical element first isolated in 1808. In the century and a half since then, strontium has the rather odd distinction of having remained one of the most nearly useless elements in the entire list.

Strontium nitrate, when heated in a flame, give that flame a bright red color, so that it is used in railroad flares and in fireworks. Strontium oxide has a minor application in sugar-refining and strontium bromide and strontium iodide have very limited medical uses. That about exhausts the list.

But strontium has one fatal property which all chemists knew about from the beginning but which no chemist ever suspected (until this decade) would have such awesome consequences for the human race.

Strontium, you see, has chemical properties that are very similar to the more familiar and infinitely more useful element, calcium. The strontium atom is a little over twice as heavy as the calcium atom but that is the only difference worth mentioning. Almost anything the calcium atom will do, the strontium atom, in more lumbering fashion, will also do.

Living creatures have learned to utilize calcium compounds in a number of ways. Calcium is an indispensable factor in the clotting of blood and in the cement that keeps cells glued together. The bones of all vertebrates (including man) are made up chiefly of calcium phosphate. The shells of molluscs and of birds' eggs are calcium carbonate.

Presumably, living things might have learned to use strontium compounds as easily and have done about as well, except that there seems no point to it. Strontium atoms occur in the soil and ocean much less commonly than do calcium atoms. In fact, in the Earth's crust generally there is only one strontium

Source: Isaac Asimov, "I Feel It in My Bones," *Fantasy and Science Fiction*, 13:6 (December, 1957). Copyright © 1957 by Mercury Press, Inc. Reprinted by permission from the December 1957, issue of *The Magazine of Fantasy and Science Fiction.*

Editors' Note: Except for minor deletions (made by the author) this is the original article. The fact that it first appeared some years ago should be borne in mind by the reader. However, in our judgment, the essentials of the argument are as valid today as they were then.

atom for every four hundred calcium atoms. Why bother looking for that one strontium when there are four hundred calciums available?[1]

So strontium is not necessary to life and is not found in living tissue except as an accidental contaminant.

In fact, no chemistry textbook, except the largest and most comprehensive, ever devoted more than a paragraph to strontium; and a paragraph is all it was worth.

That is, until 1944.

Now for the "90" part of strontium-90. Every strontium atom has in its nucleus exactly 38 protons, no more and no less. In addition, the nucleus contains a certain number of neutrons. The neutron number, however, is not fixed, but varies from atom to atom. Some strontium atoms contain 46 neutrons in their nucleus, some contain 48, some 49 and some 50. If we count in the 38 protons present in each case, it means that some strontium atoms have a total of 84 particles in the nucleus, some 86, some 87 and some 88.

To distinguish these varieties of strontium atoms, the nuclear chemist speaks of strontium-84, strontium-86, strontium-87 and strontium-88.[2] To the ordinary chemist, however, these varieties (called *isotopes*) are strictly yawnworthy. The four strontium isotopes are practically identical in chemical behavior. All four are equally useless.

Only these four strontium isotopes exist in nature. Nuclear chemists, however, by bombarding atoms with speeding sub-atomic particles have managed to put together strontium atoms with anywhere from 43 to 59 neutrons.

None of these additional strontium isotopes, these man-made varieties, are stable. The nucleus of one of these artificial isotopes will, even if left strictly alone, explode in various ways and emit particles. In doing so, it changes its nuclear composition to some stable arrangement of protons and neutrons. Then, and only then, does the atom quiet down, and when it does so, it is no longer strontium of any variety.

Now strontium-90 is one of the man-made strontium isotopes. Its nucleus contains 38 protons and 52 neutrons ($38 + 52 = 90$). One of the ways in which this isotope may be man-made is through man-arranged uranium fission.

A uranium-235 atom, when struck by a neutron under the proper conditions, breaks approximately in half. It doesn't always break in exactly the same way, so that up to 170 different isotopes are formed in the process with anywhere

---

[1] And yet just to show that it can be done and that old Mother Nature is still the best science fiction writer of them all, there is a species of shellfish in the Great Lakes (so I am told) that fashions its shell out of strontium carbonate. Why it should go to the bother of sieving the rare strontium out of the waters and how it manages to latch on to it, to the exclusion of the so-similar calcium, no one knows.

[2] Every sample of strontium or its compounds contains some of each of these varieties. Out of every 10,000 strontium atoms chosen at random, the inquiring chemist would find 8,256 strontium-88 atoms, 987 strontium-86 atoms, 702 strontium-87 atoms and 55 strontium-84 atoms.

from 72 to 161 particles in their nuclei. One of these isotopes is strontium-90 and, as a matter of fact, it is one of the more frequent isotopes formed, making up about 5 per cent of the total.

All the isotopes so formed, the *fission fragments*, including strontium-90, are unstable. All emit energetic particles, changing their atomic identity as they do so.

As long as the subject of uranium fission has arisen, let's follow it up. It will lead us back to strontium-90; you can be sure of that.

The explosion of a nuclear bomb presents the population in the vicinity with three kinds of immediate danger, and the population of the Earth generally with a fourth kind of delayed danger. The three immediate dangers are (1) blast, (2) heat, and (3) radiation.

Blast and heat are the familiar accompaniments of ordinary bombs, but are much magnified in nuclear bombs. The radiation is something newer and uglier. It consists of x-rays and gamma rays speeding outward from the explosion, shouldering their way through any living tissue that they strike and often disrupting vital chemical processes in doing so. If disruption is sufficient, *radiation sickness* is the result and, in extreme cases, death. It depends on the dose.

However, the burst of dangerous radiation that accompanies a nuclear bomb explosion lasts only a minute or so.

That leaves the fourth danger, the delayed danger, the great danger.

The unstable (*i.e., radioactive*) fission fragments formed by an exploding nuclear bomb are blown up into the atmosphere by the familiar fireball and mushroom cloud we have all seen on television or in photographs. Eventually, the fragments come to Earth again and it is this settling back of fission fragments that is called *fallout*.

There are three types of fallout, depending on the size of the bomb and its position when exploded. If a nuclear bomb is exploded at ground level, the fission fragments are all bound up with relatively large particles of soil and settle back to Earth speedily, and usually within a hundred miles of the blast. This is *local fallout*.

A bomb exploded in the air will, if it is a small one in the *kiloton* range (that is, equivalent in explosive force to a mere thousand tons or so of dynamite), send its radioactive debris into the lower atmosphere (the *troposphere*) unmixed with soil particles. The prevailing westerly winds will carry it eastward for hundreds or even thousands of miles and it will settle out within one or two months, mainly in the latitude in which the bomb was originally exploded. This is the *tropospheric fallout*.

A large bomb exploded in the air, one in the *megaton range* (that is, equivalent in explosive force to a million tons or more of dynamite), will send radioactive material still higher. The stratosphere will be reached. Once in the stratosphere, the fission fragments will remain there for years, being carried by the jet streams to all corners of the Earth and slowly, little by little, coming to Earth again—everywhere. This is the *stratospheric fallout*.[3]

Now what are the dangers of fallout?

The radioactive fission fragments produced in a nuclear explosion become stable by emitting very energetic electrons from the nucleus (and sometimes gamma rays as well). The collision of those electrons with living tissue can produce radiation sickness and, depending on the dose, death.

The danger of a particular type of unstable atom depends upon the force with which those electrons are sprayed outward and the number being emitted in a given time.

Some atoms are very unstable and break down rapidly; some are less unstable and breakdown rather slowly. The measure of the instability of a particular type of atom is its *half-life*; that is, the time it takes for half the atoms in a quantity of a particular type to break down.

All things being equal, a heap of atoms with short half-lives spray more electrons (or other particles or radiation) into the surrounding space than does a similar heap of atoms with long half-lives. Thus, it would seem that a short-lived atom would be more likely to cause radiation sickness than would a long-lived atom.

So it would . . . at first.

The very energy and enthusiasm with which short-lived atoms break up means that after a while none or practically none is left. Atoms with half-lives of only a few seconds (which includes many of the fission fragments) are gone with the fireball and so can do no damage to anyone not so close to the explosion as to be consumed by blast and heat at once.

Even atoms that have half-lives of a few days or weeks can have only local effects. They are gone by the time tropospheric fallout comes to Earth. The electrons have been expended harmlessly several miles up and it is the stable descendants of those atoms that settle down.

But there are also long-lived atoms among the fission fragments and these must also be considered. Their radiations are weaker and they are less dangerous than the short-lived atoms to begin with. But the long-lived atoms hang around. An atom with a half-life of six weeks, say, will still be around in fair quantities when the tropospheric fallout comes to Earth. An atom with a half-life of ten years will linger in dangerous amounts when even the stratospheric fallout comes

---

[3] There has been talk of developing "clean" H-bombs; that is, H-bombs that will, on explosion, yield a non-radioactive fallout.

Hydrogen fusion itself does not result in any radioactivity to speak of. However, in order to get hydrogen atoms to fuse to helium, they must first be heated to millions of degrees Centigrade. The way that is done is to use a uranium fission bomb to produce the heat and act as a trigger for the hydrogen fusion bomb. It is from the exploding fission bomb that radioactive fragments are derived.

To reduce the radioactivity, we must figure out a way to reduce the size of the uranium fission bomb trigger. Better still, a method might be devised for reaching the required temperatures by some means other than uranium fission. (Alternate methods do exist in theory.)

to Earth. An atom with a half-life of thirty years will not only be around when the stratospheric fallout comes down, but will be still with us in annoying quantity a century after it comes down.

If the half-life were *too* long, say, a few thousand years, the radiation effects would last enormously long but would be so weak as to constitute little if any danger.

This is the way it works out, then:

1. Fission fragments with *very short* half-lives are extremely intense radiators but are not dangerous because they don't last long. (Not dangerous, that is, to mankind as a whole.)
2. Fission fragments with *very long* half-lives last a long time but are not dangerous because they are very weak radiators.
3. Fission fragments with *intermediate* half-lives are strong enough radiators to be dangerous and last long enough to be dangerous, too.

It is the third category that we must worry about.

There are just two types of fission fragments that fit neatly into category three. These are cesium-137 and strontium-90. And of these two, strontium-90 is by far the more dangerous, for several reasons.

Cesium-137 and strontium-90 have about equal half-lives (30 years for cesium-137 and 28 years for strontium-90) so that one might think they were equally dangerous. A cesium-137 atom, however, breaks down by emitting one electron, becoming in this fashion a stable atom of barium-137.

A strontium-90 atom, on the other hand, breaks down by emitting *two* electrons, becoming in this fashion a stable atom of zirconium-90. The double dose of strontium-90 electrons is even worse than it sounds since the strontium-90 electrons are individually more energetic than the cesium-137 electrons and can therefore do more damage.[4]

Secondly, if cesium-137 happens to get into the body (where, being right in the center of things, it can do the most damage), it doesn't stay there long. Cesium atoms do not occur naturally in the body and the body has no use for them.

----

[4] A still more damaging isotope that many of us have heard of is *cobalt-60*. The cobalt-60 atom emits only a single electron in breaking to the stable nickel-60 atom. However, its half-life is 5.3 years so that a quantity of cobalt-60 would be emitting just over $2\frac{1}{2}$ times as many electrons as would a similar quantity of strontium-90. This, perhaps, does not sound *too* bad, especially when you consider that the cobalt-60 electrons are less energetic than the strontium-90 electrons.

But cobalt-60 does something that strontium-90 does not do. Cobalt-60 emits gamma rays in addition to electrons, and unusually energetic gamma rays at that. Gamma rays are much more penetrating and can do much more damage than the speeding electrons could.

Fortunately, cobalt-60 is *not* among the fission fragments of ordinary nuclear explosions. However, the grisly suggestion has already been made that a nuclear bomb can be encased in matter that would, under the intense radioactive bombardment of the concentrated fission fragments formed in the first moments of nuclear explosion, be converted to cobalt-60. This would then be spread far and wide in a "super-dirty" fallout.

To be sure, cesium atoms bear a strong chemical resemblance to the much smaller sodium and potassium atoms (which do occur in the body and are necessary to its functioning) but these related atoms undergo rapid turnover. That is, they are taken in and eliminated by the body fairly rapidly so that while sizable amounts of sodium and potassium are always in the body, any particular sodium or potassium atom doesn't stay in the body very long.

Therefore, even if the cesium-137 tried to get by on its relationship to sodium and potassium, it wouldn't linger in the body. The level of cesium-137 in the body at any particular moment would remain very low; so low that the danger of the speeding electrons it emits would be virtually zero.

How different for strontium-90. Here is where the similarity to calcium is devastating. There is a turnover of calcium in the body, too, just as in the case of sodium or potassium. However, 99.5 per cent of the body's relatively large supply of calcium (which may be as much as 3 pounds or more) is in the bones. Bone is a sluggish tissue and while turnover of atoms in it exists, it is very slow. A particular calcium atom in bone may remain there a long time, even years.

The method by which strontium-90 gets into the body is simple enough. To begin with, the strontium-90 settles onto the soil along with the rest of the fallout. Vegetation growing in the soil absorbs the strontium-90 along with the calcium it is really after. Animals (including man, of course) which eat the vegetation then take up the strontium-90 along with the calcium they are really after.[5]

When strontium-90 enters the body, the chemical mechanisms of the body make little distinction between it and the very similar calcium. It, too, is deposited in the bones.

And there the strontium-90 atoms remain for years.

And there the strontium-90 atoms accumulate.

Until twenty years ago, strontium-90 existed nowhere on Earth, except perhaps in exceedingly small quantities in the special equipment of a few nuclear physicists. Until twenty years ago, no creature on Earth, in all the long history of life, had any strontium-90 at all in its bones.

Today strontium-90 exists everywhere. An estimated total of 400 pounds of it is spread out over the surface of the Earth while another 1,000 pounds is still floating about in the stratosphere.

Of course, this is pretty thin spreading in actual fact and to talk about quantities of strontium-90 in individual human beings, scientists find it convenient to use a much smaller unit of weight than the pound. They use the *Sunshine Unit*, which they abbreviate S.U. (This is so called because the AEC studies of fallout were termed "Project Sunshine.")

---

[5] Actually, the major source of calcium in the American diet is milk and cheese. It is therefore also the major source of strontium-90 in the diet. The cow picks up strontium-90 from the grass it eats and pumps the radioactive atoms into the milk along with the calcium that belongs there. The milk industry is as concerned these days about public fears of strontium-90 as is the tobacco industry about its fears of lung cancer.

One micromicrocurie of strontium-90 for every gram of calcium in one's body is what is meant by 1 S.U. The *curie* is a unit not of mass but of radiation. It was originally defined as the radiation given off by a gram of radium in equilibrium with its emanation (radon). (A gram is about one twenty-eighth of an ounce.) It is now more generally calculated as meaning 37 billion disintegrations per second.

A *micromicrocurie* is one one-trillionth of a curie, or 2.12 disintegrations per minute. This number of disintegrations would result from 45 million atoms of strontium-90.

The body of the average adult male contains 1,400 grams of calcium. So a man with 1 S.U. (which, I should add, nobody has reached yet) would have 63 billion atoms of strontium-90, or one two-trillionth of an ounce. Because the S.U. is a unit of radiation-mass ratio, it should be clear that a child, with less mass, can have a smaller amount of strontium-90 than a man but a higher S.U. figure. (And children also acquire strontium-90 more readily, because they deposit calcium in their growing bones more rapidly than adults do.)

Now then, every adult human being on Earth today contains about 0.1 to 0.2 S.U. of strontium-90 scattered throughout the bones of his body. Children have as much as 0.5 S.U. (Much the same goes for any animal with bones, by the way, not just humans.)

Furthermore, the quantity of strontium-90 in bones must increase, even if all nuclear bomb testing stopped today. There is still the thousand pounds of strontium-90 in the atmosphere that is slowly settling out.

As the body absorbs more strontium-90, a point will be reached where the strontium-90 in the bones will be excreted or will break down at a rate just equal to that at which new strontium-90 is being absorbed. In this way, an equilibrium will be attained.

If no more nuclear bomb testing takes place, this equilibrium will be reached (it is estimated) in about 5 to 10 years and bones will then contain 2 to 3 S.U. If, however, nuclear testing continues at the present rate of about 10 megatons per year, then the equilibrium (it is estimated) won't be reached for fifty or sixty years and bones will then contain somewhere between 16 and 40 S.U. of strontium-90.

All right, so we have less than half an S.U. of strontium-90 in our bones right now. How bad is that?

In some ways, it might seem to be not bad at all. After all, we are exposed continuously to all sorts of energetic radiation and speeding sub-atomic particles just by virtue of being on Earth. When these other radiations are measured in Sunshine Units, the term first devised for measuring strontium-90 absorption, the meaning of 1 S.U. is "the amount of radiation you would get from the equivalent quantity (defined above) of strontium-90."

For instance, the soil is slightly radioactive.[6] If you live in a building, you will

---

[6] The radioactivity of the soil is not just because it contains a scattering of uranium and thorium. Every bit of the soil contains the very common element, potassium, and one of the potassium isotopes, potassium-40, is weakly radioactive. A carbon isotope, carbon-14, is formed in small quantities in the atmosphere by cosmic ray action, and it is radioactive. Both potassium-40 and carbon-14 are in our bodies from birth to death as a consequence.

pick up the equivalent of 17 S.U. a year more than the amount you would pick up if you lived in a frame house, because brick has higher natural radioactivity than wood has. If your town is a mile high in altitude you will collect the equivalent of 8 S.U. more per year than if you lived at sea-level, because of the additional bombardment of cosmic rays. All in all, the average man picks up a total of 50 S.U. per year from all sources.

Well, then what's another few tenths of an S.U.? Why worry?

The worry, it seems, is in the *location* of the strontium-90 and the fact that it stays put in that location. Radiation and particles from all other natural sources bombard the body from outside (or from a moving position inside) in random fashion. Few significant hits are made (It's like shooting blindfold at a few flies buzzing about in Grand Central Station.)

The strontium-90, however, concentrates all its fire in the region of the bones and the bones have a particularly sensitive spot. The red blood cells and some of the white blood cells are formed in the marrow of certain bones and the continuous bombardment of the marrow by high-speed electrons could result in knocking the cell-forming mechanisms awry.

One form of awry-ness will produce the disease known as *leukemia*, a kind of cancer of the blood in which the bone marrow is forming excessive quantities of immature white blood cells. The condition gets progressively worse as these useless white blood cells crowd out the necessary red blood cells and death follows inevitably. As far as we know today, the condition is incurable.

Now it is known that radiation, in general, will cause leukemia. Radiologists (that is, doctors who specialize in x-ray therapy and such things) have an incidence of leukemia ten times that of other doctors.

In 1954, 10,000 people died in the United States of leukemia. Dr. Edward Lewis of California Institute of Technology estimates that about 1,000 of these cases were caused by the effects of the general radiation of our environment. (What caused the other 9,000? Ha, don't we wish we knew.)

But, were any of the deaths caused by the strontium-90 blasting away at the bone marrow at point-blank range?

That is where the major disagreement among experts lies. Some say strontium-90 has already caused leukemia and some say not. The arguments depend on whether a *threshold of action* does or does not exist.

What do we mean by a threshold of action?

Suppose we have a brick resting on the sidewalk. Push it very gently. Nothing happens. The force of your push is insufficient to overcome the frictional forces between brick and cement.

Push the brick harder. Still nothing. Push it still harder. Ah—now it begins to move.

It takes a certain minimum push to make the brick move at all. After that minimum has been reached, the harder you push the faster the brick moves, but as long as you don't reach the minimum, the brick doesn't move at all. The minimum push required to move the brick is the threshold of action.

The moving-the-brick-on-cement case is an example of an action with a pronounced threshold of action. Suppose, instead, you had a billiard ball on a perfectly smooth glassy surface. The lightest push will set it rolling. You couldn't push it so lightly as not to make it move. (Of course, an exceedingly light push will cause it to roll exceedingly slowly.)

All right, then, consider electrons bombarding the bone marrow. If there is a sizable threshold to this action, it means that as long as there are fewer electrons than a certain minimum, there will be no effect at all on the bone marrow. Only when total electron energy raises itself above that minimum will action start and leukemia become a possibility.

Average Age at Death	
Physicians having no known contact with radiation	65.7 years
Specialists having some exposure to radiation (dermatologists, urologists, etc.)	63.3 years
Radiologists	60.5 years
U.S. Population over 25 years of age	65.6 years

Source: "Summary Report of the Committee on Pathologic Effects," p. 35, in National Academy of Sciences-National Research Council, *The Biological Effects of Atomic Radiation* (Washington, D.C., 1956), pp. 33–43.

The National Academy of Sciences Committee on Internal Emitters has suggested that a quantity of strontium-90 as high as 100 S.U. may represent such a threshold. If this were the case, then strontium-90 is not endangering human beings now and won't be even if H-bomb testing were continued at the present rate.

Ah, but is 100 S.U. the threshold? Actually, it may be simply a plausible (or, perhaps, wishful-thinking) guess. There are a number of scientists who seem convinced that there is a very low threshold of action to the strontium-90 effect.

If that were so then strontium-90 is a killer right now. If 1,000 people died of leukemia in 1954 as a result of the 50 S.U. they picked up from natural radioactivity, then the 0.5 S.U. (maximum) of strontium-90 in the bones now may have caused 1 per cent of those deaths. That would mean that strontium-90 was killing 10 Americans a year with leukemia. (Exactly which particular American would die would depend on which particular American had the unlucky hit scored upon the proper points in the proper cells by the speeding electrons. It's a kind of huge shooting gallery with ourselves the ducks.)

From a cold-blooded and objective standpoint, 10 deaths a year may not seem much of a price to pay for the possible good that may be derived from H-bomb research. Even a rise to 800 deaths a year as the strontium-90 level reaches as high as 40 S.U. may not seem excessive. After all, the pleasure car kills some 40,000 Americans a year.

Unfortunately, we don't know that the leukemia effect is necessarily one of simple direct proportion.

Thus, to bring up an analogy, a concentration of carbon monoxide in the air of less than 0.01 per cent is harmless. No effect and no symptoms. We are below the threshold of action.

A concentration of 0.05 per cent of carbon monoxide will, however, give you a headache within an hour. A concentration of 0.1 per cent will give you a worse headache and a concentration of 0.2 per cent a still worse headache. Raise it to 0.3 per cent, however, and it's no longer a question of the headache getting still worse. You're dead.

Now, then, as strontium-90 goes up in concentration, is it just a question of the leukemia incidence rising with it in direct proportion, or is there a point which is another boundary line, another threshold of action, beyond which everybody gets leukemia? If so where is it?

No one knows about that either.[7]

Now why should there be this disagreement about the thresholds of action of strontium-90 and leukemia?

One reason lies in the difficulty of conducting long-term experiments on human beings in a matter of this sort. (It is always difficult to tell for sure how far animal experiments might apply.)

The logical thing would be to take a large number of human beings and subject them to carefully graded doses of radiation or feed them carefully measured quantities of strontium-90, observe them for fifty years or so and note how many develop leukemia—running appropriate controls, of course.

Well, who's going to volunteer for such an experiment? Or conduct one? Not I. Not anybody.

A lot of the information upon which scientists are depending goes back to the cases of the few unfortunate women who got radium poisoning back in the twenties while working on radium-dial watches (and pointing the brushes they used with their lips, if I remember correctly). The radium, which is another member of the calcium family, also got stored in the bones. Those studies seem to show a quite high threshold of action, but the number of cases were few and the experimental methods of handling radioactive data were primitive, then. It would be unsafe to rely on those data.

So we're left uncertain, with a very poor gamble on our hands. At best, we break even; no harm done. At worst, we may lose everything; literally everything. . . .

---

[7] An even more subtle danger to the human race than leukemia is the question of mutations. It is known that radiation causes mutations and that increasing the intensity of radiation increases the number of mutations and that most mutations are for the worst. And as far as mutations are concerned, most authorities are agreed that there is no threshold to speak of. So it is quite conceivable that the human race has been done tremendous damage already that may not show up in all its ugliness for several generations.

Theses for the Atomic Age

GÜNTHER ANDERS

▬

1. HIROSHIMA AS WORLD CONDITION: On August 6, 1945, the Day of Hiroshima, a New Age began: the age in which at any given moment we have the power to transform any given place on our planet, and even our planet itself, into a Hiroshima. On that day we became, at least "modo negativo," omnipotent; but since, on the other hand, we can be wiped out at any given moment, we also became totally impotent. However long this age may last, even if it should last forever, it is "The Last Age": for there is no possibility that its "differentia specifica," the possibility of our self-extinction, can ever end—but by the end itself.

2. THE TIME OF THE END VERSUS THE END OF TIME: Thus, by its very nature, this age is a "respite," and our "mode of being" in this age must be defined as "not yet being non-existing," "not quite yet being non-existing." Thus the basic moral question of former times must be radically reformulated: instead of asking "*How* should we live?" we now must ask "*Will* we live?" For us, who are "not yet non-existing" in this Age of Respite, there is but one answer: although at any moment The Time of the End could turn into The End of Time, we must do everything in our power to make The End Time endless. Since we believe in the possibility of The End of Time, we are Apocalyptics, but since we fight against this man-made Apocalypse, we are—and this has never existed before—"Anti-Apocalyptics."

3. NOT ATOMIC WEAPONS IN THE POLITICAL SITUATION, BUT POLITICAL ACTIONS IN THE ATOMIC SITUATION: Although it sounds absolutely plausible, it is misleading to say that atomic weapons exist in our political situation. This statement has to be turned upside down in order to become true. As the situation today is determined and defined exclusively by the existence of "atomic weapons," we have to state: political actions and developments are taking place within the atomic situation.

4. NOT WEAPON, BUT ENEMY: What we are fighting is not this or that enemy who could be attacked or liquidated by atomic means, but the atomic

---

Source: Günther Anders, "Theses for the Atomic Age," *The Massachusetts Review* (Spring 1962), pp. 493–505. Reprinted by permission.

Editors' Note: In February, 1959, at the Free University of Berlin, Günther Anders conducted a two-day seminar on "The Moral Implications of the Atomic Age." At its conclusion, the students asked Anders for a short text which could serve them as a basis for further discussion. Anders dictated these "theses," which later appeared as "Thesen zum Atomzeitalter," *Berliner Hefte* (1960), pp. 16–22. The translation here printed is by Mr. Anders.

situation as such. Since this enemy is the enemy of all people, those who, up to now, had considered each other to be enemies, have now to become allies against the common menace. Peace actions from which we exclude those with whom we wish to live in peace amount to hypocrisy, self-righteousness and a waste of time.

5. TO THREATEN WITH ATOMIC WEAPONS IS TOTALITARIAN: A pet theory broad enough to be embraced by subtle philosophers as well as by brutal politicians, by Jaspers as well as by Strauss, runs: "If it were not for our ability to threaten with total annihilation, we would be unable to hold the totalitarian menace in check." This is a sham argument for the following reasons: (1) The atom bomb *has* been used, although those who used it were not in danger of falling victim to a totalitarian power. (2) This argument is a fossil from the "ancient" days of atomic monopoly and has become suicidal today. (3) The catchword "totalitarian" is taken from a political situation which not only *has* already fundamentally changed, but will continue to change; atomic war, on the other hand, excludes all chance of such a change. (4) By threatening with atomic war, thus with liquidation, we cannot help being totalitarian; for this threat amounts to blackmail and transforms our globe into one vast concentration camp from which there is no way out. Thus, whoever bases the legitimacy of this extreme deprivation of freedom upon the alleged interests of freedom is a hypocrite.

6. EXPANSION OF OUR HORIZON: Since radioactive clouds do not bother about milestones, national boundaries or curtains, distances are abolished. Thus in this Time of the End everybody is in deadly reach of everybody else. If we do not wish to lag behind the effects of our products—to do so would be not only a deadly shame but a shameful death—we have to try to widen our horizon of responsibility until it equals that horizon within which we can destroy everybody and be destroyed by everybody—in short, till it becomes global. Any distinction between near and far, neighbors and foreigners, has become invalid; today we are all "proximi."

7. "THE UNITED GENERATIONS": Not only our horizon of space must be widened, but also that of time. Since acts committed today (test explosions, for instance) affect future generations just as perniciously as our own, the future belongs within the scope of our present. "The future has already begun"[1]— since tomorrow's thunder belongs to today's lightning. The distinction between the generations of today and of tomorrow has become meaningless; we can even speak of a *League of Generations* to which our grandchildren belong, just as automatically as we ourselves. They are our *"neighbors in time."* By setting fire to *our* house, we cannot help but make the flames leap over into the cities of the future, and the not-yet-built homes of the not-yet-born generations will fall to ashes together with our homes. Even our ancestors are full-fledged members of this League: for by dying we would make them die, too—a second

---

[1] This formula is taken from the title of Robert Jungk's book, *Die Zukunft hat schon begonnen.*

time, so to speak; and after this second death everything would be as if they had never been.

8. NOTHINGNESS—THE EFFECT OF THE NOT-IMAGINED NOTHINGNESS: The apocalyptic danger is all the more menacing because we are unable to picture the immensity of such a catastrophe. It is difficult enough to visualize someone as not-being, a beloved friend as dead; but compared with the task our fantasy has to fulfil now, it is child's play. For what we have to visualize today is not the not-being of something particular within a framework, the existence of which can be taken for granted, but the nonexistence of this framework itself, of the world as a whole, at least of the world as mankind. Such "total abstraction" (which, as a mental performance, would correspond to our performance of total destruction) surpasses the capacity of our natural power of imagination: "Transcendence of the Negative." But since, as "homines fabri," we are capable of actually producing nothingness, we cannot surrender to the fact of our limited capacity of imagination: the attempt, at least, must be made to visualize this nothingness.

9. "WE ARE INVERTED UTOPIANS": The basic dilemma of our age is that, "We are smaller than ourselves," incapable of mentally realizing the realities which we ourselves have produced. Therefore we might call ourselves "inverted Utopians": while ordinary Utopians are unable to actually produce what they are able to visualize, we are unable to visualize what we are actually producing.

10. "THE PROMETHEAN DISCREPANCY"[2]: This inverted Utopianism is not simply one fact among many, but the outstanding one, for it defines the moral situation of man today. The dualism to which we are sentenced is no longer that of spirit against flesh or of duty against inclination, is neither Christian nor Kantian, but that of our capacity to produce as opposed to our power to imagine.

11. THE SUPRA-LIMINAL: Not only has imagination ceased to live up to production, but feeling has ceased to live up to responsibility. It may still be possible to imagine or to repent the murdering of one fellow man, or even to shoulder responsibility for it; but to picture the liquidation of one hundred thousand fellow men definitely surpasses our power of imagination. The greater the possible effect of our actions, the less are we able to visualize it, to repent of it or to feel responsible for it; the wider the gap, the weaker the brake-mechanism. To do away with one hundred thousand people by pressing a button is incomparably easier than to slay one individual. The "subliminal," the stimulus too small to produce any reaction, is recognized in psychology; more significant, however, though never seen, let alone analyzed, is the "supra-liminal": the stimulus too big to produce any reaction or to activate any brake-mechanism.

---

[2] The elaboration of this category is given in the author's *Die Antiquiertheit des Menschen*, 3rd ed. (Munich: C. H. Beck, 1961), pp. 21–95.

THE DOOMSDAY MACHINE

Assume that for, say, $10 billion we could build a device whose only function is to destroy all human life. The device is protected from enemy action (perhaps by being thousands of feet underground) and then connected to a computer which is in turn connected, by a reliable communication system, to hundreds of sensory devices all over the United States. The computer would then be programmed so that if, say, five nuclear bombs exploded over the United States, the device would be triggered and the earth destroyed.... [The mechanism used would most likely not involve the breaking up of the earth, but the creation of really large amounts of radioactivity or the causing of major climatic changes or, less likely, the extreme use of thermal effects.] ... If Khrushchev should order an attack, both Khrushchev and the Soviet population would be automatically and efficiently annihilated.

Source: Herman Kahn, *On Thermonuclear War* (Princeton, N.J.: Princeton University Press, 1961), p. 145. Reprinted by permission.
Editors' Note: Mr. Kahn does not advocate the kind of strategy that would call for the building of a Doomsday Machine, nor does he think it likely in any event that one will be built. His aim, as he says, is to clarify current thinking on the subject. It is of interest to the general reader, nevertheless, to know that it is neither infeasible nor irrational (given assumptions widely and seriously held) to threaten to destroy all life on earth.

12. SENSES DISTORT SENSE. FANTASY IS REALISTIC: Since our pragmatic life horizon (sec. 6), the one within which we can reach and be reached, has become limitless, we must try to visualize this limitlessness, although by trying to do so we would evidently violate the "natural narrowness" of our imagination. Although insufficient by its very nature, there is nothing other than imagination which could be considered as an organon of truth. Certainly not perception. Perception is a "false witness," in a far more radical sense than Greek philosophy meant when warning against it. For the senses are myopic, their horizon is "senselessly" narrow. It is not in the wide land of imagination that escapists of today like to hide, but in the ivory tower of perception.[3]

13. THE COURAGE TO FEAR: When speaking of the "imagining of nothingness," the act meant is not identical with what psychology imagines to be imagination, for I speak of fear, which *is* the imagining of nothingness "in concreto." Therefore we can improve the formulations of the last paragraphs by saying: it is our capacity to fear which is too small and which does not correspond to the magnitude of today's danger. As a matter of fact, nothing

---

[3] No wonder that we feel uneasy in front of these normal pictures which are painted according to the conventional rules of perspective. Though realistic in the ordinary sense of the word, they are actually utterly unrealistic since they ignore the limitless horizon of today's world.

is more deceitful than to say, "We live in the Age of Anxiety anyway." This slogan is not a statement but a tool manufactured by the fellow travellers of those who wish to prevent us from becoming really afraid, of those who are afraid that we once may produce the fear commensurate to the magnitude of the real danger. On the contrary, we are living in the Age of Inability to Fear. Our imperative: "Expand the capacity of your imagination," means, in concreto: "Increase your capacity of fear." Therefore: don't fear fear, have the courage to be frightened,[4] and to frighten others, too. Frighten thy neighbor as thyself. This fear, of course, must be of a special kind: (1) a fearless fear, since it excludes fearing those who might deride us as cowards, (2) a stirring fear, since it should drive us into the streets instead of under cover, (3) a loving fear, not fear *of* the danger ahead but *for* the generations to come.

14. PRODUCTIVE FRUSTRATION: Time and again our efforts to comply with the imperative, "Widen your capacity to fear and make it commensurate with the immensity of the effects of your activities," will be frustrated. It is even possible that our efforts will make no progress whatsoever. But even this failure should not intimidate us; repeated frustration does not refute the need for repeating the effort. On the contrary, every new failure bears fruit, for it makes us vigilant against our initiating further actions whose affects transcend our capacity to fear.

15. "DISPLACED DISTANCE": If we combine our statement about the abolition of distances (sec. 6) with that about the Promethean discrepancy (sec. 10)—and only this combination makes the picture of our situation complete—we reach the following result: the "abolition" of time and space distances does not amount to abolition of distances altogether, for today we are confronted with the daily increasing distance between production and imagination.

16. END OF THE COMPARATIVE: Our products and their effects surpass not only the maximum size of what we are able to visualize or to feel, but even the size of what we are able to *use*. It is common knowledge that our production and supply often exceed our demand and produce the need for the production of new needs and new demands. But this is not all: today we have reached the situation in which products are manufactured which simply contradict the very concept of need, products which simply *cannot* be needed, which are too big in an absolute sense. In this stage our own products are being domesticated as if they were forces of nature. Today's efforts to produce so-called "clean weapons" are attempts of a unique kind: for what man is now trying is to increase the quality of his products by decreasing their effects.

If the number and the possible performance of the already existing stock of weapons are sufficient to reach the absurd aim of the annihilation of mankind, then today's increase in production is even more absurd and proves that the

---

[4] It is not Roosevelt's "Freedom *from* Fear" for which we have to strive, but the Freedom *to* fear.

producers do not understand at all what they are actually doing. The comparative, the principle of progress and competition, has lost its sense. *Death is the boundary line of the comparative: one cannot be deader than dead and one cannot be made deader than dead.*

17. APPEAL TO COMPETENCE PROVES MORAL INCOMPETENCE: We have no reason to presuppose (as, for instance, Jaspers does) that those in power are better able to imagine the immensity of the danger or that they realize the imperatives of the atomic age better than we ordinary "morituri." This presupposition is even irresponsible. And it would be far more justified to suspect them of having not even the slightest inkling of what is at stake. We have only to think of Adenauer, who dared to berate eighteen of the greatest physicists of today, telling them that they are incompetent in the "field of atomic armament and atomic weapons questions," and that they should talk shop instead and not "meddle" with those issues. It is precisely by using these vocables that he and his kind demonstrate their moral incompetence. For there is no more final and no more fatal proof of moral blindness than to deal with the Apocalypse as if it were a "special field," and to believe that rank is identical with the monopoly to decide the "to be or not to be" of mankind. Some of those who stress competence are doing so solely in order to disguise the anti-democratic elements of their monopoly. By no means should we be taken in by this camouflage. After all, we are living in allegedly democratic states. If the word "Democracy" has any sense at all, then it means that precisely the province *beyond* our professional competence should concern us, that we are not only entitled, but obliged —not as specialists but as citizens and human beings—to participate in deciding about the affairs of the "res publica." Since, after all, we *are* the "res publica," the reproach that we are "meddling" amounts to the ridiculous accusation that we are interfering with our own business. There has never been and will never be an affair more "publica" than today's decision about our survival. By renouncing "interference," we not only fail to fulfill our democratic duties, but we risk our collective suicide.

18. ABOLITION OF "ACTION": The possible annihilation of mankind seems to be an "action." Therefore those who contribute to it seem to be "acting." They are not. Why not? Because there is hardly anything left which, by a behaviorist, could be classified as "acting." For activities which formerly had occurred *as* actions and were meant and understood as such by the acting subjects themselves, now have been replaced by other variants of activity: (1) by working, (2) by "triggering."

(1) Work: Substitute for Action: The employees in Hitler's death factories did, so to speak, "nothing," thought they had done nothing, because they had done "nothing but work." By "nothing but work" I mean that kind of performance (generally considered to be the natural and only type of operation today) in which the *eidos* of the end-product remains invisible to the operator— no, does not even matter to him—no, is not even supposed to matter to him—no,

ultimately is not even permitted to matter to him. Typical of today's work is its seeming moral neutrality; *non olet*; no work-goal, however evil, can defile the worker. Nearly all jobs assigned to and performed by man today now are understood as belonging to this universally accepted and monocratic type of operation. Work—the camouflaged form of action. This camouflage exempts even the mass murderer from his guilt, since, according to today's standards, the worker is not only "freed" from responsibility for his work, but he simply *cannot* be made guilty by his work.

Consequence: once we have realized that today's fatal equation runs, "All action is work," we have to have the courage to invert it and to formulate: "*All work is action.*"

(2) "*Triggering*"—*Substitute for Work:* What is true of work applies even more to "triggering," for in triggering, the specific characteristics of work— effort and consciousness of effort—are diminished, if not nullified. Triggering— the camouflaged form of work. As a matter of fact, there exists hardly anything today which cannot be achieved through triggering. It can even happen that one first push of a button sets in motion a whole chain of secondary triggerings—till the end-result—never intended, never imagined, by the first button-pusher— consists of millions of corpses. Seen behavioristically, such a manipulation would be considered neither work nor action. Although seemingly no one would have done anything, this "doing nothing" would actually produce annihilation and nothingness. No button-pusher (if such a minimum-operator is still required at all) feels *that* he is acting. And since the scene of the act and the scene of the suffering no longer coincide, since cause and effect are torn apart, no one can perceive what he is doing—"*schizotopia*" by analogy with "schizophrenia."

Evident again (see above): only he who continuously tries to visualize the effect of his doings, however far away in space or in time the scene of his effects may be, has the chance of truth; perception "falls short."

This variant of camouflage is unique. While formerly it had always been the aim of camouflaging to prevent the prospective victim from recognizing the danger, or to protect the doer from the enemy, now camouflaging is meant to prevent the doer himself from recognizing what he is doing. Therefore today's doer is also a victim. Eatherly[5] belongs to those whom he has destroyed.

19. THE DECEITFUL FORM OF TODAY'S LIE: The examples of camouflage teach us something about the present-day type of lie. For today the lie no longer needs to dress itself in the costume of an assertion; ideologies are no longer required. Victorious today is that type of lie which prevents us from even suspecting that it *could* be a lie; and this victory has become possible because today lying no longer needs to assume the disguise of assertions. For whereas until now, in "honest hypocrisy," lies had pretended to be truths, they now are camouflaging themselves in a completely different costume.

[5] See *Burning Conscience, The Case of the Hiroshima Pilot, Claude Eatherly, Told in His Letters to Günther Anders* (New York: Monthly Review, 1962).

(1) Instead of appearing in the form of assertions, they now appear in that of naked *individual words* which, although seemingly saying nothing, secretly already contain their deceitful predicate. Example: since the term "atomic weapon" makes us believe that what it designates may be classified as a weapon, it already *is* an assertion, and as such a lie.[6]

(2) Instead of appearing in the form of false assertions, they appear in that of *falsified reality*. Example: once an action appears in the disguise of "work," its action-character becomes invisible; and so much so that it no longer reveals, not even to the doer himself, that ultimately he is acting; and thus the worker, although working conscientiously, enjoys the chance of renouncing conscience with a clean conscience.

(3) Instead of appearing in the form of false assertions, lies appear in that of *things*. In the last example it is still man who is active, although he misinterprets his acting as working. But even this minimum can disappear—and this, the supreme triumph of lying, has already begun. For during the last decade action has shifted (of course through human action) from the province of man to another region: to that of machines and instruments. These have become, so to speak, "incarnated" or "reified actions." Example: through the mere fact of its existence, the atom bomb is an uninterrupted blackmailing—and that black-mailing has to be classified as an "action" is, after all, indisputable. Since we have shifted our activities and responsibilities to the system of our products, we believe ourselves able to keep our hands clean, to remain "decent people." But it is, of course, just this surrender of responsibility that is the climax of irresponsibility.

This, then, is our absurd situation: in the very moment in which we have become capable of the most monstrous action, the destruction of the world, "actions" seem to have disappeared. Since the mere existence of our products already proves to be action, the trivial question, how we should use our products for action (whether, for instance, for deterrence), is an almost fraudulent one, since this question obscures the fact that the products, by their mere existence, already *have* acted.

20. NOT REIFICATION BUT PSEUDO-PERSONALIZATION: One cannot adequately interpret the phenomenon by giving it the Marxian label of "reification," for this term designates exclusively the fact that man is reduced to a thing-function. We are stressing, however, the fact that the qualities and functions taken away from man by his reification are now becoming qualities and functions of the products themselves, that they transform themselves into

---

[6] For a discussion of why the atomic bomb cannot be classified as a weapon, see the author's *Die Antiquiertheit des Menschen*, 247 ff., *Der Mann auf der Brücke* (Munich: C. H. Beck, 1959), 95 ff., and *Off limits für das Gewissen* (Rowohlt, 1961), 30 (English edition: London: Weidenfeld and Nicolson, 1962, p. 15). The main argument runs: a weapon is a means. Means are defined by dissolving in their ends, ends by their surviving the means. This cannot be applied to atomic weapons, since there is no end which could survive the use of weapons and no end conceivable which could justify such an absurd means.

pseudo-persons, since, through their mere existence, they are acting. This second phenomenon has been ignored by philosophy, although it is impossible to understand our situation without seeing both sides of the process simultaneously.

21. THE MAXIMS OF PSEUDO-PERSONS: These pseudo-persons have rigid principles of their own. The principle of "atomic weapons," for example, is pure nihilism, because, if they could speak, they would say: "Whatever we destroy, it's all the same to us." In them, nihilism has reached its climax and has become naked "Annihilism." [7]

Since action has shifted from man to work and products, examination of our conscience today cannot confine itself to listening to the voice of our heart. It is far more important to listen to the mute voice of our products in order to know their principles and maxims—in other words, the "shift" has to be reversed and revoked. Therefore, today's imperative runs: have and use only those things, the inherent maxims of which could become your own maxims and thus the maxims of a general law.

22. MACABRE ABOLITION OF HATRED: If (sec. 18) the scene of action and the scene of suffering are torn apart—if the suffering does not occur at the place of the act, if acting becomes acting without visible effect, if suffering becomes suffering without identifiable cause—hatred disappears, although in a totally delusive way.

Atomic war will be waged with less hatred than any war before: attacker and victims will not hate each other since they will not see each other. There is nothing more macabre than this disappearance of hatred which, of course, has nothing to do with peacefulness or love. It is striking how rarely, and with how little hatred, Hiroshima victims mention those who have caused their suffering. This, however, does not mean that hatred will play no part in the next war: since it will be considered indispensable for psychological warfare, the production of hatred will, no doubt, be organized. In order to nourish what a perverted age calls "morale," identifiable and visible objects of hatred will be exhibited, in emergency cases invented—"Jews" of all kinds. Since hatred can bloom only if the objects of hatred are visible and can fall into the hater's hand, it will be the domestic scene from which one will choose scapegoats. Since the targets of this artificially manufactured hatred and the target of the military attacks will be totally different, the war mentality will become actually schizophrenic.

I have published these words in order to prevent them from becoming true. If we do not stubbornly keep in mind the strong probability of the disaster, and if we do not act accordingly, we will be unable to find a way out. There is nothing more frightful than to be right.—And if some, paralyzed by the gloomy likelihood of the catastrophe, have already lost courage, they still have a chance to

---

[7] Even this climax of nihilism has been surpassed, for the principle of the neutron bomb would run: "Whomever we destroy, it's all the same to us. The world of objects, however, has to remain sacrosanct. *Products should not kill other products.*" As a matter of fact, this is the most radical perversion of moral principles which has ever existed.

prove their love of man by heeding the cynical maxim: "Let's go on working as though we had the right to hope. Our despair is none of our business."

"A MODEST PROPOSAL"

To the Editor of The Washington Post:

I address myself to the Eminences and the Serenities. I make them a Modest Proposal. Let our children go.

A nuclear war, which day by day seems more likely may very well end human life. But suppose, more cheerfully, that only the people of the Northern Hemisphere are exterminated; that in the Southern Hemisphere it will still be possible, some how, for some persons to survive. Why should we not transport our young children to these regions as a refuge? The merits and advantages of the Proposal are obvious and many as well as of the highest importance.

For first, as I cannot conceive any sane person capable of human feeling would challenge, the war to come, if war comes, is not the children's concern. Our quarrels, our bitterness, our hatreds, our fears do not possess them. Our heroes and our devils are not theirs. They have barely begun their lives, they are not ready to end them for Causes. They are too innocent and foolish to realize that death is preferable to life under alien creeds. I recall a story which Carl Sandburg told of a little girl, perhaps his granddaughter, who, after hearing his description of a battle of the Civil War, observed, "Suppose they gave a war and no one came." There is no reason to suppose that children, unless forced, would come to our war.

Secondly, the conduct of the war would be so much less Burdensome if the children were removed. It would be unnecessary to yield to niceties, to observe amenities, to nurse the sick, to shield the weak, to spare the infirm. With the children gone, without the distractions and temptations of their cries and complaints, we could give ourselves over completely to the serious business at hand. There would be many fewer mouths to feed, less need for water and air and bandages and whole blood. Children are notoriously subject to epidemic diseases; thus a prolific source of infection would be eliminated.

The savings in money alone would be immense, and would not only pay to transport the children and maintain them until they could fend for themselves, but would leave a handsome margin for use in vigorous prosecution of the war. I have made a rough calculation for U.S. children which bears on the point. Say we take many of the children from the ages of two to twelve—the younger are too frail, the older are more stable and could be useful to us at home—then we shall have about 25 million to transport and keep. For this purpose, allow $1,000 a head. The total is $25 billion, a sum well under half our annual military appropriation. Surely this is not too much to spend, considering the advantages to be gained.

Thirdly, we rid ourselves once for all of the Incubus of a shelter program. What a relief no longer to have to pretend! What a comfort simply to face the facts! No sensible person, even among scientists, believes in the efficacy of shelters. Down one goes to the well-stocked, cozy hole. Then what? There is the gentle patter of fallout on the roof; one is shielded from the blast; the light of a thousand suns (or is it now a million suns?) does not penetrate. The Lares and Penates are there. The family is snug. Father is pedalling the air-pump. Mother is preparing a tuna-fish casserole. The radio is on. Splendid. But when does one come up and what is there to come up to? Anarchy? Cannibalism? The living dead? Bloated corpses? Troublesome questions. And even more troublesome is the effect of fire and heat, a subject which none of the experts and no one in the Establishment has seen fit to discuss. I lay this omission, of course, to delicate feelings. It would, I believe, undermine morale to be reminded of the fire storms over Tokyo, Hamburg, Dresden, where a mere few thousands of tons of high explosives produced atmospheric convulsions.

Now with weapons, each of which may yield the equivalent of ten, or fifty, or 100 million tons of high explosives, the fire storm produced by a single bomb will, I am reliably informed by an article in Scientific American, vaporize the structures and burn off the vegetation of an area of at least 15,000 square miles. Even in a deep shelter the occupants will be quickly barbecued. What a dreadful thing to contemplate. It is enough to make cowards of us all. The necrophiles, the bitter ones, the incandescent patriots, those among the aged and ailing who take comfort in the thought that their demise will coincide with that of mankind: these endorse the view that shelters will give shelter. But secretly they laugh at our innocence. We must not encourage them. If we are to die for the Cause, let us not cheapen and betray the sacrifice: Away with the shelters, and all will become clear.

Fourthly, there is the grave moral issue of suicide. The law forbids it to the individual. On a national scale, however, is it apparently acceptable. Do we not, after all, make the law? Thus we may write its exceptions. Still, the question nags us, can we require the suicide of those who have no voice in the making of the laws, viz children? It is a fine point, and none would venture to say how our leaders would feel compelled to decide it. My Proposal disencumbers them of this obligation.

Fifthly, there must be many who, like myself, have a Weakness for children. In format and freshness they are much preferable to the larger editions, their parents. Children are unwrinkled, unwarped. They are healthy. They smell nice. They are not cynical. They suppose life to be an end in itself. Properly nourished, watered and cared for, they grow up. When grown they can breed. The dead do not breed. Quite recently the eminent geneticist Herman Muller described a scheme for setting up large-scale sperm banks. Sperm could be stored indefinitely; it could be classified according to the characteristics of the males who produced it. Human evolution would thus, in a sense, come under man's own control. Yet the scheme presupposes the continuance of women. It is my impression that sperm by itself will yield no fruit. Here again the Proposal is vindicated; for there will be female as well as male children: instead of storing germ plasm we will be storing the young themselves and thus assure the future.

For the moment I have said enough. I am anxious that Wise men consider my Proposal. Is it Feasible? (Less feasible, say than a journey to the planets?) Is it visionary? (More visionary than the preservation of Freedom by a nuclear war?) Is it too Costly? Is there yet time to execute it—in part at least if not in whole? Could it be made a matter of International Cooperation? Is a country without children worth living in? Perhaps not. In that case some better course must be found. Let the Wise men define it.

JAMES R. NEWMAN
Chevy Chase, Md.
Sept. 20, 1961.

Source: The Washington Post (Monday, September 25, 1961). Reprinted by permission.

The Nuclear Revolution in Military Power—Overkill*

SEYMOUR MELMAN

Conventional (Pre-Overkill) Military Assumptions	*Strategic Changes Due to Overkill Capability*
1. Addition to offensive capability increases military power (or deterrence).	1. Addition to offensive capability in the overkill range does not add to military power (or deterrence): overkill of 1,000 is not greater than overkill of 100, or 1.
2. Defensive systems can effectively protect sufficient numbers to insure an on-going society.	2. All defensive strategies and technologies can be saturated, overwhelmed or evaded by variety and quantity of offensive power. A 99% effective defense against overkill of more than 100 leaves overkill.
3. With plausible technological breakthroughs the shores of the United States can be shielded against military assault.	3. See proposition 2.

Source: Seymour Melman, *Our Depleted Society* (New York: Dell, 1965), pp. 45–47. Reprinted by permission.

Editors' Note: Since this analysis was prepared, in 1964, overkill capacity has continued to increase. The Soviet Union now has something over 900 missiles emplaced in hardened sites or in submarines; the United States has about 1,700. Both have firm plans, or so it appears, to deploy "thin" anti-missile-missile defense systems, and both have developed multiple warhead attack missiles capable of saturating such systems. (The Soviets' version can be launched from a suborbital capsule. Because it has a very short trajectory it is much more difficult to track and intercept than a ballistic missile. The American "space bus" version carries a load of warheads that can be dropped off one by one, each with its own target.) It has been speculated that these "thin" defense systems are designed to counter the growing Chinese nuclear capability.

* These notes were prepared in collaboration with Alan L. Madian.

Conventional (Pre-Overkill) *Military Assumptions*	*Strategic Changes Due to* *Overkill Capability*
4. With sufficient nuclear delivery capability, the military power of the USSR could be destroyed and the U.S. spared a counter-blow.	4. Hardened missile sites and submarine based missiles on both sides renders this strategy inoperative.
5. A nuclear war would be composed of a series of calculated, controlled nuclear weapons exchanges.	5. Major portion of military communication networks would be destroyed. Under stress of combat some military and civilian leaders could be expected to react independently, releasing the nuclear weapons at their command. (For example, the Commander of a Polaris Submarine has control of 16 missiles carrying the equivalent of 16 megatons of TNT.)
6. For military security a lead must be held in all relevant research and technology, together with a preponderance of military material.	6. This assumption is nullified by propositions 1 and 2 (above).
7. The total strength of our military system is maximized by improving the strength of each component.	7. Our total military power cannot be defined as the sum of the parts. Suboptimization—making a better warhead, a better antimissile missile, a better vehicle—is the prevailing approach of the Department of Defense, despite its nullification by propositions 1 and 2 (above).
8. We must be competent to cope with all military contingencies.	8. The United States is a wealthy society but not an infinitely wealthy society. For example, incomplete protection from fallout, which could cost 250 to 300 billion dollars, can be gained only at the expense of generating economic weakness which, in turn, weakens the security of the United States.

Conventional (Pre-Overkill) *Military Assumptions*	*Strategic Changes Due to* *Overkill Capability*
9. The United States must be prepared to absorb a nuclear first strike and have sufficient reserve power to strike back, punish the aggressor, and stop hostilities.	9. In 1960, Dr. Jerome Weisner advised that studies by the U.S. Army and Navy indicated that 200 secured missiles would be an adequate deterrent. We now possess 1,378 such missiles. The assumption that we need additional weapons to destroy Soviet missiles and allied weapons overlooks the relatively small Soviet delivery capability (and the relatively invulnerable hardened sites, and Soviet Polaris-type submarines). The Soviets would have to use their entire strength in a first blow in order to minimize the power of the counterattack. Our counter-attack on military targets would be on empty holes.
10. Pre-eminent military power is the decisive requirement for successful conduct of American foreign policy.	10. When potential opponents each possess more than 100 times overkill, neither can be pre-eminent. Over 600 million Chinese went under Communist rule while the West had a nuclear monopoly. Industrial-economic power is crucial for shaping the social and political systems of developing nations.

PART TWO

APPROACHES

Social scientists usually decry monistic causal theories as logically fallacious, incomplete, biased, and untestable. However, despite (or possibly because of) scientific protest, most people, in their attempts to comprehend or to solve a problem, favor some sort of monism. This is particularly so when the problem comes to be regarded as socially significant.

Most of us feel uncomfortable unless we can reduce complex realities to a single dimension. Thus we are tempted to seize on categorical labels for phenomena that are not easily understood. Most teachers are familiar with resistance to careful analysis. Too many students substitute such categories as psychological, economic, sociological, and biological determinism for analysis—as if labelling explained anything.

We do not make this charge only against students. Unfortunately the prestige of scientific labels has led to general reliance on a kind of magical nominalism that is felt to explain away problematic aspects of social life, whether these be mass terror or political dishonesty. The following pages of this section are devoted to a description and dissection of various mystiques, adopted by scientists and laymen alike as modes of thinking about social problems, both trivial and profound. Some of these approaches are fairly well discarded, whereas others are very much alive and in the vanguard of contemporary "scientific" sociological concern.

The distinguished contemporary sociologist Robert K. Merton once observed of his science that it was characterized by many approaches—and few arrivals. His witticism applies with special force to that part of sociology with which we are concerned in this book.

Herewith we offer a limited miscellany of those approaches to social pathology that, although they have led us nowhere, still attract a host of laymen, many scholars, and a golden flow of money. Research funds for the further exploration of sterile hypotheses seem to be inexhaustible. Apparently the resourceful man can always scare up enough backing for yet another inquiry into the alleged relationship between anatomy and criminality or between body chemistry and psychosis. Of course, we are not now, and probably never will be, able to disprove the relationship. But, as Leslie White[1] used to say, neither are we able to disprove the existence of Santa Claus. And he would add that sometimes science progresses not so much by disproving theories as by outgrowing them.

---

[1] A well-known anthropologist now retired from the faculty of the University of Michigan.

One could have said until July 20, 1969, that the moon was made of green cheese (science can never dismiss any unexplored possibility). Yet if an astrophysicist had proposed to spend huge sums for the investigation of such lunar phenomena, he would have been laughed out of court and consigned to scientific oblivion. Suppose he found support, undertook his expensive study, and failed to establish that the moon was made of green cheese. Wouldn't that be the end of it for a long time? Couldn't he or his scientific betters go on to something else? Not if our man and those who followed him down to the same dead end, generation after generation, had been gripped by a will to believe.

Must we enter the twenty-first century before the *idée fixe* that first possessed Cesare Lombroso[2] is finally relinquished—the notion that criminals are biologically different from other men? In our time that idea has been cherished by the physical anthropologist Ernest Hooton (p. 193) and by William Sheldon, Sheldon and Eleanor Glueck, and their many admirers. Clyde Kluckhohn declares in his prize-winning *Mirror for Man* (described on its cover by Margaret Mead as "the best contemporary introduction to modern anthropology"):

> One of the most famous studies in constitutional anthropology is that by Professor Hooton on the American criminal. His finding that criminals are, in general, biologically inferior has been disputed. Most reviewers have concluded that he took insufficient account of socioeconomic factors. Hooton makes it perfectly clear that criminals "do not bear the brand of Cain nor any specific physical stigmata whereby they can be identified at a glance." However, he presents a good evidence for certain associations. For example, among criminals as a group, those convicted of burglary and larceny are likely to be short and slender; those convicted of sex crimes are likely to be short and fat.
>
> For many of Hooton's major assertions the cautious reader must probably render the Scotch verdict of "not proven." On the other hand, a demonstration that some of Hooton's methods were unsatisfactory does not mean a constitutional factor in criminality can be ruled out. . . . The hard facts . . . suggest that the biological factor deserves further study.[3]

And further (still inconclusive) study is just what it has been given, for example, by William Sheldon, a student of human body types, or *somatotypes* elaborately correlated with various forms of psychopathic and sociopathic human conduct. Of this work, Kluckhohn says, "Somatotyping must be regarded as a valuable technique still in the exploratory stage."

Sheldon, in *Varieties of Delinquent Youth* (a formidable volume that looks ominously "scientific"), purports to explain delinquent behavior not by an uncritical equation of physique and deviance, but by observing the frequency with which youngsters' so-called D (for Disappointingness) scores correlate with a triple rating of somatotypes. The method is impressive. Put to use for some other purpose it might even interest statisticians. Nevertheless, his

---

[2] A nineteenth-century Italian criminologist.
[3] Clyde Kluckhohn, *Mirror for Man* (New York: Fawcett, 1959), p. 74.

analysis is on the level of magical nominalism mercilessly anatomized by Lynn Thorndyke in *The History of Magic and Experimental Science*. Thorndyke's book is replete with informative accounts of naive biological determinism with its single-minded stress on morphological, genetic, and physiological traits, that now comes to us in the form of a refined category used as a substitute for explanation.

Sheldon finds that for his most delinquent boys, a husky *mesomorphic* type is the statistical mean. He concludes that this type is most markedly disposed to delinquency. The precise relationship is never revealed; it is only asserted. He does not tell us why ectomorphic and endomorphic children (of less athletic build) should be less inclined to break laws. Some critics have contended that mesomorphic boys may be socially induced to display greater aggression than their punier mates. Notice that neither morphological determination nor social inducement can be established (by any plausible argument) as truly or basically causal.

It should not have to be repeated—but evidently it does—that empirical data that inform us about the association between two phenomena do not necessarily inform us about causation. We may be misled into confusing plausibility with necessity, and therefore into ignoring alternative hypotheses. Furthermore, continued preoccupation with biology, especially as the basis of crime and madness, may have a function transcending the goals of science —specifically, a systematic displacement of interest from potentially troublesome and controversial areas of social inquiry. This tendency also appears in other kinds of monistic nominalism.

After William Sheldon, the Drs. Sheldon and Eleanor Glueck, long famous as criminologists, drew out their calipers and applied them to the anatomy of many certified juvenile delinquents. Although their work was still in the exploratory stage, they nevertheless reported their findings in an influential book entitled *Unraveling Juvenile Delinquency*. The results, although scientifically indefensible, made a real mark—which shows no sign of being fully effaced as yet—on an assortment of social workers, field personnel, and family counselors. A syndicated column in the daily press written by Dr. Frances L. Ilg and Dr. Louise B. Ames offers a synthesis of constitutional psychology (the Hootonian or Sheldonian view) and developmental psychology (out of a Yale laboratory where every phase of growth, from birth to age fifteen, has been carefully observed and unhelpfully "averaged").

In attacking this school, one does not beat a dead horse. Yet a barnyard figure of speech may not be inappropriate, for it has been said of people pursuing this strange line of inquiry that they show less flexibility than the hen who will sit on a rock in the belief that it is an egg, but for only so long. After a while she gives up. Those bearing the banner of Lombroso cannot seem to give up. Nothing hatches, but they keep sitting on the same rock, protesting after more than a hundred years, that really, it may turn out to be an egg. Let the reader decide, once he has sampled Hooton and Hooton's critics, whether it is worthwhile to encourage more somatotyping.

In one form or another, the heredity theory, according to which criminals and other "deviants" are born, not made, is still with us. It dies hard. Next in durability, at least with laymen (and teachers, preachers, planners, reformers), if not with criminologists, is the poverty theory. Jean Valjean, as a decent but hungry man driven to steal, excites the public imagination more than a robber baron who may never have experienced anything but affluence. We now know that crime occurs at every level of society; it is as common in the upperworld as it is in the underworld. No one did as much as the sociologist Edwin Sutherland (p. 216) to destroy the idea that only poor people are habitual lawbreakers. He focused our attention on businessmen and professional men, the most respectable of them and not their disreputable confreres, who repeatedly violate the criminal code. Like racial identification, socioeconomic class turns out to explain a good deal about why some people are punished for their crimes, but very little about why they commit them. As a theory of crime causation, economic determinism is useless if only because many people in poverty are not criminals, and many of the well-to-do are. From Bonger (p. 212) to Sutherland is a major step in the direction of banishing a powerful myth.

If biologism and economism are unacceptable, so is psychologism.[4] Psychologistic explanations fashioned out of "mechanisms" said to operate only in the individual are a favorite refuge of detached scholars and active administrators interested in social problems.

The champions of psychological determinism, when they invoke it to account for any and all human phenomena, profess to have found a master key in the unique individual that will unlock all doors and thereby dispel every behavioral mystery. This is a great piece of presumption, not because psychologists are unable to throw light on the individual, but because that light might blind us to the collectivity, to society and *its* problems.

It would be preposterous to deny the psychologist his province (or for him to deny sociologists theirs). Neither is this to say that disciplinary frontiers should never be crossed. We do not hesitate to shift from one type of abstraction to another, nor to appropriate useful data from any source, including that of behaviorist and depth psychology. The issue is actually that of finding limits to psychologically slanted explanations. How far can one go with them if they are not located within a broader cultural framework?

The phenomenon of personal injuries, accidents, and casualties can be used as a hypothetical case in point. When the psychologist applies himself

---

[4] And all these "isms" are simply manifestations of the basic fallacy of *reductivism*, a fallacy whose equally unsatisfactory antithesis is the vague and weightless concept of *multiple causation* that implies, "No, not just this, but this and that—and that and that and, well, everything."

to this problem in the spirit of magical nominalism what may emerge is a theory of accident-proneness, or sadomasochism, or cardiomotor disability or the need to compensate for frustration. The emphasis is always individualistic and behavioristic. We, on the other hand, would feel obliged to consider the possibility that accidents are derived from a sociocultural context, that they are reflected in accident *rates*, and that group and subgroup differences must be taken into account. Sex, age, ethnicity, class, and occupation are the significant variables to a sociologist examining the differential distribution of accident rates—or suicide rates, divorce rates, and crime rates. If from this perspective one can specify the location of high and low incidence, he will then perhaps be well advised to enrich his analysis by recourse to psychology for interpreting residual differences. Thus it might be that men tend to have more accidents than women, but when we correct our male and female rates for age, it becomes obvious that young men have more accidents than older men. If so, the original male-female differences becomes a function of age distribution. Then, the residual difference *may be attributable* to psychological patterns present in the younger and older male but absent in the younger and older female.

This fictitious example is meant only to suggest the possible link between psychological and sociological analysis. It is better illustrated in Durkheim's *Suicide*, a masterpiece of early empirical and theoretical sociology, still unsurpassed in its subtlety. While eager to establish the independence of sociology, Durkheim recognized and utilized social psychology as a discipline, comparable to biochemistry, combining elements from two other sciences to achieve its own point of view. That point of view is more often hopelessly confused than creatively fused with others.

The small group is a practical, self-selected unit of study for social psychologists like Charles Horton Cooley (p. 240), Kurt Lewin, and their contemporary followers. The material in this section on primary-group and small-group research is less a critique of these men than of a widespread propensity to generalize from their microcosmic laboratory to the macrocosm of society at large. When this is done in the area of social pathology, the consequences are particularly unfortunate. The small group is only one step removed from the individual and, its study, however, ingenious, can tell us only about the small group. The area is legitimate, its scope considerable. We can only be indebted to the social psychologist who teaches us about interaction in the family—and deceived if he claims that every social problem can be traced to the family without asking, "How did the family get that way?"—a question which is beyond his purview.

The sociologist is beset by other pitfalls, some of his own creation. More than twenty years ago, C. Wright Mills (p. 253) set forth the nature of these pitfalls and sketched their topography. He presented his findings in a classic essay called, "The Professional Ideology of Social Pathologists," which we have reproduced in its entirety. Mills' findings were based on a thorough examination of textbooks then in use; Emil Bend and Martin Vogelfanger (p. 271) have replicated Mills' study for this book, making some of the same objections, withdrawing some, and adding a few of their own; they have inspected textbooks now widely in use.

The texts of today are undoubtedly more sophisticated than those in use two decades ago. For this, their authors have many men to thank, not the least is Robert K. Merton. Merton's brilliant quasi-Durkheimian conception of social problems stemming from "Social Structure and Anomie" (the title of his famous article) (p. 282) gently helps sociology to formulate more meaningful hypotheses. We take it as a healthy sign that not even this important contribution is invulnerable to serious criticism. Many investigators have lately discovered that it is difficult for them to conceptualize their data around Merton's schema. Among these are Bernard Rosenberg and Harry Silverstein (p. 294). They offer modifications that promise to be fruitful.

To end there would be to leave the reader on a positive note very far from our intention in these chapters, which have actually been assembled for a destructive purpose: to suggest what is wrong, to raise every kind of doubt about existing approaches—the better to make way for future arrivals. Therefore, our next-to-the-final selection is a skillful summary of Barbara Wootton's work (p. 290). Miss Wootton has scoured the literature of criminology and observed its judicial application as a juvenile court judge. She finds that though there is a plethora of studies, none has as yet demonstrated with any rigor that the twelve commonest, or "hypothetically causative," factors of crime and delinquency have any real bearing on the question. Evidently we must start anew. Meanwhile, demolition of old and useless theories as well as the rehabilitation of those that show some promise must continue. We take it that this is an act of creative destruction.

CHAPTER 1

BIOLOGISM

Crime and the Man

EARNEST ALBERT HOOTON

▬

If one considers in order sane civilians, sane criminals, insane civilians, and insane criminals, he finds that each succeeding group tends to manifest greater ignorance, lowlier occupational status, and more depressing evidence of all-around worthlessness. The same hierarchy of degeneration is evidenced in physical characteristics. The lower class civilian population is anthropologically fair to middling; the sane criminals are vastly inferior, the insane civilians considerably worse than sane criminals, and the insane criminals worst of all. It would be a rash person who would venture to assert that these parallelisms of increasing inferiority in sociological and anthropological characters are fortuitous and unrelated. The specific criminal proclivities found in certain races and nationalities among the sane prisoners are carried over, to a great extent, into the offenses committed by insane criminals, of the same ethnic or religious origin. . . . (P. 382)

So I think that inherently inferior organisms are, for the most part, those which succumb to the adversities of temptations of their social environment and fall into antisocial behavior, and that it is impossible to improve and correct environment to a point at which these flawed and degenerate human beings will be able to succeed in honest social competition. The bad organism sullies a good environment and transforms it into one which is evil. Of course, I should by no means argue that man should cease to attempt to ameliorate his social environment, but, when he entirely neglects the improvement of his own organism, he condemns his environmental efforts to futility.

That racial background of inheritance which determines our skin color, our hair form, and numerous anatomical features, may also in some vague and general way influence mental and temperamental characteristics, emotional sets, and so on. But race does not make the human animal criminalistic. All existing races have survived through scores of thousands of years the vicissitudes of

Source: Reprinted by permission of the publishers from Earnest Albert Hooton, *Crime and the Man.* Cambridge, Mass.: Harvard University Press, Copyright, 1939, by The President and Fellows of Harvard College.

natural and social selection and are mentally and physically sound at the core. But race undoubtedly influences choice of crime in those organic inferiors which are all too numerous within each racial group. It is the individual and familial inheritance which produce the deteriorated organism which cannot withstand environmental adversity. When a whole race is environmentally depressed, either because of coercion by other races or through inability to cope with the environment to which it has become adapted, we need not expect it to proliferate in antisocial or criminal behavior. Crime is not rampant in savage and retarded human societies. Crime flourishes rather in rich cultures where production is varied and abundant, so that constitutional inferiors are coddled and fostered, inevitably to bite the hands which have fed them. . . . (Pp. 388–89)

It may be well to state bluntly here that I have not spent the greater part of twelve years in studying criminals from any humanitarian zeal for the rehabilitation of offenders, or from any deep interest in the treatment of incarcerated felons. Such motives are laudable and the efforts of those who engage in criminological work are usually disinterested and sometimes efficacious. More power to their elbows! I wish to disabuse everyone of the idea that the function of the general human biologist is that of the family physician—to comfort or to cure individual patients. The anthropologist studies the adult male incarcerated felon as the medical research scientist would study the manifestations of cancer in its advanced stages, so that he may obtain an accurate knowledge of the most pronounced, far-reaching, and exaggerated effects of the disease. I have selected the criminal for study principally because the extreme outrageousness of criminal conduct makes the delinquent a most suitable subject for an exploration of the relation between the quality of the organism and its behavior. No scientific criminologist or penologist, however optimistic he may be of the good effects of a favorable environment and of education and moral suasion, has any particular hope of rehabilitating hardened adult criminals *en bloc*. Crime prevention is centered upon the treatment of juveniles and when it gets to be really scientific, it will have to start earlier still and concern itself with familial heredity. . . . (Pp. 390–91)

I may now, at length, confess that to the biological anthropologist the entire question of crime and the criminal bulks very small indeed in comparison with the enormous problem of checking the degenerative trends in human evolution which are producing millions of animals of our species inferior in mind and body. I deem human deterioration to be ultimately responsible not only for crime, but the evils of war, the oppression of the populace by totalitarian states, and for all of the social cataclysms which are rocking the world and under which civilization is tottering. . . . (P. 393)

I confidently predict that it will be a comparatively easy and short matter to determine the correlations of human body types with disease. At the same time it is equally necessary, and even more necessary, to relate gross anatomical structure to physiological and mental variation in the large mass of the so-called "normal" human beings—those who are not ill, or who, in blissful ignorance of the fact that they are ill, nevertheless go on functioning and living as if they were well. Since the individual behavior of the human being is indissolubly connected with the quality of his organism and its health functioning, the study of human conduct must not be divorced from the simultaneous attack of anthropology, medicine, and psychology upon the individual. The sociologist, or if you prefer, the social anthropologist, is wholly indispensable in the cooperative effort. For our ultimate purpose is to improve human behavior through the study of the organism which produces behavior.

Intelligent and intensive work should yield in a decade a fairly detailed and accurate knowledge of the associations of manifold human types of structure with the normal variations of physiological functions, with pathological susceptibilities and immunities, with mental range and capacity, and with patterns of social behavior. We should then have learned what types of human beings are worthless and irreclaimable, and what types are superior and capable of biological and educational improvement.

By the time we shall have secured exact data upon physico-psycho-sociological correlates from the study of constitution in all of its broader implications, it is possible that the human geneticists will be able to furnish us with more than an inkling of the manner whereby desirable and undesirable human combinations are produced through the mechanism of heredity. If nature can evolve better and more complicated animal organisms through the blind processes of trial and error, natural selection, and fortuitous variation, surely man with his comparatively high animal intelligence, with the transmitted cultural knowledge of thousands of years, and with a purpose hardened by the realization that the fate of his own species is at stake, can learn the mechanism of human heredity. We can direct and control the progress of human evolution by breeding better types and by the ruthless elimination of inferior types, if only we are willing to found and to practise a science of human genetics. With sound and progressively evolving human organisms in the majority of our species, problems of human behavior will be minimized, and there will be improved educability. Crime can be eradicated, war can be forgotten.

The theory of democratic government is noble and the practise of it offers the greatest opportunities for human happiness, if only the mass of the human individuals within the democracy is sound in body and in mind, and consequently social and to some extent unselfish in behavior. Progressive biological deterioration of the people leads inevitably to anarchy and dictatorships. More than ever, in the light of recent events, we have come to pin all of our faith for the future of civilization and of man on democracy. Like Noah we have builded an ark, the rains have come, and the deluge is upon us. Do we hope to take refuge in that ark of democracy, with our sons and our sons' wives, and survive the flood? We can succeed in this hope only if we leave out some of the noxious animals who are boring from within and making that ark dangerously leaky. So it behooves us to learn our human parasitology and human entomology, to practise an artificial and scientific selection with intelligence, if we wish to save our skins. . . . (Pp. 395–98)

Crime and the Anthropologist
ROBERT K. MERTON AND M. F. ASHLEY-MONTAGU

▬

> Of all the cants which are canted in this canting world, . . . the cant of criticism is the most tormenting.—Laurence Sterne, *Tristram Shandy*.

> I await these squallings with equanimity.
> —Earnest A. Hooton, *Crime and the Man*.

Professor Hooton in two works recently published in the combined fields of physical anthropology and criminology[1] has propounded some highly unorthodox theories and stated some startling conclusions. Already the popular press is heralding the more lurid of these conclusions and it may no doubt be expected that additional publicity of this sort will follow upon the appearance of the two succeeding volumes of *The American Criminal*. In this massive report, Hooton has presented the results of twelve years of research representing the most extensive investigation of the physical characters of a criminal series of populations as compared with civilian populations that has yet appeared. It may at once be stated that this work will occupy as conspicuous a place in the history of criminology as the works of his predecessors in the field, Lombroso and Goring. It is the mantle of Lombroso, patched with some pieces from that of Max Nordau, rather than that of Goring—which Hooton spurns—that has descended upon the shoulders of Hooton. He wears it most gracefully. We are convinced that this vigorously tendentious study of the American criminal will have a most stimulating effect upon that largely neglected branch of human biology which is concerned to discover the relations between body, mind, and

Source: Robert K. Merton and M. F. Ashley-Montagu, "Crime and the Anthropologist," *American Anthropologist*, 42:3 (July–September, 1940), pp. 384–408. Reprinted by permission.
[1] Earnest Albert Hooton, *Crime and the Man* (Cambridge, Mass.: Harvard University Press, 1939) and *The American Criminal: An Anthropological Study* (Cambridge, Mass.: Harvard University Press, 1939).

society; or shall we say heredity, conduct, and culture? It is a work which simply bristles with controversial points.

Since Hooton's work seems destined to exert an appreciable effect upon the thought of all those who make themselves acquainted with it, as well as upon the thought of many who do not, it is desirable that the significance of his results be critically examined from as many aspects as possible, for its implications are of the greatest importance. The study is of such magnitude that even the present forerunners of what promises to be a monumental report cannot be adequately discussed in a paper of this length. At most all that we can venture to do here is to consider some features of the framework of the research, some of its more general conclusions, and certain methodological assumptions which have been adopted. We shall hereafter refer to *The American Criminal* (the first of "three ponderous volumes, each positively bristling with statistical documentation") as *AC*, and to *Crime and the Man* (the summary volume of Lowell Institute Lectures) as *CM*.

As a consequence of his researches Hooton has been forced into the un-American position of espousing the cause of the angels. It may seem from what we say here that we have been forced into the opposite extreme of embracing the cause of the criminals. That is only apparently so. Actually, what we wish to do here is to suggest that the differences between the angels and the criminals are only skin deep; that the criminals may not have sprouted wings as the angels have done, not because it was not in them to do so, but because their wings were clipped before they were ready to try them.

Both of Hooton's works are introduced with ingenious attacks upon anticipated criticism and a series of *ad hominem* rejoinders-in-advance to any who may venture to voice their disagreement with the author's conclusions. "The categorical denials of hereditary influences in crime which are commonly emitted by sociologists" (*AC*, 4) and other "humanitarian practitioners" who "have poured out so much blood and treasure upon the investigation of the causes of crime" have not led us any nearer to a solution of the causative elements in criminal behavior. Hence, it is implied, the author's categorical affirmations that "criminals are organically inferior" and that "the primary cause of crime is biological inferiority" are more likely to do so. The statement of the case in terms of these mutually exclusive alternatives adds considerably to the dialectical flavor of the argument if not to our knowledge of the causation of crime. As we shall have occasion to see, this posing of false dilemmas is one of the more frequent polemical devices which Hooton utilizes in the analysis of his data.

Hooton defines a criminal as "a person who is under sentence in a penal institution, having been convicted for an antisocial act punishable by commitment to such an institution." (*AC*, 7.) He points out that "Crimes are obviously infractions of more or less arbitrary social rules, and whether an act is or is not accounted a crime, depends not only upon the nature of that act, but also upon the attitude of society toward it, which may differ radically from time to time and in diversely constituted political, social, and ethnic groups." (*AC*, 7.) "The criminal is a person distinguished by the commission of an overt act against society and he exemplifies for us an extreme of human conduct, thus making himself an excellent subject for the investigation of the relation of physique to behavior." (*AC*, 8.)

It is because the criminal exemplifies an "extreme" of human conduct that he was selected by Hooton for the investigation of the possible relation of physique to conduct. The object of the investigation is stated at the conclusion of the second chapter (*CM*, 33), which is significantly entitled *The Organic Basis of Crime*, as being "Specifically [the examination of] the physical characteristics of a large series of anti-social individuals in order to find out whether their varied types of delinquency are associated with their anthropological characters, and whether they are physically distinguished from those of us who are, perhaps temporarily, at large, and at least, putatively, law-abiding."

An indication of Hooton's dispassionate approach—in contrast, presumably, to Goring's "emotional preconception" which Hooton decries—is afforded by his initial comment "upon one stupid objection . . . to the effect that it is useless to study incarcerated criminals because they represent only the failures of those habitually and purposefully engaged in anti-social pursuits." (*AC*, 10.) In such an extreme form, this objection, whether "stupid" or not, would rule out most studies of criminals, since only those who are incarcerated are usually available for study. But it is still possible, and for some purposes relevant, that incarcerated criminals are not a representative sample (with respect to intelligence, economic status, race, nationality and rural-urban composition) of those who commit crimes. Selective arrests, and more importantly, selective commitments in terms of economic status and race are attested by many conversant with the facts; the differential in the case of Negroes seems to be especially marked. Hooton himself finds it convenient to adduce possible differentials in "rates of apprehension and conviction" between rural and urban criminals when he writes that "in rural life sparsity of population and restricted criminal opportunity lead . . . to easy detection and apprehension of persons responsible for crimes" in relative contrast to urban offenders. (*AC*, 288.) Criminologists have indicated additional selective elements in this connexion.) It is at least possible, then, that some of the apparent sociological and physical differentials between criminals and civilians would be eliminated, were allowances made for the selective elements in commitment. Hooton is of course at liberty to define the "criminal" as he wishes, but he is not free to assume as an unchallengeable axiom that prisoners are in all relevant respects representative of the total population of those who have committed one or more illegal acts. To insinuate an axiom is not to demonstrate a fact. This consideration is mentioned here, not so much for its intrinsic importance—the fact remains that unconfined criminals and the anthropometrist's calipers have little chance to meet—but simply to bring out the author's tendency to demolish exaggerated propositions and hence to obscure the essential issue.[2]

The study of the *Old American Criminal* reports on 4212 native white prisoners of native white parentage from nine states and a civilian (non-criminal) check sample of 313 (146 Nashville firemen and 167 residents of Massachusetts). Observations included at least 33 anthropometric measurements and indices, ten sociological categories and 33 morphological categories for each person. It should be noted that almost one-half of the civilian check group are firemen; in an occupation for which, Hooton observes, "the physical qualifications are rather stringent." He also notes that the "the principal objection to them is that they are inclined to be fat," but feels compelled to add that they have the further liabilities of being of uniform social and economic status, in contrast to the criminal sample, and that their urban residence contrasts with the dominantly rural residence of the criminals when not incarcerated. In other words, as far as half the crucial check sample is concerned, the civilians are in many respects distinctly selected. However, it is comforting to learn that the Nashville civilians and the Tennessee villains are at least ethnically comparable.

Another part of the check group consists of Massachusetts militiamen and "in as much as enlistment in the militia is contingent upon the passing of a physical examination, it may be assumed that its members are, on the whole, of superior physique to the criminals" who, presumably, do not need to pass a formal physical examination. (*AC*, 34.) One may readily sympathize with Hooton's difficulty in obtaining a suitable check sample, but the fact still remains that a research of this magnitude proceeded with a clearly loaded check group. That the Tennessee civilian sample, with its various physical and social idiosyncrasies, proves disturbing to Hooton may be inferred from the frequency of such remarks as: "the Tennessee firemen show an unduly high mean," "the Tennessee firemen are perhaps broader in the face than an unselected (*sic*) civilian group would be," "the plump and sedentary fire-fighters," "the big-jowled firemen," "the excess weight of the Tennessee firemen," etc. (*AC*, 208 *ff.*) Despite all this, we are told that the Tennessee series probably "affords the more reliable results," "for the Massachusetts criminal series includes a brachycephalic French element almost absent from the civilian series." (*AC*,

---

[2] It is interesting to confront Hooton's remarks with the observations of a criminologist on the question of prison samples of criminal populations. "It is probable that arrests for serious crimes are less than 10 per cent of the serious crimes actually committed in large cities. Out of 1,000 consecutive burglaries and robberies of chain grocery stores in Chicago in 1930–1931, only two resulted directly in arrests." "Many types of offenses are widespread but seldom result in prosecution." "The selective nature of arrest and of imprisonment make these statistics an inadequate source of information regarding the characteristics of criminals, but it is difficult to develop statistics regarding criminals who are not recorded in some manner. Apparently, therefore, the best that can be done at present is to recognize the bias in the statistics of arrests or of prisons and attempt to secure statistics in other ways regarding the classes which are not adequately represented." E. H. Sutherland, *Principles of Criminology* (Philadelphia, 1939), pp. 29, 37, 45. The various writings of Thorsten Sellin on crime indexes should further be consulted in this connexion.

216.) Another liability of the Massachusetts civilian series is the intrusion of the personal equation of "Observer C" with respect to some morphological items. Thus, the Tennessee civilian sample is the more reliable, and if this be so, then rough indeed is this roughly comparable setting of civilians." To what extent are observed "biological" differences attributable to the bias of the sample? In view of some of the inferences which Hooton later feels justified in drawing, this bias becomes a grievous inadequacy, to say the least. It should be noticed, however, that Hooton has zealously ascertained and emphasized some of these sources of bias, both slight and pronounced in his data.

An exhaustive statistical analysis of the data leads to the "important conclusion that native White criminals of native parentage are not only distinguished from each other by offense groups in sociological characteristics, but also in anthropometric and morphological features. Thus it is suggested that crime is not an exclusively sociological phenomenon, but is also biological." (*CM*, 75.) Concerning the nature of Hooton's statistical analysis we shall have something to say hereafter, but even if this were unexceptionable, we may here recall the words of Wilhelm Ostwald.

Among scientific articles there are to be found not a few wherein the logic and mathematics are faultless but which are for all that worthless, because the assumptions and hypotheses upon which the faultless logic and mathematics rest do not correspond to actuality.

But Hooton's logic, if not his mathematics, is far from faultless.

Hooton finds that "on the whole, the biological superiority of the civilian to the delinquent is quite as certain as his sociological superiority." (*CM*, 376.) "The evidence," he writes, "that the criminals are derived from the baser biological stuff of their various ethnic stocks seems to me to be conclusive, although" he adds, "it might be argued that they came from families which are the anthropological victims of environmental depression." (*CM*, 379.)

Hooton finds that the "First generation criminals seem to adhere more closely than first generation civilians to the squat, broad-faced types which are often characteristic of the foreign born emigrant from Europe," and he goes on to make the astonishing suggestion that "It seems possible that such biological inadaptability, such phylogenetic conservatism, is responsible for the association of primitive features with retarded culture in modern savages." (*CM*, 379.)

It need hardly be said that for this suggestion there exists not the slightest factual support, but unexceptionally the evidence completely and unequivocally proves the contrary; that modern "savages" are biologically at least as perfectly adapted to the environments in which they live as the white man is to his. With respect to culture, it apparently requires to be pointed out that the culture of "savages," with rare exceptions, is anything but "retarded." It is a misunderstanding of the nature of culture, and of the history of our own, to speak of the culture of simpler peoples as retarded. Primitive cultures are no less complex and developed in their own ways than our own; unless, of course, we set out with the assumption that the standards of thought and material organization which Western culture has attained, as a consequence of the countless fertilizing cross currents and eddies of other cultures to which Western man has for the past few thousand years been exposed, are the measures of all cultures. Is it necessary to point out that not more than two thousand years ago, many peoples now esteemed "retarded" by us, might have judged the ancestors of all the potential and actual readers of this article as irremediably physically and culturally retarded, with quite as much justice as is implicit in Hooton's suggestion? It would seem that Hooton might profitably include an historical dimension in his biologistic judgments.

What, furthermore, it would be interesting to know, are the "primitive features" which are thought to be associated with the "retarded culture" of "modern savages"? As far as the physical structure of "modern savages" is concerned, there is no ground whatever for the belief that it is characterized by quantitatively or qualitatively more "primitive features" than is the physical structure of Western man. It is in such pronouncements as these that Hooton reveals his strong bias in favor of the belief that certain kinds of physical characters are probably associated with certain kinds of mental and social functioning.

Two distinct interpretative tendencies run throughout the work: one, a cautious and admirably restrained effort to assay the significance of biological factors in the determination of the incidence of criminal behavior; the other, a pugnacious and flamboyant insistence on the biological determination of crime. These two views do not rest comfortably in the same book but, conveniently enough, they are usually segregated. Thus, we have such careful disclaimers of extreme biological determinism as these:

This is very far from an insistence upon the direct causal relationship between the physical minutiae of an animal and his psychological processes—much less his behavior. All of these are varied expressions of the organism bound up together in their common heredity and modified in their several directions by the common environment. (*AC*, 6.)

Similarly, it may be worth while to examine the physical characteristics of large groups of criminals to discover whether they are in any sense physically homogeneous, and if so whether they are distinguishable from non-criminals. Here again there is no necessary implication of causality—at least in the sense of a direct relationship between the physical characteristics of criminals and their antisocial conduct. (*AC*, 8.)

The lawless habits of a racial or ethnic group may be persistently linked with its hereditary physique, although in a mainly non-causal relationship. (*AC*, 296.)

These straightforward formulations of problems in criminal anthropology seem to us to be unexceptionable. But these moderate statements are soon forgotten in the fervor of formulating conclusions. In spite of all these laudable protestations that a statistical association is not to be confused with a causal relationship, Hooton insists that "the variation in physique and body build is *certainly causally* related to nature of offense." (*AC*, 296; italics inserted.) And this, despite the absence of adequate evidence to demonstrate the causal connexion which he holds to be incontestable. In an equally forthright fashion, Hooton tells his Lowell Institute audience: "You may say that this is tantamount to a declaration that the *primary cause* of crime is biological inferiority—and this is exactly what I mean." (*CM*, 130; italics inserted.) In fact, as he warms to his subject, he evidently means much more than that. Hooton believes that he now has sufficient evidence for the following dictum:

> I deem human [biological] deterioration to be ultimately responsible not only for crime, but for the evils of war, the oppression of the populace by totalitarian states, and for all of the social cataclysms which are rocking the world and under which civilization is tottering. (*CM*, 393.)

He does not tell us whether the recent "bear market" on the Stock Exchange is likewise attributable to this same biological degeneration. The sibylline abandon with which one of our most eminent physical anthropologists bestows these *obiter dicta* upon a Lowell Institute audience augurs ill for the more exact correlation between fact, inference and conclusion which we have assumed to characterize the scientific method. Extrapolations such as these pique the imagination and bedevil the intellect. One of Hooton's more interesting implications is that we either accept and act upon these views or sink back into our self-constituted caverns of democratic ignorance and despair to await the impending collapse of civilization. (See his concluding remarks in *CM*.) If we are to escape the day of Biological Judgment we must act—before too long. Only the "ruthless elimination of inferior types" can save us. The concluding words of Hooton's monograph are these:

> Criminals are organically inferior. Crime is the resultant of the impact of environment upon low grade human organisms. It follows that the elimination of crime can be effected only by the extirpation of the physically, mentally and morally unfit, or by their complete segregation in a socially aseptic environment. (*AC*, 309.)

In his call to arms, Hooton is especially prone to such horrendous catchwords as "biological inferiority," "organic degeneration," "biological deterioration." Thus, we are told that "criminals present a united front of biological inferiority," (*AC*, 300) and that "criminals as a group represent an aggregate of sociologically inferior and biologically inferior individuals." (*AC*, 304.) Without holding any particular brief for criminals, one may nevertheless inquire: what does Hooton concretely mean by inferiority in these connexions? As we shall see, his "answers" are either contradictory, equivocal or darkly implicit. In comparing his criminal and civilian samples—the latter, be it remembered, consist of exactly 313 persons (146 Nashville firemen and 167 Massachusetts militiamen and Boston out-patients)—he finds seven metrical and indicial items in which there are unquestionably significant *differences*[3]

---

[3] Significant differences = 3 or more times the probable error (not the standard error).

(which persist when civilian and criminal aggregates are compared as a whole and when intra-state comparisons of civilians and criminals are made). What are these *differences* which, we must infer, unquestionably signify *inferiority*? The first is age. The criminals are 3.80 years younger than the civilians. Youth, presumably, is to be included in this homespun category of biological inferiority. "The hoary head is a crown of glory." (*Proverbs*, xvi, 31.) It hardly comes as an unheralded discovery that the age-group of maximum criminality is in the young-adult period and that this age-group varies with the type of offense. The study of crime statistics had long ago led to this finding.

The second term involving statistically significant differences between the civilians and criminals is weight: the criminals are 11.70 pounds lighter, on the average, and this difference is 10.83 p.e. Presumably, deficiency of weight as compared with the "roly-poly" firemen, et al., is a mark of biological inferiority. In view of the frequently observed associations between body weight and socio-economic status, might it not be advisable to equate the status of the criminal and check samples, before treating differences of weight as "biological" differences? Or are we to make the further assumption that socio-economic status is also biologically determined?

The five other indubitable differences involve the criminals' deficiencies in chest breadth, head circumference, upper face height, nose height and ear length. One awaits with some impatience the demonstration that these deficiencies represent biological inferiority, as one awaits the proof that these "significant differences" mean anything more than a difference between two statistics computed from separate samples of such a magnitude that the probability that the samples were drawn from the same universe is inappreciable. We already know that Hooton's samples were drawn from different universes, and what we would be interested to know is why Hooton fastened upon a difference of a biological nature, rather than upon the many other characters of difference which are socio-economically known to exist between the civilians and criminals, as the causative factor in criminality. Statistically significant differences tell us no more than that the statistics involved are of different values; they do not tell us *why* or how they came to be so. The extrapolation of the "biological" factor, to the exclusion of all others, may satisfy Hooton's critical sense, but it does not satisfy ours. Furthermore, since some of Hooton's "significant differences" between the civilians and criminals are no more than 3 or 4 times the probable error, this renders those particular differences less clearly significant. It may be mentioned here that the employment of the critical ratio, i.e., difference/standard error of difference, rather than the difference/probable error of difference as used by Hooton, would have constituted a critically more exacting index of "statistical significance" of such differences as were found to exist between criminals and civilians. But in any event, the demonstration is altogether lacking that such differences as the criminals exhibit are marks of "inherited inferiority" which inevitably militates against the living of a legally acceptable life.

If one turns to the fourteen morphological items which involve unequivocal statistical differences (Table XII–12 *ff.*) [the table does not appear in this
book], these are found to include an excess proportion of criminals with small
hair quantity (beard) and a deficiency of those with medium quantity; likewise,
an excess proportion of criminals with straight hair-form and a deficiency of
those with low waves; a deficiency of those with blue eye color, with gray and
white hair color, with medium (length and breadth) necks and an excess of those
with long, thin necks. These, and six other marks of biological inferiority constitute some of the major differences upon which Hooton bases his imputation
of organic inferiority. To be sure, with respect to morphological, indicial and
metrical items, there are other differences as well, though not as clearcut as the
foregoing. It remains for Hooton to reassess the utility of his control group and
to make more explicit the exact implications of the "inferiorities"—or shall we
say, differences?—to which he attaches so much anthropological significance.
Finally, it remains for him to demonstrate that the differences which survive a
reexamination of his check sample are in no way attributable to environmental
differences since he often tends to identify "the organism" and "heredity."
("... although scientifically competent persons without exception admit the
importance of the organism as a determiner of its own behavior, it is expedient
for them to stress rather the contribution of environment to that behavior. This
is because the heredity of an existing individual cannot be altered. ...")
(*AC*, 252.)

As we have seen, Hooton speaks much of biological inferiority. To our
knowledge, in only one passage does he specifically state what he means by this
term. This statement is a truly remarkable example of *petitio principii*. Hooton
is quite clear as to the characters which are biological inferiorities; namely, *any
of the characters which are distinctive of the criminal aggregate when compared
with the civilian sample*. In effect all differential characters of the criminal
population are by fiat inferiorities.[4] It is by virtue of a clearly circular definition
that Hooton can arrive at the "indubitable" conclusion that "criminals are
biologically inferior." The exact defining statements, placed within their
original context, are deserving of repetition.

Differences between individuals or groups can be ascertained and appraised without
the necessity of pronouncing judgments as to inferiority or superiority. These latter
may be wholly subjective and undesirable. Certainly that is true of racial differences ...
But, when we compare convicted felons ... with law-abiding citizens of the same race,
we are contrasting the social liabilities with the social assets, and we deliberately
judge criminals to be undesirable and of lesser worth than economically efficient and
socially-minded men. *Thus, if we find felons to manifest physical differences* (sic) *from
civilians, we are justified in adjudging as undesirable biological characters those which*

---

[4] In terms of such logic, the male of the species with a rate of imprisonment often tenfold
that of the female is hopelessly inferior. Here indeed is a "biological" difference associated
with a difference in rate of commitment. On Hooton's logic, as Sutherland has indicated, the
all-too-wicked male "should be weeded out of the population."

are associated in the organism with antisocial behavior . . . It is the organic complex which must be estimated inferior or superior on the basis of the type of behavior emanating from such a combination of parts functioning as a unit. (*CM*, 342–353; italics inserted.)

* * *

What the significant deviation in greater nose breadth among the criminals may mean we do not know, but we should be strongly disinclined to look upon such a character as a mark of organic inferiority. With respect to the significance of this character Hooton is silent, but not so when it comes to small-headedness, for in this connexion he remarks that "Presumably or possibly, the smaller head sizes of the criminals may be associated with their indubitably inferior intelligence." (*CM*, 368.)

To leave the discussion of the anthropometric-indicial characters for a moment, what, we may well ask, does Hooton mean by the "indubitably inferior intelligence" of the criminal? It may be pointed out that "indubitable" means "clear or certain beyond question." Hooton's statement concerning the un-questionably inferior intelligence of the criminal is explicitly based upon two sets of data: the intelligence ratings of 154 cases (inmates of the Concord Reformatory) in his criminal series and upon Sheldon and Eleanor Glueck's intelligence ratings of 466 former inmates of this Reformatory. The first series of 154 Concord matriculants is notably dull-witted, for only 19.48 per cent possess a "normal intelligence" (I.Q. 96 or above). The Gluecks found that of their 466 subjects 33 per cent had a normal I.Q. (90–110), 24.1 per cent were dull (I.Q. 80–90), 22.3 per cent borderline (I.Q. 70–80), and 20.6 feeble-minded (I.Q. 50–70). It is not our purpose to question these results. What is in question is Hooton's implied suggestion that such "intelligence tests" measure native intelligence or ability exclusively. The fact is that intelligence tests, so-called, measure innumerable factors among which native intelligence is presumably one. Whatever they may be claimed to be, intelligence tests are not a measure of that single factor alone. For children and college students it has been shown time and again that these tests do not measure native ability or intelligence apart from schooling, that the tests are largely measures of scholastic or experiential attainment. What these tests measure is an expression of the experience-capacity equation.

Altogether apart from these considerations, the Gluecks' findings are by no means invariably substantiated by other studies. In view of the widely differing techniques and "results" in this field, as recent surveys have shown, the one conclusion which seems wholly out of place is that of the 'indubitably' inferior intelligence of the criminal aggregate.[5] Murchison found, after a comparison of

---

[5] See E. H. Sutherland, *Mental Deficiency and Crime*, in Kimball Young (ed.), *Social Attitudes* (New York, 1931); L. D. Zeleny, "*Feeblemindedness and Criminal Conduct*," *American Journal of Sociology* (1933), pp. 38, 564–578; S. H. Tulchin, *Intelligence and Crime* (Chicago, 1939); W. C. Reckless, *Criminal Behavior* (New York, 1940).

the Army Alpha ratings of soldiers with prisoners of the same states, that the scores of the prison population were a representative sample of the community from which the subjects were drawn.[6] With respect to juvenile delinquents, competent observers such as Healy, Slawson, Burt and Willemse, while agreeing that some delinquents are feebleminded also agree that delinquents as a whole do not exhibit differences in intelligence which would be capable of explaining the fact of their delinquency.[7] Thus, Burt found only eight per cent of delinquents "who were backward in intelligence by at least three-tenths of their ages."[8]

Of course, authorities could be multiplied on both sides, but our purpose here has been to suggest that native intelligence is not what the intelligence tests measure, and that it is far from indubitable that criminals and delinquents are of inferior native intelligence.

As for the suggested possible or presumed relationship between head size and intelligence, it has been clearly established by the work of Pearson, Murdock and Sullivan, Reid and Mulligan, and others that there is no relation whatever between head size and intelligence or scholastic achievement.[9]

And here we may return to Hooton's characters of assumed physical inferiority. We have already seen with respect to the majority of the so-called primitive or inferior characters in the anthropometric-indicial series, that these are few in number and that they are far exceeded in number by characters of an agreed advanced and neutral or indifferent nature. When we turn to consider the 16 "primitive" characters which characterize the morphological grouping, as shown in Table III [the table does not appear in this book], we must frankly confess that we fail to see in any one of them any sign which may be interpreted as a mark of physical or organic inferiority, although by the arbitrary standard which we have adopted as a measure of the developmental status of such characters, these characters must remain in the "primitive" category. But there are only 32.0 per cent of these characters in this group as against 56.0 per cent of "advanced" characters. A more significant figure is obtained by taking these 16 primitive characters together with the two characters of the same class from the anthropometric-indicial series and expressing them as a percentage of the total number of combined anthropometric-indicial-morphological characters, which amounts to 101. In this way we find that only 17.8 per cent of characters

---

[6] Carl Murchison, *Criminal Intelligence* (Boston, 1926). See also H. M. Adler and M. R. Worthington, *"The Scope of the Problem of Delinquency and Crime As Related to Mental Deficiency,"* *Journal of Psycho-Asthenics* (1925), pp. 30, 47–56.

[7] John Slawson, *The Delinquent Boy* (Boston, 1926); Cyril Burt, *The Youth Delinquent*, (London, 1925); W. A. Willemse, *Constitutional Types in Delinquency* (New York, 1932).

[8] Burt, *op. cit.*, p. 300.

[9] K. Pearson, *Relationship of Intelligence to Size and Shape of the Head and Other Mental and Physical Characters* (Biometrika, 1906), pp. 5, 105–146; R. Pearl, *"On the Correlation Between Intelligence and the Size of the Head,"* *Journal of Comparative Neurology and Psychology* (1906), pp. 189–199; K. Murdock and L. R. Sullivan, *"A Contribution to the Study of Mental and Physical Measurements in Normal Children,"* *American Physical Education Review* (1923), pp. 28, 209–215; 276–280; 328; R. W. Reid and J. H. Mulligan, *"Relation of Cranial Capacity to Intelligence,"* *Journal of the Royal Anthropological Institute* (1923), pp. 53, 322–332.

fall into the primitive class as compared with 49.5 per cent in the advanced class. In the light of these findings, then, is it a tenable hypothesis that the criminal is an organically inferior being? We think not. We believe it to be undemonstrated that such differences as we do find are marks of genetic or biological inferiority. We believe that Hooton's own findings, when subjected to a developmental analysis such as we have attempted, do not support his conclusion that "The evidence that the criminals are derived from the baser biological stuff of their various ethnic stock seems . . . to be conclusive."

Hooton also imputes "sociological inferiority" to the criminal aggregate. It may be suggested, however, that his summary of significant sociological differences between the criminal and civilian samples attests above all the glaring inadequacy, in some respects, of the check sample (Table XII–126, ff.) [the table does not appear in this book]. This may be seen by examining the specific marks of sociological "inferiority." With respect to marital status, the excess of single men among criminals, and correlatively, the deficiency of married criminals, is acknowledged to be "partially attributable to the lower mean age of the criminals." Some differences persist, however, apart from this factor of age. The criminals' excess of divorced men is allegedly due in part "to probable suppression of divorce on the part of civilians" (for not a single divorced person appears in the civilian check sample!). *All* of the differences in occupational distribution are exaggerated, Hooton acknowledges, by the disproportionate number of public service workers (those Nashville firemen again) in the check sample. To the naive reader it would seem that the occupational distribution (and perhaps other social and physical characteristics) of the criminal sample would have appeared even more "abnormal" and "inferior" if the entire civilian sample, instead of only some 50 per cent, were constituted by the "stout" firemen.

When it comes to the third set of clearcut social differences, namely, education, the criminals are found to be, as expected, clearly deficient in duration of formal schooling. However, here again the gross results must be interpreted cautiously in view of the fact that 60 per cent of the criminal sample come from Tennessee, Kentucky and Texas. In fact, when comparison is made between the Tennessee criminal and the Tennessee firemen, some of these differences are sharply attentuated, if not reversed in direction (e.g., the criminals have a marked excess of those who have had from one to two years of high school training and a statistically insignificant excess of college men). All this is not to suggest that there are no social differences between the criminal and civilian populations—on the contrary, other exacting studies have shown many such differences—but simply to indicate the inadequacy of the particular samples utilized in this study.

Moreover, there still remains the question as to what is meant by the oft-repeated phrase, "sociological inferiority" of the criminal sample. The possibility of selective commitment on the basis of social and economic status is not explored here for the ample reason that the relevant evidence is not available. Thus, granted the reliability of the observed differences, what is concretely meant by the unqualified imputation of sociological inferiority? Fortunately, Hooton is explicit on this point. "Excess of single men and of divorced men indicate an inability or unwillingness to undertake successfully the normal family responsibilities of the adult male." (*AC*, 304.) The introduction of Hooton's personal attitude toward divorce and celibacy is illuminating, perhaps interesting, but hardly relevant. If those of us who have given hostages to Fortune are more kindly disposed toward benedicts than toward celibates, well and good; but is this a considered judgment resting in part upon twelve years of anthropological research concerning the American criminal or is its source some arcanum into which we may not be admitted? In any event, if this evaluation is to be accepted at its face value, one must also conclude that the Massachusetts civilians are in this respect "sociologically inferior" to the Tennessee civilians inasmuch as 86 per cent of the latter are married whereas only 32 per cent of the Bay State representatives have attained this superior status. Moreover, on the same logic, the Massachusetts civilians are likewise inferior to the criminal aggregate since 45 per cent of the latter are confessed benedicts. The not wholly irrelevant point is that Hooton's conclusion of ingrained biological and sociological inferiority of the criminal will be and has been heralded as a finding derived by an unquestionably eminent scientist from a comprehensive analysis of objective data. In view of the painstaking and exact nature of a great part of the study, it is unfortunate that the interpretation is marred by such dicta.

Hooton continues with the proposition that "deficient education and low occupational status are bound up with mental inferiority, lack of industry and stability and general weakness of character." (*AC*, 304–305.) Within the context of Hooton's general point of view, all of these, presumably, are biologically determined. At the risk of unleashing a favorite *ad hominem* thesis of the author —critics of his extreme position are simply voicing their adherence to the "democratic doctrine of human equality" and thereby insisting that all men are created biologically equal—one might suggest that this unauthenticated statement might well await more intensive study before claiming general acceptance. The exacting researches by Gray and Moshinsky[10]—pertaining to England, to be sure, but not wholly irrelevant to Hooton's expansive assertion— find that (in a sample of 9,000) 59 per cent of the children with an I.Q. of 130 and over do not enjoy the opportunity of a higher education. It must be confessed that these investigators do not examine differences in "general weakness of character," which, it must be assumed, either Hooton or others must have done.

---

[10] J. L. Gray and P. Moshinsky, *Ability and Educational Opportunity in Relation to Parental Occupation* in L. Hogben (ed.), *Political Arithmetic* (New York, 1938), pp. 376–417. See also L. Isserlis, *On the Relation between Home Conditions and the Intelligence of School Children* (H.M. Stationery Office, London, 1923).

Hooton's causal imputations and his varied attempts to attribute to the criminal "inferiorities" of one type or another can be questioned in greater detail, but the general consideration is clear. By neglecting a close, systematic examination of social, economic and cultural differences between his criminal and civilian samples,—such differences being attributed by fiat to biological causes—by using a check sample which is highly selective in many respects and by extrapolating far beyond the data which he has so meticulously assembled, he comes to a series of conclusions which are to the largest extent questionable.

The extent to which Hooton's convictions color not only his interpretation but also his procedure may be gathered from the following statement.

A considerable part of the sociological differentiation of the body build types may be due to the inequality of their individual derivations from the nine states represented in our criminal series. Thus, short and slender men are particularly common among the Massachusetts and Wisconsin criminals, while tall-heavy men are unduly represented in the Texas sample, and tall-slender men in Tennessee and Kentucky. In Wisconsin and Massachusetts educational facilities are excellent, while the same cannot be said of Tennessee and Kentucky. Again, Massachusetts is a state with a large urban population, whereas most of the other states in our series are predominantly rural. *It is all too clear that the several state environments, physical and cultural, are quite diverse.* It may then occur to my readers that it would be possible to eliminate the complicating effects of state environment from this study of body build type by applying a correction for state sampling, such as was done in testing the physical differentiation of offense groups. *I have not applied such corrections for state sampling, because I maintain that it is the organism which creates social environment and not the reverse.* Only if each of the states possessed an exclusive physical environment and an exclusive physical type with its own particular and unvarying culture, could we conclude that environment is the common cause of body build and sociological status . . . But *if short, fat men commit rape and come from Texas, I for present purposes, am inclined to relate their criminal predilection to their bodily constitution and not to the sexuality of the Lone Star State.* (*CM*, 99; italics inserted.)

This interesting formulation once again presents the issue in terms of a dilemma: either "the organism creates the social environment" or the social environment creates the organism. An alternative view that homicidal patterns, for example, may be more definitely an integral part of one local culture in contrast to another and that a larger proportion of "organisms" reared in this culture may assimilate these cultural values—e.g., "the unwritten law" pattern —and act accordingly, receives no attention. On Hooton's view, to take an extreme case for illustration, head-hunting practices in New Guinea can be quite simply interpreted as manifestations of the particular bodily constitutions of the population. A critical examination of the quoted passage from Hooton's book shows most clearly the limited purview of his sociological framework of analysis.

Yet in another particular context—and it is this discriminatory inclusion of cultural considerations in one instance and not in others which appears especially indefensible—Hooton finds it advisable to distinguish between bootleggers from rural districts (largely those in the present sample) where "moon-shining" is a traditional private avocation and the metropolitan bootlegger who is generally foreign-born or of foreign parentage. Likewise, when confronted with the fact that Negro and Negroid criminals are "not unequivocally inferior in physique to the humbler non-college civilians, but only to the collegians, and, in their case, the criminal inferiority is restricted to stature and some few other metric features," Hooton decides that it is the "rigid social and economic straitjacket in which the Negro is confined" which "confuses" the (imputable or expectable) anthropological differences between the Negro criminal and civilian. (*CM*, 386.) In other words, when the expected differences do not occur, socio-economic factors may be at times involved; when they do occur, socio-economic factors are on the whole irrelevant and the differences are biologically determined. *In neither case, be it noted, is there a close examination of the actual role of these non-biological factors; they are introduced or neglected in accord with the disposition of the investigator.* If socio-economic factors "obscure" (putative) biological differences between the Negro criminal and civilian, why not investigate further to see whether or not they "accentuate" apparently biological differences in other instances? Of what avail is an accurate, refined and chaste anthropometry when interpretation devolves into a "medley of *ad hoc hypotheses*"? An occasional, unpredictable nod in the direction of social and economic factors is not an adequate substitute for their systematic appraisal.

The peculiar procedure adopted by Hooton may possibly be due to the uncertain status of sociological elements in his interpretative scheme. Thus, we find him remarking that "Opportunities for theft and temptations to homicide are alike, or virtually alike, for the blond and brunet, for the Negro and the White. It is therefore remarkable that we should be able to demonstrate even a minor organic factor in the intricate web of crime causation." (*AC*, 298; in this passage the author temporarily reverts to the modest position that the organic factor is only of minor importance.) Clearly it is only in an equivocal and misleading sense that "temptations to homicide" (a formulation which largely obscures the issue) are alike for the White from a bourgeois cultural area in Massachusetts, let us say, and the lower class Negro in rural Texas or, for that matter, the White of corresponding status and origin. Or does Hooton believe himself to have demonstrated that biological differences between the two samples explain the 24:1 ratio of Kentucky to Massachusetts criminals convicted of first degree murder? And may we likewise assume biological determinants of the fact that there are proportionately five times as many Texas criminals convicted of forgery and fraud as in the Massachusetts sample? Are these discrepancies readily ascribable to biological, quite apart from the sociocultural, differences between the native white populations of the two states?[11] Is it not significant that the

---

[11] In this connexion it would be profitable to consult H. C. Brearley, *Homicide in the United States* (Chapel Hill, N.C.: 1932).

forgery-and-fraud group among Negro and Negroid as well as among White criminals stem largely from Texas? Possibly that "glib and oily art" of stock-swindling is less a matter of bodily type than of petroliferous regions and an established pattern of promoting chimerical "gushers."

ECONOMISM

Crime and Poverty

W. A. BONGER

▬

What are the conclusions to be drawn from what has gone before? When we sum up the results that we have obtained it becomes plain that economic conditions occupy a much more important place in the etiology of crime than most authors have given them.

First we have seen that the present economic system and its consequences weaken the social feelings. The basis of the economic system of our day being exchange, the economic interests of men are necessarily found to be in opposition. This is a trait that capitalism has in common with other modes of production. But its principal characteristic is that the means of production are in the hands of a few, and most men are altogether deprived of them. Consequently, persons who do not possess the means of production are forced to sell their labor to those who do, and these, in consequence of their economic preponderance, force them to make the exchange for the mere necessaries of life, and to work as much as their strength permits.

This state of things especially stifles men's social instincts; it develops, on the part of those with power, the spirit of domination, and of insensibility to the ills of others, while it awakens jealousy and servility on the part of those who depend upon them. Further the contrary interests of those who have property, and the idle and luxurious life of some of them, also contribute to the weakening of the social instincts.

The material condition, and consequently the intellectual condition, of the proletariat are also a reason why the moral plane of that class is not high. The work of children brings them into contact with persons to associate with whom is fatal to their morals. Long working hours and monotonous labor brutalize those who are forced into them; bad housing conditions contribute also to debase the moral sense, as do the uncertainty of existence, and finally absolute poverty, the frequent consequence of sickness and unemployment. Ignorance and lack of training of any kind also contribute their quota. Most demoralizing of all is the status of the lower proletariat.

Source: W. A. Bonger, *Crime and Economic Conditions* (Boston: Little, 1916), pp. 667–672.

The economic position of woman contributes also to the weakening of the social instincts.

The present organization of the family has great importance as regards criminality. It charges the legitimate parents with the care of the education of the child; the community concerns itself with the matter very little. It follows that a great number of children are brought up by persons who are totally incapable of doing it properly. As regards the children of the proletariat, there can be no question of the education properly so-called, on account of the lack of means and the forced absence of one or both of the parents. The school tends to remedy this state of things, but the results do not go far enough. The harmful consequences of the present organization of the family make themselves felt especially in the case of the children of the lower proletariat, orphans, and illegitimate children. For these the community does but little, though their need of adequate help is the greatest.

Prostitution, alcoholism, and militarism, which result, in the last analysis, from the present social order, are phenomena that have demoralizing consequences.

As to the different kinds of crime, we have shown that the very important group of economic criminality finds its origin on the one side in the absolute poverty and the cupidity brought about by the present economic environment, and on the other in the moral abandonment and bad education of the children of the poorer classes. Then, professional criminals are principally recruited from the class of occasional criminals, who, finding themselves rejected everywhere after their liberation, fall lower and lower. The last group of economic crimes (fraudulent bankruptcy, etc.) is so intimately connected with our present mode of production, that it would not be possible to commit it under another.

The relation between sexual crimes and economic conditions is less direct; nevertheless these also give evidence of the decisive influence of these conditions. We have called attention to the four following points.

First, there is a direct connection between the crime of adultery and the present organization of society, which requires that the legal dissolution of a marriage should be impossible or very difficult.

Second, sexual crimes upon adults are committed especially by unmarried men; and since the number of marriages depends in its turn upon the economic situation, the connection is clear; and those who commit these crimes are further almost exclusively illiterate, coarse, raised in an environment almost without sexual morality, and regard the sexual life from the wholly animal side.

Third, the causes of sexual crime upon children are partly the same as those of which we have been speaking, with the addition of prostitution.

Fourth, alcoholism greatly encourages sexual assaults.

As to the relation between crimes of vengeance and the present constitution of society, we have noted that it produces conflicts without number; statistics have shown that those who commit them are almost without exception poor and uncivilized, and that alcoholism is among the most important causes of these crimes.

Infanticide is caused in part by poverty, and in part by the opprobrium incurred by the unmarried mother (an opprobrium resulting from the social utility of marriage).

Political criminality comes solely from the economic system and its consequences.

Finally, economic and social conditions are also important factors in the etiology of degeneracy, which is in its turn a cause of crime.

Upon the basis of what has gone before, we have a right to say that the part played by economic conditions in criminality is preponderant, even decisive.

This conclusion is of the highest importance for the prevention of crime. If it were principally the consequence of innate human qualities (atavism, for example), the pessimistic conclusion that crime is a phenomenon inseparably bound up with the social life would be well founded. But the facts show that it is rather the optimistic conclusion that we must draw, that where crime is the consequence of economic and social conditions, we can combat it by changing those conditions.

However important crime may be as a social phenomenon, however terrible may be the injuries and the evil that it brings upon humanity, the development of society will not depend upon the question as to what are the conditions which could restrain crime or make it disappear, if possible; the evolution of society will proceed independently of this question.

What is the direction that society will take under these continual modifications? This is not the place to treat fully of this subject. In my opinion the facts indicate quite clearly what the direction will be. The productivity of labor has increased to an unheard of degree, and will assuredly increase in the future. The concentration of the means of production into the hands of a few progresses continually; in many branches it has reached such a degree that the fundamental principle of the present economic system, competition, is excluded, and has been replaced by monopoly. On the other hand the working class is becoming more and more organized, and the opinion is very generally held among working-men that the causes of material and intellectual poverty can be eliminated only by having the means of production held in common.

Supposing that this were actually realized, what would be the consequences as regards criminality? Let us take up this question for a moment. Although we can give only personal opinions as to the details of such a society, the general outlines can be traced with certainty.

The chief difference between a society based upon the community of the means of production and our own is that material poverty would be no longer known. Thus one great part of economic criminality (as also one part of infanticide) would be rendered impossible, and one of the greatest demoralizing forces of our present society would be eliminated. And then, in this way those social phenomena so productive of crime, prostitution and alcoholism, would lose one of their principal factors. Child labor and overdriving would no longer take place, and bad housing, the source of much physical and moral evil, would no longer exist.

With material poverty there would disappear also that intellectual poverty which weighs so heavily upon the proletariat; culture would no longer be the privilege of some, but a possession common to all. The consequences of this upon criminality would be very important, for we have seen that even in our present society with its numerous conflicts, the members of the propertied classes, who have often but a veneer of civilization, are almost never guilty of crimes of vengeance. There is the more reason to admit that in a society where interests were not opposed, and where civilization was universal, these crimes would be no longer present, especially since alcoholism also proceeds in large part from the intellectual poverty of the poorer classes. And what is true of crimes of vengeance, is equally true of sexual crimes in so far as they have the same etiology.

A large part of the economic criminality (and also prostitution to a certain extent) has its origin in the cupidity excited by the present economic environment. In a society based upon the community of the means of production, great contrasts of fortune would, like commercial capital, be lacking, and thus cupidity would find no food. These crimes will not totally disappear so long as there has not been a redistribution of property according to the maxim, "to each according to his needs," something that will probably be realized, but not in the immediate future.

The changes in the position of woman which are taking place in our present society, will lead, under this future mode of production, to her economic independence, and consequently to her social independence as well. It is accordingly probable that the criminality of woman will increase in comparison with that of man during the transition period. But the final result will be the disappearance of the harmful effects of the economic and social preponderance of man.

As to the education of children under these new conditions it is difficult to be definite. However, it is certain that the community will concern itself seriously with their welfare. It will see to it that the children whose parents cannot or will not be responsible for them, are well cared for. By acting in this way it will remove one of the most important causes of crime. There is no doubt that the community will exercise also a strict control over the education of children; it cannot be affirmed, however, that the time will come when the children of a number of parents will be brought up together by capable persons; this will depend principally upon the intensity that the social sentiments may attain.

As soon as the interests of all are no longer opposed to each other, as they are in our present society, there will no longer be a question either of politics ("*a fortiori*" of political *crimes*) or of militarism.

Such a society will not only remove the causes which now make men egoistic, but will awaken, on the contrary, a strong feeling of altruism. We have seen that this was already the case with the primitive peoples, where their economic interests were not in opposition. In a larger measure this will be realized under a mode of production in common, the interests of all being the same.

In such a society there can be no question of crime properly so called. The eminent criminologist, Manouvrier, in treating of the prevention of crime expresses himself thus: "The maxim to apply is, act so that every man shall always have more interest in being useful to his fellows than in harming them." It is precisely in a society where the community of the means of production has been realized that this maxim will obtain its complete application. There will be crimes committed by pathological individuals, but this will come rather within the sphere of the physician than that of the judge. And then we may even reach a state where these cases will decrease in large measure, since the social causes of degeneracy will disappear, and procreation by degenerates be checked through the increased knowledge of the laws of heredity and the increasing sense of moral responsibility.

"It is society that prepares the crime," says the true adage of Quetelet. For all those who have reached this conclusion, and are not insensible to the sufferings of humanity, this statement is sad, but contains a ground of hope. It is sad, because society punishes severely those who commit the crime which she has herself prepared. It contains a ground of hope, since it promises to humanity the possibility of some day delivering itself from one of its most terrible scourges.

White-Collar Criminality

EDWIN H. SUTHERLAND

This paper is concerned with crime in relation to business. The economists are well acquainted with business methods but not accustomed to consider them from the point of view of crime; many sociologists are well acquainted with crime but not accustomed to consider it as expressed in business. This paper is an attempt to integrate these two bodies of knowledge. More accurately stated, it is a comparison of crime in the upper or white-collar class, composed of

Source: Edwin H. Sutherland, "White Collar Criminality," American Sociological Review, 5 (February, 1940), pp. 1–12. Reprinted by permission.

respectable or at least respected business and professional men, and crime in the lower class, composed of persons of low socioeconomic status. This comparison is made for the purpose of developing the theories of criminal behavior, not for the purpose of muckraking or of reforming anything except criminology.

The criminal statistics show unequivocally that crime, *as popularly conceived and officially measured,* has a high incidence in the lower class and a low incidence in the upper class; less than two percent of the persons committed to prisons in a year belong to the upper class. These statistics refer to criminals handled by the police, the criminal and juvenile courts, and the prisons, and to such crimes as murder, assault, burglary, robbery, larceny, sex offenses, and drunkenness, but exclude traffic violations.

The criminologists have used the case histories and criminal statistics derived from these agencies of criminal justice as their principal data. From them, they have derived general theories of criminal behavior. These theories are that, since crime is concentrated in the lower class, it is caused by poverty or by personal and social characteristics believed to be associated statistically with poverty, including feeblemindedness, psychopathic deviations, slum neighborhoods, and "deteriorated" families. This statement, of course, does not do justice to the qualifications and variations in the conventional theories of criminal behavior, but it presents correctly their central tendency.

The thesis of this paper is that the conception and explanations of crime which have just been described are misleading and incorrect, that crime is in fact not closely correlated with poverty or with the psychopathic and sociopathic conditions associated with poverty, and that an adequate explanation of criminal behavior must proceed along quite different lines. The conventional explanations are invalid principally because they are derived from biased samples. The samples are biased in that they have not included vast areas of criminal behavior of persons not in the lower class. One of these neglected areas is the criminal behavior of business and professional men, which will be analyzed in this paper.

The "robber barons" of the last half of the nineteenth century were white-collar criminals, as practically everyone now agrees. Their attitudes are illustrated by these statements: Colonel Vanderbilt asked, "You don't suppose you can run a railroad in accordance with the statutes, do you?" A. B. Stickney, a railroad president, said to sixteen other railroad presidents in the home of J. P. Morgan in 1890, "I have the utmost respect for you gentlemen, individually, but as railroad presidents I wouldn't trust you with my watch out of my sight." Charles Francis Adams said, "The difficulty in railroad management . . . lies in the covetousness, want of good faith, and low moral tone of railway managers, in the complete absence of any high standard of commercial honesty."

The present-day white-collar criminals, who are more suave and deceptive than the "robber barons," are represented by Krueger, Stavisky, Whitney, Mitchell, Foshay, Insull, the Van Sweringens, Musica-Coster, Fall, Sinclair, and many other merchant princes and captains of finance and industry, and by a host of lesser followers. Their criminality has been demonstrated again and again in the investigations of land offices, railways, insurance, munitions, banking, public utilities, stock exchanges, the oil industry, real estate, reorganization committees, receiverships, bankruptcies, and politics. Individual cases of such criminality are reported frequently, and in many periods more important crime news may be found on the financial pages of newspapers than on the front pages. White-collar criminality is found in every occupation, as can be discovered readily in casual conversation with a representative of an occupation by asking him, "What crooked practices are found in your occupation?"

White-collar criminality in business is expressed most frequently in the form of misrepresentation in financial statements of corporations, manipulation in the stock exchange, commercial bribery, bribery of public officials directly or indirectly in order to secure favorable contracts and legislation, misrepresentation in advertising and salesmanship, embezzlement and misapplication of funds, short weights and measures and misgrading of commodities, tax frauds, misapplication of funds in receiverships and bankruptcies. These are what Al Capone called "the legitimate rackets." These and many others are found in abundance in the business world.

In the medical profession, which is here used as an example because it is probably less criminalistic than some other professions, are found illegal sale of alcohol and narcotics, abortion, illegal services to underworld criminals, fraudulent reports and testimony in accident cases, extreme cases of unnecessary treatment, fake specialists, restriction of competition, and fee-splitting. Fee-splitting is a violation of a specific law in many states and a violation of the conditions of admission to the practice of medicine in all. The physician who participates in fee-splitting tends to send his patients to the surgeon who will give him the largest fee rather than to the surgeon who will do the best work. It has been reported that two thirds of the surgeons in New York City split fees, and that more than one half of the physicians in a central western city who answered a questionnaire on this point favored fee-splitting.

These varied types of white-collar crimes in business and the professions consist principally of violation of delegated or implied trust, and many of them can be reduced to two categories: misrepresentation of asset values and duplicity in the manipulation of power. The first is approximately the same as fraud or swindling; the second is similar to the double-cross. The latter is illustrated by the corporation director who, acting on inside information, purchases land which the corporation will need and sells it at a fantastic profit to his corporation. The principle of this duplicity is that the offender holds two antagonistic positions, one of which is a position of trust, which is violated, generally by misapplication of funds, in the interest of the other position. A football coach, permitted to referee a game in which his own team was playing, would illustrate this antagonism of positions. Such situations cannot be completely avoided in a complicated business structure, but many concerns make a practice of assuming such antagonistic functions and regularly violating the trust thus delegated to them. When compelled by law to make a separation of their functions, they make a nominal separation and continue by subterfuge to maintain the two positions.

An accurate statistical comparison of the crimes of the two classes is not available. The most extensive evidence regarding the nature and prevalence of white-collar criminality is found in the reports of the larger investigations to which reference was made. Because of its scattered character, that evidence is assumed rather than summarized here. A few statements will be presented, as illustrations rather than as proof of the prevalence of this criminality.

The Federal Trade Commission in 1920 reported that commercial bribery was a prevalent and common practice in many industries. In certain chain stores, the net shortage in weights was sufficient to pay 3.4 per cent on the investment in those commodities. Of the cans of ether sold to the Army in 1923–1925, 70 per cent were rejected because of impurities. In Indiana, during the summer of 1934, 40 per cent of the ice cream samples tested in a routine manner by the Division of Public Health were in violation of law. The Comptroller of the Currency in 1908 reported that violations of law were found in 75 per cent of the banks examined in a three months' period. Lie detector tests of all employees in several Chicago banks, supported in almost all cases by confessions, showed that 20 per cent of them had stolen bank property. A public accountant estimated, in the period prior to the Securities and Exchange Commission, that 80 per cent of the financial statements of corporations were misleading. James M. Beck said, "Diogenes would have been hard put to it to find an honest man in the Wall Street which I knew as a corporation lawyer" in (1916).

White-collar criminality in politics, which is generally recognized as fairly prevalent, has been used by some as a rough gauge by which to measure white-collar criminality in business. James A. Farley said, "The standards of conduct are as high among officeholders and politicians as they are in commercial life," and Cermak, while mayor of Chicago, said, "There is less graft in politics than in business." John Flynn wrote, "The average politician is the merest amateur in the gentle art of graft, compared with his brother in the field of business." And Walter Lippmann wrote, "Poor as they are, the standards of public life are so much more social than those of business that financiers who enter politics regard themselves as philanthropists."

These statements obviously do not give a precise measurement of the relative criminality of the white-collar class, but they are adequate evidence that crime is not so highly concentrated in the lower class as the usual statistics indicate. Also, these statements obviously do not mean that every business and professional man is a criminal, just as the usual theories do not mean that every man in the lower class is a criminal. On the other hand, the preceding statements refer in many cases to the leading corporations in America and are not restricted to the disreputable business and professional men who are called quacks, ambulance chasers, bucket-shop operators, dead-beats, and fly-by-night swindlers.[1]

The financial cost of white-collar crime is probably several times as great as the financial cost of all the crimes which are customarily regarded as the "crime problem." An officer of a chain grocery store in one year embezzled $600,000, which was six times as much as the annual losses from five hundred burglaries and robberies of the stores in that chain. Public enemies numbered one to six secured $130,000 by burglary and robbery in 1938, while the sum stolen by Krueger is estimated at $250,000,000, or nearly two thousand times as much. *The New York Times* in 1931 reported four cases of embezzlement in the United States with a loss of more than a million dollars each and a combined loss of nine million dollars. Although a million-dollar burglar or robber is practically unheard of, these million-dollar embezzlers are small-fry among white-collar criminals. The estimated loss to investors in one investment trust from 1929 to 1935 was $580,000,000, due primarily to the fact that 75 per cent of the values in the portfolios were in securities of affiliated companies, although it advertised the importance of diversification in investments and its expert services in selecting safe securities. In Chicago, the claim was made six years ago that householders had lost $54,000,000 in two years during the administration of a city sealer who granted immunity from inspection to stores which provided Christmas baskets for his constituents.

The financial loss from white-collar crime, great as it is, is less important than the damage to social relations. White-collar crimes violate trust and therefore create distrust, which lowers social morale and produces social disorganization on a large scale. Other crimes produce relatively little effect on social institutions or social organization.

White-collar crime is real crime. It is not ordinarily called crime, and calling it by this name does not make it worse, just as refraining from calling it crime does not make it better than it otherwise would be. It is called crime here in order to bring it within the scope of criminology, which is justified because it is in violation of the criminal law. The crucial question in this analysis is the criterion of violation of the criminal law. Conviction in the criminal court, which is sometimes suggested as the criterion, is not adequate because a large proportion of those who commit crimes are not convicted in criminal courts. This criterion, therefore, needs to be supplemented. When it is supplemented, the criterion of the crimes of one class must be kept consistent in general terms with the criterion of the crimes of the other class. The definition should not be

[1] Perhaps it should be repeated that "white-collar" (upper) and "lower" classes merely designate persons of high and low socioeconomic status. Income and amount of money involved in the crime are not the sole criteria. Many persons of "low" socioeconomic status are "white-collar" criminals in the sense that they are well-dressed, well-educated, and have high incomes, but "white-collar" as used in this paper means "respected," "socially accepted and approved," "looked up to." Some people in this class may not be well-dressed or well-educated, nor have high incomes, although the "upper" usually exceed the "lower" classes in these respects as well as in social status.

the spirit of the law for white-collar crimes and the letter of the law for other crimes, or in other respects be more liberal for one class than for the other. Since this discussion is concerned with the conventional theories of the criminologists, the criterion of white-collar crime must be justified in terms of the procedures of those criminologists in dealing with other crimes. The criterion of white-collar crimes, as here proposed, supplements convictions in the criminal courts in four respects, in each of which the extension is justified because the criminologists who present the conventional theories of criminal behavior make the same extension in principle.

First, other agencies than the criminal court must be included, for the criminal court is not the only agency which makes official decisions regarding violations of the criminal law. The juvenile court, dealing largely with offenses of the children of the poor, in many states is not under the criminal jurisdiction. The criminologists have made much use of case histories and statistics of juvenile delinquents in constructing their theories of criminal behavior. This justifies the inclusion of agencies other than the criminal court which deal with white-collar offenses. The most important of these agencies are the administrative boards, bureaus, or commissions, and much of their work, although certainly not all, consists of cases which are in violation of the criminal law. The Federal Trade Commission recently ordered several automobile companies to stop advertising their interest rate on installment purchases as 6 per cent, since it was actually $11\frac{1}{2}$ per cent. Also it filed complaint against *Good Housekeeping*, one of the Hearst publications, charging that its seals led the public to believe that all products bearing those seals had been tested in their laboratories, which was contrary to fact. Each of these involves a charge of dishonesty, which might have been tried in a criminal court as fraud. A large proportion of the cases before these boards should be included in the data of the criminologists. Failure to do so is a principal reason for the bias in their samples and the errors in their generalizations.

Second, for both classes, behavior which would have a reasonable expectancy of conviction if tried in a criminal court or substitute agency should be defined as criminal. In this respect, convictability rather than actual conviction should be the criterion of criminality. The criminologists would not hesitate to accept as data a verified case history of a person who was a criminal but had never been convicted. Similarly, it is justifiable to include white-collar criminals who have not been convicted, provided reliable evidence is available. Evidence regarding such cases appears in many civil suits, such as stockholders' suits and patent-infringement suits. These cases might have been referred to the criminal court but they were referred to the civil court because the injured party was more interested in securing damages than in seeing punishment inflicted. This also happens in embezzlement cases, regarding which surety companies have much evidence. In a short consecutive series of embezzlements known to a surety company, 90 per cent were not prosecuted because prosecution would interfere with restitution or salvage. The evidence in cases of embezzlement is generally conclusive, and would probably have been sufficient to justify conviction in all of the cases in this series.

Third, behavior should be defined as criminal if conviction is avoided merely because of pressure which is brought to bear on the court or substitute agency. Gangsters and racketeers have been relatively immune in many cities because of their pressure on prospective witnesses and public officials, and professional thieves, such as pickpockets and confidence men who do not use strong-arm methods, are even more frequently immune. The conventional criminologists do not hesitate to include the life histories of such criminals as data, because they understand the generic relation of the pressures to the failure to convict. Similarly, white-collar criminals are relatively immune because of the class bias of the courts and the power of their class to influence the implementation and administration of the law. This class bias affects not merely present-day courts but to a much greater degree affected the earlier courts which established the precedents and rules of procedure of the present-day courts. Consequently, it is justifiable to interpret the actual or potential failures of conviction in the light of known facts regarding the pressures brought to bear on the agencies which deal with offenders.

Fourth, persons who are accessory to a crime should be included among white-collar criminals as they are among other criminals. When the Federal Bureau of Investigation deals with a case of kidnapping, it is not content with catching the offenders who carried away the victim; they may catch and the court may convict twenty-five other persons who assisted by secreting the victim, negotiating the ransom, or putting the ransom money into circulation. On the other hand, the prosecution of white-collar criminals frequently stops with one offender. Political graft almost always involves collusion between politicians and business men but prosecutions are generally limited to the politicians. Judge Manton was found guilty of accepting $664,000 in bribes, but the six or eight important commercial concerns that paid the bribes have not been prosecuted. Pendergast, the late boss of Kansas City, was convicted for failure to report as a part of his income $315,000 received in bribes from insurance companies but the insurance companies which paid the bribes have not been prosecuted. In an investigation of an embezzlement by the president of a bank, at least a dozen other violations of law which were related to this embezzlement and involved most of the other officers of the bank and the officers of the clearing house, were discovered but none of the others was prosecuted.

This analysis of the criterion of white-collar criminality results in the conclusion that a description of white-collar criminality in general terms will be also a description of the criminality of the lower class. The respects in which the crimes of the two classes differ are the incidentals rather than the essentials of criminality. They differ principally in the implementation of the criminal laws which apply to them. The crimes of the lower class are handled by policemen, prosecutors, and judges, with penal sanctions in the form of fines, imprisonment, and death. The crimes of the upper class either result in no official action at all, or result in suits for damages in civil courts, or are handled by inspectors, and by administrative boards or commissions, with penal sanctions in the form of warnings, orders to cease and desist, occasionally the loss of a license, and only in extreme cases by fines or prison sentences. Thus, the white-collar criminals are segregated administratively from other criminals, and largely as a consequence of this are not regarded as real criminals by themselves, the general public, or the criminologists.

This difference in the implementation of the criminal law is due principally to the difference in the social position of the two types of offenders. Judge Woodward, when imposing sentence upon the officials of the H. O. Stone and Company, bankrupt real estate firm in Chicago, who had been convicted in 1933 of the use of the mails to defraud, said to them, "You are men of affairs, of experience, of refinement and culture, of excellent reputation and standing in the business and social world." That statement might be used as a general characterization of white-collar criminals for they are oriented basically to legitimate and respectable careers. Because of their social status they have a loud voice in determining what goes into the statutes and how the criminal law as it affects themselves is implemented and administered. This may be illustrated from the Pure Food and Drug Law. Between 1879 and 1906, 140 pure food and drug bills were presented in Congress and all failed because of the importance of the persons who would be affected. It took a highly dramatic performance by Dr. Wiley in 1906 to induce Congress to enact the law. That law, however, did not create a new crime, just as the federal Lindbergh kidnapping law did not create a new crime; it merely provided a more efficient implementation of a principle which had been formulated previously in state laws. When an amendment to this law, which would bring within the scope of its agents fraudulent statements made over the radio or in the press, was presented to Congress, the publishers and advertisers organized support and sent a lobby to Washington which successfully fought the amendment principally under the slogans of "freedom of the press" and "dangers of bureaucracy." This proposed amendment, also, would not have created a new crime, for the state laws already prohibited fraudulent statements over the radio or in the press; it would have implemented the law so it could have been enforced. Finally, the Administration has not been able to enforce the law as it has desired because of the pressures by the offenders against the law, sometimes brought to bear through the head of the Department of Agriculture, sometimes through congressmen who threaten cuts in the appropriation, and sometimes by others. The statement of Daniel Drew, a pious old fraud, describes the criminal law with some accuracy, "Law is like a cobweb; it's made for flies and the smaller kinds of insects, so to speak, but lets the big bumblebees break through. When technicalities of the law stood in my way, I have always been able to brush them aside easy as anything."

The preceding analysis should be regarded neither as an assertion that all efforts to influence legislation and its administration are reprehensible nor as a particularistic interpretation of the criminal law. It means only that the upper class has greater influence in moulding the criminal law and its administration to its own interests than does the lower class. The privileged position of white-collar criminals before the law results to a slight extent from bribery and political pressures, principally from the respect in which they are held and without special effort on their part. The most powerful group in medieval society secured relative immunity by "benefit of clergy," and now our most powerful groups secure relative immunity by "benefit of business or profession."

In contrast with the power of the white-collar criminals is the weakness of their victims. Consumers, investors, and stockholders are unorganized, lack technical knowledge, and cannot protect themselves. Daniel Drew, after taking a large sum of money by sharp practice from Vanderbilt in the Erie deal, concluded that it was a mistake to take money from a powerful man on the same level as himself and declared that in the future he would confine his efforts to outsiders, scattered all over the country, who wouldn't be able to organize and fight back. White-collar criminality flourishes at points where powerful business and professional men come in contact with persons who are weak. In this respect, it is similar to stealing candy from a baby. Many of the crimes of the lower class, on the other hand, are committed against persons of wealth and power in the form of burglary and robbery. Because of this difference in the comparative power of the victims, the white-collar criminals enjoy relative immunity.

Embezzlement is an interesting exception to white-collar criminality in this respect. Embezzlement is usually theft from an employer by an employee, and the employee is less capable of manipulating social and legal forces in his own interest than is the employer. As might have been expected, the laws regarding embezzlement were formulated long before laws for the protection of investors and consumers.

The theory that criminal behavior in general is due either to poverty or to the psychopathic and sociopathic conditions associated with poverty can now be shown to be invalid for three reasons. First, the generalization is based on a biased sample which omits almost entirely the behavior of white-collar criminals. The criminologists have restricted their data, for reasons of convenience and ignorance rather than of principle, largely to cases dealt with in criminal courts and juvenile courts, and these agencies are used principally for criminals from the lower economic strata. Consequently, their data are grossly biased from the point of view of the economic status of criminals and their generalization that criminality is closely associated with poverty is not justified.

Second, the generalization that criminality is closely associated with poverty obviously does not apply to white-collar criminals. With a small number of exceptions, they are not in poverty, were not reared in slums or badly deteriorated families, and are not feebleminded or psychopathic. They were seldom problem children in their earlier years and did not appear in juvenile courts or child guidance clinics. The proposition, derived from the data used by the conventional criminologists, that "the criminal of today was the problem child of yesterday" is seldom true of white-collar criminals. The idea that the causes of criminality are to be found almost exclusively in childhood similarly is fallacious. Even if poverty is extended to include the economic stresses which afflict business in a period of depression, it is not closely correlated with white-collar criminality. Probably at no time within fifty years have white-collar crimes in the field of investments and of corporate management been so extensive as during the boom period of the twenties.

Third, the conventional theories do not even explain lower class criminality. The sociopathic and psychopathic factors which have been emphasized doubtless have something to do with crime causation, but these factors have not been related to a general process which is found both in white-collar criminality and lower class criminality and therefore they do not explain the criminality of either class. They may explain the manner or method of crime—why lower class criminals commit burglary or robbery rather than false pretenses.

In view of these defects in the conventional theories, an hypothesis that will explain both white-collar criminality and lower class criminality is needed. For reasons of economy, simplicity, and logic, the hypothesis should apply to both classes, for this will make possible the analysis of causal factors freed from the encumbrances of the administrative devices which have led criminologists astray. Shaw and McKay and others, working exclusively in the field of lower class crime, have found the conventional theories inadequate to account for variations within the data of lower class crime and from that point of view have been working toward an explanation of crime in terms of a more general social process. Such efforts will be greatly aided by the procedure which has been described.

The hypothesis which is here suggested as a substitute for the conventional theories is that white-collar criminality, just as other systematic criminality, is learned; that it is learned in direct or indirect associations with those who already practice the behavior; and that those who learn this criminal behavior are segregated from frequent and intimate contacts with law-abiding behavior. Whether a person becomes a criminal or not is determined largely by the comparative frequency and intimacy of his contacts with the two types of behavior. This may be called the process of differential association. It is a genetic explanation both of white-collar criminality and lower class criminality. Those who become white-collar criminals generally start their careers in good neighborhoods and good homes, graduate from colleges with some idealism, and with little selection on their part, get into particular business situations in which criminality is practically a folkway and are inducted into that system of behavior just as into any other folkway. The lower class criminals generally start their careers in deteriorated neighborhoods and families, find delinquents at hand from whom they acquire the attitudes toward, and techniques of, crime through association with delinquents and in partial segregation from law-abiding people. The essentials of the process are the same for the two classes of criminals. This is not entirely a process of assimilation, for inventions are frequently made, perhaps more frequently in white-collar crime than in lower class crime. The inventive geniuses for the lower class criminals are generally professional criminals, while the inventive geniuses for many kinds of white-collar crime are generally lawyers.

A second general process is social disorganization in the community. Differential association culminates in crime because the community is not organized solidly against that behavior. The law is pressing in one direction, and other forces are pressing in the opposite direction. In business, the "rules of the game" conflict with the legal rules. A business man who wants to obey the law is driven by his competitors to adopt their methods. This is well illustrated by the persistence of commercial bribery in spite of the strenuous efforts of business organizations to eliminate it. Groups and individuals are individuated; they are more concerned with their specialized group or individual interests than with the larger welfare. Consequently, it is not possible for the community to present a solid front in opposition to crime. The Better Business Bureaus and Crime Commissions, composed of business and professional men, attack burglary, robbery, and cheap swindles, but overlook the crimes of their own members. The forces which impinge on the lower class are similarly in conflict. Social disorganization affects the two classes in similar ways.

I have presented a brief and general description of white-collar criminality on a framework of argument regarding theories of criminal behavior. That argument, stripped of the description, may be stated in the following propositions:

1. White-collar criminality is real criminality, being in all cases in violation of the criminal law.

2. White-collar criminality differs from lower class criminality principally in an implementation of the criminal law which segregates white-collar criminals administratively from other criminals.

3. The theories of the criminologists that crime is due to poverty or to psychopathic and sociopathic conditions statistically associated with poverty are invalid because, first, they are derived from samples which are grossly biased with respect to socioeconomic status; second, they do not apply to the white-collar criminals; and third, they do not even explain the criminality of the lower class, since the factors are not related to a general process characteristic of all criminality.

4. A theory of criminal behavior which will explain both white-collar criminality and lower class criminality is needed.

5. An hypothesis of this nature is suggested in terms of differential association and social disorganization.

CHAPTER 3

PSYCHOLOGISM

Crime and the Psychoanalyst
FRANZ ALEXANDER

▬

The psychoanalytic study of unconscious psychic life leads to the conviction that every part of the human personality, which is socially adjusted, represents a later and comparatively labile product of a special evolution.

However, within the innermost nucleus of the personality, which is both quantitatively and dynamically much more powerful, it is impossible to differentiate normal from criminal impulses. The human being enters the world as a criminal, i.e., socially not adjusted. During the first years of his life, the human individual preserves his criminality to the fullest degree. His actual social adjustment begins only at the time after the Œdipus complex is overcome. This happens during the so-called latency period which was described by Freud. This period begins between the ages of four and six, and ends at puberty. It is at this period that the development of the criminal begins to differentiate itself from that of the normal. The future normal individual succeeds (mostly in the latency period) in partly repressing his genuine criminal instinctual drives, and thus cuts them out of motor expression and partly in transforming them into socially acceptable striving; the future criminal more or less fails in carrying out this adjustment.

The criminal carries out in his actions his natural unbridled instinctual drives; he acts as the child would act if it only could. The repressed, and therefore unconscious criminality of the normal man finds a few socially harmless outlets, like the dream and phantasy life, neurotic symptoms and also some transitional forms of behavior which are less harmless, like duelling, boxing, bull fights and, occasionally, the free expression of one's criminality in war.

No better proof for the general criminality of mankind could be found than the proof which would be brought about by the daring experiment of depriving, say, the Spanish nation of its bull fights, the Americans of their boxing and football games, old Europe of its soldier game and the world of its penal codes.

Source: Reprinted with permission of the publisher from *The Criminal, the Judge and the Public* by Franz Alexander, Copyright 1931 by The Macmillan Company. Copyright 1956 by the Free Press, A Corporation. Pp. 34–41.

The universal criminality of man of to-day demands violent, purely physical outlets; without them it would become transformed into a battle of all against all.

The only difference between the criminal and the normal individual is that the normal man partially controls his criminal drives and finds outlets for them in socially harmless activities. This power of controlling, and of the domestication of the primitive, unsocial tendencies is acquired by the individual as a result of education. In other words, criminality, generally speaking, is not a congenital defect but a defect in the bringing up; this statement does not cover certain borderline cases which should be considered separately. Our contention will become clearer if we could imagine that all the children of the world between the ages of two to six should suddenly become physically superior to the adult and were thus able to dominate the adult to the same degree as the adult dominates the child. These children, let us imagine further, would then set themselves to act out all their phantasies. These Gulliverian giant children dominating a world of dwarf-like adults would present a hundred-per-cent criminality in action.

The first drive in relation to the outside world which the newly born individual experiences is the drive to grasp, to dominate. This drive in its earliest expression appears in the form of the cannibalistic possession of the breast of the mother, a sort of a partial eating up of the mother. The psychic content of this drive on this level is known in the psychoanalytic theory of instinctual drives as the *oral-sadistic* phase of development of the individual. The pregenital sexuality of the suckling finds its satisfaction in the mouth activity while sucking the mother's breast, the nipple or the bottle or the thumb. In this phase one is naturally unable to find any trace of the future social attitude, i.e., the tendency to consider the interests of others.

Disturbances in the normal functioning during this instinctual phase, particularly any educational mistake in the process of weaning, might influence the educability of the individual along the lines of social relationships. Individuals who at every frustration of a wish show a tendency to violent action, who react to any postponement of a pleasure with uncontrollable impatience, prove frequently to have been orally spoiled children; these individuals serve as a proof of how exceptionally long indulgence during the period of sucking reappears with a vengeance in an adult.[1] But weaning must inevitably come some day, and such spoiled babies respond to it with spiteful resistance; they do not want to give up a rightfully acquired habit. Abraham and Alexander[2] consider that the deepest roots of kleptomania are to be found in the history of this period.

The child finds itself compelled for the first time to submit to the wishes of the adult when it begins to be taught habits of cleanliness. At first the child

[1] Cf. Abraham—*Collected Papers*, London, 1927.
[2] Cf. Alexander—*Castration Complex and Character*, 1922.

experiences a definite pleasure in relation to its excretory functions; this pleasure consists either of holding back or expressing the excreta; this pleasure, as well as the coprophilic tendencies of the child, is considerably interfered with when the adult begins to present demands for orderliness, cleanliness, and propriety.

Interference with its primitive instinctual drives brings the child to the realization that its sovereignty is badly encroached upon; it becomes impossible for the child to utilize the excretory processes whenever and in whatever manner it wishes, and thus to derive pleasure from them whenever it wishes, in whatever manner and degree it wishes. One of the chief characteristics of this anal erotism is that it gives one a sense of power, a feeling that one's pleasures do not depend upon others; for, in contrast to breast or bottle, which can and are always taken away and therefore are connected with a feeling of insecurity, the excrements are products created by the child itself, and take the place of the breast or bottle as a source of pleasure. In other words, the source of oral pleasure is always in the hands of the adult, while the fecal masses, hidden within the body, are outside the reach of grown-ups who want to dominate.

The psychoanalytic literature has not yet considered with sufficient detail this strong drive for independence, the spite with which it is connected, and the high self-esteem of the anal phase of development. It was first recognized by Freud as stubbornness of the anal erotic; it is a sort of overcompensation for the sad experiences met with in the oral phase in which the child depended for pleasure on the whim of the mother.

However, sooner or later, the child learns to control and regulate its sphincter activity, because it is afraid of being censured and punished by the adults. The first crime which all humans, without exception, sooner or later commit is the violation of the prescription for cleanliness. Under the rule of this penal code of the nursery, man for the first time becomes acquainted with the punishment which the world metes out to individual transgressors. Ferenczi,[3] therefore, is right when he speaks of the "sphincter morality" as the beginning and foundation of adult human morality. As a prototype of certain refractory criminals who persist in their spiteful rejection of social demands, one can imagine a baby sitting on its little chamber pot persistently rejecting any demands coming from the outside; it sits in this sovereign position and feels superior to the grownups.

At the moment when the child begins to impose inhibitions on the demands of its own sphincter, it makes the first decisive step toward the adjustment to the outside world; at that moment it creates an inhibitory agency within its own personality, and this agency from now on demands from within what the outside world demanded heretofore. In other words, a definite part of the child's personality identifies itself with the demands of the person who is bringing it up. We thus deal here with an identification with a *demand*; i.e., a partial identification with a person; at a later phase the child will identify itself with an adult *person* as a whole instead of with a demand only.

---

[3] Ferenczi, *Psychoanalysis of Sexual Habits* in *Collected Papers*.

This education to cleanliness becomes a prototype for the future restrictions of instinctual life; a disturbance during this phase of development may naturally serve as a cause of a future disturbance in one's social adjustment.

The anal character traits which were described by Freud, Jones, and Abraham, in their exaggerated form present a number of anti-social and criminal characteristics.

The exaggerated, unsocial, stubborn bluntness of some violators of the law corresponds to the unyielding persistence of infantile anal spite. The characteristic self-centered stubbornness of the anal character acquires in the majority of criminals the form of proud, inaccessible spite, which is directed against all humanity.

In the course of the development of every child we find that its interests gradually broaden, and in addition to its relationship to its own physiological processes it tries to establish a relationship with the outer world. The instinctual drives in the phases of oral and anal development which were just mentioned were psychologically concerned with intake of food and its elimination; instinctual pleasure was derived from these two processes. However, in view of the fact that they begin to be directed toward objects of the outer world, they approach for the first time a psychological level of the adult individual. As is to be expected, the first objects of the outside world toward which the child's interest is directed are the immediate members of the family. Thus, the relationship of the child to father, mother, brothers and sisters, becomes the central problem of the future adult individual. The psychological management of these relationships on the part of the growing human being becomes definitely the decisive factor in the whole development and functioning of the adult person. After thirty years of therapeutic work and psychoanalytical research this point may be considered definitely proved. The way in which the child overcomes the conflicts arising from this situation determines whether it will develop into a healthy or sick individual, or whether his general behavior will be that of a socially adjusted person or that of a criminal. We should like to emphasize now, and we shall be able to prove later in these pages, that psychoneurosis and criminality are defects in one's social adjustment; they hardly differ from one another in their respective psychological contents; the differences are those of psychological dynamics. Both the neurotic and the criminal fell victims to their incapacity of finding a socially acceptable solution of the conflicts which the relationships to the various members of the family engendered. The neurotic expresses symbolically by means of his symptoms, which are socially innocuous, the same things which the criminal does by means of real actions. This important fact opens to us a promising method of study; we can understand the psychological content of a criminal act through the psychoanalysis of the neuroses.

We thus come to the fundamental problem as to which are the circumstances responsible for the fact that, in some individuals, the unconscious criminal phantasy finds it sufficient to come to expression in the substitution form of a neurotic symptom, while in other individuals it demands the motor expression in the form of criminal acts. This problem requires the consideration of the economic and structural characteristics of the psychic apparatus; it is a problem dealing with the relative strength of inhibitory psychic agencies as compared with the pressure coming from the undomesticated remnants of our instinctual drives. We shall be able to throw light on the problem if we consider the data acquired by psychoanalysis with regard to the structural and dynamic development of the human personality.

It is self-evident that, in order to gain an understanding of criminality, we shall have to investigate the process by means of which a socially adjusted Ego develops out of a great homogeneous reservoir of instincts which originally were unsocial; this reservoir of instinctual drives is called the Id.

The two pregenital phases of adjustment which were described above, oral and anal, are but preparatory to the first great necessity, which demands that the object relationship to parents and siblings be transformed into relationships of a social nature.

Psychoanalysis and Crime

DAVID FELDMAN

▬▬

Psychoanalysis is, of course, best known for its contributions to the understanding and treatment of mental disorders. Yet, almost from its inception, psychoanalytic theory was conceived by Sigmund Freud as having equal explanatory value in areas quite beyond what is usually considered the realm of the psychopathological. And in accordance with this conception, psychoanalysts have, over the years, expanded their theoretical interests to include very nearly every facet of the subject-matters treated in the social sciences and arts.[1] But perhaps the most assiduously cultivated extracurricular interest for psychoanalysis has been the problem of criminal behavior. Indeed, what may be called psychoanalytic criminology is already close to half a century in age and remains still among the foremost influences in shaping current programs of dealing with criminal and delinquent offenders. However, as has been the case in all of the behavioral disciplines, the fundamental theoretical framework of psychoanalysis has received differential interpretations, resulting in the

Source: Prepared especially for this volume.

[1] See, e.g., the range of subject-matters covered in S. Lorand (ed.), *Psychoanalysis Today* (New York, 1944) and in G. Roheim (ed.), *Psychoanalysis and the Social Sciences* (New York, 1947).

development of diverse psychoanalytic accounts of criminality. In this survey of psychoanalytic criminology what follows, then, is, first, a brief sketch of its underlying theoretical orientation and, second, a consideration of some of the important recent trends in the various applications of that orientation.

Logically, psychoanalytic theory starts out with the commonplace, but crucial, assumption that all human behavior is motivated and, hence, goal-oriented or teleological in character. To begin with, this means that human behavior is functional, that it is undertaken to fulfill a given need or desire, and that it has consequences for other patterns of behavior. But since the same action can have many different purposes, it follows that neither the motives nor the functions of any given act can be ascertained by observing the overt action itself. This implies that, as a matter of general principle, a proper grasp of human behavior requires that this behavior be understood in terms of the subjective meanings and significances which the actor himself attaches to his action. This principal of subjective understanding now occupies a well-established, though not undisputed, position in contemporary sociological theory. But for psychoanalysis the situation is further complicated by its concept that the subjective meaning which an actor attaches to his action may be quite unconscious, so that the actor himself is consciously unaware of the functions he imputes to his own action. Thus, in addition to any manifest functions which an overt act may have for the actor, the same act can also have latent functions which, while of equal or more importance, remain unconscious.[2]

With respect to the problem of criminal behavior, this principle of motivational functionalism implies that a concentration of analysis on the manifest criminal act itself cannot hope to provide a proper etiological understanding of the crime. For like any other behavior, criminal behavior is a form of self-expression and what is intended to be expressed in the act of crime is not only unobservable in the act itself, but also may even be beyond the awareness of the criminal actor himself. So, for example, an overt criminal act of stealing may be undertaken for the attainment of purposes which are far removed from, and even contrary to, that of simple illegal aggrandizement; indeed, it may even be, as shall be seen in the sequel, that the criminal, in stealing, seeks not material gain by self-punishment. The etiological basis of a criminal act can, therefore, be understood only in terms of the functions, latent as well as manifest, which the act was intended to accomplish.[3]

---

[2] It is worth emphasizing that the distinction between manifest and latent functions, currently something of an issue in sociological discussion, was not imported for use in the present context. The distinction is actually very much a part of the psychoanalytic conception of motivation and was originated by Freud in his theory of dreams. In fact, it was Merton who popularized the notion in sociology and borrowed the terms from Freud. See R. K. Merton, *Social Theory and Social Structure* (Glencoe, Ill., rev. ed., 1957), p. 60 ff.

[3] The concept of motivational functionalism is most explicitly formulated in psychoanalytic criminology in W. Healy and A. Bronner, *New Light on Delinquency and Its Treatment* (New Haven, Conn., 1936). Today, of course, functionalism is highly fashionable, and it is no longer required to be a Freudian to think of crime in terms of its latent functions. See, e.g., A. K. Cohen, *Delinquent Boys* (Glencoe, Ill., 1955), which sets down a theory of the latent functions of gang delinquency.

But, of course, to know that a criminal act is functional and may have both manifest and latent functions is not yet to know anything about the specific causal determinants of that act. Accordingly, the methodological principle of motivational functionalism has to be supplemented with substantive concepts of the actual functions involved. Now crime, however it is defined, represents a behavioral violation of one or more social norms. Since the cognition of, and conformity to, social norms are resultants of the socialization process, it follows that the individual who engages in a pattern of criminal behavior has, in some sense, been defectively socialized or that the norms demanding his conformity are themselves, in some sense, defective. In either case, it also follows that pre-requisite to a resolution of the problem of crime causation is a theoretical explication of the processes comprising the socialization of the individual. And such an analysis is precisely what constitutes the heart of the psychoanalytic conception of ego psychology.

In a gross way, it may be said that, as an analytic schema of the socialization process, psychoanalytic ego psychology revolves around, and reflects, the fact that the human individual, born into a family, group, and class, has in some way to come to terms with the operative norms which are arbitrarily imposed upon him as regulators of his behavior. Thus there is a certain tension built up within the individual as a result of the competing requirements of the social group and his own private and original impulses. In the Freudian view, these original impulses are part of the biological equipment of the individual and are essentially antisocial in nature, consisting of the sexual, aggressive, and de-structive "instinct."[4] Left to his own devices, therefore, the individual would necessarily undertake actions which, in substance and aim, run counter to the normative demands of his social group. But since he is not allowed such license and is, moreover, for a long time after his birth, in a physical condition of total helplessness and dependency, thereby making him highly susceptible to both the danger of his environment and the threat of punishment, the individual has little choice in the matter and must find means of adapting himself to the "reality" of his situation. And he must do so because his needs for the support, protection, and acceptance of his family and group are far more urgent than are his needs to satisfy his antisocial drives.

However, one fundamental aspect of being born dependent and powerless is that the individual is, willy-nilly, subjected to an inexorable process of indoctrina-tion in the group norms under a pedagogical technique consisting largely of a differential application of reward and punishment (love and rejection) and relying heavily on the individual's role-taking capacity. The individual manages his adaptation in primarily two ways: on the one hand, he resorts to reasoned

---

[4] It should be noted that Freud's German term for "instinct" is "trieb," which, as Freudians are forever pointing out, does not have the connotations of rigidity and immutability associated with the English usage of "instinct." See, e.g., the discussion in O. Fenichel, *The Psychoanalytic Theory of Neurosis* (New York, 1945), pp. 12 f, 54 ff.

calculations and compromises of what can and cannot be done, which of his original impulses he may seek to satisfy with impunity and which he must not act upon lest he suffer penalty. And, on the other hand, he incorporates and accepts for himself the group norms and evaluates his own impulses in their terms. This he does by means of identification, involving what Mead called "taking the role of the other," first with the immediate authority figures in his life, then with an expanding number of "significant others," and lastly with the social group as a whole representing the "generalized others." [5]

In short, there are three basic psychological processes operating within the individual comprising the original impulses, the mechanisms of adjustment, and the internalized group norms. Each of these processes tends to be in potential or active conflict with the others, and the individual is able to maintain a stable existence only to the extent that a viable "balance of power" obtains among them and functions to temper the conflicts and prevent an explosive eruption. And this balance, in turn, depends upon a minimally favorable equilibrium between the kinds and amounts of compensatory gratifications and enforced renunciations the individual experiences. [6]

Combining now the principle of motivational functionalism and the socialization schema of ego psychology, the basic etiological formula of psychoanalytic criminology becomes apparent; it simply states that criminality is undertaken as a means of maintaining psychic balance or as an effort to rectify a psychic balance which has been disrupted. On this general formula, a substantial consensus of opinion has been attained among psychoanalytic criminologists. At the same time, however, a considerable diversity of views has developed as to exactly what it is in the socialization of the individual which compels him to resort to crime and as to precisely how criminal behavior fulfills the function of helping retain psychic balance. In fact, there are at present at least five more or less contrasting psychoanalytic views available for consideration.

Among the first and still persistently maintained interpretations of the etiological formula is the view that criminality is a form of neurosis. The criminal is a person suffering from a neurotic illness which, in no fundamental way, differs from any of the other forms of neurotic phenomena. Psychodynamically, so it is held, the only difference between the common symptomatic neurosis and criminal neurosis is merely that the latter is alloplastically manifested in overt acts, while the former finds expression in the autoplastic

---

[5] G. H. Mead, *Mind, Self, and Society* (Chicago, 1934), chs. III and IV.

[6] In Freudian theory the three psychic processes are referred to as id, ego, and superego, respectively. But, of course, these analytic categories entail a good deal more than has here been set down. The primary sources of ego psychology are S. Freud, *The Ego and The Id* (London, 1947) and S. Freud, *The Problem of Anxiety* (New York, 1936); less technical discussions are contained in S. Freud, *New Introductory Lectures on Psychoanalysis* (New York, 1933) and S. Freud, *An Outline of Psychoanalysis* (New York, 1936). The Freudian schema of socialization has been taken over practically intact by contemporary structural-functionalism in sociology and has already found expression in the textbook literature. See the interesting discussion in H. M. Johnson, *Sociology: A Systematic Introduction* (New York, 1960), ch. 5.

symbolism of symptom formation. But exactly like the symptoms of the sympto-matic neurosis, the criminal acts of the criminal neurosis have the function of providing neurotic gratifications and resolutions of unconscious conflicts over which the individual has partially lost control. Generally, it is believed that the criminal neurotic suffers from a compulsive need for punishment to alleviate intolerable guilt feelings stemming from unconscious, and poorly sublimated, incestuous strivings. Thus the criminal engages in illegal activity so that he may be apprehended and penalized for his crimes. From the subjective standpoint of the criminal, the real crime demanding punishment is his incestuous wish; but by a form of neurotic compromise, the punishment he receives for his overt crimes functions to expiate his guilt and ameliorate the debilitating effects of his emotional conflicts.[7]

A more recent, and contrasting, conception of the etiological formula holds that, far from suffering guilt and needing punishment, the criminal feels no guilt and strenuously avoids being subjected to penalty. On this view, the criminal is an "antisocial character" who has been defectively socialized so that he is unable to cope properly with the normative requirements of his external situation. Realistically, every individual is frequently compelled to postpone gratification of his needs or to modify them in a manner more accept-able to his group and to himself. But the antisocial character, due to certain deformities in his rearing, is chronically unable to orient his conduct in accord-ance with the dictates of this "reality principle." He simply cannot endure temporary frustrations and he cannot postpone the quest for satisfaction, and so he impulsively engages in antisocial, criminal behavior as a means of seeking immediate gratification. Because the internalization of social norms is, for the antisocial character, in a weakened state, he has no strong internal guides to evaluate his actions; and because his mechanisms of adjustment are poorly developed, he permits himself kinds of activities which a properly socialized individual would not undertake. Basically, he regards his behavior and his relationships to others sheerly in terms of pleasure and penalty. If actions can provide pleasure without penalty he will perform them, and if, upon mis-judgment, he is penalized for these actions, he does not react with remorse but with hatred and frustration at having to put up with displeasure.[8]

A third, and extremely influential, interpretation of the etiological formula is that criminal activity is undertaken as a means of obtaining substitutive and compensatory gratifications of needs and desires which would ordinarily be met and fulfilled within the network of familial relationships. These are the needs

[7] An early and still influential statement of this view is F. Alexander and H. Staub, *The Criminal, The Judge, and the Public* (Glencoe, Ill., rev. ed., 1956). The original edition was published in translation in 1931.

[8] The concept of the antisocial character is most closely associated with K. Friedlander, *The Psychoanalytical Approach to Juvenile Delinquency* (New York, 1945); a briefer statement is K. Friedlander, "Latent Delinquency and Ego Development," in K. R. Eissler (ed.), *Searchlights on Delinquency* (New York, 1949).

and desires which are fundamental in determining the nature of the individual's maturation and involve such matters as the inherent needs for security, recognition, acceptance, adequacy, status, and self-assertion. When the individual finds that these basic needs are frustrated in the interpersonal channels of his family environment, he inevitably experiences painful feelings of being thwarted and deprived. In these circumstances, it is a natural response for the individual to divert his activities into the illegal channels of delinquency and crime as a means of securing some substitute satisfactions and to pacify his frustrations. Where his family fails, the delinquent gang can succeed in giving the individual the necessary sense of acceptance, recognition, and adequacy; and if the family cannot, or will not, allow outlets for the individual's expression of independence, self-assertion, and self-direction, he may wreak his vengeance and demonstrate his inner capacities to his own satisfaction in the act of crime. Criminality, therefore, is a consequence of a disturbance in the psychic balance and the criminal or delinquent is an emotionally frustrated and perturbed individual who unconsciously seeks in his offensive actions a resolution to his emotional problems in the form of compensatory satisfactions which have been denied him in his familial relationships.[9]

A quite recently developed fourth conception of the etiological formula is somewhat akin to the idea of the criminal as an antisocial character. However, according to this newer view the deficiency within the criminal stems not from impoverished mechanisms of adjustment and internalized norms, but from the unconscious permissiveness of parental figures who are themselves ambivalent towards the acceptance of the norms prohibiting criminality. The delinquent or criminal, it is held, suffers from "superego lacunae," or unformed segments in his normative orientation; he may be fully oriented toward acceptance of most social norms, while toward some other norms he has not evolved an orientation of acceptance and conformity. These lacunae derive from similar defective normative orientations in his parents who unconsciously encourage criminal activities in their child as a means of obtaining vicarious gratifications for their own unconscious strivings. Thus the child, seeking the approbation of his parents, engages in delinquent acts because he believes that his delinquencies would be gratifying to them or because he rightly senses that such actions can be used as a weapon in his relations with his family.[10]

The concept of superego lacunae seems to hint slightly at a notion that the norms prohibiting criminal behavior are not strongly or consistently maintained as regulators of conduct; there is at least something of an implication that, aside from any psychological deficiencies within the criminal, criminality may also ensue from the internalization of defective norms. This implication has

---

[9] The most prominent statement of this position is W. Healy and A. Bronner, *op. cit.*, which has practically become a classic of psychoanalytic criminology.

[10] For an exposition of this view, see A. M. Johnson, "Sanctions for Superego Lacunae of Adolescents," in K. R. Eissler, *op. cit.*, and A. M. Johnson, "Juvenile Delinquency," in S. Arieti (ed.), *American Handbook of Psychiatry* (New York, 1959), Vol. I.

recently received some further development in yet a fifth interpretation of the etiological formula which, in many respects, bears a close resemblance to the theory of anomie currently so popular in sociological circles.[11] According to this psychoanalytic conception of anomie, criminal behavior occurs in the context of a social situation in which an extremely high value is placed on the individual achievement of economic success, but which, at the same time, stringently limits the legitimate means of obtaining this goal. The value of individual initiative and success, it is maintained, is an historical hangover from the period of the open frontier, when the emphasis on personal effort and achievement was feasible economically and, therefore, a natural ideological outgrowth of the prevailing conditions. Since that period, however, the available opportunities for achieving success have been progressively exhausted, and a heavy expenditure of individual initiative can no longer be expected to be rewarded by economic success. But while the underlying socioeconomic conditions for achieving success have changed, the ideological superstructure has been retained. In these circumstances, there must develop definite tensions for the individual who has been socialized to incorporate the norms of personal initiative and achievement and who finds himself placed socially in a situation of deprivation or poverty where the legitimate exercise of these values can only lead to frustration and failure. Yet this discrepancy between social structure and cultural norms does not uniformly affect all individuals in like degree; it will, instead, have its greatest psychological impact upon those individuals who are least equipped psychically to undertake the unrewarding pursuit of success. Such individuals who are, by nature, more passive, compliant, and dependent than the average are trapped in an intolerable conflict with their internalization of the norms of personal achievement. Compelled to define their passivity and dependency as personal weakness and incompetence, they will tend to repress these qualities and, by the process of reaction-formation, overconform to the social norms by adopting an excessively individualistic aggressiveness. But barred from success by their social position and the social structure, this exaggerated individualism will naturally find outlet in criminal behavior, which serves the dual purpose of denying their unconscious dependency while accruing material benefits. And so it is the social structure which generates tendencies towards criminality among select individuals who, as a result of a combination of social position and psychic nature, are unable to make the necessary adjustments.[12]

Now looking over these variant interpretations of the same basic etiological formula, it is readily noted that they form something of a sequence ranging in scope from an exclusive emphasis on internal factors operating within the

---

[11] The sociological theory of anomie was originally developed by Durkheim and further extended by Merton. See R. K. Merton, *op. cit.*, chs. IV and V.

[12] A clear statement of the psychoanalytic conception of anomie can be found in F. Alexander, *Our Age of Unreason*, p. 301 ff. An earlier adumbration of this view is F. Alexander and W. Healy, *The Roots of Crime* (New York, 1935).

psychological constitution of the criminal to a fairly liberal concentration on external situational conditions confronting him. Partially, at least, this shift in perspective probably derives from the obvious vulnerability of the idea that all of the etiological sources of criminality are to be located in the personality of the criminal. Thus the notion of the neurotic criminal compulsively intent on self-punishment is plainly vitiated by the fact that most criminals seem to expend a great deal of energy and effort on escaping the clutches of the law and, on the whole, as is commonly acknowledged, are inordinately successful at it. Moreover, available evidence of the mental states of convicted criminals unmistakably points to the conclusion that the vastly major portion of them are simply not neurotic.[13] Again, the concept of the criminals as an antisocial character bent on obtaining immediate gratifications patently ignores the commonplace fact that criminality frequently demands much laborious training and planning of techniques and strategies, all of which belie the naive idea that the criminal is psychologically unable to endure temporary frustrations. And, indeed, if professional, organized, and white-collar crime are to be given their due, it must be acknowledged that much, if not most, criminality rather strongly adheres to the "reality principle" of Freudian theory.

Empirical considerations of this and other cognate sorts have, no doubt, persuaded many psychoanalytic criminologists to attempt an integration of sociological materials. Yet even the psychoanalytic conception of anomie, which probably comes as close to a distinctively sociological perspective as psychoanalysis has yet achieved, remains rooted in the idea that there must be something special and different about the personality of the criminal which induces him to behave in a criminal fashion. And while it cannot be said that criminological research has definitively disposed of this idea, evidence accumulated to date strongly suggests that the distribution of normality, pathology, and general personality traits among criminals is in approximately the same proportion as that found for the rest of the noncriminal population.[14] Thus it would seem that there is nothing in the criminal personality, apart from his criminality, to differentiate him from the noncriminal. And if this is so, it must follow that criminality is not to be considered a function of the psychic state of the individual.

Nor has the psychoanalytic criminology taken sufficient cognizance of the fact that the criminal does not spontaneously invent patterns of criminality.

---

[13] See, e.g., the important study by W. Bromberg and C. B. Thompson, "The Relation of Psychosis, Mental Defect, and Personality Types to Crime," in *Journal of Criminal Law & Criminology*, Vol. 28. Studying a random sample of close to ten thousand convicted criminals, Bromberg and Thompson found that 82.0 per cent were "average or normal."

[14] See the excellent review of research in this area by L. G. Lowrey, "Delinquent and Criminal Personalities," in J. M. Hunt (ed.), *Personality and the Behavior Disorders* (New York, 1944), Vol. II; see also K. F. Schuessler and D. R. Cressey, "Personality Characteristics of Criminals," in *American Journal of Sociology*, Vol. 55, and M. B. Clinard, "Criminological Research," in R. K. Merton, *et al.*, (eds.), *Sociology Today* (New York, 1959), p. 515 ff.

Criminal behavior, it hardly needs saying, is a social phenomenon, and a learning process has, therefore, to intervene between the personality of the criminal and his criminal actions. Typically, this learning process entails a wide assortment of techniques, ideas, and skills, all of which take time and practice to master and assimilate. Moreover, this learning process requires the individual's participation in the formation and maintenance of relationships with others who dispose of the necessary knowledge and put it to use. It is in the context of these relationships that the individual learns his criminality and adopts for himself distinctive criminalistic attitudes and precepts. Presumably, the experiences of such a learning process must have an effect on the personality of the individual undergoing them. Yet this reciprocating influence of criminal experience on the personality of the criminal appears to have received no consideration in psychoanalytic criminology. Indeed, all the interpretations of the basic etiological formula share this common implicit assumption that the personality differentials to which causal status is attributed are temporally antecedent to the individual's participation in criminal activity. Nevertheless, it is, at least, a plausible alternative possibility that such personality differentials are consequential precipitants of the individual's induction into criminality. And in failing to take this possibility into account, the entire structure of psychoanalytic criminology becomes vulnerable to the charge that it merely begs the question from the outset.

CHAPTER 4

SOCIAL PSYCHOLOGISM

The Primacy of Primary Groups

CHARLES H. COOLEY

■■■■

By primary groups I mean those characterized by intimate face-to-face association and cooperation. They are primary in several senses, but chiefly in that they are fundamental in forming the social nature and ideals of the individual. The result of intimate association, psychologically, is a certain fusion of individuals in a common whole, so that one's very self, for many purposes at least, is the common life and purpose of the group. Perhaps the simplest way of describing this wholeness is by saying that it is a "we"; it involves the sort of sympathy and mutual identification for which "we" is the natural expression. One lives in the feeling of the whole and finds the chief aim of his will in that feeling.

It is not to be supposed that the unity of the primary group is one of mere harmony and love. It is always a differentiated and usually a competitive unity, admitting of self-assertion and various appropriate passions; but these passions are socialized by sympathy, and come, or tend to come, under the discipline of the common spirit. The individual will be ambitious, but the chief object of his ambition will be some desired place in the thought of the others, and he will feel allegiance to common standards of service and fair play. So the boy will dispute with his fellows a place on the team, but above such disputes will place the common glory of his class and school.

The most important spheres of this intimate association and cooperation—though by no means the only ones—are the family, the play-group of children, and the neighborhood or community group of elders. These are practically universal, belonging to all times and all stages of development; and are accordingly a chief basis of what is universal in human nature and human ideals. The best comparative studies of the family, such as those of Westermarck[1] or

---

Source: Charles Horton Cooley, *Social Organization* (New York: Scribner, 1925), pp. 23–31.
[1] *The History of Human Marriage.*

Howard,[2] show it to us as not only a universal institution, but as more alike the world over than the exaggeration of exceptional customs by an earlier school had led us to suppose. Nor can anyone doubt the general prevalence of play-groups among their elders. Such associations are clearly the nursery of human nature in the world about us, and there is no apparent reason to suppose that the case has anywhere or at any time been essentially different.

As regards play, I might, were it not a matter of common observation, multiply illustrations of the universality and spontaneity of the group discussion and cooperation to which it gives rise. The general fact is that children, especially boys after about their twelfth year, live in fellowships in which their sympathy, ambition, and honor are engaged even more often than they are in the family. Most of us can recall examples of the endurance by boys of injustice and even cruelty, rather than appeal from their fellows to parents or teachers—as, for instance, in the hazing so prevalent at schools, and so difficult, for this very reason, to repress. And how elaborate the discussion, how cogent the public opinion, how hot the ambitions in these fellowships.

Nor is this facility of juvenile association, as is sometimes supposed, a trait peculiar to English and American boys; since experience among our immigrant population seems to show that the offspring of the more restrictive civilizations of the continent of Europe form self-governing play-groups with almost equal readiness. Thus Miss Jane Addams, after pointing out that the "gang" is almost universal, speaks of the interminable discussion which every detail of the gang's activity receives, remarking that "in these social folkmotes, so to speak, the young citizen learns to act upon his own determination." [3]

Of the neighborhood group it may be said, in general, that from the time men formed permanent settlements upon the land, down, at least to, the rise of modern industrial cities, it has played a main part in the primary, heart-to-heart life of the people. Among our Teutonic forefathers the village community was apparently the chief sphere of sympathy and mutual aid for the commons all through the "dark" and middle ages, and for many purposes it remains so in rural districts at the present day. In some countries we still find it with all its ancient vitality, notably in Russia, where the mir, or self-governing village group, is the main theatre of life, along with the family, for perhaps fifty millions of peasants.

In our own life the intimacy of the neighborhood has been broken up by the growth of an intricate mesh of wider contacts which leaves us strangers to people who live in the same house. And even in the country the same principle is at work, though less obviously, diminishing our economic and spiritual community with our neighbors. How far this change is a healthy development, and how far a disease, is perhaps still uncertain.

Besides these almost universal kinds of primary association, there are many

---

[2] *A History of Matrimonial Institutions.*
[3] *Newer Ideals of Peace*, 177.

others whose form depends upon the particular state of civilization; the only essential thing, as I have said, being a certain intimacy and fusion of personalities. In our own society, being little bound by place, people easily form clubs, fraternal societies and the like, based on congeniality, which may give rise to real intimacy. Many such relations are formed at school and college, and among men and women brought together in the first instance by their occupations—as workmen in the same trade, or the like. Where there is a little common interest and activity, kindness grows like weeds by the roadside.

But the fact that the family and neighborhood groups are ascendant in the open and plastic time of childhood makes them even now incomparably more influential than all the rest.

Primary groups are primary in the sense that they give the individual his earliest and completest experience of social unity, and also in the sense that they do not change in the same degree as more elaborate relations, but form a comparatively permanent source out of which the latter are ever springing. Of course they are not independent of the larger society, but to some extent reflect its spirit; as the German family and the German school bear somewhat distinctly the print of German militarism. But this, after all, is like the tide setting back into creeks, and does not commonly go very far. Among the German, and still more among the Russian, peasantry are found habits of free cooperation and discussion almost uninfluenced by the character of the state; and it is a familiar and well-supported view that the village commune, self-governing as regards local affairs and habituated to discussion, is a very widespread institution in settled communities, and the continuator of a similar autonomy previously existing in the clan. "It is a man who makes monarchies and establishes republics, but the commune seems to come directly from the hand of God." [4]

In our own cities the crowded tenements and the general economic and social confusion have sorely wounded the family and the neighborhood, but it is remarkable, in view of these conditions what vitality they show; and there is nothing upon which the conscience of the time is more determined than upon restoring them to health.

These groups, then, are springs of life, not only for the individual but for social institutions. They are only in part moulded by special traditions, and, in larger degree, express a universal nature. The religion or government of other civilizations may seem alien to us, but the children or the family group wear the common life, and with them we can always make ourselves at home.

By human nature, I suppose, we may understand those sentiments and impulses that are human in being superior to those of lower animals, and also in the sense that they belong to mankind at large, and not to any particular race or time. It means, particularly, sympathy and the innumerable sentiments into

---

[4] De Tocqueville, *Democracy in America*, vol. i, Chap. 5.

which sympathy enters, such as love, resentment, ambition, vanity, hero-worship, and the feeling of social right and wrong.[5]

Human nature in this sense is justly regarded as a comparatively permanent element in society. Always and everywhere men seek honor and dread ridicule, defer to public opinion, cherish their goods and their children, and admire courage, generosity, and success. It is always safe to assume that people are and have been human.

It is true, no doubt, that there are differences of race capacity, so great that a large part of mankind is possibly incapable of any high kind of social organization. But these differences, like those among individuals of the same race, are subtle, depending upon some obscure intellectual deficiency, some want of vigor, or slackness of moral fibre, and do not involve unlikeness in the generic impulses of human nature. In these all races are very much alike. The more insight one gets into the life of savages, even those that are reckoned the lowest, the more human, the more like ourselves, they appear. Take for instance the natives of central Australia, as described by Spencer and Gillen,[6] tribes having no definite government or worship and scarcely able to count to five. They are generous to one another, emulous of virtue as they understand it, kind to their children and to the aged, and by no means harsh to women. Their faces as shown in the photographs are wholly human and many of them attractive.

And when we come to a comparison between different stages in the development of the same race, between ourselves, for instance, and the Teutonic tribes of the time of Caesar, the difference is neither in human nature nor in capacity, but in organization, in the range and complexity of relations, in the diverse expression of powers and passions essentially much the same.

There is no better proof of this generic likeness of human nature than in the ease and joy with which the modern man makes himself at home in literature depicting the most remote and varied phases of life—in Homer, in the Nibelung tales, in the Hebrew Scriptures, in the legends of the American Indians, in stories of frontier life, of soldiers and sailors, of criminals and tramps, and so on. The more penetratingly any phase of human life is studied the more an essential likeness to ourselves is revealed.

To return to primary groups: the view here maintained is that human nature is not something existing separately in the individual, but a *group-nature or primary phase of society*, a relatively simple and general condition of the social mind. It is something more, on the one hand, than the mere instinct that is born in us—though that enters into it—and something less, on the other, than the more elaborate development of ideas and sentiments that makes up institutions.

---

[5] These matters are expounded at some length in the writer's *Human Nature and the Social Order*.

[6] *The Native Tribes of Central Australia*. Compare also Darwin's views and examples given in ch. 7 of his *Descent of Man*.

It is the nature which is developed and expressed in those simple, face-to-face groups that are somewhat alike in all societies; groups of the family, the playground, and the neighborhood. In the essential similarity of these is to be found the basis, in experience, for similar ideas and sentiments in the human mind. In these, everywhere human nature comes into existence. Man does not have it at birth; he cannot acquire it except through fellowship, and it decays in isolation.

If this view does not recommend itself to commonsense I do not know that elaboration of it will be of much avail. It simply means the application at this point of the idea that society and individuals are inseparable phases of a common whole, so that wherever we find an individual fact we may look for a social fact to go with it. If there is a universal nature in persons there must be something universal in association to correspond to it.

What else can human nature be than a trait of primary groups? Surely not an attribute of the separate individual—supposing there were any such thing— since its typical characteristics, such as affection, ambition, vanity, and resentment, are inconceivable apart from society. If it belongs, then, to man in association, what kind or degree of association is required to develop it? Evidently nothing elaborate, because elaborate phases of society are transient and diverse, while human nature is comparatively stable and universal. In short the family and neighborhood life is essential to its genesis and nothing more is.

Here as everywhere in the study of society we must learn to see mankind in psychical wholes, rather than in artificial separation. We must see and feel the communal life of family and local groups as immediate facts, not as combinations of something else. And perhaps we shall do this best by recalling our own experience and extending it through sympathetic observation. What, in our life, is the family and the fellowship; what do we know of the we-feeling? Thought of this kind may help us to get a concrete perception of that primary group-nature of which everything social is the outgrowth.

The Functions of Small-Group Research

LEWIS A. COSER

Research in *small groups* has grown tremendously in recent years. A specialized bibliography (12) indicates that not fewer than three items per week are now being "produced" while from 1930 to 1939 a total of two hundred ten items were published in this field; in the four-year period from 1950 to 1953 roughly as many small-group studies have appeared as in the whole twenty-year span from 1930 to 1950. For the forty years from 1890 to 1929 as many items are listed as are now published during a single year.

A recent issue of the *American Sociological Review* (1) was in its entirety devoted to small-group studies; a collection of small-group papers has proved to be a scientific best seller (2); another collection is about to be published. One is led to agree with the editor of the aforementioned special issue of the *American Sociological Review* that small-group research has experienced in recent years a "runaway growth."

Sociologists are wont to direct their attention to the rise of new social movements, fashions, or cults which arise in the society at large, but they have been rather reluctant to direct their efforts at an examination of similar phenomena within their own discipline. Yet such an analysis would seem to be both scientifically profitable and critically important. A science which does not employ its research tools for a self-critical analysis of its own structure and functions lays itself open to justified reproach.

Sociologists have been eager to study the growth of religious movements and to link their rise to specified functions that they perform for their practitioners. It is our purpose in the following pages to study in a similar way the rise of small-group analysis within the sociological discipline. For a sociologically sophisticated audience it should hardly be necessary to *stress that analysis of such a movement in no way aims to throw light upon the validity of its findings.* Just as the sociologist concerned with the analysis of religious phenomena is not making judgments as to the merits of specific religious views and attitudes, so the analyst of the rise of schools within a scientific discipline is not concerned with the validity of their results. Since small-group study claims to be part of the

Source: Lewis A. Coser, "The Functions of Small-Group Research," *Social Problems* 3:1 (July, 1955), pp. 1–6. Reprinted by permission.

province of sociology, the validity of its *findings* should also come under the sociologists' scrutiny, but we are not concerned with this task here, important though it may be.

Small-group research has proceeded under the guidance of variant and divergent theoretical assumptions and it is fragmented into various "schools" which often seem to take little notice of each other. Under these conditions it is difficult to make valid generalizations about the whole "movement." We have therefore limited ourselves in the following to those small-group analysts who are primarily concerned with the laboratory study of small experimentally created groups. In order to further restrict our focus, we shall in the main be concerned with the contributions to the above-mentioned special issue of *The American Sociological Review*. It seems justified to concentrate on this publication since the editors of the official organ of the American Sociological Society apparently took these contributions to be representative of the work of sociological interest now going on in the small-group field.

The functional analysis of an item requires the description of the activity involved as well as the description of the participants in structural terms so as to locate them in their interconnected social statuses (8, p. 56).

Small-group research, to judge from the recent issue of the *American Sociological Review* (1), consists essentially of the observational study of small experimentally created groups. Most of these studies are carried on in larger universities with special laboratory facilities such as microphones, one-way vision screens, tape recorders, etc. Most of the studies reported are carried out with college or high-school students as subjects: of eleven experimental studies reported, seven had college or high-school groups as their subjects and an additional study used twelve-year-old boys. Subjects usually are manipulated to create conditions for the testing of specific hypotheses as to the behavior in the experimental situation. To give just one example, in a study by Godfrey M. Hochbaum (4), it "was attempted to create four conditions in different individuals by first creating self-confidence regarding the task assigned to the experimental groups in about half the subjects, and feelings of inadequacy concerning the task in the other half. About half of the subjects in each of these two conditions were then made to conceive themselves as deviates." (4, p. 679.)

Moving now to the analysis of the status of those engaged in the behavior under scrutiny, what strikes one immediately is the relative youth of small-group analysts. The average age of the authors of the papers published in the recent issue of the *American Sociological Review* is in the low thirties. It thus differs significantly from the average age of the total membership of the American Sociological Society. Since it is usually between the ages of thirty and thirty-two that individuals enter the academic hierarchy (13, p. 58) as instructors, we can further assume that a high proportion of practitioners of small-group research are as yet occupying lower-staff statuses within the academy.

Having thus roughly located practitioners of small-group research within the social structure of the academic community in which their behavior is to be observed, we may now move to a tentative discussion of their motives.

As Logan Wilson and other observers have remarked, ascent on the academic ladder is marked by serious strains and anxieties. Among the main strains for the junior men in the academic hierarchy is the uncertainty as to criteria for advancement. The junior member is under pressure to "make good" and neither the wish for security nor the wish for recognition is adequately met (13, p. 63). The temporary insecurity for the individual may subserve positive functions for the university but it has serious dysfunctional consequences for the junior member involved. This is especially so in those major universities in which a high premium is put on the quantity of publication as a criterion for advancement. "Publish or perish" seems to be the unwritten maxim governing the advancement process (13, p. 201). Yet in the early years of an academic career the teaching activities of the junior members are likely to take a disproportionate amount of their time, thus impeding the necessary preparation for scholarly research. Also in those early years of a scholarly career, the young practitioner is not yet likely to have fully absorbed the available literature in his field and to have fully appropriated the theoretical inheritance of his discipline. Pressure to publish in a hurry is thus likely to lead to overzealous attempts to rush into print even though adequate preparation may as yet be lacking.

Furthermore, long established areas of investigation usually are preempted by senior members of the discipline so that entry into these areas of research is likely to involve prolonged periods of apprenticeship during which younger members attach themselves for a considerable time to senior members and slowly gain the recognition which enables them finally to stake out research claims of their own.

The pattern of sociological work in earlier periods was typically that of a researcher writing a book from library sources. But with the increasing complexity of sociological research in the more recent period, the refinement of method and the attendant growth of necessary apparatus, sociologists have found it more and more difficult to engage in research without considerable outside aid. The young scholar is not likely to have much access to such research funds and thus tends to be considerably hampered in his research activities; he generally is forced to attach himself to a "collaborative" project headed by a senior member who has access to different types of fund granting organizations.

Since library research is no longer prestigeful and work in a large-scale collaborative project headed by a senior member does not usually lead to rapid prestige, the junior member's access to the legitimate means for success within the academic structure is impeded. Under such conditions he is likely to be motivated to look for types of innovation which will allow him to attain the institutionally rewarded success by alternative means (8, p. 73).

Small-group research seems to be well suited for this purpose. Publication in this field need not be preceded by the kind of elaborate theoretical preparation that is requisite, although not always actually displayed, in more settled areas of investigation. The field is new and theoretical preparation, according to the standards applied within it, involves only an acquaintance with publications that have appeared within roughly the last fifteen years. Of the many hundred references in the special issue of the *American Sociological Review*, only seventeen referred to articles or books published before 1937! (1)

It might be said that analysis of small groups has, in fact, a very ancient history, going back, indeed, to classical Greek and Chinese philosophy, but this is irrelevant in our context since we are not concerned here with objective reality but with the ways the field has been defined by its practitioners. By *their* standards the writings of even the most recent forerunners of their movement, are judged irrelevant. Thus in the aforementioned bibliography of small-group work we note twenty-seven entries under Moreno, nineteen under Festinger, fifteen under Kurt Lewin, but only one under Freud. *The Polish Peasant* by W. I. Thomas and F. Znaniecki is not listed at all (12).

Mention has already been made of the difficulties that await the young scholar who attempts to gain access to research funds and tools of research. But such conditions are not likely to prevail in the small-group field where the research apparatus is not as yet very elaborate. This is indeed a field on the frontier, where individuals can still stake out large claims of their own without being restricted by the settled jurisdictions prevailing in older territories. Since there are very few senior members now engaged in small-group research, younger members of the discipline can move ahead much faster, unencumbered by the many restrictions and controls which are likely to prevail in other areas of research.

As C. Wright Mills has observed, "The graduate school is often organized as a feudal system: the student trades his loyalty to one professor for protection against the other professors" (10, p. 130). But in a new field such feudal patterns have not yet been established; on the contrary, the pattern of organization may be compared to that of a band of pioneers linked by common rejection of the thought ways of the settled community, by contempt for the old and enthusiasm for the achievements of the members of the brotherhood. We already have commented upon the fact that small-group research, to judge from the evidence of bibliographies, seems to have little regard for work which is not contemporary or near-contemporary; we might add here that it is also characterized by in-group solidarity. When nine judges, mostly well-known small-group researchers, were asked by Strodtbeck and Hare to rate the most significant articles in the field since 1950, they chose twelve articles, five of which had been written by the judges themselves. These same judges considered the work of George Herbert Mead as "not important," felt it unnecessary to cite more than one work by Freud, did not list any work by Jean Piaget and mentioned only one article by Malinowski, which they judged "not important," while not only listing all the writings of the "in-group members" but even decorating them profusely with double and triple asterisks indicating that these were of the greatest importance (12). We are reminded of Logan Wilson's description of cultism in the academic community: "As long as the cult thrives, particularism flourishes. Members of the in-group are favored by one another in book reviews; complimentary references are made only to the writings of authors with 'approved' points of view." (13, p. 209.)

In summary, while in the older-areas of research the junior member remains for long periods a "marginal man" whose anticipatory socialization becomes dysfunctional for him since it leads him to become the victim of aspirations he cannot achieve, the relative openness of the structure within new areas of research may be said to be functional for the individual involved to the degree that it helps him to achieve the social status toward which he aspires (9, p. 88).

Though some technical paraphernalia for small-group research are relatively costly, these costs are generally borne by the university or fund-granting organizations and are still insignificant in comparison with field research. Moreover, where no special research equipment is available, the research design can be simplified so that less elaborate technical facilities can be used. Furthermore, many of the studies are conducted for clients in large-scale bureaucratic organizations which provide the requisite laboratory facilities: both the Air Force and the Navy possess their own small-group laboratories and so does the RAND Corporation. Two out of eleven studies reported in the *American Sociological Review* were conducted with Navy or Air Force subjects and four out of eleven were financed by Air Force or Navy grants.*

Subjects for small-group studies are easily available since, as has been noted, they can be taken from classes of college students or personnel of the armed forces. In small-group research the difficulties which stand in the way of field work are minimized. Expenses generally are much smaller than those involved in field work; difficulties in obtaining data are likewise minimized since the small-group researcher manufactures the data with which he operates through manipulation of subjects who are easily available and offer little resistance, being to a large extent students subordinated to their teachers or personnel of the armed forces subordinated to the clients of the researchers. It may be noted in passing that small-group researchers recently have turned their attention to techniques on how to improve manipulative devices so as to facilitate the process of recruiting college student "volunteers" for experiments. Thus Schachter and Hall (11) report that, among other things, recruitment of volunteers could be increased by requesting volunteers to raise their hands and having half the class pre-instructed to respond as if volunteering.

Not only does small-group research minimize expenditures of funds, it also minimizes expenditure of time. Results can be attained rather quickly and without the tantalizing expense of time that is so often involved in field work.

---

* Eight out of forty-one studies reported in the Cartwright and Zander volume (2) were likewise supported by grants from either the Navy or the Air Force.

While a community study or an interview program may involve several months or even years of work, a small experimental group study may only require several weeks or even days for its execution. There are no preliminary delays in which such preparatory work as sampling has to be undertaken since the sample to be studied *is* the universe.

In short, easy availability of subjects, minimization of expenses in money and time, and the frontier territory are all advantages which recommend such research to those members of the academic hierarchies who, for the reasons outlined above, are under pressure to produce "results" in a hurry.

Having examined some of the internal reasons which have made research in small groups attractive to its practitioners, we might now turn to the question why small group research seems to enjoy high prestige among non-practitioners.

In recent years higher prestige has accrued to quantifiable than to qualitative results in the social sciences and precision has been rated higher than significance (5, 7). Since findings in small-group research are typically reported in seemingly precise quantitative terms, often in mathematical formalization, they are well suited to bring prestige. In so far as sociologists as well as clients of sociology have been fascinated by natural science methods, the methodological ascetism and the seeming precision of small-group findings are likely to impress various decision-makers both inside and outside the academy. Surrounded as they are by the magic aura of "science," the products of such research seem more easily saleable than work using less precise methods and more complex sets of variables, many of which may not as yet be susceptible to quantification. Such precise formulations are likely to appeal to people who are not able to "take" the uncertainties and complexities in work in the uncontrolled world.

Karl Mannheim once remarked that "typical American studies start from questions in nowise connected with those problems which arouse our passions in everyday political and social struggle." (6, p. 191.) This remark may be applicable to much research carried on in America today but it eminently characterizes experimental small-group work. Research in this field seems indeed to be carried on under antiseptic conditions in which preoccupation with and contamination by the world at large are rigorously excluded. Such isolation from large-scale questions of import for political and social structure is a decided advantage for the practitioner. In an age of political insecurity and fear, the small group provides an area of research so far removed from the concrete issues of the day and at so high a level of abstraction that it may be considered entirely "safe." While the research in the field, especially in larger groups and organizations, is only too likely to encounter resistance and attack from vested interests or decision makers, while such research might find it hard to get support from foundations which are under Congressional or other scrutiny for their alleged orientation toward reform, small-group research is free from such dangers. Since it does not deal with specific variables operative in the real world outside of the laboratory, it is also not in danger of offending real suscepti-bilities. Yet it seems that much of small-group research, while conceived on a high level of abstraction is, in the selection of its problems, tied to the solution of immediate problems of various types of bureaucratic decision makers, whether Army, Navy, factory managers or welfare agencies. Small-group research appeals to those decision makers in large-scale organizations who need re-searchers who do not question or discuss the impact of the organizations' structures but who focus instead on small segments within these structures. The Navy, for example, is not likely to be interested in studies of the bureaucratiza-tion of decision making in top echelons or in the relation between the process of militarization and democratic values, but it may want to know more about conformity producing mechanisms. Mr. John R. P. French, a leading small-group expert, discussing field research, has formulated the problem with com-mendable frankness: "The dominant objective of industry is production and this objective cannot be subordinated to the research objectives of a field experi-ment. The freedom of the field experimenter is limited to those types of experi-ments which do not conflict with the goal of the organization with which he works. . . . It means that the researcher must be flexible in choosing appropriate problems, in a field setting. Most fundamentally, it means that he must render a service which helps the practitioner to achieve his practical objectives." (3, p. 91.) Mr. Strodtbeck expresses the same idea somewhat differently when he writes: "The growth of social science research and the availability of agencies willing to invest resources in the solution of *their* (emphasis mine, L.A.C.) problem, are inseparably linked." (1, p. 652.)

While small-group research predisposes the practitioners to selective inatten-tion to large-scale organizational problems and habitually keys its research to a high level of abstraction in which contamination with the problems of society is successively minimized, it is, on the other hand, well suited to serve the decision maker in the practical problems that he encounters in administration. Just because this research operates on a high level of abstraction, it can easily be tailored according to the specifications of decision makers and clients. Moreover, since small-group researchers often, although not always, claim that results attained in groups of boy scouts or college students are valid beyond the juvenile universe and can be transferred to society at large, this may seem to the decision maker a convenient way of reaching macroscopic results with micro-scopic expenses.

In conclusion, we might ask whether channeling of a high proportion of personnel into small-group research does not have significantly dysfunctional consequences for the development of sociology as a discipline. The social functions of small-group research help determine its structure, including the recruitment of personnel, but the structure of small-group research also affects its function (8, pp. 80–81). The general research orientation of the small-group school enables its members to acquire a public among the managerial elites of

American society and this orientation and public is likely to lead them to neglect crucial societal variables. To the extent that the recent vogue of small-group research leads to the neglect of problems of social structure in favor of pre-occupation with the social psychology of adjustment, it may be said to have serious dysfunctional consequences for the development of a mature science of society.

REFERENCES

1. *American Sociological Review*, 19 (December, 1954).
2. Cartwright, Dorwin and Zander, Alvin, Eds., *Group-Dynamics*, Evanston: Row, Peterson & Co., 1953.
3. French, John R. P., "Field Experiments: Changing Group Productivity," in *Experiments in Social Process*, Ed. Jas. G. Miller, New York: McGraw Hill, 1950.
4. Hochbaum, Godfrey M., "The Relation between Group Members' Self-Confidence and Their Reactions to Group Pressures to Uniformity," *American Sociological Review*, 19 (1954), 678–687.
5. Lee, Alfred McClung, "Individual and Organizational Research in Sociology," *American Sociological Review*, 16 (1951), 701–707.
6. Mannheim, Karl, *Essays on Sociology and Social Psychology*, New York: Oxford University Press, 1953.
7. Maslow, Abraham H., "Problem-centering vs. Means-centering in Science," *Philosophy of Science*, 13 (1946), 326–331.
8. Merton, Robert K., *Social Theory and Social Structure*, Glencoe: The Free Press, 1949.
9. Merton, Robert K. and Kitt, Alice S., "Contributions to the Theory of Reference Group Behavior," in *Continuities in Social Research*, Eds., Merton, Robert K. and Lazarsfeld, Paul F., Glencoe: The Free Press, 1950.
10. Mills, C. Wright, *White Collar*, New York: Oxford University Press, 1951.
11. Schachter, S. and Hall, R., "Group-Derived Restraints and Audience Participation," *Human Relations*, 5 (1952), 397–406.
12. Strodtbeck, Fred L. and Hare, A. Paul, "Bibliography of Small Group Research," *Sociometry*, 17 (1954), 107–178.
13. Wilson, Logan, *The Academic Man*, New York: Oxford University Press, 1942.

CHAPTER 5

SOCIOLOGISM

The Professional Ideology of
Social Pathologists

C. WRIGHT MILLS

▬

An analysis of textbooks in the field of social disorganization reveals a common style of thought which is open to social imputation. By grasping the social orientation of this general perspective we can understand why thinkers in this field should select and handle problems in the manner in which they have.

By virtue of the mechanism of sales and distribution, textbooks tend to embody a content agreed upon by the academic group using them. In some cases texts have been written only after an informal poll was taken of professional opinion as to what should be included, and other texts are consulted in the writing of a new one. Since one test of their success is wide adoption, the very spread of the public for which they are written tends to insure a textbook tolerance of the commonplace. Although the conceptual framework of a pathologist's textbook is not usually significantly different from that of such monographs as he may write, this essay is not concerned with the "complete thought" or with the "intentions" of individual authors; it is a study of a professional ideology variously exhibited in a set of textbooks.[1] Yet, because

Source: Reprinted from "The Professional Ideology of Social Pathologists," in *American Journal of Sociology*, 49 (September, 1943), by C. Wright Mills by permission of the University of Chicago Press, publisher. Copyright, 1943 by C. Wright Mills.

[1] No attempt has been made to trace specific concepts to their intellectual origins. Only elements admitted into the more stable textbook formulations have come within my view: the aim is to grasp typical perspectives and key concepts. Hence, no one of the texts to be quoted exemplifies *all* the concepts analyzed; certain elements are not so visible in given texts as in others, and some elements are not evidenced in certain texts at all. In general, the documentary quotations which follow in footnotes are from the later editions of the following books: W. G. Beach and E. E. Walker, *American Social Problems* (1934); J. H. S. Bossard, (*a*) *Social Change and Social Problems* (1934) and (*b*) *Problems of Social Well-Being* (1927); C. H. Cooley, (*a*) *The Social Process* (1918), (*b*) *Human Nature and the Social Order* (1902, 1922), (*c*) *Social Organization* (1909); Edward T. Devine, (*a*) *The Normal Life* (1915, 1924), (*b*) *Progressive Social Action* (1933); R. C. Dexter, *Social Adjustment* (1927); G. S. Dow, *Society and Its Problems* (1920, 1929); M. A. Elliott and F. E. Merrill, *Social Disorganization* (1934, 1941); C. A. Ellwood, (*a*) *The Social Problem, a Constructive Analysis* (1915, 1919); (*b*) *Sociology and*

of its persistent importance in the development of American sociology and its supposed proximity to the social scene, "social pathology" seems an appropriate point of entry for the examination of the style of reflection and the social-historical basis of American sociology.

The level of abstraction which characterizes these texts is so low that often they seem to be empirically confused for lack of abstraction to knit them together.[2] They display bodies of meagerly connected facts, ranging from rape in rural districts to public housing, and intellectually sanction this low level of abstraction.[3] The "informational" character of social pathology is linked with a failure to consider total social structures. Collecting and dealing in a fragmentary way with scattered problems and facts of milieux, these books are not focused on larger stratifications or upon structured wholes. Such an omission may not be accounted for merely in terms of a general "theoretical weakness." Such structural analyses have been available; yet they have not been attended to or received into the tradition of this literature. American sociologists have often asserted an interest in the "correlation of the social sciences"; nevertheless, academic departmentalization may well have been instrumental in atomizing the problems which they have addressed.[4] Sociologists have always felt that "not many representatives of the older forms of social science are ready to admit that there is a function for sociology."[5] However, neither lack of theoretical ability nor restrictive channeling through departmentalization constitutes a full explanation of the low level of abstraction and the accompanying failure to consider larger problems of social structure.

Modern Social Problems (1910–1935); H. P. Fairchild, *Outline of Applied Sociology* (1916, 1921); M. P. Follett, (a) *The New State* (1918), (b) *Creative Experience* (1924); James Ford, *Social Deviation* (1939); J. M. Gillette and J. M. Reinhardt, *Current Social Problems* (1933, 1937); J. L. Gillin, (a) *Poverty and Dependence* (1921, 1926, 1937), (b) *Social Pathology* (1933, 1939); J. L. Gillin, C. G. Dittmer, and R. J. Colbert, *Social Problems* (1928, 1932); E. C. Hayes, editor's introductions to texts in the "Lippincott Series"; W. J. Hayes and I. V. Shannon, *Visual Outline of Introductory Sociology* (1935); G. B. Mangold, *Social Pathology* (1932, 1934); H. A. Miller, *Races, Nations, and Classes* (1924); H. W. Odum, *Man's Quest for Social Guidance: The Study of Social Problems* (1927); Maurice Parmelee, *Poverty and Social Progress* (1916); H. A. Phelps, *Contemporary Social Problems* (1932, 1933, 1938); S. A. Queen and J. R. Gruener, *Social Pathology* (1940); S. A. Queen, W. B. Bodenhafer, and E. B. Harper, *Social Organization and Disorganization* (1935); C. M. Rosenquist, *Social Problems* (1940); U. G. Weatherly, *Social Progress* (1926).

[2] See Read Bain, "The Concept of Complexity," *Social Forces*, VIII, 222 and 369. K. Mannheim has called this type "isolating empiricism" ("German Sociology," *Politica*, February, 1934, p. 30).

[3] H. P. Fairchild, p. vii: "Dealing with applied sociology [this book] devotes itself to facts rather than to theories." James H. S. Bossard (a), p. xi: "In [*Problems of Social Well-Being*] an effort was made to consider chiefly in a factual vein, certain elements which seemed of basic importance. . . ." G. P. Mangold, p. viii: "The author has tried to select that which [of factual material] best illustrates problems and practical situations."
The quotations in the footnotes are merely indications of what is usual. The imputations presented must be held against the reader's total experience with the literature under purview.

[4] In Germany the academic division of specialties prior to the rise of sociology channeled sociological work into a formal emphasis. In America a somewhat comparable situation led to a fragmentation of empirical attention and especially to a channeling of work into "practical problems."

[5] A. W. Small, *American Journal of Sociology*, May, 1916, p. 785, citing an editorial in the *American Journal of Sociology*, 1907.

If the members of an academic profession are recruited from similar social contexts and if their backgrounds and careers are relatively similar, there is a tendency for them to be uniformly set for some common perspective. The common conditions of their profession often seem more important in this connection than similarity of extraction. Within such a generally homogeneous group there tend to be fewer divergent points of view which would clash over the meaning of facts and thus give rise to interpretations on a more theoretical level.[6]

The relatively homogeneous extraction and similar careers of American pathologists is a possible factor in the low level of abstraction characterizing their work. All the authors considered[7] (except one, who was foreign born) were born in small towns, or on farms near small towns, three-fourths of which were in states not industrialized during the youth of the authors. The social circles and strata in which they have severally moved are quite homogeneous; all but five have participated in similar "reform" groups and "societies" of the professional and business classes. By virtue of their being college professors (all but three are known to have the Ph.D.), of the similar type of temporary positions (other than academic) which they have held, of the sameness of the "societies" to which they have belonged and of the social positions of the persons whom they have married, the assertion as regards general similarity of social extraction, career, and circles of contact seems justified.[8]

A further determinant of the level of abstraction and lack of explicit systematization (beyond which the mentality we are examining does not easily or typically go) is the immediate purpose and the type of public for which they have presumably written. They have been teachers and their specific public has been college students: this has influenced the content and direction of their intellectual endeavors.[9] Teaching is a task which requires a type of systematization to which the textbook answers. Most of the "systematic" or "theoretical"

---

[6] Such "homogeneity" is not, however, the only condition under which some common style of thought is taken on by a group of thinkers. Compare the formal conception of "points of coincidence" advanced by H. H. Gerth in *Die sozialgeschichtliche Lage der burgerlichen Intelligenz um die Wende des 18 Jahrhunderts* (diss., Frankfurt A.M.) (V.D.I.-Verlag, G.m.b.H. Berlin, N.W. 7). The entire question of the grounding of imputations in terms of social extraction and career-lines is an unfinished set of methodological issues. In this paper the major imputations advanced do *not* proceed upon career data as much as upon the social orientation implied by general perspectives and specific concepts, and by the selection of "problems."

[7] Information concerning twenty-four of the thirty-two authors was full enough to be considered. Five of the eight not considered were junior authors collaborating with persons who are included.

[8] The order of their respective experience has not been systematically considered. All career data on contemporary persons should be held tentatively: open to revision by knowledge not now publicly available.

[9] See above. A. W. Small, p. 754: ". . . the mental experience of the teacher-explorer in the course of arriving at the present outlook of sociologists . . . has also been due to the fact that many of the advances in perception or expression have been in the course of attempts to meet students' minds at their precise point of outlook." See C. Wright Mills, "Language, Logic, and Culture," *American Sociological Review*, October, 1939, for mechanism involved in such determinations of the thinker by his public.

work in "social pathology" has been performed by teachers in textbooks for academic purposes.[10] The fact that sociology often won its academic right to existence in opposition to other departments may have increased the necessity for *textbook* systematization. Such systematization occurs in a context of presentation and of justification rather than within a context of discovery.[11] The textbook-writing and the academic profession of the writers thus figure in the character and function of systematic theory within the field.[12] Systematization of facts for the purpose of making them accessible to collegiate minds is one thing; systematization which is oriented toward crucial growing-points in a research process is quite another. An attempt to systematize on the level of the textbook makes for a taxonomic gathering of facts and a systematization of them under concepts that have already been logically defined.[13] The research possibilities of concepts are not as important as is the putting of the accumulated factual details into some sort of order.

But, even though the perspectives of these texts are usually not explicit, the facts selected for treatment are not "random." One way to grasp the perspective within which they do lie is to analyze the scope and character of their problems. What, then, are the selecting and organizing principles to be extracted from the range and content of these texts? What types of fact come within their field of attention?

The direction is definitely toward particular "practical problems"—problems of "everyday life."[14] The ideal of practicality, of not being "utopian," operated,

---

[10] This statement, as is widely recognized, holds in a measure for all American sociology. Cf., e.g., Pitirim Sorokin, "Some Contrasts in Contemporary European and American Sociology," *Social Forces*, September, 1929, pp. 57–58. "In America sociology has grown as a child nursed by the universities and colleges. . . . American literature in sociology has been composed largely out of textbooks."

[11] Cf. Hans Reichenbach, *Experience and Prediction*, chap. i. See P. Sorokin's comment, *op. cit.*, p. 59.

[12] J. L. Gillin (*a*), p. v: "My years of experience as a social worker and teacher have gone into the content and method of presentation." J. H. S. Bossard (*a*), p. 759: "In the preceding chapters, problems have been grouped on the basis of one underlying fact or condition. Obviously, this is an arbitrary procedure which can be justified only on the basis of pedagogical experience"; p. xi: "The . . . is the method followed. . . . By way of defense, this seems simple and pedagogically preferable"; p. xii: "The decision to omit them was made . . . second, because in an increasing number of colleges and universities, these particular fields are dealt with in separate courses."

[13] Cf. Fritz Mauthner, *Aristotle*, for the pedagogic character of the taxonomic logic of Aristotle. H. P. Fairchild, pp. 6–7: ". . . the essential features of the scientific method . . . are three in number. First, the accumulation of facts. . . . Second, the arrangement or classification of these facts according to some predetermined logical basis of classification. . . ." J. H. S. Bossard (*a*), p. 34: "It is the present contention that the scientific study of social problems which confines itself to mere description and classification serves a useful purpose."

[14] M. A. Elliott, *American Sociological Review*, June, 1941, p. 317: "The only problems which need concern the sociologists' theories and research are the real, practical problems of everyday living." Queen and Gruener, p. 42: "[In contradistinction to scientific problems] social problems . . . pertain directly to everyday life. . . . Their concern is usually 'practical,' and often personal." J. H. S. Bossard (*a*), p. 32: "Frankly, applied sociology is utilitarian. It is concerned with practical problems and purposes." Gillette and Reinhardt, p. 22: "The study of social problems constitutes the heart of sociology as a science. . . . Even so-called 'pure' sociology, or theoretical sociology, more and more devotes itself to these practical problems of society."

in conjunction with other factors, as a polemic against the "philosophy of history" brought into American sociology by men trained in Germany; this polemic implemented the drive to lower levels of abstraction. A view of isolated and immediate problems as the "real" problems may well be characteristic of a society rapidly growing and expanding, as America was in the nineteenth century and, ideologically, in the early twentieth century. The depictive mode of speech and the heavy journalistic "survey" are intellectual concomitants of an expanding society in which new routines are rising and cities are being built.[15] Such an approach is then sanctioned with canons of what constitutes real knowledge; the practice of the detailed and complete empiricism of the survey is justified by an epistemology of gross description. These norms of adequate knowledge linger in an academic tradition to mold the work of its bearers. The emphasis upon fragmentary,[16] practical problems tends to atomize social objectives. The studies so informed are not integrated into designs comprehensive enough to serve collective action, granted the power and intent to realize such action.

One of the pervasive ways of defining "problems" or of detecting "disorganization" is in terms of *deviation from norms*. The "norms" so used are usually held to be the standards of "society." Later we shall see to what type of society they are oriented. In the absence of studies of specific norms themselves this mode of problematization shifts the responsibility of "taking a stand" away from the thinker and gives a "democratic" rationale to his work.[17]

On the other hand, such writers as Ellwood, rising to a *very* high level of abstraction, conceive *formally* of "the social problem." C. A. Ellwood (*a*), pp. 13–14: "Some of us, at least, are beginning to perceive that the social problem is now, what it has been in all ages, namely, *the problem of the relations of men to one another*. It is the problem of human living together, and cannot be confined to any statement in economic, eugenic or other one-sided terms . . . it is as broad as humanity and human nature. . . . Such a statement [in terms of one set of factors] obscures the real nature of the problem, and may lead to dangerous, one-sided attempts at its solution." In terms of social and intellectual orientation, both ways of conceiving of "social problems" are similar in that neither is of a sort usable in collective action which proceeds against, rather than well within, more or less tolerated channels.

[15] See H. D. Lasswell, *Politics* (1936), p. 148; K. Mannheim, *op. cit.*, pp. 30–31; and *Ideology and Utopia*, pp. 228–229.

[16] Gillin, Dittmer, and Colbert, p. 44: "There are hundreds of social problems, big and little." Queen and Gruener, p. 171: "We present here some of the problems of day by day living encountered by diabetics and cardiacs." J. H. S. Bossard (*a*), p. 33: "Certain particular social problems are coming to be reserved for applied sociology. Their selection has been determined less by logic or principle than by accident and historical development"; p. 44: "The more one deals with life's problems at first hand, the more one is impressed with their concreteness, their specificity, and their infinite variety." Gillette and Reinhardt, p. 14: "From almost any point of view there must be a large number of social problems today"; p. 15: "This book is a treatise on a large number of social problems. It does not claim to consider them all. It repeatedly recognizes the plurality of problems in its treatment of the great problems."

[17] C. M. Rosenquist, p. 19: ". . . popular recognition of any social condition or process as bad, followed by any attempt to eliminate or cure it, serves as a criterion for its inclusion in a study of social problems. The writer merely accepts the judgment of public opinion. This is the method to be followed in this book." E. T. Devine (*a*), in Note to the Second Edition: "The object of Social Economy is that each shall be able to live as nearly as possible a normal life according to the standard of the period and the community."

Rationally, it would seem that those who accept this approach to "disorganization" would immediately examine these norms themselves. It is significant that, given their interest in reforming society, which is usually avowed, these writers typically assume the norms which they use and often tacitly sanction them.[18] There are few attempts to explain deviations from norms in terms of the norms themselves, and no rigorous facing of the implications of the fact that social transformations would involve shifts *in them*.

The easy way to meet the question of why norms are violated is in terms of biological impulses which break through "societal restrictions." A paste-pot eclectic psychology provides a rationale for this facile analysis.[19] Thus, more comprehensive problematization is blocked by a biological theory of social deviation. And the "explanation" of deviations can be put in terms of a requirement for more "socialization." "Socialization" is either undefined, used as a moral epithet, or implies norms which are themselves without definition. The focus on "the facts" takes no cognizance of the normative structures within which they lie.

The texts tend either to be "apolitical"[20] or to aspire to a "democratic" opportunism.[21] When the political sphere is discussed, its pathological phases

---

[18] C. M. Rosenquist, p. 19: "Perhaps we may be on solid ground through a recognition of the capitalist system and its accompaniments as normal. We may then deal with its several parts, treating as problems those which do not function smoothly. This, it seems, is what the more reputable sociologist actually does." H. P. Fairchild, p. 59: ". . . some of the social conditions which are the natural and consistent outcome of an individualistic-capitalistic organization of industry, and hence are to be considered as normal in modern societies." Examination of discussions of such items as poverty in most of the texts confirms this assertion. J. L. Gillin (*a*), p. 495: "For serious depressions carefully planned unemployment relief schemes should be formulated before the depression is felt."

[19] That is, an eclecticism that does not analyze in any adequate way the elements and theories which it seeks to combine. Cf. Reuter's critique, *American Journal of Sociology*, November, 1940, pp. 293–304.

[20] E. C. Hayes in the Introduction to H. A. Miller, p. x: "Not political action, the inadequacy of which Professor Eldridge (*Political Action*) has shown, nor revolution, the pathological character of which Professor Sorokin has demonstrated, but social interaction, the causal efficiency of human relationships, is the predominant factor in securing both order and progress."

[21] J. H. S. Bossard (*a*), pp. 14–15: "The constructive approach . . . may be summarized in one sentence: It is always possible to do something. . . . Such an approach represents in welfare work that hopelessly incurable optimism which in political life we call democracy." Gillette and Reinhardt, pp. 16–17: "There are no certain rules to be followed step by step in the discovery of the solution. Our best recourse is to employ scientific methods rigidly at every step . . . because of uncertain factors always present, we never can be sure that our conclusions are more than approximations of the truth. . . . Since we cannot completely control their activities . . . our cures must be partial and approximate." One type of link between democratic ideology and social pathology is shown in the following quotation, wherein a condition that deviates from the former is called pathological; the quotation also indicates a typical shying-away from all orders of domination other than that type legitimated traditionally, which is left open: H. A. Miller, p. 32: "When certain . . . psycho-pathological conditions are found, we may postulate an abnormal relationship as a cause . . . the particular form of pathology which is involved in our problem may be called the *oppression psychosis*. Oppression is the domination of one group by another." G. V. Price, reviewing Queen and Gruener, *Social Forces*, May, 1941, p. 566: "Without using the word democracy in the doctrinal sense the authors have shown what its utilities are in reducing pathologies."

are usually stated in terms of "the anti-social," or of "corruption," etc.[22] In another form the political is tacitly identified with the proper functioning of the current and unexamined political order; it is especially likely to be identified with a legal process or the administration of laws.[23] If the "norms" were examined, the investigator would perhaps be carried to see total structures of norms and to relate these to distributions of power. Such a structural point of sight is not usually achieved. The level of abstraction does not rise to permit examination of these normative structures themselves, or of why they come to be transgressed, or of their political implications. Instead, this literature discusses many kinds of apparently unrelated "situations."

About the time W. I. Thomas stated the vocabulary of the situational approach, a social worker was finding it congenial and useful. In M. E. Richmond's influential *Social Diagnosis* (1917) we gain a clue as to why pathologists tend to slip past structure to focus on isolated situations, why there is a tendency for problems to be considered as problems of individuals,[24] and why sequences of situations were not seen as linked into structures:

> Social diagnosis . . . may be described as the attempt to make as exact a definition as possible of the situation and personality of a human being in some social need— of his situation and personality, that is, in relation to the other human beings upon whom he in any way depends or who depend upon him, and in relation also to the social institutions of his community.[25]

This kind of formulation has been widely applied to isolated "problems" addressed by sociologists.[26] And the "situational approach" has an affinity with other elements which characterize their general perspective.[27]

Present institutions train several types of persons—such as judges and social

---

[22] M. A. Elliott and F. Merrill, p. 28: "The pathological phases of the political process include such anti-social behavior as delinquency, crime, disorder, revolt, and revolution. Corrupt political activity is an important example of such malfunctioning."

[23] Note the identification of "political action" with legislation: Gillin, Dittmer, and Colbert, p. 94: "It is an American practice to attempt to solve any and every sort of social problem through political action. As a result, our statute-books are loaded with 'dead-letter' laws that are not enforced simply because public opinion does not respect them, nor does it feel responsible for them."

[24] J. L. Gillin (*a*), p. 13: "Experience shows that rehabilitation is possible only when each case of poverty or dependency is taken separately and its difficulties handled with strict regard for all the attendant circumstances. . . . It must be done in terms of the individual, for . . . it cannot be done *en masse*."

[25] Richmond, p. 357; see also pp. 51 and 62.

[26] J. H. S. Bossard (*a*), p. 3: "Social problems consist of (*a*) a social situation, (*b*) which are. . . ." Gillette and Reinhardt, p. 15: "A social problem is a situation confronting a group. . . ."

[27] J. H. S. Bossard (*a*), p. 57: ". . . the emphasis in our social thinking upon the situation as a unit of experience, as 'an aggregate of interactive and interdependent factors of personality and circumstance,' is in essence a recognition of the idea of the emergent. . . . Queen recognizes the implications of the situational approach very clearly in these words: 'For purposes of sociological analysis, a situation consists in relationships between persons viewed as a cross section of human experience, constantly changing. . . . Thus we make of the concept "situation" and "intellectual tool"'" (S. Queen, "Some Problems of the Situational Approach," *Social Forces*, June, 1931, p. 481).

workers—to think in terms of "situations."[28] Their activities and mental outlook are set within the existent norms of society; in their professional work they
tend to have an occupationally trained incapacity to rise above series of "cases."
It is in part through such concepts as "situation" and through such methods as
"the case approach"[29] that social pathologists have been intellectually tied to
social work with its occupational position and political limitations. And, again,
the similarity of origin and the probable lack of any continuous "class experience" of the group of thinkers decrease their chances to see social structures
rather than a scatter of situations. The mediums of experience and orientation
through which they respectively view society are too similar, too homogeneous,
to permit the class of diverse angles which, through controversy, might lead to
the construction of a whole.

The paramount fact of immigration in American culture, with each wave of
immigrants displacing the lower-class position of former waves and raising the
position of the earlier immigrants, also tends to obscure structural and class
positions.[30] Thus, instead of positional issues, pathologists typically see problems in terms of an individual, such as an immigrant, "adjusting" to a milieu[31]
or being "assimilated" or Americanized. Instead of problems of class structure
involving immigration, the tendency has been to institute problems in terms of
immigration involving the nationalist assimilation of individuals. The fact that
some individuals have had opportunities to rise in the American hierarchy
decreases the chance fully to see the ceilings of class. Under these conditions such structures are seen as fluctuating and unsubstantial and are likely
to be explained not in terms of *class position* but in terms of *status
attitudes.*[32]

Another element that tends to obviate an analytic view of structure is the
emphasis upon the "processual" and "organic" character of society. In Cooley,
whose influence on these books is decisive, one gets a highly formal, many-sided
fluidity where "nothing is fixed or independent, everything is plastic and takes
influence as well as gives it."[33] From the standpoint of political action, such a
view may mean a reformism dealing with masses of detail and furthers a tendency to be apolitical. There can be no bases or points of entry for larger social
action in a structureless flux. The view is buttressed epistemologically with an
emotionalized animus against "particularism" and with the intense approval of

---

28 See K. Mannheim, *Man and Society*, p. 305.
29 Queen, Bodenhafer, and Harper, p. viii: Editor's Note by S. Eldridge: "The present
volume . . . features the case approach to social problems."
30 Note the lack of structure in the conception of "class": Gillette and Reinhardt, p. 177:
"Viewing the matter historically, then, it appears that the chief cause of rigid *class systems*
of society with their attendant evils is the prolonged concentration of wealth in the hands of a
relatively few persons."
31 See below, the concept of "adjustment."
32 Gillin, Dittmer, and Colbert, p. 59: "The most fundamental cause of class and group
conflict is the attitude of superiority on the part of one class, or group, toward another."
33 *The Social Process*, pp. 44–45.

the safe, if colorless, "multiple-factor" view of causation.[34] The liberal "multiple-factor" view does not lead to a conception of causation which would permit points of entry for broader types of action, especially political action.[35] No set of underlying structural shifts is given which might be open to manipulation, at key points, and which, like the fact of private property in a corporate economy, might be seen as efficacious in producing many "problems." If one fragmentalizes society into "factors," into elemental bits, naturally one will then need quite a few of them to account for something,[36] and one can never be sure they are all in. A formal emphasis upon "the whole" plus lack of total structural consideration plus a focus upon scattered situations does not make it easy to reform the status quo.

The "organic" orientation of liberalism has stressed all those social factors which tend to a harmonious balance of elements.[37] There is a minimization of chances for action in a social milieu where "there is always continuity with the past, and not only with any one element only of the past, but with the whole interacting organism of man."[38] In seeing everything social as continuous process, changes in pace and revolutionary dislocations are missed[39] or are taken as signs of the "pathological." The formality and the assumed unity implied by "the mores" also lower the chances to see social chasms and structural dislocations.

Typically, pathologists have not attempted to construct a structural whole. When, however, they do consider totalities, it is in terms of such concepts as "society," "the social order," or "the social organization," "the mores and institutions," and "American culture." Four things should be noted about their use of such terms: (a) The terms represent undifferentiated entities. Whatever they may indicate, it is systematically homogeneous. Uncritical use of such

---

[34] Elliott and Merrill, p. 38: "One of the most significant concepts in the understanding of social problems is the idea of multiple causation."

[35] See above comments on political relevance. C. A. Ellwood (b) p. 324: "We may, perhaps, sum up this chapter by saying that it is evident that the cure of poverty is not to be sought merely in certain economic rearrangements, but in scientific control of the whole life process of human society. This means that in order to get rid of poverty, the defects in education in government, in religion and morality, in philanthropy, and even in physical heredity, must be got rid of. Of course, this can only be done when there is a scientific understanding of the conditions necessary for normal human social life."

[36] J. L. Gillin (a), pp. 51–128: ". . . the modern theory of the causes of poverty has passed beyond any one-sided explanation to a many-sided theory." The following conditions of poverty and dependence are discussed: poor natural resources, adverse climate, adverse weather, insect pests, disasters, illness and diseases, physical inheritance, mental inheritance, adverse surroundings of children, death or disability of the earner, unemployment, lack of proper wages, traditions, customs, habits, advertising and instalment buying, fluctuations between costs of living and income, inequitable distribution of wealth and income, family marital relations, political conditions, unwise philanthropy, etc. After these discussions, *family cases* are presented as ". . . studies in causation."

[37] Whereas many socialist theories have tended to overlook the elastic elements that do exist in a society. Cf. K. Mannheim, *Politica*, pp. 25–26.

[38] C. H. Cooley (a), p. 46.

[39] Max Lerner, *It Is Later than You Think*, pp. 14–15; and *Encyclopaedia of the Social Sciences*, article "Social Progress." See documentation and consequences below.

a term as "the" permits a writer the hidden assumption in politically crucial contexts of a homogeneous and harmonious whole.[40] The large texture of "the society" will take care of itself, it is somehow and in the long run harmonious,[41] it has a "strain toward consistency" running through it;[42] or, if not this, then only the co-operation of all is needed,[43] or perhaps even a right moral feeling is taken as a solution.[44] (b) In their formal emptiness these terms are commensurate with the low level of abstraction. Their *formality* facilitates the empirical concern with "everyday" problems of (community) milieu. (c) In addition to their "descriptive" use, such terms are used normatively. The "social" becomes a good term when it is used in ethical polemics against "individualism" or against such abstract moral qualities as "selfishness," lack of "altruism," or of "antisocial" sentiments.[45] "Social" is conceived as a "co-operative" "sharing" of something or as "conducive to the general welfare."[46] The late eighteenth-century use of "society" as against "state" by the rising bourgeoisie had already endowed "society" with a "democratic" tinge which this literature

---

[40] Gillin, Dittmer, and Colbert, p. 11: "All this group life is nicely woven into a system that we call society. . . ."

[41] *Ibid.*, p. 15: "But the aim of society is ever directed to the task of bringing uniform advantages to all." C. A. Ellwood (b), p. 395: "Social organization may refer to any condition or relation of the elements of a social group; but by social order we mean a settled and harmonious relation between the individuals or the parts of a society. The problem of social order is then the problem of harmonious adaptation among the individuals of the group. . . ."

[42] It is significant that it was Sumner, with his tacit belief in "natural" order, who set forth the phrase and what it implies.

[43] Gillin, Dittmer, and Colbert, p. 13: "Since a community is made up of a number of neighborhoods, it is necessary that all cooperate in order to secure better schools, improved. . . ."

[44] J. L. Gillin (a), p. 133: "Only as a passion for social righteousness takes the place of an imperative desire for selfish advantage . . . will society do away with the conditions that now depress some classes of the population and exhalt others."

[45] C. A. Ellwood (b), p. 84: ". . . increasing altruism is necessary for the success of those more and more complex forms of cooperation which characterize higher civilization and upon which it depends." G. B. Mangold, p. 17: "Without the spirit of altruism society would be but a sorry exhibition of the collective humanity that we believe has been made in the image of God." Conversely, the "antisocial" is held to include certain abstract, moral traits of individuals. Elliott and Merrill, p. 43: "An analysis of the disorganization process suggests two types of anti-social forces: (1) the consciously directed anti-social forces and (2) the impersonal organic forces which are an outgrowth of the formalism discussed above . . . to advance their own selfish ends. These men are thoroughly aware of their antisocial attitudes. Social values have no meaning for them. . . . There has often been no socializing influence in the lives of those men. . . . Cooperation, or 'mutual aid,' the implicit counterpart of effective social organization. . . . Vice areas . . . function because of human appetites, because individual desires are more deeply rooted than any sense of the social implications. . . . The prostitute exists only because she is a means to man's sensual pleasure and satiety"; p. 44: "Sin, vice, crime, corruption, all consciously directed anti-social forces, offer a primrose. . . ." G. B. Mangold, p. 59: "Unsocial habits lead to poverty; particularly do they degrade poverty into dependency. Chief among these vices is intemperance. Before the advent of prohibition it was. . . ." Queen, Bodenhafer, and Harper, p. 4: "When there is . . . characterized by harmony, teamwork, understanding, approval, and the like, we may speak of organization. When the opposite is true and there is a . . . marked by tension, conflict, or drifting apart, we may speak of disorganization."

[46] Gillin, Dittmer, and Colbert, p. 5: "'The word [social] means conclusive to the collective welfare, and thus becomes nearly equivalent to moral' [Cooley, *Human Nature and the Social Order*, p. 4] . . . it is this . . . meaning that comes closest to our interpretation . . . —'conducive to the collective welfare'—relationships, and products of relationships that are believed to foster and promote *group life*, and to insure *group survival*."

transmits. (*d*) There is a strong tendency for the term "society" to be practically assimilated to, or conceived largely in terms of, primary groups and small homogeneous communities. Such a conception typically characterizes the literature within our purview.[47] In explaining it, we come upon an element that is highly important in understanding the total perspective.

The basis of "stability," "order," or "solidarity" is not typically analyzed in these books, but a conception of such a basis is implicitly used and sanctioned,[48] for some normative conception of a socially "healthy" and stable organization is involved in the determination of "pathological" conditions. "Pathological" behavior is not discerned in a *structural* sense (i.e., as incommensurate with an existent structural type) or in a *statistical* sense (i.e., as deviations from central tendencies). This is evidenced by the regular assertion that pathological conditions *abound* in the city.[49] If they "*abound*" therein, they cannot be "abnormal" in the statistical sense and are not likely to prevail in the structural sense. It may be proposed that the norms in terms of which "pathological"

---

[47] J. L. Gillin (*b*), p. 313: ". . . personal relationships . . . are the most important ties in the social organization. . . ." C. A. Ellwood (*b*), pp. 3–4: "The tendency in the best sociological thinking is to emphasize the importance, for the understanding of our social life, of 'primary' or face-to-face groups"; p. 77: "Primary groups . . . are of most interest sociologically, because they exhibit social life at its maximum intensity, and because they are the bearers of the most vital elements in social life, especially the traditions of civilization"; pp. 70–80: "The chief importance of primary groups in our social life, however, is that they . . . furnish the 'patterns' which we attempt to realize in our social life in general"; pp. 84–85: "All human history has, from one point of view, been a struggle to transfer altruism and solidarity of the family to successively larger and larger groups of men"; pp. 90–91: "Primary, or face-to-face groups are the key to the understanding of our social life. . . ." Gillin, Dittmer, Colbert, p. 282: ". . . the home is probably our most fundamental social institution . . ."; p. 285: "Anything that endangers the stability of the family endangers society." J. H. S. Bossard (*a*), p. 555: "Family life is the focal point of virtually all of our social problems."

[48] C. A. Ellwood (*b*), pp. 79–80: "The very ideal of social solidarity itself comes from the unity experienced in such [primary] groups." Elliott and Merrill, p. 581: "An ever-increasing number of persons living in the giant cities has become completely deracinated, cut off from all stable primary ties. They have lost not only their physical home, but often their spiritual home as well. Social disorganization breeds in these unattached masses of the urban proletariat. They furnish willing nuclei for robbery, brigandage, and revolution."

[49] J. L. Gillin (*b*), p. 411: "In the city we have a greater degree of disorganization in the sense in which we use that term"; p. 410: ". . . in the simple and well-organized ties of country life . . ."; p. 409: "Recreation in the country is largely homemade. . . . In the city it is professional. . . . The patterns of behavior . . . are here again disorganized and new patterns have to be found." Gillette and Reinhardt, p. 116: "Cities exhibit all the social problems, save those peculiar to agricultural extractive pursuits." H. P. Fairchild, p. 304: "Since there are no *natural* facilities available to the majority of the *denizens* of cities for the gratification of the desire for dancing, it inevitably follows that provision is made on a commercial basis" (my italics). C. M. Rosenquist, p. 47: "The controls which were effective in the small, settled farm community no longer suffice in . . . the city. To this fact may be traced many of the conditions we speak of as social problems. . . ." W. G. Beach and E. E. Walker, pp. 102–103: ". . . men find their life interests and values in group membership and participation. The most influential groups are those which provide intimate, face-to-face relationships, as the family, the playground, the club, the neighborhood, and the small community. . . . Any wholesome and satisfying life must provide for a continuation of such small groups and institutional forms. . . . One of the most elusive and challenging problems arising from the growth of cities is that of preventing the complete disorganization of essential social groups. In the rural community. . . ." J. H. S. Bossard (*a*), p. 113: "The marked trend of population to the city and the rapid rise of large urban centers, together with their reflex upon the rural regions, constitute the basis of virtually every problem to be discussed in this volume."

conditions are detected are "humanitarian ideals." But we must then ask for the social orientation of such ideals.[50] In this literature the operating criteria of the pathological are typically *rural* in orientation and extraction.[51]

Most of the "problems" considered arise because of the urban deterioration of certain values which can live genuinely only in a relatively homogeneous and primary rural milieu. The "problems" discussed typically concern urban behavior. When "rural problems" are discussed, they are conceived as due to encroaching urbanization.[52] The notion of disorganization is quite often merely the absence of that *type* of organization associated with the stuff of primary-group communities having Christian and Jeffersonian legitimations.[53]

Cooley, the local colorist of American sociology, was the chief publicist of this conception of normal organization. He held "the great historical task of mankind" to be the more effective and wider organization of that moral order and pattern of virtues developed in primary groups and communities.[54] Cooley took the idealists' absolute[55] and gave it the characteristics of an organic village; all the world should be an enlarged, Christian-democratic version of a rural village. He practically assimilated "society" to this primary-group com-

---

[50] This is what Waller does *not* do in his provocative discussion of "humanitarian" and "organizing mores" ("Social Problems and the Mores," *American Sociological Review*, December 1936, pp. 922–933).

[51] J. L. Gillin (*b*), p. 407: The home "developing as . . . rural" is considered "disorganized" in the city; p. 409: "[In the city] it is only the rebel, unable and unwilling to adjust himself to machine and organization, who retains personal independence. . . . The farmer, conscious that he lives by his own thinking . . . responds to his environment with a feeling of independence— a normal response. The city worker has no keen perception of his dependence upon nature." Elliott and Merrill, p. 32: "However different their approach, the basic dilemma of civilization is the fundamental disparity of values and standards of universally accepted definitions of the situation."

[52] C. A. Ellwood (*b*), p. 281: "The reflex of the city problem is the rural problem." J. L. Gillen (*b*), p. 429: "[Urbanization] which has modified the solidarity of the rural family. . . ." W. J. Hayes and I. V. Shannon, p. 22: "Contacts . . . emancipate individuals from control of primary groups . . . this leads to setting up personal norms of behavior instead of conforming to group standards." (Implies no conception of *urban* types of norms.)

[53] The intellectual consequences of the rural to urban drift are much wider than the perspectives noted in the literature of pathology. In more general American sociology the writings of a man like E. A. Ross are to be understood in terms of a reaction of those oriented to a farmer's democracy against the growth of big business, in its control of railroads, etc. Another division of American sociology in which America's rural past is *intellectually* evident is "rural sociology" itself. This field shows the positive side of the matter, for here the yearning for the values associated with rural simplicity and neighborliness is even more noticeable. In this literature a primary, rural heritage is taken as the source of "stability" and is conceived as the reservoir of "values." Such straddling concepts as "urban" function to limit recognition of the urban character of dominant contemporary social structures. In a historical sense we need not argue with these emphases: the underlying form of American democracy and religion, e.g., has drawn much from the dominance of a rural society. And a rapid urbanization may well be only a veneer upon masses of rurally oriented personalities. But the kind of structural stability in America which grew from rural patterns is historical. In the world today the kind of stability that can—indeed, in part has—emerged from the hunger for those primary contacts historically associated with ties of blood and closeness to soil is a streamlined variety.

[54] *Social Organization*, ch. v.

[55] G. H. Mead, "Cooley's Contribution to American Social Thought," *American Journal of Sociology*, XXXV, 701: "Cooley was Emersonian in finding the individual self in an oversoul." Cf. G. W. F. Hegel, *Lectures on the Philosophy of History* (London: Geo. Bell & Sons, 1884), especially pp. 39–44.

munity, and he blessed it emotionally and conceptually.[56] "There is reflected here," says T. V. Smith of Cooley—and what he says will hold for the typical social pathologist—"what is highly common in our culture, an ideal of intimacy short of which we do not rest satisfied where other people are concerned. Social distance is a dire fate, achieved with difficulty and lamented as highly unideal, not to say as immoral, in our Christian traditions. It is not enough to have saints; we must have 'communion' of the saints. In order to have social relations, we must nuzzle one another."[57]

The aim to preserve rurally oriented values and stabilities is indicated by the implicit model which operates to detect urban disorganization; it is also shown by the stress upon *community* welfare. The community is taken as a major unit, and often it sets the scope of concern and problematization.[58] It is also within the framework of ideally democratic communities that proposed solutions are to be worked out.[59] It should be noted that sometimes, although not typically or exclusively, solutions are conceived as dependent upon abstract moral

---

[56] Note the common association of urban "impersonality" and "formalism" with "disorganization." Elliott and Merrill, p. 16: ". . . lack of harmony between the various units of the social order is in a sense . . . exemplified by the impersonal nature of the social organization and the consequent process of social disorganization . . . [cf. C. H. Cooley, *Social Process*, pp. 3–29]"; p. 574: "There is a very close relationship between formalism and disorganization, although at first glance the two states appear to be opposite poles in the social process. They are in reality sequential steps in the same great movement of disorganization, which grows out of formalism. . . ."

[57] *Beyond Conscience*, p. 111.

[58] C. A. Ellwood (*b*), p. 12: "All forms of association are of interest to the sociologist, though not all are of equal importance. The natural, genetic social groups, which we may call 'communities,' serve best to exhibit sociological problems. Through the study of such simple and primary groups as the family and the neighborhood group, for example, the problems of sociology can be much better attacked than through the study of society at large or association in general"; pp. 75–77: ". . . natural groupings, such as the family, the neighborhood, the city, the state or province, and the nation. They may be, and usually are, called *communities*, since they are composed of individuals who carry on all phases of a common life. Voluntary, purposive associations always exist within some community, whether large or small. Groups which we call 'communities' are, therefore, more embracing, more stable, less artificial and specialized than purely voluntary groups. For this reason communities are of more interest to the sociologist than specialized voluntary groups, and sociology is in a peculiar sense a study of the problems of community life." J. H. S. Bossard (*a*), pp. 49–50: "Acceptance of the community as a definite unit in social work and in social theory has become general during the past fifteen years. American participation in the World War was an important factor in bringing this about, first because the community constituted the basic expression of that democratic spirit which the war engendered, and second, the community was seized upon by the various war-time activities and drives as the most effective unit for the mobilization of the spirit and resources of the nation."

[59] Gillin, Dittmer, and Colbert, p. 15: ". . . *social work*, which means, scientifically developing and adjusting human relations in a way that will secure normal life to individuals and communities and encourage individual and community progress"; p. 47: ". . . it is important to keep in mind that the central problem is that of adjusting our social life and our social institutions, so that, as individuals and as communities, we may use and enjoy the largest measure of civilization possible, and promote further progress." M. P. Follett (*a*), Part III, has suggested that neighborhood groups be organized into political units. This would permit the expression of daily life and bring to the surface live needs that they may become the substance of politics. The neighborhood as a political unit would make possible friendly acquaintance; it would socialize people and would make for "the realization of oneness."

traits or democratic surrogates of them, such as a "unanimous public will." [60]

"Cultural lag" is considered by many pathologists to be the concept with which many scattered problems may be detected and systematized. Whereas the approach by deviation from norms is oriented "ideologically" toward a rural type of order and stability, the cultural-lag model is tacitly oriented in a "utopian" [61] and progressive manner toward changing some areas of the culture or certain institutions so as to "integrate" them with the state of progressive technology. [62] We must analyze the use made by pathologists of "lag" rather than abstract formulations of it. [63]

Even though all the situations called "lags" *exist* in the present, their functional realities are referred back, away from the present. Evaluations are thus translated into a time sequence; cultural lag is an assertion of unequal "progress." It tells us what changes are "called for," what changes "ought" to have come about and didn't. In terms of various spheres of society it says what progress is, tells us how much we have had, ought to have had, didn't have, and when and where we didn't have it. The imputation of "lag" is complicated by the historical judgment in whose guise it is advanced and by the programmatic content being shoved into pseudo-objective phrases, as, for example, "called for."

It is not enough to recognize that the stating of problems in terms of cultural lag involves evaluations, however disguised. One must find the general loci of this kind of evaluation and then explain why just this form of evaluation has been so readily accepted and widely used by pathologists. The model in which institutions lag behind technology and science involves a positive evaluation of natural science and of orderly progressive change. Loosely, it derives from a liberal continuation of the enlightenment with its full rationalism, its messianic and now politically naive admiration of physical science as a kind of thinking and activity, and with its concept of time as progress. This notion of progress was carried into American colleges by the once prevalent Scottish moral philosophy. From after the Civil War through the first two or three decades of the twentieth century the expanding business and middle classes were taking over instruments of production, political power, and social prestige; and many of the academic men of the generation were recruited from these rising strata and/or actively mingled with them. Notions of progress are congenial to those who are rising in the scale of position and income.

Those sociologists who think in terms of this model have not typically

---

[60] J. L. Gillin (*b*), p. 97: "The 'liquor problem' is as acute in the United States today as it ever was in the past, perhaps even more so"; p. 101: "The solution must spring from an aroused and unanimous public will."

[61] Cf. K. Mannheim, *Ideology and Utopia*, for definitions of these terms.

[62] However, "lag" and "norms" are not unrelated: Queen, Bodenhafer, and Harper, p. 437: "Much of the discussion of cultural lags in the family assumes some kind of normal pattern which is commonly believed to have permanent validity because of the functions performed."

[63] See examples given in J. W. Woodward's "Critical Notes on the Cultural Lag Concept," *Social Forces*, March 1934, p. 388.

focused upon the conditions and interest groups underlying variant "rates of change" in different spheres. One might say that in terms of the rates of change at which sectors of culture *could* move, it is technology that is "lagging," for the specific reason of the control of patents, etc., by intrenched interests.[64] In contrast to the pathologists' use, Veblen's use of "lag, leak, and friction" is a structural analysis of industry versus business enterprise.[65] He focused on where "the lag" seemed to pinch; he attempted to show how the trained incapacity of legitimate businessmen acting within entrepreneurial canons would result in a commercial sabotage of production and efficiency in order to augment profits within a system of price and ownership. He did not like this "unworkman-like result," and he detailed its mechanism. In the pathologists' usage the conception has lost this specific and structural anchorage: it has been generalized and applied to everything fragmentarily. This generalization occurs with the aid of such blanket terms as "adaptive culture" and "material culture."[66] There is no specific focus for a program of action embodied in the application of such terms.

Another model in terms of which disorganizations are instituted is that of "social change" itself.[67] This model is not handled in any one typical way, but usually it carries the implicit assumption that human beings are "adjusted" satisfactorily to any social condition that has existed for a long time and that, when some aspect of social life changes, it may lead to a social problem.[68] The notion is oriented ideologically and yet participates in assumptions similar to those of cultural lag, which, indeed, might be considered a variant of it. Such a scheme for problematization buttresses and is buttressed by the idea of continuous process, commented on above; but here the slow, "evolutionary" pace of change is taken explicitly as normal and organized,[69] whereas "discontinuity" is taken as problematic.[70] The orientation to "rural" types of organization

---

[64] See, e.g., B. J. Stern's article in *Annals of the American Academy of Political and Social Science*, November 1938.

[65] *The Engineers and the Price System; The Theory of Business Enterprise.*

[66] J. H. S. Bossard (*a*), p. 5: ". . . as Ogburn put it [W. F. Ogburn, *Social Change* (1922)] to the extent that the adaptive culture has not kept pace with the material culture, the amount of social ill-being has increased relatively."

[67] J. L. Gillin (*b*), p. 416: "Social disorganization is a function of rapidly changing conditions in people's lives." W. J. Hayes and I. V. Shannon, p. 20: "Social disorganization is an abrupt break in the existing social arrangements or a serious alteration in the routine of group life causing maladjustment." H. W. Odum, p. 100: ". . . if one reviews the general categories of social problems already listed in previous chapters, it must be clear that most of them or their present manifestations are due to or accentuated by the process of social change."

[68] The point is made and acutely discussed by Rosenquist, pp. 8–10.

[69] Gillin, Dittmer, and Colbert, p. 48: "Social life and its products require long periods of time to develop and ripen. . . ." Gillette and Reinhardt, p. 13: "The larger proportion of social changes are small and simple, and resemble osmosis in the field of physics and organic life." This gradualism is related to the orientation to primary group relations and experiences and hence to the "sharing" conception of the social. E.g., Elliott and Merrill, p. 11: "Assimilation, on the other hand, is gradual and depends upon some degree of contact and communication, if there is to be any vital sharing of common experience (Cf. M. P. Follett, *Creative Experience*). . . ."

[70] Gillette and Reinhardt, p. 30: ". . . the need for thought about discontinuity in industry or education and about our dependence on proper training to keep society stabilized and progressive should be emphasized"; p. 21: "The habitual, daily, routine, conventional

should be recalled. In line with the stress on continuous process, the point where sanctioned order meets advisable change is not typically or structurally drawn.[71] A conception of "balance" is usual and sometimes is explicitly sanctioned.[72] The question, "Changes in what spheres induce disorganization?" is left open; the position taken is usually somewhere between extremes, both of which are held to be bad.[73] This comes out in the obvious fact that what a conservative calls *dis*organization, a radical might well call *re*organization. Without a construction of total social structures that are actually emerging, one remains caught between simple evaluations.

Besides deviation from norms, orientation to rural principles of stability, cultural lag, and social change, another conception in terms of which "problems" are typically discussed is that of adaptation or "adjustment" and their opposites.[74] The pathological or disorganized is the maladjusted. This concept, as well as that of the "normal," is usually left empty of concrete, social content;[75] or its content is, in effect, a propaganda for conformity to those norms and traits ideally associated with small-town, middle-class milieux.[76] When it is an

activities of life fortunately make up the greater part of life, most of the time. Often, however, they are broken across by social breakdowns, disturbances, and dislocations and the appearance of troublesome classes of persons." C. A. Ellwood (*a*), p. 230: ". . . revolution is not a *normal* method of social change; . . . it marks the breakdown of the normal means of social development; . . . it is not inevitable, but may be easily avoided by plasticity in social institutions and in the mental attitudes of classes and individuals. . . ."

[71] The notion of temporal contingency, at times extended to the point of historical irrationality, plays into the processual, nonstructural characteristics of the perspective; notice also its commensurability with the apolitical and one-thing-at-a-time reformism. Elliott and Merrill, p. 3: "Life is dynamic. Life is ceaseless, bewildering change, and man, armed though he is with the experience of the past, can never be certain of the future. He must recognize that the immediate present is a constantly changing frame of reference and that future problems are a matter of chance for which the past offers no sure panacea."

[72] E. C. Hayes' Editor's Introduction to U. G. Weatherly, p. xii: "Realization that progressive change is not likely to be less in the generation next to come . . . and determination . . . to promote progress, is the normal attitude for every person who is animated by generous loyalty and . . . ." Weatherly, p. 138: "Both innovation and conservatism have their value, and the balance between them, which is an ideal attitude . . ."; p. 380: "Discipline and liberation are not two antagonistic processes; they are complimentary parts of the same process, which is social equilibration. They illustrate the law of physics . . . stability is reached only by a balance of forces."

[73] A. Ellwood (*a*), p. vii: "The aim of the book is to indicate the direction which our social thinking must take if we are to avoid revolution, on the one hand, and reactions, on the other."

[74] H. P. Fairchild, p. 35: ". . . it can be safely said that maladjustments are among the most numerous and important of all forms of abnormality, frequently being so extensive as to include entire social groups or classes."

[75] Gillin, Dittmer, and Colbert, p. 536: "All social problems grow out of *the* social problem —the problem of the adjustment of man to his universe, and of the social universe to man. The maladjustments in these relationships give us all our social problems. . . ." H. P. Fairchild, p. 16: "While the word 'normal' carries a fairly definite and, for the most part, accurate implication to the mind of any intelligent person, it is nevertheless extremely difficult to define in concrete terms. . . . As commonly used to convey a definite idea, the word 'normal' means that which is in harmony with the general make-up and organization of the object under discussion—that which is consistent with other normal factors."

[76] Elliott and Merrill, p. 17, correctly assert that in "Edward T. Divine's discussion of 'the normal life' the norm is the healthy and uneventful life cycle of the average middle-class man or woman. These persons are never subjected to the temptations of great wealth. Neither do they come in contact with poverty, crime, vice, and other unpleasantly sordid aspects of life [*The Normal Life*, pp. 5–8]. His discussion is thus a consideration of the 'normal standards' for the several ages of the bourgeoisie. . . ."

individual who is thought to be maladjusted, the "social type" within which he is maladjusted is not stated. Social and moral elements are masked by a quasi-biological meaning of the term "adaptation"[77] with an entourage of apparently socially bare terms like "existence" and "survival," which seem still to draw prestige from the vogue of evolutionism.[78] Both the quasi-biological and the structureless character of the concept "adjustment" tend, by formalization, to universalize the term, thus again obscuring specific social content. Use of "adjustment" accepts the goals and the means of smaller community milieux.[79] At the most, writers using these terms suggest techniques or means believed to be less disruptive than others to attain the goals that are given. They do not typically consider whether or not certain groups or individuals caught in economically underprivileged situations can possibly obtain the current goals without drastic shifts in the basic institutions which channel and promote them. The idea of adjustment seems to be most directly applicable to a social scene in which, on the one hand, there is a society and, on the other, an individual immigrant.[80] The immigrant then "adjusts" to the new environment. The "immigrant problem" was early in the pathologist's center of focus, and the concepts used in stating it may have been carried over as the bases for a model of experience and formulations of other "problems." *The Polish Peasant* (1918), which has had a very strong influence on the books under consideration, was empirically focused upon an immigrant group.

---

[77] When it is so hidden; but note the heavily sentimental endowment the term may receive: R. C. Dexter, p. 408: ". . . few of the present generation of little ones, and fewer still of the next, will never see the sun or the green grass because of the sins of their parents or the carelessness of their physician; and thanks to our increasing provision for free public education, more and more adapted to the needs of the individual child, thousands of boys and girls will become intelligent, responsible citizens, worthy of a free nation, instead of pawns for unscrupulous politicians. All this and much more is due to social adjustments, made by the unceasing effort and sacrifice of men and women who. . . ."

[78] J. L. Gillin (*b*), p. 4: "Social pathology . . . is the study of the social patterns and processes involved in man's failure to adjust himself and his institutions to the necessities of existence to the end that he may survive and satisfy the felt needs of his nature."

[79] J. L. Gillin (*b*), p. 8: "An individual who does not approximate these [socially approved] standards is said to be *unadjusted*. If he does not concern himself with living up to them, he is said to be demoralized or disorganized." R. C. Dexter, p. 407: "In this book the term Social Adjustment has been . . . used as applying to . . . the necessary task of smoothing-off the rough edges and softening the sledge-hammer blows of an indifferent social system. The term . . . is practically synonymous with social adaptation—the fitting of man to his complete environment, physical and social alike. Until the present it has been the especially maladjusted individual or group who has receive the service of 'straighteners.'" (Note *ideological* orientation of concept.)

[80] H. P. Fairchild, p. 34: "The other form of incompetence, which may be called 'maladjustment,' does not imply any lack on the part of the individual himself. . . . The man is all right, but he is not in the right place. Our immigrants furnish abundant examples of this form of incompetence. . . . But the foreigner is not by any means the sole example of maladjustment. Our modern life, particularly our modern city life, teems with cases of this sort." J. H. S. Bossard (*a*), p. 100 (under "The Immigrant's Problem of Adjustment"): "To most persons, life consists in large measure of habitual responses to the demands of a fairly fixed environment. When man changes his environment, new and perhaps untried responses are called for. New adjustments must be made, as we say." J. L. Gillin (*b*), p. 10: "Social pathology . . . arises out of the maladjustment between the individual and the social structure." Elliott and Merrill, p. 22: "Just as an effective social organization implies a harmony between individual and social interests, so a disorganized social order must involve a conflict between individual and social points of view."

In approaching the notion of adjustment, one may analyze the specific illustrations of maladjustment that are given and from these instances infer a type of social person who in this literature is evaluated as "adjusted." The ideally adjusted man of the social pathologists is "socialized." This term seems to operate ethically as the opposite of "selfish;"[81] it implies that the adjusted man conforms to middle-class morality and motives and "participates" in the gradual progress of respectable institutions. If he is not a "joiner," he certainly gets around and into many community organizations.[82] If he is socialized, the individual thinks of others and is kindly toward them. He does not brood or mope about but is somewhat extravert, eagerly participating in his community's institutions. His mother and father were not divorced, nor was his home ever broken. He is "successful"—at least in a modest way—since he is ambitious; but he does not speculate about matters too far above his means, lest he become "a fantasy thinker," and the little men don't scramble after the big money. The less abstract the traits and fulfilled "needs" of "the adjusted man" are, the more they gravitate toward the norms of independent middle-class persons verbally living out Protestant ideals in the small towns of America.[83]

---

[81] Gillin, Dittmer, and Colbert, pp. 16–17: "By *socialization* we mean the directing of human motives toward giving to 'even the least' of the members of the social whole the benefits of cultural development. Socialization is thus practically the opposite to *aloofness*, *selfishness*, *greed*, *exploitation*, and *profiteering*. It causes the individual and the group to *feel* their *oneness* with the social whole. . . . In brief, what society regards as *moral*, i.e., good for the whole, becomes the aim of socialized individuals and groups. This being true, the improvement of society rests to a very large extent upon *moral progress*."

[82] See Queen and Gruener, *Social Pathology: Obstacles to Social Participation*. These authors would deny this mode of statement, but such verbal denials must be tested against what they have done and the framework they have actually employed in defining pathologies. Their criterion of the pathological is correctly indicated in the subtitle of their book. Elliott and Merrill, p. 580: "There are various criteria by which the degree of individual participation may be measured roughly . . . whether or not he votes at elections . . . the individual's ownership of real or personal property . . . the degree of specific interest in community activities may be roughly measured by the number and character of the institutions to which the individual belongs, as well as the voluntary community activities in which he participates. Communities in which there is a high percentage of individuals with a positive rating on the items listed above are logically those which are the most highly organized and efficient." (Note the character of the institutions, participation in which is defined as organized.)

[83] See above documentation; notice the Protestant ethical accent on *utility* and what it will do for one, apparently irrespective of social fact: Gillin, Dittmer, and Colbert, p. 106: "People who are useful, no matter what happens to be their race or color, come to be liked and respected. Consequently, the central aim of a sound educational program should be to teach people to be useful. (Hart, Hornell, *The Science of Social Relations*, 1927, pp. 521–524.)" In the following, note the norm of competitiveness: Elliott and Merrill, pp. 29–30: "Often, however, the individual cannot or will not compete. We then have the following pathological manifestations: '. . . the *dependent* . . . who is unable to compete; the *defective* . . . who is, if not unable, at least handicapped in his efforts to compete. The *criminal*, on the other hand, . . . who is perhaps unable, but at any rate refuses, to compete according to the rules which society lays down.' (Park and Burgess, *Introduction to the Science of Sociology*, p. 560)." Among the traits thought to characterize "the good life from the standpoint of the individual," Odum, pp. 50–51, cites: "patience," "specialized knowledge of some particular thing," "skill," "optimism," "love of work," "dynamic personality," "moderation," "trained will power," etc. Cf., in this connection, K. Davis, "Mental Hygiene and the Class Structure," *Psychiatry: Journal of the Biology and Pathology of Interpersonal Relations*, February 1938, pp. 55–65.

A New Look at Mills' Critique

EMIL BEND AND MARTIN VOGELFANGER

The study of social problems was one of the original areas of inquiry of American sociology, and an important impetus to its development. Today it is among the most frequently offered courses in the sociology curriculum.[1] One might guess that such a traditional and popular subject would be completely accepted within the field, and fairly well integrated with the theory it has produced. On the face of it, one might not expect much controversy over such a "veteran crowd-pleaser"[2] as social problems. Yet controversy there is, for over the study of social problems, disorganization, pathology hover some of the persistent dilemmas of sociology. Published criticism of this area either explicitly or implicitly, but invariably, touches upon such basic issues as the boundaries and goals of sociology, the professional roles of sociologists, and public images of sociology. Behind every critique of the sociology of social problems reside questions in the sociology of knowledge. In some cases, these questions remain half-hidden; in others, they are prominently displayed. The latter is true of C. Wright Mills' widely quoted article, "The Professional Ideology of Social Pathologists."[3] Mills, whose paper is summarized below, wrote: "Because of its persistent importance in the development of American sociology, and its supposed proximity to the social scene, 'social pathology' seems an appropriate point of entry for the examination of the style of reflection and the social historical basis of American sociology."[4]

The criticism of social problems that has found its way into articles and book reviews in the professional journals falls into several classes. One contains the descriptions and/or denunciations of social problems as too distant from the mainstreams of contemporary sociology. One should examine the problems of society as one would any other sociologically relevant phenomena, as a means

---

Source: Prepared especially for this volume.

[1] The terminological smog is very heavy in this region. The field has been titled "social problems," "social disorganization," "social pathology," "social deviation," and still more. Although the different approaches vary in emphasis, they essentially cover the same ground, and fit into the same niches within sociology curricula. Since this paper is concerned with this whole sector of sociology, the terms shall be used interchangeably, except when otherwise noted.

[2] Podell, Vogelfanger, and Rogers, "Sociology in American Colleges: 15 Years Later," *American Sociological Review* (February 1959). Of the 3763 undergraduate courses in the sample of 263 college catalogues, 13.9 per cent were categorized as "social problems" courses. It was noted that a number of courses dealing with social problems were placed in other categories for various reasons.

[3] *American Journal of Sociology*, 49 (September 1943), pp. 165–180.

[4] *Ibid.*, p. 165.

to the end of more and better facts and theories of social behavior. The foci of interest, modes of analysis, and underlying values in the field of social problems prevent its serving the above purpose. So runs this type of argument.

A second class of criticisms emphasizes the inability of the sociologists of social problems to solve, or perhaps even to perceive, the important problems of society. The field of social problems should apply the available resources of sociology toward the goal of understanding and ameliorating the conditions that trouble mankind. The foci of interest, and so on, of social problems prevent the achievement of that goal.

The origins of such a classification can be traced to the very early days of American sociology, to Ward's distinction between "pure" and "applied" sociology, and to the many early references to societal or scientific problems versus social or ameliorative ones.

C. Wright Mills' critique, mentioned above, contains elements of both types of criticism. Mills examined a number of social problems books of the 1920s and 1930s, and discovered great uniformities in the "typical perspectives and key concepts" of the field. He examined the life histories of the pathologists, and attributed the textbook uniformities to the overwhelming homogeneity in the social extraction, class, and career patterns of the authors. They were middle-class, rural-oriented individuals who interacted within academic and reform movement environments. The similarity in background, argued Mills, tended to lead to common unchallenged values which entered into the literature and were perpetuated.

The uniformities that Mills uncovered clustered about three points:

1. The nature of society, as seen by the pathologists.
2. The nature of social problems, as seen by the pathologists.
3. The criteria for the selection and organization of problems in textbooks utilized by the pathologists.

1. The model of social organization which the pathologists tended to adopt was that of the small town, blown up in scale. "The good society" was one where the intimacy and homogeneity of primary groups prevailed; where proper social change occurred in a slow and orderly fashion. The "good citizen" was one who joins and helps and is adjusted. Mills pointed to Cooley as one of the original architects of this model, through his emphasis on the "organic" (a harmonious balance of elements) and "processual" (continuous through time) nature of society.

2. Mills suggested that the concept of disorganization utilized by the pathologists quite often meant merely the absence of that type of organization described above. Social problems were often defined in terms of deviations by aggregates of individuals from the existing norms. They arise when numbers of individuals are unwilling or unable to conform to the status quo standards, as a result of encroaching urbanization, immigration, and so on. Norm violations were sometimes seen simply as biological impulses breaking through societal restrictions.

This analysis was supported in Mills' remembered phrase, by "a paste-pot ecletic psychology."

In addition to the "deviation from norms" approach, another popular orientation to social problems centered about the concept of social change. The assumption in this type of analysis was that stability of any social pattern inevitably results in an adjustment to it, whereas change, except for the slow, orderly variety, invariably unlocks the Pandora's box of social problems. A frequent variant of the social change approach was that of culture lag, where social problems emerge out of the unequal rates of change of the different aspects of the culture.

The solutions to social problems served up by pathologists had as their major ingredient more and better socialization. In this way, individuals with problems could be adjusted or readjusted, and the repercussions of social change could be controlled more effectively.

3. The value uniformities which led to typical notions of social organization and disorganization also determined the principles for selecting and organizing problems in texts. For example, the method of presenting social problems was greatly influenced by the case-study approach of the social worker, in that problems selected leaned to the "practical problems of everyday life," problems of individuals in specific situations. The "situational approach" of W. I. Thomas contributed greatly to this mode of problems perception. The case-study approach plus the lack of any theory resulted in books that were "fragmentary collections of scattered problems and facts" selected in a non-random fashion, and characterized by an extremely low level of abstraction.

It has already been mentioned that Mills attributed the value patterns underlying pathology books primarily to the class origins and experiences of the authors. A second determining factor, present but less fully developed in Mills' analysis, is worth mentioning because of its relevance to our analysis of the contemporary social problems literature which comprises the major portion of this paper. This deals with the various academic pressures that have shaped the development of the social problems field. Almost everything written by sociologists about social problems has been in the form of textbooks, intended for student audiences. Mills commented on some results in the student-centered orientation: "[Textbook] systematization occurs in a context of presentation and justification rather than within a context of discovery."[5] And "Since one test of [textbook] success is wide adoption, the very spread of the public for which they are written tends to insure a textbook tolerance of the common-place."[6]

What, according to Mills, have been the consequences of the middle-class, rural-oriented value uniformities shared by social pathologists?

First, they have been responsible for the lack of any sociological orientation

5 *Ibid.*, p. 167.
6 *Ibid.*, p. 168.

in social problems writings. Mills' sample of pathologists exhibited an inability to focus upon the structural bases of society, to perceive the structural origins and interrelations of the individual conditions that have been described as social problems. This lack of theory has had the effect of supporting the acceptance of the existing norms as given and therefore good, and of portraying deviation as undesirable. Pathologists could not recognize that problems can emerge not only from deviation, but from conformity as well—conformity to conflicting or changing norms. Similarly, almost all stratificational aspects of social problems have been obscured by the lack of theory.

Second, the common values have prevented pathologists from attaining their avowed goal, the amelioration of problems, the reformation of the status quo. Mills insisted that the ways problems have been perceived and analyzed, giving tacit and often open support to the status quo, made collective action oriented to their solution virtually impossible.

The above rough sketch does not do justice to the fullness and vigor of Mills' argument. With all its shortcomings, several of which Mills acknowledges in footnotes, we feel that it adequately describes a major portion of the output of American social pathologists of the post-World War I and pre-World War II period.

We would like to comment on a major problem inherent in the nonempirical type of analysis of which Mills' and the present paper are both examples. Mills does caution his readers that ". . . the aim is to grasp typical perspectives and key concepts. Hence no one of the texts . . . exemplifies *all* the concepts analyzed; certain elements are not so visible in given texts as in others, and some elements are not evidenced in certain texts at all."[7] After reading his article, one still imagines a fraternity of pathologists, befriending each other socially, and supporting each other ideologically. While it is beyond doubt that there existed a common core of values underlying the social problems literature, it must be noted that many pathologists were aware of the situation, and themselves critical of the consequences of such homogeneity. One can see this clearly in pathologists' book reviews of their "brethren's" works, or in the introductory remarks in a textbook, justifying the need for it to be published. Elliott and Merrill, whose very popular text is included in Mills' sample, wrote in 1933: "Courses in 'Social Problems' or 'Social Pathology' have been among the most popular offerings of academic sociology, yet there has seldom been any attempt to integrate the subject matter within a scheme of systematic sociology. For the most part, the approach to the conglomerate topics listed under these headings has been on a strictly common-sense level."[8]

It is interesting to see that Elliott and Merrill have, in turn, been found guilty of quite similar "textbook crimes."

---

[7] *Ibid.*, p. 168.
[8] Mabel A. Elliott and Francis E. Merrill, *Social Disorganization* (New York: Harper, 1961), 4th ed., p. ix.

The acceptance of Mills' description of the social problems literature does not commit us to accept his orientation to social pathology and pathologists. It is not difficult to see that the concepts and perspectives that Mills offers as replacements for the existing rural, middle-class oriented ones are themselves bound up in an ideology. Martindale, for example, in his excellent outline of past and present developments in the study of social problems in America, notes that "the one thing . . . all the critics—from Mills to Lemert, and many others in addition—are agreed upon is the presence of valuations in the theory of social disorganization. There is no question whatsoever about the fact that they are correct." Still, "the criticism is frequently marred . . . by the fact that the critic objects to *particular* evaluations rather than to the confusion of facts with values." [9]

The present paper focuses upon certain aspects of the modern body of writing of social pathologists. In common with Mills' article, it is not a systematic study. The content of the volumes in our sample has not been categorized or counted by formal techniques. The attempt has been to establish ideal types, which some existing works closely resemble, others, less so.

Let us stress that we are not interested in describing and evaluating the various approaches to social problems. This material can be found in the introductory chapters of a number of social problems textbooks. We are concerned with the present position and prospects of the field, much as Mills was decades ago. He asked the question, "What has the field of social problems to do with society?" The question underlying this paper is, "What has the field of social problems to do with sociology?" The values underlying that question are those of academic sociology.

We are interested in social pathology only because it has been generally recognized to be a subdivision of sociology,[10] because most such courses have been offered in sociology departments, and because much of the literature of the field has been produced by people with sociology degrees.

We make explicit the belief that the evaluation of any substantive segment or movement in sociology should be based on the answers to the following questions:

1. To what extent does segment or movement "X" utilize any of the theoretical schemes that are representative of modern sociological analysis?

2. To what extent does "X" contribute to the existing bodies of sociological facts and theories or point to possibly fruitful new directions in sociology?

About half a dozen different approaches to the study of the ills of society have been identified in the contemporary problems literature. As mentioned above, they are described in many pathology texts, as well as in the Martindale

---

[9] Don Martindale, "Social Disorganization . . ." in Howard Becker and Alvin C. Boskoff, eds., *Modern Sociological Theory* (New York: Random House, 1961), p. 348.

[10] This, of course, refers to our "professional interest." In our other statuses, we can be interested or disinterested in the problems of society for a variety of different reasons.

article.[11] We are interested in the ways the various approaches have been organized and presented to their readers. Three major organizational types can be distinguished. Beside differing in their structure, the types appear to differ in their authors' intentions, and in their attractiveness to various kinds of audiences. Although certain problems approaches have had an affinity for certain organizational types, the relationship is far from a consistent one.

The first type is the one most distant from the sociological center. As a matter of fact there is often not even the pretense of a sociological approach. This type has been called the "omnium gatherum," the collection of myriad, miscellaneous problems from Abortion to Zooerasty, with little or no attempt to relate them to a sociological framework, or, for that matter, to any framework. The problems in this collection are held together by tradition and expectation alone. There is usually some minimal preliminary material, where mention may be made of several approaches to social problems. However, such material is decidedly prefatory to the major business at hand—the description of the many, many problems of society.

This type is often the third or fourth edition of a "best-seller," originally published in the 1920s or 1930s. There are a very few books that have changed little since then. Only the dates on charts and tables given them away as "modern" texts. It is common for this organizational type to have a "social problems" as opposed to a "disorganization" or "pathology" orientation. The various problems "readers," collections of articles and fragments of articles, fit neatly into this category.[12] Books of this type are produced simply to escort many college and junior college students along social problems paths well-travelled by "satisfied" student generations of the past.[13]

The second organizational type deserves more attention, because it attempts to do more, sociologically. In this volume one finds two sections: (1) a theoretical outline, which is intended to provide a basis for analyzing (2) the assortment of problems, comprising the major portion of the book. The theoretical material often bears resemblance to modern sociological theory; structural concepts are identified, the terminology is up to date, and so on. Invariably, however, the "analysis" of the problems in the second section turns out to be the standard descriptions of the standard problems. The theory rarely reaches the problems.

---

[11] See, for example, Abbott P. Herman, *An Approach to Social Problems* (New York: Harper, 1949); Martin H. Neumeyer, *Social Problems and the Changing Society* (Princeton, N.J.: Van Nostrand, 1953); and Edwin H. Lemert, *Social Pathology* (New York: McGraw-Hill, 1951). Martindale noted the various approaches to social problems found in a number of the more important pathology textbooks.

[12] Alfred McClung Lee and E. B. Lee, eds., *Social Problems in America*: A Source Book (New York: Holt, 1949). Lee and Lee, in their reader, combine excerpts from the works of famous sociological theorists, with those of journalists, clergymen, lawyers, government officials, and so on. The representatives of the other professions contribute little to the sociology of social problems.

[13] William W. Weaver, *Social Problems* (New York: Sloan Associates, 1951). As Weaver writes, "This book is submitted with few pretensions to erudition but with the earnest hope that it may be a useful guide for undergraduate students in their study of social problems."

Where it does reach, it appears to have been squeezed in, as a concession or an afterthought.

In this type of volume are reflected some of the "cross-pressures" experienced by present-day pathologists. Problems texts are no longer written by ex-social workers, ex-ministers located in sociology departments comprised of ex-ministers and ex-social workers. Contemporary pathologists have been trained as sociologists. One's professional self-image and relations within the academic department and within the profession are undoubtedly influences in determining what kind of book one should write. On the other horn of the dilemma are the other influences involved in the writing and selling of textbooks. It is known that in all but a few colleges and universities, presocial work, pre-education, pre-nursing and predomesticity students occupy most of the seats in sociology classes. It is also known that courses in social problems and in applied sociology have always been stellar attractions for these students. It is difficult for an author to remain unmoved by this information. If unimpressed he does remain, there is always his publisher to remind him. We know of no study of the influence of publishers on the ultimate content and form of texts. We feel that the odds in favor of rejection of the hypothesis of no association are great. The image of the "good book" held by those who purchase, print, design, and market manuscripts seems to be that of a text, similar to those that are known to have done well, with a new wrinkle or two to justify publication, and to provide copy for advertising.[14]

The type of book under discussion represents a way out of the pathologist's dilemma, containing as it does the little island of theory (the sociological imprimatur) separated from the vast archipelago of problems (for students and sales).

The last major organizational category contains the more serious efforts to present theories of disorganization, deviation, and others. In this type, the theoretical material is elaborately developed, sometimes taking up as much as half the volume. Problems are generally selected with a greater care for consistency than in the other types. This is achieved by narrowing the range of problems selected for analysis, because the specific theory can only handle certain kinds of problems.

Although attempts at theory-building are to be applauded and encouraged whenever they occur in the social problems area, we find that the actual theories leave much to be desired. They contain, at best, selected sociological elements. Some are theories of psychological more than sociological disorganization. Not one can be said to be a structural theory. One is disappointed by this lack more in this type of work than in the others. The others are completely devoid of *any* theory, but, when a sociologist works hard to present a theoretical

---

[14] We do not wish to suggest that all publishers are anti-intellectual, or that all textbooks contain only pap. We are dealing with types, rather than with individuals.

system in a sociological work (thereby probobly sacrificing junior college and schools of nursing adoptions), it is to be regretted that the result isn't sociology.

One did not have to read much between the lines of the above paragraphs to discover that, although writing of differences in the literature, we were implying that in a most important way the organizational types were more or less similar. The common feature of the sociology of social problems literature of today is its nonsociological, sometimes even antisociological, character.

This is not to suggest that the extreme simplifications, the unabashed moralizing, the exhortations to reform that characterized Mills' sample are to be found in the literature of today. A quarter of a century has elapsed since most of the volumes that Mills examined were published. Writings in pathology have not remained unaffected by the advances in sociology in those 25 years.

The important question is what lies behind the shiny, new exterior of up-to-date terminology, attempts at theories, and professed value neutrality that many modern works in social problems display. Have the old values been expunged, or do they still remain, in less extreme, less explicit form, but nonetheless present? The answer is "yes" and "no." Some of the standard concepts and usages of the 1920s and 1930s have gone completely out of sociological fashion and do not appear in modern problems literature. Other uniformities noted by Mills are still quite in evidence.

Two such examples are (1) the analysis of social problems as individual problems and (2) the nonrandom selection of social problems.

1. Many of the modern pathology primers contain a subdivision titled "personal or individual problems, crises, disorganizations." In this category fall the illnesses, addictions, vices, crimes, and the like.

The first critical question concerns the relevance of many of the individual problems to a sociological analysis. To be sure, such conditions as accidents, blindness, and mental deficiency affect many individuals in the population. But there are literally hundreds of potentially threatening conditions in man's environment, to which he attempts adjustment. The study of most of these conditions neither requires sociological theory nor contributes to it. Although members of the society may acknowledge the infirmities and handicaps and modify expectations in certain statuses; and deny participation in others. These are not sociological problems, for neither their causes, nor the reasons for their persistence, can be located within the structure of relationships that make up a human society.

Quite often the conditions singled out for consideration as social problems are simply those which affect the largest numbers of individuals. As one pathologist wrote: "One question often raised in the effort to locate and define problems, is, what is the number of people who are affected by them? . . . The assumption is that any problem is of major or minor significance in accordance with its incidence. Financial costs are used for the same purpose. The implication in the use of either implement is sound." [15]

A more serious deficiency in the literature revolves about those problems that could be structurally significant, and the ways in which they are treated. Variously labelled "group," "institutional," "family," "community," and so forth, they are with few exceptions analyzed as problems of individuals. One can illustrate this by considering the limited and unrewarding way "institution" might be used in the problems literature. An "institutional problem" is a condition that affects aggregates of individuals as they participate in an area of group life known to sociologists as an institution. The label serves only to indicate where in the society the problem is visible. Therefore divorce is a family problem, corruption and graft a political problem, unemployment an economic one. How is the "institutional problem" "analyzed" in the literature? Pathologists generally describe how many people are affected, how these rates have changed, and in what ways the problem is experienced by those affected and by others in the society. What brought the problem about (either "lags," "disorganizations," or "value conflicts," or any combination of the three), and perhaps, what can be done about it. In other words, the problems that are located in areas of the group life upon which modern sociological theory has been focused are "analyzed" in the same manner as the myriad ailments of mankind (physical, geographical, economic) with which the sociologist does not even pretend to be involved.

The simple message of this paper is that the fate of present-day sociological knowledge permits so much more than this to be done.

2. Almost every author will inform his readers that there are many social problems, both big and small. Of the large number of recognized problems, a handful can be thought of as the "G.O.P." (Grand Old Problems). Veritable universals are problems of physical and mental health, crime and delinquency, marriage and family problems, and problems of some kinds of minority groups. Also quite popular are some conditions that can be located in the economic institution—poverty, unemployment, and industrial relations, as well as population problems. Political and stratification problems (beside poverty) are two examples of those less frequently offered in the works of the pathologists.

There are several reasons why some problems are textbook universals, and others are rarely discussed. One is apparent from the following statement: "... Certain social problems have been central in the concept from the very beginning. A discussion of them is expected in books and courses on social problems, and this expectation has been respected." [16]

Another can be related to the criteria pathologists utilize in their definition

---

[15] Harold A. Phelps and David Henderson, *Contemporary Social Problems*, 4th ed. (Englewood Cliffs, N.J.: Prentice-Hall, 1952).
[16] Jessie Bernard, *Social Problems at Mid-Century* (New York: Holt, Rinehart, & Winston, 1957), p. 114.

of a social problem. We mentioned above that pathologists often define problems as conditions that affect aggregates of individuals. A very popular method of ascertaining which are the important problems of a society involves scrutinizing the population for the things that worry them, the conditions they would like to change. There are all sorts of evidence to support the position that Americans are generally not concerned with world or national issues. They worry about what is closest to them, what they experience most frequently— health, family, job. These, then, become the "universals," plus a few conditions which represent clear-cut and widely censured deviations from American norms and values.

Not only are certain problems rarely included in the literature, but one also finds that certain dimensions of the "acceptable" problems are ignored or barely noted. For example, the chapters on religion or religious minorities stress the discrimination against certain religions, the contributions of religious organizations toward amelioration of social problems, and so on. Rarely are the divisive consequences of religion in America discussed. The progress of the Negro is a popular theme in the chapters on minorities, but the consequences of progress, ranging up to mixed marriages, are hastily skipped over. In the ubiquitous chapter on health, syphilis, or whatever other interesting disease, is mentioned much more frequently than the A.M.A., although several recent texts have criticized developments in medical practice.

We have tried to point out, in the language of the pathologists, there exists a great "lag" between the developments in sociological theory and those in that branch of the field known as social problems, pathology, disorganization, deviation.

Let us review some of the factors that have contributed to this situation:

1. Most students who are enrolled in undergraduate courses in sociology are not especially interested in careers in sociology, nor in courses in sociological theory.

2. Since the size of the staff and the prestige of the department in many colleges are tied to the number of students enrolled, there are pressures to make available to students courses that will attract and satisfy. It is difficult to think of any other academic department that appears as concerned with what the student wants as is sociology. Perhaps the comparatively recent origins of sociology on the campus, and the widespread ignorance of it beyond the campus, help explain this.

3. Since it is not uncommon for authors to aspire to write books that sell, the literature geared to undergraduates tends to be lean on theory and rather overweight on the uncomplicated descriptive material that has been known to sell books.

4. The question of the role of the publisher in determining the content of the pathologists' literary output was raised in the body of the paper.

5. Since the study of social problems is so overwhelmingly an undergraduate proposition, the compulsion and the opportunity to do creative work, by either faculty or student body, are not very strong.

6. In many of the smaller colleges there are no conflicts between academic and applied sociology, as the former is barely to be seen. Social awareness and adjustment are the major educational aims of the social science program.

To criticize the field of social problems as we have done is neither novel nor difficult. What is harder to do, and therefore rarer, is to suggest how to infuse the problems field with significant theoretical content. Although the works of several important modern sociologists contain theories and theory fragments relating to disorganization and deviation, it remained for a recent article by A. K. Cohen[17] to provide a first step toward a rapprochement between sociological theory and social pathology. It is also to be noted as a hopeful sign that a recent issue of the *American Sociological Review* devoted most of its pages to theoretical papers in the sociology of deviation and of disorganization.

In spite of these first steps, it will be a long time before social problems offerings to undergraduates are reconstituted as truly sociological courses. A less distant goal would be for some of the theoretical material to filter down into social pathology syllabi, and for some of the more blatantly nonsociological approaches to be transferred out of sociology departments and into some interdisciplinary artifact, such as "Problems of American Civilization" or "Problems of the Twentieth Century."

Ultimately, if we survive the "social problems" of the atomic era, we can look forward in this area to subdisciplines that are sociological, not through tradition and student expectations, but because of their ties to sociological theory and research. A sociology of deviation and one of disorganization would not only contribute to our scientific knowledge of the social behavior of man, but would also place powerful tools in the hands of those who by training and inclination are dedicated to the betterment of man's life.

---

[17] Cohen, "The Study of Social Disorganization and Deviant Behavior," in Merton, Broom, and Cottrell, *Sociology Today.*

Social Structure and Anomie

ROBERT K. MERTON

In competitive athletics, when the aim of victory is shorn of its institutional trappings and success in contests becomes construed as "winning the game" rather than "winning through circumscribed modes of activity," a premium is implicitly set upon the use of illegitimate but technically efficient means. The star of the opposing football team is surreptitiously slugged; the wrestler furtively incapacitates his opponent through ingenious but illicit techniques; university alumni covertly subsidize "students" whose talents are largely confined to the athletic field. The emphasis on the goal has so attenuated the satisfactions deriving from sheer participation in the competitive activity that these satisfactions are virtually confined to a successful outcome. Through the same process, tension generated by the desire to win in a poker game is relieved by successfully dealing oneself four aces, or, when the cult of success has become completely dominant, by sagaciously shuffling the cards in a game of solitaire. The faint twinge of uneasiness in the last instance and the surreptitious nature of public delicts indicate clearly that the institutional rules of the game *are known* to those who evade them, but that the emotional supports of these rules are largely vitiated by cultural exaggeration of the success-goal.[1] They are microcosmic images of the social macrocosm.

Of course, this process is not restricted to the realm of sport. The process whereby exaltation of the end generates a *literal demoralization*, i.e., a deinstitutionalization, of the means is one which characterizes many[2] groups in which the two phases of the social structure are not highly integrated. The

---

Source: Robert K. Merton, "Social Structure and Anomie," *American Sociological Review* (1938), pp. 672–682. Reprinted by permission.

Editors' Note: This is an excerpt of the first published version of an article that has since become a classic of sociological literature. The interested reader should consult the revised and expanded version which appears in Robert K. Merton, *Social Theory and Social Structure* (Glencoe, Ill.: Free Press, 1959).

[1] It is unlikely that interiorized norms are completely eliminated. Whatever residuum persists will induce personality tensions and conflict. The process involves a certain degree of ambivalence. A manifest rejection of the institutional norms is coupled with some latent retention of their emotional correlates. "Guilt feelings," "sense of sin," "pangs of conscience" are obvious manifestations of this unrelieved tension; symbolic adherence to the nominally repudiated values of rationalizations constitute a more subtle variety of tensional release.

[2] "Many," and not all, unintegrated groups, for the reason already mentioned. In groups where the primary emphasis shifts to institutional means, i.e., when the range of alternatives is very limited, the outcome is a type of ritualism rather than anomie.

extreme emphasis upon the accumulation of wealth as a symbol of success[3] in our own society militates against the completely effective control of institutionally regulated modes of acquiring a fortune.[4] Fraud, corruption, vice, crime, in short, the entire catalogue of proscribed behavior, becomes increasingly common when the emphasis on the *culturally induced* success-goal becomes divorced from a coordinated institutional emphasis. This observation is of crucial theoretical importance in examining the doctrine that antisocial behavior most frequently derives from biological drives breaking through the restraints imposed by society. The difference is one between a strictly utilitarian interpretation which conceives man's ends as random and an analysis which finds these ends deriving from the basic values of the culture.[5]

Our analysis can scarcely stop at this juncture. We must turn to other aspects of the social structure if we are to deal with the social genesis of the varying rates and types of deviate behavior characteristic of different societies. Thus far, we have sketched three ideal types of social orders constituted by distinctive patterns of relations between culture ends and means. Turning from these types of *culture patterning*, we find five logically possible, alternative modes of adjustment or adaptation *by individuals* within the culture-bearing society or group.[6] These are schematically presented in the following table where (+) signifies

	Culture Goals	*Institutionalized Means*
I. Conformity	+	+
II. Innovation	+	−
III. Ritualism	−	+
IV. Retreatism	−	−
V. Rebellion[a]	±	±

[a] This fifth alternative is on a plane clearly different from that of the others. It represents a *transitional* response which seeks to *institutionalize* new procedures oriented toward revamped cultural goals shared by the members of the society. It thus involves efforts to *change* the existing structure rather than to perform accommodative actions *within* this structure, and introduces additional problems with which we are not at the moment concerned.

---

[3] Money has several peculiarities which render it particularly apt to become a symbol of prestige divorced from institutional controls. As Simmel emphasized, money is highly abstract and impersonal. However acquired, through fraud or institutionally, it can be used to purchase the same goods and services. The anonymity of metropolitan culture, in conjunction with this peculiarity of money, permits wealth, the sources of which may be unknown to the community in which the plutocrat lives, to serve as a symbol of status.

[4] The emphasis upon wealth as a success-symbol is possibly reflected in the use of the term "fortune" to refer to a stock of accumulated wealth. This meaning becomes common in the late sixteenth century (Spenser and Shakespeare). A similar usage of the Latin *fortuna* comes into prominence during the first century B.C. Both these periods were marked by the rise to prestige and power of the "bourgeoisie."

[5] See Kingsley Davis, "Mental Hygiene and the Class Structure," *Psychiatry*, 1928, I, esp. 62–63; Talcott Parsons, *The Structure of Social Action*, 59–60, New York, 1937.

[6] This is a level intermediate between the two planes distinguished by Edward Sapir; namely, culture patterns and personal habit systems. See his "Contribution of Psychiatry to an Understanding of Behavior in Society," *American Journal of Sociology*, 1937, 42:862–870.

"acceptance," (−) signifies "elimination" and (±) signifies "rejection and substitution of new goals and standards."

Our discussion of the relation between these alternative responses and other phases of the social structure must be prefaced by the observation that persons may shift from one alternative to another as they engage in different social activities. These categories refer to role adjustments in specific situations, not to personality *in toto*. To treat the development of this process in various spheres of conduct would introduce a complexity unmanageable within the confines of this paper. For this reason, we shall be concerned primarily with economic activity in the broad sense, "the production, exchange, distribution, and consumption of goods and services" in our competitive society, wherein wealth has taken on a highly symbolic cast. Our task is to search out some of the factors which exert pressure upon individuals to engage in certain of these logically possible alternative responses. This choice, as we shall see, is far from random.

In every society, Adaptation I (conformity to both culture goals and means) is the most common and widely diffused. Were this not so, the stability and continuity of the society could not be maintained. The mesh of expectancies which constitutes every social order is sustained by the modal behavior of its members falling within the first category. Conventional role behavior oriented toward the basic values of the group is the rule rather than the exception. It is this fact alone which permits us to speak of a human aggregate as comprising a group or society.

Conversely, Adaptation IV (rejection of goals and means) is the least common. Persons who "adjust" (or maladjust) in this fashion are, strictly speaking, *in* the society but not *of* it. Sociologically, these constitute the true "aliens." Not sharing the common frame of orientation, they can be included within the societal population merely in a fictional sense. In this category are *some* of the activities of psychotics, psychoneurotics, chronic autists, pariahs, outcasts, vagrants, vagabonds, tramps, chronic drunkards, and drug addicts.[7] These have relinquished, in certain spheres of activity, the culturally defined goals, involving complete aim-inhibition in the polar case, and their adjustments are not in accord with institutional norms. This is not to say that in some cases the source of their behavioral adjustments is not in part the very social structure which they have in effect repudiated nor that their very existence within a social area does not constitute a problem for the socialized population.

This mode of "adjustment" occurs, as far as structural sources are concerned, when both the culture goals and institutionalized procedures have been assimilated thoroughly by the individual and imbued with affect and high positive

---

[7] Obviously, this is an elliptical statement. These individuals may maintain some orientation to the values of their particular differentiated groupings within the larger society or, in part, of the conventional society itself. Insofar as they do so, their conduct cannot be classified in the "passive rejection" category (IV). Nels Anderson's description of the behavior and attitudes of the bum, for example, can readily be recast in terms of our analytical scheme. See *The Hobo*, 93–98, *et passim*, Chicago, 1923.

value, but where those institutionalized procedures which promise a measure of successful attainment of the goals are not available to the individual. In such instances, there results a twofold mental conflict insofar as the moral obligation for adopting institutional means conflicts with the pressure to resort to illegitimate means (which may attain the goal) and inasmuch as the individual is shut off from means which are both legitimate *and* effective. The competitive order is maintained, but the frustrated and handicapped individual who cannot cope with this order drops out. Defeatism, quietism, and resignation are manifested in escape mechanisms which ultimately lead the individual to "escape" from the requirements of the society. It is an expedient which arises from continued failure to attain the goal by legitimate measures and from an inability to adopt the illegitimate route because of internalized prohibitions and institutionalized compulsives, *during which process the supreme value of the success-goal has as yet not been renounced.* The conflict is resolved by eliminating *both* precipitating elements, the goals and means. The escape is complete, the conflict is eliminated and the individual is asocialized.

Be it noted that where frustration derives from the inaccessibility of effective institutional means for attaining economic or any other type of highly valued "success," that Adaptations II, III and V (innovation, ritualism and rebellion) are also possible. The result will be determined by the particular personality, and thus, the *particular* cultural background, involved. Inadequate socialization will result in the innovation response whereby the conflict and frustration are eliminated by relinquishing the institutional means and retaining the success-aspiration; an extreme assimilation of institutional demands will lead to ritualism wherein the goal is dropped as beyond one's reach but conformity to the mores persists; and rebellion occurs when emancipation from the reigning standards, due to frustration or to marginalist perspectives, leads to the attempt to introduce a "new social order."

Our major concern is with the illegitimacy adjustment. This involves the use of conventionally proscribed but frequently effective means of attaining at least the simulacrum of culturally defined success,—wealth, power, and the like. As we have seen, this adjustment occurs when the individual has assimilated the cultural emphasis on success without equally internalizing the morally prescribed norms governing means for its attainment. The question arises, Which phases of our social structure predispose toward this mode of adjustment? We may examine a concrete instance, effectively analyzed by Lohman,[8] which provides a clue to the answer. Lohman has shown that specialized areas of vice in the near north side of Chicago constitute a "normal" response to a situation where the cultural emphasis upon pecuniary success has been absorbed, but where there is little access to conventional and legitimate means for attaining such

---

[8] Joseph D. Lohman, "The Participant Observer in Community Studies," *American Sociological Review*, 1937, 2:890–898.

success. The conventional occupational opportunities of persons in this area are almost completely limited to manual labor. Given our cultural stigmatization of manual labor, and its correlate, the prestige of white collar work, it is clear that the result is a strain toward innovational practices. The limitation of opportunity to unskilled labor and the resultant low income cannot compete *in terms of conventional standards of achievement* with the high income from organized vice.

For our purposes, this situation involves two important features. First, such antisocial behavior is in a sense "called forth" by certain conventional values of the culture *and* by the class structure involving differential access to the approved opportunities for legitimate, prestige-bearing pursuit of the culture goals. The lack of high integration between the means-and-end elements of the cultural pattern and the particular class structure combine to favor a heightened frequency of antisocial conduct in such groups. The second consideration is of equal significance. Recourse to the first of the alternative responses, legitimate effort, is limited by the fact that actual advance toward desired success-symbols through conventional channels is, despite our persisting open-class ideology,[9] relatively rare and difficult for those handicapped by little formal education and few economic resources. The dominant pressure of group standards of success is, therefore, on the gradual attenuation of legitimate, but by and large ineffective, strivings and the increasing use of illegitimate, but more or less effective, expedients of vice and crime. The cultural demands made on persons in this situation are incompatible. On the one hand, they are asked to orient their conduct toward the prospect of accumulating wealth and on the other, they are largely denied effective opportunities to do so institutionally. The consequences of such structural inconsistency are psychopathological personality, and/or antisocial conduct, and/or revolutionary activities. The equilibrium between culturally designated means and ends becomes highly unstable with the progressive emphasis on attaining the prestige-laden ends by any means whatsoever. Within this context, Capone represents the triumph of amoral intelligence over morally prescribed "failure," when the channels of vertical mobility are closed or narrowed[10] *in a society*

---

[9] The shifting historical role of this ideology is a profitable subject for exploration. The "office-boy-to-president" stereotype was once in approximate accord with the facts. Such vertical mobility was probably more common then than now, when the class structure is more rigid. (See the following note.) The ideology largely persists, however, possibly because it still performs a useful function for maintaining the *status quo*. For insofar as it is accepted by the "masses," it constitutes a useful sop for those who might rebel against the entire structure, were this consoling hope removed. This ideology now serves to lessen the probability of Adaptation V. In short, the role of this notion has changed from that of an approximately valid empirical theorem to that of an ideology in Mannheim's sense.

[10] There is a growing body of evidence, though none of it is clearly conclusive, to the effect that our class structure is becoming rigidified and that vertical mobility is declining. Taussig and Joslyn found that American business leaders are being *increasingly* recruited from the upper ranks of our society. The Lynds have also found a "diminished chance to get ahead" for the working classes in Middletown. Manifestly, these objective changes are not alone significant; the individual's subjective evaluation of the situation is a major determinant of the response. The extent to which this change in opportunity for social mobility has been recognized by the least advantaged classes is still conjectural, although the Lynds present some suggestive materials. The writer suggests that a case in point is the increasing frequency of

which places a high premium on economic affluence and social ascent for all *its members.*[11]

This last qualification is of primary importance. It suggests that other phases of the social structure besides the extreme emphasis on pecuniary success, must be considered if we are to understand the social sources of antisocial behavior. A high frequency of deviate behavior is not generated simply by "lack of opportunity" or by this exaggerated pecuniary emphasis. A comparatively rigidified class structure, a feudalistic or caste order, may limit such opportunities far beyond the point which obtains in our society today. It is only when a system of cultural values extols, virtually above all else, certain *common* symbols of success *for the population at large* while its social structure rigorously restricts or completely eliminates access to approved modes of acquiring these symbols *for a considerable part of the same population*, that antisocial behavior ensues on a considerable scale. In other words, our egalitarian ideology denies by implication the existence of noncompeting groups and individuals in the pursuit of pecuniary success. The same body of success-symbols is held to be desirable for all. These goals are held to *transcend class lines,* not to be bounded by them, yet the actual social organization is such that there exist class differentials in the accessibility of these *common* success-symbols. Frustration and thwarted aspiration lead to the search for avenues of escape from a culturally induced intolerable situation; or unrelieved ambition may eventuate in illicit attempts to acquire the dominant values.[12] The American stress on pecuniary success and ambitiousness for all thus invites exaggerated anxieties, hostilities, neuroses, and antisocial behavior.

This theoretical analysis may go far toward explaining the varying correlations between crime and poverty.[13] Poverty is not an isolated variable. It is one

---

cartoons which observe in a tragi-comic vein that "my old man says everybody can't be President. He says if ya can get three days a week steady on W.P.A. work ya ain't doin' so bad either." See F. W. Taussig and C. S. Joslyn, *American Business Leaders,* New York, 1932; R. S. and H. M. Lynd, *Middletown in Transition,* 67 ff., ch. 12, New York, 1937.

[11] The role of the Negro in this respect is of considerable theoretical interest. Certain elements of the Negro population have assimilated the dominant caste's values of pecuniary success and social advancement, but they also recognize that social ascent is at present restricted to their own caste almost exclusively. The pressures upon the Negro which would otherwise derive from the structural inconsistencies we have noticed are hence not identical with those upon lower class whites. See Kingsley Davis, *op. cit.,* 63; John Dollard, *Caste and Class in a Southern Town,* 66 ff., New Haven, 1936; Donald Young, *American Minority Peoples,* 581, New York, 1932.

[12] The psychical coordinates of these processes have been partly established by the experimental evidence concerning *Anspruchsniveaus* and levels of performance. See Kurt Lewin, *Vorsatz, Willie und Bedurfnis,* Berlin, 1926; N. F. Hoppe, "Erfolg und Misserfolg," *Psychol. Forschung,* 1930, 14:1–63; Jerome D. Frank, "Individual Differences in Certain Aspects of the Level of Aspiration," *American Journal of Psychology,* 1935, 47:119–128.

[13] Standard criminology texts summarize the data in this field. Our scheme of analysis may serve to resolve some of the theoretical contradictions which P. A. Sorokin indicates. For example, "not everywhere nor always do the poor show a greater proportion of crime . . . many poor countries have had less crime than the richer countries . . . The [economic] improvement in the second half of the nineteenth century, and the beginning of the twentieth, has not been followed by a decrease of crime." See his *Contemporary Sociological Theories,* 560–561, New York, 1928. The crucial point is, however, that poverty has varying social significance in different social structures, as we shall see. Hence, one would not expect a linear correlation between crime and poverty.

in a complex of interdependent social and cultural variables. When viewed in such a context, it represents quite different states of affairs. Poverty as such, and consequent limitation of opportunity, are not sufficient to induce a conspicuously high rate of criminal behavior. Even the often mentioned "poverty in the midst of plenty" will not necessarily lead to this result. Only insofar as poverty and associated disadvantages in competition for the culture values approved for *all* members of the society is linked with the assimilation of a cultural emphasis on monetary accumulation as a symbol of success is antisocial conduct a "normal" outcome. Thus, poverty is less highly correlated with crime in southeastern Europe than in the United States. The possibilities of vertical mobility in these European areas would seem to be fewer than in this country, so that neither poverty per se nor its association with limited opportunity is sufficient to account for the varying correlations. It is only when the full configuration is considered, poverty, limited opportunity, and a commonly shared system of success symbols, that we can explain the higher association between poverty and crime in our society than in others where rigidified class structure is coupled with *differential class symbols of achievement*.

In societies such as our own, then, the pressure of prestige-bearing success tends to eliminate the effective social constraint over means employed to this end. "The-end-justifies-the-means" doctrine becomes a guiding tenet for action when the cultural structure unduly exalts the end and the social organization unduly limits possible recourse to approved means. Otherwise put, this notion and associated behavior reflect a lack of cultural coordination. In international relations, the effects of this lack of integration are notoriously apparent. An emphasis upon national power is not readily coordinated with an inept organization of legitimate, i.e., internationally defined and accepted, means for attaining this goal. The result is a tendency toward the abrogation of international law, treaties become scraps of paper, "undeclared warfare" serves as a technical evasion, the bombing of civilian populations is rationalized,[14] just as the same societal situation induces the same sway of illegitimacy among individuals.

The social order we have described necessarily produces this "strain toward dissolution." The pressure of such an order is upon outdoing one's competitors. The choice of means within the ambit of institutional control will persist as long as the sentiments supporting a competitive system, i.e., deriving from the possibility of outranking competitors and hence enjoying the favorable response of others, are distributed throughout the entire system of activities and are not confined merely to the final result. A stable social structure demands a balanced distribution of affect among its various segments. When there occurs a shift of emphasis from the satisfactions deriving from competition itself to almost exclusive concern with successful competition, the resultant stress leads to the

---

[14] See M. W. Royse, *Aerial Bombardment and the International Regulation of War*, New York, 1928.

breakdown of the regulatory structure.[15] With the resulting attenuation of the institutional imperatives, there occurs an approximation of the situation erroneously held by utilitarians to be typical of society generally wherein calculations of advantage and fear of punishment are the sole regulating agencies. In such situations, as Hobbes observed, force and fraud come to constitute the sole virtues in view of their relative efficiency in attain goals—which were for him, of course, not culturally derived.

It should be apparent that the foregoing discussion is not pitched on a moralistic plane. Whatever the sentiments of the writer or reader concerning the ethical desirability of coordinating the means-and-goals phases of the social structure, one must agree that lack of such coordination leads to anomie. Insofar as one of the most general functions of social organization is to provide a basis for calculability and regularity of behavior, it is increasingly limited in effectiveness as these elements of the structure become dissociated. At the extreme, predictability virtually disappears and what may be properly termed cultural chaos or anomie intervenes.

This statement, being brief, is also incomplete. It has not included an exhaustive treatment of the various structural elements which predispose toward one rather than another of the alternative responses open to individuals; it has neglected, but not denied the relevance of, the factors determining the specific incidence of these responses; it has not enumerated the various concrete responses which are constituted by combinations of specific values of the analytical variables; it has omitted, or included only by implication, any consideration of the social functions performed by illicit responses; it has not tested the full explanatory power of the analytical scheme by examining a large number of group variations in the frequency of deviate and conformist behavior; it has not adequately dealt with rebellious conduct which seeks to refashion the social framework radically; it has not examined the relevance of cultural conflict for an analysis of culture-goal and institutional-means malintegration. It is suggested that these and related problems may be profitably analyzed by this scheme.

---

[15] Since our primary concern is with the socio-cultural aspects of this problem, the psychological correlates have been only implicitly considered. See Karen Horney, *The Neurotic Personality of Our Time*, New York, 1937, for a psychological discussion of this process.

Evaluating Juvenile Delinquency Research

LOUISE G. HOWTON

▬

Investigating juvenile delinquency is one of the best financed and most energetically pursued specialties in social research. Crimes and other socially impermissible acts committed by minors which bring them to the attention of the courts are highly visible and greatly regretted. Public opinion is understandably sensitive, in any society deeply committed to the value of children and the importance of protecting their welfare, to the reproof implied in a juvenile delinquency rate that rises year by year. Some respond by calling for sterner measures—a "get tough" attitude by the courts, less probation and more detention, even a return to corporal punishment in the schools. At the other extreme are those who blame society altogether and call for expanded treatment facilities, typically of the sort that rely on techniques of individual and group psychotherapy. The great liberal center responds by concluding that more research is needed in any event, and by making funds available.

Thus the specifics vary, but common to all sectors of public opinion is a sense of moral indignation and a will to act. The social scientist is provided with funds, encouragement, cooperation, plentiful and accessible records and, perhaps most important of all, a research problem that has theoretical as well as practical implications. With so many favoring circumstances one would expect to find empirically grounded knowledge of the subject to be well advanced. Examination reveals, however, that while the scale of the research effort is impressive, the findings are not. Too often they are so inconsistent as to nullify each other and bring us back practically to the zero point.

Criticism of large-scale criminological research has not been lacking in the American literature, but it remained for a British magistrate to do a critique systematic enough to be called definitive. Both as a judge sentencing youthful offenders and as a University District Head training social workers, Barbara Wootton became concerned about the failure of individual studies to be of much practical help. She undertook a systematic comparative evaluation, and found that they also fail as science. This is distressing enough but even worse, as she reports it, is that books on social work education and arguments used in

---

Source: Prepared especially for this volume. References are to Barbara Wootton, *Social Science and Social Pathology* (New York: Macmillan, 1959).

court proceedings (taking this material as a source of relevant facts is one of the features of the book) present fashionable assumptions as if they were conclusions, and the findings of study X as if they were not called into question by study Y. This escalation of error damages both the rationality of practice and the prestige of science. At best, empirically established correlates of deviant behavior are presented loosely as causes and serve to confuse discourse; at worst, questionable ideas currently in vogue gain good repute and become incorporated into the policies and training doctrine of social agencies.

The portion of Wootton's critique which is summarized here systematically compares the findings of all the "competent" major empirical studies of "the causes and characteristic features of crime and delinquency." To qualify, the studies had to meet the following standards: inclusion of at least 200 subjects; collection and analysis of facts bearing on at least half of twelve factors hypothetically causative of delinquency; ample reporting of study design and research procedure; and detailed listing of results. These are stringent limitations. All journal articles were excluded as well as some well-known book length studies.

The twelve criminological hypotheses were chosen on the basis of their prevalence in the popular and professional literature concerned with the subject. They are listed below:

Twelve Factors Hypothetically Causative
of Crime and Delinquency

 1. Size of family
 2. Presence of other criminals in family
 3. Club membership
 4. Church attendance
 5. Employment record
 6. Social status
 7. Poverty
 8. Mother employed outside the home
 9. Truancy
10. Broken home
11. Health
12. Education attained

The analysis is exhaustive—hypothesis by hypothesis, twelve examinations of each of 21 studies. Despite the formidable investment of time and resources by the researchers (21 broad, careful projects in three countries over a period of four decades), basic limitations recur: noncomparable definitions, incommensurable features in research design, overinterpretation of findings, and unexplained anomalies in estimating significance.

The array of results bearing on each of the hypotheses is bewildering in its variety. This is apparent when one attempts the usual analytical summary in tabular form. For example, consider the hypothesis specifying *broken home* as a factor. Carr-Saunders finds that 28 per cent of delinquents, compared with 16 per cent of controls, come from broken homes. Trenaman's comparable figures are 57 per cent and 12 per cent, and Wilkins reports 22 per cent and 14 per cent. The Gluecks' figures are highest in both categories: 60.4 per cent and 34.2 per cent. This brief enumeration exhausts the studies which report figures for comparable categories; the others require special notation, such as that one includes handicapped and the other does not, or that one is limited to the provinces and the other to the metropolis. One researcher unaccountably reports information on only 823 out of his 1,000 cases, another divides the rates by boys and girls, another by age at which the break in social control occurs. This material is obviously not cumulative and cannot be directly compared with the percentage figures given above. One of the basic problems, clearly, is definition. Trenaman's is unusually broad, including cases classifiable as "homeless," "from broken homes," "had parents who were chronic invalids," or "parents absent for long periods." Gibb's figures are based on the institutionalization of a child as well as the loss of a parent to the home, including the very institutionalization of the child which led to him being included in the study in the first place.

The best summary that can be presented is that, for the British studies, broken homes as a factor ranges from 22 per cent to 57 per cent for the delinquents, and 11 per cent to 17 per cent for the controls. For the American studies, the corresponding ranges are 34 per cent to 62 per cent, and 14 per cent to 34 per cent, respectively. It is noteworthy that the control figures in the American studies can be larger than the delinquent figure in the British studies. Finally, the control figure in some of the American studies is not far from equality with the delinquent figure in others.

The cited range does not represent the results altogether fairly because of the omission of items that could not be scaled. However, there is reason to suspect even the most charitable tabulation. Shaw and McKay, for example, demonstrate a marked variation in the incidence of broken homes in various ethnic groups and a slighter one with regard to boys past seventeen years of age. This shows that in addition to the definitional problem of specifying criteria by which concepts are operationalized, there is the additional one of deciding what population is to be studied.

The foregoing is only a sampling, but it should serve to convey some sense of Miss Wootton's strategy and technique of critical evaluation. She sums up as follows:

All in all, therefore, this collection of studies, although chosen for its comparative methodological merit, produces only the most meagre, and dubiously supported generalizations. On the whole, it seems that offenders come from relatively large families. Not infrequently (according to some investigators very frequently) other members of the delinquents' (variously defined) families have also been in trouble with the law. Offenders are unlikely to be regular churchgoers, but the evidence as to whether club membership discourages delinquency is wildly contradictory. If they are of an age to be employed, they are likely to be classified as "poor" rather than "good" workers. Most of them come from the lower social classes, but again the evidence as to the extent to which they can be described as exceptionally poor is conflicting; nor is there any clear indication that their delinquency is associated with the employment of their mothers outside the home. Their health is probably no worse than that of other people, but many of them have earned poor reputations at school, though these may well be prejudiced by their teachers' knowledge of their delinquencies. In their school-days they are quite likely to have truanted from school, and perhaps an unusually large proportion of them come from homes in which at some (frequently unspecified) time both parents were not, for whatever reason, living together; yet even on these points, the findings of some enquiries are negative. And beyond this we cannot go. (Pp. 134–35)

The studies are not without value, in Miss Wootton's opinion, although what they have achieved has been mostly incidental or by indirection. Most dramatically, perhaps, the results show that the assumptions still entrenched in the popular wisdom such as that poor health and working mothers cause delinquency are not substantiated. (The rate of incidence of working mothers in the families of delinquents and controls in the British studies shows a range of 4.6 per cent to 32 per cent and 7.4 per cent to 33 per cent, respectively, which is practically identical in level as well as range. A somewhat larger raw differential is found in the American studies, but it disappears when a correction is applied for social status. The same thing is true of health as a factor.) The earlier literature, especially, stresses the role of physiological and functional differences in causing deviant behavior, and some elaborate theories were spun out of poorly supported observations. What little evidence now remains of poor health in the offender group is easily accounted for as generally characteristic of the population from which it is drawn.

Wootton concludes that the type of research which assumes discoverable factors in the individual case characterizing a delinquent population has already contributed what little it can and should be abandoned. Juvenile delinquency as an all embracing category is too imprecise for research purposes. "In place of the quest for causes in the factorial sense, research needs to seek to achieve an understanding of the varieties of socialization—the ongoing life careers of young people with their frequent crises and turning points, their alternatives and choices and the patterns of the paths which develop." Research guided by short-term practical considerations, such as the needs of the magistrate in intelligently sentencing the offender, would be far more useful.

*　　*　　*

Analyzing child guidance literature over three historical periods, Martha Wolfenstein[1] concludes that while the image of the child has changed greatly there is not much evidence that he is better understood. Writing from a different perspective and generalizing from a different body of literature, Barbara Wootton finds a singular persistence in the image of the youthful offender: he

---

[1] Martha Wolfenstein, "Fun Morality: An Analysis of Recent American Child Training Literature," *Journal of Social Issues*, 7:4 (1951), pp. 15–25.

is seen mechanically, as a collection of traits, or "factors." Different clusters of traits are emphasized in different decades by different researchers, but the variation is best understood as reflecting little more than the play of fashion. In social science research, too often the image changes without warrant or stays constant even when there is reason to question it.

If knowledge of the causes of juvenile delinquency is not ahead of what it was 40 years ago, it is not because researchers have not been diligent in getting "the facts." The 21 studies constitute a record of diligence sadly misapplied. They show the futility of expecting the accumulation of facts to result automatically in the improvement of scientific knowledge. The line of inquiry assuming that what causes delinquency is something *in the individual* (psychological, biological) ought to be dropped; however, the demonstrated power of our cultural preconceptions to outride repeated failures to validate them is such that it will probably continue.

Varieties of Delinquent Experience

BERNARD ROSENBERG AND HARRY SILVERSTEIN

In American society, the rapid pace of economic and technological change has developed within the framework of an equalitarian social and political ideology. This system, under law, ostensibly affords the same opportunity to every citizen to attain the better life for himself by effort and initiative. Thus, the most popular culture hero frequently reenacts a version of the Horatio Alger theme. "Rags to riches" is consequently a staple of national imagery. Indeed, so widely has the idealization of equal opportunity and unfettered aspiration been disseminated through our mythology, that it has come to be *assumed as an unquestioned fact of American cultural and social life.*

ANOMIE AND OPPORTUNITY

In the past few decades, sociologists have focused their attention on the significance of this ideal. They have used the "drive to success" as a significant

Source: Reprinted by permission of the publisher, from Bernard Rosenberg and Harry Silverstein, *The Varieties of Delinquent Experience* (Waltham, Massachusetts: Ginn-Blaisdell, A Xerox Company, 1969), pp. 120–138.

variable in attempting to explain many endemic social problems. Two major avenues of inquiry have been pursued. We have had studies designed to examine the structural limitations of opportunity in American society. In general, they show that opportunities are severely restricted in a rather rigid class system. These studies leave no doubt that achievement possibilities are most imperfect though the society proclaims its egalitarian intentions. The excellent empirical work of Robert and Helen M. Lynd,[1] Lloyd Warner,[2] and John Dollard[3] made all this clear long ago. More recently, continued discrimination against minority groups has dramatized the degree to which segments of this society are denied access to the "open" system of opportunity.

An intersecting line of sociological inquiry has sifted the empirical evidence to buttress a theoretical explanation which holds that many types of social deviance result from the *unfulfilled, ungratified hope for material success* among underprivileged classes of people to whom the usual avenues of advancement remain closed.

Beginning with the incisively logical and now classical essay by Robert K. Merton, "Social Structure and Anomie,"[4] many sociologists in the United States have contended that there is a commonly held, society-wide level of aspiration, but that the lower strata, blocked from attaining that level, include significant numbers of people who have recourse to "innovation," that is, to crime and delinquency. No theoretical formulation has had greater impact on the work of sociologists than Merton's essay which, through successive refinements, has produced many hypotheses about the disjuncture between aspirations and opportunity and how it leads to a condition of "anomie" in modern society.

Anomie, a term introduced by Emile Durkheim to describe a state of "normlessness" in some societies,[5] presumably arises when men's hopes and aspirations exceed his ability to fulfill them. Individuals, striving for the unobtainable, are deprived of normative restraints and controls: hence, they engage in innovative, illegitimate activities. Their purpose is to overcome the obstacles which confront them and to do so by any and all available means. Where a society offers culturally acceptable goals but fails to provide legitimate means adequate to their attainment, the structural condition of that society is, perforce, anomic.

For Merton, the situation is described as follows:

A high frequency of deviant behavior is not generated merely by lack of opportunity or by this exaggerated pecuniary emphasis. A comparatively rigidified class structure,

---

[1] Robert S. and Helen M. Lynd, *Middletown in Transition* (New York: Harcourt, Brace, 1937).

[2] W. Lloyd Warner and Paul S. Lunt, *Social Life of a Modern Community* (New Haven: Yale University Press, 1941).

[3] John Dollard, *Caste and Class in a Southern Town* (New York: Harper, 1937).

[4] Robert K. Merton, "Social Structure and Anomie," reprinted in *Social Theory and Social Structure*, rev. ed., (New York: Free Press of Glencoe, 1957) pp. 161–194.

[5] Emile Durkheim, *Suicide* (New York: Free Press of Glencoe, 1951).

a caste order, may limit opportunities far beyond the point which obtains in American society today. It is only when a system of cultural values extols, virtually above all else, certain *common* success-goals *for the population at large* while the social structure rigorously restricts or completely closes access to approved modes of reaching these goals *for a considerable part of the same population*, that deviant behavior ensues on a large scale.[6]

... When we consider the full configuration—poverty, limited opportunity and the assignment of culture goals—there appears some basis for explaining the higher correlation between poverty and crime in our society than in others where rigidified class structure is coupled with *differential class symbols of success*.[7]

Merton, and other social scientists following his lead, have compiled an impressive array of arguments, all set forth with admirable rigor, suggesting that deviance is a natural byproduct of social pressures impinging upon the lower classes of American society.

At the core of this analysis, however, is an *assumption* that the value of success is a goal shared at some point by virtually all members of this society, no matter where they are located in the continuum of social stratification. Yet, despite the fact that some degree of rigidity in the class system (especially at its base and at its apex) has been established by empirical study, little evidence, in the form of measurable data, has been adduced to prove that success, as defined in the middle class, pervades all of American social life. There appears to be a general consensus that, as compared to other socioeconomic systems, ours is relatively fluid. At the same time, it is apparent that a kind of "cultural lag" has developed, so that values clustered around the poor man's desire for upward mobility far exceed the opportunities available to satisfy them. Hence, anomie. "In this setting, a cardinal American virtue, 'ambition,' promotes a cardinal American vice, 'deviant behavior.'"[8]

"Hard" data accumulated so far have been primarily suggestive and inferential. Investigators have drawn their conclusions from widely diverse sources. Sometimes they extrapolated from census tract data, and, more recently, they have induced results from highly structured scales designed to measure anomia, the individualized effect of the social–structural pressures brought to bear on specific populations. In general, almost all the data gathered, whatever their relative degree of validity, have tended to substantiate the initial assumption that pecuniary success is a totally pervasive American value. In addition, the broad criminological picture seems to lend its statistical weight to the notion that delinquency is largely a class-bound phenomena, disproportionately concentrated in, and really a mark of, the underclass. Still, theoretical calculations have greatly outraced and outpaced actual findings; unfortunately, the theory has overshadowed the research.

---

[6] Merton, "Social Structure and Anomie," p. 146.
[7] *Ibid.*, p. 147.
[8] *Ibid.*, p. 146.

Some important empirical exceptions to the alleged rule that pecuniary success is an ubiquitous American goal have only recently appeared in attempts to test the Mertonian thesis. Mizruchi in *Success and Opportunity*[9] indicates that lower-class people place greater emphasis on security than on the acquisition of wealth, a finding akin to others independently reported by Meir and Bell,[10] Hyman,[11] and Inkeles.[12] Furthermore, many of the facts that seem to support Merton may only be artifacts, and the theory, with all its speculative insight, could stand or fall on those facts. So, for example, though official statistics show much higher rates of crime among members of the lower class, most criminologists would agree that these rates are biased. They are more a product of the response of control agencies than a true index of the distribution of crime and delinquency throughout the society.[13] Our own data, already presented in the chapters on delinquency patterns, tend to support this contention, at least insofar as it pertains to lower-class communities.[14]

In the field of delinquency, an important extension of Merton's thesis was developed by Cloward and Ohlin in their influential book, *Delinquency and Opportunity*. According to these authors, a delinquent subculture will develop when legitimate means for the attainment of success goals are inaccessible: "The disparity between what lower-class youth are led to want and what is actually available to them is the source of a major problem of adjustment. Adolescents who form delinquent subcultures, we suggest, have internalized an emphasis on conventional goals, and unable to revise their aspirations downward, they experience intense frustrations; the exploration of non-conformist alternatives may be the result." [15] One alternative is the use of illegitimate means to attain conventional goals. Another involves participation in illegitimate opportunity structures. A third type of response is embodied in the retreatist gang or group, composed of those who are "double failures"—unsuccessful alike in their use of legitimate *and* illegitimate means to success (for example, drug addicts).

Moreover, in a particularly important passage bearing on their major hypothesis, Cloward and Ohlin suggest it is not necessary to show that a large proportion of persons in the lower class exhibit a high level of aspiration. Rather, ". . . it is sufficient to show that a significant number of lower-class members aspire beyond their means if it can also be demonstrated that these

---

[9] Ephraim H. Mizruchi, *Success and Opportunity* (New York: Free Press of Glencoe, 1964).

[10] Dorothy L. Meir and Wendell Bell, "Anomia and Differential Access to the Achievement of Life Goals," *American Sociological Review, XXIV* (1959), pp. 189–202.

[11] Herbert Hyman, "Reflections on Reference Groups," *Public Opinion Quarterly, XXIV* (Fall, 1960).

[12] Alex Inkeles, "Industrial Man: The Relation of Status to Experience, Perception, and Value," *American Journal of Sociology, LXVI* (July, 1960).

[13] Edwin H. Sutherland, *White Collar Crime* (New York: Dryden Press, 1949).

[14] See Bernard Rosenberg and Harry Silverstein, *The Varieties of Delinquent Experience* (Waltham, Mass.: Blaisdell Publishing Company, 1969), especially Chs. 2, 5, 6, and 7.

[15] Cloward and Ohlin, *Delinquency and Opportunity: A Theory of Delinquent Gangs* (New York: Free Press of Glencoe, 1961).

same persons contribute disproportionately to the ranks of delinquent sub-cultures." [16] And, although they offer much discussion from a variety of sources concerning their hypothesis, they adduce no new evidence with which to validate their conclusion that delinquent youth in fact are those with high aspirations who have experienced insuperable obstacles to their achievement.

This then becomes a major focus of our inquiry. We have shown that delinquency patterns vary markedly in three lower-class study areas. And so we raise the question: Are these variable patterns traceable, in any or all three of the communities, to problems stemming from unfulfilled and insatiable aspirations? On the contrary, as we will attempt to demonstrate, social and economic realism is the rule. High aspiration among the three impoverished groups of youth in our study is almost nonexistent.

THE DEPRIVATION OF IMAGINATION

In pursuing this matter, our approach is highly qualitative. Although the total number of youth interviewed in the study areas were more than sufficient for quantitative study—we decided to probe the full spectrum of aspirations, from lofty dreamlike ambitiousness to hard-headed realism.[17] We asked each respondent to "let his imagination run loose" over the full range of conceivable employment, income, and residence—not just those possibly available to him, but those a fairy godfather might offer. We expected that quite a few would reach impossibly high, and then come down to earth with a thud as reality intruded on their fantasies. It is clear that, though our poverty youth may be rich in fantasy in other ways, aspirationally they are almost painfully deprived. Where these youth aspire to a fairly high level—they represent less than 25% of the total interviewed—some at least realistically recognize that they will be able to approximate their goals only if they have taken meaningful steps toward upward achievement. These youth are essentially committed to completing their educations, and—for our purposes a most critical point—they have rarely engaged in delinquent acts.

For example, a male Negro respondent in Washington states:

Success? That's a very large word as far as I'm concerned. Well, so far, let's just say after I've gotten out of high school, say when I got this job right here, I made a

---

16 *Ibid,* page 88.

17 The three study areas from which the youth sample was drawn are relatively small "social blocks" characterized by extreme poverty. One social block was examined in New York, Washington, D.C., and Chicago. The ethnic distribution of the youth sample reflects the ethnic distribution of the entire population on each block: in New York, ethnicity predominantly Puerto Rican; in Chicago, predominantly Southern white; in Washington, D.C., exclusively Negro. References to these cities in the following material reflect only information collected about resident youth in each study block and are not references to youth throughout each city. For a more detailed discussion of the study blocks in these cities, see Rosenberg and Silverstein, *op. cit.,* Ch. 3.

little success in attaining my goal. I have myself a good job now. I can, let's say, more or less get me anything I want because I don't have any responsibilities whatsoever. . . . I think I have been successful. I had my education paid for. All I have to do is get into college right there. I think that's on the way to success.

[What kind of work would you like to be doing the rest of your life?]

The rest of my life? Well, that's why I'm trying to go to school now—to be a student first, then a lawyer second. That's what I really want to be—a lawyer. I think I'll be a pretty darn good one . . . I know first it takes four years of college, possibly three or four years of law school—because I want at least three years of law school. And after that, I'll probably stay two or three years to try to get another degree—possibly to get a doctor's degree or something like that. I'd like to shoot as high as I can go.

Other youth with high aspirations are much less optimistic. One Chicago boy who would like to be a lawyer describes his problem:

[Why would you like to be a lawyer?]

I don't know. I guess cause they talk a lot. I fit in there perfectly.

[Do you have any idea what a lawyer does?]

Yes. I have an idea of what a lawyer does. He makes good money, I can assure you of that.

[What kind of thing does he have to do on his job?]

He . . . he either condemns 'em, or . . . In other words, helps 'em to get locked up, or maybe even sent to the death house, maybe even be the one that executes 'em. Or he could be the one that gets 'em out of an execution. But, it depends on whose side you're on, who hires you for the best price, or whatever. That's just like, say, people out here hire you for a job and they don't tell you what you're running up against. That's the same way with a lawyer. He never knows what he runs up against until he's right there.

[What kind of work do you think you'll do for the rest of your life?]

Digging ditches mostly. Probably digging ditches. Or I'll be running machines— punch press, drill press, screw machine, hand screw machine, automatic screw machine—so forth like that. I figure I'll be running these types of machines. Not too good of jobs, but jobs, you know. Enough today, at least it's a job.

In this case, the aspirational comedown is severe. Allowing his fantasy to run full range, he speculates about being an attorney and, unlike our Washington youth, he has made little effort in this direction. Yet, when he is deflated, his expectations fit those that are most frequently the currency of youth in this community—to be employed as laborers or factory workers. This pattern, as we shall see, occurs in each community studied. Occupational aspirations, though differently specified in each area, tend to be culturally patterned within each community. So, in the Chicago area, factory work is the expected occupation and one to which youngsters generally aspire; in Washington and New York, skilled and semiskilled occupations, such as those of mechanic or carpenter, are both aspired to and expected. In these instances, though high aspirations obtain, the expectation is either consistent with them or much lower, but, almost always, they remain within the framework of that which is expected and patterned by the community.

Only infrequently do we encounter pure fantasy in connection with occupational success. Here a young Washington Negro male, who otherwise wishes to be a cook, responds to our question concerning success:

[What does success mean to you?]
Success?
[Success, yes.]
Couldn't tell you.
[You have no idea?]
Wheel . . . big wheel, or come a success . . . becoming a lawyer or anything like that.
[So you think success to you is becoming a big wheel?]
Yes. I think you could be a little wheel and be successful . . . anything, anything you do. Like something you been trying to do for the last five years and you finally become successful.
[What do you mean by big wheel and little wheel?]
Well, a big wheel . . . I'll tell you, got most of the money. They got, you know . . . they can go out here and do most anything and get away with it. You know, crap games or gambling. They own these big places and stuff like that, or you know . . . And they can do almost anything, speed or anything, you know, in cars. Or they don't get no tickets, you know . . . I don't think.

The same young man, when asked what a good salary would be, states: "About $85 a week. That's a good salary for someone my age, I think." Yet he does not "know" his future salary and is unable to guess about it.

At the opposite pole from that rare individual who looks to a future in one of the professions are those in a state of occupational *atonie*—an inordinate listlessness and lifelessness—a condition more severe than mere *anomie*. From this type we can evoke no more than an unemotional "No" to our questions, "Do you want to get ahead in the world?" and "Do you have any ambitions?" And no amount of indirection, exhortation, or free association will produce anything more.

Between the extremes of realistically and unrealistically ambitious and totally unambitious youth, we find most of the others. They would like to move up a notch or two above their present station. The following are typical responses from each of the three study groups.

A Puerto Rican male youth typifies the respondents from this community:

[Do you want very much to get ahead in the world?]
Yeah.
[What do you mean by get ahead?]
Well, I'd have a good job.
[Suppose you had any one of your choice—this is heaven now—any kind of job. What would you pick?]
If I had any kind of job?
[Yes.]
I would get an office job.
[You'd like to work in an office? Doing what?]
Maybe typing or . . .
[That would be the best job you could imagine? Typing?]

No, it wouldn't be the best.
[What's the best you can imagine? Dream!]
That's kind of hard.
[Can't you think of any?]
No.
[Well, what do you think you will wind up doing? In jobs? When you settle down
for the rest of your life?]
Maybe something that has to do with stock work in department stores and things
like that.
[How much do you think you'll earn?]
I won't make much. Maybe about eighty or something.

Again, a Washington male youth:

[What kind of work would you like to do for the rest of your life?]
Wash dishes.
[Wash dishes in a restaurant?]
I think that's clean. More clean, like, that's clean work.
[Anything else you would like to do?]
Cook. Cooks make pretty good money.

And in Chicago, a male white youth responds to the question about his
occupational hope:

A steel job like my dad is doing.
[You want to work at hard labor. Have to lift heavy things, move around?]
Yes.
[Would you rather work in an office and wear a shirt and tie?]
No.
[Why not?]
Cause for those kind of jobs you gotta get up too early. And there's a secretary that
tells you . . . sits in your lap . . . takes notes for you. I don't like them to come in and
sit on my lap. I saw on TV, this was a true story and this man, he was sitting down.
He had a suit on and he pushed a little button that called his secretary in. And the
clothes that she wore to work—she didn't have on! She had her nightgown on, that
you could see through it. And she came in and sat on his lap and says, "You ready?"
And that man said, "I want you to take a note for me." And he kept looking all over
her. And she set down on his lap and he started goofing off with her. And then she
got up and slapped him and walked out.

These youth appear relatively satisfied with their moderate ambitions, willing
to settle for those jobs that are realistically available to them. For most, it is
impossible to elicit discontent or to inspire them to register even a modicum
of frustration. They envision the occupational world within the framework of
that community of occupations surrounding them—so little are they inspired by
powerful success-orientation. Rather than being motivated by "relative deprivation" as Merton and his continuators maintain, they appear to settle for a social
and psychological plateau, perhaps best described by the notion of "relative
contentment," primarily influenced by the cultural setting of occupational
possibilities present in the communities where they have been reared and
socialized. Whenever those pieces of cultural success-orientation from the

external world breach their enclosed community life, they are viewed as secondary possibilities and rejected for the most part as foreign matter.

Among the poverty youth studied, both social class and the neighborhood subculture are strategic influences in prevailing occupational and pecuniary success levels. More than 70% of these ethnically diverse youth, though markedly different in their delinquency-conformist patterns in each study area, share a realistic orientation toward occupational placement in the future; this rather large proportion *aspires* to a level equivalent to *expectation*. Those who wish to be carpenters expect to achieve that goal; those who want to be secretaries expect just that; those who aspire to be factory workers also expect it will come to pass. Very little discrepancy between aspirations and expectations appears. Nor do the dominant goals appear to be unrealistic.

Of course, some are undecided about occupational choice, but their indecision is more a function of their *personal* and *idiosyncratic* dispositions than any synthetic culture conflict. For them, the level of aspiration is still relatively low. For example, a girl from our New York sample states:

I like a job where I could be on the go. Moving around, you know, doing some filing. Going from here to there. In a restaurant where you have to move with a dish here, run with a dish there. Something where I don't have to be . . . you know, where I could sit around and look at things and I won't ever get bored with it. [There was this job] where the books were about that thick. There were four books—big, gigantic. Everything I used to look at, you know . . . Like I got so used to seeing that small print that when I used to look at something, I used to see the print on people's faces, you know. Seems like everything I looked at had that small print. I got tired of it fast. Then I had to start wearing glasses and I hate them. And I quit right away.

Or, a Chicago Southern white youth who, like so many of his peers, day-dreams about cars:

I want to go around and see different parts of the United States. I don't like to stick in one place. I don't want to settle down in one place right now.
[What kind of work would you like for the rest of your life?]
It's hard to say. I wouldn't mind working . . . I don't even mind pumping gas. I like anything that has to do with a car, put it that way. I'll go sit and look at a car all day long. I'm not sure what I'll do. I may get a job and just keep it, even if I don't like it. I mean if it's easy, I'll keep it. If it isn't, then I'll find a way to get fired.

Still, some remain who are unhappy about their occupational future. They represent a very small proportion of those interviewed. To what do they attribute their discontent? Two major sources are indicated. On the one hand, the social community around them has produced almost insurmountable obstacles for attaining their goals. These youth, perceptive as they may be, stand out as a small proportion of all those who feel dissatisfied. Nevertheless, they are not pronouncedly more or less delinquent than other youth in our study. They speak with deep resignation as young people who must settle for something less than they would like. The forces of control in the social universe far exceed their capacity to manage their own objectives. This factor is decidedly more marked for girls than boys.

In New York, a Puerto Rican female youth states her dilemma:

[Do you think there's any use struggling to get ahead in the world?]
For a girl, no.
[For a guy?]
Uh-huh. Like getting a job. But sometimes I sit down and think of things. I'm going to get a high school diploma. For what? I'm going to end up getting married and getting a baby and being in a house. The high school diploma will be hanging on the wall. I ain't going to be using it.

A Puerto Rican boy points to educational deficiency as the solid rock upon which his aspirations are regularly broken. He aspires to be a lawyer. He believes his chances of succeeding are "very rare." He explains: "Because if the teacher doesn't understand me in school, they don't give you a chance to explain."

Or, as another puts it: "When you without a high school education, it's very hard." And, "That's the trouble. In school I couldn't get along. I know I couldn't get along in college. Plus I wouldn't get there."

On the other hand, the *primary* interpretation for failure to get ahead is not a perception of structural obstacles but rather a highly personal explanation. As they see it, some deficiency of their own leads them to an inevitable dead-end. A young lady in her late teens tells us:

Well, there is one thing I always wanted to be: an airline hostess. But I'm too short. That was one thing I had put in my mind I wanted to be, until someone nice and kind had to tell me that I was too short.
[What do you think you will do if you work?]
Nothing. I'm too stupid and simple. I'll never get nowhere.

If there is any single ideological consensus that pervades these communities and is shared by the majority of their youth, it is not an image of pecuniary success but an interpretation of failure, whatever the level of aspiration. Paradoxically, those youth who match their aspirations with a sense of reality, and expect nothing more, see failure overwhelmingly as a function of personal inadequacy. This value not only permeates explanations of occupational failure and success, but also extends to behavior within the deviance–conformity configuration. It appears that they have succumbed to, or been suckered into accepting American society's smug interpretation of virtue vis-à-vis vice as a highly individualistic process: to fail is to be a victim of one's own shortcomings and not the shortcomings of the system.

This ideological expression of individual inadequacy as the basis of social placement is well documented in *Mass Persuasion* by Merton and his associates.[18]

---

[18] Robert K. Merton, *Mass Persuasion: The Social Psychology of a War Bond Drive* (New York: Harper, 1946), pp. 168–169.

But to the extent to which these sentiments are echoed by those who regard themselves as "working class" or "poor class" is even more revealing. Consider, for example, an elderly housewife, with a small income and of limited grade school education, who reaffirms the legitimacy of present arrangements: "*People with good heads deserve more. If my head isn't as good as another one, why should I get the same as you?* I didn't try hard enough for it. . . . *How do people get rich? They're smarter than we are.*"

A small shopkeeper, viewing herself as poised between "the rich" and "the poor," points to the essential incapacity of the poor as the chief reason for their plight: "*I imagine poor people are poor because most of them are poor managers.* People like us, we're more in the middle class. We don't see too much hardship. I'm very sympathetic to sick people, but really poor people—it's always their own fault."

From these examples and others, Merton himself demonstrates that failure to achieve high economic levels does not necessarily lead to rebellious, withdrawn, aberrant, or criminal behavior. The system is perceived as a fair one; the individual blames himself for his failure.

Just as occupational ambitions are modest, so are income orientations. Most youth hope to earn a "living wage" somewhere between $75 and $100 per week. The income aspirations and expectations coincide with remuneration generally available in the occupations they desire. Occasionally, they wish to make more, but rarely does that figure exceed $125 per week.

When we asked them to conjure up a windfall ("What's a lot of money?"), their responses were humble, most often involving amounts from one dollar to a few hundred. And what would they do with the money? "Buy a Coke," "have a party," "get my car worked on," "buy me some clothes," and occasionally when the fantasy burgeoned, "help my mother and put some money in the bank." In other words, do pretty much the same thing that they do now, except do it a little more.

Where do they wish to live? What is the most desired residence? Despite enormous dilapidation in each of the study areas, the sense of "staying with one's kind of people," of "being at home," of gaining pleasure from one's community of persons (rather than the physical community) far outweighs residential aspirations to move "up and out."

One youth, a respondent in our New York sample, imagined coming into a sizeable fortune. He said he would like to move somewhere else, "downtown," denoting a desire to change his physical surroundings. We suggested, "Possibly Park Avenue?" (a wealthy section of New York). He responded, "No, that's too much. I would spend too much money there. I'd move down, like at First and York, to the Projects [Public Housing developments], except you can't." Here, he desires to move to a community not too far from his peers and relatives and just a cut above his present level. This same youth aspires to earn $100 per week and to be a cabinetmaker, an occupation and income he expects to achieve without too much difficulty.

ILLUSION ANCHORED IN REALITY

In all, our findings are relatively simple. We have recorded in-depth interviews with youth of low socioeconomic status in three ethnically diverse social communities, a matter of critical empirical significance. We observed their various levels of aspiration in occupations, money, and residence. And although each community of youth was shown to exhibit diverse patterns of delinquent behavior, they had in common one important attribute—a low level of aspiration. If maladaptation exists in these groups, we would venture to suggest that it is not a consequence of the disjunction between opportunity and an internalized value system disproportionately stressing "success." Our study populations exhibit a generally adaptive orientation to the economic world which they eventually will face—no matter how truncated this world may appear to be. A major reassessment seems, then, to be needed in the theory that economic "anomie" is the compelling determinant behind social deviance which manifests itself as delinquency among lower-class youth. Illegitimate "innovation," which is perhaps an explanation for some forms of deviance (the middle class may fit better in this regard), does not have much validity among disadvantaged youth.

In recapitulating our own findings, a number of fundamental issues are worth further delineation. As organized in Table 1, several aspirational–expectational types materialize.

Table 1 / An Empirical Taxonomy of Aspirations and Expectations Among Lower-Class Youth

High Aspirations (Empirically Few—Less Than 25%)			
High Expectations		Low Expectations	
Realistic	Unrealistic	Realistic	Unrealistic
+ (many)	− (few)	+ (many)	− (very few)

Low Aspirations (Empirically High—More Than 75%)			
Equivalent Expectations	Low Expectations	Atonic	Exploratory
Realistic	Realistic–Unrealistic	Unrealistic	Realistic
+ (most)	− (very few)	− (few)	− (few)

1. *High Aspiration–High Expectation–Realistic.* Of the high-aspirational group, this represents the largest proportion of youth studied. Many of the youth who aspire high have set about attempting to achieve their goals. They are fairly knowledgeable about the legitimate means by which these goals can be attained, and are aware of the obstacles which they are likely to encounter. *Paradoxically, most of this group represents distinguishably nondelinquent youth* with many of its members actively engaged in the achievement process. They characteristically regard deviant and delinquent behavior as inappropriate to their objectives and therefore as maladaptive. One might say that these youth have some predictable expectation to succeed. They, as much as anyone, truly represent the Horatio Alger pattern.

2. *High Aspiration–High Expectation–Unrealistic.* These youth are a small proportion of the high aspirational group. They engage in considerable fantasy about achievement but at this point lack substantive knowledge about their objectives and the means to attain them. We would predict that hard reality ultimately will intervene and they will lower their expectations (and aspirations) at a future time.

In order to avoid repetition when describing all the remaining categories, it should be stated that the rate of delinquency appearing in this group is *no greater than any of the others, and is roughly equivalent in each of them.* Put another way, the following six categories exhibit similar rates of delinquency, and disjunctures between aspirations and expectations, wherever they may exist, are not significantly related to delinquency among the lower class youth studied. It should again be emphasized that *nondelinquency* (or a low rate of it) appears only in Type 1.

3. *High Aspiration–Low Expectation–Realistic.* Among the high-aspiration group, these represent the second largest category. These are youth who realize the problems of achieving success and have come down with a severe jolt from their lofty ambitions. Some delinquency appears *but not disproportionately* when compared to other types. This would in all probability be the group in which, according to Merton, and Cloward and Ohlin, a large proportion of delinquency would appear. Yet we find them generally adaptive and willing to settle for less than what they once would.

4. *High Aspiration–Low Expectation–Unrealistic.* This category is extremely rare. It would include youth who had considerable ambition and for some reason lowered their expectations; yet they are those who with some effort might very well be able to achieve high goals.

5. *Low Aspiration–Equivalent Expectation–Realistic.* This type represents the largest proportion by far of those youth interviewed. They are responsive to their own cultural environment and select occupations (income, residence) which are found most often among adults in the community and set their sights on achieving similar socioeconomic status. Horatio Alger is essentially irrelevant to them and is not a "meaningful" value in the context of their community and social

life. They are aspirationally adaptive and see no great difficulty in accomplishing their aims.

6. *Low Aspiration–Low Expectation–Unrealistic.* This group is empirically quite rare. Only occasionally do we find youth who aspire to occupations commonly found in their cultural setting and expect even lower results.

7. *Low Aspiration–Atonic–Unrealistic.* Occasionally during our interviewing we encountered youth who were extraordinarily listless and had no interest or hope in occupational placement. This group may ultimately gain some measure of interest in the occupational world, or they may begin to engage in "retreat-ist" activities such as drug addiction.

8. *Low Aspiration–Exploratory–Realistic.* These are highly individualistic youth who wish to move out and try many occupations, although their sights are now set on a fairly low level. They represent a small proportion of the total number interviewed. These youth, in possibly breaking away from the specific cultural milieu in which they have been reared, ultimately may develop higher aspirations through new culture contacts and subsequently higher socioeconomic status. At this juncture, however, they remain at a relatively low level of hope and are representative of a generally existential mode. They may be those lower-class youth who occasionally crop up in "hippie" communities.

In the final analysis, even though our approach is highly qualitative, we offer the proposition that youth deviance is not a consequence of "illegitimate" innovation. Social scientists, perhaps with a view from the top, have assumed that middle class values impinge significantly upon lower class segments of society. We find little evidence to support that contention.

PART THREE

ENDEMIC CONDITIONS

The pioneer French sociologist Emile Durkheim startled scholars and scientists at the turn of the century by proposing that crime is functional in society and therefore normal. The rate at a given moment may be abnormally high or low but only in the relative sense, by comparison with the average rate in societies of a similar type. The kind of crime as well as the rate may be abnormal, but the fact of crime is not and cannot be. A society that functions without generating crime is as impossible to conceive as an internal combustion engine that runs without producing heat. Crime is *endemic* in society ; it is inherent in the condition of social order and is characteristic of it.

The importance of the Durkheimian theorem is that in the light of it any social problem has to be understood as being intertwined with some essential and possibly even desirable function of the institutional structure of society. It is not something to be solved but only ameliorated, because it is a manifestation of a condition endemic to society generally or to some particular type such as the modern, urban, industrial society of North America and Western Europe.

Broadly and conventionally speaking, a social problem is a condition most people find undesirable and that they believe can be and should be eliminated. The contribution the sociologist makes is to clarify the relationship between that problem as it is publicly defined and the character of the society that gives it birth and nurtures it.

This Part is organized into four chapters: deviance, discrimination, rationalization, and alienation.

Deviation is manifested in patterns of nonconforming behavior that are sufficiently visible and that affect the lives of others to such an extent that the deviant is likely to come to the attention of a social agency.

Criminality and delinquency are the province first of the police and then the courts—both agencies of control, although they function differently. The police selectively apprehend perpetrators of deviant acts and charge them with lawbreaking, delinquency, or mental incompetence. The court hears arguments and weighs evidence. If it finds the charge sustained it may order incarceration, for punishment or treatment, or release in the custody of parents or a probation officer. The court acts as society's agent in determining what should be done with the deviant while, ideally, safeguarding his rights and welfare.

The police and the courts and the various agencies in whose charge the deviant is placed, once he is convicted, committed, or certified, have to adjust their operations to the fact that there are different sorts of deviants. The rational thief—a professional man with expert skills and a career—is hardly to be compared with the compulsive shoplifter—perhaps a middle-aged suburban housewife with no real need for stolen goods—or with an obsessive criminal like Jean Genet (p. 313)—who describes himself as "hot for crime." The drug addict (Winick, p. 329) is another type: not rational, not compulsive, not morally dedicated, a criminal out of sheer desperate necessity. Srole (p. 320) reports findings that show mental illness in the metropolis to be shockingly high, which is significant because a good deal of deviance—by no means all—is related to mental and psychological disturbance.

Discrimination, far from being new and peculiar to modern society, began with civilization. In the early cities it was taken for granted that the birthrights of individuals differed from tribe to tribe and caste to caste and class to class; *citizenship* (membership in a voluntary association called The City) entailed rights superimposed on a layer or more of rights already held—or not held. Discrimination is conduct by agents of society, formal or informal, official or unofficial, that takes as its premise that some people naturally and justly have more privileges than others.

Discrimination has become a social problem not because it is itself new but because it is inconsistent with new values. It can no longer be reconciled credibly with the cornerstone doctrine of modern republics that all men are created equal, or with the ideal that all citizens ought to enjoy equal protection of the law as well as equal rights before it. It now seems wrong and unjust and socially harmful to permit people with power to deny, in tacit or open concert, people without power the means to live in comfort and decency and to compete on equal terms with others for society's prizes because they are black or Jewish or poor. Discrimination is particularly troublesome because in its racist form it is endemic in Western European and North American society, historically based as they are on colonization and exploitation of minority peoples.

The late Malcolm X (p. 333), prophet and ideologue of much of the black revolution in its present form, explains how what he terms "liberal myths" distort the terms of the struggle black people are waging to assert their identity and pride as a national minority in American society. Sethard Fisher (p. 354), not a movement leader but a Negro and a social scientist, reviews the literature on the social sources of the black movement and projects its future. Rosenberg and Howton (p. 341) analyze the structure of discrimination against Negroes and Puerto Ricans in Northern business firms whose executives are ideologically "ethnic liberals." Brief comment is made by Surace and Turner (p. 351) on the situation of Mexican Americans in the Los Angeles area.

Rationalization is the force underlying a congeries of social problems. In modern society organization and social relations at work are becoming increasingly bureaucratized, partly because of the imperatives created by the rationalization of production technology, and this affects the work situation of the governmental elite, white collar people, scholars and scientists, factory operatives, and even farm laborers. The process entails a break with tradition and with rule-of-thumb improvisations in work organization and procedure. Management, research and development, the processing of information by technicians and junior professionals, and production work in automated factories all are rationalized. Moreover, rationalized technology in agriculture has doomed old-fashioned stoop labor. Now the man who was the producer of the field-hand sort runs a machine, works in a packing shed, or else goes on welfare or goes hungry.

Bendix (p. 367) raises the question of whether an elite stratum of higher civil servants with a degree of social homogeneity and a culture of its own is developing in the United States. Cohen (p. 369) presents a chilling analysis of how the logic and the instruments of rationalization in a state employment service can be perverted and subverted, so that what is formally rational in procedures covers up irrationality in substance. Seligman (p. 381) questions the optimism of neoutilitarians who ignore the human waste and misery automation brings and look only at the gain in production efficiency. In each case rationalization is not itself a social problem but a creator of social problems, an endemic condition in modern society.

Alienation is endemic as well but in a different way. Rationalization is socially defined as good despite its undesirable side effects, because it fosters progress in technology and creates a quality of mind thought to be good in itself. Demystification and intellectual self-clarification, according to Max Weber, are goals sought by social science. In Freud's conception, the goal of psychoanalysis is to strengthen the rational component of the psyche, the ego, at the expense of the irrational id—"Where Id Was Let Ego Be." Alienation in the sense of the spirit of secularism, a willingness to break with tradition, is both a precondition and a consequence of rationalization and therefore an endemic condition. Like crime and mental illness it is "normal" in modern society. Nonetheless, again like crime, it is socially defined as a problem or nexus of problems because there is thought to be too much of it.

The alienated individual feels like an outsider in relation to the larger com-munity—cut off, unable to join in and share with others or to participate. Goals and means of "the others" seem to him senseless, alien, not his. Seeman (p. 428) shows this strikingly in the case of intellectuals. The nature of their work and the kind of ethical commitment and identity that follows from it predispose them to feel alienated as a social type. They adopt a perspective and a mode of expression that reflect the experience in some ways typical of an ethnic minority group.

One of the most pervasive and yet dramatic manifestations of alienation in American society is withdrawal from participation in the democratic political process. In an article written nearly twenty years ago, Riesman and Glazer (p. 399) identify and describe two types of apathetics: "indignants" and "indifferents." Both reject the electoral process, although for different reasons. Apathetic indignants care a great deal about the distribution and uses of power in society, but have very little faith in their ability to influence them with the means at hand—the institutionalized party system and the machinery of voting. Apathetic indifferents have little more than a spectators' interest in either the means or the goals of political activity.

It is illuminating to look at a typical example of the new-style "confrontation politics" of the late 1960s, as described in the Cox Commission Report (p. 442) on the disturbances on the campus of Columbia University, from the standpoint of theories of political alienation of the early 1950s. The apathetic indignants—one might say the extremists, those who want to change the power structure through direct action because they have no faith in regular channels and modes of expression and suasion—were small-town ultrarightists, then. Now they are big-city ultraleftists. The apathetic indifferents then were the great majority of the population who had neither the interest nor the nerve to stop McCarthyism (the conservatives did the job, not the moderates); now they are a fading minority as the moderates are increasingly receptive to backlash sentiment against "campus turmoil" and "crime in the streets," or ghetto rioting. The indignants then were middle-aged and elderly people who supported the use of police state tactics to harass and intimidate teachers, librarians, scientists, and government officials alleged to be "soft on Communism." The indignants now are university students and young black militants who use anarchist tactics of disruption, provocation, and sabotage to challenge institutional leadership groups they consider reactionary.

The differences in character and style between the two historical types of apathetic indignants are so great that it would seem at first that they have nothing important in common and that the Riesman-Glazer concepts are no longer relevant.

The differences are impressive, but on the balance they are outweighed by the fact that the two historical types of apathetic indignants share a sense of being alienated from the system—meaning the electoral process—and a character of moral self-righteousness that gives them the nerve to act in the spirit that the end justifies the means. This is the nub of it. Alienation in politics is still very much a social problem and a condition endemic to modern society.

CHAPTER 1

DEVIANCE

On Thieves and Flowers

JEAN GENET

■

Convicts' clothes are striped pink and white. Though it was at my heart's bidding that I chose the universe wherein I delight, I have at least the power of finding in it the many meanings I wish to find: *there is a close relationship between flowers and convicts.* The fragility and delicacy of the former are of the same nature as the brutal insensitivity of the latter.[1] Should I have to portray a convict—or a criminal—I shall so bedeck him with flowers that, as he disappears beneath them, he will himself become a flower, a gigantic and new one. Toward what is known as evil, I have, for love's sake, pursued an adventure which led me to prison. Though they may not always be handsome, men doomed to evil possess the manly virtues. Of their own volition, or through an accident which has been chosen for them, they plunge lucidly and without complaint into a reproachful, ignominious element, like that into which love, if it is profound, hurls human beings. Erotic play discloses a nameless world which is revealed by the nocturnal language of lovers. Such language is not written down. It is whispered into the ear at night in a hoarse voice. At dawn it is forgotten. Repudiating the virtues of your world, criminals agree hopelessly to organize a forbidden universe. They agree to live in it. The air there is nauseating: they can breathe it. But—criminals are remote from you—as in love, they turn away and turn me away from the world and its laws. Theirs smells of sweat, sperm and blood. In short, to my body and my thirsty soul it offers devotion. It was because it contained these erotic conditions that I was bent on evil. My adventure, never governed by rebellion or a feeling of injustice, will be merely one long mating, burdened and complicated by a heavy and strange erotic ceremonial (figurative ceremonies leading to jail and anticipating it). Though it be the sanction, in my eyes the justification too, of the foulest crime, it will be the sign of the most utter degradation. That ultimate point to which

---

Source: Jean Genet, *The Thief's Journal.* Translated from the French by Bernard Frechtman. Reprinted by permission of Grove Press, Inc. Copyright © 1964 by Grove Press, Inc.
[1] My excitement is the oscillation from one to the other.

the censure of men leads was to appear to me the ideal place for the purest, that is, the most turbid amatory harmony, where illustrious ash-weddings are celebrated. Desiring to hymn them, I use what is offered me by the form of the most exquisite natural sensibility, which is already aroused by the garb of convicts. The material evokes, and not only by its colors and roughness, certain flowers whose petals are slightly fuzzy, which detail is sufficient for me to associate the idea of strength and shame with what is most naturally precious and fragile. This association, which tells me things about myself, would not suggest itself to another mind; mine can not avoid it. Thus, I offered my tenderness to the convicts; I wanted to call them by charming names, to designate their crimes with, for modesty's sake, the subtlest metaphor (beneath which veil I would not have been unaware of the murderer's rich muscularity, of the violence of his sex). Is it not by the following image that I prefer to imagine them in Guiana: the strongest, with a horn, the "hardest," veiled by mosquito netting? And each flower within me leaves behind so solemn a sadness that all of them must signify sorrow, death. Thus, I sought love as it pertained to the penal colony. Each of my passions led me to hope for it, gave me a glimpse of it, offers me criminals, offers me to them or invites me to crime. As I write this book, the last convicts are returning to France. The newspapers have been reporting the matter. The heir of kings feels a similar emptiness if the republic deprives him of his anointment. The end of the penal colony prevents us from entering with our living minds into the mythical underground regions. Our most dramatic movement has been clipped away: our exodus, the embarkation, the procession on the sea, which was performed with bowed head. The return, this same procession in reverse, is without meaning. Within me, the destruction of the colony corresponds to a kind of punishment of punishment: I am castrated, I am shorn of my infamy. Unconcerned about beheading our dreams of their glories, they awaken us prematurely. The home prisons have their power: it is not the same. It is minor. It has none of that elegant and slightly bowed grace. The atmosphere is so heavy that you have to drag yourself about. You creep along. The home prisons are more stiffly erect, more darkly and severely; the slow and solemn agony of the penal colony was a more perfect blossoming of abjection. So that now the home jails, bloated with evil males, are black with them, as with blood which has been shot through with carbonic gas. (I have written "black." The outfit of the convicts—captives, captivity, even prisoners, words too noble to name us—forces it upon me: it is made of brown homespun). It is toward them that my desire will turn. I am aware that there is often a semblance of the burlesque in the colony or in prison. On the bulky and resonant base of their wooden shoes, the frame of the condemned men is always somewhat shaky. In front of a wheel-barrow, it suddenly breaks up rather stupidly. In the presence of a guard they lower their heads and hold in their hands the big straw sun-bonnet—which the younger ones decorate (I should prefer it so) with a stolen rose granted by the guard—or a brown homespun beret. They strike poses of wretched humility. If they are beaten, something within them must nevertheless stiffen: the coward, the crook, cowardice, crookedness are—when kept in a state of the hardest, purest cowardice and crookedness—hardened by a "dousing," as soft iron is hardened by dousing. They persist in servility, despite everything. Though I do not neglect the deformed and misshapen, it is the handsomest criminals whom my tenderness adorns.

Crime, I said to myself, had a long wait before producing such perfect successes as Pilorge and Angel Sun. In order to finish them off (the term is a cruel one!) it was necessary that a host of coincidences concur: to the handsomeness of their faces, to the strength and elegance of their bodies there had to be added their taste for crime, the circumstances which make the criminal, the moral vigor capable of accepting such a destiny, and, finally, punishment, its cruelty, the intrinsic quality which enables a criminal to glory in it, and, over all of this, areas of darkness. If the hero join combat with night and conquer it, may shreds of it remain upon him! The same hesitation, the same crystallization of good fortune governs the success of a pure sleuth. I cherished them both. But if I love their crime, it is for the punishment it involves, "the penalty" (for I can not suppose that they have not anticipated it). One of them, the former boxer Ledoux, answered smilingly: "My crimes? It's before committing them that I might have regretted them" in which I want to accompany them so that, come what may, my love may be filled to overflowing.

I do not want to conceal in this journal the other reasons which made me a thief, the simplest being the need to eat, though revolt, bitterness, anger or any such similar sentiment never entered into my choice. With fanatical care, "jealous care," I prepared for my adventure as one arranges a couch or a room for love; I was *hot* for crime.

Crime and Conformity

EMILE DURKHEIM

___

If there is any fact whose pathological character appears incontestable, that fact is crime. All criminologists are agreed on this point. Although they explain this pathology differently, they are unanimous in recognizing it. But let us see if this problem does not demand a more extended consideration.

We shall apply the foregoing rules. Crime is present not only in the majority of societies of one particular species but in all societies of all types. There is no society that is not confronted with the problem of criminality. Its form changes; the acts thus characterized are not the same everywhere; but, everywhere and always, there have been men who have behaved in such a way as to draw upon themselves penal repression. If, in proportion as societies pass from the lower to the higher types, the rate of criminality, i.e., the relation between the yearly number of crimes and the population, tended to decline, it might be believed that crime, while still normal, is tending to lose this character of normality. But we have no reason to believe that such a regression is substantiated. Many facts would seem rather to indicate a movement in the opposite direction. From the beginning of the [nineteenth] century, statistics enable us to follow the course of criminality. It has everywhere increased. In France the increase is nearly 300 per cent. There is, then, no phenomenon that presents more indisputably all the symptoms of normality, since it appears closely connected with the conditions of all collective life. To make a crime a form of social morbidity would be to admit that morbidity is not something accidental, but, on the contrary, that in certain cases it grows out of the fundamental constitution of the living organism; it would result in wiping out all distinction between the physiological and the pathological. No doubt it is possible that crime itself will have abnormal forms, as for example, when its rate is unusually high. This excess is, indeed, undoubtedly morbid in nature. What is normal, simply, is the existence of criminality, provided that it attains and does not exceed, for each social type, a certain level, which it is perhaps not impossible to fix in conformity with the preceding rules.[1]

Here we are, then, in the presence of a conclusion in appearance quite pathological. Let us make no mistake. To classify crime among the phenomena of normal sociology is not to say merely that it is an inevitable, although regrettable, phenomenon, due to the incorrigible wickedness of men; it is to affirm that it is a factor in public health, an integral part of all healthy societies. This result is, at first glance, surprising enough to have puzzled even ourselves for a long time. Once this first surprise has been overcome, however, it is not difficult to find reasons explaining this normality and at the same time confirming it.

In the first place crime is normal because a society exempt from it is utterly impossible. Crime, we have shown elsewhere, consists of an act that offends certain very strong collective sentiments. In a society in which criminal acts are no longer committed, the sentiments they offend would have to be found

---

[1] From the fact that crime is a phenomenon of normal sociology, it does not follow that the criminal is an individual normally constituted from the biological and psychological points of view. The two questions are independent of each other. This independence will be better understood when we have shown, later on, the difference between psychological and sociological facts.

without exception in all individual consciousness, and they must be found to exist with the same degree as sentiments contrary to them. Assuming that this condition could actually be realized, crime would not thereby disappear; it would only change its form, for the very cause which would thus dry up the sources of criminality would immediately open up new ones.

Indeed, for the collective sentiments which are protected by the penal law of a people at a specified moment of its history to take possession of the public conscience or for them to acquire a stronger hold where they have an insufficient grip, they must acquire an intensity greater than that which they had hitherto had. The community as a whole must experience them more vividly, for it can acquire from no other source the greater force necessary to control these individuals who formerly were the most refractory. For murderers to disappear, the horror of bloodshed must become greater in these social strata from which murderers are recruited; but, first it must become greater throughout the entire society. Moreover, the very absence of crime would directly contribute to produce this horror; because any sentiment seems much more respectable when it is always and uniformly respected.

One easily overlooks the consideration that these strong states of the common consciousness cannot be thus reinforced without reinforcing at the same time the more feeble states, whose violation previously gave birth to mere infraction of convention—since the weaker ones are only the prolongation, the attenuated form, of the stronger. Thus robbery and simple bad taste injure the same single altruistic sentiment, the respect for that which is another's. However, this same sentiment is less grievously offended by bad taste than by robbery; and since, in addition, the average consciousness has not sufficient intensity to react keenly to the bad taste, it is treated with greater tolerance. That is why the person guilty of bad taste is merely blamed, whereas the thief is punished. But, if this sentiment grows stronger, to the point of silencing in all consciousness the inclination which disposes man to steal, he will become more sensitive to the offenses which, until then, touched him but lightly. He will react against them, then, with more energy; they will be the object of greater opprobrium, which will transform certain of them from the simple moral faults that they were and give them the quality of crimes. For example, improper contracts, or contracts improperly executed, which only incur public blame or civil damages, will become offenses in law.

Imagine a society of saints, a perfect cloister of exemplary individuals. Crimes, properly so called, will there be unknown; but faults which appear venial to the layman will create there the same scandal that the ordinary offense does in ordinary consciousness. If, then, this society has the power to judge and punish, it will define these acts as criminal and will treat them as such. For the same reason, the perfect and upright man judges his smallest failings with a severity that the majority reserve for acts more truly in the nature of an offense. Formerly, acts of violence against persons were more frequent than they are today, because respect for individual dignity was less strong. As this has increased, these crimes have become more rare; and also, many acts violating this sentiment have been introduced into the penal law which were not included there in primitive times.[2]

In order to exhaust all the hypotheses logically possible, it will perhaps be asked why this unanimity does not extend to all collective sentiments without exception. Why should not even the most feeble sentiment gather enough energy to prevent all dissent? The moral consciousness of the society would be present in its entirety in all the individuals, with a vitality sufficient to prevent all acts offending it—the purely conventional faults as well as the crimes. But a uniformity so universal and absolute is utterly impossible; for the immediately physical milieu in which each one of us is placed, the hereditary antecedents, and the social influences vary from one individual to the next, and consequently diversify consciousness. It is impossible for all to be alike, if only because each one has his own organism and that these organisms occupy different areas in space. That is why, even among the lower peoples, where individual originality is very little developed, it nevertheless does exist.

Thus, since there cannot be a society in which the individuals do not differ more or less from the collective type, it is also inevitable that, among these divergencies, there are some with a criminal character. What confers this character upon them is not the intrinsic quality of a given act but that definition which the collective conscience lends them. If the collective conscience is stronger, if it has enough authority practically to suppress these divergences, it will also be more sensitive, more exacting; and, reacting against the slightest deviations with the energy it otherwise displays only against more considerable infractions, it will attribute to them the same gravity as formerly to crimes. In other words, it will designate them as criminals.

Crime is, then, necessary; it is bound up with the fundamental conditions of all social life, and by that very fact it is useful, because these conditions of which it is a part are themselves indispensable to the normal evolution of morality and law.

Indeed, it is no longer possible today to dispute the fact that law and morality vary from one social type to the next, nor that they change within the same type if the conditions of life are modified. But, in order that these transformations may be possible, the collective sentiments at the basis of morality must not be hostile to change, and consequently must have but moderate energy. If they were too strong, they would no longer be plastic. Every pattern is an obstacle to new patterns, to the extent that the first pattern is inflexible. The better a structure is articulated, the more it offers a healthy resistance to all modification; and this is equally true of functional, as of anatomical, organization. If there were no crimes, this condition could not have been fulfilled; for such a hypothe-

---

[2] Calumny, insults, slander, fraud, etc.

sis presupposes that collective sentiments have arrived at a degree of intensity unexampled in history. Nothing is good indefinitely and to an unlimited extent. The authority which the moral conscience enjoys must not be excessive; otherwise no one would dare criticize it, and it would too easily congeal into an immutable form. To make progress, individual originality must be able to express itself. In order that the originality of the idealist whose dreams transcend his century may find expression, it is necessary that the originality of the criminal, who is below the level of his time, shall also be possible. One does not occur without the other.

Nor is this all. Aside from this indirect utility, it happens that crime itself plays a useful role in this evolution. Crime implies not only that the way remains open to necessary changes but that in certain cases it directly prepares these changes. Where crime exists, collective sentiments are sufficiently flexible to take on a new form, and crime sometimes helps to determine the form they will take. How many times, indeed, it is only an anticipation of future morality—a step toward what will be! According to Athenian law, Socrates was a criminal, and his condemnation was no more than just. However, his crime, namely, the independence of this thought, rendered a service not only to humanity but to his country. It served to prepare a new morality and faith which the Athenians needed, since the traditions by which they had lived until then were no longer in harmony with the current conditions of life. Nor is the case of Socrates unique; it is reproduced periodically in history. It would never have been possible to establish the freedom of thought we now enjoy if the regulations prohibiting it had not been violated before being solemnly abrogated. At that time, however, the violation was a crime, since it was an offense against sentiments still very keen in the average conscience. And yet this crime was useful as a prelude to reforms which daily became more necessary. Liberal philosophy had as its precursors the heretics of all kinds who were justly punished by secular authorities during the entire course of the Middle Ages and until the eve of modern times.

From this point of view the fundamental facts of criminality present themselves to us in an entirely new light. Contrary to current ideas, the criminal no longer seems a totally unsociable being, a sort of parasitic element, a strange and unassimilable body, introduced into the midst of society.[3] On the contrary, he plays a definite role in social life. Crime, for its part, must no longer be conceived as an evil that cannot be too much suppressed. There is no occasion for self-congratulation when the crime rate drops noticeably below the average level, for we may be certain that this apparent progress is associated with some social disorder. Thus, the number of assault cases never falls so low as in times

---

[3] We have ourselves committed the error of speaking thus of the criminal, because of a failure to apply our rule (*Division du travail social,* pp. 395–396).

of want.[4] With the drop in the crime rate, and as a reaction to it, comes a revision, or the need of a revision in the theory of punishment. If, indeed, crime is a disease, its punishment is its remedy and cannot be otherwise conceived; thus, all the discussions it arouses bear on the point of determining what the punishment must be in order to fulfil this role of remedy. If crime is not pathological at all, the object of punishment cannot be to cure it, and its true function must be sought elsewhere.

---

[4] Although crime is a fact of normal sociology, it does not follow that we must not abhor it. Pain itself has nothing desirable about it; the individual dislikes it as society does crime, and yet it is a function of normal physiology. Not only is it necessarily derived from the very constitution of every living organism, but it plays a useful role in life, for which reason it cannot be replaced. It would, then, be a singular distortion of our thought to present it as an apology for crime. We would not even think of protesting against such an interpretation, did we not know to what strange accusations and misunderstandings one exposes oneself when one undertakes to study moral facts objectively and to speak of them in a different language from that of the layman.

Mental Health in the Metropolis

LEO SROLE, THOMAS S. LANGNER, STANLEY T. MICHAEL, MARVIN K. OPLER, AND THOMAS A. C. RENNIE

███████

HOME SURVEY SAMPLE: MENTAL HEALTH DISTRIBUTIONS

With this review of the main technical features of the Home Interview Survey, we can now turn to the sample of 1,600 Midtown adults for a first report on their standing within the gradient classification of symptom formation.[1]

Source: From *Mental Health in the Metropolis: The Midtown Study*, vol. 1, by Leo Srole, *at al.* Copyright 1962. McGraw-Hill Book Company, Inc. Reprinted by permission. Pp. 138–145.

[1] This is the number of respondents who were finally interviewed, with the results reported and discussed below. (A probability sample of 1,911 was drawn from the 110,000 persons 21 to 59 years of age estimated to reside within a delimited area of midtown Manhattan. The figure 1,660 includes those who could be reached and agreed to cooperate by giving information.) Each respondent was interviewed in his home. The interviews required about two hours, and covered such topics as life history, social functioning, and sociocultural environment as well as psychophysiological symptoms. Summaries of each interview protocol were then prepared, and two psychiatrists, working independently, rated the mental health of each respondent.

Table 1 / Home Survey Sample (Age 20–59)

Respondent's Distribution on Symptom-Formation Classification of Mental Health

Well	18.5%
Mild symptom formation	36.3
Moderate symptom formation	21.8
Marked symptom formation	13.2
Severe symptom formation	7.5
Incapacitated	2.7
Impaired[a]	23.4
$N = 100\%$	(1,660)

[a] Marked, Severe, and Incapacitated combined.

TYPES OF SYMPTOMATIC INDICATORS OF MENTAL ILLNESS

Functional	*Psychological*	*Physiological*
breathing	worry	sweats
eating	nervousness	nausea
sleeping	inertia	weakness

How can the presence and intensity of mental illness be inferred from responses to an administered questionnaire? The findings of epidemiological research are based in part on answers to questions drawn from "symptom inventories" such as the NSA (Neuropsychiatric Screening Adjunct) and MMPI (Minnesota Multiphasic Personality Inventory). Most of the eighteen items (out of a total of over a hundred) reported by the authors of *Mental Health in the Metropolis* to constitute a "core series of 'psychophysiologic manifestations of emotional disturbance'" (see pp. 42, 43) fall into the categories laid out above. Authorities generally agree that the MMPI and NSA are reliable and valid discriminators between persons who are mentally ill in the clinical sense —patients—and controls. What is less certain is that two psychiatrists, working with summaries of data only (mainly limited to verbal responses in structured questions) taken in a nonclinical setting by nonmedical interviewers, have produced a convincing, six-step rating of the mental health of the metropolis.

Editors' Note: For discussion and comment on methodological aspects of the Midtown study, see the review by August Hollingshead in the *American Sociological Review*, 27:6 (December 1962), pp. 864–866. Edgar Z. Friedenberg's observations on the possible class bias introduced by taking verbal responses at face value are also noteworthy. See his review in *Commentary*, 34:6 (December 1962), pp. 545–547.

In Table 1 we see that roughly 1 in 5 (18.5%) respondents were viewed by the team psychiatrists as free of other than inconsequential symptoms and can be regarded as essentially Well.

The Mild and Moderate categories are the most populous strata (36.3 and 21.8%, respectively), together holding a 58.1% majority of the Midtown sample. It will be remembered that these represent people who to all appearances are performing their adult responsibilities passably or better, although they carry significant loads of pathology-denoting symptoms. It seems, therefore, that these subclinical strata define the most frequent conditions in the Midtown population, and probably in the inclusive Manhattan white population as well. Whether these are also the most prevalent mental health conditions in more comprehensive segments of the American people is a question rather beyond the capabilities of our data to answer.

Although separately they are the least populated, the three Impaired categories add up to a sizable 23.4% slice of the Midtown respondents. Had we also sampled Midtown's absentee mental hospital patients in the 20 to 59 age range, they would have raised the Incapacitated category (by 0.5%) to 3.2% and the Impaired proportion to 23.9%. Applying the necessary margin for sampling error, we estimate with 95% confidence that in the Midtown population universe the mental morbidity rate stands in a range between 21.9 and 25.9%. Next, on the basis of our earlier indication that this estimate probably involves an error of understatement, it seems likely that the true rate stands closer to the high point in this range.

With the particular kinds of respondent data that were secured, the symptom-formation classification could be readily applied by the Study's psychiatrists. For reasons already discussed, such confidence could not be extended to classification of sample respondents in terms of the established psychiatric nomenclature. Nonetheless, at the beginning of the evaluation process the ultimate workability of the symptom-formation mode of classification was still uncertain. In short, it entailed an unknown risk of losing invaluable, irreplaceable time. As a form of insurance, therefore, Rennie instructed the evaluating psychiatrists to apply as best they could a second, supplementary classification system, designated as the *gross typology*. This involved nosological categories familiar in psychiatry, but their qualification with the term *probable* (more strictly speaking, *possible*) reflects the recognition that they were based on a very large leverage of psychiatric impression and intuition based on a fulcrum of data not designed for this purpose. With the utility of the symptom-severity rating system subsequently established, the reserve use of the gross typology scheme is obviated in this volume. However we yield one exception at this point, for whatever suggestive value there may be in sensing the diversive make-up of the impaired group as delineated under the symptom-formation mode of classification. Thus, analysis of the gross typology composition of the sample's 389 Impaired respondents suggests that about 1 in 20 (5.7%) falls in the probable organic (damage or deficiency) type, 1 in 4 (26.5%) in the probable psychotic type, and the remaining two-thirds (67.8%) in the probable neurotic or probable personality disorder types. Of course, the latter two types are concentrated most heavily in the Marked category of symptom formation.

MENTAL MORBIDITY RATES AND CRITERIA IN OTHER STUDIES

The 23.4% impairment rate found in the noninstitutional, in-residence sample population of Midtown may be viewed by some students as staggering in magnitude, or of dubious credibility.

We must address ourselves to such skepticism as potentially justifiable. Specifically, the credibility of the finding may be questioned on two different planes. On one level, the question may imply that the morbidity rate reported is beyond serious technical reproach, but the study population in its loading of mental pathology may be an extreme, local deviant on the American scene. On another level, the study population may not be grossly atypical, but the Midtown psychiatrists' criterion of mental morbidity could be faulty in its excessive breadth.

To get purchase on the first level, a nationwide study of mental health applying the Midtown classification of symptom formation, is lacking to us. However, the Midtown interview instrument included a series of "signs and symptoms" questions that had previously been used in the development of the Army's Neuro-psychiatric Screening Adjunct questionnaire. Toward this development in 1944, a cross-section control sample of 3,501 white enlisted men on active duty, with no overseas service (and almost entirely between the ages of 18 and 36), anonymously filled out the experimental questionnaire. Compared to the Midtown sample, this sample was of course more homogeneous in age, sex, and socioeconomic status, more heterogeneous in rural-urban and regional origins, and in general more representative of the white population in the nation at large.

Despite these differences, if Midtown adults in mental health respects are an atypical population we would expect them to show consistently larger frequencies of specific pathognomic signs than did the Army sample. For purposes of this comparison we have confined ourselves to the 18 symptom questions that were used in both studies with identical wordings. Only in two of these items did the Midtown sample appreciably exceed the Army's frequencies of "symptom positive" answers. On eight questions, it was the Army sample that exceeded Midtown's in this respect. And in eight other items, the two samples were more or less identical in their replies. Particularly significant in the latter series was the query: "Are you ever bothered by nervousness?" "Yes, often" rejoinders were given by 17% of the Army men and by 18% of the Midtown respondents.

Nothing can be extracted from this limited analysis to support the inference

that the Midtown population is any more deviant than the comparison population of relatively selected,[2] able-bodied, young, white enlisted men. A lesser but
related clue may be offered by the 2,252 New Yorkers who applied for treatment
to a new, unopened, low-cost psychiatric clinic. Scattered through the five
boroughs, they comprised a city-wide rate of 26 per 100,000 population. Mid-
towners among these applicants represented an area rate of 23 per 100,000. In
this expressed need for psychiatric help, Midtown hardly appears atypical of
New York City at large.

A second basis for questioning the magnitude of the Midtown impairment rate
can turn on the possibility that the criterion of mental morbidity it reflects was
stretched beyond resemblance to clinical realities. Rennie's calibration of the
Midtown impaired categories to the out-patients and hospital patients in his
metropolitan experience lessens this specific possibility.

The skeptics can insist, nonetheless, that the Midtown morbidity rate is out
of line with previous knowledge, drawn principally from studies of patients.
Even more to their case, they can point to two other studies involving professional evaluation of mental health in a large metropolitan sample and producing
morbidity rates patently well below that of Midtown's in both cases. One of
these was the investigation in Baltimore conducted by the Commission on
Chronic Illness.[3] The other was the wartime study of Selective Service examinees
in the Boston induction station, as reported by Hyde and Kingsley.[4]

To meet such evidence it is possible, of course, to marshal counter-indications,
e.g., the various estimates that 10 to 50% of patients seen by general practitioners and internists are "psychiatric cases."[5] Or there is the morbidity rate
of 32% uncovered in a Salt Lake City sample of 175 households, by methods
exemplifying rather less than the most advanced standards of sampling.[6]

Even if these rates were defensible, however, they would still be irrelevant to
the challenge offered the Midtown Study by the Baltimore and Boston investigations, to which we must now detour for careful examination.

The Baltimore investigation consisted of three different research operations,
the only one of pertinence here being that designated the *clinical evaluation.*
Focused on a broad spectrum of chronic and acute somatic illnesses, and also
mental disorder, this particular operation started with a drawn sample of 1,292
persons in an age range defined as reaching from "under 15 to over 65." Of

---

[2] *Selected* here refers to the fact that obvious physical and mental misfits had already been
in largest part screened out. On the other hand, it should not be overlooked that the military
environment is at a considerable sociological distance from the family and community settings
of these ex-civilians.

[3] This has been fully reported, authors undesignated, in *Chronic Illness in a Large City:
The Baltimore Study* (1957).

[4] "Studies in Medical Sociology: The Relation of Mental Disorders to Population Density,"
New Engl. J. Med., Vol. 23, No. 17 (October 26, 1944), pp. 571–577.

[5] *Third Annual Report*, Joint Commission on Mental Illness and Health (1958), p. 11.

[6] N. J. Cole, C. H. Branch, and O. M. Shaw, "Mental Illness: A Survey Assessment of
Community Rates, Attitudes and Adjustments," *A.M.A. Arch. Neurol. Psychiat.*, Vol. 77
(April 17, 1957), pp. 393–398.

these, 809 individuals, or 62.6% all told, appeared in clinic for (1) a battery of laboratory tests and (2) thorough physical examinations by one of a staff of 31 physicians, internists in the main. From this sample of participating examinees a "weighted" estimate of 10.9% was derived as the prevalence rate for mental disorder.[7] This figure has not only been extrapolated to the city of Baltimore and quoted in Federal publications addressed to the general public, but in a variety of publications has also been projected on the American population at large.

The basic fact that need concern us here is that between the reported Baltimore mental disorder frequency of 10.9% and Midtown's 23.4% impairment rate stretches a seemingly unbridgeable gulf. Before we accept this difference as lending credence to views that the Midtown Study's criterion of mental morbidity was overextended, we must first determine whether the two studies are comparable in other relevant respects.

First, the studied populations are far from demographic comparability, but this can be partially corrected by isolating the segment of the Baltimore sample that most nearly matches the Midtown respondents, at least in race and age composition. The closest Baltimore age approximation reported in the source volume[8] is the 15 to 64 age range, where the morbidity frequency is 14%. We are not told the disorder rate for examined sample people of this age span who are white, numbering 371 individuals. However, we are told that for the whites of all ages the morbidity rate is almost three-fourths higher than for nonwhites. Setting aside the nonwhites brings the mental illness frequency among the indicated subsample of 371 white persons, by our calculation, to about the 16% point.

Attention is next drawn to the Baltimore classification process. For one thing, the complete examination in clinic was made by internists (rather than psychiatrists), who had many somatic conditions to check systematically and apparently were short both in clinic time for focused psychiatric inquiry and in prior training for secure psychiatric observation, reporting, and evaluation. Explicit at least is that the Baltimore mental disorder rate is beset with potentially serious problems of underreporting, as the monograph authors are at some pains to indicate in the following passages:

1. It was recognized that the number of cases of a particular disease uncovered is closely related to the thoroughness of the examination.[9]
2. With a large number of physicians participating . . . it was not feasible to develop rules governing the recording of diagnoses. . . . The physicians were therefore asked to record all conditions, acute or chronic. . . . Under this general directive, there was,

---

[7] Such cases were classified in one of four categories, namely: (1) psychoses; (2) psychoneuroses; (3) psychophysiologic, autonomic, and visceral disorders; and (4) other mental, psychoneurotic, and personality disorders.
[8] *Chronic Illness in a Large City: The Baltimore Study* (1957), p. 97.
[9] *Ibid.*, p. 384.

as anticipated, a very wide variation in the kinds of conditions which physicians recorded (and presumably did not record) as diagnoses.[10]

3. The method of arriving at diagnoses probably is a more significant factor (affecting) the prevalence (rate) of mental disorders . . . than most other diseases discussed in this report. The examining internists diagnosed a mental disorder as they chose, with or without a psychiatric consultation or psychometric testing.[11] It was recognized that there would be differences in physicians' *interest in and willingness to diagnose mental disorders*. The records, therefore, were subsequently reviewed by a psychiatrist and classified by diagnosis and severity of impairment. . . . In this review, there became apparent substantial differences among examining physicians in the *completeness of recording of information* bearing on mental disorders. The review resulted in the deletion of about one-third of the cases which had been diagnosed (as mental disorders) by examining physicians, on the basis that the information *recorded* did not adequately support the diagnosis. To the extent that the deletion of cases by the reviewing psychiatrist was due to *incomplete recording of evidence* by the examining physician, the data presented here *understate the prevalence*. [All italics added.][12]

Thus, in the Baltimore clinical study, the recording of psychiatric diagnoses and supporting evidence depended entirely upon the motivations of the examining internists to venture a diagnosis beyond their professional competence and, if they so ventured, to inscribe the evidence in sufficient volume and detail to satisfy the specialized and exacting, but previously undefined, criteria of the reviewing psychiatrist.

Under these circumstances, it appears likely, first, that cases of mental pathology in the Baltimore sample examined went unrecognized by the physician, or, if recognized, were unrecorded. Their number is of course unknown. Second, among the many cases of recorded pathology that were subsequently rejected by the reviewing psychiatrist, it is likely that a number reflected inadequate probing for or recording of supporting details, rather than absence of mental illness. On the basis of a 16% mental morbidity rate above derived for the subsample of Baltimore age 15 to 64 whites, we can estimate that prior to such review and rejection this morbidity rate stood at about 24%.[13] Represented in the latter rate would be the "false positives" correctly rejected by the reviewing psychiatrist, but *not* the "false negatives" that were overlooked or maldiagnosed or left unrecorded by the examining internists (and unreviewed by the reviewing psychiatrist). If these two different kinds of errors should happen more or less to cancel each other out, a matter on which evidence is lacking, the estimated 24% morbidity rate would seem to stand as approximately accurate.

---

[10] *Ibid.*, p. 391.

[11] The authors report that only psychiatric consultations were sought, and for only 14 (1.7%) of the 809 examined sample subjects (*ibid.*, p. 390). Given that the examiners were internists in the main, this is not exactly a reassuring index of psychiatric interest.

[12] *Ibid.*, p. 96. Throughout the volume, the authors are critically aware of methodological problems in, and lessons to be learned from, the Baltimore investigation.

[13] This estimate assumes that the one-in-three rejection of diagnoses cases by the reviewing psychiatrist, reported for the examined sample as a whole, more or less applies to the subsample of interest here.

The original mental disorder rate of 10.9% reported for the Baltimore sample examined in clinic appears to be distant indeed from the Midtown sample finding of mental impairment in a frequency of 23.9%. We have now demonstrated that the apparent discrepancy between the two studies is not real. When the Baltimore sample is demographically matched to the Midtown sample, the illness rate, on evidence reported, must be adjusted from 10.9% to 16%. And if identifiable errors of underreporting and overreporting of mental pathology should balance out, it appears possible that the true frequency might approach 24%, or near identity with the Midtown rate.

However, any Baltimore frequency would suffer from the further damaging fact that the 44% of the Baltimore sample whites originally selected for clinical examination did *not* participate in the study.[14] With so large a defection, the bias potential in the studied sample itself is serious indeed. The Baltimore investigators' method of applying "weights" in an effort to compensate for observed biases in age, sex, and racial composition[15] altogether fails to correct for the possibility that participants in the underrepresented groups may be unrepresentative of the many non-participants on the crucial index of mental pathology rate. Specifically, if the mentally ill predominantly chose not to submit to the requested medical examination in clinic, then the 24% morbidity frequency estimated above as possible—for the Baltimore age 15 to 64 white subsample actually studied—may be an understatement by a considerable margin. All in all, in the face of this haunting unknown, it must be submitted that the Baltimore mental disorder rate is altogether too inconclusive to be used in judging the tenability of the mental morbidity finding of the Midtown Study.

A more promising benchmark may be elicited from America's World War II experience with military-age men. In the most comprehensive review of that experience made available to the date of this writing, Brill and Beebe[16] focus on "the manpower pool of about 26 million men who were in the ages of 18–37 in 1941, plus those reaching their 18th birthday in the succeeding four years." The quoted authors divide this pool of men into three segments: (1) served in Armed Forces, (2) medically disqualified for such service, and (3) granted occupational or other deferment from such service. For each segment they estimate the prevalence of "psychoneurosis, pathological personality, and other psychiatric disorders" and "psychiatric defects, mental or educational deficiency." In the three indicated segments, these total 4.7 million men (excluding the category "neurological defects") or 18.1% of the entire pool.

This datum, of course, refers to the entire national population of military-age

---

[14] *Chronic Illness in a Large City: The Baltimore Study* (1957), p. 209.

[15] That is, these varyingly underrepresented groups in the studied sample were arithmetically reconstituted to accord with their representation in the population universe. In this process it was apparently assumed that the unknown mental disorder rate of *nonparticipants* from a given demographic segment would approximate the rate known for *participants* from the same segment.

[16] N. Q. Brill and G. W. Beebe, *A Follow-up Study of War Neuroses* (1955), pp. 322–333.

men. A closer match to the Midtown male population can be drawn from wartime Selective Service rejections on psychiatric grounds at the well-documented Boston Regional Induction Station.[17] Relative to all examinees, we know that the station's psychiatric rejection rate was 10.6% during the early months of the war[18] and 21.3% in August, 1945.[19]

We also know that the national psychiatric rejection rate fluctuated appreciably through the war years with shifts in standards and military demands for manpower. We can assume that the Boston station's rate fluctuated similarly, probably around 16%—the middle point in the above range. On the basis of a 1942 study of the station's examinees we can adjust this median rate to about 17.5% for white men from the high-density areas of metropolitan Boston. If we could also take into account the unrecorded psychiatric cases screened out *before* reaching the station's examiners, and also the subsequent recorded and unrecorded psychiatric discharges from the armed services, the over-all rate would almost certainly turn out to be not less than 20%.

To achieve a better-fitting match to this military-age, white Boston population, we might look at the age 20 to 39 males in our Midtown sample. And there we find an over-all prevalence of impairment in a frequency of 19.5%. The chances are 95 in 100 that this rate stands somewhere between 15.1 and 23.9% in the corresponding segment of the Midtown population universe.

We would not be understood to attach any large significance to the seeming concordance between the Boston frequency of mental morbidity, as just worked out, and Midtown's. It is universal knowledge that initial Selective Service psychiatric examinations were usually brief and superficial, and evaluation was hardly geared to a realistic formulation of psychological balances required to cope with the military environment. From the viewpoint of military manpower needs, therefore, such screening may have discarded too many men who could have been fitted to a limited service function of some kind. However, its very superficiality and an accompanying set of intense social pressures for acceptance in the armed forces, together argue that few of these men could have been rejected except on psychiatric grounds that were sufficiently telling by the criteria of civilian experience.[20]

From this comparison of the Baltimore, Boston, and Midtown data we do *not* draw the inference that *over-all* mental morbidity rates in the three populations were demonstrably alike. Although we made several adjustments in the data to enlarge comparability, remaining uncontrolled are several large inter-

---

[17] The region covered was eastern Massachusetts.

[18] R. W. Hyde, and L. V. Kingsley, "Studies in Medical Sociology: The Relations of Mental Disorders to Population Density," *New Eng. J. Med.*, vol. 23, no. 17 (October 26, 1944), pp. 571–577.

[19] S. A. Stouffer, *et al.*, *Measurement and Prediction*, Studies in Social Psychology in World War II, Vol. iv (1950), p. 551.

[20] This probability finds particular reinforcement in the case of the Boston induction station from the fact that it was served by a corps of psychiatrists out of the area's distinguished medical schools.

community variations: (1) known differences in such elements of demographic composition as socioeconomic standing and ethnic origin—which could not be analytically controlled because of lack of necessary information; (2) known gross differences in the operating circumstances of the psychiatric examination and evaluation process; and (3) probable differences in professional criteria for differentiating the mentally ill from others. On all these counts, it remains impossible to make any generalizations about relative magnitudes of *over-all* mental pathology in the three analyzed populations.

Nonetheless, we have introduced the two comparison populations to suggest, despite appearances to the contrary, that they offer no evidence to support a view of Midtown mental morbidity rate as out of line with previous relevant research experience.

Drug Addiction: Enforcement and/or Treatment

CHARLES WINICK

———

The last few years have seen narcotics programs which are both more punitive and less punitive than has been customary, and both extremes have reported considerable success. A number of vocal exponents of permitting physicians to supply drugs to addicts at low cost have aroused considerable sentiment for their point of view (Lindesmith, 1957). It has been repeatedly urged by various legislative committees that this approach be tried on a limited basis, but to date it has not. The employment of such a procedure involves some ambiguous questions of medical ethics. Physicians have generally believed, along with the late distinguished narcotics authority, Dr. Kenneth W. Chapman, that "drugs are not good for anyone . . . giving drugs to all addicts is a last resort. . . ." Physicians would have the responsibility of deciding which addicts were incurable and what their dosage should be, and whether such a dosage should be increased if the user wanted more than the amount prescribed for him.

Another procedure for liberalizing treatment procedures, and one which has been tried experimentally with limited success, has been the psychotherapy of

———

Source: Charles Winick, "The Drug Addict and His Treatment," in Hans Toch (ed.), *Legal and Criminal Psychology* (New York: Holt, 1961), pp. 376–379. Reprinted by permission.

addicts on an ambulatory basis, while they are still on drugs. Such procedures leave the question of cessation of drug use up to the patient, with no coercion from the psychotherapist. Using such procedures, the Musicians' Clinic in New York reported that all its jazz musician-addict patients were off drugs for an average of thirty months, three years after the commencement of voluntary out-patient therapy. These patients were given treatment on an ambulatory basis, while still on drugs, and it was up to them to handle the problem of their addiction. The clinic grew out of the experience of another experiment in voluntary treatment, the Narcotic Addiction Research Project, which resulted in a working classification of addicts into two categories: those who function effectively on drugs, and those who do not function well and want to get off drugs but are "hooked" (Nyswander, Winick, et al., 1958).

At the other extreme, there have been a number of proposals for making more stringent the current practices for coping with drug addicts. One direction, followed by some states, including New Jersey, has been to make it a misdemeanor to be a drug addict. New Jersey requires a convicted narcotics offender to register with the police and to keep the police posted on changes of address. This procedure seems to have resulted in an increase in the number of narcotics arrests, with some addicts going to states with less stringent penalties. The District of Columbia has made hospitalization for addicts compulsory and has established a high-security ward for addict patients.

The city of Oakland in California has experimented with the Nalline test for determining whether a person has taken drugs prior to the administration of the test. In a person who has taken an opiate in the day or so previous to administration of the synthetic drug Nalline, there will be a measurable dilation of the pupils as well as a miniature withdrawal reaction after taking a small dosage of Nalline. In Oakland the test is used to establish whether a convicted former drug user is or is not using drugs. Some physicians have objected to its use on the ground that it is a kind of chemical conscience, and that this kind of external threat is likely to interfere with any ongoing therapeutic relationship which a former drug user may be attempting to establish. Oakland authorities, however, report not only a decline in addicts but also a sharp decline in crimes usually associated with addiction, which they feel is related to their use of the Nalline test. In the three-year period (1955–58) since they began using Nalline, for example, they report a 21 per cent decline in robberies, a 13 per cent drop in burglaries, a 47 per cent falling off in stealing from automobiles, and 25 per cent fewer prostitution offenses.

The experience of Oakland has renewed interest in a suggestion made by a number of law-enforcement officials, and especially by Commissioner Harry J. Anslinger of the Federal Bureau of Narcotics. He has suggested that there be compulsory commitment of the drug addict (Anslinger, 1957). Such a law, Commissioner Anslinger notes, "would have to be enacted by state legislatures; it could not be federal because of the Constitution. . . ." The commissioner has

JUNK: THE ALGEBRA OF NEED

I awoke from The Sickness at the age of forty-five, calm and sane, and in reasonably good health except for a weakened liver and the look of borrowed flesh common to all who survive The Sickness. . . .

I have seen the exact manner in which the junk virus operates through fifteen years of addiction. . . .

Junk yields a basic formula of "evil" virus: *The Algebra of Need*. The face of "evil" is always the face of total need. A dope fiend is a man in total need of dope. Beyond a certain frequency need knows absolutely no limit or control. In the words of total need: "Wouldn't you?" Yes you would. You would lie, cheat, inform on your friends, steal, do *anything* to satisfy total need. Because you would be in a state of total sickness, total possession, and not in a position to act in any other way. Dope fiends are sick people who cannot act other than they do. A rabid dog cannot choose but bite. Assuming a self-righteous position is nothing to the purpose unless your purpose be to keep the junk virus in operation. . . .

If you wish to alter or annihilate a pyramid of numbers in a serial relation, you alter or remove the bottom number. If we wish to annihilate the junk pyramid, we must start with the bottom of the pyramid: *the Addict in the Street*, and stop tilting quixotically for the "higher-ups" so called, all of whom are immediately replaceable. *The addict in the street who must have junk to live is the one irreplaceable factor in the junk equation.* When there are no more addicts to buy junk there will be no junk traffic. As long as junk need exists, someone will service it.

Source: William S. Burroughs, *Naked Lunch* (New York: Grove Press, 1959).

documented the extent to which very severe sentences on peddlers have led to a substantial decline in the number of addicts arrested in such states as Ohio. He has consistently opposed providing drugs to addicts on any clinic basis, pointing to his estimate of one addict in 400 in America before the passage of the Harrison Act, whereas there is now one in 3,000. This decline in the proportion of addicts, the commissioner feels, is a reflection of the efficacy of the Harrison Act and is the best retort to the critics of his bureau's procedures.

The argument for compulsory treatment has received some support from the experience of the New York State Department of Parole's experimental project for providing close supervision to a limited number of parolees who had been in prison for narcotic violations. After three years, 42 per cent of this group which received the supervision had remained off drugs, suggesting that this kind of intensive case work in an authoritarian setting may be effective with some former drug users.

Another development in the enforcement of drug-addiction laws has been the introduction, in a number of jurisdictions, of legislation which removes the judge's discretion in issuing sentences to drug users by providing for mandatory minimum sentences with no probation. This has raised the question of how police can reward the informers on whom they must depend for the bulk of arrests of other narcotics violators, if they cannot promise them a suspended sentence for cooperating and identifying their source of supply. Most arrested narcotics users will not cooperate by naming other users or sellers, but there are some who will. In some cases they may be encouraged to buy narcotics for their own use, so that police can watch them making the purchase and so arrest the seller. There have been cases in which drug-using informers were paid by the police in drugs, and thus maintained in their addiction.

Although many officials believe that it is unethical for police to promise anything to an informer, a substantial proportion of narcotics violators are arrested through such procedures. The growing inability of the police to promise informers a light sentence, because of the growing tendency toward mandatory minimum sentences, will surely focus new attention on the ethical and civil liberties aspects of arrests for drug violations as the question of how informers are to be paid becomes increasingly urgent. Recent court decisions have questioned the propriety of evidence obtained through wiretapping and have also raised important questions related to narcotics enforcement, since many narcotics arrests are based on wiretaps.

It is a sign of healthy differences in a controversial field that so many differences of opinion exist on the subject of dealing with addiction. Available facilities have, however, not kept up with the interest in discussing the addiction problem. The extent to which the problem is ignored in practice can be seen in the almost total lack of beds for adult addicts in the large cities which have the major problems of addiction. In the municipal hospitals of all three of these cities (New York, Chicago and Detroit) combined, there are not even one hundred beds for many thousands of addicts. The poor results so far obtained with treatment of addicts should not be discouraging, any more than poor results in schizophrenia or cancer research are keeping us from an extensive program of research and treatment in these fields. Unless we can mount the kind of concerted research and treatment program which ultimately led to the Sabin and Salk polio vaccines, our treatment of narcotics addiction will continue to be a rebuke to twentieth-century America. . . .

DISCRIMINATION

"White Devils" and Liberal Myths

MALCOLM X

▬

The more places I represented Mr. Muhammad on television and radio, and at colleges and elsewhere, the more letters came from people who had heard me. I'd say that ninety-five per cent of the letters were from white people.

Only a few of the letters fell into the "Dear Nigger X" category, or the death-threats. Most of my mail exposed to me the white man's two major dreads. The first one was his own private belief that God wrathfully is going to destroy this civilization. And the white man's second most pervading dread was his image of the black man entering the body of the white woman.

An amazing percentage of the white letter-writers agreed entirely with Mr. Muhammad's analysis of the problem—but not with his solution. One odd ambivalence was how some letters, otherwise all but championing Mr. Muhammad, would recoil at the expression "white devils." I tried to explain this in subsequent speeches:

"Unless we call one white man, by name, a 'devil,' we are not speaking of any *individual* white man. We are speaking of the *collective* white man's *historical* record. We are speaking of the collective white man's cruelties, and evils, and greeds, that have seen him *act* like a devil toward the nonwhite man. Any intelligent, honest, objective person cannot fail to realize that this white man's slave trade, and his subsequent devilish actions are directly *responsible* for not only the *presence* of this black man in America, but also for the *condition* in

Source: Malcolm X, *The Autobiography of Malcolm X* (New York: Grove Press, Inc., 1965), with the assistance of Alex Haley, pp. 266–274. Reprinted by permission of Grove Press, Inc. Copyright © 1964 by Alex Haley and Malcolm X. © by Alex Haley and Betty Shabazz.

Editors' Note: Malcolm X did not live to reach his fortieth birthday, or, just as he predicted, to read his own book. The reverential attitude toward Elijah Muhammed he expresses in the excerpt reprinted here changed completely a few months later, in the course of the book's preparation, when he and the Nation of Islam came to a bitter parting of the ways. A short time before his death he wrote: "... black men are watching every move I make, awaiting their chance to kill me.... I know they have their orders. Anyone who chooses not to believe what I am saying doesn't know the Muslims in the Nation of Islam." He was shot and killed by several men as he spoke before a public meeting on February 21, 1965.

which we find this black man here. You cannot find *one* black man, I do not care who he is, who has not been personally damaged in some way by the devilish acts of the collective white man!"

Nearly every day, some attack on the "Black Muslims" would appear in some newspapers. Increasingly, a focal target was something that I had said, "Malcolm X" as a "demagogue." I would grow furious reading any harsh attack upon Mr. Muhammad. I didn't care what they said about me.

Those social workers and sociologists—they tried to take me apart. Especially the black ones, for some reason. Of course, I knew the reason: the white man signed their paychecks. If I wasn't "polarizing the community," according to this bunch, I had "erroneously appraised the racial picture." Or in some statement, I had "over-generalized." Or when I had made some absolutely true point, "Malcolm X conveniently manipulated. . . ."

Once, one of my Mosque Seven Muslim brothers who worked with teenagers in a well-known Harlem community center showed me a confidential report. Some black senior social worker had been given a month off to investigate the "Black Muslims" in the Harlem area. Every paragraph sent me back to the dictionary—I guess that's why I've never forgotten one line about me. Listen to this: "The dynamic interstices of the Harlem sub-culture have been oversimplified and distorted by Malcolm X to meet his own needs."

Which of us, I wonder, knew more about that Harlem ghetto "sub-culture"? I, who had hustled for years in those streets, or that black snob status-symbol-educated social worker?

But that's not important. What's important, to my way of thinking about it, is that among America's 22 million black people so relatively few have been lucky enough to attend a college—and here was one of those who had been lucky. Here was, to my way of thinking, one of those "educated" Negroes who never had understood the true intent, or purpose, or application of education. Here was one of those stagnant educations, never used except for parading a lot of big words.

Do you realize this is one of the major reasons why America's white man has so easily contained and oppressed America's black man? Because until just lately, among the few educated Negroes scarcely any applied their education, as I am forced to say the white man does—in searching and creative thinking, to further themselves and their own kind in this competitive, materialistic, dog-eat-dog white man's world. For generations, the so-called "educated" Negroes have "led" their black brothers by echoing the white man's thinking—which naturally has been to the exploitive white man's advantage.

The white man—give him his due—has an extraordinary intelligence, an extraordinary cleverness. His world is full of proof of it. You can't name a thing the white man can't make. You can hardly name a scientific problem he can't solve. Here he is now solving the problems of sending men exploring into outer space—and returning them safely to earth.

But in the arena of dealing with human beings, the white man's working intelligence is hobbled. His intelligence will fail him altogether if the humans happen to be non-white. The white man's emotions superseded his intelligence. He will commit against non-whites the most incredible spontaneous emotional acts, so psyche-deep is his "white superiority" complex.

Where was the A-bomb dropped . . . "to save American lives"? Can the white man be so naive as to think the clear import of this *ever* will be lost upon the non-white two-thirds of the earth's population?

Before that bomb was dropped—right over here in the United States, what about the one hundred thousand loyal naturalized and native-born Japanese American citizens who were herded into camps, behind barbed wire? But how many German-born naturalized Americans were herded behind barbed wire? They were *white*!

Historically, the non-white complexion has evoked and exposed the "devil" in the very nature of the white man.

What else but a controlling emotional "devil" so blinded American white intelligence that it couldn't foresee that millions of black slaves, "freed," then permitted even limited education, would one day rise up as a terrifying monster within white America's midst?

The white man's brains that today explore space should have told the slave-master that any slave, if he is educated, will no longer fear his master. History shows that an educated slave always begins to ask, and next demand, equality with his master.

Today, in many ways the black man sees the collective white man in America better than that white man can see himself. And the 22 million blacks realize increasingly that physically, politically, economically, and even to some degree socially, the aroused black man can create a turmoil in white America's vitals—not to mention America's international image.

I had not intended to stray off. I had been telling how in 1963, I was trying to cope with the white newspaper, radio, and television reporters who were determined to defeat Mr. Muhammad's teachings.

I developed a mental image of reporters as human ferrets—steadily sniffing, darting, probing for some way to trick me, somehow to corner me in our interview exchanges.

Let some civil rights "leader" make some statement, displeasing to the white public power structure, and the reporters, in an effort to whip him back into line, would try to use me. I'll give an example. I'd get a question like this: "Mr. Malcolm X, you've often gone on record as disapproving of the sit-ins and similar Negro protest actions—what is your opinion of the Montgomery boycott that Dr. King is leading?"

Now my feeling was that although the civil rights "leaders" kept attacking us Muslims, still they were black people, still they were our own kind, and I would be most foolish to let the white man maneuver me against the civil rights movement.

When I was asked about the Montgomery boycott, I'd carefully review what led up to it. Mrs. Rosa Parks was riding home on a bus and at some bus stop the white cracker bus driver ordered Mrs. Parks to get up and give her seat to some white passenger who had just got on the bus. I'd say, "Now, just *imagine* that! This good, hard-working, Christian-believing black woman, she's paid her money, she's in her seat. Just because she's *black*, she's asked to get up! I mean, sometimes even for *me* it's hard to believe the white man's arrogance!"

Or I might say, "No one will ever know exactly what emotional ingredient made this relatively trivial incident a fuse for those Montgomery Negroes. There had been *centuries* of the worst kind of outrages against Southern black people—lynchings, rapings, shootings, beatings! But you know history has been triggered by trivial-seeming incidents. Once a little nobody Indian lawyer was put off a train, and fed up with injustice, he twisted a knot in the British Lion's tail. *His* name was Mahatma Gandhi!"

Or I might copy a trick I had seen lawyers use, both in life and on television. It was a way that lawyers would slip in before a jury something otherwise inadmissible. (Sometimes I think I really might have made it as a lawyer, as I once told that eighth-grade teacher in Mason, Michigan, I wanted to be, when he advised me to become a carpenter.) I would slide right over the reporter's question to drop into his lap a logical-extension hot potato for him.

"Well, sir, I see the same boycott reasoning for Negroes asked to join the Army, Navy, and Air Force. Why should we go off to die somewhere to preserve a so-called 'democracy' that gives a white immigrant of one day more than it gives the black man with four hundred years of slaving and serving in this country?"

Whites would prefer fifty local boycotts to having 22 million Negroes start thinking about what I had just said. I don't have to tell you that it never got printed the way I said it. It would be turned inside out if it got printed at all. And I could detect when the white reporters had gotten their heads together; they quit asking me certain questions.

If I had developed a good point, though, I'd bait a hook to get it said when I went on radio or television. I'd seem to slip and mention some recent so-called civil rights "advance." You know, where some giant industry had hired ten showpiece Negroes; some restaurant chain had begun making more money by serving Negroes; some Southern university had enrolled a black freshman without bayonets—like that. When I "slipped," the program host would leap on that bait: "Ahhh! Indeed, Mr. Malcolm X—you can't deny *that's* an advance for your race!"

I'd jerk the pole then. "I can't turn around without hearing about some 'civil rights advance'! White people seem to think the black man ought to be shouting 'hallelujah'! Four hundred years the white man has had his foot-long knife in the black man's back—and now the white man starts to *wiggle* the knife out, maybe six inches! The black man's supposed to be *grateful*? Why, if the white man jerked the knife *out*, it's still going to leave a scar!"

Similarly, just let some mayor or some city council somewhere boast of having "no Negro problem." That would get off the newsroom teletypes and it would soon be jammed right in my face. I'd say they didn't need to tell me where this was, because I knew that all it meant was that relatively very few Negroes were living there. That's true the world over, you know. Take "democratic" England —when 100,000 black West Indians got there, England stopped the black migration. Finland welcomed a Negro U.S. Ambassador. Well, let enough Negroes follow him to Finland! Or in Russia, when Khrushchev was in power, he threatened to cancel the visas of black African students whose anti-discrimination demonstration said to the world, "Russia, too. . . ."

The Deep South white press generally blacked me out. But they front-paged what I felt about Northern white and black Freedom Riders going *South* to "demonstrate." I called it "ridiculous"; their own Northern ghettoes, right at home, had enough rats and roaches to kill to keep all of the Freedom Riders busy. I said that ultra-liberal New York had more integration problems than Mississippi. If the Northern Freedom Riders wanted more to do, they could work on the roots of such ghetto evils as the little children out in the streets at midnight, with apartment keys on strings around their necks to let themselves in, and their mothers and fathers drunk, drug addicts, thieves, prostitutes. Or the Northern Freedom Riders could light some fires under Northern city halls, unions, and major industries to give more jobs to Negroes to remove so many of them from the relief and welfare rolls, which created laziness, and which deteriorated the ghettoes into steadily worse places for humans to live. It was all—it *is* all—the absolute truth; but what did I want to *say* it for? Snakes couldn't have turned on me faster than the liberal.

Yes, I will pull off that liberal's halo that he spends such efforts cultivating! The North's liberals have been for so long pointing accusing fingers at the South and getting away with it that they have fits when they are exposed as the world's worst hypocrites.

I believe my own life *mirrors* this hypocrisy. I know nothing about the South. I am a creation of the Northern white man and of his hypocritical attitude toward the Negro.

The white Southerner was always given his due by Mr. Muhammad. The white Southerner, you can say one thing—he is honest. He bares his teeth to the black man; he tells the black man, to his face, that Southern whites never will accept phony "integration." The Southern white goes further, to tell the black man that he means to fight him every inch of the way—against even the so-called "tokenism." The advantage of this is the Southern black man never has been under any illusions about the opposition he is dealing with.

You can say for many Southern white people that, individually, they have been paternalistically helpful to many individual Negroes. But the Northern white man, he grins with his teeth, and his mouth has always been full of tricks and lies of "equality" and "integration." When one day all over Aerica, am black hand touched the white man's shoulder, and the white man turned, and there stood the Negro saying "Me, too . . ." why, that Northern liberal shrank from that black man with as much guilt and dread as any Southern white man.

Actually, America's most dangerous and threatening black man is the one who has been kept sealed up by the Northerner in the black ghettoes—the Northern white power structure's system to keep talking democracy while keeping the black man out of sight somewhere, around the corner.

The word "integration" was invented by a Northern liberal. The word has no real meaning. I ask you: in the racial sense in which it's used so much today, whatever "integration" is supposed to mean, can it precisely be defined? The truth is that "integration" is an *image*, it's a foxy Northern liberal's smoke-screen that confuses the true wants of the American black man. Here in these fifty racist and neo-racist states of North America, this word "integration" has millions of white people confused, and angry, believing wrongly that the black masses want to live mixed up with the white man. That is the case only with the relative handful of these "integration"-mad Negroes.

I'm talking about these "token-integrated" Negroes who flee from their poor, downtrodden black brothers—from their own self-hate, which is what they're really trying to escape. I'm talking about these Negroes you will see who can't get enough of nuzzling up to the white man. These "chosen few" Negroes are more white-minded, more anti-black, than even the white man is.

Human rights! Respect as *human beings*! That's what America's black masses want. That's the true problem. The black masses want not to be shrunk from as though they are plague-ridden. They want not to be walled up in slums, in the ghettoes, like animals. They want to live in an open, free society where they can walk with their heads up, like men, and women!

Few white people realize that many black people today dislike and avoid spending any more time than they must around white people. This "integration" image, as it is popularly interpreted, has millions of vain, self-exalted white people convinced that black people want to sleep in bed with them—and that's a lie! Or you can't *tell* the average white man that the Negro man's prime desire isn't to have a white woman—another lie! Like a black brother recently observed to me, "Look, you ever smell one of them *wet*?"

The black masses prefer the company of their own kind. Why, even these fancy, bourgeois Negroes—when they get back home from the fancy "integrated" cocktail parties, what do they do but kick off their shoes and talk about those white liberals they just left as if the liberals were dogs. And the white liberals probably do the very same thing. I can't be sure about the whites, I am never around them in private—but the bourgeois Negroes know I'm not lying.

I'm telling it like it *is*! You *never* have to worry about me biting my tongue if something I know as truth is on my mind. Raw, naked truth exchanged between the black man and the white man is what a whole lot more of is needed in this country—to clear the air of the racial mirages, clichés, and lies that this country's very atmosphere has been filled with for four hundred years.

In many communities, especially small communities, white people have created a benevolent image of themselves as having had so much "good-will toward our Negroes," every time any "local Negro" begins suddenly letting the local whites know the truth—that the black people are sick of being hind-tit, second-class, disfranchised, that's when you hear, uttered so sadly, "Unfortunately now because of this, our whites of good-will are starting to turn against the Negroes. . . . It's so regrettable . . . progress *was* being made . . . but now our communications between the races have broken down!"

What are they talking about? There never was any *communication*. Until after World War II, there wasn't a single community in the entire United States where the white man heard from any local Negro "leaders" the truth of what Negroes felt about the conditions that the white community imposed upon Negroes.

You need some proof? Well, then, why was it that when Negroes did start revolting across America, virtually all of white America was caught up in surprise and even shock? I would hate to be general of an army as badly informed as the American white man has been about the Negro in this country. . . .

"GEORGIA HAS THE NEGRO AND HARLEM HAS THE JEW"

. . . When the Negro hates the Jew *as a Jew* he does so partly because the nation does and in much the same painful fashion that he hates himself. It is an aspect of his humiliation whittled down to a manageable size and then transferred; it is the best form the Negro has for tabulating vocally his long record of grievances against his native land.

At the same time, there is a subterranean assumption that the Jew should "know better," that he has suffered enough himself to know what suffering means. An understanding is expected of the Jew such as none but the most naive and visionary Negro has ever expected of the American Gentile. The Jew, by the nature of his own precarious position, has failed to vindicate this faith. Jews, like Negroes, must use every possible weapon in order to be accepted, and must try to cover their vulnerability by a frenzied adoption of the customs of the country; and the nation's treatment of Negroes is unquestionably a custom. The Jew has been taught—and, too often, accepts—the legend of Negro inferiority; and the Negro, on the other hand, has found nothing in his experience with Jews to counteract the legend of Semitic greed. Here the American white Gentile has two legends serving him at once: he has divided these minorities and he rules. . . .

Both the Negro and the Jew are helpless; the pressure of living is too immediate and incessant to allow time for understanding. I can conceive of no Negro native to this country who has not, by the age of puberty, been irreparably scarred by the conditions of his life. All over Harlem, Negro boys and girls are growing into stunted maturity, trying desperately to find a place to stand; and the wonder is not that so many are ruined but that so many survive. The Negro's outlets are desperately constricted. In his dilemma he turns first upon himself and then upon whatever most represents to him his own emasculation. Here the Jew is caught by the American crossfire. The Negro, facing a Jew, hates, at bottom, not his Jewishness but the color of his skin. It is not the Jewish tradition by which he has been betrayed but the tradition of his native land. But just as a society must have a scapegoat, so hatred must have a symbol. Georgia has the Negro and Harlem has the Jew.

Source: James Baldwin, "The Harlem Ghetto," in *Notes of a Native Son* (New York, Beacon, 1955), pp. 69, 71–72. Reprinted by permission of the Beacon Press, copyright © 1955 by James Baldwin. By permission of Michael Joseph, Ltd., publishers.

CRIME IN THE GHETTO STREETS

Two facts are crucial to understand the effects of high crime rates in racial ghettos: most of these crimes are committed by a small minority of the residents, and the principal victims are the residents themselves. Throughout the United States, the great majority of crimes committed by Negroes involve other Negroes as victims, just as most crimes committed by whites are against other whites. A special tabulation made by the Chicago Police Department for the President's Crime Commission indicated that over 85 per cent of the crimes committed by Negroes between September 1965 and March 1966 involved Negro victims.

As a result, the majority of law-abiding citizens who live in disadvantaged Negro areas face much higher probabilities of being victimized than residents of most higher-income areas, including almost all suburbs. For nonwhites, the probability of suffering from any index crime except larceny is 78 per cent higher than for whites. The probability of being raped is 3.7 times higher among nonwhite women, and the probability of being robbed is 3.5 times higher for nonwhites in general.

The problems associated with high crime rates generate widespread hostility toward the police in these neighborhoods for reasons described elsewhere in this Report. Thus, crime not only creates an atmosphere of insecurity and fear

Ethnic Liberalism and Employment Discrimination in the North

BERNARD ROSENBERG AND F. WILLIAM HOWTON

▬

It is more the rule than the exception that hiring and promoting in the North follows a pattern in which the better jobs are reserved for whites—just as in the South, except that there it is open and official. De facto discrimination is familiar enough in Northern schools, voluntary associations, and residential housing. What is unique about employment discrimination in the North is that it is not only usually unlawful and contrary to stated company policy, but it is also likely to be immoral by standards the company officials who make those policies say they uphold. Robert Merton has observed that "all-weather ethnic liberalism" is now practically an article of faith for the educated non-Southerner, and in this category, of course, must be included most Northern employers.[1]

How does de facto discrimination in employment work? How does the putatively liberal Northern employer resolve his problems of conscience in

Source: Bernard Rosenberg and F. William Howton, "Ethnic Liberalism and Employment Discrimination in the North," *American Journal of Economics and Sociology*, 26:4 (October 1967), pp. 387–398. Reprinted by permission.

[1] Most people took it for granted a hundred years ago that Negroes are inferior to whites in some innate, biological sense. With one or two exceptions this notion is no longer seriously defended. Educated people now all but universally concede that Negroes are capable of exercising full civil and social rights and ought to have them. Even in the South the new conventions of the public dialogue are such that demurrers to integration are generally confined to questions of means and pace. To go much beyond this and question the goal itself is to risk losing moral and intellectual respectability.

accounting for it? To what extent is he embarrassed by his involvement in what his professed values lead him to see as an immoral system? Is he ideologically ambivalent enough to make that system vulnerable to pressure for change? How can such vulnerability as there is be exploited?

We undertook to get some provisional answers to these questions by interviewing a number of employers in the New York metropolitan area. Specifically, we asked them about (a) their own attitude toward Negroes and Puerto Ricans as employees, (b) the hiring and upgrading policies in their firms, and (c) what they thought employers could do to correct discrimination if they chose to do so.[2]

I: IMAGE OF THE NEGRO AS EMPLOYEE

The new liberal consensus comes out in the interview reports through the positive eagerness with which most respondents sought to deny any feelings of personal prejudice. The one man who said he could not bring himself to hire a Negro under any circumstances was defensive about it and clearly thought of himself as exceptional—thus conceding the legitimacy of the liberal premise. None of the executives and employment managers, however they hedged, held that race as such is an acceptable consideration in hiring, assigning, or upgrading employees.

Still, race admittedly is a factor. The employers agreed that Negroes generally have poorer prospects than whites when it comes to hiring and promoting. But in their view this is due less to outright discrimination (they concede there is some) than to the "fact" that Negroes are objectively undesirable as employees: Negroes are "dirty," "shiftless," and "unsuited for skilled work," or they "tend" to be, *not because they are radically predestined to be inferior, but because they have had fewer advantages.* Thus the employers preserve a liberal line even while offering an ideological defense for an illiberal system.

1. The Negro Is "Dirty"

The respondents unhesitatingly ridiculed the folk notion that Negroes smell bad and are inherently less clean than whites. They said that white workers who object to Negroes as fellow employees frequently mention body odor as a reason, but this simply shows ignorance and prejudice. The fact is:

B.O. is . . . a front. Naturally, in a factory, and it's true of white people too, [both]

---

[2] Twenty-four depth interviews were first carried out with respondents drawn from four companies at three levels of management, two on each level. The first was a large industrial plant producing military hardware and employing about 4,000 workers. The second was a precision-instrument factory of about the same size. The third and fourth (with 2,000 and 250 workers, respectively) employed mainly technical, professional, and miscellaneous white-collar workers. All were located in suburban areas adjacent to New York City. In the second phase, questionnaires, pinpointing five particularly relevant questions, were administered to seventy-two respondents distributed among companies representing goods and services produced in the same geographical areas.

males and females . . . you will sometimes encounter it. If people want to keep clean they can avoid this. I've had trouble with some of the white people who use perfume instead of the scrub brush. They'll try camouflage.

In the same spirit another employer pointed out that "we've had . . . complaints from both Negroes and whites. . . . There are very few such cases and then the girls really are dirty."

But asked about the suitability of Negroes for white-collar jobs, especially the kind that call for a degree of physical and social closeness to themselves personally, the respondents were uneasy and defensive. One unusually introspective man remarked, candidly enough, "When you asked me about a personal secretary, I have to say that I have not advanced to the point where I could consider a Negro without conscious effort." Another seemed startled by the question and took a long time, with many hesitations, in making his reply:

I just don't know. [Pause.] The functions of a secretary are so varied and special. [Pause.] She knows a lot about your personal life. [Pause.] Not that I sit and discuss private matters, [pause] but she gets to know a lot about you, your family; [pause] on occasion she talks to my wife. [Pause.] I just don't know how I'd feel.

Several respondents explicitly drew the inference that job equality portends full social equality and this, in turn, forecasts intermarriage. "Intermarriage is bound to increase, and this is probably for the best, in the long run, but I don't want it for my child"—this is their attitude in paraphrase. It would seem that white employers are reluctant to hire Negroes for "sensitive" jobs because they fear personal contamination, or taint, which is the abstract form of what the common man literally perceives as "dirt."

2. The Negro Is "Shiftless"

In the composite view Negroes as employees lack the virtue of dependability. "Sometimes they just stay out, and when you call them up they say they didn't like it or they have another job. They don't even bother to let you know." "There are a lot of resignations. They don't stay too long." "As I said, the only thing is their attendance record is worse—why I don't know—it's odd—and of course that's considered an important qualification and part of the job."

Another character virtue seen as conspicuously lacking is initiative. "Negroes gravitate to porter jobs. Why? They don't have the desire, from their home or their education." "Home life has a lot to do with it. The colored boy is more inclined to go along with the crowd. He has less initiative." This, they say, is why in-plant education programs do not work too well for Negroes. "They may find it difficult to absorb; their desire isn't as deep." "They just swim with the crowd, but they don't get it."

But what about the minority of Negroes who are clearly inner-directed types, militants and hard strivers? These seem to their employers to sin in two ways. Either they "stick together" and form obstreperous cliques and factions, or else individuals "take advantage of their minority status . . . [and claim] everything is a 'matter of discrimination.'" For example:

There is one type of Negro we won't hire. I say Negro because he's more often Negro than white, and that's the one who comes in with a chip on his shoulder. You know, the Negro who turns the least little thing around to serve his own ends. Such people are their own worst enemies.

Evidently the "pushy Negro" is no more desirable as an employee than the more common "handkerchief head," who can be counted on to be docile if not worth much as a worker.[3] Then what does the employer want? What can be told Negro youth? One respondent was ready with an answer:

Advise them . . . [to] get out and get into the same field as the white boy. First, let the Negro believe in himself and believe that he is capable. Inspire that child to think beyond the porter stage, teach him love of country, love of God, that he has as much talent as any other person.

The second, Algeresque statement provides ironic counterpoint to the first. The Negro is told he can overcome his "tendency toward shiftlessness" and acquire suitable virtues of character if he will just try. But then if he uses his new character strength for collective rather than individual ends he will wind up being "his own worst enemy." Again, the employers' stereotype of the Negro employee—most are dumb and docile, the rest pushy—functions to rationalize inequities as simply reflecting the objective inferiority of Negroes as Negroes. That the "shiftlessness" of the general run is attributable to "sociological" rather than "biological" factors is irrelevant. For practical purposes the effect is the same: the Negro is seen as having a weak mind and character, and this handicap explains why whites surpass him in the competition for jobs and advancement.

3. The Negro Is "Incompetent"

As the employers see it, Negroes are deficient not only in character but in general ability. The Negro employee "just doesn't go for skills," as one manager put it. "The big thing is that you have to get them to study." The implication is that studying is particularly hard for Negroes. Some respondents were willing to spell it out: they "possibly have less ability to acquire learning." One went on to ask, rhetorically, "Don't you suppose you might find a difference in the [I.Q.] scores between colored and middle-class [sic] people?" (The implicit equation of "colored" with "lower class" is an example of the tendency that secure and comfortable people have of inferring merit in some absolute sense from the size of one's earned income. And they continue to do this regardless of their new ideological liberalism.)

---

[3] This illustrates the "damned-if-you-do-damned-if-you-don't" pattern serving to keep ethnic minorities of all sorts "in their place." See Robert K. Merton, "The Self-Fulfilling Prophecy," in R. K. Merton, *Social Theory and Social Structure* (New York: The Free Press of Glencoe, 1957), pp. 421–431.

Some Negroes do manage to qualify for advanced positions, however, and may show thoroughgoing competence in performing their work. Several respondents noted this with what seemed to be genuine pleasure, "Negroes are just as capable of handling work as anyone else." They are in principle if not always, regrettably, in practice. Moreover, "Things are easing up." The discrimination that still exists, these respondents felt is residual and on the wane, and as social conditions improve (since it is "something in the home situation," not "something in the genes," that handicaps them) Negroes can be expected to close the "competence gap," in time, between themselves and whites. This is the image.

Negroes in general really are "shiftless" and "incompetent," our employers think, and this mostly accounts for their underrepresentation in preferred job categories. Discrimination is vaguely admitted to play a role—in the spirit of the apology, "no system is perfect"—but not a very important one. The system of hiring and promotion is portrayed as flawed but still fundamentally just: the proof is that "exceptional" Negroes do manage to get good jobs. What is unjust without question, these employers do believe, is the disadvantaged place Negroes have in American society. The deprived "home situation" of the Negro child produced a damaged adult: an individual inferior in character and intelligence, and so unfitted for playing the more important roles the larger society holds open. In sum, as the liberal employer sees it *the problem is not so much social injustice as mental ill-health.*

The self-serving character of this formula is obvious. On grounds of its premises alone it would be very hard to identify even an instance of hard-core, entrenched, systematic discrimination as long as it is camouflaged with moderate care. The employer, more interested in apologetics than the whole truth when it comes to a question of the power arrangements within his own firm, has a material interest in fostering a version of reality in which the Negro employee, not the employment situation, is at fault.

Though driven underground and fitted with a mask, the old illiberal attitudes evidently still have life and force. The conception of "jobs Negroes have a hard time qualifying for" functions, ideologically, as the up-to-date version of "white man's work."

II: THE REALITY OF THE EMPLOYMENT SITUATION

So far we have shown that our employers share the new assumptions of ethnic liberalism which pervade the intellectual and moral climate of their world-taken-for-granted, and yet they still see the Negro as inclined to be "dirty," "shiftless," and "incompetent" as an employee. We account for this by attributing it to their need to condemn employment discrimination in general even while explaining away particular instances of it in fact as due to "personal unsuitability of the candidate." The task of this section is to make clear that Negroes really are discriminated against. Race-structured personal suitability undeniably is a factor in discrimination. But if this factor is held constant it is still true that hiring and upgrading practices institutionalized in virtually all fields of employment function to favor whites over Negroes. The main features of the discriminatory mechanisms which seem to be in force in the plants we studied are set forth below.

1. Whites Are Preferentially Hired

It is consistent with their avowed ethnic liberalism that the employers describe their firms as "not averse to hiring anyone regardless of race or color—just as we have no negative policy toward hiring the aged. We have 40-, 45-, or even 50-year-old workers newly hired. Also quite a few handicapped persons." The same applies to women and Puerto Ricans. Persons from any of these groups— "handicapped groups" all, by implication—are said to be hired on the basis of their own individual merit. Their predominance in some job lines and under-representation or total absence in others is explained as due to their tendency to be especially well suited for work that is tedious ("they have a lot of manual dexterity"), dull ("they are phlegmatic—they don't get bored"), or menial ("they know how to take orders").[4]

Official policy is one thing, however, and operating procedure is something else again. Minority group members are theoretically hirable for the better jobs and sometimes are hired, but only after their qualifications have been reviewed with unusual care. If female, is she married and therefore likely to get pregnant? If Puerto Rican, will he be able to handle the language problem? If Negro, the race problem? If any of the three, will the individual quit (because "inclined to be unstable") before the company's investment in processing and training is recovered? To ask such questions is to define the applicant as marginal, and this provides those immediately responsible for hiring and placing with an excuse to practice discrimination, if they want to, without calling it that. Motive is added to opportunity by the prevailing assumption that most white workers are reluctant to accept Negroes as equals, and by the wish of the first-line supervisor to steer away from such troublesome innovations as giving what has been defined by custom as "a white man's job" to a Negro. Our respondents tacitly admitted that this is the way it works in their plants by pointing out that Negroes are "poor risks" and, besides, "we cannot ignore the feelings of the [white] workers, much as we might deplore them."

Backward attitudes on the race question are not confined to the shop, however. There is ample evidence in the interview protocols of their politer counter-

---

[4] The tendency for particular minority-group stereotypes to overlap and form a generalized stereotype has been described most notably by Hughes (Everett C. Hughes, "Queries Concerning Industry and Society Growing out of Study of Ethnic Groups in Industry," *American Sociological Review*, Vol. 14 (1949), pp. 211–220.

part in the office. For example, our respondents were quick to express concern for the welfare of the Negro white-collar applicant and of the work group he (or more often, she) will join if hired. Will he "gain acceptance?" Will she "fit in?" If there are already several Negroes on the staff, would the addition of one more make it hard to "keep a good racial balance?"

The impression that technical and professional jobs are the one category relatively open to Negroes in Northern industry is consistent with our findings. This is largely due, no doubt, to the continuing shortage of applicants in these fields. In administrative, clerical, and production work, however, where there is no comparable problem, considerations of practical politics and "good human relations" seem to provide employers with a rationale for condoning a hiring policy that in substance favors whites over Negroes.[5]

2. Whites Are Preferentially Upgraded

Manual workers. The formal upgrading policy of the three firms employing substantial numbers of manual workers seems cut and dried.

When it's time to advance, we get together with the union—we post a notice—people apply—I don't know who they are—I pull out the cards for the names. I look at a girl's efficiency, her quality level, absentee and lateness record. If there are four or five people with good records, I take the most senior—that is policy. I don't even see them until the end.

Each worker is free to "make bids" for preferred jobs as they open up, and the final selection is determined by "qualification and seniority." Race as a factor is officially excluded. And the process throughout is open and public, with the union as a participant: "We have union contracts and all our upgrading is regulated by them."

Officially the competition is objective and impartial; in practice the norm of equal opportunity is easily evaded. How this works is illustrated in the dialogue below, reconstructed from the interview reports:

Q. How does a worker go about getting upgraded?

---

[5] The de facto exclusion of Negroes from huge areas of the white-collar job world cannot be dismissed as the simple consequence of their lack of qualifications, particularly educational qualifications, The U.S. Civil Service Commission reports that during the year ending June 1963, Negroes employed by the federal government increased 3 per cent overall. This is hardly an impressive figure. But a breakdown by grade yields the significant fact that the distribution of rate of increase is heavily and progressively skewed toward the higher echelons. In Grades GS–9 through GS–11, paying $6,667 to $10,165 a year, the increase was much larger—19.5 per cent. And in the elite grades (GS–12 to GS–18, paying $9,475 to $20,000) the figure goes up to 38.7 per cent. This is about thirteen times the over-all rate of increase. Going back to June 1961, as the base, the two-year old net increase in the elite categories is found to be no less than 88.2 per cent (*The New York Times*, March 4, 1964.) It is hardly plausible to attribute the near doubling in the number of Negroes employed in the top brackets within this relatively short period of time to a sudden increase in the supply of qualified applicants. To have been able to make this much room for Negroes in the white-collar ranks is persuasive evidence that there had been a long-standing policy of de facto discrimination in the federal civil service— just as there continues to be in sectors of the economy less vulnerable to the glare of publicity and mass political pressure.

A. He can attend schools and take shop courses. We put up notices that anyone who is qualified will be sent to school or taught on the job.
Q. How do you mean, "qualified?"
A. We give them a test.
Q. How does he get chosen to take the test? And who decides on what action is indicated by the results of the test?
A. *Progression is at the discretion of the supervisors.* (Emphasis added.) Negro production workers, like women, very often "can't seem to find the career ladder"—or, if they do, they cannot seem to climb very high.
Q. How high can a Negro worker move? As high as foremanship?
A. Oh, yes. But there aren't any Negro foremen. Negroes have become group leaders, which is a grade below foreman . . . [But that is] as high as it's possible to go *without becoming part of management.* (Emphasis added.)
Q. How about skill grade?
A. Negroes have been upgraded to Grade 3, 4, and even 6 . . . It's theoretically possible to go from 1 to 13, but actually very difficult. Top-grade people are tool makers and model makers. *You must have the necessary ability.* (Emphasis added.)

The "record," weighed with such antiseptic care to forestall bias ("I don't even see them until it's all over"), is objective only in the sense that it draws no distinction between artifacts of an entrenched system of privilege and real indicators of merit. "Progression is at the discretion of supervisors"—and the supervisor is in a position to use his discretion to reserve helpful information, advice, and recommendations for those who are "promising." This means that Negroes can effectively be denied opportunities to acquire the "necessary ability" if the predominantly white supervisors wish to do so. It falls within the scope of their prerogative.

White-collar workers. The upgrading system in effect for white-collar workers in all four plants is less formal but just as discriminatory, if not more so.

The employers recognized that Negro clerical workers are handicapped by "the discrimination problem." In order to have much chance for promotion to secretary, for example, a Negro stenographer ought to be "approximately 10 per cent above average in order to maintain her self-confidence without developing undue self-protective attitudes." She should have a background "on a place above the laborer's level," and "be very active in mixing." She should be the type who "knows the facts of life" and so is able to "cope with the resentment" her presence can be expected to generate. (There is, finally, as one respondent put it, "something undemocratic about white-collar workers.") In sum, she has to have a highly desirable set of personal qualities: tact, poise, a gracious but not insinuating manner—the whole gamut of middle-class social skills, plus tolerance and humility. Not surprisingly such a combination is rare. A characteristic employer's complaint is that instead of working extra hard to measure up and compensate for their "handicap,"

We have found . . . they are not competent . . . and they have such a lackadaisical attitude. It doesn't seem to matter to them whether they come in or not, whether they're late or not. There just doesn't seem to be the same desire to do a good job.

The Negro office worker is not upgraded because she lacks the necessary personal qualifications—again, this is the way the employers we interviewed see it. And again the picture they see is not altogether false, but neither is it altogether true. The qualities needed for white-collar advancement are even more easily monopolized by the dominant group than the qualities the production worker needs, because they are less objective, less tangible. The record is made by its keeper as well as its subject; and aside from sheer recording bias, there is the bias introduced, as before, by the way opportunities to "make a good record" are distributed.

Preferential upgrading of whites over Negroes occurs because there is a will to do so and a way to do it. The keepers of the record and of the means to show up well on it use their discretion to favor their own, thus reflecting the will and ability of the microcosmic White Power Structure to preserve its privileges. Ideologically liberal employers condone and even shore up this inequitable system because it would be difficult, even hazardous, to go against it. "Harmonious human relations" are best assured by leaving the established order alone as long as it works. Employers have a conservative bias in the area of social relationships and usually are reluctant to innovate. "Wait until it's been proved livable in somebody else's shop" is their characteristic attitude.

III : EMPLOYERS' READINESS FOR CHANGE

Q. What kind of advice would you give the executive who wants to integrate his plant?
A. My advice would be just go ahead and hire. I certainly wouldn't make an announcement. The company has the right to hire anybody. No one is going to quit just because you hire a Negro.

Northern employers condone and rationalize an illiberal system, but whether or not they prefer it to a liberal one is another matter. There are two reasons for believing they do not: it goes against their professed liberal principles in ethnic matters—"It's not right"; and it goes against the bureaucratic ethos that is the spirit of modern management—"It's not rational."

The best evidence that the employers we interviewed are ready for change is provided by the specificity and vehemence of their answers to the question of how change could be accomplished:

Make sure the lines of communication between policy makers and middle management are wide open. . . . The laws are also necessary. Coercion and conviction combine to give you a fair policy. When top management is put on the griddle, it is forced to make some basic changes. The individual is inclined to treat his fellow as a human being if he knows, "This is definitely the policy we want." Often there is so much equivocation that such a man doesn't know what to do. With the best will in the world he may still be uncertain.

"I would consult nobody," another man said. "The worst thing would be to ask—I know what the answer would be." "Education is ineffective. . . . The thing to do is just do it." "That there would be resistance down the line is to be expected, but employees . . . can be controlled." "I would not accept at face value a supervisor's objection to a Negro. I'd check to see that she got a fair and reasonable opportunity—not a prejudiced opinion." "Check . . . on why so-and-so was fired and why someone else was not." "Something that could serve as a motto . . . [is] 'If you want something down the line, *inspect.*'"

This does not necessarily mean that employers, individually, are going to initiate change. (The respondents made their brave pronouncements in a vacuum—a hypothetical answer to a hypothetical question is a commitment to values, not action.) But it does show that their allegiance to the existing order is perfunctory. They are pragmatists. When they rationalize and defend discriminatory practices they do it as functionaries, not crusaders. They would defend any system they found themselves part of, just because it is there and their job is to make it work.

The employers' commitment to ethnic liberalism is more than ideological froth, however. Whether or not a man acts on the counsel of his conscience, he does not willingly and in good spirit act against it; nor is he delighted to condone such acts of others in which he is morally implicated. The fact that the employers we interviewed were ready with precise and plausible strategies for correcting discrimination is evidence that their minds have been on this matter. And the obvious relish with which they developed their replies suggests a deep and corroding ambivalence. Like the Southern deputy sheriff who reportedly told an arrested civil rights demonstrator, "I hate to say it, but I know you guys are going to win," the Northern employers we interviewed feel that the system they improvise apologetics for is wrong and ought to be changed.

*   *   *

Thus we arrive at a twofold conclusion. On the pessimistic side it is evident that the ancient stereotype of the Negro as unclean, childlike, and mentally dull persists. His handicaps are due to environment, not race, the enlightened employer feels, but he also feels that the differences are there and they unfit the Negro for the higher types of work *just as if their source was biological and not sociological.* As the old myth is discounted, a functionally equivalent new one takes its place. Instead of "racial character" we now have "ethnic character" as an anchor for the secular theodicy. Just as before, the spokesmen and apologists for the White Power Structure have a rhetoric for explaining to the Negro that the favored positions in society are occupied by whites because they have the capacity he lacks, not because they have conspired against him.

On the optimistic side, the "sociological" myth of Negro inferiority puts those who discriminate in particular instances on the defensive, practically as well as morally. Denied official sanction, they have to work by indirection. Discrimination based on the myth of race was categorical rather than individual, and this made the whole business a good deal simpler. Moreover, in the "sociological" version Negro inferiority is caused by society, by the arrangements men enter into and for which individual men must ultimately stand responsible. In the racial version human differences are "natural" and therefore beyond human control. God is responsible, not man. The best the sociological myth can do is provide an interim rationale and thus buy time. The price of its use is what Max Weber called "world disenchantment." The educated man of our time, white or Negro, is forced to choose between living with guilt and pressing for change. In a disenchanted world fixing the blame for injustice in the social order on "God" or "Nature" is no longer credible.

We conclude that the Northern white employer—apologist and rationalizer for de facto discrimination in employment that he is—can be moved. He is ready for change because readiness for change, even hopefulness for change, is predicated on the creed to which he subscribes. The best he can say for the arrangements in which, willy-nilly, he is implicated is that things are not so bad, they are getting better, and it would be risky to speed up the pace. The important thing is that these judgments are relative and pragmatic, not absolute. In the useful phrase of practical politics, they are "negotiable."

THE "ZOOT-SUIT RIOTS"

Beginning on June 3, 1943, Los Angeles, California, was the scene of sporadic acts of violence involving principally United States naval personnel, with the support of a sympathetic Anglo community, in opposition to members of the Mexican community which have come to be known as the "zoot-suit riots." "Zooter" referred mainly to two characteristics. First, zoot suits consisted of long suit coats and trousers extremely pegged at the cuff, draped full around the knees, and terminating in deep pleats at the waist. Second, the zooters wore their hair long, full, and well greased.

During the riots many attacks and injuries were sustained by both sides. Groups of sailors were frequently reported to be assisted or accompanied by civilian mobs who "egged" them on as they roamed through downtown streets in search of victims. Zooters discovered on city streets were assaulted and forced to disrobe amid the jibes and molestations of the crowd. Streetcars and busses were stopped and searched, and zooters found therein were carried off into the streets and beaten. Cavalcades of hired taxicabs filled with sailors ranged the East Side districts of Los Angeles seeking, finding, and attacking zooters. Civilian gangs of East Side adolescents organized similar attacks against unwary naval personnel.

* * *

The symbol "zoot-suiter" evoked only the picture of a breed of persons outside the normative order, devoid of morals themselves, and consequently not entitled to fair play and due process. Indeed, the zoot-suiter came to be regarded as such an exclusively fearful threat to the community that at the height of rioting the Los Angeles City Council seriously debated an ordinance making the wearing of zoot suits a prison offense.

The "zooter" symbol had a crisis character which mere unfavorable versions of the familiar "Mexican" symbol never approximated. And the "zooter" symbol was an omnibus, drawing together the most reprehensible elements in the old unfavorable themes, namely, sex crimes, delinquency, gang attacks, draft-dodgers, and the like and was, in consequence, widely applicable.

The "zooter" symbol also supplied a tag identifying the object of attack. It could be used, when the old attitudes toward Mexicans were evoked, to differentiate Mexicans along both moral and physical lines. While the active minority were attacking Mexicans indiscriminately, and frequently including Negroes, the great sanctioning majority heard only of attacks on zoot-suiters.

Once established, the zooter theme assured its own magnification. What previously would have been reported as an adolescent gang attack would now be presented as a zoot-suit attack. Weapons found on apprehended youths were now interpreted as the building-up of arms collections in preparation for zoot-suit violence. In short, the "zooter" symbol was a recasting of many of the elements formerly present and sometimes associated with Mexicans in a new and instantly recognizable guise. This new association of ideas relieved the community of ambivalence and moral obligations and gave sanction to making the Mexicans the victims of widespread hostile crowd behavior.

Source: Ralph H. Turner and Samuel J. Surace, "Zoot-Suiters and Mexicans: Symbols in Crowd Behavior," *American Journal of Sociology* (Winter 1956), 14–20. Reprinted by permission of the University of Chicago Press, publisher, and the authors. Copyright 1956 by the University of Chicago Press.

"... A STRANGE CASE OF JUBILATION"

Late in 1960 the Department of Labor issued a study, "The Economic Situation of Negroes in the United States." It noted that in 1939, non-white workers earned, on the average, 41 per cent as much as whites, and that by 1958 had climbed to 58 per cent of that of whites. Not a little elation greeted this announcement. Some of the editorialists cited these statistics as indicating that slow and steady progress was being made. (At this rate, the Negro would reach parity with the white some time well after the year 2000.)

To begin with, the figures were somewhat more optimistic than the reality. Part of the Negro gain reflected the shift of rural Negroes to cities and Southern Negroes to the North. In both cases, the people involved increased their incomes by going into a more prosperous section of the country. But within each area their relative position remained the same at the bottom. Then, the statistics take a depression year (1939) as a base for comparison, and contrast it to a year of recession (1958). This tended to exaggerate the advance because Negroes in 1939 were particularly victimized.

Another important aspect of the problem was obscured by the sweeping comparisons most editorialists made between the 1939 and 1958 figures. Even the Department of Labor statistics themselves indicate that the major gain was made during World War II (the increase from 1939 to 1947 was from 41.4 per cent to 54.3 of the white wage). In the postwar period the rate of advance slowed to a walk. Moreover, most of the optimism was based on figures for Negro men. When the women are included, and when one takes a median family income from the Current Population Reports, Negroes rose from 51 per cent of white family income in 1947 to 57 per cent in 1952—and then declined back to the 1947 level by 1959.

But even without these qualifications, the fact is stark enough: the United States found cause for celebration in the announcement that Negro workers had reached 58 per cent of the wage level of their white co-workers. This situation is deeply imbedded in the very structure of American society. . . .

Source: Reprinted with permission of The Macmillan Company from *The Other America: Poverty in the United States* by Michael Harrington. Copyright 1962 by Michael Harrington. Pp. 72–73.

Type of Occupation	Percentage of Male Workers in Each Type of Occupation —1966		Median Earnings of All Male Civilians in Each Occupation —1965
	White	Nonwhite	
Professional, Technical, Managerial	27%	9%	$7,603[a]
Clerical and sales	14	9	$5,532[a]
Craftsmen and foremen	20	12	$6,270
Operatives	20	27	$5,046
Service Workers	6	16	$3,436
Non-farm laborers	6	20	$2,410
Farmers and farm workers	7	8	$1,699[a]

[a] Average of two categories from normal Census Bureau categories as combined in data presented in *The Social and Economic Conditions of Negroes in the United States* (BLS #332).
Source: Report of the National Advisory Commission on Civil Disorders (New York: Bantam, 1968), p. 254. © 1967 by the New York Times Company. Reprinted by permission.

Negro Life and Social Process*

SETHARD FISHER

████

Once again, cries for social justice, equality, and dignity for American Negroes have gained momentum and intensity. Once again, national policy is favorable to the "cause." Yet Negroes have been appointed to high office in earlier times. They gained the franchise many years ago and have been before the cause for massive upsurges of moral indignation. The awesome tale of exploitation, cruelty, and injustice which recounts the history of Negroes in American society has not reached the happy end which some current events may suggest. Ethnicity remains a decided hindrance rather than help to Negroes; a shameful rather than prideful matter. Blackness and dignity remain incompatible in American culture.

How strangely incongruent the Negro experience of today with the image of what it would be like held by two former slaves who became prominent advocates of the Negro cause, Frederick Douglass[1] and Booker T. Washington.[2] Following emancipation and the end of the Civil War, Douglass' work with the Anti-Slavery Society was over and his fight for the cause of free Negroes began. Seeing freedom without power as empty, he undertook the cause of enfranchisement of Negroes. The movement for Negro suffrage grew rapidly; by 1870 the Fourteenth and Fifteenth Amendments had been adopted. With passage, Douglass said: "Negro men are today invested with complete citizenship—the right to vote and be voted for in the American Republic."[3] Yet the following account appears in the recently published *Mississippi Black Paper*:

Source: Sethard Fisher, "Review Essay: Negro Life and Social Process," *Social Problems*, Vol. 13, No. 3 (Winter 1966), pp. 343–353. Reprinted by permission of The Society for the Study of Social Problems and the author.

* I want to acknowledge my debt to Sheldon L. Messinger for helpful editorial assistance and stimulating conversations about the Negro problem. I have also benefited from critical readings of the paper by Myrtha Chabran.

[1] Frederick Douglass, *The Life and Times of Frederick Douglass* (New York: Pathway Press, 1941); the book was originally published in 1892. A reprint is available: New York: Collier Books, 1963. Citations are to the 1941 edition. See also *A Star Pointed North* (New York: Harper and Row, 1965), by Edmund Fuller; Philip S. Foner, *Frederick Douglass* (New York: The Citadel Press, 1964).

[2] Booker T. Washington, *Up From Slavery: An Autobiography* (New York: Doubleday, Page & Co., 1901); reprinted: New York: Bantam Books, 1956. Citation is to the 1941 edition.

[3] Douglass, *op. cit.*, p. 438.

On Feb. 28, 1963, I attended a voter registration meeting in the office of the Student Nonviolent Coordinating Committee in Greenwood, Mississippi. . . . As we were going onto the highway [after the meeting], we noticed a white 1962 Buick that had been driving around the office coming off the highway. There were three white men in the car. . . . They followed us for about seven miles. . . . [Soon] there were no other cars in sight. They speeded up and pulled even with us. When they were right beside us, one of the men in the car opened fire with a submachine gun. He fired for about three or four seconds and then the car sped away. I felt something hit me in the neck. I said "I'm hit." Bob Moses, who was sitting beside me, grabbed the wheel from me and then I slumped in his lap. . . . I had been shot once in the neck and once in the shoulder. When our car was later examined, eleven to thirteen bullet holes were found in it. . . . At the time I was shot I was twenty years old and field secretary for SNCC.[4]

And "The New Abolitionists" have this experience in 1964:

[A twenty-three year old Negro, native of Mississippi named Guyot] . . . was questioned by a state trooper, who became enraged when Guyot refused to say "yes sir" and "no sir." The trooper slapped Guyot repeatedly, then turned him over to a group of Citizens Council members. They beat him until he couldn't lift his arms, hit him again and again in his face until his eyes were so swollen he couldn't open them.

Another SNCC worker . . . managed to get into the jail to see Annelle Ponder. She reported on her visit when she got back to Greenwood: "Annelle's face was swollen. . . . She could barely talk. She looked at me and was able to whisper only one word: FREEDOM."[5]

Booker T. Washington characterized Douglass' career as "almost wholly within the first period of the struggle in which the race problem has involved the people of this country, the period of revolution and liberation." He added, ". . . that period is now closed, we are in the period of construction and readjustment." For Washington, "construction" and "readjustment" were optimistic terms:

. . . there was never a time when I felt more hopeful for the race than I do at the present. The great human law that in the end recognizes and rewards merit is everlasting and universal. The outside world does not know, neither can it appreciate, the struggle that is constantly going on in the hearts of both the Southern White people and their former slaves to free themselves from racial prejudice. . . .[6]

His optimism included the presumption of a dying KKK. It seems a cruel miscalculation considered in the light of reports such as the *Mississippi Black Paper*, Zinn's, or William McCord's[7] on the South today. These recent accounts suggest that Douglass and Washington were themselves part of a social process which they saw only imperfectly if at all.

These accounts also suggest that the social process which has characterized the relation of Negroes to the total society is essentially different from that

---

[4] Statement by James Travis in *Mississippi Black Paper* (New York: Random House, 1965), p. 8.
[5] Howard Zinn, *SNCC: The New Abolitionists* (Boston: Beacon Press, 1964), p. 95.
[6] Washington, *op. cit.*, p. 319.
[7] William McCord, *Mississippi: The Long Hot Summer* (New York: W. W. Norton & Company, 1965).

which characterized the relation of the Irish, Italian, German, and other ethnic groups.[8] Progressive access to the centers of economic, political, and social power in American Society, and progressive accumulation of rewards, cannot be substantiated for Negroes. Negro gains in employment, education, and income have been relative rather than absolute; they have been periodically reversed, sometimes to be made again. The social process characteristic of the relation of the Negro to the wider society has been circular and repetitive; it has not taken the progressive and unilinear course characterizing the relation of other ethnic groups to the society. Broom and Glenn cite 1880 through 1915, the depression of the 1930s and the late 1950s as periods of deterioration of gains made by Negroes.[9]

The majority of Negroes during the time of Douglass and Washington spent their lives in the fields, gutters, and ghettoes of America. They continue to do so today. Two recently published autobiographies clearly indicate that Negro degradation and deprivation are confined neither to the South nor to earlier times.[10] Claude Brown and Henry Williamson provide dramatic accounts of life in urban Negro slums. Both are highly readable, although Williamson's seems less complete and less authentic.

Brown tells the story of "Sonny," a Harlem "corner boy" who went to college. His childhood and adolescence included chronic truancy, prolonged friction with his parents, gang fighting, and assorted delinquencies. Sonny was intimate with personal danger and suffered severe bodily harm. He was well known to the courts and the youth correctional houses. Although Sonny's childhood and adolescence appear to have been those of many Harlem youth, he was spared the fate of many of his friends: violent death, permanent body injury, demoralization, and fanaticism.

The life of Henry Williamson in a Negro ghetto on Chicago's south side resembled Claude Brown's life in a Harlem slum in many ways. Yet, there were essential differences. Both men lived the street life of urban Negro slums and were engaged in the violence, excitement, and illegality which characterize that life. But Henry's adolescence was in the 40s and Sonny's in the 50s. The antagonism between Henry and the agents and institutions of reform remained constant and unabated; Sonny formed meaningful, though temporary, relations with officials. Both men were deeply immersed in the underworld life of the street but they were attached in different ways. Although both were "cool studs," Henry showed little loyalty to close associates. As he puts it: "There wasn't no

---

[8] A useful definition and discussion of ethnic groups may be found in a recent publication by Tomatsu Shibutani and Kian M. Kwan. According to the authors "an ethnic group consists of those who conceive of themselves as being alike by virtue of their common ancestry, real or fictitious, and who are so regarded by others." See their *Ethnic Stratification* (New York: Macmillan, 1965), p. 47.

[9] Leonard Broom and Norval Glenn, *Transformation of the Negro American* (New York: Harper and Row, 1964), p. 186.

[10] Claude Brown, *Manchild in the Promised Land* (New York: Macmillan, 1965), and Henry Williamson, *Hustler!*, edited by R. Lincoln Keiser (New York: Doubleday, 1965).

honor amongst us. If we stole somethin' at night, didn't sell it that night, and hid it until next morning, any one of us was likely to go out there and take it. They call it gettin' burnt." [11]

Henry, further, tells of the time he accidentally knocked his girlfriend down the stairs during an argument. Her mother located him and, at gun point, brought him back to the scene where "Callie" was aborting a child. Henry was sent to buy medicine for Callie but he didn't return for two weeks.

Both Sonny and Henry quit school and became known to law enforcement officers at an early age. Both were sent by their parents to the South as a reform measure and both returned and continued their former activities. Both were wounded by bullets, although it was Henry rather than Sonny who himself nearly killed. Henry's illegal activities led progressively from delinquency to adult crime, and included robbery and theft as major means of gaining a livelihood. Fear of getting a record played a role in curtailing Sonny's illegal behavior beyond his sixteenth year. This appears to be the point at which he began his departure from the world of institutionalized illegality, a departure Henry never made.

Henry's story ends in Federal prison serving sentences of three to twenty and three to fourteen years. Caught in a robbery by a policeman, shot, and paralyzed by a bullet lodged near his spine, it was three and a half years, he says, before he could get out of bed "for any length of time. It was five and a half years before I got back on the streets." Henry learned later that the policeman who shot him had been killed "by some stud in a robbery." He comments, "I wish I coulda pissed on his grave."

Henry's language is that of the insulated northern Negro ghetto, heavily infused with a "down home" flavor. Sonny, on the other hand, is a new breed of cat. His is more the language and style of the hipster, a world so far removed from "down home" as probably to be unrecognizable there. The existence of these differences, which are probably generational, does not obscure the telling testimony of devastation, deprivation, and human misery which both volumes abundantly provide. The overwhelming majority of Negroes today continue to inhibit the bottomless pits of devastation in American society.

The career of Adam Clayton Powell is a forerunner of the now somewhat more widespread tendency for Negroes to occupy a few positions of political and economic prominence. Powell represents a deviant instance of careers among Negroes. In addition, he symbolizes that phase in the cyclic process of Negro history during which cracks in the repressive social mold appear and some gains are made.

A biographical account of Powell has recently appeared which recounts a rather illustrious career.[12] Adam Clayton Powell, Jr. was born in New Haven

---

[11] *Ibid.*, pp. 35-36.
[12] Neil Hickey and Ed Edwin, *Adam Clayton Powell and the Politics of Race* (New York: Fleet Publishing Corp., 1965).

in 1908. He grew up in Harlem and was well acquainted with the misery of ghetto life, although, being the son of a successful minister of the world's largest Baptist church, he himself was to some extent protected from its ravages. Powell graduated from Colgate University and returned to Harlem to succeed his father at Abissinnia Baptist Church in 1937.

From his power base in Harlem, Powell took up the fight for Negro equality and dignity with militancy. In 1938 he became co-chairman of the Greater New York Coordinating Committee for Unemployment, a highly successful Harlem protest group. In 1941 he was elected to the New York City Council, becoming the first Negro ever elected to that body. During World War II Powell was actively engaged in "Civil War II." He protested segregation in the Armed Forces, job discrimination against Negroes in defense plants, and continually confronted Americans with the paradox of Negroes fighting for democracy abroad and for protection of the "color-caste system" at home. He attacked the federal government for interning Japanese-Americans while not interfering with German and Italian Americans. In addition, Powell maintained a column in the *Amsterdam News*, an influential Harlem newspaper, through which he advocated the cause of Negroes for jobs, for dignity, and for mobilization in self-help activities.

Powell's protests progressively endeared him to the citizens of Harlem. In 1943 he took office as Representative to the 79th Congress, along with Franklin D. Roosevelt and Harry S. Truman. His career as Congressman has been characterized by ongoing fights with Southern legislators and an unrelenting attack on the patterns of segregation and discrimination in the nation's Capitol. In Harlem his stature continued to grow. In the 1946 elections he attained an easy victory due to the solid support of the people of Harlem.

As a new Negro leadership grew and the parade of "marching blacks" picked up momentum, Powell became somewhat antagonistic toward them as he did not have a fixed place in the Movement. "History was moving too swiftly now, and Powell stood in terrible danger of being left in its backwater." The failure of the "Big Six" (Roy Wilkins, NAACP; Whitney Young, Urban League; James Farmer, CORE; A. Phillip Randolph, Brotherhood of Sleeping Car Porters; Martin Luther King, SCLC; and John Lewis, SNCC) to accord Powell a place of prominence is said to be responsible for his periodic criticism of them and for his affinity for the Black Muslims. Chairmanship of the powerful Education and Labor Committee has thrust Powell into a position of national influence. His breach with Negro leaders in the Civil Rights movement remains, his resistance to party line politics remains, as does his tenure as the most politically influential American Negro. This atypical career line deserves further and more systematic study for it may suggest important lines of development for the Negro Movement.

The history of Negroes in American Society suggests social process of acceleration of gains, followed by a gradual grinding halt and retardation.

Certainly the human events which reflect this condition and are caused by it are several, and many are forever lost. The stories of Horace Cayton[13] and of Gideon Jackson,[14] however, illustrate how this process sets in, confounds, halts, and decimates the progressive development theretofore underway. Though covering different historical periods, they reflect essentially the same social process and its repetitive or circular character.

Horace R. Cayton's parents had college degrees at a time when most Negroes were illiterate. They resided in a wealthy white community at the turn of the century when few Negroes lived in the Pacific Northwest. Cayton's mother, a writer and school teacher with a cultivated interest in the arts, was from a "prominent family of the Negro elite." Her father, Hiram Revels (1827–1901), was elected United States Senator from Mississippi after the Civil War in 1870. Cayton's father finished college and eventually settled in Seattle where he became a prosperous newspaper owner, publisher, and real estate speculator. As Cayton suggests: "We, unlike most Negroes, lived in a tradition of success, achievement, and hope for Negro liberation." The development of this proud and successful family seems to have been progressively favorable up to Cayton's generation. The volume provides dramatic testimony to its demise, and to the consequent pain and suffering of a sensitive man.

The population of Seattle was 42,000 in 1890; it grew to 237,000 by 1910. A large influx of Negroes accompanied this population growth. With increased immigration, patterns of race relation in Seattle changed. As Cayton expresses it:

There was no longer a place for an inbetween group, and everyone became identified as either Negro or white. We were, to my knowledge, the only Negro family to feel so dramatically the impact of these social forces, and our fall from our unique position was swift and, for us, painful.[15]

With this change in social arrangements in the city as a whole, the station of the Cayton family in the community declined drastically. The *Seattle Republican*, his father's paper, failed. The horses and carriage of the family were sold, and the services of their Japanese servant discontinued. The family moved to a less wealthy area of the city and at one point his mother took a part-time job as a housekeeper. His mother's preoccupation with cultural "uplift" activities among Negroes gave way to "the hard grind of making a home for the family." His father's previous role as leader among Negroes was challenged. Cayton suggests the ensuing changes in the outlook of members of the family toward one another as the most dramatic of all:

---

[13] Horace Cayton, *Long Old Road* (New York: Trident Press, 1965).

[14] Jackson is the central character in Howard Fast's *Freedom Road* (New York: Pocket Books, Inc., 1962). Although this is a novelistic treatment and suffers some typical weaknesses of such documents, Fast gives the following account of his material: "All the essentials of this story are true. There was not one Carwell in the South at that period but thousands, both larger and smaller." The specific sources of his data are provided on pp. 263–264.

[15] Cayton, *op. cit.*, p. 23.

Early I had sensed that there was some latent conflict between my parents. Now, under the stress of adversity, these differences began to come out into the open. My mother had never quite forgotten that she was the daughter of a United States Senator and that her family belonged to the aristocracy of free Negroes, nor had she ever completely accepted the fact that Dad was not only the son of a slave but had even been a slave himself. This could be glossed over at the time when Dad had been a successful businessman and a leader in the community. But when a precarious living for the family was possible only if he worked as a janitor and she as a domestic, it was a different matter entirely.[16]

The subsequent career of Horace Cayton has been largely a frustrating suspension between a Negro world in which he felt uncomfortable and alienated, and a white world whose values he shares but satisfaction in which he could not achieve. What he says of his life at sixteen seems to hold for his later years as well:

At sixteen, my life seemed to add up to very little. I was lonesome, having neither school companions nor many Negro friends. I made several futile efforts to gain entrance to the Negro group, including an unsuccessful attempt to become a member of the Mt. Zion Baptist Church. But the services seemed to me loud and vulgar, when I contrasted them with those in the church downtown where I had always gone. . . . I was an outsider, partly because I could not give friendship and partly because I simply didn't know how to act—what to say, how to dress, what language to employ. I could find no acceptance among Negroes, and the white world had rejected me, cruelly frustrating my every attempt to belong.[17]

For a while Cayton "moved with the rising, well-to-do Negro upper class" and university intellectuals. He had several brief involvements with women. He gradually became aware of an "overpowering loneliness," and became frightened about himself, wondering "had I lost love forever?" He found his way to a psychoanalyst and continued this relationship for several years. As his description progresses one is aware of a constant and malignant intrusion of the race issue in every aspect of his life. His torment grew to such heights of intensity that gradually he withdrew from his former associates, began to drink excessively, found himself penniless, and ultimately had what he refers to as a "crack-up" five years following World War II. During these same years his mother and favorite sister died, and he had an angry confrontation with his brother who disowned him. As he expresses it, "my world collapsed; events piled up in a disorderly fashion, shaking my confidence and leaving me stripped of the will to continue."

Cayton himself recovered somewhat from the tragedy which beset his family. However, the social process to which the Cayton family became victim did not end when the family's demise was complete, nor did it originate in Seattle. *Freedom Road* tells the story of Gideon Jackson and is another reflection of the same social process operating at a different historical juncture and in a different social context.

---

[16] *Ibid.*, p. 25.
[17] *Ibid.*, p. 34.

Gideon Jackson's was one of the many families of former slaves which, after the Civil War, remained on the plantations of their former masters. Jackson, who lived on the Carwell Place, was an ignorant and unlearned man goaded on by the demand for leadership among his people. He educated himself and rose to great political heights.

As the Carwell community prospered, it came increasingly under attack by the Klan, especially when Federal troops were removed from the South. At the end, Carwell was surrounded, bombarded, and demolished by "the men who hid their faces from the sun with white hoods." Gideon Jackson's explanation of the demise of Carwell, and of this faltering, hopeful time for Negro betterment does not accord with the Social Darwinist stereotypes which later generations of interpreters have applied to it.

I want to tell you the truth now, I want you to understand why Fred McHugh lies in my house, his arms twisted from their sockets and useless to him, his wife dead, his mind gone. I want to tell you why, when my son and I came down here from Washington, we were forced to ride in a separate car marked "colored." I want to tell you why all over the South, from Texas to Virginia, cries of suffering fill the air. And most of all, I want you to know why from here on, the white man will be set against the black like a dog against a sheep; why, if they succeed, it will be a dream that there had ever been such a place as Carwell.[18]

. . . More than eight years ago, the Klan raided our people at Carwell. That was a clumsy thing, a frightened thing. They burned the barns and killed one little boy. But they were beginning then, as far back as that. From the very first, they planned to destroy us. The war was hardly over before the same people who made it set about planning for the next war, a different one this time, armies that ride in the night, underground organization, intimidation, threats, terror. Now their preparation has been completed; they're ready.[19]

And the curious part is . . . that even those things which you cling to will be forgotten. The black men who sat in the House, in the Senate; they will be forgotten, the black men who built schools and justice—all of it, my friends. We will not be men anymore. They will grind us down until we lose our humanity, until we hate the white men as truly as they hate us. They will make of us a tortured, debased people, unlike any other people on earth. And how long, my friends, before we see a little sunlight again? How long? Ask yourselves that.[20]

Southern white politicians did not simply displace Negro politicians at the end of Reconstruction. The displacement was accompanied by legal restraints and restrictions which barred Negroes from the competitive process. These events point to a more general social process, sometimes more subtly accomplished.

One of the most widely proclaimed virtues of the American political system has been its supposed responsiveness to individuals who band together to exercise pressure for self-advantageous policy formation. Rhetoric depicts this process as a free and equal scramble, regulated by "the rules of the game," and as a fundamental source of creativity and social stability. Current advocates of

---

[18] Fast, *op. cit.*, p. 201.
[19] *Ibid.*, p. 175.
[20] *Ibid.*, p. 207.

a pluralist society adhere to this view, sometimes explicitly and sometimes by implication.[21] One important error of this view is its failure to recognize the extent to which gains made through interest groups frequently become accelerated by virtue of the power realized at each point of victory: *as given interest groups achieve specific goals they frequently so alter the "rules" that further achievements are facilitated. Potential competitors are increasingly encumbered as the successful ones maneuver and manipulate from a vantage point of power.* While it may be argued that American society as a whole has prospered under this arrangement, it may also be stressed that this very process has been fundamental in retarding the progress of the American Negro. The point is that gains made through interest groups carry with them a certain degree of leverage, and if such gains are sufficiently cumulative the resulting leverage permits alteration of the rules of the game in a fundamental way.[22] This subtle process, a generic ingredient of pluralism, in combination with laissez faire economic arrangements, kept the developmental course of the American Negro circular and relative rather than unilinear and absolute. A significant portion of the so-called psychological difficulty which currently corrodes the Negro world stems from the distinctive cultural definitions which emerged as part of this process.

Elkins[23] attributes the uniquely inhumane character of U.S. slavery to the lack of influence of the church and state on a rampant capitalism. Negro subordination came to be a necessary ingredient in the long range plans of influential plantation owners, for economic gain and power. Social definitions which accompanied and grew out of this total devastation depicted the Negro as an inhuman thing; a being without a soul, outside the moral community. His image became the very antithesis of an American, both physically and morally. An important self-destructive strain among Negroes today, noted by E. Franklin Frazier[24] and others, is the desire or wish to meet the impossible demands of a white Anglo-Saxon Protestant culture which has crystallized and institutionalized images of virtue which by definition cannot be met by those with dark skins, kinky hair, or other negroid features. If blackness and dignity are ever to become compatible in American culture an assault must be made on this pathogenic white Anglo-Saxon Protestant cultural syndrome which has been reinforced by the Western colonialist heritage. But this calls for basic change in patterns of dominance among major institutions in American society.

Having the Negro as victim of this debilitating social process in American

---

[21] See C. Wright Mills' discussion of pluralism in his *The Power Elite* (New York: Oxford University Press, 1959), esp. pp. 242–268; "The Distribution of Power in American Society" by Talcott Parsons, *World Politics*, Vol. 10, October, 1957, pp. 123–143; and, articles by Todd Gitlin and Shin'ya Ona in *Studies on the Left*, Summer, 1965. These sources provide rather extensive discussion of pluralism from diverse viewpoints.

[22] This I take to be the essential meaning of what Elkins, Tannenbaum, and others tell us about the Negro situation. See Frank Tannenbaum, *Slave and Citizen* (New York: Vintage Books, A Division of Random House, 1963).

[23] Stanley M. Elkins, *Slavery* (New York: Universal Library, 1963).

[24] E. Franklin Frazier, *Black Bourgeoisie* (Glencoe: The Free Press, 1957).

society has forestalled the kind of societal reaction which might restrain and delimit it. The most humanly damaging consequences of American acquisitiveness and competition have been absorbed by the Negro. In an ethnically homogeneous United States, equal quantities of devastation would have contributed to separating the social classes and would have called forth more drastic demands for social change than have thus far appeared as a result of the Negro movement. The Negro may be seen as the inadvertent tool who in some measure blocks a more direct and straightforward corrective social response to a debilitating social process that claims Negroes as its major victims.

Within the Negro group a major consequence of built-in social retardation and subordination has been a significant degree of defection from white Anglo-Saxon Protestant culture.[25] The defection is not totally a matter of voluntary detachment but of traditional social barriers which circumscribe the degree and kind of participation Negroes are able to achieve. There is now in the Negro world, particularly among Northern Negro youth, a growing perspective of futility.[26] Negro youth, and lower class Negroes in general, are in important measure discarding conventional American society as a social sphere within which to seek acceptance. This both reflects and causes a decline in influence of the other worldly, or religious, outlook among Negroes and an increase in a secular view. This perspective of futility is reflected in a recent poem by a young Negro college student entitled "Burn, Baby, Burn!"[27]

> Sick and Tired,
> Tired of being
> Sick and Tired.
>
> Lost.
> Lost in the
>   wilderness
> Of white America.
> Are the masses asses?
> Cool.
> Said the master to the slave,
> "No problem. Don't rob an steal,
> I'll be your drivin' wheel."
> Cool.
> And he wheeled us into
>   350 years of black madness,
> To hog guts, conked hair, covadis,
> To bleaching cream and uncle thomas,
> to Watts,
> To the streets,
> To the KILL.

[25] An insightful and perceptive description of the ethical and moral aberrations occasioned by race prejudice and the manner in which they influence both Negroes and whites is provided by Howard Thurman in his *The Luminous Darkness* (New York: Harper and Row, 1965).

[26] The term "futility" is intended to suggest a lack of reorientation from which meaningful goal oriented directions might come.

[27] Marvin Jackman, *Soulbook*, Fall, 1965, p. 153.

BOMMMMM . . . . . . 2 honkeys gone.
MOTHER FUCK the police!
and parker's siter, too.
BLACK PEOPLE;
Tired
Sick and Tired,
Tired of being
Sick and tired—

Burn, baby, burn. . . . . .
Don't leave dem bosses rags,
C'mon, child, don't mind da
    tags.
Git all dat motherfucking pluck,
Git dem guns too, we 'on't give
    a fuck!
Burn, baby, burn,
Cook outta sight—
    Fineburgs,
    Whitefront,
    Wineburgs,
    Blackfront—
Burn, baby, burn,

In time

He

will learn.

The aim of social action and change on the part and in behalf of the Negro must be to alter the characteristically circular social process to which Negroes have been subject; it must be hammered into unilinear form, which means continuous, accelerated, and absolute social gain. Pettigrew[28] asserts that the Negro problem at this historical juncture is vulnerable to unprecedented improvement through unrelenting militancy of the civil rights movement. On the other hand, the view of two social scientists from the South is different. Broom and Glenn[29] amass a wealth of data on income, education, and employment among Negroes. They conclude that Negroes are not likely to reach achievement levels of whites in these areas. They add that the protest tactics of the civil rights movement must give way to more pacific and, in their view, effective measures to realize the limited possible achievement by Negroes. This surely seems a hazardous suggestion given our limited understanding of the range of alternative avenues by which such achievement could occur. Significant change of course will depend on the resourcefulness, ingenuity, and intelligence of Negroes and their allies. They must provoke and engineer a social response consisting of at least three dimensions.

---

[28] Thomas F. Pettigrew, *Profile of the American Negro* (Princeton: D. Van Nostrand Company, 1964), p. 200.
[29] Leonard Bloom and Norval Glenn, *op. cit.*, p. 190.

First, the movement for Negro betterment must involve the development of political skills, leadership, and power among Negroes themselves. This means election and appointment of Negroes to positions of influence in local, state, and national governmental bodies. Negroes would then be better equipped to defend themselves against the efforts of malevolent whites to neutralize their gains by political craft and subtlety—or by whip and gun.

Second, ties between American Negroes and the African and Asian peoples must be developed.[30] The development of bonds of mutual solidarity by Negro Americans with African and Asian peoples could serve the cause of the Negro in America and of America itself, as well as the cause of the industrializing nations of dark-skinned peoples. Such a move would internationalize the condition of the American Negro, a resource which most other ethnic groups in America always had. This achievement would win allies for Negroes and make reversals of their gains and welfare a matter of international importance, and thus less likely to occur. For the industrializing African and Asian countries this move would mean a source of new advocates for their cause who could be highly influential. The cause of skill development, education, and other needs of industrializing nations could be vastly assisted by American Negroes with a militant organization of Civil Rights, religious, and other groups with an authentic interest in promoting this kind of liaison. For white America this move could have the effect of promoting an opportunity never yet realized in this country. Whites have not developed ties of friendship and respect with Negroes as social equals. They have not taken seriously the need to dismantle and replace the pathogenic white Anglo-Saxon Protestant cultural syndrome. This is a badly needed experience which could be of great value to this country as more and more it must come to grips with its racist heritage.[31]

A third and final facet of this social response must be to challenge and counteract the rampant acquisitive and competitive tendencies in American society by seeking proscriptions on the power and influence of the dominant economic institutions from which they spring. This means building into American life certain "rules of the game" regarding economic activity which are not vulnerable to the power stratagems of competing interest groups. In this way checks and balances could be built into our economic system which would relax the grip of tenacious economic imperatives and make possible the growth of needed new definitions.

Problem-related social action can only maximize its achievements as it is informed by creative scholarly research. The complex of factors which at

---

[30] For an extensive discussion of this matter in relation to Africa see Charles E. Silberman's *Crisis in Black and White* (New York: Random House, 1964), pp. 162–188.

[31] Regarding racism I take the view expressed by Calvin C. Hernton that racism represents "learned behavior and learned emotions . . . that compel one group to conceive of and treat the other on the basis of its physical characteristics alone, as if it did not belong to the human race." See his *Sex and Racism in America* (New York: Doubleday and Company, 1965), p. 175.

different historical periods have reversed the progress of Negroes must be documented in detail so that social policy may be devised which will assure that they do not appear again. Historical and comparative data must be drawn on in pursuit of means by which legitimacy for Negro gains which are absolute, once made, may be achieved.[32] Finally, some research effort must be made to define and characterize more precisely the nature of the social process which has continually worked to stabilize the Negro in an inferior social status. Is this process a necessary component of the system of economic and political arrangements by which American society is defined and defines itself?[33] Does the accumulation of social gain by Negroes automatically mean social loss for other groups? Serious pursuit of these matters could allow new patterns of race relations to appear which promise to curtail the impending violence and destruction which must occur when a mobilized, militant black minority and a defensive, fearful white majority angrily confront one another.

---

[32] Attacking the problem of "pluralistic ignorance" is one suggestion offered by L. K. Northwood and Ernest A. T. Barth. See their *Urban Desegregation* (Seattle: University of Washington Press, 1965), esp. pp. 84–86.

[33] Pettigrew has answered this question affirmatively. He suggests that ". . . some basic structural changes in American society will have to occur before viable race relation solutions are possible. These changes include wider employment, a different taxation base, an extension of the minimum wage to cover service workers, and massive retraining. Clearly, the problem we are trying to solve transcends the boundaries of Civil Rights and reaches into the basic structure of American society." See his "White-Negro Confrontations," in the Negro Challenge to the Business Community, edited by Eli Gingberg (McGraw-Hill: New York, 1964). Other essays in this volume which deal with the economic and political aspect of the Negro problem are noteworthy.

CHAPTER 3

RATIONALIZATION

Individual Initiative and the Problem of Bureaucracy

REINHARD BENDIX

Authoritarian bureaucracy can become a clique ridden by suspicion. Its primary concern with self-preservation may result in the alienation of the public, a growing inability to operate efficiently, and the duplication of functions, which a more or less developed internal spy system necessitates.

Democratic administration may deteriorate, on the other hand, because the frustrations of administrative work deter qualified men and because suspicion of any authority goes so far as to make effective policy formulation and execution impossible.

The temptation is strong to summarize the difference between democratic and authoritarian administration by reference to Mannheim's distinction between functional and substantial rationality. Authoritarian officials would be thought of as efficient in the use of administrative techniques without proper comprehension of their role in the over-all policy decided on by the dictator (functional rationality). Democratic officials would combine, on the other hand, administrative efficiency with an understanding of the basic policies which they are called upon to implement (substantial rationality).[1] This application of Mannheim's distinction does not aid us, however, in our analysis of large-scale organizations. Mannheim himself would point out that all subordinate administrators suffer from the special incapacity which exclusive attention to the techniques of implementation entails. Democratic and authoritarian officials share in the inability of comprehending the political program which governs their actions. Besides, Mannheim's distinction suffers from overstating its case.[2]

Source: Reinhard Bendix, *Higher Civil Servants in American Society* (Boulder: University of Colorado Press, 1949), pp. 86–88. Reprinted by permission.
[1] Indeed, this distinction has been used to characterize Nazi administration. See John H. Herz "German Administration under the Nazi Regime," *American Political Science Review*, XL (August 1946), 684–686.
[2] Karl Mannheim, *Man and Society*, pp. 51–60. It is not denied, of course, that Mannheim has pointed to a constant source of friction.

It is impossible to run any large-scale organization without some provision for fitting the specialized technician into the larger framework of operation. It is not possible, however, to direct his every action; some reliance must, therefore, be placed on his own over-all comprehension of his function and on the initiative which he develops in implementing this comprehension by cooperative action. Thus both democratic and authoritarian officials must grapple with the problem of overcoming the "trained incapacity" (Veblen) of the administrative technician to see the larger policy framework.[3]

Democratic and authoritarian administrations differ, therefore, because of their respective institutions and culture-patterns, not because one is representative and inefficient, whereas the other is efficient but arbitrary. The distinction between these two types of administration is rather an outgrowth of historical experience and present circumstances. As such it affects the manner of the administrative technician, who combines obedience and efficiency with the initiative that is essential to the success of large-scale organization. It is not useful, therefore, to consider the social problems of administration in terms either of rational management or of the psychology of human relations. The problem of bureaucracy is rather in what manner technical and administrative rationality are combined with the exercise of individual initiative in the accomplishment of a common task. Men have combined their efforts in large-scale organizations throughout history. Their success today will depend on whether or not they can combine the efficiency of modern organization with a flexibility which allows the individual in that organization to use his imagination rather than do his job in a routine way.

The problem of bureaucracy is, then, not only a question of preserving freedom against the encroachments of government. Rather, we will not be able to utilize the efficiency of modern management unless we can make the initiative of the individual one of our principles of organization.

---

[3] Both will tend to use the rationalizations of their respective political philosophies, for instance, as guidance in all cases in which they need but cannot obtain a knowledge of basic policies. The behavioristic importance of political philosophies in a study of administrative conduct has not so far been sufficiently considered. See in this respect John M. Gaus, Leonard D. White, and Marshall E. Dimock, *The Frontiers of Public Administration* (Chicago: University of Chicago Press, 1936).

Some Uses and Abuses of Statistical Recording Procedures in a Government Agency

HARRY COHEN

But actually, he thought as he readjusted the Ministry of Plenty's figures, it was not even forgery. It was merely the substitution of one piece of nonsense for another. Most of the material that you were dealing with had no connection with anything in the real world, not even the kind of connection that is contained in a direct lie. Statistics were just as much a fantasy in their original version as in their rectified version. A great deal of the time you were expected to make them up out of your head.

—George Orwell*

EARLY RECORDS

Blau noted that statistical recording procedure in 1948 required only that interviewers report the number of client interviews completed during work

---

Source: Reprinted by permission from *The Demonics of Bureaucracy*, by Harry Cohen, © 1965 by the Iowa State University Press, Ames, Iowa.

* *Nineteen Eighty-Four* (New York: Harcourt, Brace and Co., Inc., 1949), pp. 41–42.

Editors' Note: The author became involved in his subject only gradually. He took a job as interviewer in 1956, shortly after he finished college, with a state employment service agency branch in a large city on the eastern seaboard. A colleague at another agency told him that a sociologist, Peter M. Blau, had made a study of a similar office a few years earlier (1948–1949). "I read Blau's book," he writes, "and found that it offered many insights into my own observations as a bureaucrat." Eventually he took further university work and turned his own experience as a participant observer (he left the agency in 1959) into a sociological inquiry. He describes it as ". . . aimed at two directions. First, comparisons and contrasts are drawn with Blau's earlier study. Secondly, the results . . . can stand alone as a case study of a specific bureaucracy, showing that bureaucrats deviate from the rules in response to special local conditions and client demands, but with end results contrary to those which might be predicted by popular opinion. Although we like to believe that deviation from rigid procedure by bureaucrats is good and that bureaucracy is inefficient because bureaucrats overconform to the rules, . . . [the materials presented in this book] will show that changes of rules can also lead to inefficiencies. . . . These processes will be called the demonics of bureaucracy, referring to flexibility and changes of procedures—*dynamics* of bureaucracy, as in the title of Professor Blau's book—but in a direction leading to pathological ends." . . .

operations. These early records are rudimentary in comparison to the more complex records that were later required.

These records led to functional consequences because they pressed officials to work faster, since the number of interviews completed was now visible to superiors who could evaluate their work. According to Blau:

> The supervisor wanted to know the number of interviews completed by each subordinate only in order to take corrective action in case any of them worked too slowly. The fact that the very counting of interviews had induced them to work faster facilitated operations by making such corrective steps superfluous. The use of statistical records not only provided superiors with information that enabled them to rectify poor performance but often obviated the need for doing so.[1]

These rudimentary records also led to dysfunctional consequences:

> Until the beginning of 1948 the number of interviews held per month was the only operation that was statistically counted for each interviewer in Department X. (Although detailed statistical reports were kept in the agency, they were presented only for departments as a whole, not for individuals.) As long as jobs were plentiful during the war, this rudimentary record seemed to suffice. However, when jobs became scarce after the war and time and effort were required to find one for a client, this count of interviews had a detrimental effect on operations. . . .
> Except for the information obtained by direct observation, the number of interviews completed by a subordinate was the only evidence the supervisor had at that time for evaluating him. The interviewer's interest in a good rating demanded that he maximize the number of interviews and therefore prohibited spending much time on locating jobs for clients. This rudimentary statistical record interfered with the agency's objective of finding jobs for clients in a period of job scarcity.[2]

The statistical reporting emphasis on the number of interviews completed, caused officials to dysfunctionally neglect important agency goals. "There existed an organizational need for a different evaluation system."[3]

DETAILED STATISTICAL RECORDS

A new department head was assigned to Agency B in March 1948. Two months after she had been assigned, she had instituted new performance records. These records were more detailed than the rudimentary records discussed above, and were issued monthly for the use of all interviewing officials.[4] Agency B interviewers now had to record:

1. The number of interviews held.
2. The number of clients referred to a job.

---

1 Peter M. Blau, *The Dynamics of Bureaucracy* (rev. ed., Chicago: University of Chicago Press, 1963), p. 38. Blau's observations at Agency B took place in 1949. However, he acquired information relating to the previous year, 1948, as well.
2 *Ibid.*
3 *Ibid.*
4 *Ibid.*, pp. 38–39.

3. The number of placements . . . made [credited when a referred client was hired by the employer].
4. The proportion of interviews resulting in referrals.
5. The proportion of referrals resulting in placements.
6. The proportion of interviews resulting in placements.
7. The number of notifications sent to the insurance office.
8. The number of application forms made out.[5]

Detailed records were still in use years later at Agency C, but these had been somewhat expanded and changed. Agency C interviewers in 1956 had to report:

1. The number of interviews held.
2. The number of clients referred to jobs.
3. The number of placements (hires) made.
4. The number of notifications of possible disqualifying conditions sent to the unemployment insurance office.
5. The number of application forms made out.

Up to this point, these are the same operations that were recorded by Agency B interviewers in 1949. However, the proportions listed by Blau were not formally required on Agency C records, although supervisory and interviewing officials also considered such proportions. While the proportions were not listed on the records or computed on paper, many officials still were inclined to "compute in their minds" approximately what the proportion was for some of the activities above. This computation was not exact, nor in numbers, but rather in the gross terms of, for example, "*too few* referrals considering the number of interviews conducted."

Agency C interviewers in 1956 recorded other activities that were not required at Agency B in 1949. These are, to continue with the listing:

6. The number of clients "called-in" to the office for service by use of application cards on file.
7. The number of counseling interviews performed.
8. Telephone solicitations made on the behalf of clients.
9. The number of job vacancies (job orders) received.
10. The number of visits to employers that were made.
11. The number of telephone calls made to employers for promotional purposes.
12. The number of interviews conducted that were "not elsewhere classified."

In addition, interviewers with special assignments had further activities to report. For example, the interviewers providing aptitude tests had to record the number of clients tested.

Thus we see that activities reported on Agency C detailed statistical records in

---

[5] *Ibid.*, p. 39.

1956 were well expanded from those required at Agency B in 1949. However, not all of these reported interviewer activities at Agency C received emphasis. For example, the number of "call-ins" made was not emphasized, and officials were inclined to neglect use of application files for calling in applicants to the office for jobs (because of special local conditions). This was despite inclusion on the records. In other words, records had expanded from the time of 1949, but some of the expansion was of recorded activities that were unimportant in local operations and were treated as such by superiors and subordinates. Hence, despite the fact that these activities were listed on records, staff did not emphasize them. This is unlike the functional aspect of the detailed records as abstracted from Blau here and discussed more fully later: "By altering the performance record . . . higher officials can induce lower echelons to change their practices immediately."[6] But under the direction of the new manager in 1959, Agency C detailed records were further modified and the number of activities to be reported was reduced. Vacancies received, telephone solicitations, and clients "called-in" were no longer to be reported by each interviewer on the detailed production records, although the other nine activities listed above were still required.

The initiation of detailed statistical production (performance) records had functional consequences as observed at Agency B in 1949. First, they led to increased productivity.[7] Blau presents data in proof of this statement, but the Agency C study finds evidence contrary to this. Full discussion of this point is made in the next chapter. Second, statistical records helped facilitate hierarchical control over operating officials. According to Blau:

> Procedures governing operations were often modified when interpreted by lower hierarchical levels. . . . If the department head had relied on rules that showed how qualified clients must be selected for referral, for example, these might have been modified by supervisors, and again by interviewers. The use of the proportion of referred clients who were hired as one element in the evaluation of subordinates enforced careful selection more effectively than rules could, because it identified the interest of interviewers with being selective in their referrals.[8]

> Third, these records enabled superiors to institute changes in operations quickly and effectively. New procedures are not always opposed, but sometimes they are, and usually a period of adaptation is required before they become fully effective. By altering the performance record or the relative emphasis on various factors, higher officials can induce lower echelons to change their practices immediately. The introduction of extensive statistical records in Department X illustrates this. . . .[9]

As we have seen, this latter function of statistical records is not fully repeated in the matter of counseling activity for Agency C. Mention has already been made of the fact that there were also some activities that were recorded in

---

[6] Blau, *Dynamics . . . op. cit.*, p. 43.
[7] *Ibid.*, pp. 39–43.
[8] *Ibid.*, p. 42.
[9] *Ibid.*, p. 43.

quantity on records but were not emphasized by superiors or interviewers. This meant that in these cases, contrary to Blau's point, officials were not induced to change their practices in performance of these activities.

In addition, emphasis on the records often did induce lower echelons to change some practices immediately at Agency C, but in a dysfunctional direction! Instead of improving service factors, there was sometimes fabrication made, or cutting corners to "improve" records.

To continue with Blau's discussion:

> Fourth, use of performance records improved the relations between supervisors and interviewers. The supervisor's responsibility for operations required him to criticize subordinates whose performance was inadequate, as a means of improving it. This task was greatly disliked, since such criticism was often resented, and resentful subordinates were less co-operative. Performance records either relieved the supervisors of this duty or reduced the resentment it created. Sometimes they were substituted for verbal criticism. . . . Even if a supervisor actually talked to an interviewer about the ways of improving his performance, the existence of statistical data transformed the nature of these discussions. Instead of telling the interviewer that *he* considered his performance inadequate, the supervisor tried to help him improve his record. Finally, the onus for giving a low rating was partly removed from the supervisor because he could transfer responsibility to the record of the official. Since these records reduced the chances for the development of conflict and antagonism, they made possible a more cordial and co-operative relationship between subordinates and their supervisor.[10]

This was not repeated at Agency C. Some practices of supervisors (see the next section and others) caused some ill feeling between supervisors and subordinates. Overemphasis of supervisors on "statistics" rather than on the service the statistics were designed to measure, also caused dysfunctions.

Blau also did not find that these detailed statistical performance records were completely functional but found some dysfunctional consequences too. He presented a case where a supervisor disregarded the high production records of a subordinate when rating him. The performance records of this interviewer had at one time been outstanding, but after the low rating of his superior, his productivity fell, remaining at a low level even after a new supervisor had been assigned. This official had been expecting a rating based on his good performance as indicated on the detailed records of production. When the previous supervisor disregarded the records in the personnel rating of his subordinate, he antagonized an interviewer, and also destroyed the effectiveness of the detailed statistical records as incentives for work. This was not only in relation to the immediate supervisor's action, but also carried over into relationships of this official with another superior to whom he had been assigned at a later date.[11] Similar inefficient administration in relation to use of records as a basis for personnel ratings also was repeated in cases at Agency C.

---

[10] *Ibid.* Italics in the original.
[11] *Ibid.*, pp. 44–45.

PROFESSORS AND PHILANTHROPOIDS

"I would take a job at X college in preference to the Hub based not on criteria of teaching over research but just that the Hub's future is not as certain as X college."

"One of the major problems here has been and continues to be the uncertainty of the budget. You have to know the scale of funds before you can plan. We got only a fraction of what we had planned for. Now we're looking for other funds, etc. We cannot recruit too well because we cannot make a firm offer. If we had a budget—a firm budget—we would have no personnel problems."

"The main problem here is doing research and justifying ourself to the foundation. The thing that's annoyed me the most is that we spend so much time looking at our navel without doing anything—except justifying our existence."

"The main problem is the uncertain environment. This is an uneasy life . . . tougher than a real university life . . . this time-uncertainty and shoestring operation. If I were given dough when I first came here—say so many thousand per annum, I may have hired not *better* people but people more akin to project needs."

"I have to spend up to 25 per cent of my time working on the foundation submission."

"The tightest pressure I've felt is the annual soul-searching with the foundation. I've been through it two years now and it wears me out."

"Ever since January, tension has been awful. Everyone has been watching, waiting, and, in general, usurping valuable time because of the terrible fear of not getting the contract renewed because of budget cuts. This takes a large part of group conversation."

Source: Warren G. Bennis, "The Effect of Academic Goods on Their Market," *American Journal of Sociology*, **LXII**, (July 1956), p. 31.

COMPETITION AS A DYSFUNCTIONAL CONSEQUENCE OF DETAILED STATISTICAL RECORDS

Another dysfunctional consequence resulting from the use, or perhaps we should say *misuse*, of detailed records that Blau reported derived from the resulting overpreoccupation with productivity, which led to competition. At Agency B this was found to be ". . . the most serious dysfunction of statistical reports," because interpersonal relationships between interviewers were affected.[12] Competition did occur at Agency C too, but was certainly not as prevalent as at Blau's agency, nor as serious.

The stress toward maximization of placement figures on records led to dysfunctional competition in the form of monopolization and hiding of job orders and created antagonisms between Agency B interviewers.[13] If a job order is hidden by the official receiving it from an employer, then only he can fill the opening for placement credit, rather than allowing co-workers a chance. This means that suitable clients may leave the agency without a job referral even though a vacancy exists, because of a chance appearance at an interviewer's desk who does not have such an opening, rather than at the desk of the person hiding it. According to formal procedure, the order was to have been placed in a common file, open to the use of all officials.

Such competition was not as frequent an occurrence at Agency C as it was at the B locale, although different kinds of competition did occur. The difference seems to have come about as a result, among other things, of several changed conditions in time, and the different skill-levels of clients serviced in the two agencies. In 1949, according to Blau, there were many more clients available for jobs than there were vacancies. Jobs were difficult to find, but the statistical records emphasized placement productivity. In such a situation some officials felt the need for monopolization of those few job orders that were available. This was to obtain the statistical referral and placement credit involved, which was difficult to attain because of local market conditions. At the C locale, monopolization of orders for most occupational categories was unnecessary, for it was the skilled client and not the job that was in demand.

Agency C officials rarely monopolized orders for skilled clients because this would have been a useless practice for the end of raising production figures. In fact, they sometimes did the opposite by helping their colleagues find openings for clients. However, competition for scarce job orders for *unskilled clients* was not completely unknown at Agency C. Local conditions affect bureaucratic behavior. At Agency B there was a demand for jobs, and at Agency C a demand for skilled clients. This was reflected in the generally different actions of the officials at the two study locales.

Another reason for the difference in the two agencies is that the Agency B department Blau studied serviced mainly unskilled clients while Agency C served mostly skilled clients. In times of job scarcity, positions requiring little skill and training are generally more difficult to obtain than are vacancies for skilled workers. As mentioned, if monopolization occurred at all at Agency C, it was

---

[12] *Ibid.*, p. 46.
[13] *Ibid.*, pp. 46–47, and pp. 57–81. It should be mentioned that some cooperative practices *did* develop in one section at Agency B, unlike the observations Blau made for another section which was the highly competitive one. The difference was due, according to Blau, to structural differences between Agency B sections. Cooperative norms had developed in one section and this made competitive practices ineffective there. See his pp. 63–74.

likely to be for unskilled job vacancies, which were still rather scarce in relation to client demand.[14]

COMPETITION FOR CLIENTS

There was great competition in a section at Blau's locale for job orders, but this was not completely so at Agency C, as has been discussed. However, there was a degree of competition for what can be called "easier" *clients* at Agency C.[15] This was in response to the demand for skilled clients (as well as the desire for increased job satisfaction), rather than demand for job openings for skilled workers.[16]

---

[14] The total Agency B locale in 1956–1959, ten years after Blau's study, was *still* known by officials for a greater degree of competitive practices than at Agency C at the same date, even though skilled clients were now in demand at *both* branches. There may be some pervasive structural differences at both agencies accounting for this continued difference in amount of competition engaged in by staff. Agency B officials during the years of 1950–60, for example, worked under a special quantitative evaluation system where different operations as reported on individual statistical records received various point scores (and weights) according to quantity. The desire to make many points, which reflects an official's value to upper levels, might lead staff toward a high level of competition.

Yet, according to the Agency B management:

"It [the point scoring system] was an evaluation devise [*sic*] to measure quantitative achievement. It was never considered as a device to induce staff to maximize production.

". . . [this] individual quantitative achievement was introduced in this office [Agency B] in 1950 and was used in one section for a period of two years. In 1952 its use was extended throughout the entire office. [It was discontinued in 1961.]" (From a letter to the author by the bureau commissioner, top state-level official of the bureaucracy. The information above was sent to the commissioner's office by the Agency B management in response to questions about various Agency B operations.)

According to the Agency B management, the scoring scheme was *not meant* to be a device to maximize production, but this seems to have occurred despite managerial intent. Perhaps this led in part to the continued high level of competition at Agency B. Agency C did not operate under such a point system, and operations were merely recorded in quantity on the daily performance records.

[15] There are no quantitative data that can be presented in proof, but it appears from careful matching of the author's experiences as a participant with Blau's report, that Agency C competition for clients was still not as great as that described for job orders at an Agency B section.

[16] Blau's data offer no extensive information on whether or not officials at Agency B competed for clients as well as for job orders. However, some inferences can be made from his work. For example, one Agency B respondent explained: "I always *try* to see non-benefit applicants. *Most people* [interviewers] *prefer* them . . . because they want to work." (Blau, *op. cit.*, p. 91. Italics added.) As shall be seen above, Agency C interviewers also tried to interview nonbenefit applicants which sometimes led to competition for these more satisfying contacts, and easier interviews. Perhaps such competition also occurred at Agency B.

Blau also did make the observation that extreme competition for *job orders* occurred at the department he studied. However: "It did not occur in other departments, in which interviewers also competed for making the best records, but not for job openings, since each handled a different occupational category, and there were no common pools of job orders." (*Ibid.*, p. 60.) There were, in other words, differences in the degree and kind of competition between different departments at Agency B. (Perhaps one kind of competition at departments other than the one studied by Blau was that of competition for clients.) Different conditions at Agencies B and C, as has been seen, can also account for the differential degree and type of competition observed at the two locales.

Blau has written (in a personal communication to the author) that there were other forms of competition at his locale, in addition to the monopolization of job orders: ". . . there was some competition by trying to avoid difficult clients as well as in various other ways. . . ." (Letter dated October 3, 1961.)

Officials generally were supposed to interview clients in the order of their arrival, but sometimes delayed or speeded work, as necessary, in order to interview an "easier" client, thereby avoiding a recognized "difficult" case. Sometimes work was delayed in an entire section while officials busied themselves with "papers" and stretched interviews, trying to avoid a recognized difficult case, until one unfortunate interviewer could no longer stretch his work and had to interview the client.

Clients complained at delays, and also when some officials went a step further, calling "easy" clients outside the order of time at which they arrived, and hence ahead of other waiting workers. This meant that colleagues had to interview the more difficult cases that were left. Interpersonal relationships between bureaucrats were affected when officials became annoyed at one another for these competitive practices.

This competition for clients was related not only to the desire to increase production listed on statistical records, but also for increased job satisfaction. Difficult clients were often argumentative, and caused other frustrating difficulties which made dealing with them a harrowing experience.

EMPHASIS ON QUANTITY AND SUPERVISORY RECEPTION SIFTING POLICY

Supervisors were trying to maintain good sectional statistical records, referring to high-level production credited by their staff. This was because each supervisor was rated in good part by his own superior, the manager, on productivity of all interviewers combined in his section.

Superiors often forced reception officials to "put more through," meaning to seat more clients of all kinds for interviews. This demand, aimed at increasing productivity, was sometimes made even if few employment vacancies were available for specific client groups.

When many clients were waiting for service, the supervisor often relieved the official at the reception counter; the reception official now performing interviewing tasks and reducing the backlog of clients. The supervisor, temporarily acting as receptionist, tended to seat even more clients for interviews without reference to service that could be given, in an attempt to maximize statistical production figures. The number of interviews, and not reception counter service, counted on statistical production records.

Visibility (to the manager) of sectional production on statistical records and production goals set for his section, caused the supervisor to want many clients seated for interviews, often without complete reference to the organizational placement and unemployment insurance goals. To be sure, some workers for whom service was possible were seated. However, the goals of the reception sifting procedure to limit the flow of clients to those who could be serviced in the time available was being neglected where others were seated without regard to service factors, but only in the hope of maximization of production figures.

At the extreme, sometimes so many people waited that all seats in the waiting area were filled and some clients had to stand until called for an interview. With a large backlog of clients, the superior appealed for help to the manager, asking him to send interviewers on loan from other sections. These officials could help reduce the backlog. When this was done, the supervisor had more interviewers and therefore more production for the records of his section.

In this way interviewers were taken from their sections where they might have better been able to provide needed services, to handle another section's clients, many of whom should have been dismissed according to procedure at the reception counter with reappointment dates. A supervisor was thus able to maximize his own records at the expense of the other sectional superior's records.

Other superiors also "stuffed their boxes," which in agency argot meant seating more clients than could be efficiently interviewed. If many clients were waiting in other sections, these superiors also could demand help from the manager, asking for temporary loans of interviewers. At the least, a large number of waiting people served as justification for section supervisors *not* to lend interviewers to other sections. Superiors were frequently observed jockeying for position at rush periods by seating more clients than necessary, and then attempting to take interviewers from other sections on loan, while the other supervisors tended to point to the fact that they too had many applicants waiting and could not provide help. Supervisors and managers walked from one section reception counter to another at these times, "weighing" in their hands the number of client booklets in each intake box (which referred to the number waiting for interviews). This was done without reference to quality of service that could be given, but rather to quantity, i.e., the total *number* waiting. Managers then tried to allocate staff accordingly.

This supervisory action was dysfunctional because it wasted the time of clients and staff for the sake of supervisory competition, a far cry from the original aims of statistical production records. This practice also removed officials from the service of those who might have really needed help. However, functional ends were gained when one segment of the clothing industry was on layoff, overloading one section with work, while other segments were still at full employment, and few clients were reporting. In such situations it occurred that in one section interviewers worked frantically to keep up with the rush, while other interviewers in other sections had little if anything to do. Where loans were made under these conditions, functional results followed. The dysfunctional results occurred when the supervisor "stuffed the box," merely to be able to request extra interviewers and improve his sectional statistics at the expense of the co-superior's statistical totals. When many supervisors engaged in this activity at the same time, and conditions were rushed, many clients waited lengthy periods for interviews, for no reason except to maximize agency statistical records.

REACTION OF INTERVIEWING OFFICIALS TO SUPERVISORY "BOX STUFFING"

Interviewing officials were not oblivious to this supervisory action. When supervisors seated too many clients, officials modified their interviewing activity in response. "Stuffing the box" caused a great backlog of people waiting for interviews and this put pressure on officials to work faster. Deliberate slowdowns resulted when it became evident that the faster one worked, the more people there were waiting for service because of the supervisor's reception sifting policy.

Various dilatory tactics were employed. Clients were engaged in personal conversation. An official searched the files of all sections, stopping to consult with colleagues, even though he knew no jobs were available for the particular client. Some engaged in personal telephone calls, pretending they were speaking to employers or conducting official business. Many other delaying tactics were engaged in and the backlog grew, while clients fidgeted and milled about, waiting impatiently to be called for interviews.

Clients complained sharply when they realized that no service could be performed for them but they were still required to wait for long periods of time for interviews. These complaints caused some interviewers who were already angry at the supervisor for his reception sifting behavior to react accordingly with hostility or annoyance. Brusque treatment of the clients sometimes followed, especially when officials were pressured in rush periods, for this tended to fray tempers over and above supervisory or client actions. This was one element making for antagonisms between applicants and staff. This antagonism added to client hostility caused by the desire of some to be "sneaked out," which had been thwarted by the supervisor's reception behavior.

Many complaints were also directed at the receptionist (the supervisor in this situation), and thus he too was subjected to hostility.[17]

---

[17] This description above focuses on supervisory action when the superior filled in for interviewers at the reception counter. There were some officials who tried to impress superiors or who were strict conformists to procedures, fearing unlike the majority of their colleagues to informally deviate from supervisory requests. These nonsupervisory officials frequently engaged in practices similar to that described above and with the same results.

Sometimes the supervisor's presence near the reception counter caused even flexible reception interviewers to seat more clients than necessary in order to meet supervisory demands. In such cases colleagues tried to dispense with some of these "excess" clients by interviewing them rapidly in succession with no attempt at service. Poor statistical referral records which then resulted were often manipulated, as will be discussed in the next chapter.

Restrictive practices occurred when this rapid "interviewing" still did not serve to reduce the client load because the superior still hovered near the reception counter and the reception official was forced to seat more clients. This restriction also troubled the supervisor, for clients complained about waiting too long, and it was his duty to maintain proper operations and calm the ire of more agitated clients.

When nonsupervisory officials seated too many without the superior's presence, restrictive practices also tended to follow. When too many clients were waiting, the supervisor often relieved the official at the reception counter, so the official could interview; this in turn meaning that he had to interview some of the very same difficult clients he had seated while he was the

The superior could not effectively speed his subordinates' work because interviews naturally varied in length of time, depending on problems of the client. The supervisor knew he had seated difficult people for interviews, and as a result there was nothing he could do except "sweat out" the numerous barbed assaults.

The supervisor had one additional worry when the time of day approached noon, for if the backlog of applicants could not be serviced completely before the lunch period for staff, he would be left with a group of complaining people who would not be serviced until his staff returned from lunch one hour later. If he requested his staff to remain during the lunch hour to service those waiting, the subordinates would still require a full lunch-time period, and he would be left with insufficient personnel to handle the one o'clock rush. These worries, if he could not secure enough extra help, obliged the superior to dismiss more without service, and hence the staff "fixed" the supervisor for his activities, at the same time reducing the amount of work they had to do.

At such a point it tended to occur that all clients reporting were dismissed, because there were too many already waiting. Applicants who could have been serviced because they had skills that employers desired were also dismissed haphazardly, only because others had earlier been haphazardly seated for interviews. Sometimes there were still too many waiting in spite of the supervisor's dismissals, and the hour was very close to the lunch period. At such times the officials tended to interview these clients very quickly and carelessly only to be finished in time for lunch. In this situation clients had been kept waiting only to be rushed through interviews which turned out to be worthless.

Reception sifting procedure was being redefined in order to maximize production figures. Had the formal reception sifting procedure been followed, service would have been increased, public relations more completely maintained, and records could have been legitimately maximized. These informal changes caused deviation from service goals, and eventual restriction of output by staff, sometimes sacrificing the maximization of figures on records originally desired through the informal supervisory redefinition.

CONCLUSIONS

In this chapter we have traced the origin of statistical records at Agencies B and C, and have seen the transformation of statistical records toward dysfunctional ends. The "dynamics of bureaucracy" became "demonics of bureaucracy" and were adversely affecting client service, whereas the original change

---

receptionist. Since this was unpleasant, there was always a constraint for the reception official to try to avoid "stuffing the box." This led some receptionists to dismiss more clients, and to such an extent, that restrictive interviewer practices (to be discussed on other pages) were furthered. Other receptionists, however, were less affected by colleague pressures, and still "stuffed the box" to meet the superior's demand.

intended improved service to clients through better agency operations. There was "too much of a good thing" here; that is, supervisors and interviewers were interested in production, but became so highly interested in it that they forgot the original aims of the procedure. "Stuffing the box" is an example. There was a displacement of goals where "an instrumental value becomes a terminal value." [18] Statistical records, figures and recording procedure, instrumental to attainment of service-oriented goals, became terminal values; ends in and of themselves. Yet these are only hints of the final results of modifications of statistical recording procedure. The following chapters trace numerous other dysfunctional consequences, which are so extreme in nature that they actually match quotations from George Orwell's fictional *Nineteen Eighty-Four*. Statistics did turn out to be ". . . just as much a fantasy in their original version as in their rectified version," and, "a great deal of the time . . . [interviewers] *were* expected to make them up out of . . . [their] head[s]."

---

[18] Robert K. Merton, *Social Theory and Social Structure* (rev. ed., Glencoe: Free Press, 1957), p. 199.

Man, Work, and the Automated Feast

BEN B. SELIGMAN

▬

Automation is said to have ancient beginnings. To be sure, the technology from which it stems goes back several centuries, at least. Automatic devices in the middle eighteenth century included a mechanical loom for the manufacture of figured silks; James Watt's steam engine utilized a fly-ball governor which controlled the speed at which his contrivance operated; and it has been suggested that automation's basic concept—the linkage of machines—is evident in the detachable harpoon head of the Eskimo. Yet to assert that automation is simply the latest link in a great chain of industrial history obscures what is patently a new phenomenon. In the old days, industrial change developed through fission: division of labor was the key to progress and work was made available to a huge pool of unskilled persons who in the main had been forced to migrate from farm to city. Today, it is precisely these unskilled, together with

---

semi-skilled and even some of management's people, who are displaced and poured back into the pool. Furthermore, automation represents a marked acceleration of change with so cumulative a force that this alone spells a profound difference from what went on before.

Automation is already moving with a rapidity that threatens to tear apart existing social and organizational structures; according to some observers, it will even alter the habits of thought that men have up to now prided themselves on. Such a prospect is perhaps not surprising when we consider the cataclysmic results of the eighteenth century's Industrial Revolution: the changes then were so swift as to constitute a whole new phenomenon. And Marx and Weber and Sombart had shown convincingly how human and social transformation accompanied technological transformation.

Now, new industrial functions, new economic forms, new work habits, and new social headaches are being created in ways that signify a kind of dialectic leap. Even John Diebold, who claims to have invented the word "automation" and whose ebullient advocacy of computer technology has done much to spread the gospel, confesses: "I believe that [automation] marks a break with past trends, a qualitative departure from the more conventional advance of technology that began with jagged pieces of flint and progressed up to the steam engine."

Why is this so? Up to recent times, technology simply sought to substitute natural force for animal or human force. In the early days, primacy of place was given to windmills and waterfalls. Then came metallurgical discoveries; and the screw and the lathe made possible the machine, essentially a contrivance which man could watch in action. But man remained at the center of the whole business, essential to both operation and control, still more or less the maker and master of materials. With automation, man not only loses irrevocably his function as *homo faber*; he no longer even possesses the character of *animal laborans*. At best, he is a sometime supervisor of a flow process. Actual control is removed from him and given to an electronic contraption whose feedbacks and servomechanisms make it possible to produce goods and manipulate information in a continuous system, without human participation.

To realize what automation implies, we must examine the kinds of machines employed and see what they do to people and organizations. Essentially, today's scientific upheaval comprises four aspects: the conversion of industrial materials into a flow; the setting of uniform standards so that output can be treated as a flow; the utilization of electronic computers with built-in feedbacks to enable the exercise of automatic control; and the application of new energy sources to the whole process. Thus, raw materials, which represent the "input" of an industry, must be handled without human hands, as in a modern meatpacking plant. Production, at one time a series of discrete steps, is completely integrated by means of transfer machines. In some cases, computers tied to cams or templates can make the producing machine follow a predetermined pattern with greater accuracy and sharper tolerances than were dreamed possible in the heyday of the skilled machinist. Computers, into which all sorts of complex information can be fed by "programmers," automatically correct errors. A wide range of goods is now produced in this startling manner—chemicals, automobiles, steel, glassware, electric bulbs, television sets, beverages, and drugs, to name a few. Factories are able to function 24 hours a day, 365 days a year, while manpower needs are reduced dramatically. And with the development of nuclear energy for industrial power, manufacturers no longer need to be near their source of raw materials; they can set up their plants closer to markets, or—if they are seeking to escape the union organizer—in the most isolated of places. Yet one industry necessarily must relate itself more intimately with the next; a seamless web envelops all the entrepreneurs and their works.

There is no lack of Panglossian attempt to assuage our concern. In the long run, we are told (who lives that long?), natural economic forces will work out the necessary adjustments. A shorter work week might stem from automation, suggest some experts; but at the thought that men might work less than the ordained forty hours a week, all kinds of people, from Secretary of Labor Arthur Goldberg down, immediately explode with great cries of anguish. Or we are told that human desires are insatiable: demand will grow, enough to reabsorb men displaced by machines—which calls to mind an apocryphal conversation between Henry Ford II and Walter Reuther. "How," said Ford, as he revealed his automatic factory, "are these machines going to pay you dues, Walter?" "How," replied Reuther, "will they buy your autos?"

We are assured that more jobs will be created by new industry, that higher skills will be required, that economic stability will be guaranteed by automation. There are pitifully few facts available to support these euphoric hopes. More likely a vast trauma awaits us all, to use Irving Howe's phrase. Then why automate? The underlying motives were exposed with unaccustomed bluntness in one of the trade journals recently when an automation advocate wrote: "[Machines] don't call in sick; they don't talk back; they work early and late and without overtime; they don't get tired; and last, but far from least, they don't line up at the cashier's window every week for a slice of the operating funds."

The automobile industry illustrates how an integrated set of machines can function. There the engine production line, for example, consists of a series of drilling, boring, and milling operations connected by transfer machines which move the engine blocks from one point to the next. Tolerances are checked automatically; if something is awry, the whole line is stopped by an electronic device. Or one can see an automatic assembly machine put the components of a television set on a printed board and then solder them into place. These are repetitive operations and their economic justification stems from the replacement market. There is not much of a style factor here and such model changes as do occur can be handled with relative ease. Yet even where variation in the product is essential, as in machine tools, the operation still can be made automatic.

The machine tool industry, mainly a congeries of small shops employing highly skilled labor, has notoriously resisted innovation. But since it is now so closely allied to Air Force and Space technology, it has been impelled willy-nilly by the needs of the armed forces to the adoption of newer techniques. Formerly, a human operator worked from blueprints, controlling his equipment with a variety of jigs and templates. To avoid waste, and perhaps because he was concerned with craftsmanship, he worked slowly. But now, all the variables can be "programmed" into computers, and with the technique known as "numerical control" these electronic brains direct the same cutting tools, handle the same jigs and templates once operated by the machinist. Most important of all, this sort of automation is economically feasible for small lots in which there are changes in product design.

The key here is feedback, the simplest case of which is the home thermostat turning a furnace on and off in order to maintain a constant room temperature. In essence, signals are sent from one part of the automated line to another, correcting errors, shifting power loads, or modifying the speed of the line. No human need adjust gauges or read thermometers or press buttons. Feedback or servomechanisms do a better control job then humans, especially when many elements are involved. Whereas the human eye can follow the motion of a gauge at about two cycles a second, a servomechanism does about 100 a second. Now, marry feedback to a computer and automation is complete. The computers, really giant adding machines and calculators, receive information from the gauges and thermometers, analyze the data, and then transmit new instructions to other gauges and instruments.

Computers, whose basic concept goes back to Blaise Pascal, were developed in their electronic form during World War II to help guns hit their targets more efficiently. There are two basic types—the analog and digital computer. The former is a kind of electronic slide rule able to apply higher mathematics to problems of rates of change in various flows. However fast it might have been, for the engineer, mathematician, and operations researcher it was not fast enough. So the digital computer was devised, a machine that employs the binary number system and consequently can only add and subtract. This is no impediment, for like an electronic abacus, the digital computer sends its impulses forward at an unbelievable speed, giving it a marked advantage over the analog machine. Moreover, digital computers have "memory" drums in which data can be stored for future use. The electrical pulses in a digital computer last less than one-millionth of a second. Information can be extracted from the memory drum in about ten-millionths of a second.

Of course, a considerable amount of human brain power is expended before the computer can be put to work. This is the science of programming. Instructions are written on a process sheet, then coded and entered on tape. That is,

English is translated into machine language. The control unit of the system then "reads" the tape, gives forth with the appropriate electrical impulses, and sets the servomechanisms to work. One writer compared the operation to an old-fashioned player piano in which the punched holes in the roller actuate the hammers to bang out either the "Basin Street Blues" or a Beethoven sonata.

Lending a nightmarish quality to these developments is the current scientific talk about artificial intelligence. Machines, it is said, can be built to recognize certain patterns and can learn to plan simple tasks. While the computer may be something of a moron, awaiting instructions from a human Ph.D., the fact that an electrical contrivance can be made to learn anything is astonishing enough. If a heuristic or generalized solution is sufficient, then a thinking computer is no longer science fiction. Chess-playing machines are at least feasible: the only problem seems to be that they would have to review the outcomes of all possible plays and that might take centuries. Perhaps that is what makes them morons.

The names one often sees bandied about—PERT, ALGOL, COBOL, GECOM, SURE—are merely abbreviations for specific programming methods, each utilizing one or more computer installations constructed by Burroughs, Bendix, Rand, or IBM. PERT, for example—Program Evaluation and Review Technique—is based on the concept of a tree network with alternatives to be considered at each node of the tree. Since the computer works so much faster than the human mind and also uses stored information, it can review the accumulating cost of a flow process at each step and then direct the sequence of decisions along the critical or least-cost pathway. PERT originated in the Polaris Missile Project when it became essential to keep track of some 11,000 contractors and subcontractors. Again, military need provided the research motive. So complex can these matters become that the Defense Department had to work out a standardized pidgin English to coordinate programming.

It is sometimes said that the considerable investment in these systems precludes all but the largest firms from employing them. This is not so. Any number of consulting services are available for smaller concerns to meet data-processing needs, and some firms have set up cooperative research centers. Span, Inc. is one such co-op doing the bookkeeping for a number of insurance companies in Hartford; Tamcor maintains brokerage records in New York, and IBM, the biggest of them all, makes its equipment available to all comers through 70 locations around the country. In fact, the latter is now compiling tape libraries, dubbed by one journal "computer laundromats." Thus, the new technology is available to anyone who wants to make use of it.

All this must be worthwhile, for rental costs run from $12,000 a year up and outright purchase of computer equipment can cost millions. Some $2 billion has been invested in computers by private companies since 1950, and this does not include what the government has spent. It is estimated that by 1970 computer sales will hit $500 million a year or about $2\frac{1}{2}$ times present outlays. When the Pennsylvania Railroad automated its Conway, Pa. yards, it expected to recoup its $34 million cost within three years. At Ford, 9 workers at 3 machines putting holes into crankshafts replaced 39 workers at 39 machines. A Philco plant reduced its work force by 25 per cent by using printed circuitry. A computer engineer once remarked that he could cut one man off the payroll for every $5,000 spent on automated equipment. And finally, the initial cost of installing a computer system, according to Wassily Leontief, comes to no more than 6 per cent of total plant investment. The value of the new technology seems undeniable.

By now "Detroit" automation is quite well known. Automatic machines, linked by transfer equipment, move engine blocks through a complete manufacturing process, performing 530 precision cutting and drilling operations in $14\frac{1}{2}$ minutes as compared to 9 hours in a conventional plant. The Chrysler Corporation's recent breakthrough on computer "balancing" of assembly lines, essentially a "combinatorial" problem, now defines each job so rigidly that little liberties like a worker's taking a few minutes out for a smoke become serious impediments to the smooth flow of cars. An automated power plant in Louisiana saved $175,000 in fuel, $100,000 in maintenance, $1.5 million in eliminating delays and mishaps, and $500,000 in labor. A Jones & Laughlin sheet-plate mill turns out strip at the speed of 70 miles an hour with no labor other than the supervision of engineers. Punch-card systems in a reversing roughing mill modify ingot shapes, and the computer even "remembers" what to do when the forms have to be changed. Foundry work, traditionally a hand operation, is now being tied to the computer. In petroleum and chemicals, the story is almost ancient: as far back as 1949 catalytic cracking plants were turning out 41,000 barrels a day with instruments and only a few workers to watch gauges. In a Texaco refinery the computer controls 26 flow rates, 72 temperatures, 3 pressure levels, and 3 gas combinations. General Electric uses segmented "automation," that is, batch production, for motors of varying models up to 30 horsepower. Ribbon machines make 800 electric bulb blanks a minute, running without end, and requiring only one worker who stands by to make an occasional adjustment.

Even in the office and retail store, one finds evidence of the new technology. Although office work has expanded tremendously since 1910 (today 17 per cent of the labor force is found in the office as compared to 5 per cent fifty years ago), it is precisely the enormous quantity of paper work and routine operation that makes automation feasible here. Banks, utilities, insurance companies, and government bureaus have eagerly made room for yards of the new equipment— so much faster is the computer than the old-fashioned bookkeeper and clerk. As a result, office work no longer is the growth industry it was—at least in terms of jobs. One California firm, studied by Mrs. Ida R. Hoos, put only two accounting operations on a computer and promptly eliminated 300 out of 3,200 office jobs and drastically altered the functions of some 980 others.

In retailing, automation starts with inventory and accounting records. Sales data are transmitted to control centers where billing, inventory, and credit information is stored. Bad credit risks are automatically checked and information returned to the sales clerk before the package can be wrapped. Sylvania and IBM have been working on automatic check-out counters for supermarkets—the number of cash registers would be reduced, as well as the number of workers. Ferris wheels, conveyor belts, chutes, and slides, all controlled by electronic computers, deliver garments from receiving platforms to stockrooms and even return the merchandise to the ground floor if necessary. Eventually we will pay our traffic penalties to a computer: in Illinois, records of driver violations are stored in a computer and the fines calculated by machine.

This, then, is the automated feast. Tasks are accomplished with unimaginable speed. Decisions are made by coded instructions and errors quickly detected. Facts are stored and extracted from memory drums. The machines learn and "perceive": they analyze stock market conditions; establish rocket flight patterns before the shot is fired into space; write television scripts that compare favorably with what is now available; compose music; translate; and play games. They combine high technical competence with just enough of an I.Q. to keep them tractable. They do precisely the kind of work to which junior executives and semi-skilled employees are usually assigned.

No slur is intended here, for in addition to the ordinary worker it is the middle manager, the backbone of the average corporation, who will be most affected by automation. He has a bleak future indeed, when computers relay information to each other, do all the scheduling, and control manufacturing from inception to the point at which the product is packaged and rolled onto a box car. It is rather the archon of industry—as Edward Ziegler has dubbed him —who ultimately wins out, for with elimination of both plant and office staff, this man at the very top gains even tighter control over the decision-making process. The sort of organizational looseness that prevailed prior to the advent of the computer is eliminated, and corporate structure becomes more formal, more "integrated," since with the computer there must be greater "cooperation." The number of links in the chain of command is reduced drastically; vice-presidents are soon out of a job. No less an authority than Herbert A. Simon of Carnegie Tech has said that by 1985 machines can dispense with all middle echelons in business. Production planning is handed over to the digital demon, while both the middle manager and the displaced worker drive taxicabs. The sociologist may very well ask, whither the American dream of status and success?

Quite often, the computer engineer tries to build his own empire within the corporation. Fresh to the ways of business life, he has unabashedly played havoc with established relations. He and his programmer cohorts, cutting across all divisions, have often ignored and undermined the authority of department heads and vice-presidents. Many middle management people in automated companies now report that they are awaiting the ax, or if more fortunate, retirement. Bright young men leave for non-automated firms, hoping to reach the top elsewhere before the computer catches up with them. Sometimes the new elite does lose out: it has not been unknown for a computer installation to be yanked as a result of corporate internecine warfare.

Usually though, archon and engineers are in complete accord. With the computer creating certain expectations, the firm must operate through a series of highly rigid sequences. Flexibility has been dispensed with, for the whole plant is now a single technical structure in which total performance must be "optimized." The engineer examines each step in the process solely in terms of efficiency—industrial logic of the most unremitting kind takes primacy of place. Under automation, the engineer or mathematician is *the* skilled man in the plant, while workers, those who remain and those who do not, are expected to adjust with equanimity to a situation for which they have had no responsibility. In fact, the engineer's attitude quite often is tough and hard, too much so for ordinary men: what the worker doesn't know, says he, won't hurt him. The scientists appreciate only "facts": the human problems of an industrial system frequently have little meaning for them. Unlike the organization men of the 50s, they are usually "inner directed," disturbers of the corporate peace, free-booters in pursuit of the idols of efficiency. Since the latter is measured by high profit and low cost, such scientific ruthlessness meets the approval of the archon. The latter really doesn't know what the scientist is doing: top management merely voices a faith based on payoff. Thus the programmer, who often assumes the aspect of a medieval alchemist, runs his own show, designing projects, cutting corporate red tape with abandon, and advising the industrial relations department that labor displacement is "none of your business." At best, the engineer can parrot some devotee of the conventional economic wisdom by repeating that automation creates new demand and new jobs, upgrades the worker and inspires everyone with its challenge. There must be a certain glory in the marvels of automation: but the men who once worked in the chemical plants, oil refineries, and steel mills are now out of sight and out of mind.

Between 1953 and 1960, a million and a half jobs disappeared. In one plant, studied by Floyd Mann of Michigan State University, automation reduced the work force by half. In the electrical industry, output increased 21 per cent between 1953 and 1961, while employment declined 10 per cent. There was a loss of 80,000 production jobs in steel during the decade of the 50s. In the shift from aircraft to missiles, 200,000 jobs went down the technological drain. For the 5-year period 1955–1960, production workers in automobile factories were down 21 per cent. All this displacement occurred in an affluent society that itself went through four postwar recessions each of which left behind an increasingly hard-core residue of unemployment—3 per cent in 1951–53; 4 per cent in 1955–57; and 5 per cent in 1959–60.

Full employment for the next 10 years means creating 12 million new jobs— 25,000 a week, or almost double the number of new openings in the 1947–57

JOB DISSATISFACTION IN AN AUTOMATED PLANT

One apparent source of *dissatisfaction* with job content in the automated plant may be labeled feelings of *alienation* (if it is possible to borrow this Marxian term without its overtones of Hegelian mysticism). The worker on the automated line is alienated in the sense that he no longer has control over the machine and the work pace, machining skills previously acquired are no longer of use, and it becomes increasingly difficult to identify what the transfer machine does as *his* work. The following quotations from interviews may illustrate this feeling:

(I don't like) the lack of feeling responsible for your work. The feeling that you're turning out more work but knowing it's *not yours really* and not as good as you could make it if you had control of the machine like before.

It's a completely different feel of work. On my old job, I controlled the machine. On my present job, the *machine controls me*.

Another source of job dissatisfaction on the automated line was the feeling of tension or anxiety reported by some workers. These increased tensions were apparently attributable to a combination of factors involving the increased speed of production, the constant attention required, and the cost of mistakes and frequency of breakdowns of automated machinery. The following comments from interviews may be cited as illustrations of this feeling:

You are very rushed on automation. You are under *pressure all the time*. That's why it's so hard to learn and some can't do it—can't stand the pressure.

(Automation is) just different all the way through. You've *got to be aware all the time* and push the right button. If you push the wrong one it could cost around $13,000 and is very dangerous. I pushed a wrong button and stuff flew all over. I was lucky but it cost the company $13,000 to fix the machine.

Source: William A. Faunce, "Automation and the Automobile Worker," *Social Problems*, 6:1 (Summer 1958).

decade. Extending the period to 1961, we find that output rose 65 per cent while the number of production and maintenance jobs declined. True, white collar workers increased 7 per cent, but now automation is making them just as insecure. If we assume that demand in the 60s will expand at the same rate as it did in 1947–57, then output by 1970 may very well be 50 per cent greater. However, if the present rate of productivity is maintained, then the number of required man-hours will have increased by 12 per cent, providing only 75 million jobs at the end of the decade. Thus, about 8 million persons, 10 per cent of the labor force, will have no work. And this is a moderate forecast, for should the secular growth rate fall below 3 per cent per annum, as is conceivable, output will have gone up about 40 per cent. Add to this the effects of automation, and the job increase by 1970 may be only 2 million, leaving a residue of perhaps 10 million persons without jobs.

Is this so weird a tale? The ever optimistic Bureau of Labor Statistics' chief, Ewan Clague, recently admitted to an Arden House conclave that 200,000 jobs a year would be lost through "disemployment by automation." He found that in 70 per cent of manufacturing industries such "disemployment" comprised four-fifths of the jobs lost. And his estimate did not include computer displacement among white collar workers.

The unions now know what automation can do to them. No matter how strong the security clause in a collective bargaining agreement, the serious drop in membership for most internationals is a harbinger of approaching catastrophe. Further, it is so much easier now for plants to escape to communities where unionism seems to represent little threat. And in such towns, management does not worry about a labor supply, for under automation what need is there for workers? There are also related problems for the unions: What happens to seniority? How about pension rights? Can traditional unionism with its roots in craft concepts cope with an industry whose shape has assumed the form of a process? Is the programmer a part of the bargaining unit? Or does his role in decision-making place him in management's ranks? And how effective is the strike when a handful of engineers can operate the whole works? This last question was answered in Port Arthur, Texas, where about 3,700 production workers walked off the job at an oil refinery, leaving 600 white collar employees and supervisors behind to run the plant at 65 per cent of capacity. One labor relations man was reported to have said: "Maybe they ought to have removed a couple of transistors."

Some have argued that the displaced can be directed to jobs in the service and white collar fields. What jobs? Automation, as we have already noted, has been moving into these fields in the last three years just as rapidly as elsewhere. In 1960, at the Census Bureau, 50 technicians plus a battery of computers did the work that it had taken over 4,000 statisticians to do in 1950. The little black code numbers now appearing on bank checks inform us that our accounts are debited, credited, and cleared by a scanning device hooked into a computer. It is poor consolation, moreover, to be told that employment adjustments will be made via the A & P route—attrition and pregnancy—for this is an admission that there really are no jobs for those who want to work.

The notion that all who have been displaced by machines will quickly find new employment is a cheerful thought, something like whistling while walking through a cemetery. Some years ago, such cheerfulness was quite common, even among labor leaders. Walter Reuther's early speeches all but embraced the computer, so high was the regard for technology, so powerful the belief in growth and progress. The Joint Economic Committee's 1955 report on automation urged laissez-faire, for no serious problems were envisioned. In the short space of seven years, hesitation and doubts have cropped up. There is no longer the ancient and well-regarded optimism that more machines mean expanded employment elsewhere or that automation will upgrade workers. It is evident, rather, that the new technology enforces a deterioration of skills for the great mass of workers and offers only the social junk pile for the unskilled and untutored.

What is the solution? Frankly, there is none, at least none of a definitive character. The numerous suggestions for dealing with the pressing problems that stem from automation are all piecemeal, pecking at a spot here and a point there. No amount of federal fiscal tinkering will meet the immediate needs of those who are attached to a dying industry. Economic growth, while essential, will not of itself put to work again the idle coal miner, ex-machinist, and troubled bookkeeper whose jobs have vanished like the first atom bomb tower. Administration economists believe that automated unemployment can be solved by turning on ordinary Keynesian tap valves: it's all a matter of failing effective demand, they assert. There seems little awareness in important circles that the American economy is undergoing deep-rooted and subtle structural changes and that it will take massive economic and social therapy to assuage the hurt.

The AFL-CIO has been advocating a series of measures, including meaningful retraining programs, especially for workers over forty, area redevelopment, better unemployment insurance, an improved national placement service, special help to relocate the "disemployed," higher pensions, and even shorter hours. But will we—American Management, American unions, Congress, the administration—really expend the necessary hard thought? Don Michael doubts it, for it is unlikely, says he, that ". . . our style of pragmatic making-do and frantic crash programs can radically change in the next few years. . . ." It is hard to disagree.

Consider the retraining effort. A case of too little, if not too late, it is hardly a roaring success. In West Virginia, the federal pilot scheme plus the state's own 22-month-old program have been able to uncover new jobs for only half the 3,000 "graduates." Most of the others simply returned to the ranks of the unemployed. In Pennsylvania, 1,760 persons enrolled in retraining courses in 1957. Of these, 884 completed their re-education, 741 obtained new jobs. The state had a half million unemployed at the time.

Where private enterprise undertakes some corrective steps, it is usually found that a labor union had been doing the prodding, as in the meat-packing industry. Yet when 433 workers were laid off in Armour's Oklahoma City plant, only 60 could qualify for retraining and those who did secure new employment had to accept a lower rate of pay. Some firms are genuinely disturbed about the effects of automation. For example, U.S. Industries, a manufacturer of electronic equipment, and the machinists union have agreed upon a jointly managed fund to study the entire question. The company's president John Snyder, at least acknowledges that each one of his machines sends 60 workers scurrying to the unemployment insurance offices. Incidentally, one of U.S. Industries' contributions is the invention of automatic equipment to train displaced workers for typing and similar tasks.

There have been other experiments in adjustment. Some take the form of liberal severance-pay allowances. One of the earliest such schemes, though not related to automation per se, was the famous 1936 Washington Agreement between the railroad companies and the unions. Displaced workers receive 60 per cent of their average pay as severance compensation for periods as long as five years whenever mergers occur. In cases of relocation, moving expenses are paid and losses resulting from forced sale of homes reimbursed. More recently, another generous plan was agreed upon by TWA and its navigators, who if replaced by automatic instruments will receive $25,000 plus $400 a month for three years as severance. In addition, the now footloose navigators will be given free lifetime travel passes on the airline. Thus they will have at least acquired mobility and will be able to search for jobs in all corners of the globe. Yet such measures offer no genuine solution: they are mere palliatives, for they fail to confront the fundamental question—what does a man do with his time, either during the temporary period of affluence, or when the windfall resources will have given out, or for that matter, even when he has not been detached from industry?

Not every arrangement exhibits a handsome concern for the displaced. In the coal fields a contemptible alliance between John L. Lewis and the operators has cast adrift almost 300,000 miners. The coal industry, caught between the grinders of competitive fuels and high operating costs, was thoroughly run-down by the mid-40s. Deciding not to worry any more about the unemployed at the pits, Lewis acquiesced in rapid technological change. Output per day rose from 6.4 tons in 1949 to 14.4 tons in 1961; one ton of coal now requires less than half the labor it did a decade ago. At the Paradise, Kentucky coal field an automatic shovel larger than the Statue of Liberty strips 200 tons of material in one scoop. In Harvey Swados's words, Lewis decided to trust to time and mortality to resolve the problem of the unemployed. And so the coal industry no longer suffers from economic decay. With a return on investment of 7.5 per cent, it compares favorably with steel and oil. To hasten the day when his union can depend upon a healthy industry for its 40-cent per ton royalty, Lewis directed the mine workers to invest in sundry mine operations and even lent $35 million to Cyrus Eaton, whose interests include peace movements as well as coal. Of course, it would have been troublesome to apprise the membership of these transactions, so all the deals were carried through with great secrecy, only to be smoked out last year in a Tennessee lawsuit. A a recent convention of the union, an innocent delegate who suggested that perhaps something might be done for the unemployed was "... verbally torn to pieces by a buckshot charge of oratory from John L. Lewis himself." Declining dues are amply compensated for by investment returns in banks, mines, railroads, and power plants. Meanwhile, 300,000 miners continue to rot in the idle towns of Pennsylvania and West Virginia.

This sort of cooperation could set a strange trend if other unions were to adopt the Lewis formula. One that did is Harry Bridges's West Coast Longshoremen's International. Several years ago, the ILWU signed an agreement with the Shipping Association that was hailed as a reply to automation. Indeed, the retirement benefits are quite munificent and the pay scale was increased somewhat, but at the same time the employers were given the go-ahead signal to install a whole range of technological improvements which will virtually exclude entire blocs of workers not yet ready to retire. Moreover, the new work rules, extracted by the employers as a price for the higher pay and liberalized pensions, have intensified work loads on the docks virtually to the human breaking point.

Thus, one comes back to an immediate step, which though not by any means a "solution," nevertheless offers a practicable way for mitigating some of the effects of automation—the shorter work week. Mere mention of this is apt to send a shudder down the backs of administration economists and devotees of the conventional wisdom. Expressing their horror at the thought that man should have even more leisure than he now enjoys, the latter urge that a shorter work week means less production and higher costs. And in the present context of growthmanship, this is unthinkable. Arthur Goldberg, whose grasp of legal subtleties contrasts sharply with his simplistic formulations of economic issues, warned the International Ladies' Garment Workers' Union recently that fewer hours per week would "... impair adversely our present stable price structure [and] make our goods less competitive both at home and abroad...." The enormous productive capacity of America's industry was conveniently forgotten, a capacity so enhanced by automation that it can more than compensate for the alleged loss of output. And this is to say nothing about the quality and content of contemporary "production"—that would require another essay. The point to observe now is the curious inner tension of an industrial system whose fundamental Puritan outlook demands an incessant, unremitting outpouring of goods (for what?) while at the same time it imposes dreary idleness and dismal futures on those to whom the cornucopia is directed. We may well ask, what is the feedback in this insane circle?

But to return to the shorter work week—a cursory review of its history would demonstrate how completely reasonable it is. Prior to 1860, the rule was dawn to dusk with as much as 72 hours as the weekly standard. Demands for a shorter span were met with the contention that 12 hours a day, 6 days a week had been divinely ordained in order to strengthen worker morality. Three decades later the work week had been shortened by 12 hours. In 1910, the average ranged from 51 to 55 hours, and at that time a work force of 34 million produced a Gross National Product of about $37 billion. The work week continued to shrink: in 1920, it was 48 hours; in 1929, 44 hours; and since 1946 40 hours. By 1955, the labor force had almost doubled while GNP increased 10-fold as compared to 1910. And all the time the work week kept declining, about 13 hours in a 45-year span, or roughly 15 minutes a year.

Was anyone hurt? Did productivity lag? Has technology been impeded? The depression years aside, whatever unemployment did occur would have been unquestionably greater without the steady drop in hours. A continuation of this secular decline would cut back the normal work week by one hour every four years. According to one estimate, this might create about a million jobs a year which, together with the normal increase in job openings, could really begin to cut into the displacement caused by automation. When Harry van Arsdale of the New York electricians' union obtained a 5-hour day, he was savagely flayed for selfishness and lack of patriotism. Even the labor movement felt embarrassed. Arsdale insisted that he was only seeking to "spread the work." Now it seems, according to Theodore Kheel, the industry's arbitrator, that well over 1,000 new jobs will be made available as a result of the union's action.

What has happened in agriculture presents, in a sense, an object lesson we ought to heed. As W. H. Ferry remarked in a perceptive paper on affluence and plenty, the farm is technology's most notorious victory. Here abundance has become an economic catastrophe. So advanced is our agricultural establishment that even the 10 per cent of the labor force it now employs is too much. Farm output increased 77 per cent between 1910 and 1954, while land used for crops went up only 15 per cent. During the same period, labor on farms as measured by man-hours dropped over 30 per cent. This suggests an almost threefold rise in productivity. According to the late John D. Black, a leading farm expert, the major element in this change unquestionably was the substitution of machine power for muscle power. Yet the economic and political thrust of our system is such that 70 to 80 per cent of the federal government's spending on agriculture goes to counteract the price impact of an ever accumulating surplus.

The parallel between farm and industry is startling. There is enough grain in storage to feed everyone from Maine to Hawaii, but some 50 million Americans barely manage to subsist, even today. The steel industry functions at 65 per cent of capacity, or thereabouts, while thousands of able-bodied men are shoved aside by automation. Strategic curtailment of production is employed, like the farm parity program, to distort the genuine capacities of our economy. Technology, rather than man, becomes the central focus of existence, and at the same time that it destroys, for example, the belief in the family farm, it seemingly ought to compel a desiccated concept of resource allocation and optimum production to retire in favor of a philosophy of distribution. But we really have no adequate social theory to deal with the latter. The ideas of a Galbraith, a C. Wright Mills, a Paul Goodman, or a Harvey Swados deal only with aspects of the problem. We await to be told what is happening to us, what we need to do. And even then we shall not listen.

It is of course a common cliché that scientific advances have outrun our capacity to deal with them. Technology, the practical and material basis of life, has acquired a tidal force of its own which threatens to inundate human thought. Moreover, modern technology, as evidenced by automation, manifests no orderly growth. Its leads and lags, its uneven development, create new power centers that result in unaccustomed strains. To be sure, this has happened before, but always at immense human cost. It is this that the high priests of automation fail to grasp, while those of us who are merely bystanders can only hope that society will eventually catch up with the engineers and scientists and archons of industry who see only a handsome profit in what the machine can do. . . .

The correspondents[1] fall into three distinct classes: (1) engineers for whom the shock of recognition induces a state of grandiloquent nitpicking and a continuing refusal to face up to automation's social consequences; (2) young professors of business administration whose training in conventional wisdom has launched them into perpetual maunderings through the bogs of post-classical economics; and (3) serious persons who while disagreeing with some of my observations have indeed sought to grapple with the core of the problem.

Let me dispose first of the engineers: (One wrote to me privately, saying: "The social problems of automation *must* be solved! They *will* be solved!" Nice sloganeering, but how?). . . . While the engineers are arguing about when is a computer not a computer, they forget all about the ultimate consequences of the new technology—the creation of a vast economic and social underworld, a subculture of poverty enclosing a fourth of the population to which automation per se now contributes to the tune of 200,000 idle souls a year. Perhaps they feel about this as did a visiting English economist who told a group of West Coast academicians: "They're only Negroes, Puerto Ricans, and itinerant farmers."

Now, according to the professor of business administration, there is no such thing as Detroit automation, computers and feedback are mere science fiction, the Cleveland auto plant is a Potemkin village built by Henry Ford II, the unemployed in Detroit and Omaha and Pittsburgh displaced by machines are out of work because they're just plain lazy or uneducated, and the initials IBM stand for something like "intercontinental ballistic missile." Seriously, where has he been, lo these last ten years? Hasn't he seen any of the new installations in industry, let alone all the data-processing equipment in offices, banks, and retail stores? Has he ever talked with a worker displaced by a machine? Is he so unaware of the research efforts of the computer manufacturers that he believes bookkeepers to be a surviving breed? Ah yes, the professor teaches middle managers. The poor professor soon won't have anyone to teach.

---

[1] Reply by Mr. Seligman to discussion of his article appearing in the Letters from Readers Department of *Commentary* (December 1962), pp. 533–534.

PRE-AUTOMATED WORK—PASTURES OF PLENTY

The Migrants

These people who travel the fields come from the classically dispossessed groups. They are Texas Mexicans, Southern Negroes, Puerto Ricans, winos from skid row, Oakies from the thirties who stayed on in the culture of poverty. On the East Coast some 50,000 move from Florida to the North, most of them Negroes. From Texas come 75,000 who travel to the Mountain States and the Northwest. These are primarily of Mexican extraction. In the rich wheat fields from Texas to Canada, 50,000 work. On the Pacific Coast another 100,000 are on the move. The Braceros number some 40,000 a year.

Taken all in all, men, women, children, and counting the Braceros there are around 2,000,000 human beings who live and work under inhuman conditions. In 1959 the Secretary of Labor computed the average Bracero wage, which is a fair index of what all of these people are paid: it came to $.50 an hour. In the same period a congressional study estimated that a family of Texas migrants, with five workers in the field, would make just over $3,000 a year. That means $600 to each worker for a full year's work. . . . (p. 55)

Life in California

California agriculture is the richest in the nation, and its agricultural suffering is perhaps the most spectacular. People work ten-, eleven-, and twelve-hour days in temperatures over one hundred degrees. Sometimes there is no drinking water; sometimes big common barrels of it are used. Women and children work on ladders and with hazardous machinery. (The Industrial Welfare Commission was told in 1961 that 500 children are maimed each year.) Babies are brought to the fields and placed in "cradles" of wood boxes. . . . (pp. 49–50)

Far to the South, in the Imperial Valley of California, the living is, if anything, more terrible than in Stockton. A friend of mine wrote me of some of the people there. One family he described lives in a shack and sleeps on flattened pasteboard boxes on the floor. There is no heat, and since the man of the house has been driven out of the fields by Braceros there is often no food. The mother is breastfeeding her infant—and her four-year-old as well—since that is the only way he will eat. (In this detail there is an eerie echo of the occasion in *The Grapes of Wrath* when the young girl breastfeeds a starving Oakie man. That scene was set almost thirty years ago.) . . . (p. 51)

Americans and Braceros

I drove past the fields with an organizer from the Agricultural Workers Organizing Committee of the AFL-CIO. He had grown up in this area and had known the field as a child. As we passed each farm, he told me who was working there. Whenever he saw a group of Braceros, his voice became sharp. "They are poor people," he said. "That is why they come here, and work for so little. The growers get them cheap, and they know that the union can't organize them. So that keeps the rates down for the American workers. We don't want to hurt these poor people; they are like us. But it is no way to help them to hurt us. Let the government work out some kind of a deal with Mexico for aid, or something like that. But let the American farm workers have a decent living without having to hate other poor people." . . . (p. 50)

Source: Reprinted with permission of The Macmillan Company from *The Other America: Poverty in the United States* by Michael Harrington. Copyright 1962 by Michael Harrington.

. . . I consider the Lewis-Bridges response despicable because of its undercurrent of desperate cynicism. [The] understandable defense of the ILWU contract does not tell us what happened to the "B" men and the casuals on the docks. These workers—several thousand of them—are not "fully registered" and therefore unable to enjoy the handsome benefits won by Bridges for his "regular" longshoremen. This may seem a great victory for the ILWU, but it sounds somewhat hollow. I should think that the sort of approach employed by the Machinists' and Packinghouse Workers' Unions in bargaining on technological change makes more sense: at least the latter were concerned with *all* their members, not solely the elite. And they are exploring such avenues as retraining and relocation. As to the evidence on work loads, I choose to take the word of Harvey Swados, who was there.

. . . Does [this correspondent] suggest that displaced workers can be upgraded to become teachers and technicians? Obviously, this is silly: the prospect rather is for massive unemployment in the lower depths and shortages elsewhere. The latter may very well continue to afflict us simply because our society does not know how to secure what it needs.

An important lesson may be drawn from a debate such as this: the willingness to drift is as patent in technology as in politics and the cold war. Such is the nature of our time and such is its tragedy.

POSTSCRIPT: The above article evidently fluttered the dovecotes of a baker's dozen of *Commentary* readers who wrote angry letters to the editor. By far the greater number of correspondents appeared to be engineers of one sort or another who, ignoring the central discussion of automation's social and economic impact, seized upon what I now realize was an ambiguous description of the analog computer. Instead of saying that the analog "operates much as a desk calculator," I should have written that it does the job of that useful office machine, but in a kind of slide rule fashion. Whereas the latter uses distances and markings to represent numbers, the analog employs voltage variations. This technical imprecision on my part was the signal for an interesting attack—interesting in its utter disregard of the main points of the discussion. Not one of the engineers addressed himself to automation and unemployment, the impact on middle management, alterations in organizational structure or the role performed by the new breed of computer scientists in the corporation. Perhaps it was the latter description that irked them. If this is indeed the case, as I suspect it is, then what a commentary on the engineer mentality today!

CHAPTER 4

ALIENATION

Apathy and Involvement in the Political Process

DAVID RIESMAN AND NATHAN GLAZER

■

Among thoughtful people today there is increasing discussion of political apathy. The discussion of apathy—and its converse, the "responsibility of the citizen"—has overflowed the boundaries of traditional political science and become the concern of the sociologist, the psychiatrist, the social psychologist, and, recently, the atomic scientists. From Gosnell's studies of nonvoting to the recent interest in the "no-opinion vote" in public opinion polls, from *Middletown* to recent studies of participation in voluntary associations, we have become increasingly aware that many millions of Americans remain aggressively unattached to the political events and discourse of their locality, their nation, and the world; that millions of others pay only casual attention; and that millions more only observe the game of politics as they would a horse race. Yet during recent decades politics has become increasingly important as a mode of conscious manipulation of the social environment; and complaints arise that people begin to flee from politics just when politics matters most for them.

It is not easy to separate from current complaints about political apathy

Source: "Criteria for Political Apathy" by David Riesman and Nathan Glazer from *Studies in Leadership*, edited by Alvin W. Gouldner. Copyright 1950 by Harper & Row, Publishers, Incorporated. Reprinted by permission of the publishers.

Authors' Note: The research project on character and political apathy in America of which this previously unpublished article is one outcome has been conducted by the senior author under the auspices of the Yale University Committee on National Policy. We are very much indebted to the Committee, and to the Carnegie Corporation which financed the work, for the opportunity to pursue these inquiries. This article has been read in an earlier version by a number of friends who made many helpful suggestions. We would like to express our appreciation particularly to Professors Reuel Denny and Herman Finer of the University of Chicago, and Dr. Henry M. Pachter of New York City, for their very careful and critical readings.

Editors' Note: This discussion was first published nearly twenty years ago. We reprint it here because we think it offers an important clue to understanding the extremism, the hyper-activism, and the confrontation politics of today. There is still alienation and there is still apathy—with respect to the meaningfulness of the electoral process and the ability of ordinary people to influence the actions of political decision makers. The underlying malaise remains the same. Only the forms of its expression have changed.

those themes which represent old problems—for instance, traditional middle-class concern with lower-class indifference to politics—and those which may represent perceptions of new types or meanings of apathy. The division between an active leadership and a passive multitude, in almost all spheres of life, has been almost universally observed; many social theories assume it is inevitable, and some that it is desirable. *Yet such a generalization may obscure differences in the relative size of the passive multitude at different times; in the reasons for its passivity; in the intensity of its indifference; and in the subjective feelings which accompany the apathy.* It is our thesis that, while the proportion of the passive may not have increased in recent decades, and even declined (Bryce commented on the passivity of the American multitude, and there is some evidence that participation, as contrasted with spectatorship, was low in the alleged heyday of the town meeting)—while, we say, the numbers of the apparently passive may not have increased, *we do believe that there have been far-reaching changes in the reasons for passivity and in the types of apathy that have resulted....*

WHAT IS POLITICAL APATHY?

THE DEVELOPMENT OF INDICES FOR APATHY. While the preceding discussion is largely based on historical-philosophical reflections, we turn now to an account of our search for the proper criteria or indices for apathy and involvement to be used in analyzing our own interview material—some 150 long interviews—as well as data gathered by public opinion researchers largely for purposes other than the study of character and apathy. We can ask people today, as we cannot ask the dead, what politics means to them—though we do not have to take what they say at face value—and we can try to see, by careful analysis of their fully recorded responses, what role politics plays in their psychic economy, at present, what role it plays in their group adjustment, and, within limits, what role it might play under changed social-psychological conditions.

Our investigation is only in its initial stage. We still do not fully grasp what apathy and involvement mean to people, let alone know how to detect these attitudes "operationally" in our interview material. Nevertheless, we feel that discussion of possible criteria may be advanced even by the report of inconclusive efforts.

Apathy in our usage refers to a fairly complex psychological orientation, closely related to historical developments both directly, through the impact of the changes we have touched on in the preceding section, and indirectly (by means of the character structures "created" or favored by a given historical setting). Faced with such complexity, the tendency in social science is to seek for a simple index or criterion which will stand for, or register, the complex phenomenon. Thus, industrial morale may be measured by absenteeism, anomie by suicide rates, the success of propaganda by bond purchases. The most apparent index for apathy is also some simple behavioral one such as voting, participation in certain political activities, attention to media transmitting political information, and so on. These behavioral indices are the first type of criterion for political apathy we will consider. As we shall see, the use of this type of index raises very sharply the danger of losing sight of the complexities of the problem to which the index points.

POLITICAL ACTIVITY AS AN INDEX OF APATHY. Four difficulties arise in equating apathy with inactivity, and in equating involvement with activity. The first is that an index based on activity does not help us to distinguish cases in which that activity is carried on for apolitical purposes. The second is the possible class bias of observation: stamping certain things the middle class does, or does more easily, as "activity." The third is the possible bias in favor of the more temperamentally energetic: the index will be an inadequate measure of varying social-psychological meanings if it is affected by physiologically-grounded factors. The fourth difficulty in using some form of activity as an index lies in the human meaninglessness of activity as such, apart from purpose: we could not infer purpose, which gives changing meaning to the activity, from the index alone.

1. *Activity and apolitical uses.* While an apathy characterized by listlessness and lethargy may have its roots in neurosis, as in the case of a person whose energies are occupied with internal conflicts, individual and social neurosis might also lead to frantic political activity, as an escape from the self—an activity which we would also tend to label as "apathetic" in view of its quality and its origins, its use of politics as a "phobic screen" for the play of irrational affects. If one of the hypotheses one wishes to consider is that such "apolitical" political activity is on the increase, or widespread, an emphasis on formal political activities as the index to apathy will be of little use.

2. *Activity and social class.* We sought for an index which would not be simply representative of middle-class judgments as to the political style of the lower class; and while we thought it altogether likely that, in any scale, the middle class would on the whole rank as less apathetic than the lower class, we wished to reduce class-relative factors to a minimum.[1]

---

[1] While Gallup and other pollers occasionally ask questions such as "do you have a cold?" or "are you happy?" that are not class-typed, little has been done in public opinion research to develop and ask questions concerning politics in the widest sense that are not class-typed. To do this would require some knowledge of all political domains and interests in all social groups. How large this order is we can estimate from Kinsey's work. Sex is something we can be pretty sure exists in every human being, and its forms and meanings on the physical level to which Kinsey confined himself are not limitless. Yet the Indiana group found they had to learn the sex-lingo and sex-style of an enormous variety of people before they could ask questions which got home to their interviewees. Beyond that, they had to convince respondents that the interview was meaningful and that Kinsey and his coworkers understood what the respondents had to say. Kinsey, moreover, did not go beyond overt sex activity, whereas a questionnaire on politics would have to encompass all the intangibles which even quite limited definitions of politics imply.

We did not need evidence from our interviews to establish the obvious fact that political activity today is a matter very largely of clique affiliation and class position. At an urban progressive school where we had a group of interviews made, virtually everybody sent telegrams to congressmen, circulated petitions, and campaigned both in the presidential election and in the off-years. But our interviews seemed to us to show that most of these young people were nonetheless apathetic, in that their relationship to politics was apolitical—a matter of desperate need for group conformity and prestige and in some instances a phobic sphere as well. In many of these cases, we think that the individual, his adolescent fling in politics behind him, will settle into his business or professional life with a decreasing political interest unless there, too, it happens to be stimulated by group pressures. On the other hand, we had a group of interviews done among seniors in an urban trade school, where virtually no one had engaged in the slightest political activity, and where the level of political information was so abysmally low that one boy did not know to what party Truman belonged. Yet in a few of these cases the respondent indicated some awareness of those political developments which mattered for him personally: the draft, the chances for war, the outlook for labor unions. For these people, their adolescence is not, as so often with the middle class, a peak of political interest; when they enter the working force, they may be brought by their unions and their life-situations into some concern with politics.

Even then, however, the lower-class adult will find himself limited in his political activity by his class position, in subtle as well as obvious ways: he is apt to be more tired in the evening, and cannot take time off for meetings in the afternoon (unless he is a shop steward); he does not have a secretary, even if he is a leader in a local union, to type memoranda and make appointments; indeed, he is often ill at ease in handling such middle-class routines as telephone calls and memoranda; lower-class women with children find it of course still more difficult to be active politically. To be sure, the spread of education, the rise of unions and of other more or less formal applications, the increase in experience with government and corporate forms and routines—these developments are increasing the ability of the lower-class person to "act middle class," and to handle himself in the formalized aspects of political activity.

Studies of participation and nonparticipation in voluntary associations provide evidence that lower-class groups are in general more "privatized" than upper-class groups, no matter what forms of interest and participation are included in measuring lower-class participation. (So far as we know, however, no one has tried to see if lower-class men participate less in clique activity centering around sports, drink, and gambling; compare William F. Whyte's *Street Corner Society* and James West's *Plainville*, U.S.A.) Low-income people have very low participation in nonpolitical groups of any formal sort, and frequently have very little interest in matters that might be said to affect them directly. The experience of the Neighborhood Center for Block Organization in East Harlem is instructive in these matters: despite two years of active effort on the part of trained psychiatrists and social workers, it proved impossible to stimulate neighborhood groups in a slum area to deal even with the most pressing problems of daily life, such as housing-law violations, lack of playground space, and police protection. Although even slight cooperative efforts were impressively successful in improving neighborhood conditions, only about 2 per cent of the residents—and these often the most psychologically disturbed—could be induced to participate in any group activity. Why this was the case is obscure— at the cordial invitation of the Center, we along with other social scientists have been trying to find out—but there would seem to be evidence that the conditions of lower-class life do not train people in the motivations and techniques, taken for granted in some sections of the middle class, which underlie cooperative activity. This is a point which converges with Ullmer and Mills' analysis of "Class Structure and Civic Leadership." Put another way, this brings us back to our earlier point, that activity, including political activity, in the lower class requires much more effort, and seems therefore much more fruitless, than in the middle class. With an index which simply measures gross activity, the lower class will simply disappear from consideration and the index will not do much to cast light on class differences in political apathy. Of course, it still remains desirable to explore further the relationships between class and clique position, on the one hand, and various types of political activity, on the other. (On class and clique determination of voting behavior, see Lazarsfeld, Berelson, and Gaudet, *The People's Choice*, excellent for its techniques and stimulating for its suggestiveness.)

3. *Activity and temperament.* Activity is relative not only to class and clique situations but also to temperament differences between individuals; we use "temperament" here to mean such things as native energy-level (apart from its directly psychic components), sanguinity, gregariousness, good health. The problem is that our focus of interest is not on apathy as a universal human phenomenon but on apathy as a social, a historical product. While the distribution of different kinds of temperament in different populations may well be connected with social and historical changes—see, for instance, the brilliant paper by Margaret Mead, "The Concept of Culture and the Psychosomatic Approach" (*Psychiatry*, 10, 1947, 57–76)—in the present state of psychosomatic knowledge, we prefer to get involved as little as possible in questions of temperament, limiting ourselves to those parts of personality and its expressions that are generally considered social in their determination. To isolate apathy as a product of social factors and history rather than of individual temperament is difficult in any case, but it would be even harder if we limited ourselves to the study of activity alone.

4. *Activity and purpose.* There is, finally, the consideration that political activity may be relative not only to a person's temperament and clique situation, but also to the context of his available political world of the moment. We can

hardly call apathetic the behavior of someone who, fully aware of and completely involved emotionally in politics, yet decides not to be active, for want of meaningful activity at the time. Inevitably, we cannot survey political activity over a lifetime, much of it not yet lived, but must ask questions about the moment, the contiguous past, and the immediate future. Dipping in with an interview, our record of activity—as any behavioral index—must be incomplete and may be misleading. Since we view apathy as, among other things, a disproportionate relationship between means and ends—too much activity as well as too little—we cannot assume, because activity goes on, that it makes any human sense. For great numbers of people today, political activity is little more than an inherited ritual or routine, varying according to class demands and psychological needs.

5. *Activity as related to affect and competence.* We can sum up the foregoing paragraphs by saying that activity may conceal as much as it reveals about political apathy. Yet it would go much too far to say that activity is irrelevant to an estimate of the political involvement of an individual We cannot use it as an independent criterion without a great deal of further clarification. But we have found that we could use the record of activity, as it was revealed in an interview, as evidence in evaluating the individual's position on two other indices, those of affect and competence. It was these more "psychological" measures of apathy, rather than the "behavioral" one of activity, that seemed to give us a closer approximation to the quality of apathy itself, as our interviews revealed it. Certainly it is harder to work with such intangibles as (in our terminology) affect and competence, than with the (apparently) hard reality of activity. Yet the fact is that apathy itself is intangible: we cannot reduce it to an operational factor which we know does not include a good part of the meaning of our original object of study. We felt we must strive for criteria commensurate with our problem rather than shape our problem to the most readily available criteria.

If we are to understand apathy as "passionless existence"—one of the definitions given in the Oxford Dictionary—we need not explain why affectlessness (in the way the term is used by psychoanalysts) can be used as a criterion of political apathy. One might ask whether affectlessness is not a synonym for apathy. However, if we look at the pole opposite to political apathy, and consider the meaning and implications of political "concern" or "involvement," we will see immediately that affect or passionate existence is not a sufficient criterion to measure what we find. Concern and involvement imply awareness, appropriateness; yet passion may be blind, disproportionate. These considerations lead us to add to affect as an index of apathy another term: competence; and, as we shall see, to classify as "apathetic" according to our criteria those who, while ranking high in affect, are low in competence. Conversely, those who possess both affect and competence we term "involved," that is, nonapathetic.

We turn in the following two sections to a discussion of these criteria of affect and competence. Thereafter, we develop an additional set of criteria which, especially for the more politicized respondents, may be helpful in differentiating among affects, and hence among apathies.

POLITICAL AFFECT AS AN INDEX OF APATHY. These two dimensions, affect and competence, are obviously closely related. Just as the affect of the competent differs from the affect of the incompetent, so the competence of those of genuine affect differs from the competence of those who lack affect; the effort at distinction here faces problems similar to those of distinguishing between "cognitive" and "emotive" elements in intelligence.

At any rate, the use of these two indices simultaneously could give us four polar relationships: (1) those high in both dimensions; (2) those low in both; (3) and (4) those high in one and low in the other. Accordingly, we defined as (1) "involved" the person who combined high and genuine affect with competence; all others we classified as "apathetic." Thus we grouped in the apathetic category those (2) whose high affect and low competence indicated an "indignant" relationship to politics (it might also be an "enthusiastic" one); those (3) who were high in competence and affectless, and whom we termed "inside-dopesters"; and those low in both affect and competence, whom we called (4) the "indifferent."

These four types were, we suspected, related both to class position and to character structure; we expected, for instance, to find "inside-dopester" in upper middle-class urban circles, "indignants" in rural and small-town Protestant areas. We do not yet have the sample that would permit us to test these hypotheses, though we have found interviews which illustrate them.

Affect is, of course, an intangible. It can be probed by projective tests such as the Rorschach, but these will not tell us very much about *political* affect, as distinguished from affect in other spheres of life. Specific answers to direct questions concerning political affect are, however, of more help than one might suppose. Thus, when we ask people what in politics gets them indignant or excited and how long they stay that way; what in politics makes them feel good or bad; whether they can get as worked up about politics as about other things in life; and so on—when we ask these direct questions, even rather non-commital answers, followed up by explanatory probes, are often quite revealing. A direct positive or negative answer to the first question bearing on affect, or to the whole series, may be belied by later answers in the series, or other parts of the interview.

For example, all the students in the progressive high school already referred to claim that politics makes a difference in the way they live, and that they get indignant about political happenings. However, the content of the answer gives us clues about the real nature of their alleged affect. We quote several responses to the question whether politics makes a difference:

Not directly, but in a way I think it does; but in discussion with friends or parents

I can usually take ideas or get facts from the discussion. In this way, these discussions make a difference.

It makes no difference physically but it changes my mind—if I met someone who violently disagreed with me on an important issue it is bothersome for friendship. It affects me in this way.

Here politics is among other things a function of social intercourse in a group which makes "politics" obligatory. The first one quoted can "take ideas or get facts from the discussion"—for him politics is perhaps a means for self-improvement. The respondent who tells us that disagreement in political matters might be "bothersome for friendship" also volunteers that "if just two people were left in the world, they would still fight."

Working, then, both with what the interviewee tells us directly about his political affects and with what he "gives" of them without meaning to, we try to reconstruct the history of the individual's political affect, much as the archaeologist, working with fragments, tries to reconstruct a culture.

An individual may rate himself high, or low, in affect in contrast to his milieu. Hence, to understand what he tells us, we have to understand something of the milieu, if we are to make comparisons which transcend a limited group. Moreover, individuals differ very much in the style by which they express affect, or repress it. Possibly we cannot avoid here the interjection of temperament factors, such as the distinction between choleric and sanguinic types—compare Jan Stapel, "The Convivial Respondent" (*Public Opinion Quarterly*, 11, 1947, p. 524). The popular folklore has it that "still waters run deep": people may feel deeply and yet not express this feeling by accepted patterns of gesture or speech. Contrariwise, the folklore would have it that easily surfaced affects are not genuine, but this too, will vary, not only with individuals, but also according to the conventionalized mode of expression of affect in the particular group. So we must know something of what may be expected in the milieu to interpret the individual's idiosyncratic modification of group styles in vaunting affect or concealing it. It follows that we need a group portrait of political affect before we can draw the lineaments of the individual.

But, of course, we learn of the group in part through the individuals who compose it, just as we learn of the individual in part from single answers to questions which then become interwoven with other answers. Thus, the method weaves back and forth, from the single answer to the whole interview, and from the single individual to the whole group of which he is a part. This is far from simple. Yet it is the kind of judgment which we constantly make in life—indeed, on which our lives and fortunes often depend—and which novelists and biographers must make when they tackle political subjects.

In this way, we try to arrive at a qualitative description of political affect, in all its subtleties and variations, as well as to judge whether it is, on the whole, high or low. The gamut of affects is wide: there is the affect of aggressive or sadistic types, who look for opportunities of releasing indignation onto politics;

the affect of people who live in a slightly paranoid and autistic world; the affect of people with little staying power and the affect of those with great explosive power; the high affect of those whose roles as political leaders of certain groups require them to maintain a chronic political stance (which may feel "sincere" to them); the high, though repressed, affect of disillusioned folk who fear political affect and therefore deny it.

One crucial issue in all this is the source of the affect displayed in politics. Harold Lasswell, in *Psychopathology and Politics*, asserted that political behavior, if it is to be understood psychologically, must be understood in terms of affects arising in the personal ("primary") sphere and becoming displaced onto available ("secondary") political symbols. In a crude form, the notion that personal frustrations and tensions are displaced onto politics has become increasingly a part of our popular folklore and science; the personal experience of everyone offers examples. Professor Lasswell's more provocative question is rather whether *all* affect expressed in a political sphere must be considered as deriving from a personal tension or frustration. Perhaps in some ultimate or definitional sense there can be no other source for affect; and yet there is no question that we can distinguish between those in whom a clear link shows between the personal tension and its political expression, and those who seem to respond with emotion to the event itself. We may, that is, distinguish between an "idling" affect which seeks for justification or rationalization in politics, and an affect which is a reaction to specific political developments; the distinction here is analogous to the one Erich Fromm draws between idling and reactive hatred in *Man For Himself*. While such a phenomenological distinction does not answer the question as to the ultimate source of affect, it does indicate that there are different kinds of political affect, and we know from our experience of life that these different kinds may have different consequences.

This was, then, the first refinement we introduced in the use of affect as an index to apathy: where the affect expressed in politics is closely and directly linked to a personal tension—where the affect is "blind," so to speak, expressed on an available political object rather than directly aroused by the object—we did not consider that subject as showing affect in the political realm. Or, more precisely, we did not consider him politically "involved" if his affect was of this sort even if he might be considered politically competent—but, obviously, this very decision leads us away from any quantitative or quasi-quantitative use of either affect or competence as isolable criteria.

Finally, we found ourselves compelled to deal with still other elusive problems of the quality of affect. Our tendency had been to call those who show a great deal of affect without corresponding competence "indignant" types, but in some cases we felt that they were more properly called "enthusiasts." Moreover, "indignation" itself can be of different sorts: it can have the quality of an outlet for idling hatred and malaise which Svend Ranulf describes in his essay *Moral Indignation and Middle Class Psychology*; or it can represent a deeply human reaction to threat or atrocity. Often the presence or absence of competence would permit us to distinguish between these two types of indignation, but this is not always so.

POLITICAL COMPETENCE AS AN INDEX OF APATHY. In dealing with affect as an index we did not raise the question of how one defines politics, though obviously the problem of displacing affects which arise elsewhere onto politics implies a distinction of spheres between what is "politics" and what is "elsewhere." However, in establishing standards for political competence, it is even more necessary to define what we mean by politics.

1. *What is "politics"?* There is a great deal to be said for a "meteorological" definition—the term is that used by Kris and Leites in the paper previously cited —perhaps an "entertainment" or "consumer's" definition: "interest in the world around one." In this sense, in terms of one's ability to react to events that do not affect one directly, but which are "interesting," one would be justified in testing for competence on the "politics" of the numbers game for the lower-class men, on tenement-house intrigues for lower-class women, and so on. In another sense, however, these things often do affect people in the lower class, at least immediately, more than a presidential election—in fact, we cannot speak of apathy, in its conventional use, in referring to someone who cannot affect the outcome of a political event, and who cannot be affected by its outcome.

An interest or consumer definition of politics would permit us to set up indices for political competence that would be relative to the interests of each social group; that is, each class or group would have a different index. As a practical matter, this would be exceedingly difficult—it would require determining what is important and interesting to a particular class, relative to that class, rather than in terms of what is important and interesting to another class. But apart from such considerations, such a definition of politics and hence of political competence would ignore our view that politics *does* determine the condition of people's lives today—including lower-class lives. And, as already stated, we believe that an awareness of those power-forces in the world which do matter for people, an awareness of the human potentialities for changing the social environment in the general interest—an awareness, that is, which transcends mere consumer's "interest," mere meteorology—is a human need whose satisfaction is important for individual psychic health. Of course there may be other, still more imperative needs.

One could also consider another type of judgment of competence which would be no less relativistic than a judgment in terms of local patterns of interest or consumption. By this test, one would be judged "competent" if one were able to perform the political tasks dictated by one's group milieu and party affiliation. Thus, the government official would be "competent" if he could handle the political news in the way demanded of him by his job, no matter how fragmentary his awareness of the long-run political forces in which his

THE VOTER AND LOCAL GOVERNMENT IN
TWO STABLE DEMOCRACIES

Although there have always been among us believers in strong central government, our governmental system, as compared to the British, has been extraordinarily weak and decentralized. This has been particularly true of state and local government. The general idea seems to have been that no one should govern, or failing that, that everyone should govern together. The principle of checks and balances and the division of power, mitigated in the Federal government by the great powers of the presidency, were carried to extreme lengths in the cities and states. As little as fifty years ago, most cities were governed by large councils, some of them bicameral, and by mayors who could do little but preside over the councils. There was no such thing as a state administration. Governors were ceremonial figures only, and state governments were mere congeries of independent boards and commissions. Before anything could be done, there had to occur a most elaborate process of give and take (often, alas, in the most literal sense) by which bits and pieces of power were gathered up temporarily, almost momentarily.

It was taken for granted that the ordinary citizen had a right—indeed, a sacred duty—to interfere in the day-to-day conduct of public affairs. Whereas in Britain the press and public have been excluded from the deliberations of official bodies, in the United States it has been common practice to require by law that all deliberations take place in meetings open to the public. Whereas in Britain the electorate is never given an opportunity to pass upon particular projects by vote, in the United States it usually is. In Los Angeles, according to James Q. Wilson, "The strategy of political conflict is more often than not based upon the assumption that the crucial decision will be made not by the City Council of Los Angeles, the Board of Supervisors of the county, or the legislature of the state, but by the voters in a referendum election."

Los Angeles is an extreme case, but the general practice of American cities, a practice required by law in many of them, is to get the voters' approval of major expenditures. The New York City government, one of the strongest, is now having to choose between building schools and making other necessary capital expenditures; it cannot do both because the voters of the state have refused to lift the constitutional limit on debt. Such a thing could not happen in London; there all such decisions are made by the authorities, *none of whom is elected at large.*

Source: Edward C. Banfield, "The Political Implications of Metropolitan Growth," *Daedalus*, 1:90 (Winter 1960), pp. 69–70. By permission of the American Academy of Arts and Sciences.

department, his class, and his country were caught. And the young Stalinist, knowledgeable on how to get Marcantonio reelected, would be "competent" by the standards of his outfit—and even "incompetent" if he possessed the grasp of Marxist fundamentals demanded of an earlier generation of Communists and feared by the present generation. But, obviously, such complete relativism as this, which would equate the "functionally rationalized" with the rational (in Karl Mannheim's terms), would again be to deny our value premise: namely, that politics matters for people, irrespective of the ideology in which it is clothed in a particular culture and time and of the tasks or busywork demanded by that ideology. Our judgments of what is apathy, and of its subcomponents, must be based upon a standard which, while relative to long-term historical developments, does not fluctuate with party politics and anti-rationalist slogans; to that extent, our definitions of politics, hence of political competence, aim at a degree of universal validity, independent of culture and class.

Thus we are led to define politics, not in terms of mere passive interest nor in terms of roles demanded by one's station in life, but in terms of the human need for understanding the social environment and even of improving it. We define it, that is, in terms of our two levels of political awareness and action: the reflective and utopian and curious one, and the day-to-day struggle for the lesser as against the greater evil; to be judged competent one must have some grasp of both these levels.

2. *Distinguishing real from spurious competence.* Even when, for practical purposes, we limited our inquiries as to competence to the more traditional fields of politics, we still found it difficult to distinguish between an individual's awareness of real forces and superficial, atomistic consumption of political data. We had to distinguish between political reality and political illusion, even if that illusion was couched in conventionally "realistic" terms; inevitably, it is we who had to decide which is which, on the basis of our own political values and comprehension.

But in important respects we felt it necessary that our judgment of competence be relative. We could not judge everyone by the standard of a professor of political science; conversely, and perhaps unfairly, we expected more of the professor than of someone with (theoretically) less opportunity to acquire competence. We asked in each individual case: what could we expect, in terms of political awareness, in view of this individual's ability to deal with rather abstract matters, an ability partly native and partly learned? We also asked: what sort of awareness would this individual *need* in order to function in a satisfying way in "his" world? We asked a small-town person about rather more localized political matters than an urban person; we tried to discount, as far as possible, local and regional differences in distribution of the mass media. In every case, we tried to reduce, except for comparative purposes, questions of specific fact or opinion, such as are usually asked on polls, and to find questions which brought out the individual's ability to evaluate political forces. Since to some degree all of us live in the same world, these questions were identical for all people we interviewed, except insofar as we modified them to give the less articulate or intelligent a chance to respond.

This effort to allow for differences between rural and urban, and between articulate and inarticulate, raises many of the same complications as the effort to allow for class differences—ethnic differences also are important—and, of course, these various sets of differences overlap. In small-town and rural Vermont, where we had a group of interviews made, people are in easy contact with local and even state officials. Social distance between the politically influential and the noninfluential is small; indeed, many of the patterns of political meaning persist which we described above as typical for the nineteenth century. As against this, urban lower-class people, in our small number of interviews, seemed ordinarily to have no face-to-face contacts with officials; some of them, however, had a kind of taxi-driver wisdom and were more "knowing" than the Vermonters—less likely, for instance, to think that the interviewer must be a Communist because he asked questions about politics. Here, too, we do not have an adequate sample to permit comparisons; and in any case, we repeat, we have not solved the technical difficulties of developing a questionnaire to tap differential meanings of politics in the barely explored variety of American subcultures—what a political cosmology, for example, is wrapped up in the phrase: "Go fight city hall!"

In an effort to do this, however, we have asked people, for instance, what image they had of a political person, and of a nonpolitical person; whether they changed their minds about politics and when and why; whether they thought war or depression easier to avoid; whether they thought experts or the man in the street had better judgment; whether they trusted people, and whom they trusted on political questions. We asked whether they thought their country, their school (for people in school), and their family was democratic, and how they could tell; what groups they felt had interests in common with themselves, and what groups antagonistic interests; and who they thought ran the country. Finally, we presented people with a series of political "dilemmas" and asked them what they would do if, for example, they came into possession of information which showed that "their" candidate in an election was corrupt, and if disclosure of such information would enable the other side to win; we said nothing about what their candidate stood for.

We did find, with our small haul of 150, that people in various social strata, urban and rural, young and old, felt they could take a crack at our questions and dilemmas. We did not have, as in the usual political questionnaire, a cluster of "don't knows" at the bottom of the socio-economic scale. Middle-class people, to be sure, had greater facility on some of the questions, but they were not likely to have thought in terms of all of them; for instance, they were usually challenged by the question as to their image or picture of a person very much interested in politics. This type of challenge is important, for it enabled us to use the interview as a sort of projective test, by seeing the kind of verbal and non-verbal (e.g., gestural) performance it elicited in sequence. It helped us, on the one hand, to get through the veneer of opinionatedness in the middle class and, on the other hand, to evoke what political competence there was in our lower-class respondents.

COMPETENCE AND AFFECT AS CRITERIA. We have worked intensively with some twenty interview protocols, and in each case made as complete a record as we could of all the grounds of our judgments, as we sought to determine apathy or involvement by the application of our criteria of competence and affect. (At the same time we made a judgment of character structure, on the basis of a typology which we do not touch on here, and compared character structure and political orientation.) We found in our use of these criteria that often we could not make separate judgments of each as easily as we could make a judgment of apathy or involvement directly. We found ourselves, moreover, moving away from primary attention to the specific questions which had been designed to reveal competence and affect respectively, and making judgments which treated the whole interview as a *Gestalt*; that is, all parts of our comprehensive questionnaire—covering popular culture, attitudes toward family and friends, philosophical values, and many other things as well as politics—entered into and enriched our judgments.[2] Moreover, when we worked with the interviews, we discovered that in addition to employing our concepts of affect and competence, we were also tempted to smuggle in other criteria that were not explicit in our initial theoretical scheme. We were in the position, so frequent in social science, where our indices, despite our care to make them adequate to the complexities we were seeking to measure, turned out in many cases to be too mechanical to cover the whole range, the nuances and subtleties, of apathy and involvement. These difficulties arose, and our scheme of affect-competence seemed least illuminating, in the case of those who had fairly elaborate political ideologies, and who lived in politically saturated milieus. There ideology itself demanded that one be concerned with political events (just as in certain other environments ideology demanded the opposite), and a certain kind of competence could be avoided only by a remarkably high impermeability to the group.[3] Because general attitudes and orientations could be assumed, the range within a given orientation became exceedingly important.

In this situation, our recourse was to develop an additional set of criteria which, taken together with affect and competence rather than replacing them, would embrace more of the interview material and of our theoretical framework.

---

[2] Cf., e.g., Werner Wolff, *The Expression of Personality* (1943), p. 9: "... specific statements about personality items are often less accurate than free descriptions."

[3] Rose Laub Coser has been engaged in analyzing for varieties of affect and competence a group of twenty-three interviews with the entire second-year class of students in a coeducational, progressive urban private school. Her preliminary analysis reveals that those who, on a series of questions, show competence and alertness vis-à-vis politics are those who also exhibit the least interpersonal tensions with their classmates.

This set of criteria was based on interview data we had originally planned virtually to disregard, namely, the detailed political ideology of the respondent. We had believed that in America—whatever might be found elsewhere— ideology is almost entirely a function of milieu, bearing little if any relation to individual character or to the psychological roots of apathy and involvement. Our view was, in other words, that party and ideological positions in America do not bespeak a psychological choice: ordinarily the individual has no choice but to take the ideology offered him in his family, class, clique, and region.

Yet our interviews showed us that while this was on the whole true, there were crucial differences in the nuance and emphasis with which the ideology was expressed by each subject in our more highly political groups of respondents. We believed these differences to be significant both for revealing character structure and revealing apathy or involvement. We therefore developed, on the basis of our study of a variegated group of interviews, some general concepts of the way in which the coloring of one's ideology—more or less irrespective of its nominal content—may be related to an underlying apathy.

A set of criteria based on nuances of political statement inevitably will not be applicable to large numbers of people: first of all, to those who present virtually no political statements or opinions—and there are many of these—and then to those in whom these statements are very simple or primitive. However, our criteria, as will be seen in a moment, refer to such general categories that they might also be applied to views on family relations, education, and similar topics which have political bearing or implications, and we have often done this, though here, too, we run into some difficulty where views are not elaborated. Nevertheless, the main use of this set of categories was to serve as a refinement on the affect-competence scheme: for most people, the affect-competence scheme described the degree of political involvement or apathy sufficiently; but for those for whom politics is a focus of interest, the affect and competence categories were too gross, and a direct analysis of ideology permitted somewhat closer approximation. Moreover, these additional criteria directly introduced into our analysis of the interviews our judgments, set forth in the preceding section, on the need for a political orientation which combined elements of detachment and of attachment to one's time-bound and culture-bound milieu.

In what we have said, the reader may feel that our use of the term "apathy" is too idiosyncratic and complex, even in the light of scientific awareness that definition is an essentially arbitrary device. And, indeed, our choice of the term "apathy" rather than a word of less common use or of our own coinage is frankly polemical. It is a way of stating our conviction that current conceptions about apathy—seen in terms of failure to vote, to send telegrams, to inform oneself about politics, etc.—greatly oversimplify the problem of finding adequate ways for relating people to politics on its various levels. To seek an increase in formal political activity and information as such, without too much concern for the meaning of that activity or information, is self-deceiving. For it may blind one to the historical changes in the significance of politics for the individual which, in our opinion, have led to an increase in unconscious apathy, an apathy arising as a result of congruent changes in social structure and character structure, as well as in the political sphere alone. These changes are reflected in slight changes of ideology and of modes of expression of affect; these are possible clues to long-term developments whose consequences in political behavior have not yet become fully manifest—clues to the latent dynamics of politics.

To be sure, not all apathies are alike, and the "apathy" of the active is obviously different from the "apathy" of the quiescent. Nevertheless, in using the same term for both, we are seeking to emphasize functional similarities— primarily the inappropriateness of the political outlook or behavior of all the apathetic ones.

It is, moreover, not only apathy which is misconceived, but its opposite which we call "involvement." Here, too, we think that changes may be under way in those individuals and groups who are seeking for possible new modes of relatedness to politics. Our effort is to formulate criteria which will permit us to distinguish inappropriate and apolitical orientations, no matter how well rationalized and disguised, from orientations which might satisfy the need of modern men to meet their altered political situation with competence and fitting affect.

FURTHER CRITERIA FOR APATHY AND INVOLVEMENT

The criteria set forth below are meant to supplement, primarily for the more politicized respondents, the criteria of affect and competence. They are not yet exhaustive. Taken together, however, they help to differentiate apathetic, apolitical approaches to politics from involved and appropriate responses. They do *not* determine the correctness or misguidedness of an individual's political position: people can be mistaken without being judged apathetic, and conversely, they can be "right" despite a basic apathy. For any political position, then: (1) concern with human ends is less apathetic than concern with institutional means; (2) concern with what has been or potentially can be personally experienced is less apathetic than concern with remote items, access to which is gained through impersonal agencies of information diffusion; likewise, the ability to personalize and concretize distant events is less apathetic than the ability to report them; (3) concern with the welfare of self-and-others is less apathetic than concern exclusively with the self or exclusively with others; (4) concern with trends and elements that are not in the focus of attention of the mass media is less apathetic than exclusive concern with what is in their momentary focus; (5) ability to take a critical or independent view of authority[4] —its assertions of fact, and claims to special treatment or consideration—is less apathetic than unquestioning acceptance or rejection of these assertions and claims because of their authoritative source.

Obviously, these criteria overlap at a number of points. We have made no attempt to use them as a scale; to say, for instance, that we judge a person nonapathetic if he ranks high on three out of five. Rather, they constitute a check list of things to be looked for in characterizing the political style of a person. We say a few words in illustration and explanation of each.

HUMAN ENDS V. INSTITUTIONAL MEANS. When we ask people what could be done to make war less likely, some answer in terms of changing people, and some in terms of changing institutions; still others, of course, say that war is inevitable. But we cannot interpret such answers directly in terms of our criterion: it is the personal variant of a given ideological frame that tells us something about individual political orientation. Thus, if a politically sophisticated respondent emphasizes nationalization of industry, centralization of planning, control over industry, breakup of cartels, etc., with what seems to us a disproportionate emphasis on the specific institutional instrument rather than the human end, we become suspicious and wonder whether his interest in the human end may not be an excuse for his desire to institute a particular set of more or less belligerent means. We cannot tell this, we repeat, from the position itself. To be sure, some ideologies are so constricted that acceptance of them amounts to a virtual choice of totalitarian means; yet we can imagine a racist who puts more emphasis on freedom for the allegedly subject race than on means for destroying or controlling an oppressor race, and we can conceive of a Nazi who, before 1939, emphasized the strength-through-joy program, the end of unemployment, new motor roads and the *Volkswagen*, and who through all-too-human error, failed to see the necessary implications of other Nazi goals.

Conversely, acceptance of an ideology that exalts ends without reference to conceivable human means may tend toward apathy, as we think is the case with some current versions of pietism and quietism. For ends cannot be too serious when the problem of implementation is lightly regarded. We do not mean, of course, that one must always have means available before one can justify speculation about ends; it is again a question of the "two levels" of political relatedness we discussed above.

Though such questions seem highly theoretical,[5] the issue boils down to a fairly simple one: does the person possess, in the realm of politics, the "normal" human ability to differentiate ends from means? To take a common instance in

---

[4] "Authority" here must be taken in terms of the individual's group and not in any general sense; obviously, the authorities to which an obedient Stalinist, Zionist, Catholic, or Democrat submits are not the same.

[5] For fuller discussions, see "Some Observations on Community Plans and Utopia" in *Yale Law Journal*, 57 (1947), 173.

everyday life, we are critical of the person who makes a compulsive ritual out of behavior that should serve convenience—keeping a house neat, for example. So, too, in political life, we find people whose aim of getting rid of "dirt"—municipal corruption, excess profits, un-American activities, etc.—has become a dangerous and compulsive ritual, blind to human priorities and consequences. Flight into politics typically uses political means without appropriate relationship to human ends.

THE PERSONALIZED AND CONCRETIZED V. THE IMPERSONAL AND REMOTE. The very nature of modern politics is such that we cannot form our political judgments on the basis of personal experience alone. If we try to do this, we will simply be applying "parataxic" frames of reference to the world. This misapplication is typical of the philistine, of the ethnocentric person who, in art, "knows what he likes," and in politics insists on judging everything that happens by the norms of his own morality, his own family, his own unquestioned way of life. Such a person is also one who makes the semantic error, discussed by S. I. Hayakawa,[6] of asserting firmly that "pigs is pigs" and can never be anything else: *he* knows a pig when he sees one. Probably the lower-class person, less sophisticated, is more likely than the upper-class person to fall prey to these fallacies.

Increasingly, however, people tend to make the opposite error, and it is with this that our second criterion deals. While the world that influences us is enormous, and while we must depend almost entirely on reports that we read or hear in order to evaluate it, we are inclined to apathy if we fail to measure these reports, wherever we can, by our personal identification with the described situation. When, for instance, we read that the Russian people have greeted with joy a decree lengthening hours of labor, because this permits them to do more for the beloved Stalin, we can use our own experience to discount the report as at least in part exaggerated. Of course, this personal reference may lead us into error: people are different; nevertheless, by means of this natural and widely used control, a large part of the political can be assimilated to personal experience.

We found in our interviews, however, a number of people—largely in the urban upper-middle class, young, and much concerned with politics—who did precisely the opposite: they were attracted by what was most abstract and remote; they parroted events and attitudes in the same forms and terms in which the mass media (for their class) present them; it never occurred to them to use their own experience, their own likes and dislikes, as a norm. We might suggest that this strand of apathy is a trained incapacity of the educated. These same people knew all about the disasters of the last years; they claimed great concern, great affect. Yet in many instances we found that the events which made an impression were those which the respondent could not possibly have

---

[6] "The Revision of Vision," *ETC.: A Review of General Semantics*, IV (1947), 258.

assimilated in terms of personal experience. In such cases we were sometimes able to see that the reason for the apparent political concern lay in anxieties about group conformity patterns or in the use of politics as an escape from exigent and unconscious problems of the self.

It is in judging such cases that the problem of differential exposure to the mass media becomes important. The ability to react to the remote may have been stimulated by, say, a vivid "March of Time" or CBS broadcast. Similarly, other sources, at school or elsewhere, might sensitize an individual to connections which will seem remote only to the less sensitive observer.

More typically, however, the mass media operate on a level of spurious personalization of events, which are made concrete and chummy by playing up personalities and local color. Thus it is apparent that this criterion is closely linked with the fourth one (see p. 419, below): concern with what is not in focus as against concern only with what is in the focus—and the conventional style of perception—of the relevant clique or media.

To avoid misunderstanding, we should emphasize that we are not equating political involvement with immediacy in time and space, and political apathy with physical or temporal remoteness. It is not apathy but its opposite to react strongly to Plato's *Apology*, for example, or to an account of misery on Okinawa. Rather, our point is simply that one's own experience, enriched by sensibility and imagination, is with all its weaknesses the only safe yardstick for judgment—paradoxically, it furnishes the only escape from solipsism. Indeed, we believe that many political disasters of our own time and of earlier times have resulted because of people's acceptance of political ideologies which their own experience might have disproved, had they trusted it or resorted to it. Programs of sacrifice and war can be put over just because people, failing to do this, act like "statesmen," applying *raison d'état*, and never, like kings, saying "*l'état: c'est moi.*"

CONCERN WITH SELF-AND-OTHERS V. CONCERN WITH SELF-OR-OTHERS. This criterion is closely linked to the one we have just discussed; it too demands that the individual see himself in the context of others and others in the context of himself. But by the use of this criterion we wish to make explicit our judgment, set forth above, that both selfishness and selflessness are obstacles to political involvement. As to the former, if we find an interview record which formulates the view that the respondent can achieve happiness for himself at whatever cost to others—or for his group or nation, at whatever cost to other groups or nations—we suspect first of all his political competence, since all experience suggests the interdependence of human beings and nations, and second, his humanity: otherwise, how could he be happy at the direct expense of others? In fact, these two judgments interlock: the respondent's lack of humanity will lead him to misjudge politics in long-run terms, no matter how effective he may be as an operator; he is apathetic because he does not penetrate to the real forces at work—certain forces, for example, which may tend after a time to reduce the power of the powerful and increase the power of the powerless—but sees politics only as the manipulable extension of his own ego and its group or territorial representatives.

If, on the other hand, we find an interview record of a person who thinks only of others, and never of himself or his group, we suspect a fear of facing or knowing the self (and the group), often coupled with a more or less unconscious desire to suffer.

One of our respondents, for instance, asked what he would do if he had six months to live and could do as he pleased, said he would use the "aura of reverence attached to one who has six months to live . . . to improve conditions." His whole interview is filled with references to the suffering of others, but he is oblivious to his own suffering, which leads to his inhuman willingness to make himself an instrument, even in his hypothetical last six months, for meeting unlimited obligations to a rather shadowy "humanity."

The case is extreme; while others among our group of interviews exhibit similar tendencies, selflessness is rationalized more typically in some hard-boiled vein. In all such circumstances, however, we feel there is something apathetic in a view of politics which fails to connect it with the speaker's own place in the world, and his own claims for happiness. As we all know, modern political leaders have become adept at exploiting the willingness of people to submit to intolerable conditions for some cause; the cause gives meaning to the followers' lives because these are completely lived in the "second sphere" of culturally-given tasks and motivations: there is insufficient attachment to life in the "first sphere" of day-to-day living, let alone sufficient detachment in the "third sphere" of transcending imagination. In much the same way, many leaders who make their careers on the basis of others' sacrifice are themselves "selfless," that is, ascetic; they, too, find meaning only in submission to a cause, though they may appear as highly egocentric.

If one thinks of earlier military heroes and their devoted followings, of earlier fanaticisms and crusades, it is not easy to see what is new in all this. Erich Fromm, in *Escape From Freedom*, pointed to resemblances between the social-psychological conditions which gave rise to the more virulent aspects of the Reformation and those which gave rise to modern fascism. If there are differences, they might be sought in the more limitless nature of modern totalitarian demands, and more effective techniques for their enforcement. Beyond that, we think there may be changes in individual psychology which have removed certain defenses people once had against the internalized voices of the peer-group; moreover, older barriers of property, theology, and class have been largely smashed. Whatever the degree of change, we can at least be sure that there is plenty of political dynamite available to those who can combine the apathy of the selfless and the apathy of the egocentric, sopping up into a political movement the affect of the incompetent and finding places for the technical but often cruel competence of the affectless.

CONCERN WITH WHAT IS NOT IN FOCUS V. CONCERN ONLY WITH WHAT IS IN FOCUS OF CLIQUE OR MEDIA. As throughout this discussion, here, too, our criteria shade into one another. Individuality of the focus of attention is related, on the one hand, to ability to put oneself (but not only oneself) into the figure-ground pattern of politics—our third criterion—and on the other hand, it is related to a critical attitude toward the (generally anonymous) authorities who tell people what their focus of attention should be, which is our fifth criterion. If we define politics in terms, *inter alia*, of efforts to change the social environment, we see that the ability to envisage such change involves originality. This can flow from the actual experiences people have, if they do experience them directly—that is, if they are able to look clear-sightedly at their own conditions and their own way of life. However, most people do not interpret their experience directly, but through the conventional, ideologized accounts of their life that are proffered them by the mass media and by other authorities. This passivity of perception, this permeability, is apathetic, no matter how frantic the concern with the flow of political news. Passivity suffocates the development of alternative and unexpected ways of handling political developments. In our culture, preoccupation with the stream of events as they are culturally perceived is praised as practical. Yet without utopian thought—thought which makes it worth while to apply human effort to the social environment rather than being overwhelmed by it—man's political inventiveness is stunted.

To be sure, not everyone can be a builder of utopias, nor do we expect originality in the sense in which the term is used in scholarship before we judge a person nonapathetic. Rather, our criterion is an effort to evaluate the mode of perception of the person—his ability, as a matter of degree, to criticize and judge pleasant and unpleasant, just and unjust, ways of social living. (Here, and generally, we have profited very much from the discussion in Erich Fromm's *Man For Himself*.) Where this ability is absent, people tend to become increasingly invaded in their individuality of judgment by what they are told, and by the stream of reportage furnished them through the mass media of communication. Increasingly, the mass media peddle the "inside dope," much like the Fascist agitator portrayed by Leo Lowenthal and Norbert Guterman in *Prophets of Deceit*. Like other opiates, it may make some people jumpy and other people quiescent, but both groups are functionally apathetic in the light of our criteria.

CRITICALNESS OF AUTHORITY V. SUBMISSIVENESS. We have already indicated, in preceding criteria, the sort of nonapathetic orientation a person may have who is able to criticize assertions and demands for attention from authoritative sources: such a person can concern himself with human ends, and can relate events to his own human experience and human desires; he can transcend, if only in slight degree, the way the mass media present political occurrences. And, on the contrary, we have spoken of the apathy indicated by an orientation to politics which is basically submissive, being concerned only with means, messages, and missions. Our fifth criterion deals explicitly with the relationship to authority. Of all our criteria, this one is probably most palpably linked to character structure; though conceivably submissiveness toward authorities of state, school, or religion may be the outcome of a rational, though mistaken, judgment, we usually expect to trace a basis in personality for the attitude.

Even so, it is necessary to distinguish various kinds of submissiveness. In one of our interviews, we came across a second-generation Italian youth, a trade school senior, who exhibited great docility to the middle-class interviewer, to the school officials, and to constituted authority generally. Yet there was nothing intense about this submission; it had the archaic quality of a fatalistic but upstanding and secure peasant, who had no characterological *need* to submit because he genuinely respected authority and took his humble place in the world for granted. Today, this attitude is rare in America, and when we find submissiveness it is usually rooted, not in respect for unquestioned authority, but in a sado-masochistic syndrome of incomplete rebellion and incomplete—and therefore all the more intense—submission. Through the examination of attitudes toward authority, we hope to be able to differentiate between rebelliousness as simply a highly critical attitude toward authority and rebelliousness as an irrational character orientation.

Intense cravings for submission, and irrational rebelliousness—these again are psychological constellations which invite the coming into power of people with destructive and harmful personalities, people who are themselves apathetic in their lack of concern for human ends and their ruthless egocentricity for self or group.

APPLICATIONS OF THE CRITERIA. Out of our 150 interviews, we have taken about 20 for intensive study in the light of our criteria of affect and competence, as well as the further criteria we have just now set forth. We have sought not only to classify the respondent as politically involved or apathetic as the case may be, but also to portray in detail his political orientation as it now appears and as we envisage its possible future courses—to give, so to speak, the political potential of the person. As is evident from the qualitative nature of the criteria, such work involves ransacking the entire interview for clues to the interpretation of the specifically political responses. Moreover, the responses are themselves qualified in meaning by our knowledge of the ideology of the group, perhaps a numerically very small group, to which the interviewee belongs; it would be absurd, for instance, to take at face value the remarks of a small child about killing people, but we would have to see where the child went beyond or gave an idiosyncratic twist to his current peer-group's lingo.[7] We must also, of

---

[7] For a fuller account of the method and its difficulties, see our discussion in "Social Structure, Character Structure, and Opinion," in *International Journal of Opinion and Attitude Research*, Vol. 2 (Winter 1948–1949), p. 512.

course, take account of the respondent's age; where, for instance, we have worked with high school students, we must allow for the fact that the political style of adolescence is often not fully formed.

We have found for ourselves that the criteria, in all their elaboration, do permit us to encompass many of the nuances and subtleties of the interview material. To be sure, there are many cases where the interview leaves us in doubt either because our questions and probes did not get beneath the surface or because politics for the individual *is* only surface—he cannot be said to have a political orientation, except embryonically, which is *his*. And of course we expect that people can fool us. We have found people who go through all the motions of affect so convincingly that, on first analysis, we have judged them nonapathic, only to see on fuller scrutiny that this was a very smooth act. And conversely, we recall one instance of a returned veteran so cynical, so anxious to deny affect, that his interview was filled with brutal remarks; fuller examination revealed the very genuine affect which he was trying desperately, but quite unsuccessfully, to crush; it was apparent, for instance, that he was not submissive, not mass-media oriented, not as selfish as he claimed.

We wish it were possible to set forth here some of our material from our interviews and to show in detail how the protocol may reveal a syndrome of apathy—"indignant," "enthusiastic," "indifferent," etc., as the case may be—in terms of the criteria. However, even one of these discussions is apt to run the length of this article and space forbids including such an illustration. This is unsatisfactory because only through the details can the reader judge the validity of the research procedure. To be sure, this is not "validity" in the technical sense of proof of our results. In a few cases we have sought such proof—never fully adequate of course—by following a respondent up to see whether he fulfills predictions we have made on the basis of the interview. In other cases, we have tried to check out interpretation against the judgments of others who have had dealings with the subject: this may help test our methods but is hardly probative as to the individual, since all concerned may be deceived.

At the present stage of our work, however, we do not see the interview material as "proving" our criteria, let alone as proving something about the apathy of the Americans. For one thing, we have worked experimentally with some more or less homogeneous groups who were not meant to be representative. For another thing, we are still far from having a satisfactory instrument, in our interviews and methods of analyzing them, for the measurement of potentials for apathy and involvement in individuals; and then, as social scientists do not need to be told, it is a long step from what we call "handicraft" work with individuals to "assembly line" work with groups and social classes. A great deal of investigation by many social scientists will be necessary before we have such tools, and before the problem of using historical categories in social-psychological studies is pushed nearer to solution.

In the meantime, however, interview material can be fruitfully used, we think, to stimulate the development of hypotheses as to historical changes of the sort we have here proposed. We were struck, for instance, to find in a small community in southern Vermont a shading of difference between the way the young people and their elders expressed themselves about national and international political developments. The elders were many of them of the type we call "indignant"—high in affect, low in competence—and their indignation had a curdled quality, not an amiable one, which reminded us of similar folk as described in Granville Hicks' *Small Town*. Despite their actual lack of participation, these elders still felt some sense of relatedness to government, though this showed often only in grievance. Thus, they would tell the interviewer that they felt they ought to take part in politics, and felt guilt for not doing so. And in referring to events, they used the pronoun "I"—"I" think, "I" want, "I" hate, etc. The young people, the teen-agers, on the other hand, had less grievance and less sense of relatedness. They took whatever government gave them, including the draft, with an almost total passivity; it never occurred to them that they *ought* to do anything about it, except obey: they would certainly pass the current loyalty tests! Moreover, their interviews on politics are almost devoid of the pronoun "I"; sometimes the reference is to a group "we," and mostly to a group "they." Perhaps more "socialized," more cooperative than their parents, they do not even make use of the privilege of the underprivileged to gripe, to react—to feel strongly—about what happens to them. They have passed from "indignation" to "indifference," with low affect to match their low competence.

Our sample is much too small to be sure of this divergence. Nor are we sure whether we deal here with changed underlying attitudes, or with age-graded conventions for expressing or repressing affect, or with self-selection of the old who choose to live in small-town Vermont. Beyond that, we cannot be sure that any contemporary matching of old versus young can be taken as establishing historical changes, though it was just for the purpose of studying "older" political styles that we decided on a survey in Vermont. But we are trying to pin down and narrow possible sources of error of this sort as we work with the Vermont material.[8] And each such investigation may be viewed as a step toward the clarification and simplification of our criteria for apathy and involvement, with the hope of settling on some which are more "diagnostic" than others of the social and psychological complex which interests us. As ever, work on the problem weaves back and forth between the field and the study with, occasionally, mutual stimulation and, equally often, mutual discouragement.

One such discouragement lies in the fact, evident from the above discussion,

---

[8] The survey was made under the direction of Professor Martin Meyerson of the University of Chicago, and his wife, Marge Meyerson. The point about divergences between the young and the old was developed in discussions with them and with Rosalie Hankey, of the University of Chicago, who collaborated on the Vermont interviewing and analysis.

that it is easier to define apathy than to define its opposite, easier to spot and describe negative political orientations and the reasons for them in individual psychology and social situation, than to describe what we feel to be *appropriate* political styles and to see where, if at all, these may be developed and encouraged. Even our few interviews make plain what many know: that there is no want of people to do the dirty work of totalitarian political movements in America; this is a potential in many who are now "indifferent" apathetic types. At the same time, we have come across, out of 150 interviewees, perhaps four or five who could be classified as actually or potentially nonapathetic, and we doubt if a more favorable picture would emerge from a more complete sampling job.

This is not surprising. Character and culture combine to generate apathy. At best, involvement becomes deviant behavior, rational and adaptive though it is in historical perspective. It is rational and adaptive for the individual because, as we have said, it helps to orient him in his world and to satisfy the human need to be political. It is rational and adaptive for the society because, ever since the disillusionments of the last decades, and ever since the discovery, made by many, that America under full employment is not a particularly happy or humanly lively land, we have needed to fire people's imaginations with the possibilities of a major leap to security and freedom. It is to the nonapathetic that we look for such utopian political inventions, and to the recognition and support of those inventions when made by others. To be sure, inventions may be suppressed or ignored; all by themselves, they will not overcome apathy. But in the fate of an invention, as in the fate of a battle, there is often an element of chance. If we take the long historical view, we know that immense consequences have occasionally followed the inventiveness of a seemingly insignificant few. And if, on our other level of awareness, we take only the view of here-and-now, we can defend political involvement because, in our handful of instances, it seems to make the individual better able to face and enjoy life.

Democracy and Political Participation in the Emerging Nations

SEYMOUR MARTIN LIPSET

▬

The characteristic pattern of the stable western democracies in the mid-20th century is that of a "post-politics" phase—there is relatively little difference between the democratic left and right, the socialists are moderates, and the conservatives accept the welfare state. In large measure this reflects the fact that in these countries the workers have won their fight for citizenship and for political access, i.e., the right to take part in all decisions of the body politic on an equal level with others.[1]

The struggle for citizenship had two aspects, political (access to power through the suffrage) and economic (institutionalization of trade union rights to share in the decisions affecting work rewards and conditions). The representatives of the lower strata are now part of the governing classes, members of the club. Political controversy has declined in the wealthier stable democracies because the basic political issue of the industrial revolution, the incorporation of the workers into the legitimate body politic, has been settled. The only key domestic issue today is collective bargaining over differences in the division of the total product within the framework of a Keynesian welfare state; and such issues do not require or precipitate extremism on either side.

In most of Latin and Eastern Europe, the struggle for working-class integration into the body politic was not settled before the Communists appeared on the scene to take over leadership of the workers. This fact drastically changed the political game, since inherently the Communists could not be absorbed within the system in the way that the Socialists have been. Communist workers,

Source: Seymour Martin Lipset, "Some Social Requisites of Democracy: Economic Development and Political Legitimacy," *American Political Science Review*, 53:1 (March 1959), pp. 100–103. Reprinted by permission.
[1] T. H. Marshall has analyzed the gradual process of incorporation of the working class into the body politic in the nineteenth century, and has seen that process as the achievement of a "basic human equality, associated with full community membership, which is not inconsistent with a superstructure of economic inequality." See his brief but brilliant book, *Citizenship and Social Class* (Cambridge University Press, 1950), pp. 77. Even though universal citizenship opens the way for the challenging of remaining social inequalities, it also provides a basis for believing that the process of social change toward equality will remain within the boundaries of allowable conflict in a democratic system.

their parties and trade unions, cannot possibly be accorded the right of access by a democratic society. The Communists' self-image and more particularly their ties to the Soviet Union lead them to accept a self-confirming hypothesis. Their self-definition prevents them from being allowed access and this in turn reinforces the sense of alienation from the system (of not being accepted by the other strata) which workers in nations with large Communist parties have. And the more conservative strata are reinforced in their belief that giving increased rights to the workers or their representatives threatens all that is good in life. Thus, the presence of Communists precludes an easy prediction that economic development will stabilize democracy in these European countries.

In the newly independent nations of Asia, the situation is somewhat different. In Europe at the beginning of modern politics, the workers were faced with the problem of winning citizenship, the right to take part in the political game, from the dominant aristocratic and business strata who controlled politics. In Asia the long-term presence of colonial rulers has identified conservatism as an ideology and the more well-to-do classes with subservience to colonialism; while leftist ideologies, usually of a Marxist variety, have been dominant, being identified with nationalism. The trade unions and the workers' parties of Asia have been part of the political process from the beginning of the democratic system. Conceivably such a situation could mean a stable democracy, except for the fact that these lower-strata rights pre-date the development of a stable economy with a large middle class and an industrial society.

The whole system stands on its head. The left in the European stable democracies grew gradually in a fight for more democracy, and gave expression to the discontents involved in early industrialization, while the right retained the support of traditionalist elements in the society, until eventually the system came into an easy balance between a modified left and right. In Asia, the left is in power during the period of population explosion and early industrialization, and must accept responsibility for all the consequent miseries. As in the poorer areas of Europe, the Communists exist to capitalize on all these discontents in completely irresponsible fashion, and currently are a major party, usually the second largest in most Asian states.

Given the existence of poverty-stricken masses, low levels of education, an elongated pyramid class structure, and the "premature" triumph of the democratic left, the prognosis for the perpetuation of political democracy in Asia and Africa is bleak. The nations which have the best prospects, Israel, Japan, Lebanon, the Philippines and Turkey, tend to resemble Europe in one or more major factors, high educational level (all except Turkey), substantial and growing middle class, and the retention of political legitimacy by nonleftist groups. The other emerging national states in Asia and Africa are committed more deeply to a certain tempo and pattern of economic development and to national independence, under whatever political form, than they are to the pattern of party politics and free elections which exemplify our model of democracy. It seems likely that in countries which avoid Communist or military dictatorship political developments will follow the pattern developing in countries such as Ghana, Tunisia or Mexico, where an educated minority uses a mass movement expressing leftist slogans to exercise effective control, and holds elections as a gesture toward ultimate, democratic objectives, and as a means of estimating public opinion, not as effective instruments for legitimate turnover in office of governing parties.[2] Given the pressure for rapid industrialization and for the immediate solution of chronic problems of poverty and famine through political agencies, it is unlikely that many of the new governments of Asia and Africa will be characterized by an open party system representing basically different class positions and values.[3]

Latin America, underdeveloped economically like Asia, is, however, politically more like Europe in the early 19th century than like Asia today. Most Latin American countries became independent states before the rise of industrialism and Marxist ideologies, and contain strongholds of traditional conservatism. The countryside is often apolitical or traditional, and the leftist movements secure support primarily from the industrial proletariat. Latin American communists, for example, have chosen the European Marxist path of organizing urban workers, rather than the "Yenan way" of Mao, seeking a peasant base.[4] If Latin America is allowed to develop on its own, and is able to increase its productivity and middle classes, there is a good chance that many Latin American countries will follow in the European direction. Recent developments, including the overthrowal of a number of dictatorships, in large measure reflect the effects of an increased middle class, growing wealth, and increased education. There is, however, also the possibility that these countries may yet follow in the French and Italian direction rather than that of northern Europe, that the communists will seize the leadership of the workers, and that the middle class will be alienated from democracy. . . . Considerably more research must be done specifying the boundaries of various societies along many dimensions before

---

[2] For an interesting brief analysis of the Mexican "one-party" system see L. V. Padgett, "Mexico's One-Party System, a Re-evaluation," this REVIEW, Vol. 51 (1957), pp. 995–1008.

[3] As this paper was being edited for publication, political crises in several poor and illiterate countries occurred, which underline again the instability of democratic government in underdeveloped areas. The government of Pakistan was overthrown peacefully on October 7, 1958, and the new self-appointed president announced that "Western-type democracy cannot function here under present conditions. We have only 16 per cent literacy. In America you have 98 per cent." (*Associated Press* release, October 9, 1958). The new government proceeded to abolish parliament and all political parties. Similar crises have occurred, almost simultaneously, in Tunisia, Ghana, and even in Burma, which since World War II has been considered one of the more stable governments in Southeast Asia, under Premier U Nu. Guinea has begun life as an independent state with a one-party system.

It is possible that the open emergence of semi-dictatorships without much democratic "front" may reflect the weakening of democratic symbols in these areas under the impact of Soviet ideology, which equates "democracy" with rapid, efficient accomplishment of the "will of the people" by an educated elite, not with particular political forms and methods.

[4] Robert J. Alexander, *Communism in Latin America* (New Brunswick, N.J.: Rutgers University Press, 1957).

reliable comparative analysis of the sort attempted here can be carried out. Although the task obviously presents tremendous difficulties, it is only through such methods that we can move beyond the conventional semi-literary methods of giving illustrative examples to support plausible interpretations.

The data available are, however, of a sufficiently consistent character to support strongly the conclusion that a more systematic and up-to-date version of Aristotle's hypothesis concerning the relationship of political forms to social structure is valid. Unfortunately, as has been indicated above, this conclusion does not justify the optimistic liberal's hope that an increase in wealth, in the size of the middle class, in education, and other related factors will necessarily mean the spread of democracy or the stabilizing of democracy. As Max Weber, in discussing the chances for democracy in Russia in the early 20th century pointed out: "The spread of Western cultural and capitalist economy did not, *ipso facto*, guarantee that Russia would also acquire the liberties which had accompanied their emergence in European history. . . . European liberty had been born in unique, perhaps unrepeatable, circumstances at a time when the intellectual and material conditions for it were exceptionally propitious."[5]

These suggestions that the peculiar concatenation of factors which gave rise to western democracy in the nineteenth century may be unique are not meant to be unduly pessimistic. Political democracy exists and has existed in a variety of circumstances, even if it is most commonly sustained by a limited cluster of conditions. To understand more fully the various conditions under which it has existed may make possible the development of democracy elsewhere. Democracy is not achieved by acts of will alone; but men's wills, through action, can shape institutions and events in directions that reduce or increase the chance for the development and survival of democracy. To aid men's actions in further democracy was in some measure Tocqueville's purpose in studying the operation of American democracy, and it remains perhaps the most important substantive intellectual task which students of politics can still set before themselves.

---

[5] Richard Pipes, "Max Weber and Russia," *World Politics*, 7 (1955), p. 383.

The Intellectual and the Language of Minorities

MELVIN SEEMAN

I

The signs of deep concern about the contemporary position of the intellectual in America are not hard to find. To be sure, as Merle Curti has stressed in his presidential address to the American Historical Society, anti-intellectualism—in one form or another—has a long history in American life.[1] But in recent years the situation of the intellectual has not resembled the mere continuation of a somewhat consistent and historically routine negativism. The current sense of urgency regarding the definition of the intellectual's role has found expression in a wide variety of places: from *Time* magazine's alarm about the "wide and unhealthy gap" between the American intellectuals and the people to a series of symposiums which have appeared in the *Journal of Social Issues*, in the book edited by Daniel Bell entitled *The New American Right*, and in the thoughtful British Journal, *Encounter*.[2]

Yet, in spite of this volume of words, and the talent of those involved, it is still possible to agree with Milton Gordon's remark that "the man of ideas and the arts has rarely been studied seriously as a social type by professional students of society."[3] Whether, as some have argued, this retreat from self-analysis reflects a basic disorder in the scientific study of man is debatable enough; but the fact is clear that the research techniques which have been applied to nearly everybody else—from the hobo to the business elite—have rarely been applied to ourselves.[4]

Source: Reprinted from "The Intellectual and the Language of Minorities," in *American Journal of Sociology*, Vol. LXIV (July, 1958), by Melvin Seeman by permission of The University of Chicago Press. Copyright, 1958, by The University of Chicago Press, pp. 25–35.

[1] "Intellectuals and Other People," *American Historical Review*, LX (1955), 259–282.

[2] Cf. S. S. Sargent and T. Brameld (eds.), "Anti-intellectualism in the United States," *Journal of Social Issues*, Vol. II, No. 3 (1955); D. Bell (ed.), *The New American Right* (New York: Criterion Books, 1955); and *Encounter*, Vols. IV and V (1955).

[3] "Social Class and American Intellectuals," *A.A.U.P. Bulletin*, XL (1955), 517.

[4] The roster of those who have recently written, more or less directly, on the problem of the intellectual would comprise a list of the contemporary great and near-great in a variety of humanistic and social science fields (not to mention the physical sciences): e.g., Schlesinger and Hofstadter in history; Parsons and Riesman in sociology; Tolman and Fromm in psychology. Two well-known older works that embody the spirit of self-study are those by

This paper is a report on one such study of ourselves, its aim being to determine how intellectuals in the current social climate deal with their identity as intellectuals and, beyond that, to suggest what difference it may make if this identity is handled in different ways.

The empirical base for this report was obtained through relatively unstructured interviews (on the average about one hour in length) with all the assistant professors teaching in the humañities and social science departments of a midwestern university.[5] These interviews were not content-analyzed in any statistica sense but were simply examined for patterns of response.

The total number of persons interviewed was forty. They came, in the number indicated, from the following departments: Economics (7), English (6), German (2), History (4), Law (1), Mathematics (3), Philosophy (4), Political Science (2), Psychology (4), Romance Languages (3), and Sociology-Anthropology (4). The sample included no one from the physical or biological sciences, from the engineering and applied fields, or from the creative arts; and, when an appropriate level in the staff hierarchy had been selected, there was no further sampling problem. Co-operation was good: of a total of forty-five persons listed in the university directory at the assistant-professor level, only one refused to be interviewed (and four were unavailable because of assignments out of the city).

The procedure in the interviews was consistent though not standardized. There was no attempt to get answers to preformed questions. We engaged, rather, in a conversation regarding a letter which outlined a plan for exploring the situation of the intellectual today. The letter was not mailed; it was read by the respondent at the start of the interview and served in this way as a common stimulus object. The body of the letter, which carried my signature, follows:

There is considerable evidence (though debatable evidence, to be sure) that the role of the intellectual has become increasingly problematic in American life. Such evidence includes: (1) the widespread expression of anti-intellectual attitudes; (2) the increasing pressure for conformity in intellectual work; and (3) the typical isolation of the intellectual in community life. These current trends are presumably matters of considerable moment to university people who are uniquely concerned with the social conditions under which intellectual activity is carried forward.

It seems to me that some effort to assess the problem among ourselves is in order; and that such an effort might proceed initially by calling together small, informal groups of faculty members to clarify issues and get an exchange of viewpoints. This letter comes as an invitation to you to participate in one of these discussions on the current

---

Znaniecki (*The Social Role of the Man of Knowledge*) and Logan Wilson (*The Academic Man*). There have, of course, been many commentaries on the intellectual, especially in the more or less Marxist journals; but I am referring here to the more formally analytic mode of investigation.

[5] It seemed wiser, with a limited sample, to hold staff level constant rather than sample all levels of permanent staff. The assistant-professor group was chosen for two reasons: (1) it was large enough to provide suitable frequencies, yet small enough to be manageable without taxing time and finances, and (2) it is, in the institution studied, basically a tenure group like the higher ranks but presumably less involved in official committee work and graduate work and therefore more likely to give the time required for interviewing.

situation of the intellectual. The discussion would include four or five other persons from the humanities and social sciences, and would take roughly one hour of your time. Since several discussions are planned, I would consider it part of my responsibility to provide you with some type of analytical summary of the sessions held—in effect, a research report.

Let me emphasize that the purpose of these discussions is not to canvass possible lines of action, but to achieve a clarification of issues on matters which are clearly controversial.

Would you indicate whether you wish to be included in the list of discussants by returning this letter to me with the appropriate notation?[6]

After the respondent had read the letter, he was encouraged to comment freely on any aspect of it; then each of the three points listed in the first paragraph of the letter was discussed; and, finally, I raised the question, "Do you classify yourself as an intellectual?"

The latter question raises for us, no less than for the respondents, the matter of definition. As a first approximation, I defined the intellectuals as a group for whom the analysis of ideas in their own right (i.e., for no pragmatic end) is a central occupation. The group I chose to interview was taken as a sample of intellectuals, in spite of the fact that some would surely not qualify on more stringent criteria (e.g., their degree of dedication to the life of the mind or the quality of their intellectual work). The sample is defensible, however, on the ground that by social definition—whether he or his colleagues prefer it or not— the university professor teaching in the humanities or social sciences is probably the prime case of intellectual endeavor (i.e., of non-pragmatic and ideological pursuits). Thus, we are concerned with the self-portrait of those who, by social definition at least, are intellectuals.[7]

---

[6] The italicized portion of this letter was underlined in the original; but in one-half of the cases a more action-oriented statement was substituted for the underlined portion given here. The two types of letters were randomly alternated in the interviewing program. In the second version, the underlined sentence read: "*Let me emphasize that the purpose of these discussions is not only to achieve a clarification of issues on matters which are clearly controversial; but also to canvass suitable lines of action.*" In all cases, at the end of the interview, the respondent was asked to comment on what his reaction to the letter would have been if the alternative not presented to him had been used. The variation in letter style is mentioned here for the sake of completeness; it is not directly relevant to the treatment of the interviews reported here. The proposed discussions never took place, owing to both the press of time and a certain lack of enthusiasm—a lack which the remainder of this paper may make more understandable.

[7] This assertion, obviously, is an assumption, since the public definition of an intellectual is not a matter of empirical record, so far as I know. One could hold, further, that, if they are not so designated, they should be—that, in the ideal university, the group I have described would be identifiable as intellectuals in the sense of my stated definition. That definition has its difficulties, to be sure. For example, one might ask why an intellectual cannot believe that (or behave as if) ideas are of more than simply aesthetic interest, that ideas have consequences, and that the analysis of them serves a "pragmatic" end. A host of names come to mind of persons who would appear to have indorsed this view and whom we would presumably not wish to dismiss as intellectuals—e.g., Marx, Lenin, Jefferson, among others. The best provisional answer to this, I should think, would be that being an intellectual is not the designation for a person but for a role and that many who play the intellectual role, and play it well, are also deeply involved with the course of societal and individual development. One does not need to say, therefore, that Marx was not an intellectual because he was also a revolutionary.

In any event, though this definition does not thoroughly solve matters, it does suggest a line of approach and clarifies, perhaps, the senses in which our sample may or may not be con-

II

In a certain sense the chief finding of this study consisted of a "surprise": the unanticipated discovery of the extent to which these intellectuals use the language and mechanisms of minority status to describe themselves and their situation. It may be suggested that this should have been no surprise—that arguments quite consistent with this have been advanced in many places. And to some degree that is true.

In a recent well-publicized paper in *Harper's*, for example, a French writer had this to say:

> It seems to me that the attitude of the American intellectual in comparison with his European counterpart is based on frustration and an inferiority complex. I am continually meeting people who tell me that the intellectual in Europe enjoys a position which, if not happier, is at least more dignified than that of the intellectual in America. ... Whose fault is this? They go on to tell me that the fault rests with the American people, who have no appreciation for things of the intellect. I wonder whether it is not also in great measure the fault of the American intellectuals themselves.[8]

In a similar vein Riesman and Glazer have commented that "the opinion leaders among the educated classes—the intellectuals and those who take their cues from them—have been silenced more by their own feelings of inadequacy and failure than by direct intimidation."[9] And Marcus Cunliffe, describing the United States intellectual for *Encounter* magazine, concludes: "Altogether, there has been an unfortunate loss of self-respect. Some intellectuals have felt that, wrong about communism, they must be occupationally prone to be wrong about everything."[10]

But the point is that comments of this kind do not constitute evidence; and, indeed, it is possible, if one questions the evidence, to treat such comments themselves as reflections of a kind of minority-style indictment of one's own group (like the Jew who agrees that "we" are too clannish, the intellectual says that "we" are too weak in will). Furthermore, the comments we have cited do not provide a systematic view of the specific forms of minority language which intellectuals employ in discussing themselves. Our empirical task here is to indicate that such minority references are surprising, indeed, in their frequency

---

sidered as members of the class. To my mind it is much less important to determine whether they are, so to speak, "in" or "out" of the category than it is to recognize that they are candidates in several senses: (1) in public definitions of them; (2) in their personal self-definitions; and (3) in the definition of a university idea. The issue is nicely captured in Randall Jarrell's fictional *Pictures from an Institution*, where he says of an academic man: "He had never been what intellectuals consider an intellectual, but other people had thought him one, and he had had to suffer the consequences of their mistake" (p. 110).

[8] R. L. Bruckberger, "An Assignment for Intellectuals," *Harper's*, CCXII (1956), 69.

[9] D. Riesman and N. Glazer, "Intellectuals and the Discontented Classes," *Partisan Review*, XXII (1955), 50.

[10] "The Intellectuals: II. The United States," *Encounter*, XX (1955), 31.

and to make a start toward a categorization of the forms these references take.[11]

The clearest of these forms may be labeled *the direct acceptance of majority stereotypes*. Like the Negroes who have accepted the whites' definition of color and who choose "light" among themselves, our respondents appear eager to validate the outsider's negative view of them. One need only read these forty protocols to emerge with a collective self-portrait of the soft, snobbish, radical, and eccentric intellectual who is asocial, unreliable, hopelessly academic, and a bit stupid to boot. It is impossible to cite here the evidence for all this; but each of the stereotypes in the previous sentence has a parallel affirmation in the interview material. These affirmations are, to be sure, frequently hedged with restrictions and limitations—we are dealing, after all, with a group of highly trained qualifiers. But the significant thing is that the respondents take this opportunity to affirm the stereotype; and this affirmation is typically set in a context which makes it clear that the stereotype, rather than the qualification, has a competing chance to govern behavior. Let me give some examples:

If there is anti-intellectualism in our community, I feel frankly we are to blame. If we can't throw off our infernal need for preaching and dictating, they have a right to damn us, and we have no answer but our human fallibility [C-1].[12]

It's pretty difficult for the intellectual to mix with people. They feel ill at ease. Many intellectuals are not very approachable; perhaps his training is not complete enough. The intellectual may be more to blame for that than anyone else [C-2].

My general attitude is that some of the intellectuals are so concerned with academic freedom that it kind of tires me. And, I think, this sometimes adds up to wanting more freedom than anybody else—the kind of freedom to be irresponsible. [And later,

---

[11] A word is in order about the meaning of "minority" and the occasion for "surprise." On the latter I am aware of the fact that many occupational groups (and certainly "notorious" ones—e.g., policemen, farmers, or traveling salesmen) develop somewhat negative images of themselves. But two special conditions make this case, it seems to me, somewhat different. First, we are dealing with a high status group (note, for example, their generally high placement in the North-Hatt prestige scale); and, second, we are dealing with a group whose very function, in good part, is the objective analysis of society and its products. On these grounds, I would argue that it is not enough to dismiss the problem by saying that all occupations reflect negative self-images or that the problem approach in the stimulus letter occasioned the results obtained. The question is: What occupations have stereotypes about them, in what degree, and how are these stereotypes handled by the incumbents, with what consequences? This is the broader problem to which this paper is addressed.

With regard to "minority": I use it here to designate a group against which categorical discrimination is practiced. A minority, in this view, is determined not by size but by the behavior of being subjected to categorical discrimination. It should be clear, however, that I am not attempting to prove that intellectuals *are* a minority in this sense but that they use the typical language and forms of the classical minority groups in their self-descriptions.

[12] The source of each quotation from the interviews is identified by an assigned case number so that the reader may note the spread of the illustrations. Departmental identifications are avoided, though these would be of some interest, to preserve anonymity. There is, I presume, every reason to believe that the frequency and subtlety of minority responses will vary among universities and departments—by region, eminence, and the like. But it also seems reasonable to believe that the bulk of American universities are not substantially different from the one involved here.

when asked whether the letter should include the action alternative, this subject said:]
It shouldn't be in there, because basically I think that except in the most long-run
sense there is not a thing you can do. Maybe we can breed a new line of professors.
[C-3].

We could go on here, if space permitted, about "the snobbishness we are all
guilty of" and about the "queer birds" who "make a profession of being
different" and "don't have sense enough to pour sand out of a boot" (these
quotations coming from four different protocols). This direct acceptance by
intellectuals of the negative stereotype regarding intellectuals follows the pattern
of the minority "self-hate" which Lewin has described in the case of the anti-
Semitic Jew[13] and which has been clearly expressed in Negro color attitudes.[14]

A second, and somewhat less extreme, variety of minority attitude may be
labeled *the concern with in-group purification*. This label points to language and
behavior which are guided by the idea that the minority's troubles are rooted
in the misguided ways of a small fraction among them. The parallel with
traditional minorities reads: for the Jews, it is the "bad" Jew—the one who is,
indeed, aggressive and loud—who breeds anti-Semitism; and, for the intellectuals, it is the the radical, asocial types who are responsible for the group's
difficulty. Thus, on the radical issue, one respondent, speaking of his effort to
establish a research contact downtown, said:

I realized we had one or two strikes against us because we were from the university.
We had to have people vouch for us. We don't enjoy the best reputation down there;
we're blamed for the actions of a few who make radical speeches and seem to over-
generalize [C-4].

Another respondent, speaking of an "extreme liberal" in his college, remarked:

I've got nothing against it, but the average man might translate this [liberalism] over
to our college. In this sense, he does a slight disservice to the college [C-5].

Similarly, on scores other than radicalism there are expressions of the view
that the position of the intellectuals turns on the "impure" behavior of the
intellectual himself. One respondent, discussing anti-intellectualism in general,
remarked that we could lick the problem:

If we had people getting out and who really did mix, as speakers and members. . . .
I've worried about this: would I be willing to be in an organization if I were only a
member? We get to be president and vice-president all the time. It doesn't do any good
to be in and be officers; in order to get over the thought of us as intellectual snobs,
we have to be satisfied to be just members [C-6].

This quotation highlights one interesting result of this concern with the
"impure"—and a result which, again, has a clear minority flavor. The intellectual

---

[13] K. Lewin, *Resolving Social Conflicts* (New York: Harper & Bros., 1948), pp. 186–200.
[14] M. Seeman, "Skin Color Values in Three All-Negro School Classes," *American Sociological Review*, XI (1946), 315–321.

becomes involved in the need to prove that the impurity really is not there (or, at the very least, that the intellectual in question is not one of the "impure" few). We are familiar with the Jewish person who is inordinately careful to demonstrate in his own behavior that Jews as a group are not what the stereotype says; and Anatole Broyard has nicely described the various forms that Negro "inauthenticity" of the same type may take (e.g., what he calls "role inversion" is a careful and extreme negation of precisely those qualities embodied in the Negro stereotype—"cool" music and passive behavior, for example, being a negation of the primitive, hot, carefree quality in the Negro stereotype).[15]

The interviews reveal a similar concern with disproving the stereotype. Thus, one respondent, discussing possible action alternatives, commented:

> We could, of course, go out and make talks to various groups—show them that intellectuals really aren't bad guys [C-7].

Another, speaking about the isolation of the intellectual, said:

> Well, in neighborhood isolation, there's a lot of it due to their initial reaction—when they find out you're a professor they slightly withdraw, but, if you continue to make connections, then they find out you're a human being [C-5].

Still another person commented:

> If we mixed more, and became known as people as well as college teachers, maybe it would be better. Frequently, the antipathy to college teachers melts when they meet you personally; though we do have a tendency to carry our classroom personality into other areas [C-8].

A third major category of minority-like response may be titled *the approval of conformity*. In a certain sense, of course, the pattern just described is a specialized form of conformity; for its main aim is to emphasize the conventional as against the divergent aspects of the intellectual's behavior. But the pressure for conformity goes beyond this. It involves the same kind of passive, conservative, and attention-avoiding behavior that Lewin has described as prototypical for minority leaders, his "leaders from the periphery."[16] And, in the long run, this pressure for conformity leads to assimilationism—to the very denial of any significant observable differences on which minority status may rest. As far as the more traditional minorities are concerned, the classic Adorno volume on prejudice and personality has put one part of the conformist case as follows:

> Since acceptance of what is like oneself and rejection of what is different is one feature of the prejudiced outlook [i.e., of the authoritarian personality], it may be that members of minority groups can in limited situations and for some period of time

---

[15] "Portrait of the Inauthentic Negro," *Commentary*, X (1950), 56–64.
[16] *Op. cit.*, p. 196.

protect themselves and gain certain advantages by conforming in outward appearance as best they can with the prevailing ways of the dominant group.[17]

As with these minorities, we find that there is considerable commitment to conformity among intellectuals and that this is expressed variously as a need to adjust, to avoid controversy, or to assimilate and deny differences entirely. Thus, one respondent, discussing the conformity question raised in the letter said:

On that, I can't say I've experienced it. I'm in a pretty safe field. . . . [He then described a book of readings he had collected and said that there was a short passage from a well-known writer which had been taken out before publication.] There's no use stirring up trouble. I don't think it was a lack of courage on my part. We thought —that is, the editor and I—that it was too touchy. It's a very beautiful thing, but we took it out [C-9].

Another individual, discussing the community life of the intellectual, noted that they often do not take an active part and added:

Part of that is good, in that they are lending the prestige of the university when they do take part, and shouldn't be doing that. I don't want to be written up in the paper as Professor X of university holding a certain opinion. I've deliberately refrained from expressing political opinion [C-5].

Still others appear to argue for conformity by denying that there is a difference to which the notion of "intellectual" points:

I don't feel any different from my electrician-neighbor [C-10].

I get a kind of inferiority complex if they call me "professor"; I know that my work with the intellect is on the same level in the eyes of the man in the street as, say, a chain-store manager [C-11].

Or else there is insistence that it is important for the intellectual to assimilate or disguise himself more successfully. Thus, one respondent, speaking of occasions when he makes public addresses, said:

When I go out and meet these people, I try to fit myself into their realm, into the climate of the various groups [C-12].

Another gave, as part of his recipe for the intellectual's behavior, the directive:

He should adjust his personality so he can mix in better with the person who isn't an intellectual [C-2].

And one I have quoted before, speaking of the intellectual's isolation in community life said:

You must make concessions. I would find it pretty hard to have contacts, for example, in places like Wilder's *Our Town* or Anderson's small Ohio town, but I couldn't accuse the people in the town of being anti-intellectual; it's probably my fault. If you make a certain amount of concession, you will find a way [C-11].

---

[17] T. W. Adorno *et al.*, *The Authoritarian Personality* (New York: Harper & Bros., 1950), p. 974.

There are other comments which are less clear in their conformist implications —for example, more than faintly guilty remarks to the effect that "my neighbors see me home in the early afternoon and wonder just what it is I do in my job" (C-13). On the whole there is considerable evidence in these protocols that the typical minority response of conformity is found in a variety of forms among intellectuals.[18]

The fourth category of response represents the extreme of minority assimilation from the standpoint of the individual, namely, *the denial of group membership*. Like the name-changing Jew and the Negro who "passes," many intellectuals find means to hide or escape their unwelcome identity. An interviewee nicely described this pattern as follows:

> One consequence of anti-intellectualism is for some intellectuals to deny that they are intellectuals. This is a behavioral denial; it's part of the psychological revolution, the adjustment trend. . . . The pressure to be well-adjusted is high, and so he becomes non-intellectual and begins to deny in some respects that he is an intellectual [C-15].

The evidence in the interviews indicates that the retreat from membership is a substantial one and takes many forms. Indeed, one of the real surprises, during the course of these interviews, was the rarity of real acceptance of intellectual status. This non-acceptance is revealed in several ways. First, there is the frequency with which this freely offered remark appears: "Intellectuals, I hate the word!" Second, there are the direct denials to the question, "Do you consider yourself an intellectual?" A complete listing of the protocol responses on this point would reveal a quite consistent, though subtly varied, pattern of maneuvering, all aimed at being counted out—the kind of "Who me?" response one gets from the obviously guilty.[19]

Thus, one respondent said:

> That's a word that always does bother me. I don't think of myself so. It's a self-conscious word that sets us apart from the rest of the population. The only thing that sets us apart, in fact, is that we have gone to school longer than some, and there are doctors who have gone longer and we don't consider them intellectuals [C-10].

Another said:

> I don't apply it to myself. I never use it myself. It's sort of snobbish [C-17].

---

[18] Two of the respondents themselves commented on this "trimming of sails" in the university setting. One, for example, after noting an increase in anti-intellectual pressures, said:
"If you work at the university, you want the outside to be as non-controversial as possible; to say, 'Look at me, I'm just like anybody else.' This is part of the general line of not hurting the university by getting in the news in negative ways" (C-14). Another person, in similar vein, remarked:
"The intellectual is assuming more of the role of the non-intellectual and seeks to be a part of the gang—denies that he's different" (C-15).

[19] Even where there is acceptance of the "intellectual" label, there is sometimes a suspicious belligerence about it. One respondent, who vigorously denied the validity of the view embodied in the stimulus letter and felt that anti-intellectualism was a fictitious problem, said: "You need to live your life as if you were proud of it—talk it up" (C-16).

And still another:

> I would [use the designation "intellectual"] in the professional sense only. . . .
> Professionally, I suppose we can't avoid it. Only in the very narrow professional sense,
> in the sense that we are trying to improve the intellect of students, I suppose it applies.
> I don't see how a university professor can escape the narrow meaning of the term
> [C-1].

And, finally, one respondent clearly recognized the social definition of himself yet reflected no eagerness in his personal definition:

> I suppose I would [consider myself an intellectual]. . . . I don't know if I am twenty-
> four hours a day, but still I suppose my work would be classified or considered an
> intellectual. . . . I teach the best I can, and certainly I'm classified as an intellectual by
> the community, my neighbors, and my colleagues [C-9].

A third kind of denial of membership is shown in the efforts that are made to avoid having one's affiliation publicly known. Thus, one respondent said:

> When I'm away from the university, I usually have plenty of dirt under my nails,
> or I'm getting a harvest. Some of us fool ourselves into believing that the stain of our
> profession doesn't follow us. I can work with a carpenter for several weeks, and he
> has no notion I'm a university professor. I take a foolish pride, I suppose, in this
> [C-1].

Another remarked:

> By training we get so we show contempt for those who overgeneralize, as in the
> Rotary, and we don't want to be in arguments all the time so we stay away. And how
> often do we go out of the way to announce that we're college professors. I don't con-
> ceal it; but I don't volunteer it. It would change your relation to the group [C-4].

Thus, in one way or another, many of our respondents indicate that they do not cherish either their name or their identity as intellectuals; and they adopt a language of evasion and anonymity which is minority-like, indeed. Though one may argue that this rejection of the name is not, after all, so terribly important it seems to me more reasonable, in this case, to see the "naming trouble" as an essential part of the status involved.[20]

The fifth, and last, category of minority-like response can be designated *the fear of group solidarity*. This label indicates behavior whose essential function is similar to the conformist response; namely behavior calculated to keep the majority's attention off the minority as such. In our intellectuals this typically takes the form of strong resistance to any clearly identifiable group action on

---

[20] On a similar point Everett Hughes has written in an essay titled "What's in a Name":
"Words are weapons. As used by some people the word 'Hebrew,' for example, is a poisoned
dart. When a word is so expressively used, we are face to face with no simple matter of social
politics, but with part of the social process itself. This is, in part, what Durkheim had in mind
in his long discussion of collective symbols and concepts. Words, he pointed out, are not merely
something that happens along with the social process, but are its very essence. Naming is
certainly part of the social process in inter-ethnic and racial relations" (*Where Peoples Meet*
[Glencoe, Ill.: Free Press, 1952], p. 139).

the group's problems; the answer lies, rather, in individual goodness. One respondent, in fact, while stating the case against group action, made the minority tie himself:

The notion of action involves the whole place of the intellectual in society. In addition, direct action puts us in the position of special pleading. It's like a Jew going out and talking about anti-Semitism [C-7].

Another said:

Individual action seems more feasible. One has to measure one's forces and deploy them properly. . . . If you try to organize a society for X, Y, or Z, and you have the right people on the letterhead, maybe you're O.K.; but otherwise you're considered radical. Many things can be carried out without anybody knowing there is an organization [C-18].

Still another remarked:

I'm frankly very much afraid of any action that has the label of the organized action of the intellectuals—not afraid of what they might do, but of public reaction. It ought to be unorganized [C-19].

Many of those interviewed seem committed to "having an effect the individual way" and are against "forming an organization that's militant." They wish, in a certain sense, to be (as one respondent [C-20] described himself) "the kind of social actionist who never appears to be one." I am interested here not in asserting that the strategy of organizational effort is a sounder strategy but in noting that the arguments against it frequently reflect a desire—common in other minorities—not to become too visible or too aggressive in one's own interest.

III

Neither the quotations nor the theories given above exhaust the minority language in these protocols. Moreover I have intentionally failed to analyze or report in any fullness the more "positive" remarks on the intellectual's role in society or on the anti-intellectualism within university life itself (as one person put it [C-21]: "the destruction of the intellectual community within the university"). It was, in fact, only after the interviews were almost completed, and the variability in self-definition became ever more striking, that it was clear we might treat intellectual status directly, as one which presents a standard problem in minority adjustment.

I have argued elsewhere that marginalities of this kind provide the opportunity for the development of perspective and creativity—an opportunity whose realization depends upon the adjustment which is made to marginal status.[21] In

---

[21] M. Seeman, "Intellectual Perspective and Adjustment to Minority Status," *Social Problems*, III (1956), 142–153.

this earlier study, using the Jews as a case in point, I found that favorable adjustment to marginality was, indeed, associated with what was called "intellectual perspective"; and it now seemed possible to apply the same general logic to this sample of intellectuals.

Certainly many have asserted that there is an inherent alienative potential— an inescapable degree of marginality—in the intellectual role; and the assertion usually follows that the individual's style of adjustment to this marginality affects his performance as an intellectual. The usual view, of course, is that those who are "frozen" by this marginality and who retreat into conformity are less creative as intellectuals. Cunliffe, almost incidentally, makes this tie between mode of adjustment and creativity in advancing his distinction between two types of American intellectuals, whom he calls the "*avant-garde*" and the "clerisy":

So, if there have been many alienated Western intellectuals since 1800, whom I will label the *avant-garde*, there have also been others, [the "clerisy"] of similar intellectual weight, though as a rule of less creative brilliance, who have remained more or less attached to their society.[22]

The discovery, in the interviews, of so many and so varied responses to this marginal aspect of the intellectual's position suggested the possibility of testing, in a small-scale empirical way, such common assertions about the consequences (or correlates) of the intellectual's adjustment to marginality. The hypothesis to be tested parallels that given in the earlier paper on the Jews as a minority; namely, that those intellectuals who have successfully adjusted to the marginal character of their role—those who, let us say, reveal a minimum of our five minority-style attitudes toward themselves as intellectuals—will be, in turn, the more creative workers in their respective crafts.

For a provisional glimpse of such a test, and to illustrate at the same time one possible utility of the descriptive categories developed in the previous section, I attempted to score the forty protocols for evidence of commitment to, or rejection of, each of the five categories. At the same time, I asked a group of persons in the various departments (in all cases, men of higher academic rank than the individual in question) to judge the professional creativity of those interviewed. Creativity here refers to the ability to make the "given" problematic: the ability to challenge the routines and to provide alternatives to the standardized "right answers" in the respective fields.

Unfortunately, though expectedly, the free-response character of the interviews led to some serious limitations as far as the present more quantitative interest is concerned. For example, on two of the five minority categories (No. 2, "concern with in-group purification," and No. 5, "fear of in-group solidarity") more than one-third of the protocols received a score of 3, which indicated a lack of substantial evidence in the interview; and, in addition, among the

---

[22] *Op. cit.*, p. 25.

remaining two-thirds of the cases, there was a very poor numerical split between "high" versus "low" adjustors on these two categories.

In view of these limitations, I shall not attempt to present what would amount to a complete, but premature, account of the adjustment ratings and creativity judgments.[23] But it is of illustrative interest to note what happened on the three remaining "minority response" categories where a more reasonable split between high versus low adjustment was obtained. "High" adjustment refers to a tendency to reject the use of the indicated minority-like modes of response in self-description; "low" adjustment refers to a tendency to embody the indicated minority-type response. Table 1 reveals what was obtained when individuals who scored 3 (no evidence) on each category were eliminated and when the high and low adjustors were compared on their average creativity. The data in Table 1 are read as follows: For the twelve persons who scored either 4 or 5 on category 1 (i.e., whose responses were antithetical to the acceptance of majority stereotypes about the intellectual), the mean creativity score was 3.27 with a standard deviation of 0.65. For the thirteen persons who scored low in adjustment on this same category (i.e., who revealed a clear tendency to accept negative stereotypes), the mean creativity score was 2.54, with a standard deviation of 1.19.

Table 1 / Mean Creativity Scores and Standard Deviations for Individuals Scored High Versus Low on Three Categories of Minority Response to Intellectual Status

Adjust-ment Group	Category 1— Acceptance of Stereotypes			Category 3— Approval of Conformity			Category 4— Denial of Membership		
	N	Mean	S.D.	N	Mean	S.D.	N	Mean	S.D.
High	12	3.27	0.65	16	2.74	0.84	13	2.48	1.02
Low	13	2.54	1.19	15	2.53	1.35	15	2.34	1.06

---

[23] I am indebted to Mrs. Frances Mischel, a graduate student in sociology and anthropology, for the two hundred "minority" ratings (five ratings on each of forty protocols). These ratings were "blind" as far as identification of individuals or specialty fields was concerned. They were done as independently as possible, as far as the five categories are concerned, to minimize "halo." A total of 120 creativity judgments by colleagues were secured; and the evidence suggests that there is substantial agreement among them. Both the adjustment and the creativity ratings were made on five-point scales. For minority adjustment, the scale read as follows: 1—very much evidence of this; 2—some evidence of this; 3—no evidence one way or the other; 4—some evidence of rejection of this mode of response; 5—clear evidence of rejection of this mode. The creativity scale ran simply from 1 ("low in creativity") to 5 ("high in creativity") and was accompanied by a full-page explanation of both the meaning of creativity in this context and the method to be used in making the ratings. It should be clear that the term "adjustment" does not refer to the standard psychological meaning of the term; it designates only whether the respondent reflects or does not reflect the five categories of response described here. Thus, "high adjustment" refers to those who scored either 4 or 5 on the given category; "low" refers to a score of 1 or 2 on the category.

The differences in creativity between adjustment groups are consistently in the direction of higher ratings for those who do not use the minority-style response to intellectual status. Though the N's are small, and the differences are not uniformly great, the trend is clear, and the difference between adjustment groups for Category 1 is statistically significant.[24]

I do not take this as an unequivocal demonstration of the hypothesis in question. For one thing, there are other variables of considerable relevance (e.g., the age of the respondent) that cannot be controlled adequately in a sample of this size; and, in addition, questions remain open about the reliability of the adjustment ratings.[25] But for purposes of illustration the trend revealed in Table 1 is of considerable interest, for it suggests that the minority orientations I have attempted to specify here may be treated (provisionally, at least) not simply as categories of description but as relevant factors in the performance of the intellectual role as such.

It is customary, of course, to conclude by noting the need for further research —in this case, research on the forms and consequences of anti-intellectualism. But there is one crucial thing.—To find, as we have, that many intellectuals adopt, without serious efforts to build a reasoned self-portrait, an essentially negative, minority view of themselves and to find, in addition, some plausible ground for believing that this failure in self-conception is not independent of role performance—gives a special cast to the usual call for research. Thus it would seem essential to recognize that this research must include, if we may call it that, an "inward" as well as an "outward" orientation—that is, we must presumably conduct two related research operations: a study of the attitudes that others take toward intellectuals as well as a more intensive study of the intellectuals' attitudes toward themselves. A serious effort along those lines might yield considerably more than the usual research project; it can become an opportunity for self-discovery.

---

[24] A test of the homogeneity of the two variances for the adjustment groups yielded an F ratio which approximated the 0.05 level of significance and raised doubt about the wisdom of pooling the variances for the two groups in computing the t test between the creativity means. The obtained t ratio for the test of Category 1 was 1.841, a figure which is significant at the 0.05 level using a one-tailed test. Neither of the two remaining categories yielded a significant t. The method used to test for homogeneity of variance and for the significance of the difference between means is given in A. Edwards, *Statistical Methods for the Behavioral Sciences* (New York: Rinehart & Co., 1954), pp. 271–274.

[25] The question of reliability of rating may not be a serious problem. The same judge who did the ratings in this case was also used in the previously mentioned study of Jewish adjustment; and in that case the ratings of two independent judges, completing a task quite similar to the rating task involved here, were quite reliable (see the paper cited in n. 21 above). I have not deemed it essential for purposes of this illustration to compute another reliability figure for the judge in question.

Crisis at Columbia

THE COX COMMISSION

███████

CHRONOLOGY: APRIL 23–30, 1968

APRIL 23: *Demonstration at the Sundial.* The Sundial is in front of Low Library, the target announced for a protest march by SDS (Students for a Democratic Society) the day before. The purpose was to dramatize SDS's demand that the University dissociate itself from the Institute for Defense Analysis and that it guarantee public hearings and "full rights of due process" to students with charges pending against them for participation in an earlier protest demonstration (on March 23). About 500 persons assembled at the Sundial on Tuesday at noon. Low was found to be locked. After some discussion a little more than half of the crowd marched on the construction site of the Park Gymnasium, where they tore down a section of the fence and clashed briefly with security guards. They then returned to the Sundial and rejoined the others.

Occupation of Hamilton Hall. At about 1:30 P.M. the demonstrators moved from the Sundial to stage a sit-in at Hamilton Hall, a classroom building that also houses administrative offices, including the office of Dean Coleman, Dean of Columbia College. When Dean Coleman returned from lunch he was detained, along with several other officials. In the course of the afternoon black militant outside groups, including SNCC (Students' Non-Violent Coordinating Committee) and Harlem CORE (Congress on Racial Equality) joined the demonstrators. By 8:00 P.M. the announcement was out that "the black community is taking over."

Occupation of Low Library. SDS and the white demonstrators exited from Hamilton, leaving the building in the hands of the black students and their allies from the Harlem community. They proceeded to Low Library and forcibly entered it by smashing a glass door. They quickly occupied the entire structure including President Kirk's office on the ground floor. They later yielded the first floor and made their headquarters on the second.

APRIL 24: *Occupation of Avery Hall.* Wednesday evening, students of the School of Architecture, on their own, without evident collaboration with SDS or SNCC, seized control of the building and barricaded the entrance.

Source: Adapted from *Crisis at Columbia*—The Cox Commission Report (New York: Vintage Books, 1968), pp. 99–143. From *Crisis at Columbia*—The Cox Commission Report. Copyright © 1968 by Random House, Inc. Reprinted by permission.

COLUMBIA
UNIVERSITY
The Center of
The Morningside Campus

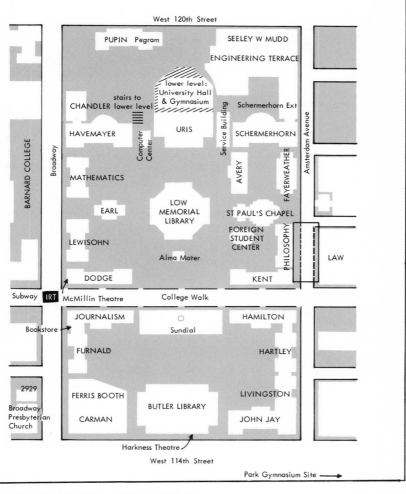

West 120th Street

PUPIN Pegram

SEELEY W MUDD

ENGINEERING TERRACE

lower level:
University Hall
& Gymnasium

stairs to
CHANDLER lower level

Schermerhorn Ext

HAVEMAYER

URIS

Computer Center

Service Building

SCHERMERHORN

Amsterdam Avenue

Broadway

MATHEMATICS

AVERY

FAYERWEATHER

BARNARD COLLEGE

EARL

LOW
MEMORIAL
LIBRARY

ST PAUL'S CHAPEL

LEWISOHN

FOREIGN
STUDENT
CENTER

PHILOSOPHY

LAW

Alma Mater

DODGE

KENT

Subway IRT McMillin Theatre

College Walk

JOURNALISM

Sundial

HAMILTON

Bookstore

FURNALD

HARTLEY

2929
Broadway
Presbyterian
Church

FERRIS BOOTH

BUTLER LIBRARY

LIVINGSTON

CARMAN

JOHN JAY

Harkness Theatre

West 114th Street

Park Gymnasium Site

SOURCE: The Cox Commission, Crisis at Columbia
(New York: Vintage, 1968), p. 2. Reprinted by permission.

THE ISSUES

A. The projected gymnasium in Morningside Park, which symbolized the shortcomings of Columbia's attitude toward her black neighbors.

B. The University's relationship to the Institute for Defense Analyses, which symbolized complicity in the war in Vietnam.

C. The imposition of discipline upon six SDS leaders, without a formal hearing, for breach of the rule against indoor demonstrations.

Source: Crisis at Columbia—The Cox Commission Report (New York: Vintage Books, 1968), p. 75. From *Crisis at Columbia*—The Cox Commission Report. Copyright © 1968 by Random House, Inc. Reprinted by permission.

APRIL 25: *Occupation of Fayerweather Hall.* Early Thursday morning about fifty students seized and occupied Fayerweather, an office and classroom building for economics, sociology, and political science. Again, it appears that this group was largely independent of SDS and SNCC.

Faculty reaction. Wednesday afternoon the faculty of Columbia College met in special session. It passed a resolution calling for suspension of work at the Park Gymnasium construction site, warning against police action to clear the occupied buildings, and proposing the creation of a tripartite committee of faculty, students, and administration to act on disciplinary matters growing out of the disturbances. A day later, on Thursday afternoon, more than one hundred members of the faculty constituted themselves informally as the Ad Hoc Faculty Group (AHFG), on the premise that as an independent body they might be effective in a role of mediation and conciliation. By 7:30 P.M. more than 150 signatures had been affixed to a resolution requesting the administration to suspend the gym construction and institute immediately the proposed tripartite disciplinary committee, requesting students to evacuate the seized buildings, and affirming their intent—this was the novel element—to "stand before the occupied buildings to prevent forcible entry by police or others."

Administration reaction. High officials of the administration tried to end the racially sensitive occupation of Hamilton Hall through negotiation. President Kirk proposed to call a meeting of the Trustees to consider the resolution adopted by the faculty earlier that afternoon recommending suspension of construction work on the gymnasium and to follow a lenient course in applying disciplinary sanctions. The proposal was rejected by the black students.

APRIL 26–30: Thursday evening through the following Monday evening was a period of negotiation, attempted conciliation, and the adoption of a policy of "public mediation" by the AHFG. A strike had been called by the students and was largely effective. Police appeared on the campus in noticeable numbers (many were in plain clothes) as early as Friday evening, but in the beginning they limited their role to monitoring exit and entrance from the campus—mainly at 116th Street, Broadway at one end of Campus Walk and Amsterdam Avenue at the other. AHFG members established cordons at the entrances of the occupied buildings, permitting people inside to leave but dissuading others from entering. The strike was managed by the SDS-influenced Strike Coordinating Committee (SCC). A new organized force, The Majority Coalition, came into being and sought to play a role by setting up its own secondary cordons in front of the AHFG cordons; its very appearance reflected the fact that a considerable body of student opinion, ranging from conservative to moderate, mistrusted the proclaimed neutrality of the AHFG. The depth of the polarization is suggested by the pejorative terms *jocks*—athletic types—and *pukes*—hippie types— that came into common use. The existence of double cordons did not prevent the outbreak of a number of clashes involving police, faculty, guards, and students on both sides. Tension continued to mount until the bust: the police were called in force on Monday afternoon, and during the early hours of Tuesday, April 30, they first cleared the buildings and then the campus. There was great violence: 692 persons were arrested; 103 persons were treated at Knickerbocker or at St. Luke's Hospitals for injuries; 70 of the injured were Columbia University faculty, staff, or students; 20 were nonstudents; and 13 were police officers.

———

I

The April uprising started and grew haphazardly. As it developed to the final academic cataclysm, its entire character was altered.

The long series of turbulent demonstrations beginning in 1965, which were tolerated by most of the University community, leaves a tragic sense of the inevitability of the final escalation. Packing the lobby of Hamilton Hall—even the somewhat ambiguous obstruction of Dean Coleman's liberty—was scarcely different from the earlier confrontation in John Jay Hall or the sit-in following the CIA demonstration. SAS's decision to evict the whites and barricade the doors in a demonstration of black student power—one of the key turning points—was a response to an occasion thrust upon the black students. With each successive day the uprising gathered its own physical and emotional momentum.

Source: Crisis at Columbia—The Cox Commission Report (New York: Vintage Books, 1968), pp. 189–199. From *Crisis at Columbia*—The Cox Commission Report. Copyright © 1968 by Random House, Inc. Reprinted by permission.

We reject the view that ascribes the April and May disturbances primarily to a conspiracy of student revolutionaries. That demonology is no less false than the naive radical doctrine that attributes all wars, racial injustices, and poverty to the machinations of a capitalist and militarist "Establishment." Student revolutionists within SDS planned turbulent confrontations and revolutionary tactics. They manipulated facts in ways that created distrust and bred unwarranted antagonism. There apparently was occasional talk of wider revolution to overthrow the present political system. A very few revolutionists may have been in dead earnest. More, we suspect, were half in dreamland, feverishly discussing romantic tactics but hardly contemplating realistic execution. Part of the responsibility for the disturbances rests upon the revolutionaries consciously seeking to subvert and destroy the University but their total number was small —much less than the full SDS membership—and their activities were only the catalyst that precipitated a deeper movement.*

II

By its final days the revolt enjoyed both wide and deep support among the students and junior faculty and in lesser degree among the senior professors. The grievances of the rebels were felt equally by a still larger number, probably a majority, of the students. The trauma of the violence that followed police intervention intensified emotions but support for the demonstrators rested upon broad discontent and widespread sympathy for their position.

The record contains ample proof of this conclusion. The very number of students arrested in the buildings—524 Columbia students in the first police action—is convincing. Many more had been in the buildings earlier. Some of the latter were doubtless curiosity seekers. For others in both groups the affair probably had many of the elements of the once-traditional spring riots and subsequent "panty raids." But even after discount is made for those elements, the extent of active participation in violent and unlawful protest is significant.

The existence of broad underlying unrest is also shown by the progress of the seizures. The action of the black students in Hamilton Hall was entirely independent of SDS. The seizure of Avery Hall by architectural students was their own movement. The occupation of Fayerweather Hall, in which a large part of graduate study in the social sciences is centered, was apparently spontaneous; no evidence of an SDS connection has come to our attention.

---

* By the same token our comments concerning the above group should not be applied to the much larger number who seek fundamental change in the established order without embracing doctrinaire revolutionary theory and tactics.

INSIDE FAYERWEATHER HALL

The demonstrators were in good spirits and very highly organized. Food was plentiful, a first aid station was set up, a lost and found office, a communications room, a newsletter was mimeographed. People slept in classroom buildings and hallways. And always meetings and more meetings lasting long into the night. Participatory democracy. There was a real community spirit; everything belonged to everybody; the building was "liberated." Girls—about 40%—were not expected to do the kitchen work alone, for this was a "liberated" area, and boys had to help. Couples slept together in public view, nobody cared, we were "liberated": here was a single commune in which adult hypocrisies did not apply any longer, where people shared and shared alike, where democracy decided everything, where people were free of adult values and codes. Fayerweather was tense, "up tight," but free and in high spirits.

Source: Crisis at Columbia—The Cox Commission Report (New York: Vintage Books, 1968), p. 186. From *Crisis at Columbia*—The Cox Commission Report. Copyright © 1968 by Random House, Inc. Reprinted by permission.

Outside the buildings the militants enjoyed visible support in the form of the thousands who watched from various points on campus, most conspicuously at the Sundial. A campus poll reportedly boycotted by those in the buildings showed that 74 per cent of the participants favored "end gym construction," 68 per cent favored severing ties with IDA, and 37 per cent even favored amnesty for all students involved in the demonstrations.

The events after the police "bust" point to the same conclusion. The emotions excited by the brutality must have polarized opinion. There would be a tendency to put unjust blame upon those who called for police intervention rather than those—chiefly from SDS—whose deliberate efforts to provoke disruptive turbulence made it almost inevitable that police action would be required. Despite these complex cross-currents, the extent and persistence of the ultimate reaction against the University Administration is adequately explained only by the presence of strong but latent dissatisfaction quickened by the violence of events.

For the future it is equally important to note that the support for the activists has come from the portions of the student body who are most energetically concerned with university and community affairs.

III

The avowed objectives of the April demonstrations, stripped of their context and symbolism, were inadequate causes for an uprising.

The University's IDA affiliation had little practical importance. It was being reviewed by the Henkin Committee as part of a larger study of Columbia's relations to outside agencies. There was not the slightest reason to doubt that the normal academic procedures could produce a reasoned and fairminded decision upon the merits. The disruptive potential of the IDA affiliation at Columbia, as at other universities, was that it enabled the large part of the intellectual community, especially students, to transfer to the campus their intense moral indignation against the Vietnam war.

The gymnasium issue was more complex, but it too was a symbolic issue. At least some black students freely acknowledge not only that the issue was over-simplified but that the public gymnasium to be built by Columbia would be more beneficial to the community than the 2.1 acres of rocky parkland, *if* the project could be judged upon that aspect alone. But the project could not be judged out of the context of Columbia's relations with its poorer neighbors and society's treatment of racial ghettos.

The third issue, the discipline of the six IDA demonstrators, had somewhat greater substance. Although most students would probably have agreed that the disruptive manner of conducting SDS demonstrations was becoming intolerable, many students were antagonized by the manner in which the "no indoor demonstration" rule was promulgated and the discipline was administered.

Since the rule came close to the area of free expression staunchly guarded by Columbia's liberal tradition, it was of intense concern to the entire University community. Nevertheless, the prohibition was promulgated by President Kirk without consultation with students, and apparently without prior discussion with faculty members. In fact, the rule ran contrary to the unanimous recommendation of a tripartite committee whose report the President withheld.

The rule, which was an obvious target for militants, was formulated in terms that hampered consistent administration and invited provocation.

Out of the 100 students who engaged in the March IDA demonstration, six SDS leaders were selected for punishment. It was difficult to persuade students that this was not a discriminatory selection even though the Dean's office explained that these six and no others were recognized.

The six IDA demonstrators were refused a public hearing and peremptorily punished. Although the older paternalistic procedures probably gave much greater protection to most student offenders, there is wide and justified campus support for the principles (1) that a student is no less entitled to due process of law than one charged with a public offense and (2) that students should share in disciplinary procedures as part of the right of participation in decisions affecting their interests.

RESOLUTION OF THE AD HOC FACULTY GROUP

28 April 1968

We believe that there is a fundamental crisis which is shaking the foundations of this University and that thus far no solution has been found. The Ad Hoc Faculty Group proposes what we believe may be the last possibility of peaceful settlement.

I. We recommend that the President establish the Tripartite Commission in the form defined in the report of the Ad Hoc Committee composed of Professors Galanter, Hovde, and Trilling.

We recommend that the University statutes be revised by the Trustees so that the Tripartite Commission serve as the body of ultimate judicial review on all matters affecting University discipline.

We believe that the dimensions and complexity of the current crisis demand that a new approach of collective responsibility be adopted, and in this light insist that uniform penalties be applied to all violators of the discipline of the University.

II. All excavation work at the gymnasium site having been suspended, we now recommend that the Trustees at their next meeting, which we urge occur within three days, request the Mayor of the City of New York urgently to convene a panel composed of:

a. representatives of the Trustees,

b. representatives of the Community appointed by the Mayor,

c. representatives of the Faculty to be chosen by the Faculty themselves.

We recommend that this panel review the gymnasium and adopt an alternative to the present plans. Should the alternative involve remaining on the present site, this plan shall be acceptable to the representatives of the Community.

III. We request that once the President indicates that he accepts these resolutions as his recommendations to the Trustees, we call upon the students now improperly occupying various buildings to vacate these buildings immediately and to submit themselves to due process as shall now be established.

IV. These proposals being in our judgment a just solution to the crisis our University is presently undergoing, we pledge that

a. If the President will not adopt these proposals, we shall take all measures within our several consciences to prevent the use of force to vacate these buildings.

b. If the President does accept our proposals but the students in the buildings refuse to evacuate these buildings, we shall refuse further to interpose ourselves between the Administration and the students.

V. We cannot believe that the Trustees, charged with the welfare of all segments of the University, will not accept a solution regarded as just by students, faculty, and the President.

VI. As members of the faculty, we are determined to do everything within our power rapidly to resume the full life of this institution in the firm expectation that our proposals will permit a climate to prevail that will once again allow reason, judgment, and order to reign.

Source: Crisis at Columbia—The Cox Commission Report (New York: Vintage Books, 1968), pp. 212–213. From *Crisis at Columbia*—The Cox Commission Report. Copyright © 1968 by Random House, Inc. Reprinted by permission.

IV

Three among the purely internal causes of unrest especially impressed us.

1. At a time when the spirit of self-determination is running strongly, the administration of Columbia's affairs too often conveyed an attitude of authoritarianism and invited distrust. In part, the appearance resulted from style: for example, it gave affront to read that an influential University official was no more interested in student opinion on matters of intense concern to students than he was in their taste for strawberries. In part, the appearance reflected the true state of affairs. The machinery of student government had been allowed to deteriorate to a point where Columbia College had no student government. The Report on Student Life was not released for seven months until CUSC members threatened publication. The President was unwilling to surrender absolute disciplinary powers. In addition, government by improvisation seems to have been not an exception, but the rule.

2. The quality of student life was inferior in living conditions and personal association.

3. Columbia, like other universities, has scarcely faced the extraordinary difficulties that face black students in the transition from a society permeated by racial injustice to one of true equality of opportunity. We recognize, of course, the difficulty of immediately remedying such deficiencies as the paucity of black teaching and administrative personnel and of appropriate courses and counseling for all students, but the indisputable fact of alienation of our black students, with all that that fact entails, makes a more active and creative search for solutions particularly urgent.

V

The fabric of Columbia was twisted and torn by the forces of political and social revolution outside the University. Columbia's geographic situation symbolizes the relation between white and black, affluence and poverty, youthful reform and established order. The University's need for physical expansion in an urban center creates inescapable tensions but its relations with the community had further deteriorated because of its apparent indifference to the needs and aspirations of its poorer neighbors. The handling of the gymnasium controversy thus came, even somewhat unfairly, to epitomize the conflict between the spirit of the civil rights movement and the attack on poverty, on the one hand, and, on the other, the ways of an *ancien régime*. Energetic and idealistic students, alienated from the older generation by an extraordinarily wide gulf in manners and interests and offended by the plethora of human suffering, were drawn to the side of change. Where they were frustrated by the massive anonymity of the government and the unmanageability of the social system, they could strike out at the more vulnerable University.

In like fashion, the University became the surrogate for all the tensions and frustrations of United States policy in Vietnam.

The desire for student power, while scarcely articulated as a cause for seizing the campus buildings, was a powerful element of the explosion. Discussion since the uprising has focused upon the methods by which students may exert more influence upon the government of an institution of which they are vital and integral parts. Participation in self-government is a natural human desire that today's students feel with greater urgency, particularly at institutions with highly selective admissions policies because they are much better educated than their predecessors, more sophisticated, in many respects more mature, and more interested in social problems than seeking out conventional careers. (Unfortunately, they are also much less disciplined.)

VI

The hurricane of social unrest struck Columbia at a time when the University was deficient in the cement that binds an institution into a cohesive unit.

Again, geography is a factor. The competing attractions of the exciting metropolitan area, coupled with the housing problems that induce a majority of the faculty to live outside Manhattan, operate as centrifugal forces. Yet the dispirited quality of student life outside the classroom is not beyond the University's power of influence.

The formal organization of both the administrative offices and the faculties apparently tends to discourage the cohesiveness that comes from shared responsibility in matters of university concern. We were struck by the constant

A THIRD-WORLD MANIFESTO

Come, then, comrades, the European game has finally ended . . .

The Third World today faces Europe like a colossal mass whose aim should be to try to resolve the problems to which Europe has not been able to find the answers. . . .

It is a question of the Third World starting a new history of Man, a history which will have regard to the sometimes prodigious theses which Europe has put forward, but which will also not forget Europe's crimes, of which the most horrible was committed in the heart of man, and consisted of the pathological tearing apart of his functions and the crumbling away of his unity. And in the framework of the collectivity there were the differentiations, the stratification and the bloodthirsty tensions fed by classes; and finally, on the immense scale of humanity, there were racial hatreds, slavery, exploitation and above all the bloodless genocide which consisted in the setting aside of fifteen thousand millions of men.

So, comrades, let us not pay tribute to Europe by creating states, institutions, and societies which draw their inspiration from her.

Humanity is waiting for something other from us than such an imitation, which would be almost an obscene caricature.

If we want to turn Africa into a new Europe, and America into a new Europe, then let us leave the destiny of our countries to Europeans. They will know how to do it better than the most gifted among us.

But if we want humanity to advance a step further, if we want to bring it up to a different level than that which Europe has shown it, then we must invent and we must make discoveries.

If we wish to live up to our peoples' expectations, we must seek the response elsewhere than in Europe.

Moreover, if we wish to reply to the expectations of the people of Europe, it is no good sending them back a reflection, even an ideal reflection, of their society and their thought with which from time to time they feel immeasurably sickened.

For Europe, for ourselves and for humanity, comrades, we must turn over a new leaf, we must work out new concepts, and try to set afoot a new man.

Source: Frantz Fanon, *The Wretched of the Earth* (New York: Grove Press, Inc., n.d.). First published in 1961, Constance Farrington, trans., p. 255.

recital of an apposition between the Administration and the faculty as rival bodies with separate interests, for it would seem to us that on educational questions the two should be essentially one. The lack of a University Senate and the division of the professors and other teachers into three or four faculties—quite apart from the professional schools—where other universities have a single Faculty of Arts and Sciences, apparently discourages faculty participation in the formulation of University policy and the improvement of student life. The central Administration to which the full burden of the quality of student life is left is not equipped for the duty. Far too few members of the University family are closely involved, outside the classroom, in the constant informal enterprises and discussions by which the values of an academic community are constantly reexamined and those which stand the test are passed on to the next generation.

Institutional coherence is also affected by the presence or lack of a spirit of institutional self-confidence. Unhappily, despite her inherent strengths, the spring crisis struck Columbia when her self-confidence was shaken by the decline in relative position in AAUP rankings of graduate departments, the exclusion from a Ford Foundation grant for improvement of graduate studies, the resignations of a number of senior professors, and the Strickman filter incident.

VII

The scale of the disturbances was greatly enlarged in numbers, intensity, and violence by the delay in calling the police—from Thursday night until Monday night—which the Ad Hoc Faculty Group forced upon the University officials. Although perhaps the effort had to be made, there was never a significant chance that the Group could negotiate a peaceful withdrawal from the buildings. Forcing the delay, by threats of physical interposition, increased the likelihood of violence and magnified the reaction by lending an air of legitimacy to use of the tactics of physical disruption as means of forcing one view of policy upon those who held another.

VIII

Our next five observations must be taken as a unit. Language requires stating them one at a time, but none can survive unless joined with the others.

A

A university is essentially a free community of scholars dedicated to the pursuit of truth and knowledge solely through reason and civility.

A privately-endowed university depends upon the experienced guidance of wise counselors and managers both inside and outside academic ranks, and also upon the financial and moral support of a large, organized body of alumni and friends. But their vital contribution must never obscure the essential quality of the institution: the university is a community of scholars, both teachers and

HELL BROKE LOOSE

The affair of May 21–22 was a phase of the confrontation that began on April 23. Clearing the buildings on the night of April 29–30 had done nothing to resolve the crisis. The issues remained. The antagonisms were deepened. There was quiet but not the usual order. The outbreak of further turbulence should not have been surprising.

* * *

Source: Crisis at Columbia—The Cox Commission Report (New York: Vintage Books, 1968), pp. 181–182. From *Crisis at Columbia*—The Cox Commission Report. Copyright © 1968 by Random House, Inc. Reprinted by permission.
Editors' Note: The events referred to occurred during the early morning hours of April 30— the police bust.

students. Any tendency to treat a university as a business enterprise with faculty as employees and students as customers diminishes its vitality and communal cohesion.

B

Resort to violence or physical harassment or obstruction is never an acceptable tactic for influencing decisions in a university. This principle does not require notions of property or legality to sustain it. It derives from three considerations.

First, force, harassment, and physical obstruction contradict the essential postulate that the university is dedicated to the search for truth by reason and civility.

Second, resort to such physical coercion tends to set in motion an uncontrollable escalation of violence. This is the plainest lesson of the rising cycle of violence that began at Columbia with the Naval ROTC demonstration in 1965 and culminated in the brutality of April 30 and May 22. The sequence of steps was not inevitable but each was the readily predictable consequence of those that went before.

Third, the survival—literally the survival—of the free university depends upon the entire community's active rejection of disruptive demonstrations. Any sizeable group, left to pursue such tactics, can destroy either the university by repeatedly disrupting its normal activities or the university's freedom by compelling the authorities to invoke overwhelming force in order that its activities may continue. The only alternative is for the entire community to reject the tactics of physical disruption with such overwhelming moral disapproval as to make them self-defeating.

This vital decision rests with the liberal and reform-minded students. They can save or destroy the institution.

C

The acceptability of the foregoing principle depends upon organization of the scholarly community in ways that produce both loyalty and the relief of grievances. The government of a university depends, even more than that of a political community, upon the consent of all the governed to accept decisions reached by its constitutional processes. The consent of the dissenters depends partly upon their knowing that their views effectively entered into the process of consensus, even though they did not prevail. They must also be convinced that the opportunities for change are open and the goals and stance of the enterprise are sufficiently right for it to deserve their loyalty despite specific points of disagreement. Administrative intractability and resistance to change contribute to the breakdown of law and order.

D

The student body is a mature and essential part of the community of scholars. This principle has more validity today than ever before in history. It is felt more keenly by a wider number of students, perhaps because of the increasing democratization of human institutions. As with all human activities, the wise division of functions and responsibilities must take into account the special skills or limitations of particular groups, as well as efficiency of operation. The process of drawing students into more vital participation in the governance of the university is infinitely complex. It cannot be resolved by either abstractions or tables of organization. It does not mean that issues must be settled by referenda. *We are convinced, however, that ways must be found, beginning now, by which students can meaningfully influence the education afforded them and other aspects of the university activities.*

The activist supporters of reform who voiced the grievances pressed by the rebels included many of the natural leaders among students—both political and intellectual leaders. They were deeply hurt by statements treating them merely as disloyal trouble-makers aligned with a small band of rebels. While their own releases, for reasons of student politics, contributed to the polarization of opinion by their lack of civility, we have not the slightest doubt that the survival of Columbia as a leading university depends upon finding ways of drawing this very large and constructive segment of the student body, which supported the strike, back into the stream of university life where it can share in the process of rebuilding.

With participation, students will surely acquire a more sophisticated under-standing of the universities' difficulties and complexities and of the necessary functions of the faculty and administration, the alumni, and the governing body. In the same process, the latter would come to an understanding they cannot otherwise acquire of the true needs and aspirations of students and values and shortcomings of current educational measures.

E

We add only that the success of those who must follow this difficult course will depend in no small measure upon the willingness of parents, alumni, and friends to recognize that the April crisis is thus being converted into a creative source of renewal.

LIFE, THE UNIVERSITY, AND "DISENCHANTMENT OF THE WORLD"

The fate of our times is characterized by rationalization and intellectualization and, above all, by the "disenchantment of the world." Precisely the ultimate and most sublime values have retreated from public life either into the transcendental realm of mystic life or into the brotherliness of direct and personal human relations. It is not accidental that our greatest art is intimate and not monumental, nor is it accidental that today only within the smallest and intimate circles, in personal human situations, in *pianissimo*, that something is pulsating that corresponds to the prophetic *pneuma*, which in former times swept through the great communities like a firebrand, welding them together. If we attempt to force and to "invent" a monumental style in art, such miserable monstrosities are produced as the many monuments of the last twenty years. If one tries intellectually to construe new religions without a new and genuine prophecy, then, in an inner sense, something similar will result, but with still worse effects. And academic prophecy, finally, will create only fanatical sects but never a genuine community.

To the person who cannot bear the fate of the times like a man, one must say: may he rather return silently, without the usual publicity build-up of renegades, but simply and plainly. The arms of the old churches are opened widely and compassionately for him. After all, they do not make it hard for him. One way or another he has to bring his "intellectual sacrifice"—that is inevitable. If he can really do it, we shall not rebuke him. For such an intellectual sacrifice in favor of an unconditional religious devotion is ethically quite a different matter than the evasion of the plain duty of intellectual integrity, which sets in if one lacks the courage to clarify one's own ultimate standpoint and rather facilitates this duty by feeble relative judgments. In my eyes, such religious return stands higher than the academic prophecy, which does not clearly realize that in the lecture-rooms of the university no other virtue holds but plain intellectual integrity. Integrity, however, compels us to state that for the many who today tarry for new prophets and saviors, the situation is the same as resounds in the beautiful Edomite watchman's song of the period of exile that has been included among Isaiah's oracles: "He calleth to me out of Seir, Watchman, what of the night? The watchman said, The morning cometh, and also the night: if ye will enquire, enquire ye: return, come."

The people to whom this was said has enquired and tarried for more than two millennia, and we are shaken when we realize its fate. From this we want to draw the lesson that nothing is gained by yearning and tarrying alone, and we shall act differently. We shall set to work and meet the "demands of the day," in human relations as well as in our vocation. This, however, is plain and simple, if each finds and obeys the demon who holds the fibers of his very life.

Source: Max Weber, "Science As a Vocation," in *From Max Weber: Essays in Sociology*, Hans H. Gerth and C. Wright Mills (eds. and trans.) (New York: Oxford University Press, 1946), p. 156.

PART FOUR

SOLUTIONS

"What should we do?" is the question put more and more clamorously to sociologists—who, for the most part and in good conscience, find it unanswerable. Still, the question, rising in volume and frequency on every hand, can scarcely be avoided.

Earlier in this book we suggested that some of our most serious problems stem from a basic pathological condition; that they may be embedded in the very structure of our society; and that disease, which is exemplified by genocide, mass terror, and thermonuclear war, goes far toward obliterating all signs of health. If our social situation is nearly as grave as we suspect, then in order to change it, desperate action would seem to be necessary. Indeed, it is perhaps already too late for any action; all "remedies" initiated now or in the near future, could fall far short of meeting our urgent need.

It is not for us as sociologists, with our limited knowledge, to say whether man will survive his "problems" or be overwhelmed by them. We can say that, although the Apocalypse may soon be upon our species, and although there is yet time, a systematic sociological appraisal of methods currently used to "solve" social problems is certainly in order. If nothing more it should help to clarify the nature of those problems and how they might better be conceptualized—while incidentally exposing the inadequate or inept means we too often adopt in our haste to resolve them.

There are many modes of remedial action that are doomed to failure from the outset, no matter how brilliantly conceived they may be. The best remedy cannot work if it is designed to cope with an inaccurately identified problem. When misidentified, the problem leads necessarily to inappropriate proposals for action. If taken, the action sometimes produces genuine problems that are also misperceived and misidentified. The original error feeds on itself ; trouble waxes; insight wanes.

Thus we commonly concern ourselves with the divorce rate, and fixated on it, lose sight of the underlying reality, that of family stability and instability in a mercurial world. What is usually called the crime problem blinds us to something else, of which it is merely a symptom, namely a chronic disparity between social control and the traditional definition of unlawful acts. Our disinclination (or our inability) to pay for effective social control of criminal behavior begets one of two parallel illusions: either that what we take for granted as criminal is "natural," and that therefore nothing can be done about it, or the converse, that crime is simply evil and must be stamped out no matter what the consequences.

Mass terror and population decimations are not necessarily isolable problems ; they might better be defined anew as events integral to certain institutional arrangements in post-modern society. These institutional features range from familial socialization to social competition; they enforce a marked tendency toward impersonal, objectified mistreatment of human beings in the interests of a given political policy.

The foregoing examples show the discrepancy between the popular definition of a social problem (by the electorate, the administrative bureaucrats, elected politicians, businessmen in vested interest associations) and the reformulation of a problem by sociological analysis. We wish to suggest a sociological scheme for delineating solutions in relation to the causal explanation, or etiology, of a problem. The schema, "Panaceas and Nostrums," is one that suggests several possible points of departure.

Given a definition of a problem at one etiological level, what are the consequences for its solution if we attack it at another level? As Thomas Gladwin reports, in the first selection reprinted subsequently, Miller's study of psychological intervention seeking to change juvenile attitudes toward authority,

Panaceas and Nostrums	
Sources Posited: Etiological Levels	*Panaceas Prescribed: Social Action Examples*
1. BIOLOGICAL (Genetic, physiological, constitutional)	MEDICAL (Eugenics, plastic surgery, vitamins, tranquilizers)
2. PSYCHOLOGICAL (Personality, regression, aggressivity, frustration, etc.)	ADJUSTMENT (Change of persons by means of therapy, psychiatry, counseling, etc.)
3. SOCIAL PSYCHOLOGICAL (Learning, reference group, interactions)	EXPERIENCE BY (a) contact with others (b) indoctrination through mass media (c) education
4. SOCIAL STATUS (Group attributes or strata attributes)	LEVELING (Expand opportunities for disadvantaged strata, e.g., group work, birth control, etc.)
5. SOCIAL INSTITUTIONS (Neighborhood, community, area aggregates)	SOCIAL REORGANIZATION (Urban renewal, political action, public health, bureaucratic reorganization, legislation, warfare)
6. SOCIAL VALUES (Norms, traditional attitudes)	INDOCTRINATION (Adult education, public relations, propaganda)

adults, school, and middle-class values in a "desirable" direction, showed no significant reduction of the delinquency rate. In terms of our schema, delinquency so conceived is a problem of level 4, but Miller's attempts to deal with it were at levels 2 and 3.

Gladwin's article demonstrates that there has to be a logical relationship between the etiological conception of a problem and intelligent attempts to do something about it.

The discrepancy already noted between a popular definition and the sociologically analyzed redefinition of social problems can be applied to a number of seemingly insoluble and generally recognized problems so serious that they might extinguish or, at least, cripple our society.

The problem of establishing and maintaining the peace of the world has been obscured in its common definition by sloganeering (Better Dead than Red, Peace with Honor) and by assigning scapegoats (It's the fault of Germans, Russians, Chinese—when not Japanese, or all foreigners). The "solutions" that follow seem simple, and they are simple-minded. For example, "If we abolish the munition makers, we could then disarm." (George Bernard Shaw, in the guise of Andrew Undershaft in *Major Barbara*, disposed of that notion some years ago.) The problem of the peace is one that has to be solved in a hard way, as Amitai Etzioni has stated in his book's sloganized title, *The Hard Way to Peace*.[1] This way involves a basic reorganization of our values and institutions. The Great Powers have to find acceptable techniques of shifting from an escalation of the arms race into a world devoted to Professor Seymour Melman's peace race.[2] This requires answering such questions as: How do we allocate the resources and energies now expended on arms to peaceful uses? Do we concentrate on underdeveloped areas, or do we focus upon raising living standards at home? Can we do both in a radioactive world where the safety levels of Strontium 90 and other poisonous products are constantly being revised upward? Indeed, the schema on p. 460 suggests that we may well be on our way to a biological solution (through genetic destruction of chromosomes and bone marrow) of a problem heretofore defined by the question: Can we survive a nuclear war?

The literature on this subject is enormous and ranges from sober evaluation of limited nuclear conflict and what our side can get out of it (for example, Herman Kahn, Edward Teller, and, we suppose, their Russian counterparts) to voices of doom warning us that we must not permit this situation to go on much longer.

In the excerpt from Moynihan's *Maximum Feasible Misunderstanding* there are some of the sources of our recent past and probable future posture on the solution of social problems. He suggests that a self-consciousness and

---

[1] Amitai Etzioni, *The Hard Way to Peace: A New Strategy* (New York: Collier Books, 1962).

[2] Seymour Melman, *The Peace Race* (New York: Ballantine Books, 1962).

awareness accompanies the "knowlege" codification of reformers, whereas Gans suggests an emphasis on social planning that involves physical environmental changes and concurrent programs for upgrading and increasing the mobility of poor people.

The roles of leaders in making decisions that are supported by their followers and actions that arise from these decisions are the topic of Seymour Leventman's selection. Here we see the successes noted by Alvin W. Gouldner in his *Studies in Leadership* and by C. Wright Mills in *The New Men of Power*. They deal with sincerely dedicated leaders committed to a mobility ethos in which personal ascent up the status ladder transcends the original aims of their action. In some such manner, all social movements—ethnic integration, universal education, trade unionism, and political action—are made rigid, get organized, and become hierarchically structured. Their leaders use the efficient bureaucratic structure to further their power goals, as well as to meet the aims of their organization. Even though this process is taken for granted in business, its presence in other areas of organized social action seems to have gone largely unnoticed.

Herbert Gans' article is constructive, but it can hardly be called optimistic. Social planning is possible, but the technical complexities and political obstacles it encounters are more likely to give pause than to fire enthusiasm. In sociological perspective, a program to be rational and effective should seek to foster what Gans names "guided mobility." Urban poverty is not going to be eliminated by physical "renewal" or psychiatrically oriented programs of social meliorism. But if guided mobility offers the best hope, ultimately, it is far harder to implement than the piecemeal programs now in vogue with city planners and social workers. This is a case in which what seems to be the least practical procedure may provide some kind of solution. To know even this much about a social problem is to have departed drastically from the conventional outlook and the conventional wisdom.

Once a social problem has been adequately defined, and seen to be amenable to solution, a policy decision must be made. We choose above all between doing something and doing nothing. A decision to act entails the further choice of the *target* of action, whether to aim at the individual or at the social and institutional organization involved in the problem. Schematically one might view it as follows:

	Target	
Action	*Individual*	*Social Structure*
+	therapeutic intervention	meliorism
−	positive neglect	laissez-faire

If the solutions proposed to real problems are not panaceas for illusory problems, all sensible action requires an estimate of the consequences of a decision to take action. If we are going to do something in order to ameliorate, abolish, allay, or aid, we must ask the following:

1. Is the action related in a specific way to the phenomenon we are trying to correct or change?
2. If it is related, how is it related?
3. What will happen if we act?
4. What will happen if we do not act?
5. If we accept a statistically normal amount of crime, divorce, mental illness, disease, disaster, political unrest, and economic dislocation, what are its limits?
6. How much pathology should we regard as normal in a given social system?
7. If we act to solve a problem as defined popularly, how much does it cost in social consequences and in money?
8. If we redefine the problem sociologically and act to solve it, how much will it cost?
9. If we do not act, what are the costs?

All ameliorative action requires decisions, and these always entail subsequent decisions based on assumptions about costs, degrees of efficiency in reaching goals, and suitability of goals. Logically and ideally, one should always—though it rarely happens—examine all proposed actions and compare them to the alternative of not acting at all. When we compare action and nonaction we can see that a considered decision to do nothing involves systematic weighing of most of the same questions associated with deciding to act.

Ways of Acting: Doing Nothing and Doing Something
Doing something involves:
1. Definition of a problem and its boundaries.
2. Specification of objectives.
3. Selection of appropriate means of attaining objectives.
4. Evaluation of effectiveness of action.

Doing nothing involves:
1. Definition of a problem and its boundaries.
2. Specification of objectives.
3. Selecting, or opting for lack of action, doing nothing as the appropriate means of attaining objectives.
4. Evaluation of the effectiveness of nonaction.

One can frequently make a rather attractive case for doing nothing, on three grounds: (1) Spontaneous recovery rates in many social problems involving behavior seem to give better results than recovery rates linked with specific actions. (2) Actions on a problem may result in undesired consequences and other problems that would not arise if we did not act. (3) Many actions based on inadequate understanding are irrelevant to the real problems.

But, in the contemporary world there are strong, although not necessarily scientific, reasons for preferring action to inaction. Political considerations, ego-satisfactions, cross-pressures of interest groups—all enter into decisions to act rather than stand pat. Utopian visions may sometimes becloud harsh realities and impel actions not consonant with careful or logical analysis of the facts. On the other hand, inaction does brake action solely for the sake of action.

An abundance of information available limits action. Given a general state of ignorance, one can act in any manner whatsoever—without fear of exposure. Much information will generally slow down decisions to act, especially so with respect to such social problems as we have considered in this volume. When our information is contradictory, inconsistent, and incomplete—and it usually is—thoughtless action may be impeded.

In part, this accounts for our capacity to make it appear that social actions are occurring when in reality they are being delayed or diverted. Studying a problem at length is a favorite method of handling pressures to act. Often the problem will change; contemplated and pressured action can then be safely forgotten; it no longer applies; the problem is redefined.

Another popular mode of avoiding action while apparently engaging in it is to remove everyone from the situation. A revolt breaks out in Hungary or Poland. Crush it and the problems that give rise to revolution, while still there, are no longer defined as such. The affected population has been destroyed. In more democratic societies, as a rule, such extreme measures are avoided. In dealing with the problem of slums, poverty, and their attendant phenomena of crime, disease, illiteracy, and disorganization, we have used urban renewal. By razing the area and thereby effectively removing the population, we solve the problem of slums by destroying them (although we send their former occupants to create a slum elsewhere).

By far, the most popular way of doing nothing by acting is to individualize problems and treat them as matters that pertain only to individuals. Thus, we tend to define problems as medical and psychiatric or as matters of individual morality. Because this means, in effect, that we are asking persons to adjust their lot while we counsel, cajole, and persuade them, the problems remain but perception of the problems is translated from the social sphere of action to the domain of individual initiative.

This seems to be the critical area of dispute in solving social problems. It pervades all matters of public concern and finds its expression in the preachments of organized religion, medicine, and law, as well as in the basic patterns of socialization at home and in school.

Adjustment is the goal, and if individuals can achieve it, then our actions or inactions are justified. There are real costs in this position because adjustment may also mean apathy, gloom, and loss of interest even in matters of social survival. Adjustment does not mean satisfaction, and because satisfactions in living are what count to most of us, it may be that we prefer to die rather than adjust to lives of dissatisfaction and frustration. So far, actions initiated by men of good and ill will have not solved our most elemental problems—those of human survival, famine, disease, senseless premature death, and widespread dissatisfaction—in an equitable manner throughout the social structure.

A case in point is the very much greater incidence of drug addiction in this country, where legislation has intensified the problem, by contrast with England and Wales, where the problem is negligible. Why should the Briton be thirty-four times less likely to use narcotics than the American? Wilkins ingeniously interprets the disparity as due (in part) to differences in social definition of narcotics addiction. It is a criminal vice, in the official American view, whereas the British have always perceived it as a sickness. Is it possible that our appraisal of need—it *must* be suppressed—has produced both the motive and the structure of opportunities (lacking in Great Britain, because drugs may be prescribed by physicians) that make for a large-scale social problem? If so, it is clear that a policy of responsible nonaction should always be held open as possibly the better alternative. The more dramatic forms of coping with deviant behavior judged by some to be intolerable may actually encourage it, and thus create a social problem where none of such magnitude existed before.

CHAPTER 1

CAUSE AND CURE: MATCHING LEVELS

Strategies in Delinquency Prevention

THOMAS GLADWIN

▬

Alarm over increases in juvenile delinquency is reaching acute proportions, and has created inescapable pressure on schools, police, social agencies, and governments to do something about delinquency. In particular, the alarm, and therefore the pressure, focuses on delinquency in lower-class urban populations. Presumably this is because delinquency is more prevalent in these populations, and also because lower-class delinquents display more of the physical violence which so distresses middle-class people. The question, then, is posed with increasing insistence: What can or should be done about delinquency in big city slums?

Current theoretical formulations on juvenile delinquency in the United States are phrased in largely sociological terms, emphasizing the interplay between personality structure and social institutions. Action programs based on these formulations select one or more strategic points around the circle of causality at which to intervene, and thereby hopefully to break the circle. Most commonly, manipulation is attempted with respect to the psychological links in the chain. Programs of this sort have largely been directed by social workers, with the assistance of psychiatrists and psychologists. The aim is to alter self-defeating attitudes and perceptions, and to redirect social energy toward more constructive goals which will hopefully prove more satisfying and less frustrating. However, in actual practice the relationship of a worker with lower-class clients is usually structured in terms of the psychoanalytically-oriented clinical training of the worker, and the goal of the relationship becomes one of draining off or deflecting acute psychological and social tensions. In essence, the worker tries to make conformity tolerable.

Source: Leonard J. Duhl (ed.), *The Urban Condition* (New York: Basic Books, Inc., 1963), pp. 267–275. Reprinted with permission.

This strategy of psychological manipulation of individuals or groups has come under increasing criticism, especially with respect to lower-class delinquency. It has been pointed out that professional intervention based on a psychothera-peutic model has little impact on the basic social and cultural conditions which channel psychological needs in troublesome directions. This criticism states in effect that lower-class people develop self-defeating attitudes because they are in fact defeated by their society.

An additional argument against this kind of psychological intervention is provided by Walter B. Miller's findings in working with lower-class gangs, that while it was possible to change many psychological attributes—attitudes toward authority, adults, education, and to some extent general middle-class values—in a desirable direction, no significant reduction was achieved in the rate of delinquent acts.[1]

However, the dilemma of the social agencies has recently led to experiments with massive assaults on the social environment. These generally propose saturation of a lower-class neighborhood with multiple and varied services intended to alleviate simultaneously all of the various social limitations which the proponent of the plan views as serious. There are numerous obvious criti-cisms which can be leveled at the strategies of this sort thus far proposed. Most are so expensive in both money and professional requirements that they offer little hope of providing in themselves a strategic model of subsequent usefulness elsewhere.

The answer to this objection is that new insights and ideas will be found and proven effective, and that these can then be applied selectively and less ex-pensively in other areas. However, the proposed programs are so global that their evaluation also tends to be global, and it becomes very unlikely that the specific impact of any single program can be isolated and measured. Therefore even if these programs are demonstrably successful, their benefits will be largely limited to the affected area or community.

Perhaps we must recognize that juvenile delinquency *as such* is not directly amenable to programs of prevention or amelioration. If we accept this, we can contemplate programs which will achieve a more critical and economical focus upon selected components of the problem of the lower-class adolescent, with the expectation that in the long run delinquency rates will drop proportionately as one after another of the forces pressuring these adolescents is relieved. Juvenile delinquency is not a distinct social disease or syndrome. It encompasses a number of different kinds of behaviors. Furthermore, the behaviors defined as delinquent are by no means the only ways in which adolescents can or do respond to their many-faceted dilemmas. Juvenile delinquents are simply those individuals or groups who happen to react to a situation in ways which the

---

[1] Miller, W. B., "The Impact of a 'Total Community' Delinquency Control Project," *Social Problems*, 10:168–191, 1962.

larger society views as threatening. In contrast, the youth who enters military service, for example, may thereby achieve temporary relief from his difficulties, but his behavior is not considered delinquent.

Equally we must recognize that the pressures and blockages are by no means perceived and experienced in the same way by everyone. One adolescent may feel frustrated and discriminated against because he cannot go to college or because he is unable to get a white-collar job, and therefore feel he must somehow vent his frustration, or at least escape from his dilemma. But another may have set his heart on being a long-haul truck driver and feel no frustration whatever.

The challenge, then, is to identify those attributes of the social environment which are perceived by the largest number of lower-class adolescents as unfair limitations upon them. If we can find realistic ways to relieve these limitations (which are usually very real) we may hope to reduce progressively a succession of those social pressures which cause some youths to react with behaviors we call delinquent.

However, any strategic alternative to a direct attack on delinquency must meet at least two conditions. One is that the alternatives be realistically feasible and within reach of available financial and professional resources. The second is that the goal of any new program must be high enough in the hierarchy of middle-class values so that the self-evident worth of the new program will justify its substitution for the original aim of simply preventing delinquency as such.

One goal meeting these requirements would be a substantial increase in the number of lower-class adolescents who complete high school and attain a regular and educationally respectable diploma. A diploma is not the cure for all the problems of any lower-class youth, and at best would be unattainable for many, but a substantial proportion of the population of our concern have the ability and would unquestionably be much better off if they could complete high school satisfactorily. It is therefore worth examining with some care the potential value and feasibility of starting the attack on the lower-class dilemma with a focus on the academic achievement of lower-class youths in high school.

Middle-class values link education not only to occupational opportunity but also to the formation of good character. High school dropouts are related in the popular view directly with delinquency—even though many adolescents leave school for the respectable purpose of entering productive employment. Similarly, the first question likely to be asked by enforcement officers or judges if a boy gets in trouble is, "How is he doing in school?" Clearly, a program goal of improving school performance and participation meets the criterion of self-evident worth as a substitute for, or an indirect approach to, delinquency prevention as such.

From what we as social scientists know of the lower-class dilemma, a valid high school diploma is clearly of ever increasing importance to an adolescent for at least two closely related reasons. It is in the first place a testimonial to "good character," and in fact during its acquisition many middle-class behaviors and attitudes are necessarily acquired. It reflects a willingness to conform.

It is also an essential, even though not in itself sufficient, key to the middle-class opportunity structure. This results from the continued dwindling of the skilled labor market and the increasing requirement of a high school diploma for consideration for even a semi-skilled job. And of course without a diploma from high school, college is also out of the question.

The difficulty is that lower-class children are lacking not so much in educational opportunities as in the capability or readiness to utilize these opportunities. Schools are available. In lower-class areas the teachers may not be quite as good but they at least meet minimum requirements. To some degree, the inability to capitalize on opportunities is recognized in planning for lower-class students. However, the response is usually an attempt to adapt the school to the child, rather than the reverse.

Thus it is frequently stated that schools demand middle-class behaviors, and that this handicaps the lower-class child. This is undoubtedly true, but the answer is not necessarily to relax the demands. If we recognize that a high school diploma acts as a badge of middle-class respectability, the schools must continue to demand middle-class behaviors. At the risk of appearing cynical, when I see a negligible relationship between the content of the average high school curriculum on the one hand, and the abilities required in the jobs for which a high school diploma is demanded on the other, I believe we are forced to conclude that the *primary* value of the diploma is as a certificate of socialization. It certifies that the holder of a diploma will respond in predictable ways to the expectations of middle-class employers.

There is a real danger in pressuring schools to meet the lower-class child at his own level. Successful school participation requires above all working fairly hard and steadily at tasks which at best are often dull, in order to achieve a very distant reward, the diploma. In other words, in order that academic learning itself be achieved, the student must accept the necessity of hard work and delay in reward and gratification—behaviors which lie at the heart of middle-class values. Equipped to work within these values, lower-class youths can and do move upward. Without them they are more than likely to fail in school and to spend their lives in underprivileged poverty.

The problem therefore is not primarily one of making the schools more accepting of lower-class adolescents and their behaviors (although certain unnecessary rigidities could be relieved), but rather of preparing lower-class children to accept and fit into middle-class society. Part of this, of course, consists in effecting changes in elementary school curricula which will develop thinking styles better adapted to the requirements of curriculum in the higher grades, but this is a separate and complex problem. Even more important, for many lower-class children, is the development of more positive values and attitudes toward schooling and teachers such that they will be willing to modify their behaviors to conform to teachers' expectations, and yet will not in the process suffer a disastrous loss of status in the eyes of their peers.

It is hard to believe that the massive reality of the meaning of a high school diploma is unknown to lower-class youth. They must all know slightly older boys, in particular, who have found the doors to good jobs permanently closed to them for lack of a diploma. The reality is constantly restated in the mass media, in recruiting and employment offices, and in a thousand other ways. Yet equally constant is the expression of negative attitudes toward schools among lower-class adolescents.

The contrast between the perceived value, even necessity, of schooling, set against consistent attitudinal devaluation of the school, almost certainly reflects a thinly veiled rationalization. The need for rationalization emerges from a belief, based on long experience and shared by many lower-class adolescents, that sooner or later their academic careers will inevitably end in failure. Their school performance has been unsatisfactory and subject to criticism. As a social experience, school has been so humiliating that there is no realistic basis for expecting personal acceptance by teachers. In other words, the lower-class student sees the cards stacked against him.

Here it is useful also to bear in mind that an increasing number of studies have pointed out the quite limited future-time orientation which obtains in much of the lower class. The inability to implement plans or hopes discourages realistic thinking about one's status in the years to come. It is more comfortable, and often psychologically essential, to live from day to day. Only by stripping the future of reality can life appear tolerable. Yet I am convinced that any program which offered some measure of meaningful help and encouragement in school, and which could demonstrate some achievement or reward in return for the expenditure of energy or the demonstration of willingness, would find acceptance among large numbers of lower-class children from junior high school onward. I also believe—despite the hostility and rejection of school by these adolescents, which we see every day—that the relief from a perhaps unconscious sense of defeat would improve their outlook and behavior in school and out. They would, in effect, become less likely to undertake the acts we call delinquent. A few examples can be cited which point tentatively in this direction.

In a primarily lower-class Negro enclave known as Ken-Gar in a middle-class white area of Montgomery County, Maryland, school achievement was revealed as conspicuously poor when the schools were integrated, and delinquency was fairly high. A group of white adults from the surrounding area organized a program on a voluntary basis to tutor and encourage the Ken-Gar children in all grades. School achievement rose rapidly, high school drop-outs decreased, adults developed more interest in the schooling of their children, and there appears to have been some decrease in juvenile delinquency. Recently the success of this venture led to the county board of education hiring a full-time director for Ken-Gar, and another person who is developing similar programs among other underprivileged groups in the county.

Neighborhood House, in a very depressed and apathetic Negro slum area of Richmond, California, instituted a Study Hall Project. They set up a center for evening study, organized as a social center but with supervision and some tutorial help with homework. Although it is not yet clear what effect this has had on academic achievement, it has resulted in a striking change among neighborhood youths with respect to homework. Whereas in the past anyone who brought books home from school was obviously a square, now one has to account for oneself if books are not brought home. It is fashionable to study, or to seem to study, and with this half the battle is won. At the same time school personnel are aware of this project and are pleased by it. This undoubtedly affects favorably the response of teachers toward these students and increases the possibility of their social acceptance by the teachers, quite aside from objective academic achievement.

Another example is provided by the Work-Study Program of the University of Southern California Youth Studies Center, conducted in the Santa Monica schools. This is a program which combines a half day of study with a half day of (often subsidized) employment and vocational counseling. This program has apparently had some success in keeping students, who were selected as imminent drop-outs, in school. But the really interesting development is that in its second year the students began complaining that the academic part of the program was not sufficiently rich.

The most ambitious undertaking of this sort to date is the Higher Horizons program in New York City schools in underprivileged neighborhoods. With its exploratory predecessor, "Project 43," this has been evolving and expanding since 1956. It has included help with school work, counseling with parents and with teachers, class trips and cultural activities, and a variety of other approaches to helping students do better in school and feel better about schooling. There has been an explicit attempt to develop in the students the idea of planning for their futures, and the recognition that education is not only a necessary but also a possible part of such planning. Starting with two high schools it has expanded into elementary schools and into additional junior high and high schools. Careful evaluation demonstrates striking gains in almost all areas of school achievement and a reduction in school misbehavior, truancy, and drop-outs. Although out-of-school behavior, including delinquency, has not been evaluated, it is hard to believe that this has not been improved also.

These examples are only straws in the wind. They certainly do not exhaust the possibilities for ingenious programs. They encourage the belief, however, that very rewarding possibilities exist for programs which will actively focus on the negative attitudes toward education which pervade and infect the lower-class adolescent subculture in most cities. Opening up the possibilities for academic success at least to the point of getting through high school, with the change in values and behavior which this implies, will certainly not solve all the problems of lower-class youth, nor even touch some of the causes of juvenile delinquency. But it does offer a real hope for increasing access to the opportunity structure of our society for substantial numbers of lower-class persons, with a very modest social agency investment. As such, it is a strategy which should receive serious attention.

The Professionalization of Reform

DANIEL P. MOYNIHAN

━━━

Thus far the origins of the community action program of the war on poverty will have appeared familiar enough. Intellectuals were doing their work—trying to make sense of the time, hoping to conceive solutions to its problems. Editors were getting it all into print; the ideas were diffusing. Now, however, a somewhat new element appears, having to do with the crucial difficulty encountered in the transition from the world of ideas to that of action. Beginning in the 1950s it becomes possible to discern the emergence of a new style—an additional style might be the more correct term—in social reform. In times past the impulse to reform and efforts in that direction had, generally speaking, risen among those groups most oppressed by existing conditions, or most likely to benefit from equitable change, or from members of the public regarding middle and upper classes who, from an enlightened and generous understanding, were able to identify their own interests with causes that benefited others in the first instance but redounded ultimately to the welfare and stability of the society as a whole. This model—if that is not too pretentious a term—of reform is one in which pressures for change arise outside the institutions that are to be changed or are capable of bringing it about. Obviously, from time to time institutions seek to reform themselves, in the sense that the effort arises from within. This is a matter of definition, almost, in terms of universal institutions such as the medieval Church. But in the electoral democracies of the Atlantic world, where at any given time only a limited number of matters are regarded as political, the effort to bring about social change has typically taken the form of seeking to add a particular issue to the political agenda of the moment, thereby, hopefully, bringing about the expenditure of public funds or the imposition of public restraints and legal sanctions to obtain the desired effect. Child labor, the sale of alcohol, the chlorination of water supplies, the beautification of highways: there .was a very long list of private concerns that were slowly translated into public issues by persons imposing pressure on the agencies of government—the courts, the legislature, the executive—capable of doing what the reformers wished done. Inasmuch as these agencies were repeatedly colonized and infiltrated by reformers there has usually been some internal pressure in favor of reforms, especially when the issue is quite general, as, for example, labor legislation, and specialized government departments can be created to further the cause. By mid-century, however, the process of external pressure and internal encouragement had acquired a degree of institutionalization and expertise that might be described as the professionalization of reform. Increasingly efforts to change the American social system for the better arose from initiatives undertaken by persons whose profession was to do just that. Whereas previously the role of organized society had been largely passive—the machinery would work if someone made it work—now the process began to acquire a self-starting capacity of its own. To borrow an exaggeration from the world of automation so much in fashion at this time, the machinery began to think for itself.

This development first became evident in the Kennedy years when the national government eagerly began to seek out new ideas and programs. Kennedy's had been a severe critique of American society, whose great weakness he in effect declared was complacency, the failure to see how many things were wrong that needed righting. His election brought to Washington as officeholders, or consultants, or just friends, a striking echelon of persons whose profession might justifiably be described as knowing what ails societies and whose art is to get treatment underway before the patient is especially aware of anything noteworthy taking place.

Writing for the British journal, *The New Society*, just prior to the assassination of President Kennedy, Nathan Glazer described the process:

Without benefit of anything like the Beveridge report to spark and focus public discussion and concern, the United States is passing through a stage of enormous expansion in the size and scope of what we may loosely call the social services—the public programs designed to help people adapt to an increasingly complex and unmanageable society. While Congress has been painfully and hesitantly trying to deal with two great measures—tax reform and a civil rights bill—and its deliberations on both have been closely covered by the mass media, it has also been working with much less publicity toward final passage of a number of bills which will contribute as much to changing American society.[1]

---

[1] Nathan Glazer, "A New Look in Social Welfare" in *New Society*, **7**, November 1963, p. 6.

The stalemate in American government was being broken. Already a number of major measures in the fields of regional development, mental health, vocational education, and manpower retraining had been enacted. Waiting in the wings, as Glazer put it, were a host of comparable measures whose headlong enactment in the twenty-four months or so following the assassination marked one of the most active legislative periods in the history of the Republic. But the most interesting thing about all this sudden expansion of social services was that behind it, as Glazer noted, there was "nothing like the powerful political pressure and long-sustained intellectual support that produced the great welfare measures of the New Deal—Social Security, Unemployment Insurance, Public Welfare, Public Housing." [2] Yet the programs moved forward. Lacking a better explanation, one must conclude that a new quantity had entered the equations of these new professionals.

It will be recalled that at this time the American poor, black and white, were surpassingly inert. The Negro civil rights movement in the South was still just that: a movement in the South for civil rights. There was almost no economic content to the protest. The American poor were not only invisible, in Michael Harrington's phrase, but they were also silent. Kennedy had ventured into West Virginia searching for Protestant votes, not for poverty. There he encountered the incredible pauperization of the mountain people, most particularly the soft-coal miners, an industrial work force whose numbers had been reduced by nearly two-thirds in the course of a decade, but with hardly a sound of protest. The miners were desperately poor, shockingly unemployed, but neither radical nor in any significant way restive. (It may be noted that in 1964, in the face of the historic Democratic sweep, Harlan County, Kentucky, returned a freshman Republican Congressman.) The Appalachian experience gave the Kennedy administration an early sensitivity to the issue of poverty and deprivation, but it was a self-imposed concern, and politically an optional one. (The decision to emphasize poverty in the 1964 legislative program, which would set the theme for the presidential year, was a close one: a strong case was made within the administration to address the 1964 campaign to problems of the suburbs, where many of the trade union members in the nation had settled.) The war on poverty was not declared at the behest of the poor: it was declared in their interest by persons confident of their own judgment in such matters. As Glazer put it, at a time when the process was not at all as visible as it was to become, the fate of poor:

. . . is in the hands of the administrators and the professional organizations of doctors, teachers, social workers, therapists, counselors, and so forth. It is these who, in a situation where the legislation and programs become ever more complex, spend the time to find out—or rather have brought home to them through their work—the effects of certain kinds of measures and programs, and who propose ever more complex programs which Congress deliberates upon in the absence of any major public interest.

---

[2] *Ibid.*

When Congress argues these programs, the chief pressures are not the people, but the organized professional interests that work with that segment of the problem, and those who will benefit from or be hurt by the legislation.[3]

Four major influences can be perceived behind this development.

1. *The econometric revolution.* Although it is still too soon to speak with full confidence, the likelihood grows that in the area of economic policy there was a genuine discontinuity associated with World War II: before it men did not know how to make an industrial economy work at high and expanding levels of activity; afterwards they did. The combination of Keynesian theory and the increasingly sophisticated and dependable quantification of economic movements, associated with such men as Wesley C. Mitchell and Simon Kuznets provided for the first time a working model of an industrial economy that permitted a very high order of successful management. That such success would be greatest in a society with no politics, and that in certain conditions of political deadlock or disorder the best model imaginable is of no practical use, need not detract from the fact that the political leaders of the 1960s in the United States *were* able to make use of this new knowledge. In the other industrial democracies of the world, or such as were left of them, memories of the political disasters that accompanied the prolonged economic depressions of the 1920s and 1930s had provided the strongest of incentives to maintain high levels of employment. (In 1964, unemployment, adjusted to conform more or less to United States definitions, was 2.9 per cent in Italy, 2.5 per cent in France and Britain, and 0.4 per cent in Germany. Consider the contrast with the unemployment that followed the First World War.) Postwar America had experienced a not less extraordinary economic growth, albeit erratic and associated with much more joblessness. Under Kennedy, however, an immensely powerful and competent political economy took hold. Growth became steady, unemployment declined, the future became predictable in a way it had never been. (The Council of Economic Advisors' forecast of Gross National Product for 1964 was off by only $400 million in a total of $623 billion, while the unemployment forecast was on the nose.) In an unbroken expansion, the longest in American economic history, the GNP grew from $503.7 billion in 1960 to $807.6 in the last quarter of 1967, with an implicit price deflator, using 1958 dollars, at the end of the period of only 118.9. What the future might hold remained as uncertain as ever, but it did become clear in this period that the American economy was moving ahead powerfully, and properly managed, could continue to do so.

The foreseeable results of this transformation were many, of which two were notable in the context of the professionalization of reform. The first is that if the economy were to continue to expand, the number of persons in economic difficulties would contract, or at least not grow. Already a minority, the poor would certainly remain one, and very likely become even more so. There would

---

[3] *Ibid.*

be less and less reason then to expect mass political support for social reform, at least to the extent that such support in the past had reflected the immediate, individual interests of an electoral majority. The principal sources of political power in a capitalist democracy being votes and money, and the poor having an insufficiency of either, it was more or less ordained that they should become in some degree clients of persons interested in their plight and professionally competent in terms of knowledge of the subject and access to power. This relationship is perhaps never more evident than when the professional reformer encourages the client to insist that only the "indigenous disadvantaged" can truly understand their problems and accordingly they should be given the power to make decisions about it.

A further and not less decisive result of the econometric revolution was the quite startling reversal of the position of the money managers of the executive branch of the Federal government. The conservative press to the contrary, the expenditure programs of the Federal government are managed on principles, or strategies, not different from those of most large organizations. The normal presumption, and the normal condition, is that resources are scarce and that the demand for them will outrun the supply. In consequence allocation is turned over to specialists, in the case of the Federal government to the Bureau of the Budget, the Council of Economic Advisors, and the Treasury, whose task, as much as anything, is to say "no." Big decisions are sorted out and reserved for the President and his staff, but typically these are matters where the necessity to prefer one set of allocations over another has such political significance as to preclude a surrogate decision by the permanent civil service. Under conditions of high and steady economic expansion, however, a quite extraordinary reversal of this process takes place. Expenditures under existing Federal programs rise at a fairly predictable rate. But revenues from the existing tax structure rise even faster. Of a sudden—by mid-decade this was clearly discernible in Washington —the immediate *supply* of resources bids fair to outrun the *demand* for them. Thus in the summer of 1965 the President's advisors publicly estimated that Federal revenues would increase by some $35 billion by 1970, starting at an annual increment of $4–5 billion and rising to about $7 billion. Without great exaggeration, it could be said that social policy during that period would be determined by the way in which the $35 billion was allocated. (Alas, almost immediately it was allocated to the war in Vietnam, but that is another tale.) The crucial point is that under the theory of fiscal management that evolved during this time, there was *no* option but to expend the surplus. The concept of "fiscal drag" held that unless the revenue increment of the Federal fisc is immediately returned to the economy it begins to have a depressing effect. This, in a word, was money you had to spend in order to get. The result was the beginning of a situation utterly without parallel in modern government: administrations that must be constantly on the lookout for new ways to expend public funds in the public interest. (In addition to various forms of tax reduction.) This is precisely the type of decision-making that is suited to the techniques of modern organization, and that ends up in the hands of persons who make a profession of it. A side effect: as such decisions become more professional, they are likely to become less political, in the sense of responding to existing power configurations.

2. *The exponential growth of knowledge.* The econometric revolution was not an isolated event: precisely to the contrary, it was part of the extraordinary growth in knowledge of the twentieth century, with all its accompanying forms of instability. The economy may yet suffer utter collapse, just as we may yet blow ourselves up: intermediary miscalculations are not only to be seen as possible, but to be expected. But the master term is that of miscalculation: fewer and fewer basic decisions in the society are made without some form of quantified knowledge being brought to bear on them. It can be said of the war on poverty that it began not because it was necessary, but because it was possible. The funds were available, not only *despite* the tax reduction of 1964, but in measure *because* of it. But this was not the only sense in which it had become possible. The same quantified knowledge of the economy which was making economic theory increasingly operational was also pointing up social problems that persisted despite the onset of persistent prosperity. In the aftermath of World War II the proposition gained favor that whereas the early stages of capitalism led to an accentuation of income inequality, the later stages reversed this trend, so that the extremes grew closer, and there was much clustering at the median. During the 1950s, however, the researches of Robert J. Lampman began to challenge this hypothesis. (Apparently a process of equalization had been going on during the war, to be reversed during the Republican years that followed. This is precisely what occurred during and after World War I.) Never without influence in Washington (his original work was widely disseminated by the Joint Committee on the Economic Report), Lampman was especially close to the economists who took office with Kennedy, and his demonstration of persisting and even worsening income maldistribution provided a powerful, and early influence on the administration to move in this direction.

But this is but one instance. Among the complexities of American life is that the American business community, during the first half of the twentieth century when it was fiercely opposed to the idea of economic or social planning, nonetheless supported, even pressed for, the development of a national statistical system that largely as a result of this support became perhaps the best in the world. This in turn made certain types of planning and regulation feasible, and in a measure, inevitable. John Kenneth Galbraith has noted the indispensable role of statisticians in modern societies, which seem never to do anything about problems until they learn to measure them, that being the special province of those applied mathematicians. Statistics are used as mountains are climbed: because they are there. If one recalls that the nation went through the entire depression of the 1930s without ever really knowing what the unemployment rate was (the statistic was then gathered once each ten years by the Census Bureau), one gains a feeling for the great expansion of knowledge in this and related fields in the quarter century that followed. By the 1960s, the monthly employment data had become a vital, sensitive, and increasingly reliable source of information about American society, and that information increasingly insisted that although the majority of Americans were prosperous indeed, a significant minority were not.

The success of the economists in mastering the problems they set themselves has been in some measure at least a reflection of investment in the field. If the natural sciences have been by far the more robust and productive, it must be noted that they have received the greater proportion of manpower and research funds. As of 1964, two-thirds of the Ph.D.'s in the United States were in the natural sciences, more than a quarter in chemistry alone. The social sciences had but 7 per cent of all Ph.D.'s, with economists outnumbering sociologists five to one. Even so, the social sciences were experiencing a roughly proportional expansion in research support. In 1964, over-all expenditure for social science research was somewhere between $500 and $600 million, a tenth of the $6 billion spent that year on the life and physical sciences, including psychology. In 1956, the Federal government had obligated a mere $4 million to social science research. By 1966, this had risen to $44 million, and reached an estimated $59 million for 1968. At such rates of expenditure it is to be expected that there would be some increase in knowledge, and almost certainly during this period there was. Nothing especially dramatic, and tending to be more descriptive than otherwise; nonetheless, it is a fact that as the resources available for social reform were increasing, so were the sources of information by which such reforms might be guided.

3. *The professionalization of the middle class.* "Everywhere in American life," Kenneth S. Lynn reports, "the professions are triumphant."[4] The period since the G.I. Bill has witnessed an extraordinary expansion of higher education. In the United States, a quarter of the teenage population now goes on to some kind of college, and among specific class and ethnic groups, the proportion is as high as three-quarters. The trend is unmistakable and probably irresistible; in the course of the coming decades some form of education beyond high school will become near to universal. But most importantly, for more and more persons the form of education will involve professional training. This is something different from mere higher education; it produces a different type of person.

That difference has been most succinctly stated by Everett C. Hughes: "Professionals *profess*. They profess to know better than others the nature of certain matters, and to know better than their clients what ails them or their affairs." And he continues:

[4] Kenneth S. Lynn: "Introduction to the Issue 'The Professions'" in *Daedalus*, Vol. 92 No. 4, Fall 1963, p. 649.

Lawyers not only give advice to clients and plead their cases for them; they also develop a philosophy of law—of its nature and its functions, and of the proper way in which to administer justice. Physicians consider it their prerogative to define the nature of disease and of health, and to determine how medical services ought to be distributed and paid for. Social workers are not content to develop a technique of case work; they concern themselves with social legislation. Every profession considers itself the proper body to set the terms in which some aspect of society, life or nature is to be thought of, and to define the general lines, or even the details, of public policy concerning it.[5]

This development is in a sense only one aspect of the general triumph of the graduate school, of which David Riesman and Christopher Jencks have written. Professors produce professionals. (In itself this is rather a new process; in the not far distant past apprenticeship was the common mode of access to many such callings.) And as the number of professionals has increased, so has the number of professions. More and more, middle-class persons are attracted to the independence of judgment, esoteric knowledge, and relative immunity to outside criticism that characterize professional occupations. Professional prerogatives are increasingly asserted in previously rather mundane fields. Again, Everett Hughes: "The YMCA secretary wants his occupation recognized not merely as that of offering young men from the country a pleasant road to Protestant righteousness in the city, but as a more universal one dealing with groups of young people. All that is learned of adolescence, of behavior in small groups, of the nature and organization of community life is considered the intellectual base of his work."[6]

There are now an extraordinary number of such professionals in America. The National Science Foundation estimates that the number of scientists and engineers alone *nearly doubled* between 1950 and 1965, a rate of growth 4.5 times that of the labor force as a whole. At mid-decade, the number of persons classified as professional and technical workers passed the nine million mark—a number greater than that of managers, officials, and proprietors, greater even than the number of craftsmen and foremen. And of this group, a considerable number are involved in various aspects of social welfare and reform. Through sheer numbers they would tend to have their way; but as professionals in a professionalizing society, they are increasingly entitled to have their way. That is how the system works. As has been said, the war on poverty resulted in the first instance from a variety of professional judgments concerning the persistence of the problem and the need for certain levels of Federal expenditure. Inevitably the content of the effort and the kind of program that resulted was similarly influenced by professional judgments. Whatever exactly is meant by the term "the poor," it will be clear enough that they had almost nothing whatever to do with the process.

---

[5] Everett C. Hughes, "Professions" in *Daedalus*, Vol. 92, No. 4, Fall 1963, pp. 656–657
[6] *Ibid.*

4. *The rise of the foundations.* Philanthropy has been a characteristic feature of American society almost from its inception. Although it began and continues to be associated with voluntary contributions of relatively small sums to religious organizations, these contributions have been in no small measure destined for social welfare purposes, and as the society has grown more secularized, so has social welfare philanthropy. In the settlement house movement of the turn of the century, philanthropy took an activist role, associating. itself not only with the cause of the poor, but also directly involving itself with the life of poor communities. With the rise of the foundations, however, a fundamental change took place. There came into being a number of organizations with immense and (within the limits of common law prohibitions) permanent financial resources, which by and large identified themselves with the advancement of knowledge and with liberal social change. The process was at first slow enough. The Carnegie Corporation and the various Rockefeller funds dominated the foundation scene and were fairly cautious. Gradually, however, a number of smaller foundations were established, many reflecting the more pronouncedly liberal traditions of Jewish politics and philosophy, which took much more adventurous and interventionist roles, especially in areas of Negro needs. The Stern Family Fund, the Field Foundation, the New World Foundation, the J. M. Kaplan Fund, the Taconic Foundation, are names that come readily to mind. But the decisive event came in 1950 when the Ford Foundation, established in 1936 "to serve the public welfare through grants for educational, scientific, and charitable purposes," largely local in nature, received a tremendous grant from the Ford family and became, in its words, "a nationwide philanthropy." Immediately Ford, with resources that in time rose above three billion dollars dominated the foundation world. In the period 1950–63, upwards of $1.9 billion in grants were made, 90 per cent to institutions within the United States, primarily colleges, universities, schools, and community organizations. This latter category represents a major innovation; it had major consequences for American society.

With the advent of Ford, the professional style in reform plunged forward. From the outset, Ford took the initiative in deciding what needed to be done. A Public Affairs Program was established as one of the nine grant-making programs of the foundation. Paul N. Ylvisaker, an energetic, creative social innovator came to head it. (The sheer size of the foundation apparently gave immense powers to the professional "philanthropoids," in Dwight Mac-Donald's phrase, who were employed by the foundation. It is reasonable to assume that on balance these were far more politically liberal than the trustees. Rather as television took editorializing away from Republican publishers and turned it over to Democratic reporters, the huge contemporary foundation has done something of the same to what once was termed charity.) From the outset, the Public Affairs Program adopted the urban theme as its motif. Speaking in 1963, Ylvisaker stated, "Hardly a grant among the $100 million we have committed over the past decade does not in one way or another address itself to urban problems and conditions." [7]

At first grants tended to emphasize research and study, but gradually these gave way to programs of direct action, the so-called "grey areas" program. A number of deteriorating central city areas were chosen, and foundation funds made available not just to help with ongoing work or to provide needed services that were not available, but rather to transform the political and social life of the community through new community organization. Ylvisaker described the effort in terms of three "tough and diverse jobs":

—of trying to mesh the policies and operations of separate public and private jurisdictions;
—of working with disadvantaged and minority groups, particularly the Negro community;
—of looking beyond old and fixed ways of doing things, to invent and evaluate new approaches in education, housing, employment, legal services, and welfare. [8]

The object, Ylvisaker boldly stated, was "to experiment with new ways of improving the social conditions of the central city and of opening new opportunities to those now living in these urban 'grey areas.'" Whereupon he claimed for the effort the distinguishing quality of the professional style in reform: the ability to anticipate problems, and to know best:

These grants were conceived and negotiated before the current wave of civil-rights protest began. They were not and are not intended as substitutes for protest, which has always been a healthy part of American politics and community improvement. Rather, they are intended to help correct the basic conditions which have led to protest, and to develop the latent potential of the human beings now crowded and often crushed at the bottom of the community's totem pole. [9]

Thus community action became one of the first major themes in this new style in social change.

---

[7] Paul N. Ylvisaker, "A Foundation Approach to City Problems," in *American Community Development*, Preliminary Reports by Directors of Projects Assisted by the Ford Foundation in Four Cities and a State, p. 5.
[8] *Ibid.*, p. 8.
[9] *Ibid.*, pp. 6–7.

Social and Physical Planning for the Elimination of Urban Poverty

HERBERT J. GANS

—

City planning has traditionally sought community betterment through so-called *physical* methods, such as the creation of efficient land use and transportation schemes, the sorting out of diverse types of land use, and the renewal of technologically obsolescent areas and buildings to achieve functional, as well as esthetically desirable, arrangements of structures and spaces. This paper deals with a new planning concept which places greater emphasis on economic and social methods of improving community life. In some places it is called human renewal; in others, community development; in yet others, social planning. Although none of the names is quite appropriate, the programs to which they refer are of crucial importance to the future of the city, for they seek to do away with—or at least to decimate—urban poverty and the deprivation that accompanies it. If these programs succeed, they are likely to have a lasting impact on city planning and on the other professions concerned with planning for community welfare.

The fight against poverty is not new, of course, and, in fact, the elimination of urban deprivation was one of the goals of the founders of modern city planning. The planning movement itself developed partly in reaction to the conditions under which the European immigrants who came to American cities in the mid-nineteenth century had to live. The reduction of their squalor was one of Frederick Law Olmstead's goals when he proposed the building of city parks so that the poor—as well as the rich—might have a substitute rural landscape in which to relax from urban life. It motivated the Boston civic leaders who first built playgrounds in the slums of that city, and the founders of the settlement house movement, notably Jane Addams, who argued strongly for city planning. It also sparked the efforts of those who built model tenements to improve

Source: Reprinted, with some revisions by its author, from *Washington University Law Quarterly* (symposium issue on land-use planning) Vol. 7 no. 1 (February 1963), pp. 2–18. An earlier version of this paper was read to the 1962 Conference of the American Institute of Planners, Los Angeles, October 17, 1962, and appears in American Institute of Planners, *Proceedings of the 1962 Conference* (Washington, D.C.: The Institute, 1963), pp. 176–190.

the housing conditions of the poor. And Ebenezer Howard had this goal in mind when he proposed to depopulate the London slums through Garden Cities.

Most of these planning efforts were not aimed directly at the reduction of poverty and deprivation, but sought to use land planning, housing codes, and occasionally zoning to eliminate slums and reduce densities in the tightly packed tenement neighborhoods. The apotheosis of this approach—slum clearance—followed upon the arrival of the newest wave of poor immigrants: the Southern Negroes, Puerto Ricans, and Mexicans who came to the city during World War II and in the post-war era. After a decade of noting the effects of the federal slum clearance program, however, some observers became concerned because while this method was eliminating slums, it was not contributing significantly to the improvement of the slum dwellers' living conditions.

In many cases, the reduction in the already short supply of low cost housing brought about by slum clearance, together with faulty or nonexistent relocation planning sent slum dwellers into adjacent slums or forced them to overcrowd declining areas elsewhere. But even where slum clearance was accompanied by adequate relocation programs, the housing of poor people in decent low cost dwellings did not solve other—and equally pressing—problems, such as poverty, unemployment, illiteracy, alcoholism, and mental illness. Nor could rehousing alone do away with crime, delinquency, prostitution, and other deviant behavior. In short, it became clear that such physical changes as urban renewal, good housing, and modern project planning were simply not enough to improve the lives of the poverty-stricken.

As a result, planners and "housers" began to look for non-physical planning approaches.[1] In this process, they made contact with other professions that are concerned with the low-income population, for example, social workers. Working in tandem with them and others, they have developed new programs, bearing the various names indicated above. Most often they have been referred to as social planning, a term that had been coined by social workers to describe the coordination of individual social agency programs carried out by such central planning and budgeting agencies as the United Fund.[2]

Although the term has already received considerable attention in city planning circles, I prefer to use another term. Insofar as the programs seek to aid low income people to change their fortunes and their ways of living, they are attempts to guide them toward the social and economic mobility that more fortunate people have achieved on their own. For this reason, the programs might best be described as planning for *guided mobility*.

---

[1] Another impetus came from the fact that several cities scheduled urban renewal projects in their skid row areas, and programs to "rehabilitate" its residents were developed as part of the relocation plan.

[2] The term has also been applied to plans which attempt to outline social—that is, non-physical—goals for the entire society, a procedure that would be more aptly called *societal* planning.

Such programs are now underway in many American cities. Some are designed as programs in juvenile delinquency prevention, which have come into being under the aegis of the President's Committee on Juvenile Delinquency and work mainly with young people.[3] Others are oriented toward low income people of all ages, and since planners have been most active in these, the rest of the article will deal primarily with such programs.[4] Although most of the programs are just getting started, some over-all similarities between them are apparent. Needless to say, any generalizations about them are preliminary, for the programs are likely to change as they progress from initial formulation to actual implementation.

The guided mobility plans and proposals which I have examined have four major programmatic emphases:

1. To develop new methods of education for children from low income and culturally deprived homes, so as to reduce functional illiteracy, school dropouts and learning disabilities which prevent such children from competing in the modern job market in adulthood;

2. To reduce unemployment by new forms of job training among the young, by the retraining of adults and by the creation of new jobs in the community;

3. To encourage self-help on an individual and group basis through community organization methods that stimulate neighborhood participation; and

4. To extend the amount and quality of social services to the low income population. Among the latter are traditional casework services, new experiments for giving professional help to the hard-to-reach, multi-problem family and the provision of modern facilities and programs of public recreation, public health, and community center activities.

The educational phase of guided mobility includes programs such as Higher Horizons, which attempt to draw bright children from the culturally restrictive context of low income environments, and to offer them the academic and cultural opportunities available to bright middle class children. There are also programs to help average and backward youngsters, using remedial reading and

---

[3] Of these, the leading program is New York's Mobilization for Youth. This is described in Mobilization for Youth, Inc., "A Proposal for the Prevention and Control of Delinquency by Expanding Opportunities" (New York, December 1961, mimeographed).

[4] Examples of the many such plans are: Action for Boston Community Development, "A Proposal for a Community Development Program in Boston" (Boston, Mass. December 1961, mimeographed); Action Housing, Inc., ". . . Urban Extension in the Pittsburgh Area" (Pittsburgh, Pa. September 1961, mimeographed); City of Oakland, "Proposal for a Program of Community Development" (City of Oakland, Cal. June and Dec. 1961, mimeographed); Community Progress, Inc., "Opening Opportunities: New Haven's Comprehensive Program for Community Progress" (New Haven, Conn. April 1962, mimeographed); and Department of City Planning, "A Plan for the Woodlawn Community: Social Planning Factors" (Chicago, Ill. January 1962, mimeographed). My comments about the plans below are based on a number of published and unpublished documents which I have examined, as well as on discussions about existing and proposed plans in which I have participated in several cities. My description of these plans is, in sociological terminology, an ideal type, and does not fit exactly any one of the plans now in existence.

other devices to guide them during the early school years, so that they will develop the skills and motivations to stay in school until high school graduation. The occupational phase of the plans includes job programs which will employ young people in useful community projects, and in quasi-apprentice programs in private industry, as well as various vocational training and retraining programs for young and old alike. Meanwhile, added effort is scheduled to attract new industries, and thus to bring new jobs to the community.

The extension of social services, and the community organization phase of the programs use decentralization as a means of reaching the high proportion of low income people who usually abstain from community contact. The provision of social services to the hard-to-reach will be attempted by bringing programs to the neighborhood level, with neighborhood directors to supervise the process. In addition, the social agencies plan to coordinate their services, so that individual agencies working with the same individual or family know what the other is doing, and duplication and contradictions can be avoided. More neighborhood facilities will also be established, including community schools, public health clinics and recreation centers, sometimes grouped in a "services center," so that people will be encouraged to come there when they need help.

The decentralizing of community organization activities is intended to create a sense of neighborhood and an interest in neighborhood self-help. Community organizers will work in the neighborhood for this purpose, and will try to involve "natural leaders" living in the area, who can act as a bridge between the professional, the city and the neighborhood population.

This is a very general description of the programs. In actuality, each community has a somewhat distinctive approach, or a different emphasis in the selection of programs, depending partly on the lineup of sponsoring agencies. But some city planners who have become interested in guided mobility programs are still preoccupied—and sometimes too much so—with traditional physical planning approaches, notably two: the realization of a neighborhood scheme— originally devised by Clarence Perry[5] and consisting of a small, clearly bounded residential area, built up at low density, with auto and pedestrian traffic carefully separated, considerable open space, and with a combination elementary school and neighborhood meeting place in its center; and the provision both in such neighborhoods and in the larger community of a standard array of public facilities for recreation, health, education, culture, and other community services.

The concern with neighborhood is of course traditional in city planning, and even the new challenge of finding non-physical ways of helping the low-income group has not diverted the planner from it. In some cities, guided mobility plans

---

[5] Clarence A. Perry, "The Neighborhood Unit," *Regional Survey of New York and Its Environs*, Vol. 7 (New York: Committee on Regional Plan of New York and Its Environs, 1929), Vol. 7, pp. 22–140.

are thus almost appendages to physical planning programs, based on the traditional belief that the rebuilding of the city into a series of separate neighborhoods to encourage a small-townish middle class form of family life is a proper solution even for poverty. Elsewhere, the program may be an appendage of urban renewal activities, the main intent still being the upgrading of the physical neighborhoods. Thus, guided mobility is used partly to organize the neighborhood into undertaking—or helping the city with—this task. But in most cases, the neighborhood emphasis is based on a genuine concern that one of the causes of urban deprivation is to be found in the poor quality of neighborhood life.

The provision of public facilities is also a traditional planning emphasis, dating back to the days when the planner was an ally of the reformers who were fighting for the establishment of these facilities. Out of this has come the belief that public facilities are crucial agencies in people's lives, that up-to-date facilities and programs will encourage intensive use of them and that this in turn will help significantly in achieving the aims of guided mobility planning.

Despite the intensity of the planner's belief in neighborhood and public facility use, there is no evidence that these two planning concepts are as important to low income people as they are to planners. Consequently, it is fair to ask whether such concepts are as crucial to the elimination of urban poverty and deprivation as is signified by their appearance in some guided mobility plans. The answer to this question requires a brief discussion of the nature of contemporary urban poverty.

II

The low-income population may be divided into two major segments, which sociologists call the *working class* and the *lower class*.[6] The former consists of semiskilled and skilled blue collar workers, who hold steady jobs, and are thus able to live under stable, if not affluent, conditions. Their way of life differs in many respects from those of the middle class; for example, in the greater role of relatives in sociability and mutual aid, in the lesser concern for self-improvement and education, and in their lack of interest in the good address, cultivation and the kinds of status that are important to middle class people. Although their ways are culturally different from the dominant middle class norms, these are not pathological, for rates of crime, mental illness, and other social ills are not significantly higher than in the middle class. This population, therefore, has little need for guided mobility programs.

---

[6] Herbert J. Gans, *The Urban Villagers* (Glencoe, Ill : Free Press, 1962), Ch. 11. See also S. M. Miller and Frank Riessman, "The Working Class Subculture: A New View," *Social Problems*, Vol. 9 (1961), pp. 86–97. The nature and extent of urban poverty is described in Michael Harrington, *The Other America* (New York: Macmillan, 1962), Chs. 2, 4, 5, 7, 8.

The lower class, on the other hand, consists of people who perform the unskilled labor and service functions in the society. Many of them lack stable jobs. They are often unemployed, or forced to move from one temporary—and underpaid—job to another. Partly because of occupational instability, their lives are beset with social and emotional instability as well, and it is among them that one finds the majority of the emotional problems and social evils that are associated with the low-income population.[7]

In past generations, the American economy had considerable need for unskilled labor, and the European immigrants who performed it were able to achieve enough occupational stability to raise themselves, or their children, to working class or even middle class ways of living. Today, however, the need for unskilled labor is constantly decreasing, and will soon be minimal. Consequently, the Negro, Puerto Rican, and Mexican newcomers who now constitute most of the American lower class find it very difficult to improve their condition.[8]

Guided mobility planning is essentially an attempt to help them solve their problems and to aid them in changing their lives. This makes it necessary to find out what causes their problems, what they themselves are striving for and how they can be helped to achieve their strivings.

The nature of the problem is not difficult to identify. For economic reasons, and for reasons of race as well, the contemporary lower class is frustrated—if not barred—from opportunities to hold well-paid, stable jobs, to receive a decent education, to live in good housing, or to get access to a whole series of choices and privileges that the white middle class takes for granted.

In addition, some lower class people lack the motivations and skills needed to participate in contemporary society, and more important, which are necessary to accept the opportunities if and when they become available. Moreover, the apathy, despair, and rejection which result from lack of access to crucial opportunities help bring about the aforementioned social and emotional difficulties.

There are a number of reasons for these reactions.[9] When men are long unemployed or underemployed, they feel useless, and eventually become marginal members of their family. This has many consequences. They may desert their families, and turn to self-destructive behavior in despair. If male instability is widespread, the woman becomes the dominant member of the

---

[7] An excellent brief description of lower class culture may be found in Walter B. Miller, "Lower Class Culture As a Generating Milieu of Gang Delinquency," *Journal of Social Issues*, Vol. 14 (1958), pp. 5–19. The everyday life of the lower class is pictured in Oscar Lewis, *Five Families* (New York: Basic Books, 1959), and *The Children of Sanchez* (New York: Random House, 1961). Although Lewis' books deal with the lower class of Mexico City, his portrait applies, with some exceptions, to American cities as well.

[8] For an analysis of the occupational history of the European immigrants and the more recent immigrants, see Oscar Handlin, *The Newcomers* (New York: Anchor Books, 1962).

[9] For a more detailed analysis, see Gans, *The Urban Villagers*, ch. 12, and Institute for Urban Studies, *Social Planning: A New Role for Sociology* (Philadelphia 1962, mimeographed). See also Mobilization for Youth, Inc., *op. cit.*, and Walter B. Miller, *op. cit.*

family, and she may live with a number of men in the hope of finding a stable mate. The result is a family type which Walter Miller calls female-based, which is marked by free unions, illegitimate children, and what middle class people consider to be broken homes.[10] Boys who grow up in such families may be deprived of needed male models, and are likely to inherit some of the feelings of uselessness and despair they see in their fathers. In addition, the children must learn at an early age how to survive in a society in which crisis is an everyday occurrence, and where violence and struggle are ever-present. Thus, they may learn how to defend themselves against enemies, and how to co-exist with an alcoholic parent, but they do not learn how to read, how to concentrate on their studies or how to relate to the teacher.[11] Those that do must defend their deviant behavior—and it is deviant in the lower class—against their peers, who, like peers in all other groups, demand that they conform to the dominant mode of adaptation. Also, many children grow up in households burdened with mental illness, and this scars their own emotional and social growth. Out of such conditions develops a lower class culture with a set of behavior patterns which is useful for the struggle to survive in a lower class milieu, but which makes it almost impossible to participate in the larger society. And since the larger society rejects the lower class individual for such behavior, he can often develop self-respect and dignity only by rejecting the larger society. He blames it for his difficulties—and with much justification—but in this process rejects many of its values as well, becoming apathetic, cynical, and hostile even toward those that seek to help him.

This overly brief analysis is at present mostly hypothetical, for we do not yet know exactly what it is that creates the lower class way of life. We know that the nature of family relationships, the influence of peers, the kind of home training, the adaptive characteristics of lower class culture, the high prevalence of mental illness, and the need to cope with one crisis after another are all important factors, but we do not yet know exactly which factors are most important, how they operate to create the way of life that they do and how they are related to the lack of opportunities that bring them about.

Similarly, we know that lower class people are striving to change their condition, but we do not know exactly for what they are striving. It is clear that they want stable jobs and higher incomes, and there is considerable evidence of an almost magical belief in education and high occupational aspirations for the children, especially among Negroes.[12] The lack of opportunity and the constant

---

[10] Walter B. Miller, *op. cit.* This family type is particularly widespread in the Negro lower class, in which it originated during slavery.

[11] The educational and other problems of the lower class child are described in more detail in Patricia C. Sexton, *Education and Income* (New York: Viking, 1961); and Frank Riessman, *The Culturally Deprived Child* (New York: Harper, 1962).

[12] For the most recent example of this finding, see R. Kleiner, S. Parker, and H. Taylor, "Social Status and Aspirations in Philadelphia's Negro Population" (Philadelphia: Commission on Human Relations, June 1962, mimeographed).

occurrence of crises frustrate most of these aspirations before they can be implemented, but they do exist, especially among the women. On the other hand, the failure of settlement houses, social workers, and other helping agencies to reach the majority of the lower class population suggests that these people either cannot or do not want to accept the middle class values which these professionals preach and which are built into the welfare activities they carry out. Such programs attract the small minority desirous of, or ready for middle class life, but they repel the rest. A number of social scientists suggest that what lower class people are striving for is the stable, family-centered life of working class culture, and at least one delinquency prevention program is based on such an assumption.[13]

These observations about the nature of lower class life have many implications for guided mobility planning. As a result of the sparsity of knowledge, much research, experiment, and evaluation of experience will be necessary in order to learn what kinds of programs will be successful. It is clear that the most urgent need is to open up presently restricted opportunities, especially in the occupational sphere. The guided mobility programs which stress the creation of new jobs, the attack on racial discrimination, education, and occupational training as highest priority items are thus on the right track. Even so, new ways of bringing industry and jobs to the community must be found, for conventional programs have not been sufficiently productive. Then, ways of channelling lower class people into new jobs, and keeping them at work even if their initial performance is not as good as that of other people, or of labor saving machines, must be invented. Racial barriers will also have to come down more quickly, especially in those spheres of life and activity most important to lower class people, so that they can begin to feel that they have some stake in society. This too is easier said than done.

Not only is desegregation difficult to implement, but the most successful programs so far have benefited middle class non-whites more than their less fortunate fellows. For lower class people, access to jobs, unions, and decent low cost housing is most important, as is the assurance of fair treatment from the police, the courts, from city hall, storeowners, and helping agencies. The integration of high priced suburban housing, expensive restaurants, or concert halls is for *them* of much less immediate significance.

Also, methods of encouraging motivations and skills, and of maintaining aspirations in the face of frustration must be found. If the matriarchal lower class family is at fault, ways of providing boys with paternal substitutes must be developed. Where the entire lower class milieu is destructive, children may have to be removed from it, especially in their formative years. Treatments for mental illness, alcoholism, and narcotics addiction that will be effective among lower class people have to be discovered, and the causes of these ills isolated so that

---

[13] Mobilization for Youth, Inc., *op. cit.*

prevention programs may be set up. Schools must be created which can involve lower class children. This means that they must teach the skills needed in a middle class society yet without the middle class symbols and other trappings that frighten or repel the lower class student.[14] Finally, it is necessary to develop urban renewal or other housing programs that will make livable dwellings available to the low income population, within its price range, and located near enough to its places of employment so as not to require unreasonable amounts of travel time and expenditures.

These program requirements demand some radical changes in our ways of doing things. For example, if lower class people are to find employment, there will need to be economic enterprises not geared solely to profit and to cost-reduction, but also to the social profits of integrating the unemployed. In short, eventually we shall have to give up the pretense that nineteenth-century free enterprise ideology can cope with twentieth-century realities, and learn to replan some economic institutions to help the low-income population, just as we are now redesigning public education to teach this population's children. Likewise, if lower class people are to become part of the larger society, there must be changes in the way the police, the courts, and political structures treat them. To cite just one instance, lower class people must be represented more adequately in local party politics, and their needs and demands must receive more adequate hearing at city hall than has heretofore been the case. Similarly, the professions that now seek to help lower class people will have to be altered so as to be more responsive to how lower class people define their needs, and this may mean the replacement of some professionals by skilled nonprofessionals who are more capable of achieving rapport with lower class clients. Also, urban renewal policy must concern itself less with "blight" removal, or with the use of new construction to solve the city's tax problems, and more with improvement of the housing conditions of the slum dwellers. Changes, such as these, which require redistribution of power, income, privileges, and the alteration of established social roles, are immensely difficult to bring out. Even so, they are necessary if urban poverty and deprivation are to be eliminated.[15]

III

Proper guided mobility planning must be based on methods that will achieve the intended goal. If the hypotheses about the causes of urban deprivation are correct, the basic components of guided mobility planning must be able to affect the economy, the political, and social structures that shore up poverty and racial

---

[14] See Sexton, *op. cit.* and Riessman, *op. cit.*

[15] For other programmatic statements, see Peter Marris, "A Report on Urban Renewal in the United States," and Leonard J. Duhl, "Planning and Poverty," in Leonard J. Duhl (ed.), *The Urban Condition* (New York: Basic Books, 1963), pp. 113–134, and 295–304, respectively. See also Harrington, *op. cit.*

—as well as class—discrimination, the foci of lower class culture that frustrate the response to opportunities, notably the family, the peer group, the milieu in which children grow up and the helping agencies that now have difficulty in reaching lower class people, especially the school. Any programs which lack these components, and cannot bring about changes in the position of the lower class population vis-à-vis the institutions named are unlikely to contribute significantly to the aim of guided mobility.[16]

The list of basic components does not include the two that have been especially emphasized by planners: the belief in neighborhood and the importance of public facilities. This omission is not accidental, for I do not believe that these two concepts are of high priority. Indeed, it is possible that they may divert guided mobility programs from the direction they ought to take.

By focusing programs on neighborhoods as spatial units, planners are naturally drawn to what is most visible in them, the land uses, buildings, and major institutions, and their attention is diverted from what is hardest to see, the people—and social conditions—with problems. It should be clear from the foregoing analysis that the program must concentrate on the people and on the social and economic forces which foster their deprivation, rather than on neighborhood conditions which are themselves consequences of these forces.

Moreover, too much concern with neighborhoods may cause the programs to seek out the wrong people: the working class segment of the low income population rather than the lower class one. This may happen for two reasons. First, the planner often finds it difficult to distinguish between areas occupied by working class people, and those occupied by lower class people, mainly because his concept of standard housing blinds him to differences between low rent areas, usually occupied predominantly by the former, and slums, which house the latter.[17] Also, working and lower class people sometimes live together in the same planning area, especially if they are non-white, and a neighborhood focus makes it difficult to reach one without the other. This is undesirable because—as I noted earlier—the working class population does not need guided mobility, whereas the lower class population needs it so badly that all resources ought to be allocated to it.

Even so, these drawbacks would not be serious if neighborhood planning could achieve the aims of guided mobility. But this is not the case, mainly because people's lives are not significantly influenced by the physical neighborhood. The important aspects of life take place within the family, the peer group and on the job, and the neighborhood does not seem to affect these greatly. Moreover, although middle and working class people do sometimes participate

---

16 For a more detailed critical analysis of current guided mobility plans, see Gans, *Social Planning.*

17 Herbert J. Gans, "The Human Implications of Current Redevelopment and Relocation Planning," *Journal of the American Institute of Planners,* Vol. 24 (1959), pp. 15–25, or *Urban Villagers,* ch. 14.

in neighborhood activities, this is not true of lower class people.[18] Not only do they shy away from organizational participation generally, but because of their great transience they do not spend much time in any one area. More important, since life is a constant struggle for survival and an endless series of crises, lower class people are often suspicious of their neighbors, and even more so of the landlord, the storeowner, the police, and the local politician. They harbor similar feelings toward most other neighborhood institutions and local public facilities.

Thus, the lower class population's involvement in the neighborhood is at best neutral, and more often, negative. Yet even if it were more positive, the components of neighborhood planning and the provision of the entire range of modern public facilities can contribute relatively little to solving the problems which concern lower class people the most. To a poverty-stricken family, the separation of car and pedestrian traffic, or the availability of park and playground within walking distance are not very crucial; their needs are much more basic.

This is not to reject the desirability of such planning concepts, but only to say that given the present condition of lower class life, they are of fairly low priority. The location and equipment of the school is much less important than the presence of the kinds of teachers who can communicate with lower class children, and a conventional public health facility is much less vital than an agency that can really help a mother deserted by her husband, or a person who must cope with mentally ill family members.

The standard neighborhood-and-facilities planning package cannot even contribute significantly to the improvement of the lower class milieu. The significant components of this milieu are other people, rather than environmental features, and until these other people are socially and economically secure enough to trust each other, the milieu is not likely to improve sufficiently to prevent the perpetuation of past deprivations on the young growing up within it.

In short, it seems clear that the kind of neighborhood scheme sought through traditional planning and zoning methods cannot be implemented among lower class people until the basic components of guided mobility programs have been effectuated. A stable, peaceful neighborhood in which there is positive feeling between neighbors assumes that people have good housing, the kind of job that frees them from worrying about where the next meal or rent money will come from, the solution of basic problems so that the landlord, the policeman or the bill collector are no longer threatening and the relief from recurring crises so that they can begin to pay some attention to the world outside the household.

---

[18] Generally speaking, middle class people participate in formal neighborhood organizations to a much greater extent than other classes, although their social life often takes place outside the neighborhood. Working class people are less likely to participate in formal organizations, but most of their social activities take place close to home. For a discussion of working class attitudes toward the neighborhood, see Marc Fried and Peggy Gleicher, "Some Sources of Residential Satisfaction in an Urban 'Slum,'" *Journal of the American Institute of Planners*, Vol. 27 (1961), pp. 305–315.

Similarly, only when people feel themselves to be part of the larger society, and when they have learned the skills needed to survive in it, will they be able to take part in school or community center activities, or to develop the ability to communicate with the staff of a health clinic. In short, the programs which the neighborhood planner proposes cannot come about until more basic problems have been solved; they are consequences of the elimination of urban poverty rather than devices for it.

Neighborhood planning is necessary, of course, but what is needed is of a social and political type which supports the community, state, and federal programs for the elimination of poverty. Thus, the methods required to help the low income population develop the skills and attitudes prerequisite to survival in a modern society must reach into the neighborhood and the street in order to recruit people who do not, for one reason or another, come by themselves into public facilities established for such programs. Also, local political activity must be stimulated so that low income people can use the one power they have—that of numbers and votes—to make their wishes heard at city hall and in Washington. This differs considerably from the need for "citizen participation" often called for by planners and community organization experts; that has usually been defined as citizen consideration of—and consent to—professionally developed programs, or civic activity which is decidedly non-political. The kind of local citizen participation that is needed is quite political, however, and since its aim must be to change the political status quo, it is unlikely that community organizers, who are after all employees of the existing political institution or of establishment-dominated welfare agencies, will be able to encourage such activity even if they are personally willing to do so. Hopefully, enlightened civic leaders and politicians will eventually realize that the low income population must be more adequately represented in the political process, but in all likelihood, they will resist any change in the existing political alignments until they have no other choice. Thus, the initiative for local political activity must come from the areas in which low income people live. But whoever the initiating agencies may be, these are the types of neighborhood planning that are required to do something about urban poverty.

IV

The incompatibility of traditional city planning aims and the basic components of guided mobility programming is not to be blamed on one or another set of planners, nor indeed is it a cause for blame at all. Rather, it stems from the history and nature of modern city planning, and from the basic assumptions in its approach. The description of two of these assumptions will also shed some light on the relationship between social and physical planning and their roles in the improvement of cities.

The first of these assumptions is the belief in the ability of change in the physical environment to bring about social change. Planners have traditionally acted on the assumption that the ordering of land uses, and improvements in the setting and design of buildings, highways, and other physical features of the community would result in far-reaching improvements in the lives of those affected. The validity of this assumption has been seriously questioned in recent years, and indeed, the rise of what has been called social planning is one expression of this questioning.[19]

But the traditional city planning approach can also be described in another way, as being *method-oriented*. By this I mean that it has developed a repertoire of methods and techniques which have become professionally accepted, and which distinguish planning from other service-giving professions. As a result, the planner concerns himself largely with improvements in these methods. In this process, however, he loses sight of the goals which his methods are intended to achieve, or the problems they are to solve. Thus, he does not ask whether the methods achieve these goals, or whether they achieve *any* goals.

This concern with method is not limited to the planning profession; it can be found in all professions. The attempt to maintain and improve existing methods is useful if the goals are traditional ones, or if the profession deals only with routine problems. But it does not work as well when new goals are sought, and when new problems arise. As I have already noted, improvements in neighborhood planning cannot contribute significantly to the new problems of the city, or to the new goal of eliminating urban poverty.

What is needed instead is a *goal-oriented* or problem-oriented approach, which begins not with methods, but with the problems to be solved or the goals to be achieved. Once these are defined and agreed upon, the methods needed to achieve them can be determined through the use of professional insight, research, and experiment until the right methods, i.e., those which will solve the problem or realize the goal, are found.[20] This approach was used in the foregoing pages, in which I questioned the usefulness of traditional planning methods and proposed instead programs to cope with the problems of the lower class population—and their causes—as well as programs which would lead toward the goals this population was seeking for itself.

This approach is more difficult to implement than a method-oriented one, because it does not respect accepted methods—unless they work—and because it rejects the claims of professional traditions or professional expertise that are

---

[19] See, for example, Irving Rosow, "The Social Effects of the Physical Environment," *Journal of the American Institute of Planners*, Vol. 27 (1961), pp. 127–133.

[20] This approach is currently receiving considerable attention in planning literature. My discussion is based on an initial formulation by Martin Meyerson, and is treated in more detail in studies conducted by him, John Dyckman, and this writer which are now being prepared for publication. For a summary statement of this approach, see Paul Davidoff and Thomas Reiner, "A Choice Theory of Planning," *Journal of the American Institute of Planners*, Vol. 28 (1962), pp. 103–115.

not supported by empirical evidence. It may require new methods and new approaches, and thus can wreak havoc with the established way of doing things. However much the goal-oriented approach may upset the profession in the short-run, in the long run it improves its efficiency and thus its expertise and status, because its methods are likely to be much more successful, thus reducing the risk of professional failure. In an effort as pioneering and difficult as guided mobility planning, a problem and goal-oriented approach is therefore absolutely essential.

The conception of method-oriented and goal-oriented planning can also aid our understanding of the relationship between physical and social planning. In the professional discussions of this relationship, the subject has frequently been posed as social planning *versus* physical training. Although it is not difficult to understand why the subject has been framed in this competitive way, the resulting dichotomy between social and physical planning is neither meaningful nor desirable. There are several reasons for rejecting this dichotomy.

First, social planning is said to deal with the human elements in the planning process. When planners talk of the human side of renewal, or of the human factors in planning, they are suggesting by implication that physical planning is inhuman, that in its concern with land use, site design, the redevelopment of cleared land and the city tax base, it has no concern for the needs of human beings. I would not blame physical planners for objecting to this implication, and am surprised that they have not done so.

But even if this implication is inaccurate, the dichotomy has led to another, even more unfortunate implication, which has some truth to it. Every planning activity, like any other form of social change, creates net benefits for some people, and net costs for others. These may be non-material as well as material. Whether intentionally or not, physical planning has tended to provide greater benefits to those who already have considerable economic resources or political power, be they redevelopers or tenants who profit from a luxury housing scheme, central business district retailers who gain, or expect to gain, from the ever-increasing number of plans to "revive downtown," or the large taxpayers who are helped most when planning's main aim is to increase municipal revenues. The interest in social planning is a direct result of this distribution of benefits, for it seeks to help the people who are forced to pay net costs in the physical planning process. Too often, these are poor people, for example, residents of a renewal or highway project who suffer when adequate relocation housing is lacking. Needless to say, this political bifurcation, in which physical planning benefits the well-to-do, and social planning the less fortunate ones, is not a desirable state of affairs either for the community or for planning.

Finally, in actual everyday usage, the dichotomy refers to skills possessed by different types of planners. Physical planning is that set of methods which uses the traditional skills of the city planner and zoning official; social planning, that set favored by sociologically trained planners, by social workers, and by other professionals concerned with welfare aims. Yet if the planning activities of each are examined more closely, it becomes evident that the terms social and physical are inaccurate labels. Zoning is considered a physical planning method, but an ordinance which determines who is to live with whom, and who is to work next to whom is as much social—as well as economic and political—as it is physical. So is a transportation scheme which decides who will find it easy to get in and out of the city, and who will find it difficult. Conversely, social planners who urge the construction of more low-rent housing, or argue for scattered units rather than projects, are proposing physical schemes even while they are ostensibly doing social planning. Since all planning activities affect people, they are inevitably social, and the dichotomy between physical and social methods turns out to be meaningless. Moreover, in actual planning practice, no problem can be solved by any one method, or any one skill. In most instances a whole variety of techniques are needed to achieve the goal.

The social-physical dichotomy is a logical consequence of viewing planning as method-oriented, because when methods are most important, there is apt to be competition between the people who are skilled in one method rather than another. All successful professions want to apply the methods they know best, for this permits them to maintain their power and social position most easily.

If planning is conceived as goal-oriented, however, goals become most important and methods are subordinated to the goal. In such a planning process, in which a large number of different methods are used in an integrated fashion, any single method loses its magical aura. Moreover, no goal can be defined so narrowly that it is only physical or only social. In a goal-oriented approach, then, there can be no social or physical planning. There is only *planning*, an approach which agrees upon the best goals and then finds the best methods to achieve them.

This way of defining planning has a number of implications for the future of the professions concerned with planning matters, as well as for the improvement of cities. If professionals continue to emphasize traditional methods, when and where it is not applicable, they can easily lose their usefulness, and their professional prerogative for participating in programs of community betterment.

But it is not only the methods which must be reconsidered. Even the goals which are built into these methods are turning out to be less important today. The neighborhood concept has received little support from the clients of planning; the same is true of the planner's insistence on a reduction in the journey to work, which has not been accepted by the journeying populace. Also, in an age of automation and increasing unemployment, the need for economic growth, even if it is disorderly, is becoming more vital than the ordering of growth, and the planner's desire for stability. It is, of course, still important to have efficient transportation schemes, and to locate noxious industry away from residences, but there is less noxious industry than ever before, and for those who are affluent, the inefficiency of the automobile seems to matter little, especially if it is politically feasible to subsidize the costs of going to work by car. And even the concern with land use per se is becoming less significant. In a technology of bulldozers and rapid transportation, the qualities of the natural environment and the location of land are less important—or rather, more easily dealt with by human intervention—and increasingly, land can be used for many alternatives. The question of what is the best use, given topography and location, is thus less important than who will benefit from one use as compared to another, and who will have to pay costs, and how is the public interest affected.

In short, so-called physical planning questions are receding in importance, and socio-economic and political ones are becoming more relevant. This is, of course, why the issue of social and physical planning has been discussed as social versus physical. In the long run, however, it seems clear that the future of city planning lies less in the reliance upon land use plans than in the development of a range of methods that will guarantee the improvement of those aspects of community life that are most in need of improvement.

V

One of the most important tasks in the improvement of cities is the elimination of urban poverty, and of the deprivations of lower class life. Poverty is fundamentally responsible for the slums we have been unable to eradicate by attacking the buildings, and for the deprivations which ultimately bring about the familiar list of social evils. Moreover, poverty and deprivation are what make cities so ugly and depressing, and they hasten the flight of more fortunate people into the suburbs. And this in turn contributes to economic decline, the difficulties of financing municipal services, political conflict, corruption, and many of the other problems of the contemporary city.

I would not want to argue that all of the city's problems can be laid at the doorstep of poverty. There are technological changes that affect its economic health, and result in the obsolescence of industrial areas and street patterns. There are political rigidities that inhibit its relations with its hinterland. And the desire of most families to raise their children in low-density surroundings suggests that suburbia is not produced solely by the flight from the city, and would exist without urban poverty. Even so, many of the suburbanites have come to hate the city because of the poverty they see there, and this in turn helps to create the hostility between city and suburb and the political conflict that frustrates schemes for metropolitan solutions.

If planners are genuinely concerned with the improvement of cities, the fight against poverty becomes a planning problem, and one that needs to be given higher priority than it has heretofore received. A beginning is being made in the guided mobility programs that are now in operation, but a much greater effort is needed, both on the local and the federal scene, before these programs can achieve their aim. If such efforts are not made, all other schemes for improving the city will surely fail.

Minority Group Leadership: The Advantages of the Disadvantages

SEYMOUR LEVENTMAN

■

THE PROBLEM

In *The Study of Sociology*, Herbert Spencer observed that social institutions tend to become self-propagating, independent of their original causes. Institutions may be maintained when they "perform some other function than that intended or no function at all."[1] Applied to the alleviation of human misery, these notions allowed Spencer to note that programs designed to solve social problems may themselves become obstacles to the problems' eventual resolution. The tendency for ameliorative movements to become problems in themselves is the general concern of this paper. We concentrate especially on minority group leadership in American society.

Minority group leadership presumably represents a force working for the good of society, especially minority group members. Frequently, however, these leaders display a propensity to perpetuate the social inferiority of their own people. We are interested in the nature of such leadership as it affects and is a product of relations between particular minority and majority groups. The major contention is that minority leaders tend to become alienated from the groups and ideals they allegedly represent. They work instead to protect their exclusive enjoyment of certain privileges and advantages resulting from the continued inferiority of their own people. Minority leaders continually must seek new *raisons d'être* as they act to eliminate the initial conditions that brought about their existence. We emphasize that these patterns are not necessarily the

---

Source: Prepared especially for the first edition of this volume.
[1] Herbert Spencer, *The Study of Sociology* (New York, 1896), pp. 17–18.

result of insidious plots by evil-minded leaders to undermine their peoples' highest aspirations. Rather, the tendency to protect their "vested interests"[2] in the "advantages of the disadvantages"[3] is a function of the strains and tensions built into the role of minority leader itself.

These strains are produced by the conflicting principles on which the role is based. The minority leader must be acceptable to his own people, but his position depends ultimately on his acceptance by the majority. He "leads" but is the most led of persons. In his tenuous position he must pacify both groups. He must integrate their conflicting demands, those of the minority group requiring commitment to its most cherished values, including claims for social equality, and those of the majority group requiring acceptance of its values, including maintenance of its dominant position. The minority leader must negotiate between "selling out" his own people by overcompromising their demands and threatening the power of the majority by over-demanding social equality. Although his position rests on "two centers of gravity," it is the majority group whose judgment of his acceptability ultimately matters. In making the demands of both groups palatable to each other, the minority leader therefore must pay more homage to the majority since it is the group that "runs things" in society.

TYPES OF MINORITY GROUP LEADERSHIP

We will examine three types of minority group leaders: the *charismatic*,[4] the *functional*,[5] and the *professional*. The charismatic minority leader is endowed with special personal characteristics that set him apart from his people and qualify him to lead them out of bondage or to adjust to it satisfactorily. The performance of this self-styled role to which the leader was "called" requires considerable virtuosity, especially in handling the more mundane affairs of politics and economics. He has a vision of social equality, a mission to lead his people toward that nirvanic state, and the ability to successfully transmit his zeal for his goals to a following of minority group aspirants as well as majority group members who want to be assured of the temperate nature of the leader's claims to social ascendancy. Leadership here depends upon a mergence of highly personal qualities and appropriate social conditions that reinforce and

---

[2] To the author's knowledge, E. Franklin Frazier was the first to call attention to the "vested interests" of minority leaders in his article, "Human All Too Human," *Survey Graphic*, 36 (1947), pp. 74–75, 99–100.

[3] A phrase originated by H. B. Frissell, second principal of Hampton Institute. Quoted in Gunnar Myrdal, *An American Dilemma* (New York, 1944), p. 794.

[4] See Max Weber, *The Theory of Social and Economic Organization*, trans. by A. M. Henderson and T. Parsons (New York, 1947), pp. 358–363, for a discussion of charismatic leadership. See also pp. 353–363 for a discussion of the routinization of charisma, which is especially pertinent to the present treatment.

[5] For a discussion of this type, see E. Franklin Frazier, *The Negro in America* (New York, 1959), pp. 547–548.

legitimize the leader's right to his position. Booker T. Washington is an interesting example since, though he was initially charismatic, he eventually developed features of the other two types.

The role of the functional leader depends on his position in an association or activity devoted to such neutral or nonracial causes as education, religion, or the protection of economic interests of particular groups or classes. Because of the prestige, power, and contacts with the wider society gained from such a position, he is drawn into the fray and becomes a race leader. A. Philip Randolph, head of the Brotherhood of Sleeping Car Porters, is an example of this type. When personal qualities become even less important and leadership becomes a career based on specialized training and skill, the professional emerges. This type of leader is likely to be a human relations expert adept at a rational application of general principles to a variety of minority situations. This individual, with a college degree in minority leadership, is apt to be an anonymous employee or director of a social agency rather than an eminent public figure. Such a leader is to be found in any number of Jewish defense agencies, particularly the Anti-Defamation League.

Several general features of this typology may be noted. All types share the same alleged goal—the social advancement of the groups they represent. But the types vary in tactics, from the personal exhortations of the charismatic leader serving as the moral conscience of society to the rational methods of the career-oriented expert. Furthermore, these types are by-products of particular minority groups and their characteristic statuses in society. We might hypothesize that the lower the status of the minority group, the greater the likelihood of its leadership being the charismatic type. The higher the status, the greater the probability for its leadership to be professional. The American Negro has gone through the charismatic stage, is now largely in the functional stage, and is approaching the professional. The American Jew is now in the professional stage and has already experienced an even more advanced development—the bureaucratization of leadership.

Early in the history of a minority group, when its structure is not fully crystallized, there is a leadership vacuum. This was the case of the post-Emancipation Negro who was free but had no awareness of the course of action to take to implement his freedom and relieve his plight as a second-class citizen. It remained for a leader to emerge who promised advancement to the Negro while making "safe" demands that did not threaten the racial status quo favoring the whites. This set the stage for the ascendancy of Booker T. Washington. It is significant that his name is known and revered by all school children, few of whom are familiar with such names as W. E. B. DuBois. In fact, the *only* Negro leaders who are generally recognized as such are those acceptable to the whites. The "real leaders"[6] are to be found at the grass roots level and include countless

---

[6] James Baldwin, "The Dangerous Road Before Martin Luther King," *Harper's* (February 1961), p. 40.

numbers of anonymous individuals whose demands for direct action to bring about full equality render them "unsafe" to carry on the work of the racial status quo. As Frazier puts it, "Only those Negroes who fit into the white man's conception of the Negro will be built into giants."[7]

THE CHARISMATIC LEADER

Booker T. Washington was one of these "giants." Born into slavery, Washington taught himself to read and write before entering Hampton Institute at the age of sixteen. At this institution, a Negro college founded by the American Missionary Society, he acquired a unique combination of pietistic practicality and mistrust of scholarly learning that became the guiding principles in his life's work of teaching Negroes to be "good people." Hard work, frugality, and Christian character were the cornerstones of his personal philosophy, while he tempered the Negro protest by emphasizing duty over right and pragmatic power bargains over demands for full-scale equality. Believing that the Negro's heart and hand should receive priority over his mind, Washington founded Tuskegee Institute in 1891 to provide vocational and moral training for Negroes.[8] Minimizing the potentiality of the intellect in education, Washington claimed that Negroes profit most by conforming to white preconceptions as much as possible. The major result of his approach was to educate Negroes to contentment as second-class citizens.

An adept fund-raiser, Washington befriended many of the leading public figures of his day, such as Presidents Roosevelt and Cleveland and philanthropists Carnegie, Eastman, and Rosenwald. To obtain and maintain their support, he argued for Negro equality in particularly appeasing tones. Characteristically, his speeches portrayed not the "sins" of the white man but the faults of his own race. His tactical philosophy was especially well expressed in the Atlanta speech of 1895. Addressing himself to Negroes, Washington exhorted them to "cast down your bucket where you are. . . . It is at the bottom of life that we must begin not at the top. No race can prosper till it learns there is as much dignity in tilling a field as writing a poem."[9]

Addressing whites, Washington assured them, "In all the things that are purely social we can be separate as the fingers, yet, one as the hand in all things essential to mutual progress."[10] He added, "The wisest in my race understand that agitation of questions of social equality is the extremist folly in that progress in the enjoyment of all the privileges that will come to us must be the result of severe and constant struggle rather than of artificial forcing."[11]

---

[7] E. F. Frazier, *The Negro in America*, p. 569.
[8] Oliver C. Cox, "Negro Leadership in the United States," in Alvin Gouldner (ed.), *Studies in Leadership* (New York, 1950), pp. 235–239. G. Myrdal, *op. cit.*, pp. 726–727, 739–742.
[9] Booker T. Washington, *Up from Slavery* (New York, 1956), p. 155.
[10] *Ibid.*, p. 157.
[11] *Ibid.*, p. 158.

Washington's remarkable ability to please all sides made him a "natural" leader. To whites, his position represented acceptance of Negro subordination, while to Negroes his skill as racial arbitrator resulted in obtaining favors and concessions from whites. Small but significant opposition came from a group of Negro intellectuals led by W. E. B. DuBois, who admonished Washington for "selling out" and advised Negroes to stay out of his "dangerous net" which stood for "submission and slavery."[12] Rejecting Washington's conciliatory attitude, DuBois and his followers formed the Niagara Movement in 1905, which demanded full social and political equality for Negroes as well as complete cultural assimilation. Foreshadowing a strategy that was to develop a half century later, the movement was short-lived and eventually led to the formation of the National Association for the Advancement of Colored People in 1910. As Myrdal says, "Its main importance was that it brought into open conflict and wide public debate two types of Negro strategy, one stressing accommodation and the other raising the Negro protest."[13]

Realistic as Washington's tactics may have been for his day, he influenced two important areas of Negro life, education and leadership, in ways that did not entirely improve the condition of the Negro in American society. His educational philosophy led to a Negro school system which, as Lomax puts it, ". . . produced a flood of miseducated Negroes who, almost by second instinct, acquiesced in segregation and all the indignities that went with it."[14] Washington also established precedents at the racial bargaining table for generations of Negro leaders. Whatever concessions the leaders carried away was done with the understanding that they in turn would influence the Negro masses in the direction desired by the dominant white group. Cox and Myrdal both indicate that Washington's control of the choice of Negro leaders was so great he literally monopolized national Negro leadership for several decades.[15]

Washington's influence waned as the Negro population became more differentiated, making it less possible for a single individual to represent the entire group. The period between the two World Wars saw great changes in the situation of the American Negro, due especially to urban migration and industrial employment. These critical forces created economic and social cleavages among Negroes to an extent never before known. Negro classes emerged whose members' concern with economic and power interests often exceeded their concern for racial matters from which they had become estranged. One such individual is A. Philip Randolph, head of the Brotherhood of Sleeping Car Porters.

---

[12] O. C. Cox, *op. cit.*, p. 260.
[13] G. Myrdal, *op. cit.*, pp. 742–743. See also Elliott Rudwick, *W. E. B. DuBois: A Study in Minority Group Leadership* (Philadelphia, 1961).
[14] Louis Lomax, *The Negro Revolt* (New York, 1962), p. 36.
[15] O. C. Cox, *op. cit.*, p. 259; G. Myrdal, *op. cit.*, p. 741.

THE FUNCTIONAL LEADER

In January, 1941, Randolph proposed that 10,000 Negroes march on Washington to demand an end to discrimination in defense employment and in the military services. July 1 was set as the date, but after months of announcements, promises, and threats, Randolph called off the march as President Roosevelt established a Fair Employment Practices Commission. Herbert Garfinkle notes, "A. Philip Randolph had a large stake in the success of the FEPC. As head of the Brotherhood of Sleeping Car Porters, the FEPC provided a governmental weapon in his effort to expand the union's jurisdiction over new categories of railroad workers." [16] Randolph threatened a mass protest movement in the hope of pressuring the President into helping him achieve his goal. After prolonged negotiation, the President apparently conceded, but, in so doing, crushed the movement by establishing a toothless FEPC with no enforcement powers.

Randolph voiced his protests through channels which brought him back "into formal alliance with the established organizational leadership, Negro and white." [17] His role shifted from mass action leader to member of the National Council for a Permanent FEPC. The movement eventually lost its mass character and became "one more organization competing for public attention in an increasingly apathetic market." [18] In effect, Randolph participated with the majority group in a carefully regulated, yet game-like, test of its power. The result was a reaffirmation of the power of the majority. An important result of minority group leadership, therefore, is the reinforcement of the dominant power structure which has so weakened as to permit an organized protest of the subordinate group. Protest leadership is possible and effective mainly under conditions of flux in the power structure regulating minority-majority relations.

Recently, we have witnessed precisely this development. The traditional Negro leadership, as represented by the NAACP for example, was more oriented toward the dominant white group than toward its own people. The leader paid lip service to the plight of the "masses," but his actions indicated a greater interest in preserving his own status and that of the "talented tenth" or "exceptional" Negro. But, especially since the end of World War II, a complex of social, political, and economic changes have created a crisis for this kind of leader. As Lomax describes it, ". . . . the Negro masses are demanding action, immediately, and leadership organizations are being circumvented when they hesitate or stand in the way." [19] The leadership of Martin Luther King is one response to the crisis.

King is no exception to our typology but overlaps several categories. He is

---

[16] Herbert Garfinkle, *When Negroes March* (Glencoe, Ill., 1959), p. 148.
[17] *Ibid.*, p. 149.
[18] *Ibid.*, p. 117.
[19] L. Lomax, *op. cit.*, p. 157.

charismatic, but this quality stems largely from his position as religious functionary. His occupation and self-controlled benignity give special force and dignity to his actions, so that, for the first time in Negro history, open protest has become respectable. In accounting for King's effectiveness, we should not overlook the traditional power of the Negro Church and the climate of opinion in contemporary American society that favors religion and religious motivations for social actions. King leads a protest movement with the ideological trapping of a spiritual mission.

King achieved prominence as a guiding force behind the Montgomery bus boycott[20] of 1955–1956. For the first time, a grass-roots movement of Negroes succeeded in altering certain aspects of the racial balance of power. Yet these changes were more apparent than real since the basic power structure remained unaltered. Though threatening white dominance, the incident may have strengthened this power by publicly suggesting that the dominant group is sufficiently secure to permit the subordinate group's gaining an occasional advantage. Negroes now sit next to whites on buses but travel to their usual low paying, low status "Negro" jobs. Neither schools, parks, playgrounds, nor other public facilities in Montgomery are integrated. Despite a temporary lapse, the dominant group did not relinquish its power but continues to control the most critical life chances of the Negro minority. Such a deep-seated movement as the Montgomery boycott apparently resulted in nothing more than the integration of buses.

King's effectiveness in this and other movements may lead to eventual estrangement from his followers rather than to identification with them. As he becomes a force to reckon with, King is drawn into a complex network of intergroup relations in which he is likely to be co-opted by the "brotherly love" and status offerings of the dominant group. Simmel observes that social mobility results in the draining off of the minority group's reservoir of talent and leadership. He describes a situation in Spanish-Colonial America in which the Spanish offered gifted and troublesome native rebel leaders legal patents to join white society. Once assimilated into the ruling class, the native leader's superiority over his fellows is replaced by apparent equality with the dominant group.[21] King may confront a similar situation, though his ties to the Negro community remain strong as interaction and apparent acceptance by whites reinforces his status among Negroes.

Nevertheless, success brings him closer to the periphery of the Negro community where, subject to increasing majority controls, he becomes a "nominal" leader with reduced efficiency at improving the lot of his people.[22] Meanwhile, pressures emanating from his own community are already beginning to modify

---

[20] N. W. Walton, "Walking City—A History of the Montgomery Boycott," *Negro Historical Bulletin*, 20:16–20, 27–33, 102–110, 147–152; 21:75–76.

[21] Kurt Wolff (trans.), *The Sociology of Georg Simmel* (Glencoe, Ill., 1950), p. 281.

[22] See Kurt Lewin for a discussion of the "leader from the periphery," *Resolving Social Conflicts* (New York: Harper, 1948), p. 193.

his effectiveness. After Montgomery, King returned to his home community of Atlanta under an apparent agreement which calls for him to concentrate largely on national matters and leave local affairs to the entrenched Negro power structure.[23] Furthermore, his connection with the Southern Christian Leadership Conference, an organization of Southern (Negro) clergymen dedicated to instigating nonviolent protest in Southern cities, has created new conflicts for him. In reality, there are two Kings, the "symbolic leader" and the "organization man." As symbolic leader, he inspired one of the most important revolts in Negro history. As organization man, he acceded to pressures exerted by Adam Clayton Powell in a personnel disagreement forcing the resignation from the Southern Christian Leadership Conference of one of King's most able associates.[24] He inspired the Albany, Georgia, desegregation movement in 1962, but after being jailed and promising to remain there till changes occurred, he came out on bond. This action dealt a severe blow to the spirit of revolt in Albany.[25] However, the most important consideration of all may be King's role in narrowing the gap between "official" leadership, such as that of the NAACP and grass-roots movements of young Negroes.

THE PROFESSIONAL LEADER

Negro leadership tends to be a nonprofessional activity of persons recruited from the upper strata of Negroes. King and others are "amateurs" compared to the professional leaders of Jewish defense agencies that protect the social reputation of Jews in the general community. In the ghettos of Eastern Europe, leadership depended upon sacred learning and scholarship. In the acculturated American Jewish community, leadership depends upon wealth and prestige derived from such secularized activities as fund-raising.[26] But there is a new leader, a special type of organization man. He is particularly skilled at converting complex race issues into neat, marketable commodities to be packaged, publicized, and sold under the label "Brotherhood." Rarely is he a native of the community in which he works which represents only a temporary stop in a career pattern of occupational mobility. As "strangers," professional leaders act as detached observers protected against community pressures by their expertise and the national organizations they represent. But high status Jews influence the strategies of professional leaders by controlling the latter's access to the power and pursestrings of the local community. This results in an alliance between lay and professional leaders whereby the professionals serve as spokesmen for their high status brothers in various affairs of status. Generally, the

---

[23] L. Lomax, *op. cit.*, p. 84.
[24] J. Baldwin, *op. cit.*, p. 42.
[25] L. Lomax, *op. cit.*, p. 99.
[26] See Judith R. Kramer and Seymour Leventman, *Children of the Gilded Ghetto* (New Haven, Conn., 1961), pp. 99–101.

concerns of professional leaders are those of high status Jews, for example, social discrimination in clubs, organizations, and exclusive resorts. Problems of low status Jews, such as discrimination in jobs and schools, are neglected as "passé," no longer critical in a successful middle-class community.

The decline of anti-Semitism and the improved status of Jews threaten the persistence of professional Jewish leaders unless they discover new *raisons d'être* in the plight of other minorities. In so doing, they are not likely to forget that "The best way of retaining the masses' attention and making them proud of their leaders is the provocation of persecution incidents rather than far flung issues." [27] Synagogue bombings or other displays of anti-Semitism may be "bad" for the Jews but "good" for defense agencies which thrive in hostile situations. The strategy these agencies sometimes utilize is illustrated in a recent school crisis in Virginia. The Richmond Anti-Defamation League disseminated pro-integration literature, thus involving Richmond Jews in the desegregation issue. An editorial in the *Richmond News* charged the ADL with deliberately associating all Jewry with compulsory integration. The editorial claimed the ADL would (as it did) take subsequent criticism of its position as evidence of anti-Semitism. And having thus "stirred up defamation of the Jews, it could then combat it with gusto, uncovering anti-Semitism under every segregated school." [28]

The instructions of the national ADL opposed the wishes of local Jews who desired to remain silent on the question of desegregation. Though sympathetic to Negroes, Southern Jews are unwilling to set themselves off from the dominant white society to which they aspire. The desegregation issue is secondary to that of community status. Jews have spent years working in Community Chest and other civic activities in an "effort to show their Christian neighbors that they too belong. If Jews now stand apart from the dominant group, they fear they may jeopardize the prestige and position they have worked so long to secure." [29]

The professional leader uses the community to enhance the prestige he derives from his occupation. He is adept at clarifying issues and guaranteeing that his services will be required to solve minority problems. However, he cannot solve these problems so efficiently as to threaten the persistence of this community which he needs to test and display his human relations skills. The leader thus may perpetuate his role by engaging in activities independent of (though not necessarily opposed to) his original functions.

SUMMARY AND CONCLUSIONS

Minority group leadership can be a social problem in its own right. The leader's role is such that often he perpetuates rather than resolves the problem

---

[27] Robert Michels, *Political Parties* (Glencoe, Ill., 1949), p. 166.
[28] Murray Freedman, "Virginia Jewry in the School Crisis," *Commentary*, 47:20–21.
[29] *Ibid.*, pp. 18–19.

that brought about his existence. The most serious problem he faces is the successful achievement of his avowed goal of social equality for his people. Indeed, he may lose sight of this goal because of intervening and conflicting interests. Due to its dependent power position, any rights the minority group attains are "favors" granted by the majority. Attempting to gain these favors, minority leaders must use tactics and ideologies acceptable to the majority. The distinction between favors granted to the minority and those to the leader himself are often blurred. In time, minority leaders form a separate stratum that bridge the minority and the majority communities and claim for themselves exclusive rights to the critical values of both communities.

While solidifying their personal gains, minority leaders thus become increasingly alienated from their own groups, often representing class interests having little relation to their original purpose. This is especially the case as minority leadership becomes increasingly professionalized, subsequently, distinctions between "radical" and "conservative" leaders are no longer relevant; "trained" and "nontrained" are more accurate designations.

The consequences but not necessarily the intentions of minority leadership are often detrimental to the minority group. Intergroup relations are too complex for any person or stratum to plan and control the outcome of a particular tactic, even a manipulatory one. Just as many advantages accruing to minority groups are fortuitous and unplanned, so are the negative effects of their leadership. Structural factors, such as changing economic and political institutions, often are more crucial than the subjective intentions of particular individuals.

ACTION AND NONACTION: APPRAISING NEED

Some Sociological Factors in Drug Addiction Control in England and Wales

LESLIE T. WILKINS

The majority of students of the problem of drug addiction in this country have, at different times, expressed interest in the fact that the British claim that they have no real problems in this area. Some have doubted this claim.

Although I have carried out considerable research projects in prisons, borstals,[1] and approved schools—not to mention probation—and have been concerned with Criminal Statistics for ten or more years, I can say that I have never met any person in the British penal system who has been worried about the use of drugs. The number of addicts who find their ways into prison is extremely small, even if one includes those who smoke the occasional reefer. According to Schur,[2] whose work on the problem of drug control in England is well known, there are about 500 addicts registered. I have no reason to doubt this figure, nor do I doubt his statement that a disproportionate number of these addicts are associated with the medical profession. His description of the facts as he found them accords with my own experience.

Disagreement begins when the "systems" or machinery for addiction control are discussed and when the so called "British system" is interpreted. I do not want to add to the controversy, but to try to throw some light on the problems of interpretation which seem to be posed by those who look favorably on the "British system" and those who do not. I do not want to suggest that there is

---

Source: Prepared especially for this volume.
[1] British reformatories for delinquents.
[2] E. M. Schur, *Narcotic Addiction in Britain and America* (Bloomington, Ind.: Indiana University Press, 1962).

anything that this country [the United States] could learn from the British. I do not think we have been particularly clever. It is possible that conditions could change in Britain and that we might be able to learn from the work which is being done in this country. But the fact remains that we in Britain have been extremely fortunate in avoiding the problems of addiction in the last half century or more.

I will assume that the standard publications giving the official details of the British system of control are known. I can honestly say, as a social scientist, that I have no knowledge whatsoever of any factors which might tend to suggest in any way that these official statements are biased or incorrect in any detail.[3]

Drug addiction in Britain is regarded as a medical matter, and the medical profession has very considerable freedom to prescribe for any ailment (including addiction) any forms of medical attention, drugs, or treatments that are considered to be desirable for the welfare of the patient. Almost all the population is covered and takes advantage of the National Health Insurance Scheme. I have not seen any recent figures, but I know that the proportion of private patients is so small that it is statistically difficult to obtain a reliable estimate. But the National Health Insurance Scheme cannot be credited with the control of drug addiction, because there were very few addicts before the Scheme became operational. It is possible that the future control of addiction might be facilitated by the Scheme, but that would not be the sort of explanation to interest readers of this book. I could mention, however, that the Ministry of Health maintains a check on "excessive prescribing" by medical practitioners, and will send experts to advise any really outstanding cases. This control covers cost as well as other factors of medical significance.

In the arguments between those interested in addiction control in the United States from various angles, I have noted that much is made of the fact that the British register of addicts is not based on a statutory provision requiring registration. I assume that this "voluntary" nature of the register is often thought to imply that it is hopelessly incomplete. This does not follow. There are many voluntary systems in Britain which seem to work better, even in terms of completeness, than compulsory schemes! Even the Central Criminal Record Office cannot claim statutory provisions for the notification of offenders to New Scotland Yard, but many tests of this register reveal that it is as complete as any enforced scheme would be expected to be, and, indeed it contains somewhat more information than that requested in the proposed list of finger-printable offenses which serve as an informal basis for its compilation. The reason for the voluntary nature of the Criminal Records Office is, of course, that the British policy has always been against any national police force, and although Scotland Yard is often thought of as a national center, in actual fact it is part of the

---

[3] *Departmental Committee on Morphine and Heroin Addiction* (London: H.M.S.O., 1926); Ministry of Health Report, *Interdepartmental Committee on Drug Addiction* (London: H.M.S.O., 1961).

Metropolitan Police who cover most of the London area. The Metropolitan Police, unlike other police forces throughout the country, are responsible to the Secretary of State for Home Affairs. Apart from a Conference of Chief Constables, central control of the local police forces is not exercised; although there are Inspectors of Constabulary, the Chief Constables of the local authorities regulate their own behavior through their Conference. If officials can be persuaded that a particular routine is in the national interest, they normally accept this fact as controlling their own behavior, and enforcement by statute is unnecessary.

This acceptance of national interest as a regulator of official and professional behavior is helpful in the administration in many sectors. I suppose it may spring from the fact that although Britain has no Constitution, we behave in a manner which is, if anything, more strictly in accord with the "unwritten constitution" than we might if one were written. I recall finding the "unwritten constitution" philosophy rather difficult to comprehend when I first began my duties in a government department. That was some eighteen years ago, but I am still not quite used to the idea, perhaps because I get a brainwashing over here in this country from time to time! I recall asking my chief at that time for my terms of reference, and to my surprise I was told that there were none. I was to take due note of precedent, but I could always suggest a modification of precedent if I could think of a good enough reason and back it up with considered argument.

To some extent, I think it is fair to summarize what has been called "the British system" as a lack of system, but I realize that as soon as I use those words they will convey a different meaning to those whose background of experience of systems and lack of systems is derived from a different culture. Precedent, when it is supported by written evidence laid before one at the time of making a decision, is a heavy control, especially when the names included in the files are some of the great names of our history. Perhaps even the informality of the notes on the "minute sheets" (a system not in use in administrative departments here) even adds to the power of conviction of the argument. I remember being concerned a year or so ago with a Parliamentary Question in the House regarding attempted suicide which was still on the statute book at that time as an offense. Some research had been carried out, and the facts were to be presented in the course of the Minister's reply. When the file containing the question came to my office, it came tied with the files containing the precedents. It was a large pile, and, somewhere near the center of the pile was a file in which Winston Churchill had written a minute (an informal note) when he was Parliamentary Under-Secretary to the Home Office. That, I may say, was some little time ago! And there were many earlier papers as well as later ones. None of these precedents were compulsory considerations—one just considers them!

So perhaps the "British system," lack of encoded system though it is, provides a powerful control. Whether it will continue to operate in the same way, it is difficult to say. I rather tend to think that it is a good "lack of system" to hold on to so long as it continues to work. It should enable changes to be made without too much difficulty when changes are needed.

THE PUBLIC IMAGE

I do not think that the unofficial official system which is lacking(!) is the explanation of the absence of addicts in Britain. There are other reasons. May I first make one short and inadequate summary of the theory of perceptual processes upon which my later arguments will be based.

All knowledge is obtained indirectly. The signals we receive through our senses are "codes" which we decode into our experience in different ways. Perception is the process of observing, recording, and organizing the experience one has with people and things. People do not behave with respect to things as *they are*, but to things as they perceive them to be. Indeed, it is doubtful that there is any meaning to discussing "things as they are." There may be some measures of consensus between observers which come to be regarded as "truth," but there are degrees of subjectivity rather than a dichotomy between subjectivity and objectivity. If a coffee table is perceived by a visitor to your home to be a chair or a stool (a mistake one can make with modern furnishings), he may well be expected to sit upon it!

Brill[4] records that Dr. G. Larrimore and he on a visit to England were "... unable to find any indication that in fact there exists anywhere in that country the practice of medically maintaining indefinitely otherwise healthy persons on continued doses of opiates under medical supervision." It might be that the perception of the "otherwise healthy person" differs between the observers. Each medical practitioner has his own views on medical matters, and these views are respected in both administration and law. Personally, I doubt that the concept of a person being at the same time "healthy" and an "addict" would fit the British perception of health and addiction. Addiction is by definition, an illness, and tends to be perceived as such by all authorities. This perception may be the most substantial difference between our countries: not even a crook goes out of his way to get *sick*, although the image of being *wicked* may even seem attractive. Brill continues, "It was clear that the British practice with respect to addicts was not fundamentally different from our own, nor did the British medical views on treatment of addicts differ from our own." I assume that this lack of difference relates only to "medical" factors, for certainly the penal treatments differ and so does public opinion. Perhaps the

---

[4] H. Brill, *Great Britain's Treatment Approach to Narcotic Addiction*, White House Conference Paper (September 27–28, 1963), Washington, D.C.

perceptual differences explain rather more than the procedural differences, even if there are procedural differences. Public opinion may be more important than public policy.

It is, of course, more probable that when an individual takes drugs for the first time his behavior is determined by his *perception* of drug-taking rather than the actual results of drug addiction. It seems unlikely that he would perceive himself as taking on a most expensive habit which will have the consequences it in fact does. Most studies of addiction which I have seen discuss the problems of addiction in terms of the actual function of drug-taking, that is, its function as seen by normal people or the medical profession. But does the perception of the addict, when he is acting in a more or less voluntary manner, agree with this opinion? Cloward and Ohlin,[5] for example, suggest that it is the two-time losers—those who have failed to make a success either of criminal activities or of legitimate ones—who turn to drugs as an *escape*. But are drugs actually *perceived* as providing an escape by the would-be users? If not, how *is* their use perceived? Not what function do they fulfill, but what function are they *perceived* as fulfilling, seems to be the better question. It is, of course, difficult or impossible to find out in retrospect by questioning addicts, and perhaps equally difficult to assess who is likely to turn to drug use in the immediate future and to validate the results of predictive research. But I wish to try to stay with the perceptual model.

In a current work, Freeman[6] suggests that the *perception* of the function of alcoholic liquors differs markedly between those who subsequently become alcoholics and those who do not. Commercial advertisers know how to use the concept of the "image" of their products to make sales, and perhaps the "image" of drugs in Britain explains a large part of the difference. The difference in image may be rather unsubstantial, but it is something we are getting to know more and more about. If, for any reason, the image were to change in Britain, we might have a serious problem on our hands in absolutely no time at all, and our procedures might avail nothing. But this might be a circular argument; perhaps the procedures operate through the image, rather than with respect to matters of more substance?

DRUGS AND ALCOHOLISM

Brill suggests that the difference in addiction rates between the two countries "may be part of a broader question in comparative psychiatry which, for example, also indicates that rates for alcoholism and alcoholic psychosis are lower in the United Kingdom than in the United States." It is certain that the

---

[5] R. S. Cloward and L. E. Ohlin, *Illegitimate Means and Delinquent Sub-cultures: Delinquency and Opportunity* (Glencoe, Ill.: Free Press, 1961).

[6] H. Freeman, Private communication.

rates for alcoholism are very much lower in England, but exactly how much lower it is difficult to say. Different estimates can be derived from different types of comparisons. Mental hospital admissions in New York State for alcoholic psychosis in 1959 are reported to have been 1,929, while Great Britain had only 531 with a population two and one-half times that of New York State. On this basis, this indicator suggests that the rate for alcoholism is about one-tenth of the rate in the United States.

It is interesting also to note that the Jellinek formula, which estimates alcoholism from various other indices, does not provide good estimates for the United Kingdom. Thus it would seem that the usual correlates of alcoholism do not apply in Great Britain, and it might be assumed that the usual correlates with drug addiction would not apply. If the usual correlates do not apply, it seems highly probable that the concept of image and the basis of perceptual processes may afford some sort of explanation of the phenomenon. There must be an explanation of large differences of this kind.

Does this mean, as Brill suggests, a broad question "in comparative psychiatry" or is it a social phenomenon? Or, like many other problems, is it one which runs across a number of disciplines in behavioral science? I think that the latter may be the case. I want, in the remainder of this paper, to try to make some contribution to scholarly thinking on this problem. I do not suggest that the observations I shall make will afford a complete explanation of the differences between the British and American cultures and the relationship between the cultural differences and drug and alcoholic addiction, but I think there may be something in some of the features of culture and human behavior which I will try to bring together into a general theory of deviance.

There are a number of postulates which, initially, may seem unrelated to each other upon which I have to rely for the general nature of the argument. In the space available, I shall have to seem somewhat dogmatic.

OPPORTUNITY THEORY

Let me begin by making a statement with which, I hope, all observers of the British "system" will agree. The *opportunities* for obtaining by legitimate means certain quantities of drugs are greater in the United Kingdom than in this country. In this country, the illegitimate opportunities for obtaining drugs are greater than in the United Kingdom. It is generally agreed that the pusher is very rare (or, I think, almost unknown) in Britain. He is not unknown here. Hence in this country, whatever may be said about the legitimate opportunities, it seems fair to conclude that the illegitimate opportunities for obtaining drugs are rather greater than in the United Kingdom. I do not wish to consider the legitimate and illegitimate opportunities in any absolute terms, but only the balance between them. I think it may be said with reasonable certainty that the *balance* between legitimate and illegitimate opportunities differs between our two countries. If one could express the illegitimate opportunities as a percentage of all opportunities, this country would show the higher ratio. I wish, therefore, to consider the likely effect of differential balance between legitimate and illegitimate opportunities in a completely general way in the first instance; then I wish to develop a theory of self-regulatory systems which may explain how a *very small* difference in the *balance* between *types of opportunities* may have a *very considerable effect* on the outcome in respect of many forms of human behavior; and, finally, I will try to apply this general theory to deviant behavior and to drug addiction.

My first postulate is that where the *balance* between legitimate and illegitimate opportunities remains constant, the amount of crime will tend to remain proportional to the *opportunities*.

My second postulate is related to the theory of strategy and states that people do not "play expected values," and in particular, the cultures from which drug addicts tend to come, there will be observed other forms of behavior which indicate a poor appreciation of "utilities" due to distortions of the "expected values." I shall illustrate what I mean by these terms by examples.

My third postulate is that definitions are made by cultures and that cultures vary in their perception of forms of behavior, and that some definitions are vestigial traces of different cultures.

Fourth, since perceptions influence behavior, the definitions (perceptions) of the culture have an influence on behavior of the culture and the subcultures as perceived and defined by the culture itself.

Finally, a model is proposed which reveals an unstable relationship of the nature of a positive feed-back loop. A kind of "servo-system" is produced such that a small amount of difference in the balance will build up to create a large difference in the state of the organization. (This is much the same sort of situation as is utilized in the engineering designs for power steering of cars or control surfaces in aircraft and in many other ways; a negative feedback tends towards stability and damping of the distorting effects however generated, whereas a positive feed-back tends towards instability and an increase in the distorting forces.)

Postulate 1

IF THE BALANCE BETWEEN LEGITIMATE AND ILLEGITIMATE OPPOR-TUNITIES REMAINS CONSTANT, THE AMOUNT OF CRIME WILL TEND TO REMAIN PROPORTIONAL TO THE OPPORTUNITIES. It is often stated that we live in an affluent society. The amount of wealth is continuously increasing, and with it the amount of crime continues to increase. But gross correlations of this kind are not very convincing. It is difficult to find any crime which is defined sufficiently in terms of behavior characteristics that it would provide a good measure for comparison with increases in opportunities. One fairly

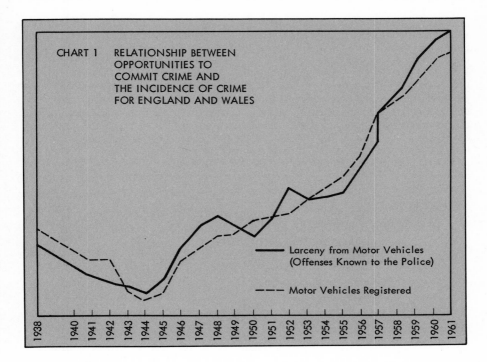

CHART 1   RELATIONSHIP BETWEEN OPPORTUNITIES TO COMMIT CRIME AND THE INCIDENCE OF CRIME FOR ENGLAND AND WALES

—— Larceny from Motor Vehicles (Offenses Known to the Police)

– – – Motor Vehicles Registered

satisfactory index of the increase in "opportunities" may be provided by the number of private cars on the roads of a country, and a crime which might be examined to see whether the increase in opportunity was accompanied by an increase in illegal activity might be the number of thefts from cars. Table 1 shows the data for England and Wales for the years 1938–1961, and Chart 1 reveals that the trends follow each other almost too closely. It cannot be held that our moral values have deteriorated in a manner strictly proportional to the increases and decreases in the number of cars on the roads! A more reasonable explanation seems to be that if opportunities increase (that is the sum of legitimate and illegitimate opportunities) the balance between the taking of illegitimate opportunities and legitimate opportunities will remain constant. The more transfers of money in total, the more legal *and* illegal transfers of money; the more cars, the more thefts from cars, unless the *balance* is changed.

Postulate 2

PEOPLE DO NOT PLAY EXPECTED VALUES. An "expected value" is that derived from the product of the probability and the sum of money or value involved. As Herman Kahn has explained in his exposition of the theory of war in the nuclear age, nations do not play expected values. In a recent broadcast lecture he said:

There is one characteristic many decision-makers have—they do not play expected values. Let me illustrate: Suppose you were Premier of Clotland, and you were told, and believed, that under policy A it was dead certain that you would lose $3,000, but under policy B there was one chance in ten you would lose $300,000, the expected loss is $30,000. Policy C, say, has a one-hundredth chance of losing $300,000,000, expected loss $300,000. If you were a reasonable person you would choose policy A over policy B and policy B over policy C. But if you are a diplomat working on these sorts of diplomatic exchanges where prestige gets committed, where you have all kinds of public humiliation, you are apt to argue that under policy C there are ninety-nine chances in a hundred that you will get away with it. Therefore, forget about the expected loss! There is a real tendency to underestimate the risk simply because . . . people do not know how to deal with low probability events; they tend to assume they are zero.

Table 1 / Showing the Number of Motor Vehicles Registered and the Number of Thefts from Motor Vehicles Known to the Police between 1938 and 1961. (England and Wales)

Year	Motor Vehicles (In Thousands)	Larceny from Motor Vehicles
1938	1944	25,281
1939	—	—
1940	1423	11,849
1941	1503	15,672
1942	858	12,180
1943	718	11,084
1944	755	14,509
1945	1487	26,520
1946	1770	32,546
1947	1943	33,984
1948	1961	32,665
1949	2131	30,297
1950	2258	33,156
1951	2380	43,127
1952	2508	41,125
1953	2762	39,739
1954	3100	39,398
1955	3526	43,304
1956	3888	50,782
1957	4187	54,937
1958	4549	68,466
1959	4966	79,899
1960	5526	92,704
1961	5979	112,671

In this connection it is interesting also to note the reciprocal of this type of strategy in the attraction of football pools for the majority of the population in Great Britain. Investment (as it is called!) in such pools has only a very small probability of a very large gain, yet the majority of people seem to consider only the size of the prize—the extremely small probability of winning attracts millions of persons and pounds to a most profitable industry to those who run it. No chairman of a board of directors of any company could satisfy his shareholders (or, for that matter, the law) by an explanation of his company's investment policy in the same economic terms as those used by football pool investors. But this does not mean that we must regard the behavior of pools investors as either unpredictable or, given certain modifications in the variables, irrational. A different set of utilities characterizes the different behaviors. It is possible that a similar set of modified utilities characterizes many criminal acts. The remote chance of winning a large prize, the thrill of participation, considerations of prestige, and involvement in the criminal culture doubtless influence criminal strategies in a manner too strikingly similar to the field of politics!

Postulate 3

DEFINITIONS ARE MADE BY CULTURES, AND CULTURES VARY IN THEIR PERCEPTIONS OF FORMS OF BEHAVIOR. THERE ARE VESTIGIAL TRACES OF DIFFERENT CULTURES WITHIN A CURRENT CULTURE. If all persons behaved in exactly the same way within a society, no matter what the form of that behavior, none of the behavior would be defined as criminal, even if by some external standard all the behavior was criminal. A nomadic society has no difficulties within a culture which accepts the nomadic way of life, but this way of life becomes quite unacceptable to a society where land is defined as belonging to people or organizations.

Distinctions between what is perceived as legitimate and illegitimate are made culturally and legally, and the legal definitions tend to follow the cultural definitions. Nonetheless, there are distinctions which are made culturally but not legally, and legal distinctions which are not accepted culturally. This statement excludes those criminal acts which are due to persons whose mental state is such that they would be defined as deviant by *any* form of society and dealt with by some form of exclusion from that society, that is, persons whose acts are defined as not within their control. These persons would be dealt with by medical definitions and not by social definitions, but even in this category social determinants control many definitions and will continue to do so until psychiatric medicine has become more precise.

In general, a religious society will define deviance from the religious norms as heresy, and if perceived as sufficiently deviant, will prescribe some form of punishment; a socialist society will define deviance with respect to its theoretical concepts of collectivism; and an economic society will define certain forms of economic behavior as sufficiently deviant to isolate the offender from the remainder of the society. On a convict island, some of the behavior would still be likely to be defined as deviant and in need of the attention of that society; similarly, in a monastery of saints, some behavior would be defined as deviant. It is clear that all people have some idea of what they regard as deviant or rare events, but no one has any prior knowledge of normality. We have only the sum of our experience against which to measure the unusual or deviant events and to serve as a basis for differential classification. It is as though the human mind had a storage system linked with some classificatory and integrating device which was used for purposes of subjective prediction of behavior and in accordance with levels of expectation.

Any rare event, perceived as either "good" or "bad," say, with a probability of occurrence of less than one in 5,000, is most likely to be perceived as a rare event. Such an event is almost certain to be remarked upon; indeed, it may well be described as "remarkable." Such events will usually call for some action, an action which is also somewhat unusual. Depending upon the way in which the rare event is perceived, and perhaps some personality factors also, the person experiencing the event may write to a newspaper, hold a party, say some special prayers, or demand revenge or punishment. If the event is perceived also by other members of the society as being a rare event, such behavior on the part of the subject will be accepted as "normal," provided that it is perceived as matching the situation. The event was unusual and the response was accepted to be unusual, also. If I am unaccustomed to eating without wearing a jacket and tie, I will perceive a person so acting as acting "abnormally," and, according to my interpretation of the culture patterns and my status within the culture, I will merely take a different seat at the restaurant, go to a different restaurant, or demand that the person be arrested!

It is difficult for a society to retain on its statute books as a law (which is enforced) any concept which is accepted as "normal" behavior by the majority of the population. A society in which 90 per cent of the population are given to gambling will tend to permit gambling, not defining it as deviant but possibly even incorporating gambling (known by a different term!) into its administrative economic system. On the other hand, a society in which a small proportion of the population indulge in behavior which is defined as gambling may well define it as illegal and force those who would participate into illegal opportunity structures. The concept of "local option" whereby laws regarding the sale of alcoholic beverages are determined by local referenda illustrates this point. Here it has been formalized into a system. The divergence between "democratic definitions" and "legal" definitions cannot be maintained at too great a distance for too long.[7] It must be noted, however, that it is not only the actual behavior which conditions the definitions, but also the attitudes of the public toward the definitions. That is to say, laws may remain unamended because they reflect some idealized behavior patterns to which the majority have been per-

---

[7] The history of prohibition in the United States provides a good example of this fact.

suaded to give lip service. Similarly, although we live today in an economic society, some laws reflect vestigial traces of older religious societies, and indeed older forms of economic society also. Taxi drivers are, within certain cities, still required by law to carry a broom and shovel, and to remain within 15 feet of their "hack"—laws which are still applied to motor vehicles, although remaining from earlier forms of transport.

Let us try to construct a suitable mathematical model of this system of "democratic" and "legal" definition concept. Crime is human behavior. Human actions do not divide into bad and good, black and white, crime and no crime. It is possible to suppose a distribution of human actions as a continuum from very saintly to very sinful. In our society, there are very few acts which are defined as extremely saintly or extremely sinful; the majority of actions are just "normal," and within the limits tolerated by our culture. It is accordingly possible to draw a distribution very similar to that used to describe measurements of general intelligence. In the case of intelligence, very few people are classified as geniuses, and very few as mentally subnormal. (A diagram of the familiar distribution is given as Chart 2.)

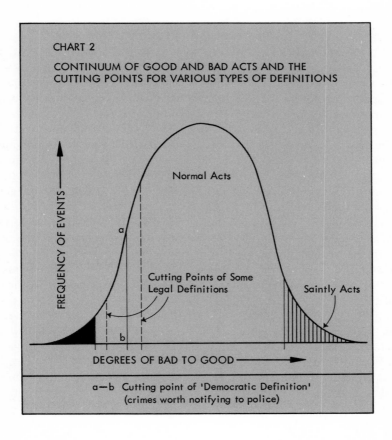

CHART 2

CONTINUUM OF GOOD AND BAD ACTS AND THE
CUTTING POINTS FOR VARIOUS TYPES OF DEFINITIONS

Normal Acts

a

Cutting Points of Some
Legal Definitions

Saintly Acts

FREQUENCY OF EVENTS

b

DEGREES OF BAD TO GOOD

a—b Cutting point of 'Democratic Definition'
(crimes worth notifying to police)

Crimes in the main will be represented by actions at the "bad" end of the scale. It will be obvious that the number of incidents defined as crimes will depend on the point of cutoff. There will be no doubt about the classification of actions which are extremely deviant, but these extremely deviant acts form a rather small proportion of the distribution.

Legal definitions of offenses are quite clear, and there is no intention in this discussion to criticize them when they are used for legal purposes. There is, however, a sense in which all (or nearly all) members of the population could be described as having committed some crime. It is important to note that the cutting point determined by some legal definitions of some crimes will be perceived by some members of the population as being further towards normal than by others, and similarly the majority of the population will perceive some crimes as being nearer to normal than some other crimes. The dotted lines on Chart 2 illustrate the cutting points for certain definitions of crime according to the law, and the line *a–b* represents the cutting point as it might be perceived by the normal middle-class citizen. There are obviously some incidents which are technically described as crimes which the average citizen would not define as anything worth telling the police about.

Postulate 4

SINCE PERCEPTIONS INFLUENCE BEHAVIOR, THE DEFINITIONS MADE BY THE CULTURE HAVE AN INFLUENCE ON THE BEHAVIOR OF MEMBERS OF THE CULTURE AND SUBCULTURES. Perhaps the best way to present some brief support for this postulate is to illustrate the difference between urban and rural cultures, using the model of the normal distribution.

In a village culture, as a community, there is greater tolerance of deviance than in urban cultures, but the deviance permitted to any one individual is greatly restricted. The roles of each member of the village community are specified in considerable detail. A model, somewhat similar to the model provided by the normal distribution, may be used to compare the urban and rural culture. The roles of each member of the village community are specified in considerable detail. There is conduct appropriate to the village blacksmith and the village banker and the village idiot. The blacksmith may not behave like the banker even in his spare time (he may perhaps blow the village church organ on Sunday, but it would be inappropriate for him to play it). If for any reason any member of the village culture deviates from the defined role, his behavior will be interpreted by the village and he will be helped, if help is perceived to be needed, or controlled, if social pressures seem to be required, to re-establish the *status quo*. In the village, each member has information regarding the roles of all other individuals, and the boundary conditions for work and leisure are narrowly defined by the culture. Each narrowly defined role is perceived to have a specific place in the culture; indeed, the tolerance of deviance from the role set for the individual may relate to the tolerance of a wide variety of roles (*y*) within the culture. Each piece of the mosaic is accepted so long as it stays the same shape. If its shape does not vary greatly, it is easy to see how it fits into the whole, but, if the blacksmith "changes his shape" (that is, fails to stay within the narrow limits of his role), then the structure is seen to be threatened. In the urban culture, far greater variation in role is permitted to each member, but members who are too far out of line are rejected.

Dentler[8] studied deviance and social controls in small work groups in Quaker work camps. These groups were in face-to-face communication. The level of communication was very much greater than that to be expected in the village culture. Dentler's findings confirm the hypotheses suggested in our theory—small groups have specific roles for each member, whereas large groups tend toward anonymity. Dentler suggested that his groups demonstrated that (1) deviant behavior tends to be induced, permitted, and sustained, by a given group; (2) deviant behavior functions to help maintain group equilibrium; and (3) groups resist any trend towards alienation of a member whose behavior is deviant.

However, the perception of deviance and the function of deviance differ between large and small groups. The rural culture consists of persons whose roles are known, but the information available to other members of the culture includes more than a knowledge of the role. The individual in the village may be named Smith, and he may be the village blacksmith. In his role he does very useful work for the village community. If Smith died, his son might take over the forge, but if it were sold to a stranger, the stranger ("foreigner") would find it difficult to attract business and the confidence of the villagers. In the urban culture, anybody can be the blacksmith, and anybody may be Smith. In the village culture, the *individual* seems essential to the functioning of the organization in much the same way as Dentler described for his work camps. He notes that the individuals who were perceived as deviant in his groups caused great efforts to be expended on the part of other members of the work group to retain them within the system, although they could leave if they wished. In the urban culture, individuals are expendable if they are replaceable in terms of their *roles*. In the urban culture, it is not Mr. Smith the blacksmith but a "pool of labor" which may or may not include somebody (anybody) possessing the necessary skills.

In the village, "Jack" the village idiot is integrated into the culture, but in the urban culture it is not "Jack" who is dealt with, but the role or stereotype which is perceived. Each member of the village receives some training in the sociology of the village by observation and informal "training on the job." A form of apprenticeship in group management and parish politics is given to all. The training may be in a primitive form of government, but there is a system of passing on of information regarding the role expectations of all within the

---

[8] R. A. Dentler, and K. T. Erikson, "The Function of Deviance in Groups," *Social Problems*, 7:98–107.

social system. It is an individualized sociology at the level of anecdote and folk lore, but *information about the system is fed into the system*. And perhaps, even more important, the information covers the whole system, and this information is seen to be relevant. By contrast, the information available to the urban dweller, as part of his experience, is more restricted. The information available to members of the village culture enables them to make predictions of behavior over a wider range of events than the information available to the urban resident. They know that the village idiot drools, but they knew his father, and they know that he has never done anybody any harm, and so on. Transfer the village idiot to an urban setting, and he will have to be removed and cared for professionally. Maybe he is better cared for, but the community has lost *information* which was available to the villagers.

Thus there are systems which can tolerate (deal with) wider ranges of behavior than others. In terms of the probability calculus, the value of x in $x\sigma$ differs with respect to individuals and systems. In the village, x is small for individuals but larger for the system, whereas, within the urban culture, x is larger for individuals and smaller for the system. This model must now be extended from the static to the dynamic frame of reference.

PROGRESSIONS—BAD AND GOOD

It has been noted that definitions of deviance relate to information and cultural experiences of individuals and types of systems. It has also been noted that communities of both saints and sinners would tend to define a certain quantity of behavior as deviant. The degree of deviance $x\sigma$ would, in general, determine the nature of the action taken, and the value of x was likely to vary between individuals and cultures.

It appears, however, that once a subsection of the general distribution has been cut off by definition as not being within the system, the cutoff sector begins to form its own distribution of values, and to define $x\sigma$ values with respect to its own central tendency. The model proposed is illustrated by Chart 3. The cutoff sector of the general distributions seems to develop a centrifugal force which drives the new subset further apart from the parent population.

This is an important feature of the general model, but it is possible to give only one or two illustrations of the working of this principle. Mannheim and Wilkins[9] showed that treatment in "open" borstal institutions appeared to be more successful in reducing recidivism than treatment in closed (secure) institutions, after making full allowance for the fact that the "open" institutions received better risk groups. Croft and Grygier,[10] using sociometric analysis,

---

[9] H. Mannheim, and L. T. Wilkins, *Prediction Methods in Relation to Borstal Training* (London: H.M.S.O., 1955).

[10] I. J. Croft, and T. Grygier, (1956) "Social Relationships of Truants and Juvenile Delinquents," *Human Relations*, 9 (1956), pp. 439–466.

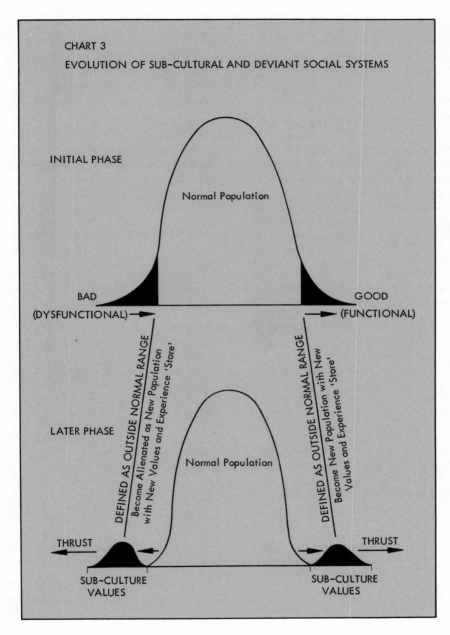

CHART 3

EVOLUTION OF SUB-CULTURAL AND DEVIANT SOCIAL SYSTEMS

INITIAL PHASE

Normal Population

BAD
(DYSFUNCTIONAL) →

GOOD
→ (FUNCTIONAL)

DEFINED AS OUTSIDE NORMAL RANGE
Become Alienated as New Population
with New Values and Experience 'Store'

DEFINED AS OUTSIDE NORMAL RANGE
Become New Population with New
Values and Experience 'Store'

LATER PHASE

Normal Population

← THRUST

THRUST →

SUB-CULTURE
VALUES

SUB-CULTURE
VALUES

found that, in most classes in the schools they studied, delinquent boys were rejected by others (had more enemies), that truants were isolated (had few friends), and that the boys rated by the teachers as behaving badly were disliked by other boys. In other words, in most cases they found that the choices on their sociometric scales tended to follow the values of the teachers. But, in the classes reserved for "backward" children, the situation was different. Conforming behavior was unrelated to sociometric status. Both truants and delinquents were more popular in the "backward" classes. Moreno and Jennings had earlier reported that in prisons and reformatories the most popular individuals tended to have had an outstanding record of antisocial activity.

It would appear that a group which has been *defined* to be, or defines itself to be, cut off from the general "norms" develops its own norms which tend to reveal some centrifugal force away from the distribution of values from which they have themselves been rejected. The definitions, as we have noted earlier, relate to both systems and to perceptions of individuals.

THE GENERAL MODEL

Although it is realized that the arguments put forward in presenting the model have been inadequate to support the theory in any detail, the following dynamic system may be proposed:

1. Certain types of information and certain systems lead to more acts being defined as deviant to the extent that the individual is "cut off" from the values of the parent system.
2. The definition leads to more action taken against those perceived as deviant, and the individuals so labelled begin to perceive themselves as deviant.
3. The self-perception and the action taken by the general society lead to isolation and alienation of the groups defined as deviant.
4. The deviant groups develop their own values running counter to the values of the parent system, which has defined them as "outlaws."
5. The centrifugal forces thus developed within the deviant group lead to more deviant behavior by the alienated groups.
6. The increased deviance demonstrated by the deviant groups (resulting from the centrifugal force, results in more forceful action by the conforming groups against the nonconformists.
7. Thus information of this kind received by the conforming groups about the behavior of the nonconformists (as in 6) leads to more acts and back to (1) and round and round again.

This is not too surprising. Indeed it would be surprising if people who are excluded by a system were to continue to regard themselves as part of the system excluding them. But if this is a fair model of the system, some surprising deductions can be made from the theory.

It would, for example, appear that the sanctions applied by a society to its deviants may seem to them to be so extreme that they become alienated from that society. The rejection of an $x\sigma$ deviant, if the value of x is not large, may act as an information set modifying his own tolerance ($x\sigma$) through his "store" —that is, his experience of the culture. If a society truncates its "normal" distribution at low values of x, it seems that it will reduce the cohesiveness of its own social order. Or simply, lack of tolerance by a society for behavior which is not completely intolerable may defeat its own ends, not only through the devaluation of sanctions (although this is important) but by inducing a self-definition of deviance where such a definition is not justified in terms of the social dysfunction of the behavior.

The lower class may find defenses against middle-class value systems which cannot have any meaning for them, by setting up other value systems. They will insulate themselves from those value systems in which they cannot hope to achieve and establish systems which will determine for them some needed hierarchical structure. It may be at this point that the balance between the legitimate and illegitimate opportunities begins to have a second, and perhaps even more powerful, effect than that relating to definitions.

A POSITIVE FEED-BACK SYSTEM

If these forces exist, it is not necessary to show that they are large. The important feature of this type of model is that it represents an *unstable system*. Small, initial differences in the network can build up of their own momentum into quite large forces. Very small forces which tend to regulate towards stability can similarly make very large adjustments in the total situation. The aircraft pilot exerts only a small force on his control column to produce minor changes in the control surfaces which are then fed back to build up much larger forces. Until quite recently, there was often trouble with lateral instability with early marks of designs due to the critical nature of feed-back systems.

How may this theory relate to the difference between the problem of drug addiction in Great Britain and the United States of America? The following are possibilities:

1. The "image" of the use of drugs in Great Britain is different, and the "image" of the addict differs.
2. The "image" of the police is also certainly different.
3. Small differences in the control systems could generate a large difference in "image," which could amplify the effects of the official controls.
4. Less action is defined as "crime" in Great Britain, and fewer people are defined as "criminal," whatever the "objective" differences may be.
5. The *balance* between legitimate and illegitimate means for obtaining drugs differs.
6. The information "set" (or folk lore—it does not have to be true!) modifies behavior. It may be, as Dr. Brill points out, quite untrue that there are

differences in the systems of controls between our two countries (I do not wish to debate this point), but the existence of a different set of *beliefs* is quite enough to change behavior.

It is possible, then, that the success of Great Britain in limiting the use of drugs to a very small proportion of the population is built upon some very slender foundations. I am not myself convinced that "perceptual processes" and "images" are slender foundations. Advertising agents know how difficult it is to change the image that the public may have formed of their products and those of their competitors, even though the manufacturing processes and all other details may be exactly similar. The difference between Great Britain and this country may be based on something like the same basis that determines which sort of gas one buys for his car, or the brand of cigarettes one smokes. Looked at one way, these determinants are slender, but they are extremely strong.

CONCLUSIONS

I said I would not presume to offer advice. I will not offer differential advice. but I would suggest that if this theory of deviance is true, or even substantially true, then there are certain factors which might assist any society to control deviance.

The following could be the best strategy:

1. Define as "deviant" the minimum number of actions which are regarded as dysfunctional, and hence reduce the number of people who are defined as "deviants."
2. Consider the "image" presented at different levels of social integration of the control systems which that society employs.
3. Insure that its social controls, and particularly its sanctions, do not become devalued (in the same way as money becomes devalued).
4. Try to insure that all levels of society are able to select legitimate means to obtain legitimate ends.

I would suggest that these points of strategy follow from the theory and are completely general. How right they are depends upon the strength of the theory when subjected to rigorous testing in terms of its practical consequences.

Finally, one light-hearted comment to emphasize the main content of my thinking. I am not (yet!) a member of the Athenaeum[11]; my image of that club is doubtless distorted. Certainly, I do not feel myself bound to follow its rules and regulations unless and until I am elected to membership. If I had been "black-balled" from any club, I should, I am sure, take an even lesser interest in its rules and regulations! Perhaps a society can control effectively only those who perceive themselves to be members of it.

---

[11] The highest status club in the United Kingdom.